MEMOIRS

Of the Extraordinary

LIFE, WORKS, and DISCOVERIES

OF

MARTINUS SCRIBLERUS

MEMOIRS

Of the Extraordinary
LIFE, WORKS, and DISCOVERIES
OF
MARTINUS SCRIBLERUS

Written in Collaboration by the Members
of the
SCRIBLERUS CLUB
John Arbuthnot   Alexander Pope
Jonathan Swift   John Gay
Thomas Parnell

AND

Robert Harley, *Earl of Oxford*

Edited by
CHARLES KERBY-MILLER

New York   Oxford
OXFORD UNIVERSITY PRESS
1988

Oxford University Press

Oxford   New York   Toronto
Delhi   Bombay   Calcutta   Madras   Karachi
Petaling Jaya   Singapore   Hong Kong   Tokyo
Nairobi   Dar es Salaam   Cape Town
Melbourne   Auckland

and associated companies in
Berlin   Ibadan

First published in 1950 by Yale University Press
New Haven, Connecticut 06520

Reissued in 1988 by Oxford University Press, Inc.
200 Madison Avenue, New York, New York 10016

Oxford is a registered trademark of Oxford University Press

Library of Congress Cataloging-in-Publication Data
Memoirs of the extraordinary life, works, and discoveries
of Martinus Scriblerus / written in collaboration by the members
of the Scriblerus Club, John Arbuthnot . . . [et al.]; edited by
Charles Kerby-Miller. p.   cm.
''The text of this edition has been taken from . . .
Works of Alexander Pope, vol. III, part II, published in 1742''—p.
Reprint. Originally published: New Haven:
Published for Wellesley College by Yale University Press, 1950.
Includes bibliographies and index.
ISBN 0-19-520647-9   ISBN 0-19-520648-7
I. Arbuthnot, John, 1667-1735.   II. Kerby-Miller, Charles.
III. Pope, Alexander, 1688-1744.   IV. Scriblerus Club.
823'.5—dc19   PR3630.M4 1988   87-34767   CIP

1 3 5 7 9 8 6 4 2

Printed in the United States of America
on acid-free paper

I have often endeavoured to establish a friendship among all men of genius, and would fain have it done. They are seldom above three or four contemporaries, and, if they could be united, would drive the world before them.

Swift to Pope
September 20, 1723

FOREWORD

The reputation of the *Memoirs,* like most things connected with the Scriblerus project, has followed an unconventional pattern. So delayed in its publication that when it finally appeared, somewhat more than two centuries ago, in the second volume of Pope's collected prose works, it was regarded more as a curiosity than as a piece of living literature, it rose slowly in general estimation until in the early part of the nineteenth century it began to be referred to by distinguished critics as a classic which was "universally known." At this stage Hazlitt called the piece inimitable; Dugald Stewart spoke of its chapters devoted to logic and metaphysics as contributions to philosophy, while contemporaries testified that the Chancellor, Lord Brougham, and his opponents frequently quoted from it in Parliamentary debates.

During the past hundred years, though reprinted on several occasions, the *Memoirs* has steadily become less well known. Scholars have continued to refer to it respectfully, but, on the whole, less out of a recognition of its intrinsic merit or significance as a literary document than because of the famous names attached to it. Undoubtedly the chief reason for this lack of real interest in the piece has been the increasing difficulty of understanding its satire. Intensely topical in its allusions, it was even at the time of its first publication fully understood only by exceptionally well-informed readers. The two succeeding centuries have buried its learned humor deeper and deeper until today whole sections of the satire may be read without any awareness of the pointed and finely turned wit they display.

Much the same situation has obtained with regard to the club which gave birth to the *Memoirs.* A hundred years ago those well acquainted with the literature of the early eighteenth century were very conscious of the interest and significance of the association between, to use Cowper's phrase, "the most celebrated collection of clever fellows this country ever saw." The frequently reprinted Swift-Pope *Miscellanies,* which contained several of the Scriblerus satires as well as a good many pieces by the individual Scriblerians, had had the effect, as Pope planned that they should, of showing the friends "walking down hand in hand to posterity." Moreover, as comparatively little was known about the lives of Dr. Arbuthnot, Gay, and Parnell, there was a general tendency to relate them very closely to the Swift-Pope circle. During the intervening time, however, a long series of scholarly studies devoted to the individual men, while steadily increasing our store of facts about the association, have tended to lessen the sense of its interest and significance. The complex lives and achievements of the individuals have not allowed students much time for the examination of cross influences, and biographers have not unnaturally been inclined to underestimate the effect which the other Scriblerians and the club had upon their figure.

In the meantime, however, another type of scholarly investigation has developed which may serve to hasten a revival of interest in the Scriblerus Club and its project. In recent decades a very considerable effort has been made to understand the cultural and intellectual milieu in which learned and literary men have lived and worked. The early eighteenth century has been of particular interest in this connection. It was the historic function of the men of this time to sort out from the vast heap of conflicting ideas piled up by the creative but tempestuous seventeenth century a basis for a stable, orderly, and rational world. Since the results of their efforts were to endure for so long a time, the turns and developments of thought during this era are matters of very considerable historical interest and importance. Partly consciously and partly unconsciously the Scriblerians produced in the *Memoirs* a most exceptionally valuable document for the study of attitudes and beliefs during the central years of this transitional period. The essence of the Scriblerus program was an attack on "all false taste in learning." Believing, as did many of their contemporaries, that learning in its broadest sense was being hampered by the continued survival of various follies, they proposed in the club project to eliminate these or render them harmless by means of ridicule. One factor that contributed greatly to the value of the result from the historical point of view was that they extended their satire into many fields, such as music, philosophy, classical learning, education, and science, which are seldom treated effectively by social satirists. Another was that they were all well-informed men and that they possessed in Dr. Arbuthnot a man of great learning as well as wit. In consequence their satire has a depth and authority rarely to be met with in literature. The fact that they were collaborating as a group also had its advantages. Since the Scriblerians differed widely in temperament, education, and experience, the common ground on which they met was that of the educated people of the day, and their views may be taken as typical of a relatively large and influential section of society. And, finally, their method of satire is of the kind most useful to historians. The satire

FOREWORD

ix

of the *Memoirs* is for the most part direct, concrete, and timely; as a result, therefore, it not only makes clear many of the general attitudes of the Scriblerians but provides us with specific judgments concerning many ideas, activities, and people.

Opinions as to the literary merit of the *Memoirs* will no doubt continue to vary greatly. Many, repelled by the somewhat static quality of its wit, the obscurity of its allusions, and the generally esoteric character of much of its subject matter, will join with Dr. Johnson in his harsh judgment of it. To them the piece will remain a prime example of the limitations of topical satire and of the fact that joint authorship among men of genius tends to produce disappointing results. Others with a taste for learned wit will share Warton's enthusiasm for the "exquisite humour" of the piece and will rate the *Memoirs* high in an admittedly limited genre. In any case, the *Memoirs* is assured of a lasting place in the history of English literature. A project and a piece which produced such offspring as *Gulliver's Travels,* the *Dunciad,* and, more indirectly, the *Beggar's Opera,* as well as a whole series of lesser satires, will continue to command the attention of those interested in the literature of the period.

In the course of working on the Scriblerus group and in the preparation of this edition I have incurred many debts which it is a pleasure to record here. The project was begun some years ago under the encouragement of Professor George W. Sherburn, and it has profited much, as have so many other studies, by his learning and his generosity. Professor Marjorie Nicolson has contributed substantially to the completion of the work by her counsel and aid, which are most gratefully acknowledged. Very warm thanks are also due to my colleague, Professor Walter Houghton, who has been good enough to go over much of the material with me and to offer me the benefit of his knowledge and judgment on many points. My wife, too, has served as consultant as well as helpmate in carrying forward the work of the edition. Among others to whom I am indebted are Professor R. S. Crane, Professor R. H. Griffith, Professor L. M. Beattie, Miss Sylvia Berkman, and various members of the staff of the Widener Library, the British Museum, and other libraries in this country and in England who have helped me to obtain material. Finally, perhaps, a word of appreciation might be devoted to the Scriblerians themselves. Their wit, their learning, and their literary genius have seemed to grow steadily under examination. And over the years, despite the barrier of two centuries, they have proved to be most delightful and stimulating companions.

CONTENTS

PREFACE

THE SCRIBLERUS CLUB AND ITS PROJECT

An account of the Scriblerus Club and its scheme must cover a long period of time and deal with many complex matters involving the personal, political, and literary activities of the six notable figures who formed its membership. From their earliest beginning to the publication of the principal piece, the activities which may be labeled Scriblerian spanned a period of almost three decades. During this time the fortunes of the scheme swelled and ebbed several times and its influence worked itself out in many different ways through the individual and collective productions of the members of the club. Because of its many ramifications and secondary effects, definite limits and boundaries are difficult to establish. Scriblerus was only one factor in the long and fruitful association of the men and it merges insensibly into other literary and social factors. By following the central thread of Scriblerus activity, however, we can trace the germination and development of the scheme and note some of its principal results.

The story of the club itself is a familiar one. Each of the biographers of the half dozen men involved has repeated the principal known facts and quoted from the famous letters exchanged by the members during the summer of 1714. But our knowledge of the club is still meager and even in the work of recent scholars there has been confusion about such fundamental matters as the date of its founding and the names of its members. Moreover, the relatively brief existence of the club is only a part of the Scriblerus story; much happened to bring the club about, much resulted from it. In an account of the Scriblerus association and its project, the club period therefore tends to take the form of a focal point toward which forces worked and from which complex consequences followed.

The founding of the club was far from a simple, spontaneous matter. Social clubs and literary associations were commonplace in the early eighteenth century, but the Scriblerus group was not a typical gathering of like-minded men. It was the result of a merger of two literary groups, one led by Swift and the other by Pope. These groups were very different in their character, and the motives of their leaders in joining forces were by no means similar. The elder group, consisting of Swift, Dr. Arbuthnot, Parnell, and the Earl of Oxford, brought to the common project prestige, experience, learning, humor —and a very strong Tory coloring; the other section, composed of Pope and Gay, brought wit, youth, and ambition. To understand how the association of these men came about and why the club took the form it did, we need to trace briefly the rise of these groups and note the factors which made their merger possible.

I THE BACKGROUND OF THE CLUB

Swift's Isolation

The history of the Swift group begins in the autumn of the year 1710 when Swift made his famous change of politics and became associated with the ministry of Robert Harley, later the Earl of Oxford. The account of its growth is largely a record of his alienation from his former Whig friends, his efforts to find a congenial group among the Tories, and his ambition to use his influence to aid literature and literary men. Its development, as well as that of the Scriblerus Club into which it grew, was, of course, greatly influenced by the fortunes of the Oxford-Bolingbroke ministry, with whose triumph, internal disintegration, and ultimate collapse Swift was intimately associated.

Swift's loss of his former friends began even before he had openly changed sides. He had returned to London on September 7 in an angry mood and, after being treated coldly by Godolphin, had become outspoken against the Whig leaders.[1] When, therefore, it became known that the new ministry had made advances to him which he had not rejected, he became suspect. The key figure among his Whig friends was Joseph Addison, with whom Swift had very strong bonds of mutual esteem and affection. They had been together in Dublin during the summer and after Swift's arrival in London had met frequently. During the time when Swift was making up his mind to accept Harley's offers they saw each other almost daily.[2]

The immediate cause of their break was their mutual friend Richard Steele, whose intemperate Whiggism had got him into difficulties with Harley;[3] however, political feeling was running so high in London and Addison's position with the Whigs was such that a continuation of their close friendship after Swift had joined the Tories was in any case almost impossible. There was no open quarrel; an air of coolness on Addison's part was enough to touch Swift's pride and bring about an increasing estrangement. By the middle of January, 1710/11, Swift was noting in his letters to Stella that "all our friendship and dearness are off: we are civil acquaintance, talk words of course, of when we shall meet, and that's all."[4]

It was natural that the split should have been followed by some feeling of

1. *Journal to Stella,* September 9, 10, 1710. Hereafter referred to as *Journ.* The full titles of works cited by abbreviations may be found on pp. 173–5.

2. *Journ.,* October 19–November 10, 1710.

3. In a generous effort to aid Steele, Swift blundered into a complex maneuver in which Harley was trying to win over Steele by threatening his government posts. Swift approached Addison in the matter and was received so coldly he was nettled. *Journ.,* October 22, 1710.

4. *Journ.,* January 14, 1710/11.

rivalry, particularly on Swift's part. Thereafter it became a matter of personal pride as well as of political policy for Swift to attempt to form a group of Tory wits that would eventually match in reputation and influence Addison's band of Whig writers. When, therefore, Steele abruptly laid down the *Tatler* on January 2, Swift promptly moved to set up a continuation of it under Tory auspices. He himself was too busy with the *Examiner,* which he had taken over, to attempt the task himself, and no doubt he did not wish to risk his own reputation directly, so he set up a young protégé, William Harrison, to carry it on.[5] Despite the aid of Swift and other Tory writers such as Prior and Dr. Freind, however, the project was not a success. As Swift feared, Harrison proved not equal to the task and the whole project limped into failure.[6]

The defeat of Swift's first effort was highlighted by a new and dazzling success achieved by his former intimates. Though Swift did not know it, Steele, before dropping the *Tatler,* had laid plans for another journal on a somewhat different basis, which incidentally would owe nothing to Swift, as had the original plan for the *Tatler.* The first issue of the *Spectator* appeared on March 1 and in a short time the new periodical dominated the whole literary scene in London to such an extent that effective rivalry was out of the question.

The result of these circumstances and a growing ill feeling between the political parties was to isolate Swift from his former large circle of friends and acquaintances. With Addison and Steele ruling the world of wit it was no longer possible for him to visit on an easy footing such coffeehouses as Will's and the St. James's, where literary men met.[7] As a result he failed to become acquainted with promising young newcomers, such as Alexander Pope and John Gay, and began to lose contact with many of his former associates.[8] In compensation he turned more and more exclusively toward his new friends and sought companionship in Tory circles and clubs.

The first of the Tory groups which Swift joined, the Saturday Club, had so brief and informal an existence that it was a "club" probably only in Swift's mind. It grew out of the future Earl of Oxford's custom of entertaining his two chief lieutenants, Sir Simon Harcourt and Henry St. John, later Viscount Bolingbroke, each week at his house for a discussion of strategy. On February 16, 1710/11 Swift, who had lately been much concerned about his personal standing with the ministry, reported to Stella with a mock petulance

5. *Journ.,* January 11, 1710/11; for a time Swift devoted two evenings a week to it. *Journ.,* February 11, 1710/11.

6. *Journ.,* January 15, March 14, 15, 1710/11.

7. "I never go to a coffeehouse," Swift wrote in May. *Journ.,* May 29, 1711. He first began to indicate a growing distaste for coffeehouses at the time when the new ministry was wooing him. *Journ.,* November 1, 1710. Since Stella's letters continued to be addressed to a coffeehouse for some time, his not going involved the frequent sending of a servant. *Journ.,* May 4, 1711.

8. "You hear no more of Addison, Steele, Henley, Lady Lucy, Mrs. Finch, Lord Somers, Lord Halifax, &c." *Journ.,* May 29, 1711.

that did not conceal his elation that "at last they have consented to let me among them." The obvious motive of the group in admitting Swift was further to bind him to their service and to increase his usefulness as a political writer by keeping him acquainted with and sympathetic toward the policies which the ministry proposed to follow. However, it is clear from Swift's accounts of the meetings he attended and from the inclusion in the group (along with Swift) of Earl Rivers that the gatherings were no longer as highly confidential as they once had been.

For a time after he had joined the Saturday group it seemed as if Swift had won his way into it only in order to have an inside view of the ministry's collapse. In February the condition of the government was so perilous that even Harley was despondent. After one meeting of the group, Swift noted gloomily in the *Journal to Stella*, "They are able seamen, but the tempest is too great, the ship too rotten, and the crew all against them." [9] Only four days after this despairing verdict, however, a dramatic event suddenly altered the whole complexion of affairs. The stabbing of Harley by Guiscard on March 8 brought about a great swing in popular feeling. The joy of the Queen and the nation in Harley's escape and rapid recovery gave his government real stability for the first time since it had been brought into existence by backstairs intrigue during the preceding summer.

The change brought an end to the little group; with political prosperity it lost its cohesion and began to change its character. There were only three "Saturday Club" meetings after Harley's recovery, the first on May 5 and the others on the following weeks.[10] At the last two the principal topic of conversation was the approaching elevation of Harley and Harcourt to the peerage as the Earl of Oxford and Mortimer and Baron Harcourt. The dinners were revived during the following season but a much larger and more mixed company was invited to them.[11] Swift was welcome at these gatherings but they were not to his taste. On January 9, 1712/13, in noting for Stella that he intended to dine the next day, a Saturday, with Oxford, he added:

I was of the original club, when only poor Lord Rivers, Lord-Keeper, and Lord Bolingbroke came; but now Ormond, Anglesey, Lord-Steward, Dartmouth, and other rabble intrude, and I scold at it; but now they pretend as good a title as I; and, indeed, many Saturdays I am not there.

Eventually, as his relations with the members of his government had grown cool, Oxford also had come to dislike these dinners and to call them his "whipping-day" because, as Swift said, "we do indeed usually rally him

9. March 4, 1710/11.
10. Swift was not invited to the first of the dinners and had to ask St. John's permission to rejoin the group. *Journ.*, May 5, 12, 1711.
11. Swift, *Works*, v, 384–5.

about his faults on that day." At the start of the London season in February, 1713/14, therefore, he did not revive them and the period each week was open for the Scriblerus Club.

The Brothers Club

Another factor in the dropping of the Saturday Club was the formation of a much larger and more colorful group in which two of the little Saturday circle were leading members. The sudden change in their political situation in the spring of 1711 enabled the ministers to relax a little and to plan their activities on something more than an emergency basis. It was clear that if the ministry was to continue, it needed greater internal unity and general prestige. Contrasted with the Whig circles which had dominated the court and the town for most of a generation, the new group seemed mixed and unimpressive. St. John, with whom Swift had been working closely, saw a means of remedying this situation to some degree by founding a Tory counterpart to the famous Kit-Cat Club. In a letter to Lord Orrery, dated June 12, 1711, he sketched out his idea:

We shall begin to meet in a small number, and that will be composed of some who have wit and learning to recommend them; of others who, from their own situations, or from their relations, have power and influence, and of others who, from accidental reasons, may properly be taken in. The first regulation proposed, and that which must be inviolably kept, is decency. None of the extravagance of the kit-cat, none of the drunkenness of the beef-stake is to be endured. The improvement of friendship, and the encouragement of letters, are to be the two great ends of our society. A number of valuable people will be kept in the same mind, and others will be made converts to their opinions.[12]

Swift was out of town for a fortnight's visit with Lord Shelburn at Wycombe while the club was being formed. On June 21, the day after his return, however, he dined with the group at Sir William Wyndham's and reported to Stella,

It seems in my absence they had erected a club, and made me one; and we made some laws to-day, which I am to digest, and add to, against next meeting. Our meetings are to be every Thursday: . . . We take in none but men of wit or men of interest; and if we go on as we begin, no other club in this town will be worth talking of.[13]

Starting with a nucleus of twelve, the club gradually increased its size until it reached a total of twenty out of a proposed twenty-one. Its membership was the most brilliant the ministry could muster. Most of the cabinet

12. Bolingbroke, *Letters*, G. Parke, ed. (1798), I, 246–7.
13. *Journ.*, June 21, 1711.

became members, as did several leading Tory peers. The four who owed their places not to their influence but their "wit" were Swift, Matthew Prior, Dr. Arbuthnot, and Dr. Freind.[14]

Among those proposed for membership at the start were the other two principal figures in the Saturday Club, the Earl of Oxford and Lord Harcourt, but Swift reported that he was against them, adding, "and so was Mr. Secretary, though their sons are of it, and so they are excluded."[15] The ostensible reasons for not including in a sociable group the top chiefs of government are clear but the move worked so directly in favor of St. John that it is difficult not to suspect that he managed the matter deliberately, using Swift as his means.[16] Without the presence of the elder statesmen he was undisputed leader of the group, with an extraordinary opportunity not only for increasing his personal prestige but of disseminating his views and increasing his influence among the lesser Tory leaders. Oxford and Harcourt were not in a position to object since their sons were freely admitted, but Oxford's later failure to support the program of the club is probably to be traced at least in part to a feeling that his growing rival was profiting from it.

The name chosen by the group was "The Society," but from the practice of its members of addressing each other as "Brother," it came more commonly to be thought of as the "Brothers Club," and in modern times it has become known almost exclusively by that title. It was presided over each week by a new president, who entertained the company at dinner and had the privilege of naming his successor. After the club had been established, young Harcourt was made secretary, but from Swift's account it is clear that most of the time many of the burdens of that office fell upon him.

The club started so late in the season of 1711 that only a few meetings could be held before the members scattered for the summer. Several informal gatherings took place later in the summer at Windsor but the regular meet-

14. Others who had some standing as men of wit were the Earl of Orrery and George Granville, the Secretary at War. Those who were made members because of their situation or influence included St. John, Sir William Wyndham, Sir Robert Raymond (the Solicitor-General), the Duke of Ormond (Lord-Lieutenant of Ireland), and Robert Benson (Chancellor of the Exchequer). Seven were chosen because of their family connections: Edward Harley, Viscount Dupplin, and Thomas Harley (members of the Lord Treasurer's family), Samuel Masham and Col. Jack Hill (husband and brother of the influential bedchamber woman to the Queen), Simon Harcourt (son of the Lord Keeper), and the Earl of Arran (brother of the Duke of Ormond). Those who apparently were made members for general or "accidental" reasons were the Duke of Beaufort (a very rich young Tory), Allen Bathurst (soon to be one of the new Tory peers), and Colonel Disney (described by Swift as "a fellow of abundance of humour; an old battered rake" whom they all loved mightily. *Journ.*, March 14, 15, 1712/13). Though elected, the Duke of Shrewsbury never became a member. The Earl of Jersey and the Earl of Danby were proposed for membership but were rejected.

15. *Journ.*, June 21, 1711.

16. Swift must have first heard about the club from St. John in the latter's office just before they went to the first meeting and hence would have had no time to work the matter out himself.

ings did not begin until the last week in November. From that time on, however, the club met almost every week until late in the following spring. This pace Swift and apparently many of the other members found oppressive; so when several members of the club gathered the next winter, on December 18, 1712, it was decided to meet only fortnightly. Since the first of the dinners did not take place until the end of January, 1712/13, there was time for only half a dozen meetings before the end of the spring season. Primarily because of the tense political situation no effort seems to have been made to revive the club the following year.

A very successful feature of the club was the regular attendance of Swift's printer, who came each week after dinner with copies of Swift's latest piece or, failing that, anything new from his presses. The club's more serious program of aiding deserving authors, however, did not accomplish much. The group notably lacked men, like Halifax and Somers among the Whigs, who could by their own fortunes and interest directly aid writers, and the club's hopes that Oxford would provide it with money and patronage to dispense were never realized. Twice in 1712 and once in 1713 the club took up a collection among its members to give poets,[17] and finally in February, 1712/13, Oxford was prevailed upon to send a hundred pounds. But the gift came too late to alter Swift's view that the club was doing no good, and any pleasure that he might have had in disposing of even this sum in the name of the club was destroyed by the discovery that Harrison, the man for whom he intended it, had just died.[18]

During its last season Swift was actively discontented with the whole club. References to it in the *Journal to Stella* show less and less interest and on some occasions he simply did not attend. The extravagance of the club and its failure to accomplish anything were partly responsible for his attitude, but equally important was his weariness of the large mixed gatherings. On February 26, 1712/13, he told Stella, "Duke of Ormond chid me for not being at the Society to-day, and said sixteen were there. I said I never knew sixteen people good company in my life; no, fais, nor eight either."

This attitude was one of the legacies of the Brothers Club to the Scriblerus group, as was Swift's realization that effective aid for writers could only stem from the direct patronage of the head of the government.

Swift's Plan for an Academy

There was still another factor in Swift's attitude toward the Brothers Club which also has significance in the background of the Scriblerus association.

17. *Journ.*, January 10, 1711/12, March 21, 1711/12, and January 29, 1712/13.

18. *Journ.*, February 14, 1712/13. On the previous day Swift had visited the poet Diaper, whom he found "in a nasty garret, very sick," to present him with 20 guineas from Lord Bolingbroke and had also distributed 60 guineas raised by the Society between two other authors.

All during the life of the Society Swift was engaged in trying to found a group of a very different character, one both nobler in purpose and more congenial for him in membership. Swift had long held strong views on the constant change and continued vulgarization of the English language; he was deeply impressed, as were many writers of the time, with the fact that in contrast to the masterpieces of classical literature those written in English, such as the works of Chaucer, rapidly became unintelligible to the average reader. France had been at work on this problem for almost a century and its means of fixing and refining the language, the *Académie française,* had already begun to have an appreciable effect. The *Académie* had also succeeded in bringing honor and financial rewards to its members. To Swift, who earnestly believed that the government should aid worthy writers, it seemed that the establishment of a somewhat similar academy in England would be a useful and splendid act for the Queen's ministry.

The sudden political prosperity which led St. John to establish the Society encouraged Swift to advance his proposal. On the day following his first dinner with the Brothers, he wrote to Stella:

I am proposing to my lord to erect a society or academy for correcting and settling our language, that we may not perpetually be changing as we do. He enters mightily into it, so does the Dean of Carlisle [Francis Atterbury]; and I design to write a letter to Lord-Treasurer with the proposals of it, and publish it; and so I told my lord, and he approves of it.[19]

Apparently, however, he was advised not to press matters immediately, for he did not complete the letter until February 22, 1711/12.[20] He then sent it promptly to Oxford, who passed it on to Matthew Prior for examination. Prior's slowness and other delays kept the manuscript from going to the printers until early May and it was not until the middle of the month that the *Proposal* was put on sale. The general reaction was neither very favorable nor extremely adverse. The scheme was promptly attacked in the public prints by John Oldmixon and others, but the motivation of these attacks was largely political and they probably carried little weight. More serious was the lack of a strong favorable response. If any enthusiasm was expressed in literary circles it does not seem to have come to Swift's attention or to have appeared in print.[21] Probably whatever interest was aroused by the proposal was tempered by the objection that a time of war was not a propitious moment for starting such a project and by some feeling that the proposed academy was modeled too closely on that of an enemy land.

19. *Journ.,* June 22, 1711.
20. *Journ.;* the printed *Proposal* carries this date.
21. Swift had won the approval of Addison when he told him about it in the summer of 1711 (*Spectator,* No. 135, for August 4, 1711, and Swift's *Works,* XI, 17; cf. *Journ.,* July 26, 1711), but Addison made no open move to support the idea after the publication of Swift's *Proposal.*

Swift, however, continued to hope. Toward the end of June, 1712, he wrote to Archbishop King:

My Lord Treasurer has often promised he will advance my design of an academy; so have my Lord Keeper [Harcourt], and all the Ministers; but they are now too busy to think of anything beside what they have upon the anvil.[22]

In the autumn his expectations were again high. The matter "upon the anvil," peace with France, had begun to take definite shape with St. John's visit to France in August. Success seemed only a matter of time; "Lord-Treasurer promises the academy for reforming our language shall soon go forward," he reported to Stella at the end of October.[23]

It does not in any way derogate from Swift's sincerity and high motives in pursuing his plan for an academy to realize that he had a very high personal stake in the matter. The proposed institution would be above the level of politics; in it he could again find common ground with the Whig friends from whom he was estranged. And if it were established, he, both as its proposer and as the intimate friend of the head of the government which had set it up and which might provide pensions for its members, would undoubtedly be the most powerful literary figure in London.

How far, with Oxford's encouragement, he carried the project in his own mind is shown by the fact that he and Oxford early determined the names of the twenty men of both parties who were to be its first members.[24] Unfortunately for historians their selections are not known; the list would be a most useful document in measuring contemporary reputations and, incidentally, in indicating Swift's ability to rise above political and personal animosities. A far less proud man than Swift might have taken pleasure in this sorting of the sheep from the goats and in the prospect of earning the respect and gratitude of his own and succeeding generations for what he believed would be a great service to literature.

Early in the spring of 1713 Swift had additional cause for optimism. At that time, though Prior remained discouraging,[25] it began to seem possible that the leading Whig writers might become favorable to the scheme. The certainty of the approaching peace had led to some lessening of political tension and the atmosphere between Whig and Tory writers was more cordial than at any time since the beginning of the Oxford ministry. Several writers with Tory sympathies were contributing to Steele's *Guardian* and at the end of March Addison, who was anxious that the forthcoming production of his play *Cato* should be well received, began to exchange friendly courtesies with Swift. On the twenty-eighth of March he called upon Swift,[26]

22. *Corres.*, I, 331.
23. *Journ.*, October 30, 1712.
24. *Corres.*, I, 325, 331.
25. *Corres.*, II, 18.
26. *Journ.*

who as a return compliment seems to have persuaded Bolingbroke to invite him to dinner on April 3.[27] Three days later Swift watched a rehearsal of *Cato* and later dined privately with Addison.[28] The great success of the play was generally regarded as a Whig triumph, but on the first night Bolingbroke, in a famous gesture, balanced the score for the Tories by presenting fifty guineas to Booth, the actor who played Cato, for defending the cause of liberty so well against a perpetual dictator—a reference to the ambitions of the Whig hero Marlborough.[29] In such an atmosphere a friendly association of writers might at least have seemed possible.

Before Swift left for Ireland in June, however, all remaining hope for the academy had been swept away in a fashion that left Swift not only defeated but bitter. During the weeks of intense worry while the question of his personal reward was being determined Swift learned that the opposition to him was very strong and that his friends, notably Oxford, lacked the will and the strength to carry out their promises to him. It also became clear that the internal rifts in the ministry were becoming so great that united action, even on noncontroversial matters, was unlikely. Finally Swift discovered that the recent friendliness of Addison did not mean that politics were not to be allowed to separate literary men. In the *Guardian* for May 12 Steele attacked Swift in strong terms as the author of the *Examiner*. Swift protested indignantly to Addison that, as was commonly known, he had had nothing to do with the *Examiner* for some time, but Addison, instead of composing the quarrel, merely turned the letter over to Steele, who wrote an insolent and provocative reply. Swift's return letter was a dignified justification of himself and an explanation of what he had tried to do for Steele, but it brought from Steele only a few equivocal expressions of gratitude and a strong statement of his own nobility and independence.[30] The result of the exchange was to leave both men and their partisans increasingly hostile. Thereafter there could be no real hope of cooperation between the literary groups, even in matters where both would profit.

Arbuthnot and Parnell

When this renewed estrangement from his onetime associates took place, Swift's position was very different from what it had been two years before. Now he was the sought-after friend and intimate of statesmen, courtiers, and duchesses. He still had not been able to establish a Tory circle of writers, but his efforts to aid writers were generally known and he had acquired

27. *Journ.*
28. *Journ.*, April 6, 1713.
29. Pope, E. & C., VI, 7–8.
30. *Corres.*, II, 26–7, 29–30, 33–5, 37–9.

two literary protégés of such quality that the addition of only two recruits at the start of the following season was to make his circle one of the most brilliant in English history.

The abler of Swift's literary followers was the learned, witty, and kindly Dr. John Arbuthnot, the Scottish physician-in-ordinary to the Queen. The two men probably first became acquainted during the winter of 1710–11 when Swift was being introduced around the court, but their friendship did not begin until the following summer when they spent a good deal of time in each other's company during Swift's visits to Windsor. Thereafter they saw much of each other during the whole period of the Brothers Club, establishing ties of affection and respect which survived throughout the remainder of their lives.

By the summer of 1711 Dr. Arbuthnot, who was then forty-four, the same age as Swift, had won for himself a distinguished reputation as a doctor, scientist, and mathematician. Member of the Royal Society since 1704, Fellow of the College of Surgeons, author of several modest but valuable mathematical and scientific works, he was active in learned circles and the friend of the leading scientists of the time. In addition, he was rightly credited with possessing some influence at court as a shrewd adviser and as a friend of the Queen's favorite, Mrs. Masham.[31] Despite his learning and versatility of mind, however, any suggestion at the time he met Swift that he would in the next few years acquire enduring literary fame would no doubt have struck him as entirely incredible. That he did do so was due to a rich fund of humor which animated his wide learning and led him to spend some of his leisure time in the exercise of his wit and ingenuity; it was also due in no small measure to the aid and encouragement of Swift. This began in the early days at Windsor when the two carried out a jest by taking up a sham subscription for a proposed *History of the Maids of Honour since Harry the Eighth*.[32] During the winter he had a hand in at least one of the many ballads Swift and his group were turning out [33] and began writing his famous John Bull pamphlets. The first of these, *Law Is a Bottomless-Pit*, which was probably all he originally intended to write, was published on March 6, 1711/12. Before it was in print, however, he must have begun on the second, for a sequel, *John Bull in His Senses*, was on sale within a fortnight. Thereafter, additional parts appeared on March 17, April 17, May 9,

---

31. *Wentworth Papers*, J. J. Cartwright, ed. (1883), p. 138. His general reputation at this period of his life is illustrated by George Berkeley's description of him in April, 1713: "He is the Queen's domestic physician, and in great esteem with the whole Court. Nor is he less valuable for his learning, being a great philosopher, and reckoned among the first mathematicians of the age. Besides which he has likewise the character of very uncommon virtue and probity." *Berkeley and Percival*, B. Rand, ed. [Cambridge, 1914], p. 114.

32. *Journ.*, September 19, 23, October 5, 1711.

33. *Journ.*, January 4, 1711/12.

and July 31. The whole series was exceedingly popular, the first part being reprinted six times in London alone and the others going rapidly into several editions.

All the pamphlets appeared anonymously and, since Dr. Arbuthnot was wholly unknown as a literary man, they were widely attributed to Swift. Swift's explicit denials to Stella and the equally plain statements of Pope and Berkeley, who knew both men well, make Arbuthnot's authorship certain, but there can be little doubt that Swift and others had a hand in them. The doctor's whole temperament inclined him to consult openly and freely with others and all through his life he took more pleasure in presenting ideas to friends than in publishing them. Moreover, he needed advice and aid in correcting his rough drafts. A comparison of the pamphlets shows that the first one was revised much more carefully than the others, and it seems likely that this one benefited especially from Swift's expert assistance.

In the John Bull pamphlets may be seen many of the characteristics of Dr. Arbuthnot's mind, literary method, and habits of work which were to mark his later literary pieces and play a significant role in the Scriblerus project. The most striking quality exhibited is the cleverness displayed in the main concept and the unflagging ingenuity and inventiveness with which details of the allegory are worked out. The execution, however, bears many evidences of haste and inexperience. There is no coherence of plan in the series, and the individual pamphlets, especially the later ones, are very irregular in literary method and uneven in merit. Among the most admirable qualities in the work is the continuous use of realistic and homely detail which gives vigor and color to the narrative. For this element it seems wise to grant some credit to the influence of Swift since he was such a notable artist in this respect. Also abundantly evident in the pamphlets are the widespread learning, the grasp of affairs, and the high good humor untinged by bitterness or malice which the doctor brought to his work.

After completing the John Bull series, Arbuthnot began to run dry as an author. In October, 1712, he sent to Swift the manuscript of a clever little satire in the form of a burlesque proposal for the publishing of a treatise entitled *The Art of Political Lying*.[34] Thereafter, however, he produced nothing of a literary character until the Scriblerus Club had been founded. Clearly he needed the stimulus and aid of a group of appreciative friends.

Swift's other literary protégé was Thomas Parnell, who, like Swift, was an Irishman of English descent, a man of letters, and a member of the Church of Ireland. Like Swift, he, too, made occasional trips to London for the church and to advance his own fortunes. However, he differed greatly from his older and more powerful friend in temperament, in energy, and

34. Swift thought it a "pretty Discourse" and made the arrangements for its printing. *Journ.*, October 9, 1712.

in the early possession of a comfortable income and a family. None of his friends has left a satisfactory account of his character, which was a complex one. Possessed of a well-stored and well-trained mind but not endowed with great vigor or independence of spirit, humorous and witty without being naturally cheerful, social and dependent on company but inclined toward retreat and melancholy, he seems to have been much affected by his immediate environment. In Ireland, under the guidance of such men as Archbishop King and the influence of a happy marriage, he led, until the age of thirty-three, a quiet, modest life, taking an unassertive role in church affairs and writing poetry of a conventional and religious character, which he did not bring to the point of publication.[35] During the next few years in London, under very strong stimulus, he became a wit of some distinction, a poet whose verse was to remain in favor for most of a century, the favored companion of famous authors and great men, and a beloved and regretted friend. On his return to Ireland, affected by ill-health, an increasing melancholy, and an all too apparent distaste for his rural Irish exile, he was to acquire a local reputation for moroseness and isolation in strong contrast to the memory held of him by his English friends.

Most of the poetry for which he has been known was produced or heavily revised during the five years of his friendship with his fellow Scriblerians. During this time he tried a number of forms, from anacreontics and learned burlesques to elaborate subject pieces, and a variety of styles from something approximating the deft, colloquial realism of Swift to the elevated classical tone of Pope. His most characteristic verse, which drew its inspiration largely from his reading, is marked by a graceful ease, a moral tone, a felicity of imagery, and what later critics called a sweetness of diction. Some of it was marked by a softness and melancholy which a later taste was to find appealing.

Swift had known Parnell in Ireland, but it was not until they met again in England during the summer of 1712 that they became intimate. Parnell's health and spirits had been severely affected by the death of his wife the year before and he had spent the winter and spring at Bath and in traveling. After his arrival in London, Swift, whose sympathies were aroused, tried to arrange a further change of scene by obtaining for him a post with the commission that was to accept the surrender of Dunkirk,[36] but this plan fell through. Instead, Parnell spent the autumn in London, passing his time by contributing two allegorical pieces to the *Spectator* and drafting an ambitious poem entitled *An Essay on the Different Stiles of Poetry*.

In December, 1712, when Parnell first showed him this poem, Swift was at the height of his power, and he determined to do all he could to advance the fortunes of his fellow countryman. Having persuaded Parnell to intro-

35. Swift declared he "hardly passed for anything in Ireland." *Journ.*, January 6, 1712/13.
36. *Journ.*, July 1, 1712.

duce into the poem some complimentary lines to Bolingbroke, Swift gave
the poem to his lordship, who was much pleased and read parts of it aloud to
the Earl of Oxford.[37] Thereafter, Swift arranged for the poet to dine several
times with Bolingbroke and on one occasion staged a little scene at court
for his benefit, in which Oxford came over publicly to ask for an introduction and to invite the poet to his house.[38] And finally, toward the end of the
following March, when the poem, after much correction, had come from the
presses, he planned for Parnell to present it to both lords at court.[39]

During the spring of 1713 Parnell continued his literary activity, partly
at least under Swift's direction. The Treaty of Utrecht, which was finally
signed on March 31, o.s., was an obvious subject for those who sought favor
with the Tory government, and Parnell was one of several who turned out
uninspired verse in celebration of it. In addition, he contributed two vision
pieces to the *Guardian,* one of which appeared in the issue for May 15 and
the other in that for May 27.[40]

Though he had succeeded in advancing Parnell's public reputation to a
notable degree, Swift was by spring well aware that he was not likely to
accomplish much more under the present circumstances of the ministry.
As soon, therefore, as he had been made Dean of St. Patrick's, he tried to
obtain for Parnell his own small prebend there in the hope that he might
in the future be of service to him. Even this modest project was defeated,
however, by the fact that Swift's elevation had long been assumed and his
place promised to another.[41]

Pope's Plan

The first direct move toward the formation of the Scriblerus Club was
made in October, 1713, when Alexander Pope approached Swift with a proposal that they and their friends collaborate on a burlesque monthly periodical in which follies in learning and criticism would be satirized in ironic
reviews that depreciated works of merit and cried up the productions of
Grub Street.[42] The idea for such a journal had apparently been in Pope's
mind for some time. A year before he had sketched out a plan for it in a
letter contributed to the *Spectator.*[43] In this letter, having reminded his read-

37. *Journ.,* December 22, 1712.
38. *Journ.,* January 31, 1712/13.
39. *Journ.,* March 20, 1712/13.
40. Though these appeared after Steele's attack on Swift in the issue for May 12, both no
doubt were written and accepted during the era of good feeling which preceded it and do not,
therefore, represent neutrality on Parnell's part in the subsequent quarrel.
41. *Corres.,* II, 23, 32, 36–7, 51 n.
42. E. & C., VII, 412; cf. below, p. 20.
43. No. 457 for August 14, 1712. Mr. Sherburn was the first to call attention to this letter
as anticipating Pope's proposal to Swift. Sherburn, pp. 74–5.

ers of the famous monthly abstract, *The History of the Works of the Learned,* he declared,

Now, Sir, it is my Design to Publish every Month, *An Account of the Works of the Unlearned.* Several late Productions of my own Country-men, who many of them make a very Eminent Figure in the Illiterate World, encourage me in this Undertaking. I may, in this Work, possibly make a Review of several Pieces which have appeared in the Foreign *Accounts* above-mentioned, tho' they ought not to have been taken Notice of in Works which bear such a Title. I may, likewise, take into Consideration such Pieces as appear, from time to time, under the Names of those Gentlemen who Complement one another in Publick Assemblies, by the Title of the *Learned Gentlemen.* Our Party-Authors will also afford me a great Variety of Subjects, not to mention Editors, Commentators, and others, who are often Men of no Learning, or what is as bad, of no Knowledge. I shall not enlarge upon this Hint; but if you think any thing can be made of it, I shall set about it with all the Pains and Application that so useful a Work deserves.

Though the outlines of the scheme which he sketches here appear to be substantially the same as those he suggested to Swift, it seems unlikely that at the time he wrote the *Spectator* paper Pope took his idea seriously. The major part of the letter containing the suggestion is devoted to an obviously facetious proposal for a *News-Letter of Whispers* and the author identifies himself as the proposer in a previous *Spectator* paper of an equally facetious plan for a paper devoted to trivial facts and gossip. Even if he privately thought the idea had possibilities, Pope was not, in 1712, in a position to try it out. The project obviously required more wit and learning than one man could provide steadily, and Pope, though he had a rising reputation as the result of his pastorals and *Essay on Criticism,* was at the age of twenty-four too young, too inexperienced, and too recently established in literary circles to promote a group undertaking of such a sophisticated character.

No real opportunity for advancing the idea occurred during the succeeding season, but in the course of the following months Pope acquired additional incentive for a satirical project and some of the prestige necessary to win a hearing for it. The prestige was in a large measure due to the interest of Addison and Steele, who during the winter of 1712–13 actively sponsored him. In November, 1712, when it had been determined to give up the *Spectator,* Steele asked for Pope's assistance in his next project, the *Guardian,*[44] and paid him something like advance royalty by including him in a list of major contributors published in the last issue of the *Spectator,* though Pope's actual contribution had been relatively slight. With such backing Pope rapidly became a man of importance in literary circles. By February he was able to boast to his friend Caryll,

44. E. & C., VI, 395.

I have ten different employments at once that distract me every hour. Five or six authors have seized upon me, whose pieces, of quite different natures, I am obliged to consider, or falsify the trust they repose in me; and my own poem to correct too, besides an affair with Mr. Steele, that takes up much consultation daily . . .[45]

During the next two months the publication of his poem *Windsor Forest,* his active share in the newly founded *Guardian,*[46] and the honor Addison bestowed upon him by asking him to contribute the prologue to his play *Cato* all served to fix his reputation at a very high level.

However, despite this success, or perhaps as the result of the self-confidence it engendered, Pope was restless in his association with the Whig leaders and writers. Politics was probably not a major factor; his Tory friends no doubt continued to protest against his friendship with Steele on political grounds, but their objections had not prevented their association from becoming established on a closer and closer footing. One source of trouble seems to have been the general atmosphere at the chief meeting place of the Whig group, Button's Coffee House, which was perhaps too lavish in its praise of fellow members and too worshipful in its attitude toward Addison to suit Pope's taste. But probably much more important was the lack of an effective outlet for his literary talents. Despite his part in its advance planning, and daily conferences about it, the *Guardian* did not prove a congenial medium for him. When it came down to the actual writing of the papers, he either lacked interest or could not please Steele. Of the first sixty issues he seems to have written only three, and in the whole series there are only eight that can be identified as his with any certainty.[47] It seems likely that after the first enthusiasm for the venture had passed, he realized that the two hundred and seventy-one issues of the *Tatler* and the five hundred and fifty-five issues of the *Spectator* had exhausted most of the good veins of material. And no doubt he came increasingly to realize that the system of anonymous contributions was far from advantageous to an ambitious young man since the good pieces would generally be credited to Steele or Addison while the weak ones would be attributed to the new hands.

Meanwhile, some critical attacks on his poetry had fostered a combative spirit in Pope. When in 1711 John Dennis had fiercely criticized the *Essay on Criticism,* Pope had only with difficulty kept himself from replying.[48] Later he had watched with concern a steady stream of praise for Ambrose

45. E. & C., VI, 182–3.
46. Its first number was issued March 12, 1712/13.
47. Mr. Norman Ault, struck by the scarcity of Pope's contributions, has made an attempt to discover Pope's hand in other *Guardian* papers. As the result of his studies, he has included six additional ones in his edition of the *Prose Works of Alexander Pope* (Oxford, 1936). Even if we accept these on the basis of the somewhat slender internal evidence which Mr. Ault has discovered, Pope's share in writing the essays still seems astonishingly small.
48. Mr. Ault believes that he did in fact make a reply in an obscure little pamphlet, *The Critical Specimen* (1711), pp. xv–xviii. If so, the counterattack fell far short of evening the score.

Philips' pastorals to the neglect of his own. When this puffing reached the point of a series of articles in the *Guardian* that praised Philips' poems to the skies and barely mentioned his own, Pope slipped in his famous ironic paper on the subject,[49] a "bite" which caused much laughter and some hard feelings. He also got a delayed revenge on Dennis by using the critic's ill-advised attack on Addison's *Cato* as an excuse for a harsh satire entitled *The Narrative of Dr. Robert Norris* in which he used the Bickerstaffian device of writing in the name of a well-known custodian of lunatics.[50]

In this frame of mind Pope apparently began to search for a more regular and effective means of carrying on his attacks against those he considered guilty of bad criticism and foolish learning. The answer he found was his project for a *Works of the Unlearned*.

The person on whom Pope could safely try out his idea for a burlesque periodical before advancing it publicly was his friend John Gay. The two had been friends since 1711 and during the season of 1712–13 had apparently seen a good deal of each other. Gay, who was only three years older than Pope and of a most sociable and compliant disposition, had more or less attached himself to the young poet, whose superior genius he was both intelligent and generous enough to recognize. In April, 1712, he had answered Dennis' attack on Pope's *Essay on Criticism* by an ironic dedication of his farce *The Mohocks* to the critic, and the following winter had again given public demonstration of his warm friendship by inscribing to him in flattering terms his poem *Rural Sports*.[51]

Like Pope, Gay had not yet found his directions as a literary man. *Rural Sports* contains some effective descriptions of hunting and fishing, but as a whole was not an impressive piece, and a new play, *The Wife of Bath,* which had the misfortune to follow *Cato* on the stage, was not written with sufficient skill to be successful. During the remainder of the spring of 1713 he contributed several numbers to the *Guardian* and began the composition of an ambitious poem, *The Fan,* but in none of these pieces did he strike the happy vein that characterized his later work. When approached by Pope with the idea of the burlesque journal, he seems to have fallen in readily with the scheme and to have encouraged Pope to push it. His own qualifications for taking part in the project were modest in comparison with those of his later colleagues, but he was well read and, as shown by his pamphlet *The Present State of Wit,* unusually familiar with the periodicals of the time. In addition, he had had through his association with Aaron Hill's pretentious question-and-answer sheet *The British Apollo,* a chance to acquire much dubious learning and to become well acquainted with Grub Street and its denizens.

49. No. 40 for April 27, 1713.
50. This pamphlet was published late in July or early in August, 1713.
51. Published on January 13, 1712/13.

Pope Advances His Plan

Pope's first real opportunity to advance his plan came early in the autumn. On the first day of October Steele abruptly laid down the *Guardian* in order to start the *Englishman,* a frankly partisan paper more in keeping with his current preoccupation with politics. The effect of this change was to free literary London for the first time in many years. Like its predecessor, though to a lesser degree, the *Guardian* had drained London of its best wit; even such Tories as Parnell and Berkeley had contributed to it. With it gone and neither Addison nor Steele bidding for immediate support in another literary venture, a real opportunity for a new project was open. Pope, who was still on friendly terms with Steele and may well have had some advance warning of the change, stepped forward to make his bid.[52]

Since there was nothing political in his plan, Pope no doubt hoped to gather a mixed group of Whigs and Tories. We do not know what exact steps he took, but his account of the Scriblerus Club given to Spence many years later indicates that among those he approached were Congreve and Addison.[53] The choice of Congreve was an obvious one; no literary man of the time was more universally beloved and admired. Obtaining his support was, however, largely a matter of mutual compliment since for several years he had been inactive so far as literary affairs were concerned.[54] The effort to enlist Addison may also have been somewhat nominal if, as biographers have suggested, the irritation which was later manifested by both Addison and Pope had begun to be felt. In any case, a direct offer to Addison of an opportunity to take part was obligatory; Pope had been too closely associated with Addison and Steele to pass them over without giving serious offense. Since there was much to be gained from Addison's aid and little to be lost if he were willing to join the project without taking the dominant role, Pope's attempt to interest him was probably sincere.

Addison was in a most difficult position. Even if he had thought that the right type of satiric journal might win favor and do some good in literary circles, a doubtful supposition in view of his character and tastes, he could not have been blind to some of the weaknesses in Pope's plan from a literary point of view. Nor could he have overlooked the probable results to himself personally and to his position as Whig "press chief" of engaging in

52. Pope had spent the summer in London learning to paint. On September 20, after returning from a week's visit to Binfield with Rowe, he wrote Caryll that he had no new literary projects in hand. E. & C., VI, 195.

53. Spence, p. 8. That Pope tried to interest these men as well as Atterbury at this time seems the most logical interpretation of the garbled version of the facts which Spence recorded; see Appendix III.

54. Swift noted in the *Journal* on October 26, 1710, that Congreve was growing blind with cataracts. One of his last pieces was a *Tatler* paper written for Harrison at Swift's request. *Journ.,* February 13, 1710/11.

a large scale and continuous attack upon inferior authors. And, perhaps most important, he must have been well aware that he would not have the unquestioned leadership to which he was accustomed in a group which Pope had gathered. On the other hand, Pope, who now had a reputation to reckon with, had shown his restlessness; to refuse to join his project might drive him into the arms of the Tories and leave a resentment which he had shown he would not be afraid to display in print. It would surely be much safer to be the ally of a man who was proposing to set up a very effective means of paying off scores on a monthly basis.[55] Addison's solution was a master-piece of tact; he left Pope with the impression that he liked the scheme "very well, and was not disinclined to come in to it." [56]

Pope also approached several Tories. One was Parnell, with whom he probably had become acquainted during the preceding spring while work-ing with Steele on the *Guardian,* to which Parnell had been contributing. In the autumn, not long after Parnell's return from Ireland, Pope got in touch with him to solicit contributions for a miscellany that he was assisting Steele to gather for Jacob Tonson. He used this occasion to present his own project. Parnell was agreeable to both suggestions; "he enters heartily into our design," Pope reported to Gay.[57]

Another Tory in the group listed by Spence was Francis Atterbury, Bishop of Rochester. It is possible that the inclusion of the bishop refers to one of the later periods of Scriblerus activity at a time when Pope and Atterbury were intimate friends, but there seems no reason why Pope should not have approached him in the autumn of 1713. Atterbury was on the surface well suited to the plan. Brilliant, learned, and courageous, he had won a repu-tation in the field of letters as the leader of the Christ Church wits in their war with the famed Richard Bentley over the epistles of Phalaris. Later he had devoted his energy and polemical skill to church affairs and had become one of the recognized leaders of the High Church group. By successive pro-motions he had become Dean of Christ Church, Oxford, and, in the pre-ceding spring at the time of Swift's elevation, Bishop of Rochester and Dean of Westminster. The latter post, which involved supervision over the famous Westminster School as well as the Abbey, kept him readily available in Lon-don during the winter season. Proud of his learning and judgment as a critic, fond of such company as that of Swift, Prior, and Pope, and combative in spirit, he may well have been attracted by the proposed scheme.

55. How carefully Addison was treating Pope at this time is to be seen in his curious way of expressing disapproval of Pope's attack on John Dennis in the *Narrative of Dr. Robert Norris.* Instead of dealing directly either with the author or the victim, he had Steele write to Bernard Lintot, the publisher, that Mr. Addison wholly disapproved of the pamphlet. Such cautious in-direction gave Dennis some satisfaction without providing Pope or the town with anything inflammatory—or quotable.

56. Spence, p. 8; cf. Appendix III.

57. E. & C., VII, 412.

The most important of the Tory prospects, of course, was Swift. How long Pope and he had known each other and on what terms of friendship they were at this time is a matter of some interest which cannot be fully settled. The only reference to Pope in Swift's correspondence before the autumn of 1713 is a single reference in the *Journal to Stella* for March 9, 1712/13. It indicates no personal acquaintance, saying merely, "Mr. Pope has published a fine poem, called Windsor Forest. Read it." On Pope's side the first reference occurs six months later, while Swift was still in Dublin after being installed as Dean of St. Patrick's, and its terms suggest that a friendship had already been established. Writing to Caryll on August 31, 1713, from Jervas' studio in Cleveland Court where he had been studying, he says that he had found his hand "most successful in drawing of friends, and those I most esteem, insomuch that my masterpieces have been one of Dr. Swift, and one of Mr. Betterton." [58] Presumably some time during late April and May when the *Journal* ceased to be a complete account of Swift's activities, they were brought together, perhaps by Parnell, and began their famous friendship.[59]

The response Pope obtained from Swift when he presented his plan was all that he could have hoped. In the same letter to Gay which told of Parnell's acceptance, Pope wrote, "Dr. Swift much approves what I proposed, even to the very title, which I design shall be, The Works of the Unlearned, published monthly . . ." [60]

Swift's Motives in Accepting the Plan

Since Swift's acceptance of Pope's plan was to bring about the Scriblerus Club, we need to consider why he should have received the idea so cordially when he could hardly have been any less aware than Addison of the difficulties it presented. Such satire was, of course, much more congenial to him and, as Pope no doubt reminded him in a flattering way, he had used burlesque and irony of a similar kind with great effectiveness in many pieces. Moreover, Swift would have no fear of stirring up Grub Street against himself since he had no friends there. Such unqualified approval as Pope

58. E. & C., VI, 193.

59. They had some opportunity to increase their acquaintance in the early autumn. Swift reached London on September 9 (*Post Boy,* September 12, 1713; cf. *Corres.,* II, 66, n. 4), but Pope was out of town from about that time until the twentieth. Both were in London for the following week or ten days, during the period from October 5 to 15, and from October 20 until the end of the first week in November. However, if any real intimacy had developed during the first two periods, it seems likely that Pope would have mentioned the fact in his letter to Caryll on October 17, in which he is at some pains to explain his connection with Steele.

60. E. & C., VII, 412. Mr. Sherburn wishes to date this letter October 23, 1712, instead of 1713 (Sherburn, p. 75), but the weight of evidence seems to be in favor of the date usually given for it.

reports, however, indicates a positive enthusiasm beyond a mere willingness to take part in the plan.

One factor in his attitude was the current situation in which he found himself. By October the Oxford ministry, long under tension, had become fatally split. Bolingbroke was now clearly trying to build a strong Tory following for himself, while Oxford, distrusting his lieutenant and a narrow party policy, was playing a mixed game which the extreme Tories feared might lead to a broad-bottomed ministry with the Whigs. In the heat of their personal resentment both men were obviously pushing the ministry toward inevitable destruction.[61] Only a Tory victory in the autumn elections and the indecision of the Queen kept the ministry afloat. Drawn back from Ireland against his will to attempt a reconciliation between his two friends, Swift soon discovered he could do little. Highly aroused emotionally by the dangers he foresaw and without a regular outlet for his energy other than occasional political pieces and poems,[62] "heartily weary of Courts and Ministers, and politics," [63] and lacking a group of congenial friends such as he had had in his old clubs, he had reason to welcome a proposal which would provide some change and relaxation.

Swift's persistent and honorable desire to aid literary men also provided a motive. During the past year he had felt keenly that one of the chief justifications for his course of life was that he should help others. "This I think I am bound to, in honour and conscience, to use all my little credit toward helping forward men of worth in the world," he had written Stella during the spring in connection with the philosopher George Berkeley,[64] and in dealing with Steele he had made much of his efforts to aid Steele and other writers with the ministry.[65] In the past years he had recommended Addison, Congreve, Rowe, and Berkeley, had solicited for Steele, Philips, and Parnell, and had managed some concrete aid for Harrison, King, and Diaper, as well as helping such clergymen authors as Fiddes and Trapp. However, he had not in point of fact actually accomplished much. Pope and his plan provided one more opportunity for being useful to literary men both by direct aid with the project and by getting patronage for the group. Pope especially needed support; young, from modest family circumstances, and ineligible for any public office because of his Catholic faith, he

61. Publicly and to a surprising extent in private contact, however, they remained on cordial terms through all the crises until the following July; hence the ability of Swift and others to remain on close terms with both.

62. He had finished his history of affairs leading up to the Treaty of Utrecht the previous spring before leaving for Ireland (*Journ.*, May 16, 1713) and was still eager to obtain the post of historiographer in order that he might carry on his historical writing officially, but all such work seems to have been at a standstill during the autumn and winter of 1713–14.

63. *Corres.*, ii, 69; cf. pp. 72, 78.

64. *Journ.*, April 12, 1713.

65. *Corres.*, ii, 33–5, 38–9; cf. *Journ.*, December 27, 1712, *Corres.*, iii, 117–18.

was seeking a means of livelihood by translation and had just issued his proposals for an English version of the *Iliad*. Swift did not neglect the chance to be of service. Swearing that "the author shall not begin to print till I have a thousand guineas for him," he vigorously solicited subscriptions for him at court.[66] It was in this cordial atmosphere that he promised to support Pope's other idea.

It is hard not to believe that one of Swift's strongest reasons for not raising at least some objections at the start was the opportunity which Pope's scheme provided of winning over Pope and his follower Gay from their connections with Addison and Steele. If such a rising young poet as Pope were to change his allegiance publicly, the balance of prestige in London literary circles would shift. With these two new recruits added to his friends in a cooperative venture, Swift could feel that the Tories might at last be winning a position in the world of letters in keeping with their status at court and in the country.

Swift's acceptance of Pope's idea marks the beginning of the Scriblerus association. It may be assumed that thereafter active steps were being taken toward the future Scriblerus scheme. Pope and Swift, together with Parnell, were in a position to see much of each other, and they must early have canvassed the possibilities of the proposed burlesque monthly and have discussed possible contributors. Such conversations could not be carried on long without the drawing up of some concrete plans, and we may date the active collaboration of the Scriblerians from this time. However, it seems likely that no great progress was made during these weeks. Pope was planning to return to his home in Binfield within a short time and in the meantime was busy with his Homer subscription and his revisions of the *Rape of the Lock*. The fact that the court was still at Windsor meant that Dr. Arbuthnot, one of the obvious prospects for a collaborator, was not available and that Swift himself would be out of town for several days every fortnight. Nor could Gay take part in "our design" at this time.[67] On the whole, therefore, it seems probable that regular work on the plan was postponed until after Christmas.[68]

66. John Nichols, *Literary Anecdotes of the Eighteenth Century* (1812–16), I, 400 n.

67. Pope's letter to Gay on October 23 indicates that Gay was not expected in town in the near future. E. & C., VII, 413. However, Gay's poem *The Fan* was published on December 8, and presumably he must have come to town some time before that date in order to correct proof.

68. Pope's famous letter to Swift declining to change his religion, which is dated from Binfield on December 8, contains no reference to the project, but this letter has not survived in manuscript form and the version first printed by Lord Orrery has so obviously been revised for literary purposes that no inference may be drawn from Pope's failure to mention the new scheme.

II THE CLUB AND ITS PROGRAM OF SATIRES

The Emergence of the Club

Sometime before the beginning of the London season in February, 1714, the scheme for a *Works of the Unlearned* underwent a drastic change. What Pope had apparently intended to be a loose literary association of the type commonly used for getting out periodicals evolved into a tight little social club with a strong Tory coloring, and the plan for a burlesque monthly publication developed into a complex scheme for satirizing a great variety of follies. We have no record of the exact way in which these changes came about but we can recognize some of the major factors which occasioned them.

The idea of a club may well have been a spontaneous one growing out of the increasing intimacy of the men who were planning satires together, but Swift was such a key figure in the group and the form the club took fitted so well with his known preferences that it seems likely that he was responsible for setting it up. There can be no doubt that from the time of his acceptance of Pope's plan he dominated the situation. His standing as a writer, his influence, and his imperiousness of will made him the natural leader, while his generosity in forwarding the interests of others, his experience in club affairs, and his high humor made the others willingly defer to him.

Some narrowing of Pope's original group was an almost inevitable result of Swift's agreement to take an active part in the plan. Political feeling was much too high, and the Dean much too controversial a figure for Whig writers who wished to remain well with the party to associate with. Pope was soon to learn how difficult it was for anyone connected with Swift to preserve a public neutrality. His increasing intimacy with him soon brought a tactful letter of remonstrance from Addison which expressed a hope—with an implied threat—that Pope would not content himself with the praise of half the nation.[69] Politics was even a factor within the Tory ranks. By January, 1713/14, the split in the ministry had reached such proportions that it would have been difficult to avoid political difficulties if those most openly opposed to Oxford became members. Thus if Atterbury had been asked by Pope to take part in his plan for a burlesque the matter was probably allowed to drop quietly after Swift took over.

Any such limiting of the associates would please Swift. His experience with the Brothers Club had, as we have seen, convinced him that large groups with mixed interests made poor company[70] and probably from the

69. E. & C., VI, 401–02.
70. See above, p. 7.

first he hoped to center the collaboration in a relatively small circle of active literary men. A small group would have greater unity and it could meet frequently without formality or great expense. The latter was a matter of some moment; neither Swift nor Pope, nor their literary friends, had enough money to afford anything but the most modest lodgings. If the group was to meet in private—and the activities they planned could hardly be carried on openly in coffeehouses—it must be small enough to gather in upstairs rooms. And if, as was certain to be the case, there were dinners and "treats," they must be on a modest scale.

In the end the group that was gathered to form the club consisted only of the two leaders and their immediate followers—with one notable exception. Swift no doubt from the start worked to enlist Dr. Arbuthnot, whom Pope probably did not know, while Pope sponsored his friend Gay, with whom Swift appears not to have been personally acquainted. Parnell as the friend of both and one of Pope's first recruits naturally was included. The exception, who was to make the sixth member of this financially modest if spirited group, was the Lord Treasurer of the kingdom.

Oxford's interest in the Scriblerus project is certainly to be traced to Swift. No doubt the Dean began telling him about Pope's scheme soon after it was proposed to him and it seems more than likely that discussions of it were used to help pass away some of the many tedious hours of the coach trip out and back from Windsor which Swift took every fortnight with Oxford in order to keep him company. Politics may have occupied much of the time on some of the early trips, but tact and weariness in covering the same topics over and over would prompt Swift to turn to so pleasant a new topic repeatedly. It is safe to assume in addition that he genuinely wished to interest Oxford in the group. Though Oxford was not himself wealthy he had recently become connected by marriage with some of the richest families in the kingdom and through his hands as Lord Treasurer went an immense amount of patronage. If only he could be persuaded to act, he might easily have found a lucrative sinecure for every needy member of the group.

Oxford Becomes a Member

It would be interesting to know at what stage and under what conditions Oxford became a recognized Scriblerian. Presumably he began as a sort of patron but soon became so familiar with the group and so interested in its schemes that he was made in effect a member. He did not, of course, join on the same footing as the others and never looked upon himself or was regarded by the others as a principal contributor to the satires, but the evidence indicates that he attended many of the meetings and made some effort to contribute toward the humor. That he was a welcome companion even apart from his high position we need not doubt. His extreme simplicity, friendliness, equanimity, and humor,[71] which had long ago won Swift's affection, made him an easy companion, and he had both the learning and the intellectual capacity to appreciate such company. In summing up his character not long afterward Swift said of him: "He had the greatest variety of knowledge that I have any where met; was a perfect master of the learned languages, and well skilled in divinity. He had a prodigious memory, and a most exact judgment." [72] Other observers, notably in later years Bolingbroke and Pope, were less generous in their estimates of Oxford's abilities [73] but Swift, though perhaps partial to him out of friendship and loyalty, was too intimate an acquaintance and too sharp an observer to have been grossly deceived. Nor was Oxford's learning his only qualification; his love of books as shown by his fine library, his wide acquaintance with scholars begun in his early career and kept up by his librarian Humphrey Wanley, and his taste for "mad" writings of various sorts [74] show that he was not out of place among the other Scriblerians. He was, it is true, lacking in literary talent; some of his attempts at verse make very clear that Swift had not uncovered in him any hidden talents such as he had found in Dr. Arbuthnot, but there is no reason for doubting that he was able to bring grist to others' mills.

From the point of view of the historian his activity with the Scriblerus group is of special interest as an indication of the impasse that he had reached in his career. A statesman of the older generation, like Godolphin, the man he dispossessed as first minister, politics were to him largely a matter of personal ambition and power. Detesting parties and without a clear policy, he had sought power largely for its own sake and for the purpose of establishing his family fortune. By the autumn of 1713 he had won almost everything he could hope for; his high office and his earldom represented practically the pinnacle of what he could achieve politically and the marriage of his son and both his daughters into families of very great wealth solved the future of his family, though he himself remained in modest circumstances. Thereafter his chief motivations seem to have been an unwillingness to give up even the shadow of power after its substance had gone and his jealous determination not to give way to his former lieutenant and now hated rival, Bolingbroke.[75] During the days of the club he was steering a doubtful course on a rough sea; it was typical of his remarkable intrepidity that when his

71. In describing his character in 1711 Swift stated that he was of "a very mild and affable disposition" and that "in private company, he is wholly disengaged, and very facetious, like one who has no business at all." *Corres.*, I, 280.

72. *Works*, v, 432; cf. *Corres.*, III, 117.

73. Bolingbroke, *Works* (1753–75), vii, 40 ff.; Spence, pp. 152, 258.

74. Cf. Historical Manuscripts Commission, *Portland MSS*, vii, 36.

75. Before he gave up his staff the following summer there were rumors that he was to receive a dukedom and £4,000 a year (*Corres.*, II, 192) and he may have hoped for some such consolation. He obviously failed to appreciate how his delay and double dealing had cost him credit in every quarter.

political fortunes were at stake he should have spent much time on the Scriblerus scheme with every appearance of pleasure and interest.

The inclusion of so notable a recruit had some important effects on the club. The Lord Treasurer's presence gave the little group a distinction and glamor which the younger members especially must have felt keenly. The project itself required secrecy, and Oxford's participation made caution doubly necessary, so there could be no boasting even in a covert way. However, when Pope, Gay, and Parnell returned, as they occasionally did, to visit their Whig friends at Button's they must have revealed a pride in their new connections that was all the more irritating because not discussed openly. Another effect must have been to make the club more formal, at least on some occasions. The five friends might, and often did, meet most casually but if the Lord Treasurer was to attend, advance arrangements would have to be made and some decorum maintained. Among these arrangements would be plans to entertain their distinguished friend and we may assume that not infrequently the energies of the group were directed as much toward this end as toward their literary goal. Finally Oxford's membership no doubt acted both as an incentive toward setting up a more ambitious project in keeping with the dignity of the club and as a check on hasty or high-spirited publications which might cause embarrassing criticism.

Meetings of the Club

It seems likely that the first active steps to set up the club were taken shortly after the end of the Christmas season when most of the future members became available. Parnell had, so far as we know, stayed in London over the holidays, Pope had returned from Binfield during the first days of January [76] and the approaching season had brought in the Duchess of Monmouth and with her John Gay. Oxford and Swift, though they still had at least two of their coach trips to make before the court moved, were freer. Only Dr. Arbuthnot was absent, held in Windsor by his attendance on the Queen.

Events during the Christmas season had brought changes in the political situation which much affected the environment in which the club began its meetings. During the holidays the Queen had become so dangerously ill that rumors of her death had circulated. In the face of what appeared to be immediate and complete ruin, the ministry and the Tories at court were for a time in the utmost consternation. So great had been the alarm that Oxford and Bolingbroke were persuaded to patch up a truce. The subsequent recovery of the Queen lifted the Tories to the heights. With the min-

76. On January 9 in a letter to Caryll he mentioned that Oxford had already read the revised *Rape of the Lock* which he had brought to London with him. E. & C., vi, 201.

istry seemingly united, the approaching Parliament apparently under control, and the Queen heartily angry at the Whigs for their reported celebrations at her rumored death, the tide seemed now to be running strongly in favor of the Tories. Even those behind the scenes who, like Swift, knew how shaky the fabric was, became temporarily optimistic.[77] Thus the club started its work in a general atmosphere of confidence and high spirits.

Much of the work and the social life of the club seems to have been carried on informally in the lodgings of the members. After the arrival of the court in London, however, the favorite place was probably Arbuthnot's room in St. James's Palace. This was convenient for all, and meetings could be held there while the doctor was on duty as physician to the Queen. Meetings were frequent; the circle was so small and intimate that a quorum of the club was together much of the time and a mere turn of the conversation might produce a Scriblerus session. Even Oxford was a frequent attender; in after years Pope told Spence, no doubt with much exaggeration, that he used to send verses from court to the club almost every day and come and talk with them almost every night.[78]

At regular intervals the club met more formally to dine and "sit upon" their project. The evidence indicates that Saturday was the usual day for these meetings and that Oxford used for Scriblerus the time he had once reserved for the "Saturday club" and later used for cabinet dinners. On several occasions the other members entertained Oxford, but we may assume that the more regular custom was for the Earl to play host to the writers. When they entertained it was the pleasant custom of the latter to summon their distinguished colleague by means of rhymed invitations, several of which have survived. The first, in the handwriting of Swift, is dated from the doctor's chamber and was sent on March 20, 1713/14; it begins,

> The Doctor and Dean, Pope, Parnell and Gay
> In manner submissive most humbly do pray,
> That your Lordship would once let your Cares all alone
> And Climb the dark Stairs to your Friends who have none . . .

Another is signed "by order of ye Club," and for a third each of the writers composed and signed a couplet.[79] Oxford answered these invitations in kind. The surviving examples of his verse are of modest merit, but in reporting to Swift a Scriblerus meeting after he had left town, Dr. Arbuthnot declared, "The Dragon . . . sent us really a most excellent copy of verses. I really believe when he lays down [his office], he will prove a very good poet."[80]

It is to be assumed that the business of the formal meetings was to shape

77. *Works*, v, 451.
78. Spence, p. 152; Appendix III.
79. The text of these invitations is given in Appendix I.
80. *Corres.*, II, 151.

the project as a whole and to pass upon the suggestions and drafts offered by individual members. According to Pope, Gay "often held the pen" for the group,[81] a task for which his youth and his post with the Duchess made him an obvious choice, but it is doubtful if he did more than make fair copies of manuscripts and record suggestions, criticisms, and passing witticisms. The real work must have been done between the meetings, with the task of weaving material together left in the hands of the more experienced writers such as Swift.

Of the success of the social side of the club there can be no question. Few ages could produce an equal company for wit and companionship. Swift, Dr. Arbuthnot, and Pope were conversationalists of the first rank, while Parnell and Gay were both so witty, amiable, fun loving, and appreciative as to be highly prized for their company. All were alike in their devotion to wine, wit, and fellowship, yet there was enough variety among them in temperament and interests to make continued association stimulating and enlarging. All, including the Earl of Oxford, loved the jesting spirit and were fertile in stratagems and *jeux d'esprit*.

Goldsmith in his life of Parnell relates two anecdotes, which he believed to rest on good authority, that illustrate the spirit in which the group met. Before the revised form of the *Rape of the Lock* was completed, Pope was reading it to Swift. Parnell overheard part of it and later from memory translated a section into Latin verse. The next day when Pope was reading the poem to others, Parnell insisted he had stolen the description of the Toilet from an old monkish manuscript, and he then produced the evidence. Not until some time later was Pope freed from the embarrassment which the charge produced.[82] On another occasion, presumably in the spring, the Scriblerians agreed to walk out into the country to the home of Lord Bathurst for dinner and to stay all night. Swift, who liked to walk rapidly, hurried on ahead. Suspecting that he would claim the best bed, Parnell took horse and, arriving first, persuaded their host to send out a servant to warn the Dean that there was smallpox in the house. While the others feasted, Swift was being served a cold supper and preparing to spend the night in a summer house. Eventually, on his promise to reform in the matter of beds, they told him the truth and allowed him to join the company.[83]

Such superb company, however, had its drawbacks from the point of view of accomplishment. Clearly one of the reasons why more progress was not made toward the completion of their scheme during the spring of 1714 was that they met too often and did not have time to prepare materials

81. Spence, p. 8; cf. E. & C., VII, 472.

82. Goldsmith, *The Life of Thomas Parnell, D.D.* (1770), pp. 45–6. This incident is said to be the origin of the Latin translation of the description of the Toilet published among Parnell's poems.

83. *Ibid.*, pp. 35–7.

fully before offering them to their colleagues. Nor was there opportunity to fill out, revise, and polish accepted sketches before new ideas thrust them aside. Hints, sketches, fragments, inspired jests piled up, but the history and ultimate character of the *Memoirs* indicates that much of the hard work was put off.

The Scriblerus Scheme

During the days when the club was being formed Pope's scheme for satire underwent as great a change as did his proposed association of writers, but here the direction was toward expansion rather than contraction. With half a dozen active minds turning up new ideas and opening up fresh subjects for exploitation, the range of satire became more and more enlarged until the horizons were reached and the group found itself embarked on a program not merely of ridiculing the follies of party writers, critics, editors, and commentators but of satirizing all follies among men of learning, whether philosophers or artists, antiquarians or travelers, teachers or poets, lawyers or dancing masters.

Since a monthly burlesque of the now defunct *Works of the Learned* would be an inadequate vehicle for so far-reaching a program, the Scriblerians abandoned this idea and searched for a way of publishing a variety of burlesques and satires. Some framework providing unity, continuity, and narrative interest was obviously necessary and the club members hit upon the idea of creating a fictitious character and publishing in his name. Such a scheme would, of course, only be effective if the Scriblerians, and eventually the public, had a definite sense of the character and identity of the phantom personage, so the club set out to build up their figure and plan his career.

In its final form the Scriblerus scheme involved three broad lines of satire. The principal work of the club was to be a full dress biography of their hero in which they would introduce him to the public and lay the foundation for any future exploits they might devise. In addition, they planned to publish a series of works by their hero either under his own name or under pseudonyms. And finally, as a sort of cream of the jest, they proposed from time to time to claim as his work various publications, discoveries, and projects advanced by others which they wished to ridicule.

The heart to this program was its ostensible solemnity and frequent use of real material. By the double process of putting out apparently serious works by their hero under his own and other names, and at the same time claiming for him things actually done by real people, they planned further to obscure the already dubious line between authentic and spurious publications until the reading public became bewildered.[84] Thus gullible people could be trapped

84. Because custom kept many authors from putting their true names on works and loose copy-

into accepting absurdities, as they had in the case of the Partridge papers and many other pieces by various authors, including the individual Scriblerians themselves, while the critical and wary would learn to scan every new production in the learned and literary world that seemed in any way ridiculous with a skeptical eye, ready to charge it with being another work by the mysterious Scriblerus.

A most valuable aspect of this plan was its great scope and flexibility. There was almost no limit to the range of its satire and, apart from the central biography, the individual Scriblerus pieces could take almost any form of poetry or prose. In fact, since an important part of the effectiveness of the whole scheme was that the club's pieces should not be too easily identified, a premium was put upon the ingenious and unexpected.

The greatest difficulties lay in the biography, on whose humor and power rested the success of the whole project. The most complex problems here lay in the character of their hero. As the protagonist of folly he had, of course, to be a fool; however, to be capable of producing the pieces which they proposed to write for him or claim in his name, he had to be something approaching a universal, if misguided, genius. Again, though he must be a definite person who is identified with real activities, he must remain sufficiently shadowy in outline so that new qualities and unexpected activities could be attributed to him. And in some way a means had to be found of satirizing through him follies of somewhat opposite character without making him seem too fantastic or inconsistent.

The solution of these and other problems the Scriblerians found in the creation of a Don Quixote-like character whom Pope summed up later as "a man of capacity enough; that had dipped into every art and science, but injudiciously in each." [85] The biography of this person they planned to present in the form of his *Memoirs,* which they conceived to have become public in a somewhat mysterious way while their hero was still alive, the possibility of future activities not yet chronicled being thus left open. This figure they provided with two major foils, a father who could represent the follies of the older generation of learned men and a servant who, like Sancho Panza, could represent either naïveté or common sense. Since their hero was to be above all a "scribler," [86] they chose a last name for him by simply latinizing that much used term of contempt, and for a first name to match they selected that of Sir Martin Mar-All, the famous figure in Dryden's comedy whose amiable

---

right practices enabled less reputable authors and publishers to pirate identities as well as texts, the public during the reign of Queen Anne was very often in the dark as to the true authorship of even popular pieces. Coffeehouse gossips were, of course, always ready to "name the pen" as well as to identify the victims of a libel or satire but they were not infrequently duped by deliberately planted rumors; cf. below, pp. 182–3, note 22.

85. Spence, p. 8; Appendix III.
86. Contemporaries spelled the word with either one or two b's.

absurdities had made "Sir Martin" a common name for the comic blunderer.[87]

With their scheme set up the Scriblerians began collecting material of all sorts. Major attention was devoted to the *Memoirs* since it was necessary to get this in print before the whole scheme could be made to work, but apparently very early some individuals and smaller groups began to consider the possibilities for side pieces and a number of these began to develop along with the principal work.

Scriblerian Satire

In part the Scriblerus scheme and its satires were good fun, designed to amuse the writers and the future readers, but the project had a serious purpose which made it seem worthy of the time which the group devoted to it. The tone of their references to the plan, the persistence of their interest in it, and the character of the pieces themselves all show that they expected to produce works not only of literary merit but of significant value to the progress of learning in their day. Bishop Warburton, who had his account of the club and its purposes directly from Pope, in later years gave a simplified account of their program by saying,

They had observed [that] . . . *abuses* [of learning] still kept their ground against all that the ablest and gravest Authors could say to discredit them; they concluded therefore, the force of ridicule was wanting to quicken their disgrace; which was here in its place, when the abuses had been already detected by sober reasoning; and *Truth* in no danger to suffer by the *premature* use of so powerful an instrument.[88]

The nature of these abuses and the reasons why the Scriblerians should have thought them of sufficient importance to have devoted their combined energies to curb and destroy them needs some consideration. Follies are perhaps not uncommon among learned men, but except for a tendency to put a higher value upon the subjects of their interest than laymen think warranted and some other universal characteristics which humorists have exploited from time immemorial, their errors are generally of an individual character and normally of little interest to the public at large. It is, therefore, a very striking

87. Cf. e.g., "Though Silence in a sort may a while pass for Wisdom, yet sooner or later Sir *Martin* peeps through the Disguise to undo all," "*Dr.* Gwither's *Discourse of* Physiognomy," *Phil. Trans.*, xviii (1694), 120. In his edition of the first forty letters to Stella in 1768, Deane Swift suggested in a note to the entry for October 11, 1711, that the name was taken from a jest by Oxford who, according to Swift, had been playfully calling him "Dr. Martin, because martin is a sort of a swallow, and so is a swift." This origin has been generally accepted, but it does not seem likely that the Scriblerians would resort to so feeble a jest or that they would adopt any name which would link Swift with their learned fool.

88. *The Works of Alexander Pope* (1751), vi, 96 n.

fact that six such men, several of whom displayed great genius in producing satires of a particularly timely and effective character, should have agreed to focus their combined energies on the follies of the "learned" in their time, even though the word was used in that time to cover those engaged in literary and artistic as well as scholarly and scientific activities. It is even more surprising in the light of what happened, for the "abuses" which the Scriblerians waged war upon proved indeed to be passing and future generations were to forget they had ever existed.

The answer, of course, lies in the times. The reign of Queen Anne and that of her successor constituted a period of transition from the great ferment of the seventeenth century to the relative stability which characterized the age of Johnson. During the first quarter of the eighteenth century there was a great settling down and sorting out of values. A new outlook was developing and the intellectual world had to be reorganized in accordance with it. The great developments brought about by the intellectual, political, and social revolutions of the preceding half century had to be absorbed; the useless part of the old had to be discarded, the false and dangerous part of the new had to be curbed.

How great the task was can be seen by reminding ourselves of some of the developments within the lifetimes of the Scriblerians. The three eldest members of the group were born less than a decade after the Restoration and began their careers in London in the last years of the 1680's. During the years when their intellectual characters and outlook were being formed there took place a great political revolution which ultimately altered men's concept of government, the church began to change its character as an increasing proportion of its bishoprics were filled with Low Churchmen, new developments in finance and trade began to alter economic thinking, and such progress was made in scholarship and science that a new era is dated from that time.

In general retrospect all these changes seem to have taken place with astonishing rapidity and clarity. But the people of the time, deeply engaged in current problems, had not the power to see the wide significance of what was happening. They did not invite William over to inaugurate a new philosophy of government but to free them from Roman Catholic despotism; they did not welcome the resignation of the nonjurors and the filling of episcopal sees with Latitudinarians as steps toward toleration but as buttresses to the Protestant succession; they did not regard the establishment of a national bank and the encouragement of trade as steps toward a new economy but as a means of raising revenues to defeat the ambitions of Louis.

Only gradually did the more important values become clearly established. In the meantime theory, practice, and prejudice were often strikingly at odds, and apparently conflicting views were often to be found within the same group and even within the individual; not a few High Churchmen loyally supported the Protestant succession without having renounced passive obedience; occasional conformists and dissenters at times voted for stringent test acts; an important wing of the Jacobites planned to require the Pretender to change his religion and sign a bill of rights; while some Whigs were Tories in church affairs and many Tories were Whigs at heart in domestic politics.

Only gradually, too, did the passions aroused by a half century of conflict calm down. Throughout the reigns of William and Anne tempers remained high. Controversies of all sorts were carried on with a virulence which is now difficult to comprehend. High and Low Churchmen attacked each other in print and in the convocations with a violence of language scarcely above billingsgate; tyrannous bills were introduced into Parliament and debated with a violence of temper which no other people but the English could engage in without bloodshed; the London mobs were easily aroused to burn effigies or attack meetinghouses. This height of feeling, which was to be found in one form or another on every hand, is illustrated, as we have seen, in such men as Swift and Steele. Both of these men were notable for the affection they inspired and gave, both sincerely and vigorously decried faction and dispute, neither was inspired by a deep or burning dogma, yet both, and many like them, engaged in controversies with the greatest bitterness. Only by recognizing the heat of feelings on these subjects in his younger days can one reconcile Swift's fierce hatred of Scotchmen, papists, and dissenters with the fact that two of his best friends were a Scot and a papist, and a third, Oxford, brought up a dissenter.

Though less dramatic, developments comparable to those in religion and politics were taking place at the same time in the realm of learning, with similarly complex results. In the last years of the seventeenth century science, philosophy, and scholarship were moving forward with giant steps. Within a few years of the arrival of Arbuthnot and Swift in London, Newton published his *Principia* and Locke his *Essay,* while Halley, Flamsteed, Woodward, Bentley, and many others made notable advances in their several fields. But these men and the little group which surrounded and supported them were pioneers, in advance of their generation and beyond the intellectual vision of some older men whose intellectual outlook antedated almost the whole movement of new ideas that swept over the world of learning in the middle and latter part of the century.

After Newton's death in 1727 Pope wrote for his epitaph the famous lines,

> Nature and Nature's Laws lay hid in Night:
> GOD said, *Let Newton be!* and all was Light.

To the generation that first became acquainted with the *Principia,* however, it had not seemed quite so simple; no rosy dawn suddenly began to glow in the skies when the work issued from the press in 1687. Newton himself so dreaded the acrimonious controversies which he knew it would arouse that only with difficulty was he persuaded to allow it to appear in print. Nor did the other great achievements of the era come like claps of thunder. The greatness of Locke's work was obscured for some time by the arguments it engendered; Bentley's career as a scholar commenced in an atmosphere of controversy in which he was generally believed to have had the worst of matters; the achievements of Hooke, Flamsteed, and many others were at times overshadowed by the ridicule stirred up by some of their activities and theories.

In the meantime, the follies of a former time continued to flourish with apparent health. In the days of Queen Anne there still were learned men who believed that the world had declined since ancient times and that the modern could not hope to equal the wonders created during the youth of mankind; there were still very able scientists who built very elaborate theories concerning natural phenomena on dubious interpretations of Biblical texts; and there were still a not inconsiderable number of people who believed in witchcraft.[89] Men like Richard Steele continued to spend fortunes on such exploded chimeras as the philosopher's stone;[90] such able and informed people as Shaftesbury were known to be superstitious, while a faith in astrology still survived among some educated people after a century and a half of ridicule. The schools and universities were not exempt from the intellectual lag; the philosophy still being taught was Aristotelian logic and metaphysics, though for more than a generation there had been a general recognition that this type of reasoning had become sterile; the small amount of science being taught was Cartesian in character, though some of the men that taught it were themselves Newtonians; and classical learning was heavily burdened by pedantry and antiquarianism.

The continuing follies of the past were, of course, not the only hindrances to contemporary learning. The impetus which produced the great advance in science also gave rise to much that was useless and ridiculous. Natural philosophy was plagued by amateurism and a naïve love of wonders. New systems and theories based upon inadequate evidence and unsound in reasoning were offered in a steady stream, while projectors, proprietors of magic nostrums, and quacks of many sorts imposed upon the public. Though many of these new follies died with the seasons, some persisted with a hardiness which made them a serious nuisance.

Such a situation was a happy one for satire. With the old and the new, the good and the bad, interwoven in bright colors and with informed opinion moving forward at a vigorous pace, satire was a most effective weapon, the more especially because it fitted well with the general mood. Increasingly

89. Mrs. Mary Hicks and her eleven-year-old daughter were hanged for witchcraft on July 17, 1716. The statute punishing witchcraft by death was not repealed until 1736.

90. Newton, Boyle, and Locke had searched for the *arcana magna,* as had other able men of their generation; by Scriblerian times, however, the futility of such searches was generally recognized. Cf. below, p. 182, note 19.

weary of long drawn-out wranglings, but critical and impatient, the educated
men welcomed satire on intellectual folly as the general public relished the
more gentle ridicule of false taste and manners in the *Tatler, Spectator,* and
Guardian.

The audience for learned satire was, of course, relatively limited. It included, however, a much larger proportion of the reading public than was to
be the case even a generation later. The excitement occasioned by the opening
up of new worlds of learning was still widespread and an increasing recognition of the magnitude of the advances made kept public interest high. During
the reign of Queen Anne, Sir Isaac Newton became a national hero of un-
precedented proportions. Few really understood such works as the *Principia*
but the period of the specialist had not arrived and there were as yet no gulfs
between theology, science, literature, and art. Most men of learning were
active along several lines; it was typical rather than exceptional that Newton
should devote much time to theology and chronology as well as physics and
chemistry, that Clarke should be respected as a metaphysician, theologian,
and expounder of science, that Dr. Mead, the most successful doctor of his
day, should be an excellent scholar and antiquarian, and that Dr. Arbuthnot
should hold a respected place in the fields of medicine, science, antiquarian
learning, literature, and music. And those who were not active still might
hope to be judicious and well informed about most current activities of a
humanistic or scientific character. Halifax was president of the Royal Society, the patron of Newton and other learned men, an author and patron
of men of letters, an able economist, an encourager of the arts, and a leading
politician without occasioning any particular wonder at his versatility as such.

Learning was, moreover, still circumscribed geographically. Though work
was being done elsewhere, especially in the universities, London was
very much the center of learned activity and the paths of the men engaged
in it frequently crossed. By visiting four or five coffeehouses one might
meet most of the leading scientists, theologians, and writers of the day—
and hear talk about the others. What was being done at Gresham College
was a topic of conversation in much the same way, if by no means to the
same degree, as the latest activity of the Socinians, or the publication of a
new volume of miscellanies. And in a day such a man as Addison might
converse with or bow to a dozen men with reputation for intellectual achievement.

Under such circumstances satire on the follies of learning such as the
Scriblerians planned would not lack for an appreciative audience, nor if it
were well done would it fail to be salutory in its effect. It would not only
be read but be discussed at length; critics would assay its merits, expounders
would repeat and enlarge upon its jests, coffeehouse commentators would
elucidate its obscure points, gossips would relate the reactions of those

attacked, sober men would discourse upon other follies—and everyone would wonder who next might feel the point of the satirists' pen. If its humor provoked laughter and its strictures were believed to be sound, it might well aid learning by crystallizing and enforcing public opinion. The Scriblerians could not hope to reach so large an audience as the essayists of the time did, but they might reasonably have expected to win applause from a much more serious, discriminating, and influential one.

The Breaking Up of the Club

Though the Scriblerus scheme showed recurring signs of life for more than a decade and a half, the original club was destined to be in existence only a few months. Throughout the latter part of the winter and the early part of the spring the club carried on its activities on a full scale; then as the end of the London season approached members began to leave town. By the middle of June the club was disbanded for the summer, though some activity on the project was continued in preparation for the resumption of work in the autumn. Before that time, however, the death of the Queen dramatically brought an end to the plans of the group by scattering its members.

Scriblerus was, of course, only one of the activities of its members. During the club period the London season was at its height and all the Scriblerians had many social ties and engagements. In addition most were engaged in other affairs than their joint project. Dr. Arbuthnot had his court duties and medical practice; Gay, who was still secretary to the Duchess of Monmouth, was completing and seeing through the press his *Shepherd's Week*,[91] while Pope, having published the revised *Rape of the Lock* on March 4, became progressively more involved in his translation of Homer. After the beginning of Parliament in the middle of February, Oxford was heavily engaged by his treasurership and his management of the House of Lords, while Swift, who was under the additional handicap of being greatly disturbed over the Oxford-Bolingbroke quarrel, soon got himself into serious difficulties by publishing, anonymously, on February 23, a virulent political tract entitled *The Publick Spirit of the Whigs,* in the course of which he harshly attacked the Scottish peers. The matter was promptly taken up in the House of Lords and a reward of £300 was offered for the discovery of the author of the piece. Swift's powerful friends were able to protect him, but for a time he was so frightened that he contemplated flight.

The first real break in the ranks of the club, however, did not occur until the end of April. On the twenty-first of that month Pope set out for Binfield, to get the peace and quiet necessary for the completion of a sample

91. It was published on April 15.

of his translation.[92] He took Parnell with him, but after a comparatively short visit the latter returned to town in the hope of obtaining from Oxford the post of chaplain in an embassy to Hanover which the ministry was planning to send as part of an effort to persuade the future king of its loyalty to the Protestant succession. Pope himself returned about the first of June with a finished version of the first book of the *Iliad,* ready to take part in the club activities again. Just before he arrived, however, the club lost its chief member, Swift. All during the spring as he became increasingly angry and despairing at the actions of both Bolingbroke and Oxford, but especially the latter, Swift had contemplated withdrawing from the scene. Finally on the first of June he left London for a retreat at Upper Letcombe in Berkshire.

After Swift's departure, meetings of the club were held on the first two Saturdays in June. The first of these, on June 5, attended by the Lord Treasurer, was reported to Swift by John Gay in a grateful letter announcing that his powerful friends had obtained for him the post of secretary to the Hanover embassy. Dr. Arbuthnot also told the absent member about it in a letter on the twelfth, which explained that though the embassy was to leave in two days' time, Gay still had not been able to obtain money from Oxford for equipping himself, and Parnell still did not know whether he was going to be appointed chaplain to Lord Clarendon, the head of the mission. Gay eventually got a hundred pounds and went away a happy man, but Parnell was disappointed. Dr. Arbuthnot later reported to Swift that he had continued to solicit both Bolingbroke and Oxford for Parnell and that the Lord Treasurer spoke "mighty affectionately" of him. But, added the doctor, as Swift knew, that was "an ill sign in ecclesiastical preferments." [93]

Scriblerus continued to be a topic of interest to those who remained in town, particularly to Dr. Arbuthnot who, after the departure of Swift, seems to have become the informal leader of the group. In a jesting letter to Swift about the explanations being given around town for his departure, Pope declared,

Dr. Arbuthnot is singular in his opinion, and imagines your only design is to attend at full leisure to the life and adventures of Scriblerus. This, indeed, must be granted of greater importance than all the rest, and I wish I could promise so well of you. The top of my own ambition is to contribute to that great work, and I shall translate Homer by the by.[94]

---

92. Pope suffered from ill-health during this period, as he did so frequently in his life. In a letter to Caryll on February 25 he mentioned an illness which had kept him in his chamber a day or two, and on March 12 he declared, "I hope in a little time to get into the country, for it begins to be necessary to me, my headaches increasing daily." E. & C., VI, 204.

93. *Corres.,* II, 158. Swift replied, "It is as you say, if the Dragon [Oxford] speaks kindly of Parnell, he is gone." P. 162.

94. *Corres.,* II, 155.

The doctor's idea was no doubt a suggestion, conveyed indirectly, that Swift divert his mind from the fear and vexations which the doctor knew were troubling him. A few days later he made a more direct effort, saying, "Pray, remember Martin, who is an innocent fellow and will not disturb your solitude." In order to arouse Swift's interest he sketched out several ideas of his own dealing with medical and scientific topics and noted that "Pope has been collecting high flights of poetry, which are very good; they are to be solemn nonsense." He added, "I do not give you these hints to divert you, but that you may have your thoughts, and work upon them." [95]

Unfortunately for his happiness Swift was not tempted. His retirement was a physical absence rather than mental disengagement. He was receiving news regularly from several sources and was engaged on two pamphlets dealing with the current state of affairs. His reply to Arbuthnot made clear that he was in no mood for Scriblerus; the doctor's hints regarding medicine, he declared, were admirable and he marveled at his having a mind so *dégagé* in a court where there were so many millions of things to vex him. Clearly the doctor was the one to carry on with the project. He himself was "a vexed unsettled vagabond" whose thoughts were turned toward other things he was working on; the most he could do for Scriblerus was to rework and edit.[96]

Despite some prompting from the doctor, Pope and Parnell also set aside the project for the time being. After the departure of Gay, Pope took his friend to Binfield to help work on Homer. From there, about the first of July, the two journeyed to Letcombe to spend several days with Swift. Apparently Swift's lack of enthusiasm for immediate work on Scriblerus infected Pope. On the way to Letcombe he and Parnell had composed some verses in the Scriblerian manner, but after returning home, he declared in a report on the visit to Arbuthnot, written on July 11, that the hot weather, which had been causing him many headaches,[97] was "not a time for us to make others live, when we can hardly live ourselves; so Scriblerus, contrary to other maggots, must lie dead all the summer, and wait till winter shall revive him." This postponement, he believed, would be of no disadvantage to the scheme since "mankind will be playing the fool in all weathers, and affording us materials for that life, which every mortal contributes his quota to. . . ." [98]

Gay's experiences with statecraft during the summer did not do much to forward the fortunes either of Scriblerus or John Gay. In accordance with

95. *Corres.*, II, 158–60.
96. *Corres.*, II, 162–3; cf. below, pp. 57–8.
97. These were very real and troubled him severely; he wrote Caryll on July 25, "I am perpetually afflicted with headaches that very much affect my sight; and indeed since my coming hither I have scarce passed an hour agreeably." E. & C., VI, 215.
98. E. & C., VII, 468–71.

Swift's parting instructions he spent part of his wearisome time on the mission reading books of statecraft and on the basis of these and other contacts with diplomacy he essayed a witty letter on the subject somewhat in the Scriblerian manner, which he addressed "For Dr. Arbuthnot or the Dean of St. Patrick's." The letter, however, though not without its amusing points, is chiefly of interest as indicating that diplomacy was not Gay's forte either as a profession or a source of wit.[99]

In the middle of the summer all plans for the following season were upset by a succession of momentous events. On July 27 Oxford was at last forced to relinquish the lord treasurership. Though he was heartily angry at him for his conduct in office, Swift loyally wrote to renew an offer to accompany him into retirement. Oxford accepted, but his letter had hardly arrived before news came, on the first day of August, that the Queen was dead. For a short time the Tories hoped that the event would not be a complete catastrophe for them; Oxford believed he might be made part of a junto, Bolingbroke kept up his spirits, and there was a general hope that the new king might keep some Tories in power to provide a balance. Swift, knowing how fatally divided the Tories were among themselves, had no hope; he wrote Bolingbroke that if they wanted him he would return to London at the beginning of winter but his letter was deeply pessimistic, and events soon proved his doubts more than justified.

The members of the little club were hard hit by the change in affairs. In the middle of August Swift left for Dublin in order to take the oath of allegiance, but well aware that he was going into a form of exile. Dr. Arbuthnot, among those affected by the failure of the Queen to sign her will, moved to Chelsea, where he had a modest post in the Chelsea Hospital, in itself not too secure. Parnell, too, planned to return to Ireland, and Gay was soon to arrive back from Hanover without his post in the Monmouth household or any immediate prospects. Only Pope, politically neutral and secure in Homer, was relatively unaffected.

In the midst of the "hurry of spirits" which all the events occasioned, the friends exchanged letters of affection and regret in which the resolve to keep Scriblerus alive was expressed. In a joint letter to Arbuthnot with Pope from Binfield, Parnell wrote,

It is a pleasure to us to recollect the satisfaction we enjoyed in your company, when we used to meet the dean and Gay with you; and greatness itself [Oxford] condescended to look in at the door to us. Then it was that the immortal Scriblerus smiled upon our endeavours, who now hangs his head in an obscure corner, pining for his friends that are scattering over the face of the earth. Yet art thou still, if thou art alive O Scriblerus, as deserving of our lucubrations,—*tua sectus orbis nomina ducet,* still shall half the learned world be called after thy name.

99. *Corres.,* II, 218–21.

In his section of the letter Pope added,

I hope the revolutions of state will not affect learning so much as to deprive mankind of the lucubrations of Martin, to the increase of which I will watch all next
winter, and grow pale over the midnight candle. . . . Our friend Gay will still
continue secretary, to Martin at least, [and] though I could be more glad he had
a better master for his profit,—for his glory he can have no better.[100]

The doctor's reply shows how closely he had come to identifying himself
with the project:

This blow has so roused Scriblerus that he has recovered his senses, and thinks and
talks like other men. From being frolicsome and gay he is turned grave and
morose. His lucubrations lie neglected amongst old news-papers, cases, petitions,
and abundance of unanswerable letters. . . . Martin's office is now the second
door on the left hand in Dover street, where he will be glad to see Dr. Parnell,
Mr. Pope, and his old friends, to whom he can still afford a half-pint of claret. It
is with some pleasure that he contemplates the world still busy, and all mankind
at work for him.[101]

There was at least one more meeting of the Scriblerians before the group
dispersed. Sometime in November the members remaining in town gathered
at the house of Charles Ford [102] and began a joint epistle to Swift, which
the doctor forwarded to him in a firm-spirited but melancholy letter. The
time obviously was not propitious for further Scriblerus activity. Parnell, who
had been ill, was about to leave England for the Boeotia he hated almost
as much as Swift did, while poor Gay, advised by his friends to make his
court by a poem addressed to Princess Caroline was, in the doctor's words,
"in such a grovelling condition, as to the affairs of the world, that his Muse
would not stoop to visit him," [103] and only succeeded in producing a poem
by versifying his difficulties in finding inspiration. Even the doctor, observing
the ruin of his friends and finding himself threatened with the loss of his
"little preferment" at the hospital, could not regain his mirth and thought
only to live quietly for a while.

Moreover, the political situation made a continuance of the club inad-
visable for the time being. Though it had in fact been nonpolitical, the group
had been very closely associated with the Tory leadership. Now the Whigs,
completely triumphant, were busy preparing their revenge. Everyone knew
that Oxford and other Tory leaders would be struck at and that even such
men as Swift and Dr. Arbuthnot were not safe. Though there was never

100. E. & C., VII, 471–2.
101. E. & C., VII, 473.
102. Charles Ford, who had been gazetteer, was a close friend of Swift's. The Scriblerians had
apparently seen much of him in the spring since Pope and Parnell asked to be remembered to
him in their letter to Gay from Binfield on May 4.
103. *Corres.*, II, 247.

any question of deserting their friends, Pope and Gay needed to emphasize their Whig connections in order to re-establish their political neutrality; Scriblerus could wait.

It is difficult to assess the accomplishments of the club during the period of its formal existence. So slight is our information about what the Scriblerians were working on and so great were the additions and revisions of later years that we can only surmise in a broad way what was achieved. It is clear that the club devoted itself primarily to the writing of the *Memoirs* and, as will be seen later in the discussion of the composition of that work, it seems probable that a considerable portion of the work, as we now have it, was composed during the year 1714. In addition, one minor Scriblerus piece, *The Origine of Sciences,* a learned little treatise in which Martinus, writing from the "Deserts of Nubia," seeks to prove that modern man derived the arts and sciences from the ancient pygmies, seems to have been substantially completed by Pope, Parnell, and Dr. Arbuthnot.[104] The beginnings of another Scriblerus work, the *Peri Bathous: Of the Art of Sinking in Poetry,* are also to be traced to this period, though the version of the piece that was finally printed was composed many years later.[105]

In addition we may safely assume that many ideas were gathered and drafts begun. No doubt most of these were among the fragments of the *Memoirs* which Pope before his death ordered destroyed, but many of them not directly connected with the central Scriblerus piece were developed as individual or collaborative pieces during the next few years by Pope, Gay, Arbuthnot, and Parnell. As is indicated in the following section, some of these can be identified. No doubt there are many others whose Scriblerian origin has not been noticed and can never be proved, but Pope, as is well known, never threw away a good line—or a good idea.

III THE CONTINUATION OF SCRIBLERUS ACTIVITY

Though the Scriblerus Club as such was never formally revived, the forces it set in motion continued to operate for nearly two more decades. During that time the Scriblerus project was twice revived and the Scriblerus spirit was to inspire many collaborations and individual pieces, from some of the enduring masterpieces of our literature down to trivial *jeux d'esprit.*[106]

104. This was first published in 1732; cf. below, p. 56.
105. See below, pp. 54–5.
106. A detailed account of the very interesting relationships and activities of the Scriblerus group in the remaining years belongs properly with a study of the later Scriblerus pieces. What follows here is a brief summary intended primarily to fill out the history of the *Memoirs.*

Pope and Gay Maintain the Scriblerus Spirit

For a time after the breakup of the club only Pope and Gay continued producing Scriblerian satire. During the winter of 1714-15 these two engaged in a lively war of wit with the members of Addison's "little Senate at Button's,"[107] and each published a piece of Scriblerian character. Pope's was a very clever pamphlet entitled *A Key To The Lock. Or, A Treatise proving, beyond all Contradiction, the dangerous Tendency of a late Poem, entituled, The Rape of the Lock, To Government and Religion. By Esdras Barnivelt, Apoth.,* and Gay's was his famous one-act play, *The What D'ye Call It: A Tragi-Comi-Pastoral Farce,* in which by combining solemn speeches with absurd action he burlesqued various famous tragedies, notably Addison's *Cato.* Had the *Memoirs* been published according to plan, both of these would no doubt have been ascribed to Martinus Scriblerus. Both were entirely within the scope of the general plan and both would have gained in humor by bearing the Scriblerus imprint.

The *Key to the Lock* was first written during the height of the club activity in the preceding year and was probably in its original form a Scriblerus piece in which all the members had a part.[108] After the death of the Queen, Pope had to revise it extensively to fit the much altered political situation, and it thus may have become substantially his own work.[109] There would, of course, have been no point in publishing it under the name of Scriblerus until Martin's identity and character were known; nor could the publication of so topical a piece be delayed to await a problematical revival of the scheme. Hence its appearance on April 25 as by Esdras Barnivelt.[110] Attached to the *Key* were an "Epistle Dedicatory to Mr. Pope" and four commendatory verses, signed by the pen names of Pope's and Gay's adversaries, which probably were written by Arbuthnot and Gay.

Gay's play seems to have stemmed from Pope's collection of high flown

107. For an account of this "war," see Sherburn, pp. 114–48, and Norman Ault, "Pope and Addison," *RES,* XVII (1941), 428–51.

108. In his letter to Pope on September 7, 1714, Dr. Arbuthnot mentions the piece in a Scriblerus connection. Declaring that the Scriblerus papers in his possessions lie neglected among other papers he says, "I wish to God they had been amongst the papers of a noble lord [Bolingbroke] sealed up. Then might Scriblerus have passed for the pretender, and it would have been a most excellent and laborious work for the Flying Post, or some such author, to have allegorised all his adventures into a plot, and found out mysteries somewhat like the Key to the Lock." E. & C., VII, 473. On June 28, 1715, Swift, who had just seen a copy of the printed version, wrote to Pope, "I think you have changed it a good deal, to adapt it to the present times." *Corres.,* II, 287. It is perhaps worth noting that neither uses the word "your" in referring to the piece.

109. The work was republished in the second volume of the 1727 *Miscellanies* and was not identified by Pope as his until 1741. *Prose Works,* II, vi.

110. It seems likely that Pope carried on in the Partridge-Dr. Robert Norris tradition by using the name of a real apothecary, but Barnivelt has not been identified.

verse, an obvious source for which would have been the tragedies of the time. It may be supposed that the other Scriblerians, especially Gay and Parnell, helped Pope with this pleasant search and that Gay was thus led to the idea of the burlesque drama. It is not unlikely that all the Scriblerians had a finger in the play in its early stage.[111] In any case, Pope seems to have had a substantial share in the final version, a fact that even at the time was suspected.[112] The motive for producing it promptly under Gay's name was an obvious and powerful one—Gay needed the money.[113]

An interesting offshoot of the play was the publication about the first of April of *A Complete Key To the last New Farce The What D'ye Call It. To Which is prefix'd a Hypercritical Preface on the Nature of Burlesque, and the Poets Design*.[114] There is reason for thinking that this, too, was largely, if not wholly, the work of Pope and Gay. It is an elaborate piece, longer than the farce itself, in which more than threescore allusions are explained or commented upon. The total effect was very much to enhance the humor and significance of the play. The two Scriblerians did not, of course, admit any part of the authorship of the *Key* since such an admission would have spoiled much of the effect and stirred up a hornet's nest of criticism. On the contrary Gay, in writing to Caryll, treated it as a hostile work, saying that the author "with much judgment and learning calls me a blockhead, and Mr. Pope a knave." [115] Twenty years later Pope declared the piece to be "by Griffin a Player, supervis'd by Mr. Th—— [i.e. Theobald]." [116]

Some contemporaries were skeptical; Tom Burnet in the *Grumbler* for May 2–3, 1715, accused Pope of having written the recently published *Key to the Lock* and added, "The same Arch Wag, a little before this, gave us

111. The tradition of joint authorship survived. The poet Cowper, in a letter written in 1783, said, "What can be prettier than Gay's ballad, or rather Swift's, Arbuthnot's, Pope's, and Gay's, in the *What d'ye Call It?*—' 'Twas when the seas were roaring?' I have been well informed that they all contributed, and that the most celebrated association of clever fellows this country ever saw did not think it beneath them to unite their strength and abilities in the composition of a song." *The Correspondence of William Cowper*, Thomas Wright, ed. (1904), II, 92. Mr. W. H. Irving points out that Cowper's source is not known and justly argues that the credit for the charming piece belongs to Gay. But the fact that Swift had been in Ireland for some months when the play was produced is not, as he suggests, an argument against his having had any part in the play at all. Irving, p. 117. Mr. Sherburn believes that Cowper's source may have been his aunt, Judith Cowper Madan, who was a friend and correspondent of Pope's.

112. See a discussion of the play and its authorship in Irving, pp. 107–17. The play was produced at Drury Lane on February 23.

113. On March 3 Pope wrote to Caryll that Gay would make £100 by it. E. & C., VI, 223. Pope's letter indicates the efforts made to fill the house on Gay's benefit night.

114. It was advertised as "Just published" in the *Evening Post* for April 2. It had not been previously advertised in the *Post* or other papers, though Roberts, the publisher, had advertised other pieces on preceding days. The humor of the piece for the spectators came from the combination of solemn action with absurd speeches. Had the *Key* not appeared only a few of the specific burlesques cited there could have been recognized by playgoers.

115. E. & C., VI, 227. Gay's statement is an exaggeration.

116. In Appendix III of the 1735 edition of the *Dunciad*.

a Compleat Key to his Farce." And one of Pope's nineteenth century biographers, Robert Carruthers, came to the conclusion that Pope's "hand may be seen in it." [117] But more recent Pope and Gay scholars, though admitting doubt, have tended to absolve Pope.[118]

An analysis of the pamphlet seems to support the idea that it was the product of the same hands as the play. It is true, as Gay told Caryll, that some of the references in it to the authors of the play (the plural is used) are not complimentary, but the total effect is distinctly favorable. A basic problem is how all the allusions could have been traced out. A few of the suggested sources are fairly obvious and half a dozen others are so far fetched that anyone might have added them. Something like a score, however, are specific identifications which only a person endowed with an unusual knowledge and patience could have discovered and still another score are so esoteric and slanted in their application that it does not seem possible for a person who did not know what was intended to have discovered the original passages.

Pope's attribution of the work to Griffin and Theobald is hard to take seriously. Why Benjamin Griffin, a glazier's apprentice who only three years before had become an actor and only recently written his first plays, should combine with Lewis Theobald, who was just publishing his *The Cave of Poverty* (it appeared March 24) and otherwise was deeply engaged in a series of translations, should labor so mightily to produce an anonymous sixpenny pamphlet for the purpose of proving what a clever fellow John Gay was is in itself a mystery. How they could have accomplished the task in the available time is just as difficult to understand. The text of the play would not normally have been available to them until it was printed on March 19. Griffin was not an actor in the piece or in the Drury Lane company [119] and it does not seem likely that the prompt copy could have been surreptitiously borrowed while the play was being given almost every night. If Griffin and Theobald had used the printed copy, they would have had only two weeks in which to prepare the key and get it published. Some of this time would, of course, have been needed by the printers, so that the obliging pamphleteers must have pushed their researches vigorously. In the meantime, one wonders what Gay and Pope did with all the material which they had collected for the piece. Would they not have found it lying heavy on their hands while audiences and readers missed many of the fine bits of

---

117. *Life of Alexander Pope* (2d ed., 1857), p. 155.

118. Sherburn, p. 138; Irving, p. 113; cf. R. F. Jones, *Lewis Theobald* (New York, 1919), pp. 16–17. An argument against Pope's having had a hand in it is that he later had the piece bound up with other genuine attacks on him which he wished to keep in justification of his counterattacks in the *Dunciad*. Since the *Key* was well known and its absence from the collection might have been noted by some of his well-informed visitors, its inclusion would seem to be clear proof only that he still did not wish to admit a part in it.

119. He was acting at the time in Rich's company at Lincoln's Inn Fields. *DNB*.

burlesque that had been worked in so cleverly? Knowing the Scriblerians, one suspects that the preparation of the *Key* was not left to chance or outsiders and that even if Griffin was employed to see it through the press, much, if not all, the material for the key came from Scriblerus sources.[120]

The First Revival

In the late summer of 1715 Pope and Arbuthnot made a horseback journey to Oxford and Bath, where they met Gay and other town wits. The occasion seems to have marked the end of the doctor's retirement [121] and thereafter he joined his friends in producing satires. His renewed activity naturally brought about a revival of interest in the old Scriblerus plans. During the early part of the following London season Pope and Gay were apparently too busy with individual works to devote time to the scheme,[122] but later in the spring the three began active collaboration along Scriblerian lines.

On April 20 Pope wrote to his friend Caryll that he had recently been occupied, among other things, with some "new designs with some of my friends for a satirical work [i.e. the *Memoirs*], which I must have formerly mentioned to you." [123] At the time he wrote, Pope himself could not have done much work on the project, for during the preceding weeks he had been employed in moving his family from Binfield to Chiswick.[124] The move, however, by bringing Pope within easy distance of his friends, greatly facilitated collaboration and during the following year the three did a good deal of work together.

The surviving correspondence of the men during this period reveals very little about their joint activities and nothing concerning their "new designs" for the *Memoirs*. We can, however, date the original draft or a major re-

120. If Griffin was not used arrangements may have been handled either by a member of the Drury Lane company or by J. Roberts, the publisher, who later in the month issued the anonymous *Key to the Lock*. Perhaps the biters were bit and some of the reflections in the piece against the authors were slipped in by those who last had the manuscript.

It is perhaps worth noting that something like an apology is offered to the only friend of Pope's and Gay's whose plays are made use of in the *Key*. After one of the many citations from Rowe's *Jane Shore* the *Key* says, "This is reckoned only fair Play, for Wits always are free with their Friends." P. 15.

121. Arbuthnot's brother Robert, a banker at Rouen, had been deeply involved in the Pretender's invasion of Scotland in the spring—a circumstance which must have been a source of grave anxiety to the doctor. In a letter to Swift at the time of the journey, however, he shows that he has regained a calm and optimistic frame of mind. *Corres.*, II, 296–8.

122. On January 26, 1715/16, Gay published his *Trivia* and on March 22 Pope issued the second volume of his translation of the *Iliad*. Sometime in February or March, Gay, Dr. Arbuthnot, and Pope, together with Jervas, "clubbed" a letter to Parnell telling him how much he and Swift were missed. E. & C., VII, 458–61. The absence of any reference to Scriblerus in this letter suggests that the project had not yet been revived.

123. E. & C., VI, 241.

124. *Ibid.*

working of the "Double Mistress" episode from this period and internal evidence suggests that several other chapters were also composed at this time.[125] The *Memoirs* was, however, by no means the sole concern of the collaborators. During the remainder of the year 1716 they produced several non-Scriblerian *jeux d'esprit* [126] and probably at least one minor Scriblerus piece, *Stradling versus Stiles,* a satire on legal jargon and quibbling which Pope later declared he wrote in collaboration with William Fortescue, a lawyer friend of the group.[127]

The friends also turned their hands to drama and during the summer and autumn composed a full-length farce, *Three Hours after Marriage,* which was acted in Drury Lane Theater for seven nights beginning on January 16.[128] Though, for obvious reasons, the play was not, strictly speaking, a part of the Scriblerus project, its connection with the club scheme was both direct and strong. The action of the piece in general follows the well-established patterns of farce at the time, the plot revolving around the efforts of two young bloods to cuckold an antiquarian virtuoso on the very evening of his marriage to a young lady of the town, but the chief character, Dr. Fossile (who was intended to ridicule a favorite Scriblerian butt—Dr. John Woodward), is clearly modeled on Martinus Scriblerus and considerable sections of the dialogue echo Scriblerian satire on learned fools and critics. Though Gay publicly assumed the authorship of the play, which was unfairly ridiculed by contemporary critics, there is ample reason for believing that it was a genuine collaboration in which all the friends had about equal shares.[129]

The joint activities of the three Scriblerians seems to have continued until the summer of 1717. In July of that year the group separated, Gay setting out on an extended visit to France with Pulteney, and Pope beginning his regular round of summer visits. There probably was no attempt to revive the collaboration in the autumn. Gay was still absent and the death of Pope's father in October both depressed the poet's spirits and involved him in a good deal of family business, which, together with his Homer translation, kept him busy for some time.

In the summer of 1718 one of the Irish "exiles" returned for a brief visit.

125. Spence, p. 109.
126. Only one piece, *God's Revenge against Punning,* was later acknowledged (it was republished in the "Third Volume" of the Swift-Pope *Miscellanies* in 1732), but it seems probable that the friends were also responsible for *An Heroi-comical Epistle from a certain Doctor to a certain Gentlewoman, in Defence of the most antient Art of Punning* and *Mr. Joanidion Fielding, His True and Faithful Account of the Strange and miraculous Comet which was Seen by the Mufti of Constantinople.* Cf. Sherburn, pp. 182–3.
127. Spence, p. 109. It seems probable that the burlesque was inspired by the lawsuit in the Double Mistress episode. The friends were in particularly close touch with Fortescue at this time. E. & C., IX, 486, n. 2; cf. VIII, 13, 15.
128. It was published on January 21, 1716/17.
129. Cf. G. W. Sherburn, "The Fortunes and Misfortunes of *Three Hours after Marriage,*" *MP,* XXIV (1926), 91–109.

Parnell had often been urged by his friends to come back to London again, but he had been for several years unable or unwilling to do so. On Pope's urging he had, however, played a part in the recent burst of Scriblerian activity by sending over a translation of the pseudo-Homeric "Battle of the Frogs and Mice" with the "Remarks" of Zoilus and a prefatory life of that critic. The translation had been begun in the club period, partly in connection with the Scriblerus project (the "Remarks" serving as a satire on critics) and partly as an offshoot of Pope's translation. After Parnell's departure his friends —especially Pope, who wished to use the piece as a reply to the critics of his *Iliad*—had repeatedly pleaded with him to complete it and send it over for publication.[130] Eventually he had done so and it had been published on May 16, 1717, somewhat late for Pope's original purpose but in time to provide a useful counterstroke in the "battle" stirred up by *Three Hours after Marriage*.[131]

Parnell's return brought together most of the members of the club and on July 8, in a reminiscent mood, Pope, Parnell, and Gay sent some doggerel verses to Oxford asking him to receive them—to which Oxford replied in kind as he had in the old days.[132] The reunion was brief, however, for later in the month Pope and Gay moved out to Stanton Harcourt, where Pope remained until shortly before Parnell started for Ireland in October. Parnell never reached his destination; on the road he was taken fatally ill and on October 24 he was buried at Chester.

One Scriblerus piece is perhaps to be traced to this summer period. Nearly ten years later Pope published in the second volume of the Swift-Pope *Miscellanies* a piece entitled "Memoirs of P. P. Clerk of This Parish" in which the excessive egotism and gossiping style of memoir writers were amusingly burlesqued. Since the most discussed memoirs of the time were those of Bishop Burnet, the first volume of which had been published in 1724, it was assumed by Pope's enemies that a ridicule of the *History of His Own Time* was intended. Pope denied the accusation, saying that it was "known to divers that these memoirs were written at the seat of the Lord *Harcourt* in *Oxfordshire* before that excellent person (Bish. *Burnet*'s) death, and many years before the appearance of that History of which they are pretended to be an abuse."[133] In 1741, when reprinting the work among the other Scriblerus pieces, he declared that he had been assisted in its composition by Gay.[134] As the only time that Pope and Gay were at Stanton Harcourt for any length of time was in the summer of 1718, these statements seem to fix the date of composition at that time. This date, however, leaves unsolved

130. E. & C., vii, 455, 456, 459, 460.
131. E. & C., vii, 464.
132. See below, pp. 358–9.
133. 1729 quarto *Dunciad*, p. 13 in the second series of page numbers.
134. *Prose Works*, ii (1741), vi.

the conflict between the statement that the piece was written before Burnet's death (he died in 1715) and the charge that it satirizes the style of his still unpublished *History*. This conflict is less real than Pope would have us believe. It was widely known during his lifetime that Burnet was writing his memoirs and a number of people had read parts of the manuscript. Since the burlesque in "Memoirs of P. P." is very broad, it seems perfectly possible that the Scriblerians based their satire upon descriptions of the Bishop's work by those who had seen it. Probably the idea of burlesquing such self-important writers of memoirs as the Bishop went back to the club days and the piece was completed by Pope and Gay in later years under the circumstances Pope relates.

An Interim—in which Gulliver Is Written

After the year 1718 there was a lull of nearly eight years in Scriblerus activity. Pope, Gay, and Arbuthnot continued to spend much time in each other's company, but they seem to have grown weary of satire and only a few pieces connected with the project can be traced to this time. Late in 1722 one or more of the group—probably Arbuthnot and Pope [135]—wrote a clever little pamphlet entitled *Annus Mirabilis: Or, The Wonderful Effects of the approaching Conjunction of the Planets Jupiter, Mars, and Saturn,* in which the prediction is made that when this celestial phenomenon occurs on December 29 men and women will suddenly change their sexes.[136] In anticipation of this event the author, "Abraham Gunter, *Philomath.* A Well-Wisher to the Mathematicks" (who was later identified as Martinus Scriblerus) [137] offers advice to those who find themselves in this predicament. As a sequel to this piece one or more of the Scriblerians—probably Arbuthnot and Gay [138]—wrote a somewhat coarse poem with the title *An Epistle To the most Learned Doctor W—d——d; From A Prude, That was unfortunately Metamorphos'd on Saturday December 29, 1722.*

During this same period a curious incident in connection with the Scriblerus project took place. In February, 1722/23, there was published a small pamphlet with the title *Memoirs Of The Life Of Scriblerus,* said to be "by D. S——t" and to have been "Printed from the Original Copy from *Dublin."* The piece, which is reprinted in an appendix to this volume, is certainly

135. The work was ascribed to Arbuthnot and Pope in the second volume (1742) of the Bathurst-Gilliver *Miscellanies.* At the time of its publication it was believed to be by Pope. Sherburn, p. 272.

136. It was advertised as "This day published" in the *Post Boy* for December 22, 1722.

137. In the "Third Volume" (1732) of the Swift-Pope *Miscellanies.*

138. G. C. Faber is inclined to attribute the poem to Arbuthnot rather than Gay on the grounds of its coarseness and malice toward Woodward (*Poetical Works of John Gay* [1926], pp. xxxi–ii), but neither of these qualities would militate against Gay's authorship. The versification seems too facile and rollicking for Arbuthnot alone.

not by Swift or any other of the Scriblerians and it has almost no connection with the real *Memoirs,* the chief point of similarity in plot between the two being that in both pieces the mother of the hero has a dream before the birth of her son which prognosticates his future greatness as a writer. Neither the style nor the turn of humor in this false *Memoirs* is like that in the true work and most of the satire in the piece is aimed at Swift. It seems likely that it is the result of some accidental leakage about the Scriblerus scheme which a Grub Street writer sought to turn to his advantage.[139] Its publication was probably one of the pricks which inspired Pope to commence about this time a mock-heroic poem of Scriblerian character on the "Progress of Dulness" which would provide a means of revenge against all hostile writers.[140]

On May 21, 1724, the original group suffered a second loss with the death of the Earl of Oxford. Oxford had played no part in Scriblerus affairs since the club days. Throughout the whole of the 1716–17 revival he had been in the Tower under charges of treason and during most of the remaining time he had lived in retirement. His friends had remained faithful to him during his confinement and in 1721 Pope had dedicated his edition of Parnell's poems to him in generous phrases that recalled Scriblerian days. For Parnell, wrote the poet,

> thou oft hast bid the World attend,
> Fond to forget the Statesman in the Friend;
> For *Swift* and him, despis'd the Farce of State,
> The sober Follies of the Wise and Great;
> Dextrous, the craving, fawning Crowd to quit,
> And pleas'd to 'scape from Flattery to Wit.

To Pope's request for permission to use these verses, Oxford had replied, "I look back indeed to those evenings I have usefully and pleasantly spent, with Mr. Pope, Mr. Parnell, Dean Swift, the doctor, &c. I should be glad the world knew you admitted me to your friendship." [141] But all real association with him had ceased and the only close ties remaining were through his son, the second earl, with whom Pope, Gay, and Arbuthnot later became very intimate.

In the meantime other important Scriblerus activity had been taking place across the Irish Sea. When he left for Ireland Swift was aware that his friends expected him to go on with—to use his own phrase—"the important history of Martin." A year later, while the memory of Bolingbroke's flight to France was still fresh and the Whigs were prosecuting Oxford, Prior, and other Tory

139. See below, pp. 374–5.
140. See below, p. 53.
141. E. & C., VIII, 189.

leaders for treason, he excused himself again on the same grounds he had used in the summer of 1714, saying in a letter to Pope, "truly I must be a little easy in my mind before I can think of Scriblerus." [142] We know from a later statement and other evidence that something like three years passed before his peace of mind was established. He then apparently began to consider contributing to the scheme which his friends in England had recently brought back to life. The part of the project on which he started work was the travels of Scriblerus, and the result, by an evolutionary process, was *Gulliver's Travels.*[143] When the work was complete in 1725 Swift began actively to plan a journey to London to see his friends and to make arrangements for its publication.

The reasons for Swift's long delay in visiting England were in large part political. For many years after his return to Ireland he had frankly been afraid of persecution because of his connection with the Oxford ministry.[144] The end of Bolingbroke's very real exile in 1723 proved conclusively that any such danger had by that time passed, but meanwhile Swift had got himself thoroughly embroiled in Irish affairs, particularly with his Drapier's letters, and for some time he did not wish to call any more attention to himself than he could help. The triumph of the Drapier and his cause in 1725, together with Swift's great popularity with the Irish people, both freed him from any threat of prosecution and gave him something of the prestige which he urgently desired before returning to the scene of his onetime greatness. He therefore set out for England early in the spring of 1726.

All his former friends, but chiefly his fellow Scriblerians, hailed his return with delight. The long passage of time since they had last seen him, far from diminishing their affection, had served to increase it. In recent years statements of their esteem for him and desire to see him again had grown steadily stronger, and the knowledge of his approaching visit, bringing his *Travels,* brought forth a vigorous renewal of the old club spirit. On September 14, 1725, Pope, who was still in ignorance of the nature of the great *Travels,* wrote of his pleasure at the prospect of a visit, declaring,

After so many dispersions and so many divisions, two or three of us may yet be gathered together; not to plot, not to contrive silly schemes of ambition, or to vex our own or others' hearts with busy vanities, such as, perhaps, at one time of life or other, take their tour in every man, but to divert ourselves, and the world too if it pleases; or at worst, to laugh at others as innocently and as unhurtfully as at ourselves.[145]

Swift was in no such mild and benevolent mood. In reply he wrote,

142. June 28, 1715; *Corres.,* II, 288.
143. Cf. below, general note to Chap. XVI.
144. Cf., e.g., *Corres.,* III, 175, 180.
145. *Corres.,* III, 269.

I like the scheme of our meeting after distresses and dispersions; but the chief end I propose to myself in all my labours is to vex the world rather than divert it; and if I could compass that design, without hurting my own person or fortune, I would be the most indefatigable writer you have ever seen . . .[146]

The promptness of Swift's answer delighted Pope and on October 15 he wrote again to tell the Dean how much he was loved and how eagerly his friends awaited him, especially Arbuthnot who was just "recovered from the jaws of death, and more pleased with the hope of seeing you again, than of reviewing a world he has long despised every part of, but what is made up of a few men like yourself." [147] Pope had planned to leave a part of his letter for the doctor to fill but Arbuthnot needed more space in which to express his feelings. In a warmly affectionate letter, he said, "I cannot help imagining some of our old club met together like mariners after a storm. For God's sake do not tantalize your friends any more." As for his book he has framed such an idea of it that he is persuaded that there is "no doing any good upon mankind without it" and he will set the type for it himself rather than not have it published. But, he added, "before you put the finishing hand to it, it is really necessary to be acquainted with some new improvements of mankind, that have appeared of late, and are daily appearing." And once again he repeated what was almost a motto of the club: "Mankind has an inexhaustible source of invention in the way of folly and madness." [148]

Swift's Visits to England

Swift arrived in London in the middle of March and took up residence in Bury Street, where he was visited by his many friends.[149] After a few weeks he went to live with Pope at Twickenham, continuing there, except for occasional trips with Pope and Gay, until the first of August when he returned to town for a short stay with Gay at Whitehall before setting out for Ireland on the fifteenth of the month.[150] He was, therefore, during practically the whole of his time in England in the company of one or more of his fellow Scriblerians.[151] On the whole, save for Swift's extreme concern

146. *Corres.*, III, 276.
147. *Corres.*, III, 281.
148. *Corres.*, III, 284.
149. *Corres.*, III, 303 n.
150. *Corres.*, III, 325, 327.
151. He probably saw less of Arbuthnot than the others, since the doctor, in addition to his family and medical responsibilities, must have spent much of his free time with his brother Robert, the banker at Rouen, who was married in London on July 17 to an English lady. *Corres.*, III, 320.

over Stella's health at the end of the summer, the reunion seems to have been a happy one for all concerned.

The period of Swift's visit was one of publication rather than composition for all the former club members. Arbuthnot was completing and seeing through the press his *Tables of Ancient Coins,* on which he had worked intermittently for many years; [152] Gay was putting the finishing touches on the first volume of his *Fables,* out of which he still hoped to win a court sinecure; [153] and Pope was finally ridding himself of the last volumes of his translation of the *Odyssey*.[154] The most important publication problem during the time was, of course, that of *Gulliver's Travels*. Though Swift's work must naturally have been the chief topic of conversation among the friends throughout the summer, word of it, for obvious reasons, was kept closely within the group, and it was not until very shortly before Swift set out for Ireland that secret negotiations with Benjamin Motte were begun.[155] In addition to these individual publications, plans were also made for issuing several volumes of miscellanies in which were to be gathered the previously uncollected pieces of the group.[156] Though not Scriblerian in character, these volumes are significant in connection with the project as publicly marking the close association of the four writers [157] and as a medium of publication for a number of Scriblerus pieces.

It seems certain that during the course of Swift's visit the whole Scriblerus scheme was discussed at length, all the additions to it since Swift had left in 1714 being laid before him and proposals for carrying it on being considered. Swift apparently showed no real interest in reviving the project. As he wrote to Pope later about the *Dunciad,* he had "long observed that twenty miles from London nobody understands hints, initial letters, or town facts and passages, and in a few years not even those who live in London." [158] He must therefore have regarded much of the Scriblerus material, parts of which were now a dozen years old, as being irretrievably outdated. More-

152. It was published early in the following year.

153. After long delays (cf. *Corres.,* III, 341, 352, 368, 382) the volume was finally published the following March.

154. The fourth and fifth volumes appeared together in June, 1726.

155. *Corres.,* III, 328.

156. *Corres.,* III, 349, 358, 372, 380 ff. The first two volumes of these were published the following June, the preface being signed by Swift and Pope, with the date "Twickenham, May 27, 1727." A third volume was added in March, 1728, and a fourth in October, 1732 (cf. below, pp. 55–6.

157. Pope wrote to Swift, on February 18, 1727, "I am prodigiously pleased with this joint volume, in which methinks we look like friends, side by side, serious and merry by turns, conversing interchangeably, and walking down hand in hand to posterity, not in the stiff forms of learned authors, flattering each other, and setting the rest of mankind at nought, but in a free, unimportant, natural, easy manner; diverting others just as we diverted ourselves." *Corres.,* III, 380.

158. July 16, 1728; *Corres.,* IV, 38–9.

over, he could hardly have helped feeling that the publication of the *Memoirs* would interfere with *Gulliver's Travels,* to the detriment of both.

Of one bit of Scribleriana Swift did approve. When in 1725 Pope had mentioned in a letter to Swift that he was working on a verse satire to be called the "Progress of Dulness," Swift had been cool toward the project.[159] During his stay at Twickenham, however, he prevented Pope from throwing the drafts of the poem into the fire and encouraged him to go on with it.[160] Pope did and the poem became his famous *Dunciad.*

In the following spring Swift again returned to London. Once more, after a short visit in town with Gay, he moved out to Pope's home at Twickenham.[161] Though the enormous success of *Gulliver's Travels* made him the literary lion of the day among those who knew him to be its author (a group which included all his friends and the court circles), the visit was a far less happy one for Swift than the one of the preceding year. The death of the King in June prevented, at the last minute, a trip to France to which Swift had been looking forward,[162] and brought about a complex and, for Swift and his friends, a distressing political situation. Later in the summer the combination of a severe attack of vertigo and deafness, the illness of his host, and the irritation of a constant stream of visitors made his stay at Twickenham so unpleasant that he finally moved into more secluded lodgings with a cousin.[163] Only a short time after he had done so news of the approaching death of Stella destroyed the last vestiges of his peace of mind and his pleasure in his English surroundings. On the eighteenth of September he abruptly left for Ireland, leaving a note of farewell to Pope with John Gay.[164]

If Swift's second visit was neither a fruitful nor a happy one for him, it was a very stimulating one for his friends, who were now free to engage in new literary activities. During the time that Swift was in England, Pope finished the first version of the *Dunciad* and Gay composed the *Beggar's Opera.* Both of these pieces have an interesting relationship with Scriblerus. Pope's poem was a direct by-product of the project. As a burlesque epic dedicated to the mock glorification of dullness it clearly derived from the great scheme and it seems not unlikely that it was first sketched out during one of the periods of group activity. It was soon to achieve an even

159. *Corres.,* III, 281–2, 293, 295.
160. 1729 quarto *Dunciad,* p. 87 n.; *Corres.,* IV, 49.
161. *Corres.,* III, 386, n. 2.
162. *Corres.,* III, 393–9, 403–07.
163. *Corres.,* III, 409–10, 415–17.
164. *Corres.,* III, 419 ff. Less than a week before he had felt himself too ill to travel and had written to Worrall to obtain an extension of his license. He requested that this be for six months and declared that if he learned of Stella's death he would, if his health permitted, travel in France in order to forget himself.

closer link with the learned phantom in the variorum edition, where his efforts as editor and commentator figure heavily. The relationship of the *Beggar's Opera* was more indirect. It has been frequently pointed out that the idea for the comic opera came from a suggestion for a Newgate piece which Swift made to Gay in 1716 and seems to have urged on him again during his 1726 visit.[165] The play, as Pope told Spence, was written while Swift and Gay were staying with him at Twickenham and there can be no doubt that, though written by Gay, it profited by his friends' advice and corrections.[166] The enormous success of the play has somewhat obscured its original character. The play was not designed to be a political satire or a vehicle for delightful music, or simply fresh and amusing farce—though it was all those things. It was composed as a burlesque piece in which low characters were to imitate the sentiments and actions of great figures. In this it had a certain resemblance to *The What D'ye Call It*, and like it was probably intended to imitate certain famous speeches and scenes in drama.[167] It thus went back in mechanism as well as spirit to the club year, and if not a brother of those other offspring, *Gulliver's Travels* and the *Dunciad*, is a not very distant cousin.

The Revival of Scriblerus Activity

The activities of the period also included a direct revival of the Scriblerus project. Pope's labors as an editor of Shakespeare, in which he had been helped by Gay [168] and probably also by Arbuthnot, had aroused the interest of the group in textual emendation and criticism. The interest was sharpened into satiric activity by the harsh criticism which Pope's Shakespeare met on publication. Pope's major gun in his counterattack was the *Dunciad,* in which he elevated Lewis Theobald, his chief critic, to the throne as King of the Dunces. As in the old days of the warfare with the Little Senate at Button's, however, he enlisted the aid of his friends. Together with Arbuthnot he revived an old club project for a burlesque of essays on the sublime and a satire on the modern poets in the form of a treatise on the "profound," or—in the words of the title—"the Art of Sinking in Poetry." [169] It seems probable that while he was himself engaged on the *Dunciad,* which he intended to publish in the third volume of the *Miscellanies,* Pope left the revising and developing of the burlesque treatise to Arbuthnot. As the

165. *Corres.,* II, 330; Spence, p. 120.

166. Spence, pp. 110, 120; cf. *Corres.,* III, 427; IV, 20. Arbuthnot, no doubt to his sorrow, had no chance to contribute hints. *Corres.,* IV, 12.

167. We get an indication of this in Swift's letter to Gay after he had seen a printed copy: "I did not understand that the scene of Lockit and Peachum's quarrel was an imitation of one between Brutus and Cassius, till I was told. I wish Macheath, when he was going to be hanged, had imitated Alexander the Great when he was dying." *Corres.,* IV, 20.

168. Gay was paid £35 17s. 6d. for his help. *Gentleman's Magazine,* LVII (1787), 76.

169. *Corres.,* II, 160; see above, pp. 38, 41.

Dunciad developed, however, Pope began to doubt the wisdom of publicly acknowledging its authorship on its first appearance. He therefore decided not to include the piece in the *Miscellanies,* but to print the Scriblerus piece in its place.[170] Hence he put pressure on Arbuthnot to complete it and when the doctor failed to do so took it over himself, thoroughly revising and methodizing it.[171] By the end of December he had finished his work and the piece duly appeared at the end of the "last volume" of the *Miscellanies,* which was published on March 8, 1728.

The *Peri Bathous: Of the Art of Sinking in Poetry* is, next to the *Memoirs,* the most important of the Scriblerus pieces and in reputation it has perhaps exceeded the parent work. The treatise begins with a formal consideration of the nature and "necessity" of the "profound." Having argued that the profound is an art, it proceeds in a series of chapters to analyze its various kinds and figures, giving copious illustrations from the works of contemporary poets. It concludes with a project for the advancement of the profound, directions for making epic poems,[172] dedications, etc., and a chapter on the stage. The work is notable not only for its clever burlesque and satire but for its interesting and illuminating analysis of errors in poetry. Pope himself thought highly of it, saying to Spence, *"The Profound,* though written in so ludicrous a way, may be very well worth reading seriously, as an art of rhetoric." [173] Modern critical opinion has agreed with him and placed the piece high among the satires of the period.[174]

Another Scriblerus piece dealing with criticism is also probably to be traced to this period. This is *Virgilius Restauratus,* a burlesque by Arbuthnot on Bentley's textual methods as exemplified in his recent edition of the fables of Phaedrus (1726).[175] Called in its published form a "Specimen," it was probably originally drafted as a mock proposal for an edition—a type of satire of which Arbuthnot was especially fond. Not completed sufficiently to warrant independent publication, it was included by Pope in his enlarged edition of the *Dunciad.*[176]

The Scriblerian activity of the time also included still further work on the *Memoirs.* The use of Martinus' name on the *Art of Sinking* made it highly desirable that the long delayed work should at last be put before the

170. E. & C., IX, 524–5. It was the original intention to include the *Art of Sinking* in another volume of prose. *Ibid.*

171. *Corres.,* IV, 4; cf. III, 440.

172. Chap. xv, "A Receipt to Make an Epic Poem," was originally written by Pope as a *Guardian* paper (No. 78, for June 10, 1713).

173. Spence, p. 133.

174. It apparently was widely read in France during the eighteenth century. Audra lists a translation by Van Effen, dated 1733, which went through many editions—*Les Traductions françaises de Pope* (Paris, 1931), p. 7.

175. Cf. below, p. 269, note 5.

176. 1729 quarto *Dunciad,* pp. 99–103.

public, and there is evidence that such was the intention of the authors.[177] In a note to the *Art of Sinking* they speak of Martinus' German extraction and refer the reader to "his *Life* and *Memoirs,* which will speedily be published." [178] Internal evidence indicates that three chapters, including the two that bring the work to a conclusion, date from these years.[179] At the same time the drafts of a second book of the *Memoirs* were begun. These drafts, however, were never completed or published.[180]

One more Scriblerus collaboration was begun in the year 1728. Having brought a torrent of abuse on himself and his friends by the *Art of Sinking* and the *Dunciad,* Pope decided to reply to his attackers by preparing an elaborate "critical" edition of the poem attended with *Proeme, Prolegomena, Testimonia Scriptorum, Index Authorum,* and Notes *Variorum,* in which piddling editorship, verbal criticism, and all those who wrote against Mr. Pope would be harshly dealt with. For aid in this project he turned to his fellow Scriblerians, including Swift, to whom he wrote on June 28, 1728, asking for contributions.[181] Pope said nothing to Swift about making Martinus Scriblerus the editor and other friends besides the Scriblerians made contributions, so that it is probable that the decision to attribute the edition to him was not made until later. In any case, when the *Dunciad Variorum* was finally printed in March of 1729, after having been in the press since the preceding summer, the name of Scriblerus bulked large in it.

Four more milestones mark the concluding stages of the long history of the Scriblerus project. On October 2, 1732, a fourth volume of *Miscellanies* was issued by Pope in which the *Origine of Sciences* was published for the first time and *Annus Mirabilis* identified as by Martinus. Two months later, on December 4, the little group of intimate friends was broken by the death of John Gay. Swift learned the news in a joint letter from Dr. Arbuthnot and Pope, which, "foreboding some misfortune," he laid aside unopened for several days. In his letter Pope prophesied sadly, "I shall never see you again now, I believe." On February 27, 1735, death, by ending the career of the beloved doctor, eliminated the possibility of further collaboration. Thus, more than twenty-one years after its founding but with its principal piece still unpublished, came to an end a literary group which if it did not, as its founders hoped, drive the world before it left imperishable monuments of its friendship and its wit. Six more years were to elapse before the *Memoirs* finally appeared in print.

177. It was apparently at this time that Pope told Spence about the club and its project; cf. below, p. 363.
178. *Miscellanies,* "The Last Volume" (1728), p. [5].
179. See below, p. 61.
180. See below, p. 62.
181. *Corres.,* IV, 35–6.

THE AUTHORSHIP, COMPOSITION, AND PUBLICATION
OF THE *MEMOIRS*

Though no doubt ideas were stored up between times, the actual composition of the *Memoirs* seems to have taken place during the three periods of Scriblerus activity: the club year in 1714, the Pope-Arbuthnot-Gay revival in 1716–18, and the second revival during and following Swift's visits in 1726 and 1727. To the first period obviously belong the general plan of the piece and the opening chapters which get the work under way. This preliminary material probably includes the Introduction and the block of chapters from one to seven which tell of Martinus' birth and education. The fact that the Freethinkers' letter to Martinus is dated "May 7," a time when we know the Scriblerians were active in 1714, together with the fact that agitation against the Freethinkers was at its height in this year, strongly suggests that the twelfth chapter was also written at this time, though the first part of the chapter dealing with the seat of the soul was probably added afterward.[182] To the same period, in addition, presumably belong the tenth chapter dealing with the diseases of the mind,[183] considerable parts of the list of Martinus' activities contained in the seventeenth chapter,[184] the unpublished episode of the music master,[185] and a number of "hints" and sketches for carrying on the *Memoirs* which Pope ordered burned.[186]

In estimating the parts played by the individual Scriblerians in working on their piece during this first period we encounter the usual difficulties involved in dividing credit among collaborators, in this case made worse by the absence of any concrete information. Fortunately, however, we have a very sharp analysis of the capacities of the members written by Swift while he was at Letcombe. In answer to Dr. Arbuthnot's suggestion that he spend some of his time on the project, Swift declared,

To talk of Martin in any hands but yours, is a folly. You every day give better hints than all of us together could do in a twelvemonth; and to say the truth, Pope who first thought of the hint has no genius at all to it, in my mind. Gay is too young; Parnell has some ideas of it, but is idle; I could put together, and lard, and strike out well enough, but all that relates to the sciences must be from you.[187]

182. In a letter to Swift on June 26, 1714, Arbuthnot sketched out an idea for ridiculing the theories of some German physicians regarding the soul. *Corres.*, II, 160–1; below, p. 361. Since his plan does not at all resemble the Scriblerians' treatment of the soul in the first part of Chapter XII, the latter would seem to have been devised at a later period.

183. It seems reasonable to suppose that this chapter was among Arbuthnot's first efforts to satirize the follies of his own field of medicine.

184. See below, p. 323.

185. See below, p. 62.

186. See below, pp. 61–2.

187. *Corres.*, II, 162–3.

This judgment, coming from such a source and matching as it does other evidence concerning the talents of the people involved, carries with it great weight, but it needs some interpretation. Swift, as we have seen, was at the time in no mood to work upon the satire and was, in effect, urging his friend to take over the project. He naturally therefore stressed the points that would serve that end.

That Swift's role in the planning and even the writing of the *Memoirs* is far greater than he suggests by his offer to do editing is a safe guess. Probably, in fact, he was chiefly responsible for changing Pope's plan into the Scriblerus scheme and for setting up the basic style of humor in the *Memoirs,* which has several significant points in common with some of Swift's earlier burlesques. Undoubtedly he began to lose interest in the club in the course of the spring as his personal situation in relation to the political leaders became more and more unendurable, and it is plain that he had ceased to contribute to the project some time before he left for Letcombe. It is, however, most unlikely that he failed to take an active and constructive part in the scheme during the early days when it was being got under way, and his name therefore belongs high on the list of contributors to the original piece.

That Dr. Arbuthnot was always the most fertile in ideas we might well have guessed without the benefit of Swift's statement. His preeminence in this regard is indicated by the hints he sent to Swift in the course of the summer and is supported by his reputation for wit throughout his life. The fragmentary character of the ideas he offered, however, together with the fact that most of them were never incorporated into the *Memoirs,* indicates what the remainder of his literary career bears out, that his ability to produce suggestions is not to be confused with actual authorship. The task of building his clever suggestions into completed sections of the *Memoirs* fell largely upon others, and in crediting the doctor with certain parts of the work we should not fail to recognize the share that others had in them also.

Swift's opinion that Parnell had "some ideas of it" but was lazy suggests that the latter had been delegated to work out either his own or others' ideas more fully into draft form but had been slow in doing so. That the others expected something considerable of him is indicated by Pope's statement in their joint letter to Dr. Arbuthnot in September that Parnell is "conscious to himself how much the memory of that learned phantom which is to be immortal, is neglected by him at present." [188] Perhaps, since no one else seems to have had the responsibility at this stage, he was supposed to pull the collected materials together into a coherent form.[189] This job might originally have been assigned to Gay, but he was absent and Swift's com-

188. E. & C., VII, 472.

189. It may, however, be that the work Parnell was neglecting was his translation of Homer's "Battle of the Frogs and Mice," above, p. 47.

ment that he is too young makes clear that he was not playing a major role. Gay obviously had many opportunities to contribute in small ways, however, and no doubt he did so. Oxford, too, could hardly have been present at many sessions without expressing judgments and making suggestions, so that we may assume him to have had at least some share in the humor.[190]

The collaborator whose role during this period is most difficult to assess is Pope. Swift's harsh judgment that though he had originated the project, he had "no genius at all for it," shows that Pope was at odds with the others in his conception of the humor and style of it. This difficulty is, perhaps, to be traced chiefly to differences in temperament and literary training. Pope's great satires lay years ahead and they were to be in style and humor very unlike the type of thing Swift and Arbuthnot had been doing before the Scriblerus period. But one might make a shrewd guess that a not inconsiderable factor in the situation was that Pope was still under the influence of his original plan and, perhaps unconsciously, found it difficult to adapt himself to the radical revisions in it. It is also to be noted that Swift's opinion follows established lines of friendship and age, the two older men having their conception of the humor involved and, we may assume by inference, the younger friends theirs, with Parnell in the middle ground. The crux of the difficulty probably lay in the narrative elements in the satire. The Scriblerus scheme called for a Cervantes-like story, filled with humorous episodes, which to be effective would need broad touches of characterization and realistic detail. Pope's plan called for straight burlesque, for which his neat, brisk, and sharp style of humor was better fitted. Though he had experimented with humorous narrative in his Dr. Norris pamphlet, Pope never did learn to handle this type of writing and his efforts to do so for Scriblerus may not have been in a happy vein.

Pope's limitations are of critical significance for the *Memoirs* and the whole Scriblerus project because, as has been indicated, he became the leader of the project after Swift's departure and all that the club had done or was to do underwent extensive revision at his hands. Hence, though he may have contributed relatively little to the first drafts of the sections completed in 1714 he properly listed himself as one of their principal authors in their present form.

Not much can be done in the way of dividing the authorship of chapters among the Scriblerians according to special interests or knowledge. All the Scriblerians were very well educated and widely informed; hence, with the exception of the parts dealing with science,[191] which are probably to be credited principally to the doctor, most of the *Memoirs* might have been

190. Oxford's library, particularly his collection of "mad" books, no doubt was very useful to the Scriblerians.
191. Notably the passages on diet in Chapter IV, on Martin's cure for the diseases of the mind in Chapter X, and on his activities as a natural philosopher in Chapter XVII.

written by any one or any combination of the Scriblerians. The fact that
Pope, Gay, and Oxford had not had much formal training in philosophy and
that Swift detested metaphysical thinking of all sorts so much that he probably would not engage in it even for the purposes of burlesque seems to limit
the major authorship of chapter seven (on logic and metaphysics) and chapter twelve (on the Freethinkers) to Arbuthnot and Parnell, with heavy odds
on the former. But beyond this we are in the realm of doubtful speculation.
Dr. Arbuthnot's family of growing children and his lifelong interest in music
may lead us to suspect that he was chiefly responsible for the fourth, fifth,
and sixth chapters, which deal with education, playthings, and music. There
is, however, no solid reason for supposing that any one of the others might
not have had an equal or a principal share in the composition of any of
these chapters.

Among the "new designs" for the *Memoirs* which Pope mentioned in his
letter to Caryll on May 17, 1716 [192] we can identify only one with any confidence. The discovery of a fragment of the Double Mistress episode among
manuscripts that can be dated in 1717 [193] provides evidence that the Scriblerians were at work on these chapters at that time. We may assume, however,
from Pope's use of the plural and from the fact that the first revival of Scriblerus activity lasted at least a year, that still other parts were added to the
Memoirs at this time. Various bits of evidence give us some key as to which
these were. The Scriblerians' great interest in punning during the year
1716,[194] together with the fact that in writing the Double Mistress episode they
had turned to narrative, suggests that the original chapters eight and nine
which tell of Crambe's mishap with a corpse and of his punning defense of
himself before the magistrate and his master Martinus were either written
or extensively revised during this period.[195] And the noticeably different
style of chapter eleven (on the young nobleman at court), the extensive use
in it of Ovid (in whom Pope and Gay were interested in 1716),[196] and
the fact that the two young men had in the years 1715 and 1716 spent much
time in court circles all argue that this chapter, too, was worked on at this
time. Since the revival of the project would seem to imply that the col-

192. E. & C., vi, 241; cf. above, p. 45.
193. See below, Appendix iv.
194. See above, p. 46 n.
195. The dating of these chapters in this period is supported by a reference in the original
Chapter ix to "this 24th of June." On that date in 1714 the Scriblerians had already separated.
They were, however, together at that time in 1716. Another bit of evidence is perhaps to be
found in the fact that in the same text is found the question, "What divides good Christians but
the words Transubstantiation, Consubstantiation, and Nonsubstantiation." While not squeamish,
neither of the two churchmen, Swift and Parnell, would have been likely to have taken responsibility for this ultraliberal view and Pope himself (probably on the advice of another clergyman, Warburton) later eliminated it. Cf. general note to Chapter viii.
196. Both contributed to Garth's *Ovid*, which was published in 1717.

laborators intended to complete the *Memoirs* sufficiently for publication, it seems probable that in addition to writing new chapters for the work they completed and revised what had already been done, no doubt adding new touches here and there.

The problem of authorship during this first revival period is much less difficult than during the club year. The group was now limited to three— Pope, Gay, and Arbuthnot. Of these Gay was almost certainly the least active in enlarging the *Memoirs*. Though affable and always willing to join in with the others, he never throughout his life displayed much interest in prose satire of the Scriblerian type. During the year 1716 he very probably devoted most of his literary energy to his part in the collaboration on *Three Hours after Marriage* and to his own poems. Between Pope and Arbuthnot there seems to have been something like a regular division of labor—Arbuthnot sketching out ideas and Pope completing them into finished pieces. Evidence of the way in which they worked is provided by the Double Mistress fragment, which is in Arbuthnot's handwriting with heavy corrections in the hand of Pope. The possible exception to this arrangement among the pieces which can be tentatively identified as belonging to this period is the chapter on the young nobleman at court. This does not seem to be in Arbuthnot's characteristic vein of humor and its *Spectator-Guardian* style suggests the authorship of Pope.

The additions made to the *Memoirs* during the second revival of the project between 1726 and 1729 were both brief and comparatively weak. They include the very short chapter nine on Martinus as a critic, the sixteenth chapter in which Martinus' travels are identified as those of Gulliver, and the last part of chapter seventeen in which Martinus' activities in music, the fine arts, and political writing are listed.[197] It is obvious that all of these were prepared hastily and that the chief effort at the time was to get the *Memoirs* into shape for publication. The weaknesses of these chapters are probably to be traced to Pope. The ideas in them, which are no doubt chiefly Arbuthnot's, are sufficiently numerous and good, but they have not been developed so fully and richly as they deserved. The truth of the matter probably was that while Arbuthnot was still overflowing with ideas, Pope had lost interest in the *Memoirs*. Swift's lack of enthusiasm for the old project would be likely to dampen his own, and in any case all Pope's energies at the time were being devoted to the *Dunciad*. Whatever work he did on the *Memoirs,* therefore, he probably did chiefly to oblige the doctor.

Shortly before Pope's death Spence recorded the fact that among the papers Pope ordered to be burnt were "the pieces for carrying on the Memoirs of Scriblerus" [198] and in his memorandum book for 1755 he quotes Warburton,

197. See the general notes to these chapters.
198. Spence, p. 219; Appendix III.

Pope's literary executor, as saying that these pieces had been destroyed.[199] It is most unfortunate that not even a description of these additional parts of the *Memoirs* has survived, as even the briefest statement of their contents would throw much light on the whole project and perhaps give us a key to some of Pope's editorial policies with regard to the *Memoirs*.

We are, however, not entirely without evidence as to the nature of these papers. In giving an account of the club to Spence some time in the years 1728 to 1731 Pope said, "It was Anthony Henley who wrote 'the life of his music master Tom Durfey;' a chapter by way of episode," [200] and Warburton later mentioned this episode as part of the Scriblerus papers that had been destroyed.[201] Since the only Anthony Henley to whom it seems at all possible Pope could be referring died some two years before the club was founded, this episode must be regarded as something of a mystery. It was possibly an independent burlesque piece by Henley which fitted well enough into the Scriblerians' scheme for them to have thought of including it in the *Memoirs*.[202] A passing reference in the text suggests that another episode among the destroyed papers may have dealt with Martinus' military exploits. There is no other direct evidence to support the theory that such an episode was drafted but in the light of the Scriblerians' attitude toward war it seems not unlikely that they attempted some satire on the subject in connection with the Scriblerus project.[203] Still another key to the nature of the additional materials is provided by the very interesting advertisement appended to one of the early editions. This promises the speedy publication of a second volume in which his travels, i.e. *Gulliver's Travels,* is "Vindicated to their True Author" and a third book which contains his journey to the Court of Ethiopia and to China. Intermixed with these travels, says the advertisement, will be extracts from the journal of an Eastern prince who has been traveling through all the courts of Europe. Though we cannot be sure that this advertisement is anything more than a final jest to round out the book, its description of the third book is so definite and plausible that it is easy to believe that we are here being given a hint concerning a real project and that these travels constituted the bulk of the papers Pope ordered destroyed.[204]

Something of the character of Pope's editorial labors on the *Memoirs* can be gathered from the piece itself. The *Memoirs* was by its nature and by the circumstances of its composition very much of a patchwork. As such it might very well be expected to display very considerable differences of tempo, style, and quality. That on the whole it does not, but maintains throughout a

199. Spence, p. 279; below, Appendix III.
200. Spence, p. 8; below, Appendix III.
201. Spence, p. 279; below, Appendix III.
202. Cf. below, Appendix III.
203. See below, pp. 195–6.
204. See text, p. 172, and notes, p. 349.

high quality and reasonably uniform style, must be attributed to his efforts. The high quality could only have been achieved by the vigorous use of scissors. These, as he amply demonstrated in suppressing a large part of Parnell's poetical work, Pope knew how to apply heroically on occasion and we can be quite sure that what we now have of the *Memoirs* is only a fraction of the materials piled up for it.

Apparently the first serious effort to prepare the *Memoirs* for publication was made not long after Swift's second visit to England. Probably the hope was to get the piece before the public while the *Art of Sinking* was still fresh and before the appearance of the *Dunciad Variorum,* in which Martinus was to figure prominently as an editor. The plan was apparently defeated by the same difficulties that had beset the project before—a plethora of ideas on the part of the doctor and an unwillingness on his or anyone else's part to devote the large amount of time needed to develop them into a full and effective text. Pope was more determined about his own work; material for the *Dunciad Variorum* was gathered from the doctor and others in a vigorous way, and the completed work was published without waiting for the *Memoirs* to appear, just as the *Art of Sinking* had been.

Having missed its big chance for an opportune publication, the *Memoirs* was allowed to lie over quietly until after the death of the doctor in February, 1735, when apparently all of the Scriblerus papers came into Pope's hands. At that time he told Spence, "I have so much of the materials for the Memoirs of Scriblerus ready, that I could complete the first part in three or four days." [205] Several considerations may have kept him from doing so and getting at least part of the aging manuscript into print. He may have wished to build up the piece by completing the second book and he also may have felt that the time had come when the *Memoirs,* if it was to appear as living satire, would need annotations of the kind that had been so lavishly used in the *Dunciad Variorum.* Still busy with his great satires, Pope no doubt was unwilling to devote the necessary energy to such work. Moreover, he may well have believed that the time was not propitious for introducing the public to the *Memoirs.* Scriblerus had stirred up a host of adversaries through the *Art of Sinking* and the *Dunciad Variorum,* and these enemies were certain to attack hotly the long-awaited central piece of the Scriblerus project. Pope must have wondered if the *Memoirs* could have stood up under a deluge of malicious criticism. In its day the *Memoirs* would have needed no defense and only the foolhardy would have run the risk of taunting its witty authors. But Pope was now alone, and every year in the long delay in publication, in addition to dulling the humor and satiric force of the work, had given it a more and more formidable reputation to live up to. The literary circles of London in 1735 knew in advance that the *Memoirs* was a grandiose attempt to ridicule false

205. Spence, p. 133; Appendix III.

taste in many branches of learning and that it had been worked on intermittently for a decade and a half by several of the ablest writers of the day. Against such a magnificent background the slender little volume of the *Memoirs* might have been made to seem inadequate in the minds of those who would not trouble to understand its recondite wit. Whatever his reasons, Pope decided to put off the publication of the piece until it could be issued simply as an interesting relic of earlier times.

Eventually Pope concluded that the most appropriate occasion for the appearance of this by-product of an already celebrated group of friendships would be in connection with the publication of his correspondence with Swift.[206] Despite the efforts of many able scholars, all the intricacies of Pope's diplomacy in getting these letters in print have still not been entirely unraveled. We now know, however, that he carried on a most delicate and complex intrigue for half a dozen years to make certain that the letters appeared under his editorship. It is not certain at what point Pope determined to link the *Memoirs* with this correspondence. That it was being deliberately held back for some purpose is clear from a letter of William Warburton's written in 1740. On May 15 of that year he informed a friend that he had just returned from a week's visit at Twickenham, in the course of which he and Pope had read the *Memoirs* together. "The first Vol. in a little 8vo or 4," he wrote, "will be published in about a Year I believe; in which the History is conducted to the Times that *Scriblerus* sets up his Resolution to go to Travel." [207] In the following autumn Pope made his motives more clear to his future editor; on October 29 he wrote to him, *"Scriblerus* will or will not be published, according to the event of some other papers coming, or not coming out, which it will be my utmost endeavour to hinder." [208]

Pope finally succeeded in his real purpose with regard to the Swift letters and on April 16 in the year 1741 they were printed in a volume entitled *The Works of Mr. Alexander Pope, in Prose. Vol. II.* In the second half of this volume, with a new set of page numbers, appeared the *Memoirs Of the Extraordinary Life, Works, and Discoveries of Martinus Scriblerus.* Fol-

206. Pope passed over a somewhat similar opportunity in 1737 when he published the first volume of his Letters. He gave this volume the general title of *The Prose Works of Alexander Pope,* and we know from a letter to Ralph Allen, dated May 14, 1737 (Egerton 1947, f. 17), that he hoped to include in it, under the title of "Tracts," his prose pieces and all that he had written "in conjunction with any others"—i.e. the previously published Scriblerus pieces. Since he did not own the copyright to this material, he tried to arrange simultaneous and matching editions of the Letters and Tracts so that they might be bound together under the general title, but this plan failed. Despite his statement to Allen that the addition of the Tracts to the 1737 volume would make the edition complete "with Every Fragment, If I may so say, of my writing," it does not appear that he had the *Memoirs* in mind or contemplated publishing it at that time.

207. A manuscript letter to Robert Taylor, in the possession of Professor R. H. Griffith of the University of Texas.

208. E. & C., IX, 212.

lowing this, under the half title of "Tracts of Martinus Scriblerus and other Miscellaneous Pieces," came most of the previously published Scriblerian satires.[209] Later in the same year the *Memoirs* was published in Dublin as a separate little volume by George Faulkner and in the following two years it was issued by Pope, together with the fourth book of the *Dunciad*, as part of an octavo edition of his works. In all these editions the work was identified as by Pope and Dr. Arbuthnot.

After the *Memoirs* had been published in 1741 Pope still continued to plan the publication of more Scriblerus material. On August 29 of that year he wrote to the publisher Bathurst, "I shall print some things more of Scriblerus, and add to what is already done; but it will be in 4to, and the new part of the vol. be above two-thirds of the old. I don't care to alienate the property, but if you have any mind to treat for the impression I will give you the refusal." [210] Nothing, however, ever came of his plans.[211]

Having first been printed among the works of Alexander Pope, the *Memoirs* continued to be published there, first as the result of copyright and later in accordance with tradition. As has been pointed out, the association has proved a serious handicap to the piece. Buried among the comparatively unimportant prose writings of a distinguished poet, it has tended to come chiefly to the attention of those whose interest was already pledged in other directions, not only among the readers but among the editors. Pope's poetical works lent themselves to, and indeed required, extensive annotation. This work has naturally absorbed the major attention of successive editors. What energy was left was apt to be devoted to Pope's correspondence, which from the poet's own days has been in a chaotic state. Under such circumstances a stepchild such as the *Memoirs* was not likely to, and certainly did not, receive adequate attention.

The first edition of the *Memoirs* after Pope's death, that of Bishop William Warburton in his edition of Pope's works published in 1751, was a disastrous one from the point of view of the reputation of the piece. Seeking only to annotate the *Memoirs* sufficiently to make good his claim to the copyright

209. The pieces not included are *Annus Mirabilis, Stradling versus Stiles,* and the notes and prolegomena to the *Dunciad*. Perhaps the first two were not included because of copyright difficulties.

210. E. & C., IX, 532.

211. The missing travels of Martinus were, however, provided a decade later by Richard Owen Cambridge in *The Scribleriad*. In this long burlesque poem, written in heroic couplets, Cambridge recounts various adventures of the great Scriblerus in search of the petrified city in Africa and on other trips. The poem ends with Martinus' discovery of the philosopher's stone and his beatification by the alchemists at Münster. The poet recognized the need for annotation and the handsome edition of the work, which was published by Dodsley in six parts between January 26 and April 24, 1751, contained many explanatory notes. Though not without some interest and merit in its own right, the burlesque added nothing to the Scriblerus scheme. Cambridge lacked both the wit and the knowledge to carry on the biography of Martinus on the original level and he makes of the Scriblerian's hero merely a fabulous eccentric.

on it under the terms of Pope's will, Warburton confined his efforts to a few brief notes and some drastic excisions. The notes, which were so hasty and superficial in character that at times it is doubtful whether the Bishop had read with care the text he was annotating, were worse than grossly insufficient; they were positively damaging. Coming from the intimate friend and literary executor of Pope they strongly suggested that what the learned Bishop had not commented upon or explained was not worth his or the reader's trouble in understanding. His excisions had still worse an effect. In dropping, on moral grounds,[212] the vulgar but highly entertaining Double Mistress episode, he removed one of the few parts of the *Memoirs* which could be enjoyed without extensive explanations and the one, therefore, which might have kept alive public interest in the piece until a more satisfactory edition appeared.

To the inadequacies of Warburton's edition may be traced, in part at least, Johnson's sweeping and ill-considered judgment of the piece in his life of Pope, in which he declared that "the follies which the writer ridicules are so little practised, that they are not known" and that "no man could be wiser, better, or merrier by remembering it." [213]

It was not until the end of the eighteenth century that the *Memoirs* obtained any further editorial attention. When Joseph Warton prepared his new edition of Pope he made a real attempt to understand the *Memoirs* and developed an appreciation of some of its excellent qualities. He restored the parts Warburton had omitted and added many notes of an explanatory and appreciative character which called attention to its merits. There is scarcely a chapter in which he did not find some passage whose "exquisite humor" and "fine ridicule" he believed to be delightful. Especially praised were the speech of Cornelius over his son, some of the satire on ancient music in chapter six, the Double Mistress episode, the case of a young nobleman at court, and the chapter on Martinus' efforts to find the seat of the soul. Of the latter two Warton said that the humor in them "is so exquisite, that it is difficult to know which to prefer." [214]

Warton's edition greatly enhanced the reputation of the *Memoirs* and stimulated interest in it. During the next several decades it seems to have been widely read and to have won the admiration of discerning critics. Hazlitt, for example, refers to the *Memoirs* in one of his lectures as "inimitable and praise-worthy." [215] And the distinguished philosopher, Dugald Stewart, paid high tribute to the acuteness and sagacity displayed in the

212. Warburton himself seems to have thoroughly enjoyed the humor of the episode. In describing the *Memoirs* to his friend Robert Taylor (in the letter previously cited—above, p. 64) he devoted most of his space to an account of it. He was not then a bishop, however.

213. *Works* (1801), XI, 136.

214. *Works of Alexander Pope* (1797), VI, 141 n.

215. *Works,* A. R. Waller and A. Glover, eds. (1902–06), V, 104.

sections dealing with metaphysics.[216] Another notable admirer of the piece was Lord Brougham. A contemporary tells us that he "as well as his opponents in Parliament and out of it, at the present day, repeatedly avail themselves of quotations from this book, and allude to the 'History' [i.e. Memoirs] as one which is classical and well-known to the people." [217]

With the coming of the Victorian era the fortunes of the piece began to sink. Roscoe in 1824 returned to Warburton's text, dropping the Double Mistress episode, and this policy was followed by Courthope in the Elwin and Courthope edition of Pope and later by Aitken in editing the piece for inclusion among Dr. Arbuthnot's works. These editors retained some of Warton's explanatory notes but discarded almost all of his appreciative ones. Since they themselves did relatively little to increase the understanding of the piece, the effect of their treatment was greatly to reduce interest in it. As a result, it was for a long period almost forgotten. Increased interest in the period and the figures who composed the Scriblerus Club has again called it to the attention of scholars, and references to it in recent decades have become increasingly frequent and respectful. It has, however, never regained the reputation it held during the early years of the nineteenth century and more than one hundred and forty years have gone by since the public was offered an edition with an unmutilated text.

216. Works, Sir William Hamilton, ed. (Edinburgh, 1877), I, 604.

217. F. C. Schlosser, History of the Eighteenth Century, D. Davison, tr. (1843), I, 79. Schlosser himself is of Johnson's opinion about the Memoirs. Stewart also testifies to the widespread reputation of the work, saying its "happy ridicule of scholastic logic and metaphysics is universally known." Op. cit., I, 542, n. I.

THE LITERARY BACKGROUND OF THE *MEMOIRS*

It might be expected that a work which ranges over so many fields of knowledge and draws material for its satire so freely from contemporary publications would be eclectic in its literary inspirations; and such is, to a certain degree, the case. In the general design of the *Memoirs* and in several of its particular parts are to be found a number of previously developed themes and devices. This broad eclecticism, though it kept the work from developing along highly individual lines, was not without compensating features; by drawing from many sources, the Scriblerians avoided any direct debts of an extensive character, and by reflecting a variety of literary influences they were able to create a piece which achieves a considerable degree of originality.

Several interesting suggestions as to the literary sources and background of the *Memoirs* have been advanced by editors and critics. The first of these may have come from, or at least had the sanction of, Pope himself. On May 15, 1740, a year before the *Memoirs* first appeared in print, William Warburton wrote to his friend Robert Taylor that he had just returned from a week's visit at Twickenham, in the course of which he had "read together" with Pope "a pleasant Drole History in imitation of Don Quixote & Sancho to ridicule all false Learning." "Scriblerus," he continued, "is the Hero & his Man *Crambe* puns as much as Sancho strings proverbs." [218] A decade later, in his edition of the *Memoirs,* Warburton described the relationship of the piece to Cervantes' work more cautiously, saying, by way of explanation of the Scriblerus project,

Mr. Pope, Dr. Arbuthnot, and Dr. Swift projected to write a satire, in conjunction, *on the abuses of human learning;* and to make it the better received, they proposed to do it in the manner of Cervantes (the original author of this species of satire) under the history of some feigned adventures.[219]

The general influence of Cervantes on the central project of the club is clear and it seems not unlikely that *Don Quixote* came to mind more than once during, at least, the first planning stage. Cervantes was a favorite author of Swift and probably of several other Scriblerians; [220] and there are some

218. See above, p. 64.
219. *Op. cit.,* VI, 96 n.
220. Cf. the references to *Don Quixote* in Swift's *Works* and *Corres.* Charles Jervas, who translated Cervantes' work, was a close friend of Pope and the other Scriblerians in the club days. Though Jervas' English version was completed in 1725, it was not published until 1742, more than two years after his death. Both Pope and Warburton were concerned in the publication of the translation, a fact which no doubt accounts in part for the latter's emphasis on the relationship of the pieces.

resemblances between the two works, especially in the character of Cornelius, whose reverence for the lore of ancient times and extravagant actions are at times reminiscent of Don Quixote,[221] of which the Scriblerians could hardly have been unconscious. However, it is easy to exaggerate the degree of direct influence and indebtedness. The figure and exploits of Martinus himself cannot be traced to any particular passages in Cervantes' work; Crambe resembles many other comic servants as well as Sancho; and Cornelius, taken as a whole, seems more a product of the well-developed tradition of the comic virtuoso than a direct offspring of the knight of Mancha.

An additional source for the *Memoirs* was suggested by Samuel Johnson. In his harsh estimate of the piece, he declared that its "design cannot boast of much originality; for, besides its general resemblance to Don Quixote, there will be found in it particular imitations of the History of Mr. Ouffle." [222] This curious and now almost forgotten work by the Abbé Laurent Bordelon was first published in Paris in 1710 and was translated into English in the following year.[223] Its hero is a man of boundless credulity who has spent a great part of his life reading books on magic, witchcraft, astrology, and various superstitious practices. The slight and episodic narrative of the piece, which deals with the results of Oufle's follies, the attempts of his daughter and valet to trick him, and the efforts of his wife and brother to bring him to reason, is intermixed with a whole series of elaborate dissertations on various subjects. The treatises are documented so heavily with extracts and citations that the footnotes total almost two-thirds of the whole work. The literary merit of the work is negligible and such interest as it aroused was occasioned chiefly by the large amount of strange and fabulous material which Bordelon packed into it.

That some of the Scriblerians were acquainted with Bordelon's book seems

221. The resemblance reaches its height in Chapter VI when Cornelius, lyre in hand, leaps out onto the balcony to demonstrate the power of ancient music by quelling the quarrel of the apple women.

222. *Op. cit.,* XI, 137. Cf. above, p. 66.

223. The title of the English translation was: *A History Of The Ridiculous Extravagancies Of Monsieur Oufle; Occasion'd by his reading Books treating of* Magick, *the* Black-Art, Dæmoniacks, Conjurers, Witches, Hobgoblins, Incubus's, Succubus's, *and the* Diabolical-Sabbath; *of* Elves, Fairies, Wanton Spirits, Genius's, Spectres *and* Ghosts; *of* Dreams, *the* Philosopher's-Stone, Judicial Astrology, Horoscopes, Talismans, Lucky *and* Unlucky Days, Eclipses, Comets, *and all sorts of* Apparitions, Divinations, Charms, Enchantments, *and other* Superstitious Practices. *With Notes containing a multitude of* Quotations *out of those Books, which have either Caused such* Extravagant Imaginations, *or may serve to Cure them.* Written Originally in *French,* by the Abbot B———; and now Translated into *English.* There were other French editions of the work in 1712 and 1754.

Laurent Bordelon (1653–1730) was a copious French author of very mediocre talents, who possessed the rare virtue of recognizing the inferiority of his works, which he called *"ses péchés mortels, dont le public faisait la pénitence."* To those who criticized his writings he replied, *"Je sais que je suis un mauvais auteur, mais du moins je suis un honnête homme."*

probable,[224] but that they derived any significant amount of literary inspiration from its turgid pages is difficult to believe. One searches it and the *Memoirs* in vain for those "particular imitations" of which Johnson speaks. The only real points of similarity between the two, apart from the fact that both display learning on the part of the authors, are that both Cornelius and Oufle are given to extravagance and credulity and that both possess a wife and brother who seek to curb their follies. It seems more likely, in view of Bordelon's obvious failure to combine humor and learning, that any memory of his work would have acted as a deterrent rather than an inspiration.

Following Johnson, Warton in his edition of Pope's works pointed out that "There are three or four celebrated works that bear a great resemblance, and have a turn of satire similar to that of these Memoirs."[225] Those that he lists are the *Barbon* of Balzac, the life of Montmaur by Ménage and others, the *Chef d'oeuvre d'un inconnu* of Mathanase; and the *De Charlataneria eruditorum* of Mencke. The suggested similarity between these pieces and the *Memoirs* is very interesting but any actual relationship is distant. The first two,[226] written in Paris during the 1640's, were part of a literary war against Pierre de Montmaur, the professor of Greek who had became celebrated for his wit, his rancor, his avarice, and his shameless parasitism. Since they were personal satire, aimed more at the man than at the follies, they do not belong in the same tradition as the Scriblerus piece and the resemblances which result from the use of the biographic form are not of any real significance. The case is otherwise with the remaining two works on Warton's lists, both of which were contemporary with Scriblerus. Mencke's *De Charlataneria*[227] is a sharp satirical exposé of the tricks of quack scholars in obtaining false reputations, written by a man who, as the editor of the *Acta eruditorum*, had ample opportunity to gather material, and the *Chef d'oeuvre d'un inconnu* by Saint-Hyacinthe[228] is a clever burlesque of learned editing in which a childish little poem of five stanzas is treated with great reverence and surrounded with a vast amount of scholarly pomp in the form of notes, commentaries, congratulatory epistles to the editor, etc., all done under the character of "Dr. Chrysostomus Mathanasius." So solemn

224. The translation was published by John Morphew, with whom Swift was in close touch. Both Oxford and Arbuthnot had a taste for works of this sort and Pope may well have come across it in working up the machinery for the *Rape of the Lock*.

225. *Op. cit.,* VI, 63.

226. J. L. Guez de Balzac's *Le Barbon* (Paris, 1648) and Gilles Ménage's *Vita Gargilii Mamurrae, parasito-pedagogi*. Circulated first in pamphlet form, the latter was reprinted in Ménage's *Miscellanea* (1652). It was included by Albert de Sallengre in his *Histoire de Pierre de Montmaur* (The Hague, 1715), where Warton probably encountered it.

227. Johann Burkhard Mencke, *De Charlataneria eruditorum* (Leipzig, 1715). A French translation was published at The Hague in 1721.

228. Hyacinthe Cordonnier, known as Chevalier de Thémiseul de Saint-Hyacinthe, *Le Chef d'oeuvre d'un inconnu* (The Hague, 1714). It went through a number of editions.

and thorough is the burlesque that an engraved portrait of the distinguished doctor is included. Both of the works were successful satires in the same general vein of humor as the *Memoirs,* and both undoubtedly were familiar to the Scriblerians. Neither, however, could have had any influence upon the original design of the Scriblerus satires, since Saint-Hyacinthe's book, though published in 1714, first appeared at The Hague after the club had begun to split up and Mencke's *Charlataneria* was not published until the following year. The Scriblerians borrowed no ideas from them in later years; they always had a larger supply of original hints than they could use. But the success of these Continental pieces no doubt was influential in keeping Arbuthnot and Pope at work on Scriblerus during the long life of the project.

In surveying Continental influences on the Scriblerians, Rabelais should not be overlooked. In common with much of the burlesque humor of the seventeenth and eighteenth centuries, the *Memoirs* owes a general debt to the great French humorist. The direct influence might have been greater had Swift's tastes prevailed. He was a lifelong devotee of Rabelais and no doubt would have liked the biography of the group's hero to have been written with some of the richness, color, and broad humor that characterizes the adventures of Gargantua and Pantagruel. Pope, however, had no patience with the extravagances and obscurities of the Frenchman and ultimately offset any early pressure from Swift. Perhaps to its cost, the *Memoirs* as we have it derives little directly from him.

Much more important in the immediate literary background of the *Memoirs* than any of the foreign works were several native and contemporary influences which played a direct role in developing Scriblerian satire. The most direct and powerful of these were, of course, the previous works of the Scriblerians themselves—especially those of Swift. As has been pointed out, Swift brought to the project a wealth of experience in handling the kind of satire which the club proposed. His *Tale of a Tub* and *Battle of the Books* had satirized a variety of "abuses of learning" and a considerable list of scholars and critics. Philosophic and religious theories and systems had been touched on repeatedly in various tracts. The humorous and satirical possibilities of the pseudoserious treatise had been tried out and developed in a series of tracts including the *Meditation upon a Broom-Stick* and the *Argument against Abolishing Christianity,* and parody of pseudophilosophical works had been experimented with in the *Tritical Essay upon the Faculties of the Mind.* In addition, the idea of writing a man's works for him had been exploited with great success in the Bickerstaff papers. In short, most of the directions in which the Scriblerus project was to develop had been explored by Swift in the decade and a half preceding the founding of the club, and there can be no doubt that his experience, operating both through his guiding hand and through a knowledge and appreciation of his works on the part of the other Scriblerians, exercised a very extensive influence. The brief experience of Arbuthnot in the John Bull series and in his mock proposal for a treatise on the *Art of Political Lying* is also to be reckoned with as part of the background.

Outside their own circle lay a rich field of English satire. The Scriblerians were latecomers on such subjects as antiquarianism, scholastic logic and metaphysics, freethinking, and the new science, and they were naturally therefore much affected by the work of their predecessors. In both the figures and the exploits of Cornelius and Martinus can be found many traces of earlier satires, comedies, and character sketches. Of particular interest is the influence of the two satirists, William King and Samuel Butler.

To King, their contemporary, the Scriblerians owed some direct though not very extensive debts.[229] In 1709 King published several issues of a journal entitled *Useful Transactions in Philosophy, And Other Sorts of Learning* in which he burlesqued with some learning and wit the *Philosophical Transactions of the Royal Society*. King's particular butt was Hans Sloane, the secretary of the Society, whose editing of the *Transactions* he had severely satirized some years before in the *Transactioneer* and whose recent book, *A Voyage to the Islands of Madera . . . and Jamaica* (1707) he elaborately ridiculed in the third and final number of his short-lived journal, but in the first two issues he attempted a wider scope and produced fairly elaborate burlesques of the Society's publication. These issues contain "letters" and "contributions" on a variety of subjects from the migration of cuckoos to the question of whether or not a woman may lay a child to a eunuch, all of which parody specific articles in the real *Transactions*.

These issues of the *Useful Transactions* anticipated and no doubt influenced the Scriblerians in several ways. Pope's idea for a burlesque *Works of the Learned* [230] is too much like King's original plan not to have derived some impetus from it and the Scriblerian scheme of actually writing some pseudo-scientific and learned works in the name of their hero probably derived some inspiration and encouragement from King's amusing little burlesque treatises. The Scriblerians' most striking debt, however, is to be found in chapter five of the *Memoirs*. Cornelius' learned dissertation on playthings appears to have been directly derived from an "Account of Meursius's Book of the Plays of the Grecian Boys" which King published in the first issue of the *Useful Transactions*. The Scriblerians' treatment of the idea is much more fully developed and humorous—but unless one believes Arbuthnot had a finger

229. King, a Tory and High Churchman, was a friend of Swift, though not a close one. In December, 1711, Swift obtained for him the post of Gazetteer (*Works*, II, 309; *Corres.*, I, 315–16) after the declining fortunes of the humorist had landed him in Fleet prison for debt (cf. Gay's *Present State of Wit*). He died in 1712.

230. See above, pp. 14–15.

in the earlier piece, King must be given credit for priority.[231] From a broader point of view King also deserves credit for showing some of the possibilities of burlesque in the field of science. His journal was not a success, but its failure was due in part to his inability to produce enough copy to keep it going.[232]

Of greater significance in the background of the Scriblerus scheme than King is the author of *Hudibras*. The spirit of Samuel Butler is strong throughout the *Memoirs*. The point of view of the great Restoration satirist and of the Scriblerians, speaking of them collectively and with the dominance of Arbuthnot and Swift over the group in mind, is remarkably the same. Both possessed the same vigorous and skeptical common sense; both were alike in their scorn for cant, hypocrisy, and enthusiasm, their fear of disorder and unbridled innovation, their distrust of projectors and schematists, and their contempt for metaphysical systems. They were also similar in their exceptionally well-informed minds, in their extraordinarily rich sense of the ridiculous, in their ingenious fancy, and in their copious wit. Such similarities make the question of influence exceedingly difficult to determine. Since they possessed these qualities in common and lived in a generally similar environment, it is to be expected that they would produce satires which had many elements in common even if there were no direct influence involved. How great the effect of these general likenesses may be is seen by comparing the *Memoirs* with the characters, satires, and fragments of Butler which Thyer edited in 1759. These previously unpublished pieces display a point of view and turn of satire so like that of the club members that had they been in print while the Scriblerians were at work it would have been difficult to avoid the supposition that they had some of them in mind. Cornelius is Butler's "Antiquary," with additions from "A Philosopher," "A Curious Man," and "An Astrologer." Martinus is his "Projector," amplified by touches taken from his "A Humourist," "A Mathematician," and "An Hermetic Philosopher." Even Crambe is to be found among the sketches under the character of "A Quibbler." And the following lines from a fragment express the Scriblerian view so well that Thyer might as plausibly have stated that he found them among the unpublished manuscripts of Scriblerus as those of Butler:

> 'Tis strange how stubbornly industrious
> Some men are found t'appeare Preposterous,
> That spare no Drudgery, and Paines
> To wast their little stock of Braines,
> All Arts and Sciences perplex,

231. See below, pp. 221–2.

232. King's use of material in his first two issues was extravagant. It is obvious that he could have maintained this pace only by extraordinary exertions on his part or the support of a group of friends. King was too easygoing to keep up the effort and the £5 he was paid for each issue by the publisher was not enough to share with anyone else. Sales were, of course, not large.

And, with a thousand idle Freakes,
The Government of Nature vex,
And like Fanatiques in their Hearts
Have visions, and New lights in Arts;
From old Designes of water-engines
Steal Gifts, and Lights of New Inventions,
Make Pumps for water, and their wit,
To Rayse 'em both so many feet,
And forge their Gimcracks at the Rate
Fanatiques use in Church, and State,
And out of Antique Theorems
New Jiggambobs of Light and Dreames.[233]

For the direct link between Butler and the Scriblerians we must, of course, turn to *Hudibras*. That all the Scriblerians knew the poem well is beyond question; if the others could not recite whole sections of it by heart as could Swift, they at least knew its contents well and could recite a good many tags from it. Though most of *Hudibras* is fairly far removed in theme and style from what the Scriblerians were attempting, there is some common ground. In the first part of the poem, written before the founding of the Royal Society, there are many reflections on the follies of the "old learning," such as astrology, metaphysics, antiquarianism, pedantry, and love of monstrosities, which anticipate some parts of Cornelius' character, while in the second and third parts, published in 1664 and 1678, there are many satiric attacks on the projects, the inventions, the piddling studies, and the ten-a-penny wonders of the new virtuosi which are in the same vein as the Scriblerians' account of Martinus' learned efforts and inventions.

Butler's satire in the field of science, however, differed in one very important respect from that of the Scriblerians. Writing at a time when the Royal Society had few accomplishments of which to boast, lacking a real knowledge of what was being attempted, and probably more than a little influenced by personal malice, he displayed a definite antagonism toward the whole "new method of philosophizing." In his portrait of Sidrophel in *Hudibras,* in his *Elephant in the Moon,* in his *Satyr upon the Royal Society,* and in his characters and fragments he ridiculed the virtuosi and their activities so harshly that it is clear that he held the whole body of scientists in contempt and expected nothing of solid value to come from their efforts.

Another important influence which we must take into account in the background of the Scriblerian scheme was the comedy of their own and the preceding generation. This influence is, of course, most clearly to be seen in their own farce, *Three Hours after Marriage,* but traces of it are observable in the *Memoirs,* particularly in the characters of the two principal figures,

233. *Satires and Miscellaneous Poetry and Prose*, R. Lamar, ed. (Cambridge, 1928), p. 163.

a large part of whose literary ancestry lies in the race of the comic virtuosi which had been developed on the stage dûring the last part of the seventeenth century.

The follies of the learned and the pretenders to learning were, of course, an old source of humor in comedy. The pedant, the antiquary, the astrologer, and the quack were all familiar figures to the audiences of the late sixteenth and seventeenth centuries, as was the device of the pretender to astrological or medical learning becoming involved in a series of farcical situations in an effort to maintain his character. In 1676 Thomas Shadwell gave a new turn to this old material.[234] Always, as was his boast, in search of new "humours" around which to build his Jonsonian comedies,[235] Shadwell, probably on the suggestion of his friend Samuel Butler,[236] decided to make use of the current interest in the new science. In his comedy *The Virtuoso,* he created the figure of a ridiculous "new philosopher," Sir Nicholas Gimcrack, whose amusing *reductio ad absurdum* of the efforts of the learned men of the Royal Society was a popular success.

Shadwell's treatment of the new science differs from Butler's in that it is, on the whole, good humored and intended primarily for amusement. Sir Nicholas is not presented as a typical "new philosopher," but as a fantastic fool who carries things to extremes. Even when at the end of the play, penniless and deserted by all, he decides that "now 'tis time to study for use," it is to finding the philosopher's stone that he intends to devote his efforts. He is not a member of the Royal Society and his wife declares that he is despised there.[237] Thus, though Shadwell drew much of his material from scientific publications,[238] the humor of the play was more likely to amuse than offend

234. As Mr. Borgman has pointed out, Shadwell was not the first dramatist to use the new science for comedy, St. Serfe having ridiculed the scientific virtuosi a number of years before in one scene of his *Tarugo's Wiles.* A. S. Borgman, *Thomas Shadwell* (New York, 1928), pp. 165–6.

235. "I ne'er produc'd a Comedy that had not some natural Humour in it not represented before, nor I hope ever shall." Dedication of *The Virtuoso* to the Duke of Newcastle; *Complete Works of Thomas Shadwell,* Montague Summers, ed. (1927), III, 101.

236. That Butler influenced Shadwell in the writing of *The Virtuoso* has not, I believe, been suggested before. Since Shadwell displayed no interest in the new science before 1676, it seems likely that about that time something or somebody called his attention to the possibilities for satire in it. Shadwell and Butler were friends—as is shown by the fact that Shadwell was one of the pallbearers at the satirist's funeral in 1680 (Aubrey's *Brief Lives,* A. Clark, ed. [1898], I, 136–7)—and it seems reasonable to suppose that they discussed each other's work. That Shadwell was familiar with some of Butler's unpublished writings in which he attacked the new scientists is indicated by Sir Nicholas' statement that he has seen elephants on the moon and that there are wars there in which elephants and castles are used (Shadwell, *op. cit.,* III, 165), an idea which Butler exploited in his unpublished *The Elephant in the Moon* (cf. II, 133–52). Most of the scientific activities satirized in Shadwell's comedy were also ridiculed by Butler, several of them in the second part of *Hudibras* which appeared a dozen years before *The Virtuoso.*

237. Shadwell, *op. cit.,* III, 178.

238. Mr. Carson S. Duncan pointed out that Shadwell drew on the *Philosophical Transactions* for some material (*The New Science and English Literature* [Menasha, Wis., 1913], pp. 101–02) and Mr. Borgman has shown that he also made use of Hooke's *Micrographia* (*op. cit.,* pp. 171–3).

the genuine scientists of the day. That no offense was intended, or taken, is indicated by Shadwell's statement in his dedication of the play to the Duke of Newcastle (whose mother had been a famous "virtuosa") that the "Humours" of the play "have been approved by Men of the best Sense and Learning." He declares that he has not heard of "any profest Enemies to the Play, but some Women, and some Men of Feminine understandings, who like slight Plays onely, that represent a little tattle sort of Conversation, like their own." [239]

Though Shadwell had found a new "humour" for Sir Nicholas, he was not entirely successful in exploiting its possibilities. The plot of *The Virtuoso* is a conventional blend of crossed young lovers, tricks played on a character who has disguised himself to further his courtship, a foolish suitor tricked into marrying his mistress' maid, and so on. In this main action Sir Nicholas is simply the gulled husband and guardian; his interest in science does not affect the course of events and the scenes in which his "humour" is developed might be dropped from the play without important alterations in the plot.[240] These scenes, however, were fresh and amusing; together with the brisk farce of the main action they won the play a popularity which it continued to hold for more than a quarter of a century—until, in fact, the scientific allusions had lost their topical effectiveness and the figure of the comic virtuoso had taken his place among the standard characters in comedy.[241]

The vein opened up by Shadwell was not neglected. In the following years the virtuoso in one form or another, including feminine versions, developed into a more or less stock comedy character. Shadwell himself used various evidences of the virtuoso spirit as a means of characterization in his later plays. Other playwrights, however, lacked enough knowledge of the activities of the scientists to exploit the current interest in natural philosophy effectively, and the comic characters they created were for the most part merely stock figures of quacks, pedants, or astrologers with a few added touches based upon the new learning. Dr. Baliardo in Mrs. Behn's *The Emperor of the Moon* (1687), for instance, is simply the old astrologer furbished over. His obsession about the world in the moon is the result of reading Lucian's *Dialogues* and some of the imaginary voyages rather than through any fondness for the new science, though there are a number of passing references to the activities of the Royal Society in the play.

239. Shadwell, *op. cit.*, III, 102.
240. Pope said of the play, "The Virtuoso of Shadwell does not maintain his character with equal strength to the end: and this was that writer's general fault. Wycherley used to say of him: 'That he knew how to start a fool very well; but that he was never able to run him down.'" Spence, p. 10.
241. Gildon said of it in 1699 that it had "always found success." It apparently was acted for the last time March 31, 1705, at Lincoln's Inn Fields.

As has been pointed out, the influence of the virtuoso type, and especially of Shadwell's play, may be most clearly seen in *Three Hours after Marriage*. There is, however, one instance in the *Memoirs* of a direct borrowing from *The Virtuoso* [242] and the spirit of Sir Nicholas Gimcrack and his brethren can be felt in several parts of the piece. Cornelius and Martinus are much more than conventional comic types, but their individuality arises not from freshness of conception but from the fact that the Scriblerians were able to draw widely on the learned world for material and condense a great deal of wit into a small compass.

242. See below, p. 345, note 34.

A BIBLIOGRAPHY OF THE PRINCIPAL EDITIONS

OF

THE MEMOIRS OF MARTINUS SCRIBLERUS

I Editions from 1741 to 1751

1. April 16, 1741   Text A
The/Works/Of/Mr. Alexander Pope,/In Prose./—/Vol. II./—/[Ornament]/ = //London:/Printed for J. and P. Knapton, C. Bathurst, and/ R. Dodsley, M.DCC.XLI.
Sm. folio
Griffith No. 529 [1]

The *Memoirs* occupies signatures B–T (in 2's) and is paged separately; [1] half-title, [2] blank, [3]–70 text, [71–2] table of contents.

Other Scriblerus pieces included in the volume are: *The Art of Sinking in Poetry, Virgilius Restauratus, The Origine of Sciences,* and *Memoirs of P. P.*

The volume also contains Letters to and from Dr. Swift, Thoughts on Various Subjects, Pope's *Guardian* papers, and *A Key to the Lock*.

This and the two following editions were issued on the same day and it has been impossible to determine which of the three should properly be called the first. The text in this edition contains sixteen chapters, numbered I–XII, XIV–XVII, while the table of contents lists seventeen, numbered I–XVII. The missing chapter is not number XIII but an original Chapter IX ("How Crambe had some Words with his Master") which Pope had drastically cut and combined with Chapter VIII. The fact, on the one hand, that the table of contents and the numbers of the last four chapters have not been corrected and, on the other, that there is no gap in the page numbers indicates that Pope's editing was done after the manuscript had been set up in type but before the type had been made up into forms. Presumably Pope made his corrections on a block of proof sheets covering Chapters VIII–XIII, leaving the subsequent adjustments to the printer, who neglected to make them.

2. April 16, 1741   Text A
[The same as the above.]
L. P. folio
Griffith No. 530
Printed from the same setting of type as No. 1.

1. R. H. Griffith, *Alexander Pope: A Bibliography* (Austin, Texas, 1922–27), Vol. I, Pt. II.

3. April 16, 1741   Text A

The/Works/Of/Mr. Alexander Pope,/In Prose./—/Vol. II./—/[Portrait of Pope in profile]/London:/Printed for J. and P. Knapton, C. Bathurst, and/R. Dodsley, M.DCC.XLI.

4to

Griffith No. 531

The *Memoirs* occupies signatures B–K (in 4's), L1–3, and is paged separately; [1] half-title, [2] blank, [3]–75 text (p. 59 being misnumbered 95), [76–7] table of contents, [78] blank.

The other contents of the volume are the same as in No. 1.

Printed from the same setting of type as No. 1, but with different ornaments and paging.

4. 1741   Text A

Memoirs/Of the Extraordinary/Life,/Works,/And/Discoveries/Of/Martinus Scriblerus./=/By Mr. Pope./=/Dublin:/Printed by and for George Faulkner./—/M.DCC.XLI.

12mo, in half-sheets

Griffith No. 538

Sig.: 1 leaf, a, B–O (in 6's), P1–5. Pp.: 2 pp., [1]–12, 1–165, [166] table of contents.

The text was taken from one of the editions listed above. Aside from a few printer's errors and minor corrections of spelling and punctuation, the only difference between this and the earlier editions lies in the fact that in this edition much of the conversation is set in italic.

5. July 8, 1742   Text B

The/Works/Of/Alexander Pope, Esq;/—/Vol. III. Part II./—/Containing the/Dunciad, Book IV./And The/Memoirs of Scriblerus./—/Never before Printed./=/London:/Printed for R. Dodsley, and Sold by/T. Cooper, MDCCXLII.

Sm. 8vo

Griffith No. 566

The *Memoirs* occupies signature F8 (half-title) and a second series of signatures A2–8, B–H (in 8's), I1–2. It is separately paged; [1] half-title, [2] blank, 3–128 text, 261 (probably a pied 129) list of works by Scriblerus, [130] advertisement of additional books of the *Memoirs*.

The volume also contains the fourth book of the *Dunciad* and an Appendix of pieces relating to the poem.

This edition varies so extensively from the preceding folios and quarto that it appears to have been set up from another manuscript. In addition to a large number of differences in spelling and punctuation, it contains more than a hundred minor variations in wording, many of which too clearly involve editorial judgment to have been introduced by printers while setting up the type from the printed text or the original manuscript. Cf. Appendix V. Moreover, as originally printed, this edition contained the first versions of Chapters VIII and IX—a circumstance which, taken in conjunction with the other variations in the text, seems to add weight to the theory that another manuscript was involved. In order to eliminate Chapter IX and bring the text of this edition in line with its companion issue (No. 6), it was decided to cancel two leaves, containing pp. 61–4, and to insert in their place a single leaf carrying the revised text. This leaf was marked p. 61 on the recto and p. 64 on the verso. In all the copies of this edition I have examined, however, only the second of the two original leaves had actually been excised, with the result that the pagination in these copies ran 61, 62, 61, 64. By this means a considerable portion of the original version of Chapter IX was recovered. Cf. general note to Chapter VIII. This edition is the only one to contain the very interesting advertisement of additional books of the *Memoirs*.

6. 1742   Text A'
The/Works/Of/Alexander Pope, Esq;/—/Vol. III. Part II./—/Containing the/Dunciad, Book IV./And The/Memoirs of Scriblerus./—/Never before Printed./=/London:/Printed for R. Dodsley, and Sold by/T. Cooper, /M DCC XLII.

Sm. 8vo

Griffith No. 567

The *Memoirs* occupies a second series of signatures, A–H (in 8's), I1–2, and is separately paged; [i] half-title, [ii] blank, [iii–iv] table of contents, v–x and 11–132 text, 132 list of works by Scriblerus.

The volume also contains the fourth book of the *Dunciad,* but not the Appendix.

This edition follows the 1741 folios and quarto and like them its text contains sixteen chapters, numbered I–XII, XIV–XVII, while its table of contents lists seventeen, numbered I–XVII. It represents an advance over those editions, however, in that its spelling has been modernized (as, for example, *extremely* for *extreamly, desert* for *desart,* and *o'clock* for *a clock*) and its punctuation much improved throughout. See Appendix V. The improvements in punctuation are so extensive and consistent that it is clear a real effort was made to improve the readability of the text. This edition was presumably published concurrently with or shortly after No. 5. The fact that this and No. 5 have different settings of type is to be explained by the desire of Pope and his publishers to have a considerably larger number of copies than could, by regulation, be printed from a single setting of type. That they either overestimated the public demand or deliberately had printed extra copies for use in later editions is indicated by the use of remainder sheets from this printing in the next edition (No. 7). The chain lines in this edition are horizontal, suggesting that the octavo forms were printed on extra-sized half-sheets.

Since the text of this edition was the last and most perfect to appear in Pope's lifetime, it is the one used in the present edition.

7. November, 1743   Text A'
The/Works/Of/Alexander Pope, Esq;/—/Vol. III. Part II./—/Containing the/Dunciad, Book IV./And The/Memoirs of Scriblerus./—/Never before Printed./=/London:/Printed for R. Dodsley, and Sold by/T. Cooper, /M DCC XLII.
Sm. 8vo
Griffith No. 579
The sheets of the *Memoirs* are remainders from the edition described directly above (No. 6) and have the same collation.
The fourth book of the *Dunciad* is also remainder sheets with a number of cancellations and substitutions. A much enlarged Appendix to the *Dunciad* follows the *Memoirs*.

8. June, 1751   Text C
The/Works/Of/Alexander Pope Esq./In Nine Volumes Complete./ With His Last/Corrections, Additions,/And/Improvements./Published by/ Mr. Warburton./With/Occasional Notes./=/London,/Printed for J. and P. Knapton, H. Lintot,/J. and R. Tonson, and S. Draper./—/M DCC LI.

——————— Volume VI./Containing His/Miscellaneous Pieces/In/Verse and Prose./=/London,/Printed for J. and P. Knapton in Ludgate-Street, /—/M DCC LI.
8vo
Griffith No. 648
The *Memoirs* occupies signatures H4–8, I–N (in 8's), O1, and pages [103] half-title, [104] blank, 105–94 text.
The other Scriblerus pieces contained in the volume are the same as in No. 1.
The volume also contains Pope's Imitations, Epistles, Epitaphs, Of the Poet Laureate, *Guardian* papers, and Prefaces to the *Iliad* and to Shakespeare.
Warburton based his text upon that of the 1741 folios and 4to, but he omitted the whole of Chapters XIV and XV, containing the Double Mistress episode, and the opening paragraphs of Chapters XVI and XVII, which refer to it. No notice is given of any of these omissions and the chapter numbers are altered to avoid a gap. The table of contents, the list of pieces by Scriblerus, and the advertisement of further books of the *Memoirs* are also missing from this edition. Warburton corrected and improved the punctua-

tion and spelling of the original text, but not so carefully or thoroughly as did Pope or his assistants for edition No. 6. Warburton's contributions as a commentator consist of seventeen short notes.

This edition was reprinted at least twenty-three times in London, Edinburgh, Dublin, and elsewhere during the next four decades.

II   Major Editions since 1751

9. 1769   Text C
  The Works of Alexander Pope. With a life of the author by Owen Ruffhead.

The *Memoirs* is printed in Volume III, pp. [77]–145. The volume also contains the other Scriblerus pieces included in No. 1.

This edition was begun merely as a four-volume reprint of Warburton's edition, but later it was decided to include in it Rúffhead's life of Pope, and a new general title page was added to cover this enlargement. The text of the *Memoirs* and the notes are the same as Warburton's, except that the note at the end of Chapter XIII, declaring *Gulliver's Travels* to have been originally planned as part of the *Memoirs,* was rephrased and a new note calling the reader's attention to the satire on attempts to discover the cause of gravity in the note to line 643 of the fourth book of the *Dunciad* was added to the final chapter.

10. 1791   Text C + A
  The Works of Alexander Pope. Edited by Joseph Warton.

The *Memoirs* appears in Volume VI (pp. [61]–191), which also contains the other Scriblerus pieces listed under No. 1.

Warton used Warburton's text, but he decided to restore the Double Mistress episode. The text of the episode he obtained from the 1741 quarto (No. 3). Instead of maintaining the original chapter divisions and numbers, however, he lumped the whole episode (including the first three paragraphs of the original Chapter XVI, which refer to it) into one long chapter, which he numbered XIII. In making the restoration, he overlooked Warburton's excision of the first paragraph of the last chapter (which also refers to the episode) and this remains missing in his edition. In addition to reprinting all of Warburton's notes, Warton added a number of his own, chiefly of an appreciative character.

This edition was reprinted in 1822.

11. 1807   Text C + A
  The Works of Alexander Pope. Edited by William Lisle Bowles.

The *Memoirs* appears in Volume VI (pp. [45]–180), which also contains the other Scriblerus pieces listed under No. 1.

Bowles's edition of the *Memoirs* is simply a reprint of Warton's, with the addition of a dozen notes and comments by Bowles and five by the Reverend Mr. Bannister.

12. 1824   Text C

The Works of Alexander Pope. Edited by William Roscoe.

The *Memoirs* appears in Volume VII (pp. [1]–97), which also contains the other Scriblerus pieces listed under No. 1.

Roscoe returned to Warburton's text, dropping the Double Mistress episode without comment. He added no new notes of his own, contenting himself with reprinting those of Warburton, a considerable number of Warton's, and two each of Bowles's and Bannister's.

13. 1886   Text C

The Works of Alexander Pope. Edited by Whitwell Elwin and W. J. Courthope.

The *Memoirs* appears in Volume X (pp. [271]–343), which also contains the other Scriblerus pieces listed under No. 1.

This volume was edited by Courthope (IX, vi). Following the example of Roscoe, he, "for obvious reasons" (*ibid.*), omitted all of the Double Mistress material which Warton had gathered into his Chapter XIII. In addition to Warburton's notes, he reprinted the best of Warton's and added a number of his own. His contributions (which seem somewhat more important than they were because Warburton is not properly credited in four instances and Warton in four others) consist in a comment on the date of the composition of the *Memoirs,* three notes to the satire on Dr. Woodward's shield, and an addition of a line from the *Dunciad* to Warburton's note on Horneck in Chapter VI.

14. 1892   Text C

The Life and Works of John Arbuthnot. Edited by G. A. Aitken.

The *Memoirs* occupies pages [305]–359. The other Scriblerus pieces included in the volume are *The Origine of Sciences* and *Virgilius Restauratus.*

Aitken left out the Double Mistress material but added a note indicating the omission and giving some account of the missing material (p. 354). He reprinted only a few of his predecessors' notes, rephrasing or adding to a number of them, and added nine of his own.

15. 1932   Text C

Satires and Personal Writings by Jonathan Swift. Edited by W. A. Eddy.

The *Memoirs* occupies pages [103]–139. The volume also contains the false 1723 *Memoirs.*

The text is Warburton's, collated with one of the 1741 editions of Pope's *Prose Works,* Vol. II. The Introduction, Chapters VII–X, Chapter XII, and the Double Mistress episode are all omitted. Only Pope's original notes on the parts of the text given, one note by Warburton, and Aitken's explanation of the missing Double Mistress episode are reprinted.

THE TEXT

The text of this edition has been taken from No. 6 in the Bibliography of Principal Editions (one of the two octavo editions of the *Works of Alexander Pope,* Vol. III, Part II, published in 1742). Typographical mistakes noted in the Errata have been corrected; otherwise the original text has been reproduced exactly. The advertisement at the end of the *Memoirs,* which does not appear in No. 6, has been added from its companion edition, No. 5.

Ornatissimo Doctissimoq; Viro JOANNI WOODWARDO, *Medicinæ Doctori, ejusdem Facultatis in Collegio Greshamensi Professori, & Societatis Regalis Socio, Ectypum istud Clypei antiqui in Museo ejus conservati, observantiæ et grati animi ergo, dicat consecratque* THO. HEARNE.

Courtesy of the British Museum

THE SHIELD OF CORNELIUS

"It was not long after purchas'd by Dr. Woodward, who, by the assistance of Mr. Kemp incrusted it with a new Rust, and is the same whereof a Cut hath been engraved, and exhibited to the great Contentation of the learned."

Memoirs, p. 105

MEMOIRS

Of the Extraordinary

LIFE, WORKS,

AND

DISCOVERIES

OF

MARTINUS SCRIBLERUS.

Written by Dr. ARBUTHNOT
and Mr. POPE.

CONTENTS

INTRODUCTION

To the READER.

IN the Reign of Queen Anne (which, notwithstanding those
happy Times which succeeded, every Englishman has not for-
5 got) thou may'st possibly, gentle Reader, have seen a certain
Venerable Person, who frequented the Out-side of the Palace of
St. James's; and who, by the Gravity of his Deportment and
Habit, was generally taken for a decay'd Gentleman of Spain.
His stature was tall, his visage long, his complexion olive, his
10 brows were black and even, his eyes hollow yet piercing, his nose
inclin'd to aquiline, his beard neglected and mix'd with grey: All
this contributed to spread a solemn Melancholy over his countenance. Pythagoras was not more silent, Pyrrho more motionless,
nor Zeno more austere. His Wig was as black and smooth as the
15 plumes of a Raven, and hung as strait as the hair of a River-God
rising from the water. His Cloak so completely covered his
whole person, that whether or no he had any other cloaths
(much less any linen) / under it, I shall not say; but his sword vi
appear'd a full yard behind him, and his manner of wearing it
20 was so stiff, that it seem'd grown to his Thigh. His whole figure
was so utterly unlike any thing of this world, that it was not natural for any man to ask him a question without blessing himself
first. Those who never saw a *Jesuit* took him for one, and others
believed him some *High Priest of the Jews.*
25   But under this macerated form was conceal'd a Mind replete
with Science, burning with a Zeal of benefiting his fellow-
creatures, and filled with an honest conscious Pride, mixt with
a scorn of doing or suffering the least thing beneath the dignity
of a Philosopher. Accordingly he had a soul that would not let
30 him accept of any offers of Charity, at the same time that his
body seem'd but too much to require it. His lodging was in a
small chamber up four pair of stairs, where he regularly payed
for what he had when he eat or drank, and he was often observed
wholly to abstain from both. He declin'd speaking to any one,
35 except the Queen, or her first Minister, to whom he attempted to
make some applications; but his real business or intentions were

utterly unknown to all men. Thus much is certain, that he was
obnoxious to the Queen's Ministry; who either out of Jealousy or
Envy, had him spirited away, and carried abroad as a dangerous
person, without any regard to the known Laws of the King-
5 dom. /   vii
      One day, as this Gentleman was walking about dinner-time
alone in the Mall, it happen'd that a Manuscript dropt from
under his cloak, which my servant pick'd up, and brought to me.
It was written in the Latin tongue, and contain'd many most pro-
10 found Secrets, in an unusual turn of reasoning and style. The
first leaf was inscribed with these words, *Codicillus, seu Liber
Memorialis, Martini Scribleri.* The Book was of so wonderful a
nature, that it is incredible what a desire I conceiv'd that moment
to be acquainted with the Author, who, I clearly perceived, was
15 some great Philosopher in disguise. I several times endeavour'd
to speak to him, which he as often industriously avoided. At
length I found an opportunity (as he stood under the Piazza by
the Dancing-room in St. James's) to acquaint him in the Latin
tongue, that his Manuscript was fallen into my hands; and say-
20 ing this, I presented it to him, with great Encomiums on the
learned Author. Hereupon he took me aside, survey'd me over
with a fixt attention, and opening the clasps of the Parchment
cover, spoke (to my great surprize) in English, as follows.

      "Courteous stranger, whoever thou art, I embrace thee as my
25 "best friend; for either the Stars and my Art are deceitful, or the
"destin'd time is come which is to manifest Martinus Scriblerus
"to the world, and thou the person chosen by Fate / for this task. viii
"What thou seest in me is a body exhausted by the labours of the
"mind. I have found in Dame Nature not indeed an unkind, but
30 "a very coy Mistress: Watchful nights, anxious days, slender
"meals, and endless labours must be the lot of all who pursue her,
"through her labyrinths and meanders. My first vital air I drew
"in this Island (a soil fruitful of Philosophers) but my complex-
"ion is become adust, and my body arid, by visiting lands (as the
35 "Poet has it) *alio sub sole calentes.* I have, through my whole life,
"passed under several disguises and unknown names, to skreen
"myself from the envy and malice which mankind express
"against those who are possessed of the *Arcanum Magnum.* But

"at present I am forc'd to take Sanctuary in the British Court, to
"avoid the Revenge of a cruel Spaniard, who has pursued me al-
"most through the whole terraqueous globe. Being about four
"years ago in the City of Madrid, in quest of natural knowledge,
5 "I was informed of a Lady who was marked with a Pomegranate
"upon the inside of her right Thigh, which blossom'd, and, as
"it were, seem'd to ripen in the due season. Forthwith was I pos-
"sessed with an insatiable curiosity to view this wonderful Phæ-
"nomenon. I felt the ardour of my passion encrease as the season
10 "advanced, till in the month of July I could no longer contain. I
"bribed her Duenna, was ad- / mitted to the Bath, saw her un- ix
"dress'd, and the wonder display'd. This was soon after dis-
"covered by the Husband, who finding some letters I had writ to
"the Duenna, containing expressions of a doubtful meaning, sus-
15 "pected me of a crime most alien from the Purity of my
"Thoughts. Incontinently I left Madrid by the advice of friends;
"have been pursued, dogg'd, and waylaid through several Na-
"tions; and even now scarce think myself secure within the
"sacred walls of this Palace. It has been my good fortune to have
20 "seen all the grand Phænomena of Nature, excepting an Earth-
"quake, which I waited for in Naples three years in vain; and
"now, by means of some British ship (whose Colours no Span-
"iard dares approach) I impatiently expect a safe passage to Ja-
"maica, for that benefit. To thee, my Friend, whom Fate has
25 "marked for my Historiographer, I leave these my Commen-
"taries, and others of my works. No more—be faithful and im-
"partial.

He soon after performed his promise, and left me the Commentaries, giving me also further lights by many Conferences;
30 when he was unfortunately snatch'd away (as I before related)
by the jealousy of the Queen's Ministry.
Tho' I was thus to my eternal grief depriv'd of his conversation, he for some years continued his / Correspondence, and x
communicated to me many of his Projects for the benefit of man-
35 kind. He sent me some of his Writings, and recommended to my
care the recovery of others, straggling about the world, and assumed by other men. The last time I heard from him was on occasion of his Strictures on the Dunciad; since when, several years

being elaps'd, I have reason to believe this excellent Person is either dead, or carry'd by his vehement thirst of knowledge into some remote, or perhaps undiscover'd Region of the world. In either case, I think it a debt no longer to be delay'd, to reveal what 5 I know of this Prodigy of Science, and to give the History of his life, and of his extensive merits, to mankind; in which I dare promise the Reader, that, whenever he begins to think any one Chapter dull, the style will be immediately changed in the next.

MEMOIRS

OF

MARTINUS SCRIBLERUS.

BOOK I.

CHAP. I.

Of the Parentage and Family of Scriblerus, *how he was begot, what Care was taken of him before he was born, and what Prodigies attended his Birth.*

IN the City of Munster in Germany, lived a grave and learned
10 Gentleman, by Profession an Antiquary; who, among all his invaluable Curiosities, esteemed none more highly than a Skin of the true Pergamenian Parchment, which hung at the upper-end of his hall. On this was curiously traced the ancient Pedigree of the *Scribleri,* with all their Alliances and collateral Re- / lations   12
15 (among which were reckon'd Albertus Magnus, Paracelsus Bombastus, and the famous Scaligers, in old time Princes of Verona) and deduced even from the Times of the Elder Pliny to Cornelius Scriblerus: For such was the name of this venerable Personage; whose glory it was, that, by the singular Virtue of the
20 Women, not one had a Head of a different Cast from his family.
His wife was a Lady of singular beauty, whom not for that reason only he espoused, but because she was undoubted daughter either of the great Scriverius, or of Gaspar Barthius. It happen'd on a time, the said Gaspar made a visit to Scriverius at Haerlem;
25 taking with him a comely Lady of his acquaintance who was skilful in the Greek Tongue; of whom the learned Scriverius became so enamour'd, as to inebriate his friend, and be familiar with his Mistress. I am not ignorant of what [a] Columesius affirms, that the learned Barthius was not so overtaken but he per-
30 ceiv'd it, and in Revenge suffer'd this unfortunate Gentlewoman to be drowned in the Rhine at her return: But Mrs. Scriblerus

[a] Columesius relates this from Isaac Vossius, in his Opuscul. p. 102.

(the issue of that Amour) was a living proof of the falshood of
this Report. Dr. Cornelius was further induced to his marriage
from the certain information, that the aforesaid Lady, the
mother of / his wife, was related to Cardan on the father's side,   13
5 and to Aldrovandus on the mother's: Besides which, her Ancestors had been professors of Physick, Astrology, or Chemistry, in
German Universities, from generation to generation.

   With this fair Gentlewoman had our Doctor lived in a comfortable Union for about ten years: But this our sober and orderly
10 pair, without any natural infirmity, and with a constant and
frequent compliance to the chief duty of conjugal life, were yet
unhappy, in that Heaven had not blessed them with any issue.
This was the utmost grief to the good man; especially considering what exact Precautions and Methods he had used to procure
15 that Blessing: For he never had cohabitation with his spouse,
but he ponder'd on the Rules of the Ancients, for the generation
of Children of Wit. He ordered his diet according to the prescription of Galen, confining himself and his wife for almost the
whole first year to ᵇGoat's Milk and Honey. It unfortunately
20 befel her, when she was about four months gone with child, to
long for somewhat which that author inveighs against, as prejudicial to the understanding of the Infant: This her husband
thought fit to deny her, affirming, it was better to be childless
than to become the Parent of a Fool. His Wife miscarried; but as
25 the Abortion proved only a female Foetus, he / comforted him-   14
self, that, had it arrived to perfection, it would not have answer'd
his account; his heart being wholly fixed upon the learned Sex.
However he disdained not to treasure up the Embryo in a Vial,
among the curiosities of his family.
30   Having discovered that Galen's prescription could not determine the sex, he forthwith betook himself to Aristotle. Accordingly he withheld the nuptial embrace when the wind was
in any point of the South; this ᵈAuthor asserting that the grossness and moisture of the southerly winds occasion the procrea-
35 tion of females, and not of males. But he redoubled his diligence
when the wind was at West; a wind on which that great Philosopher bestowed the Encomiums of Fatner of the Earth, Breath of
the Elysian Fields, and other glorious Elogies. For our learned

ᵇ Galen Lib. de Cibis boni & mali succi, cap. 3.   ᵈ Arist. Sect. 14. Prob. 5.

man was clearly of opinion, that the Semina out of which Animals are produced, are Animalcula ready formed, and received
in with the Air e.

Under these regulations, his wife, to his unexpressible joy,
5 grew pregnant a second time; and, (what was no small addition
to his happiness) he just then came to the possession of a considerable Estate by the death of her Uncle, a wealthy Jew who resided at London. This made it necessary for him to take a journey to England; nor would the / care of his posterity let him 15
10 suffer his Wife to remain behind him. During the voyage, he
was perpetually taken up on the one hand, how to employ his
great Riches; and on the other, how to educate his Child. He had
already determin'd to set apart several annual Sums, for the recovery of *Manuscripts,* the effossion of *Coins,* the procuring of
15 *Mummies;* and for all those curious discoveries by which he
hoped to become (as himself was wont to say) a second *Peireskius.* He had already chalked out all possible schemes for the improvement of a male child; yet was so far prepar'd for the worst
that could happen, that before the nine months were expired, he
20 had composed two Treatises of Education; the one he called
A Daughter's Mirrour, and the other *A Son's Monitor.*

This is all we can find relating to Martinus, while he was in his
Mother's womb: excepting that he was entertained there with a
Consort of Musick once in twenty four hours, according to the
25 Custom of the Magi; and that on a f particular day, he was ob-
served to leap and kick exceedingly, which was on the first of
April, the birth-day of the great *Basilius Valentinus.*

The Truth of this, and every preceding Fact, may be depended
upon, being taken literally from the Memoirs. But I must be so
30 ingenuous as to own, that the Accounts are not so certain of the / 16
exact time and place of his birth. As to the first, he had the common frailty of old men, to conceal his age; as to the second, I only
remember to have heard him say, that he first saw the light in
St. Giles's Parish. But in the investigation of this point Fortune
35 hath favoured our diligence. For one day, as I was passing by the
Seven Dials, I over-heard a dispute concerning the place of Nativity of a great Astrologer, which each man alledged to have
been in his own street. The circumstances of the time, and the

e Religion of Nature, Sect. 5. Parag. 15.   f Ramsey's Cyrus.

description of the person, made me imagine it might be that universal Genius whose life I am writing. I returned home, and having maturely considered their several arguments, which I found to be of equal weight, I quieted my curiosity with this
5 natural conclusion, that he was born in some point common to all the seven streets; which must be that on which the Column is now erected. And it is with infinite pleasure that I since find my Conjecture confirmed, by the following passage in the Codicil to Mr. Neale's Will.

10   *I appoint my Executors to engrave the following Inscription on the Column in the Center of the seven Streets which I erected.*

LOC. NAT. INCLUT. PHILOS. MAR. SCR.

But Mr. Neale's Order was never performed, because the Execu-
15 tors durst not administer. /   17

Nor was the Birth of this great man unattended with *Prodigies:* He himself has often told me, that, on the night before he was born, Mrs. Scriblerus dream'd she was brought to bed of a huge *Ink-horn,* out of which issued several large streams of Ink,
20 as it had been a fountain: This dream was by her husband thought to signify, that the child should prove a very voluminous Writer. Likewise a ᵍ *Crab-tree* that had been hitherto barren, appeared on a sudden laden with a vast quantity of Crabs: This sign also the old gentleman imagined to be a prognostic of the
25 acuteness of his Wit. A great swarm of ʰ *Wasps* play'd round his Cradle without hurting him, but were very troublesome to all in the room besides: This seemed a certain presage of the effects of his Satire. A Dunghill was seen within the space of one night to be covered all over with *Mushrooms:* This some interpreted to
30 promise the infant great fertility of fancy, but no long duration to his works; but the Father was of another opinion.

But what was of all most wonderful, was a thing that seemed a monstrous *Fowl,* which just then dropt through the sky-light, near his wife's apartment. It had a large body, two little dispro-
35 portioned wings, a prodigious tail, but no head. As its colour was white, he took it at first sight for a Swan, and was concluding his

ᵍ Virgil's Laurel. DONAT.   ʰ Plato, Lucan, &c.

son would be a Poet; but on a nearer view, he perceived it to be speckled with black, in / the form of letters; and that it was indeed a Paper kite which had broke its leash by the impetuosity of the wind. His back was armed with the Art Military, his belly was filled with Physick, his wings were the wings of Quarles and Withers, the several Nodes of his voluminous tail were diversify'd with several branches of science; where the Doctor beheld with great joy a knot of Logick, a knot of Metaphysick, a knot of Casuistry, a knot of Polemical Divinity, and a knot of Common Law, with a *Lanthorn* of *Jacob Behmen*.

There went a Report in the family, that as soon as he was born he uttered the voice of nine several animals. He cry'd like a Calf, bleated like a Sheep, chattered like a Mag-pye, grunted like a Hog, neighed like a Foal, croaked like a Raven, mewed like a Cat, gabbled like a Goose, and bray'd like an Ass. And the next morning he was found playing in his bed with two Owls, which came down the chimney. His Father greatly rejoyced at all these signs, which betokened the variety of his Eloquence, and the extent of his Learning; but he was more particularly pleased with the last, as it nearly resembled what happen'd at the birth of [a] Homer. /

[a] Vid. Eustath. in Odyss. l. 12. ex Alex. Paphio, & Leo Allat. de patr. Hom. pag. 45.

CHAP. II.

The Speech of Cornelius *over his Son, at the Hour of his Birth.*

NO sooner was the cry of the Infant heard, but the old gentleman rushed into the Room, and snatching it in his arms, examin'd every limb with attention. He was infinitely pleas'd to
find, that the Child had the Wart of Cicero, the wry Neck of
Alexander, knots upon his legs like Marius, and one of them
shorter than the other like Agesilaus. The good Cornelius also
hoped he would come to stammer like Demosthenes, in order
to be as eloquent; and in time arrive at many other Defects of
famous men. He held the child so long, that the Midwife grown
out of all patience, snatch'd it from his arms, in order to swaddle
it. "Swaddle him! (quoth he) far be it from me to submit to such
"a pernicious Custom. Is not my son a Man? and is not Man the
"Lord of the Universe? Is it thus you use this Monarch at his first
"arrival in his dominions, to manacle and shackle him hand and
"foot? Is this what you call to be free-born? If you have no re-
"gard to his natural Liberty, at least have some to his natural
"Faculties. Behold with what agility he spreadeth his Toes, and
"moveth them with as great variety / as his Fingers! a power,
"which in the small circle of a year may be totally abolish'd, by
"the enormous confinement of shoes and stockings. His Ears
"(which other animals turn with great advantage towards the
"sonorous object) may, by the ministry of some accursed Nurse,
"for ever lie flat and immoveable. Not so the Ancients, they could
"move them at pleasure, and accordingly are often describ'd
"*arrectis auribus.*" "What a devil (quoth the Midwife) would
"you have your son move his Ears like a Drill?" "Yes, fool (said
"he) why should he not have the perfection of a Drill, or of any
"other animal?" Mrs. Scriblerus, who lay all this while fretting
at her husband's discourse, at last broke out to this purpose:
"My dear, I have had many disputes with you upon this subject
"before I was a month gone: We have but one child, and cannot
"afford to throw him away upon experiments. I'll have my boy
"bred up like other gentlemen, at home, and always under my

"own eye." All the Gossips with one voice, cry'd, Ay, ay; but Cornelius broke out in this manner: "What, bred at home! Have "I taken all this pains for a creature that is to lead the inglorious "life of a Cabbage, to suck the nutritious juices from the spot 5 "where he was first planted? No; to perambulate this terraque- "ous Globe is too small a Range; were it permitted, he should "at least make the Tour of the / whole System of the Sun. Let 21 "other Mortals pore upon Maps, and swallow the legends of ly- "ing travellers; the son of Cornelius shall make his own Legs his 10 "Compasses; with those he shall measure Continents, Islands, "Capes, Bays, Streights and Isthmus's: He shall himself take the "altitude of the highest mountains, from the peak of Derby to the "peak of Teneriff; when he has visited the top of Taurus, Imaus, "Caucasus, and the famous Ararat where Noah's Ark first 15 "moor'd, he may take a slight view of the snowy Riphæans; nor "would I have him neglect Athos and Olympus, renowned for "poetical fictions. Those that vomit fire will deserve a more par- "ticular attention: I will therefore have him observe with great "care Vesuvius, Ætna, the burning mountain of Java, but chiefly 20 "Hecla the greatest rarity in the Northern Regions. Then he may "likewise contemplate the wonders of the Mephitick cave. When "he has div'd into the bowels of the earth, and survey'd the "works of Nature under ground, and instructed himself fully in "the nature of Vulcanos, Earthquakes, Thunders, Tempests, and 25 "Hurricanes, I hope he will bless the world with a more exact "survey of the deserts of Arabia and Tartary, than as yet we are "able to obtain: Then will I have him cross the seven Gulphs, "measure the currents in the fifteen famous Streights, and search "for those fountains of / fresh water that are at the bottom of 22 30 "the Ocean."—At these last words Mrs. Scriblerus fell into a trembling: The description of this terrible Scene made too violent an impression upon a woman in her condition, and threw her into a strong hysteric Fit; which might have prov'd dangerous, if Cornelius had not been push'd out of the room by the 35 united force of the women.

CHAP. III.

Shewing what befel the Doctor's Son, and his Shield,
on the Day of the Christ'ning.

THE day of the Christ'ning being come, and the house filled
5   with Gossips, the Levity of whose conversation suited but ill with
the Gravity of Dr. Cornelius, he cast about how to pass this day
more agreeably to his Character; that is to say, not without some
Profitable Conference, nor wholly without observance of some
Ancient Custom.

10   He remembered to have read in Theocritus, that the Cradle of
Hercules was a Shield; and being possess'd of an antique
Buckler, which he held as a most inestimable Relick, he determined to have the infant laid therein, and in that manner
brought into the Study, to be shown to certain learned men of

15   his acquaintance. /   23

The regard he had for this Shield, had caused him formerly to
compile a Dissertation concerning it, proving from the several
properties, and particularly the colour of the Rust, the exact
chronology thereof.

20   With this Treatise, and a moderate supper, he proposed to entertain his Guests; tho' he had also another design, to have their
assistance in the calculation of his Son's *Nativity.*

He therefore took the Buckler out of a Case (in which he always kept it, lest it might contract any modern rust) and en-

25   trusted it to his House-maid, with orders, that when the company
was come she should lay the Child carefully in it, cover'd with
a mantle of blue Sattin.

The Guests were no sooner seated, but they entered into a
warm Debate about the *Triclinium* and the manner of *Decubitus*

30   of the Ancients, which Cornelius broke off in this manner:

"This day, my Friends, I purpose to exhibit my son before you;
"a Child not wholly unworthy of Inspection, as he is descended
"from a Race of Virtuosi. Let the Physiognomists examine his
"features; let the Chirographists behold his Palm; but above all

35   "let us consult for the calculation of his Nativity. To this end, as
"the child is not vulgar, I will not present him unto you in a vul-

"gar manner. He shall be cradled in my Ancient Shield, so
"famous through the Universities / of Europe. You all know   24
"how I purchas'd that invaluable piece of Antiquity at the great
"(though indeed inadequate) expence of all the Plate of our
5 "family, how happily I carried it off, and how triumphantly I
"transported it hither, to the inexpressible grief of all Germany.
"Happy in every circumstance, but that it broke the heart of the
"great Melchior Insipidus!"

Here he stopp'd his Speech, upon sight of the Maid, who
10 enter'd the room with the Child: He took it in his arms and proceeded:

"Behold then my Child, but first behold the Shield: Behold
"this Rust,—or rather let me call it this precious Ærugo,—behold
"this beautiful Varnish of Time,—this venerable Verdure of so
15 "many Ages—

In speaking these words, he slowly lifted up the Mantle, which
cover'd it, inch by inch; but at every inch he uncovered, his
cheeks grew paler, his hand trembled, his nerves failed, till on
sight of the whole the Tremor became universal: The Shield and
20 the Infant both dropt to the ground, and he had only strength
enough to cry out, "O God! my Shield, my Shield!

The Truth was, the Maid (extremely concern'd for the reputation of her own cleanliness, and her young master's honour) had
scoured it as clean as her Andirons. /   25
25   Cornelius sunk back on a chair, the Guests stood astonished,
the infant squawl'd, the maid ran in, snatch'd it up again in her
arms, flew into her mistress's room, and told what had happen'd.
Down stairs in an instant hurried all the Gossips, where they
found the Doctor in a Trance: Hungary water, Hartshorn, and
30 the confus'd noise of shrill voices, at length awaken'd him: when
opening his eyes, he saw the Shield in the hands of the House-
maid. "O Woman! Woman! (he cry'd, and snatch'd it violently
"from her) was it to thy ignorance that this Relick owes its ruin?
"Where, where is the beautiful Crust that cover'd thee so long?
35 "where those Traces of Time, and *Fingers* as it were of An-
"tiquity? where all those beautiful obscurities, the cause of much
"delightful disputation, where doubt and curiosity went hand
"in hand, and eternally exercised the speculations of the learned?
"All this the rude Touch of an ignorant woman hath done away!

"The *curious Prominence* at the belly of that figure, which some
"taking for the *Cuspis* of a sword, denominated a Roman Sol-
"dier; others accounting the *Insignia Virilia,* pronounc'd to be
"one of the *Dii Termini;* behold she hath cleaned it in like
5 "shameful sort, and shown to be the head of a Nail. O my Shield!
"my Shield! well may I say with Horace, *non bene relicta Par-*
"*mula.*" /   26

The Gossips, not at all inquiring into the cause of his sorrow,
only asked, if the Child had no hurt? and cried, "Come, come, all
10 "is well, what has the Woman done but her duty? a tight cleanly
"wench I warrant her; what a stir a man makes about a *Bason,*
"that an hour ago, before this labour was bestowed upon it, a
"Country Barber would not have hung at his shop door." "A
"*Bason!* (cry'd another) no such matter, 'tis nothing but a
15 "paultry old *Sconce,* with the nozzle broke off." The learned
Gentlemen, who till now had stood speechless, hereupon looking narrowly on the Shield, declar'd their Assent to this latter
opinion; and desir'd Cornelius to be comforted, assuring him it
was a *Sconce* and no other. But this, instead of comforting, threw
20 the Doctor into such a violent Fit of passion, that he was carried
off groaning and speechless to bed; where, being quite spent, he
fell into a kind of slumber.

CHAP. IV.

Of the Suction and Nutrition of the Great Scriblerus *in his Infancy, and of the first Rudiments of his Learning.*

AS soon as Cornelius awaked, he rais'd himself on his elbow,
5 and casting his eye on Mrs. Scriblerus, spoke as follows: "Wisely
"was it said by Homer, that in the Cellar of Jupiter are two bar-
"rels, the one of good, the other of evil, which he never bestows
"on mortals separately, but constantly mingles them together.
"Thus at the same time hath Heav'n bless'd me with the birth of
10 "a Son, and afflicted me with the scouring of my Shield. Yet let
"us not repine at his Dispensations, who gives and who takes
"away; but rather join in prayer, that the Rust of Antiquity,
"which he hath been pleas'd to take from my Shield, may be
"added to my Son; and that so much of it as it is my purpose he
15 "shall contract in his Education, may never be destroy'd by any
"Modern Polishing."

He cou'd no longer bear the sight of the Shield, but order'd it
should be remov'd for ever from his eyes. It was not long after
purchas'd by Dr. Woodward, who, by the assistance of Mr.
20 Kemp incrusted it with a new Rust, and is the same whereof a
Cut / hath been engraved, and exhibited to the great Contenta-   28
tion of the learned.

Cornelius now began to regulate the Suction of his child. Seldom did there pass a day without disputes between him and the
25 Mother, or the Nurse, concerning the nature of Aliment. The
poor woman never dined but he denied her some dish or other,
which he judg'd prejudicial to her milk. One day she had a long-
ing desire to a piece of beef, and as she stretch'd her hand towards
it, the old gentleman drew it away, and spoke to this effect:
30 "Hadst thou read the Ancients, O Nurse, thou would'st prefer
"the welfare of the Infant which thou nourishest, to the indulg-
"ing of an irregular and voracious Appetite. Beef, it is true, may
"confer a Robustness on the limbs of my son, but will hebetate
"and clogg his Intellectuals." While he spoke this, the Nurse
35 look'd upon him with much anger, and now and then cast a
wishful eye upon the Beef— "Passion (continued the Doctor,

"still holding the dish) throws the mind into too violent a fer-
"mentation; it is a kind of Fever of the soul, or as Horace ex-
"presses it, a *Short Madness*. Consider, Woman, that this day's
"Suction of my son may cause him to imbibe many ungovernable
5 "Passions, and in a manner spoil him for the temper of a Philoso-
"pher. Romulus by sucking a Wolf, became of a fierce and sav-
"age disposition; and were I to breed some Ottoman Em- / peror   29
"or Founder of a Military Commonwealth, perhaps I might in-
"dulge thee in this carnivorous Appetite"—What, interrupted
10 the Nurse, Beef spoil the understanding? that's fine indeed—
how then could our Parson preach as he does upon Beef, and
Pudding too, if you go to that? Don't tell me of your Ancients,
had not you almost kill'd the poor babe with a dish of Dæmonial
black Broth?—"Lacedæmonian black Broth, thou would'st say
15 "(replied Cornelius) but I cannot allow the surfeit to have been
"occasioned by that diet, since it was recommended by the
"Divine Lycurgus. No, Nurse, thou must certainly have eaten
"some meats of ill digestion the day before, and that was the real
"cause of his disorder. Consider, Woman, the different Tempera-
20 "ments of different Nations: What makes the English Phleg-
"matick and melancholy but Beef? what renders the Welsh so
"hot and cholerick, but cheese and leeks? the French derive their
"levity from their Soups, Frogs, and mushrooms: I would not
"let my Son dine like an Italian, lest, like an Italian, he should
25 "be jealous and revengeful: The warm and solid diet of Spain
"may be more beneficial, as it might endue him with a profound
"Gravity, but at the same time he might suck in with their food
"their intolerable Vice of Pride. Therefore, Nurse, in short, I
"hold it requisite to deny you at present, not only Beef, but like-
30 "wise / whatsoever any of those Nations eat." During this   30
speech, the Nurse remain'd pouting and marking her plate with
the knife, nor would she touch a bit during the whole dinner.
This the old Gentleman observing, order'd that the Child, to
avoid the risque of imbibing ill humours, should be kept from
35 her breast all that day, and be fed with Butter mix'd with Honey,
according to a Prescription he had met with somewhere in
Eustathius upon Homer. This indeed gave the Child a great
looseness, but he was not concern'd at it, in the opinion that
whatever harm it might do his body, would be amply recom-

penced by the improvements of his understanding. But from
thenceforth he insisted every day upon a particular Diet to be observed by the Nurse; under which having been long uneasy, she
at last parted from the family, on his ordering her for dinner
5 the *Paps* of a *Sow* with Pig; taking it as the highest indignity,
and a direct Insult upon her Sex and Calling.

Four years of young Martin's life pass'd away in squabbles of
this nature. Mrs. Scriblerus consider'd it was now time to instruct him in the fundamentals of Religion, and to that end took
10 no small pains in teaching him his *Catechism:* But Cornelius
look'd upon this as a tedious way of Instruction, and therefore
employ'd his head to find out more pleasing methods, the better
to induce him to be fond of learning. He would frequently carry
him to the / *Puppet-Shew* of the Creation of the world, where   31
15 the Child with exceeding delight gain'd a notion of the History
of the Bible. His first rudiments in profane history were acquired by seeing of *Raree-shews,* where he was brought acquainted with all the Princes of Europe. In short the old Gentleman so contriv'd it, to make every thing contribute to the
20 improvement of his knowledge, even to his very Dress. He
invented for him a Geographical suit of cloaths, which might
give him some hints of that Science, and likewise some knowledge of the Commerce of different Nations. He had a French
Hat with an African Feather, Holland Shirts and Flanders Lace,
25 English Cloth lin'd with Indian Silk, his Gloves were Italian,
and his Shoes were Spanish: He was made to observe this, and
daily catechis'd thereupon, which his Father was wont to call
"Travelling at home." He never gave him a Fig or an Orange but
he obliged him to give an account from what Country it came.
30 In Natural history he was much assisted by his Curiosity in
Sign-Posts, insomuch that he hath often confess'd he owed to
them the knowledge of many Creatures which he never found
since in any Author, such as White Lions, Golden Dragons, &c.
He once thought the same of Green Men, but had since found
35 them mention'd by Kircherus, and verified in the History of William of Newbury [a]. /   32

His disposition to the Mathematicks was discover'd very early,
by his drawing [b] parallel lines on his bread and butter, and inter-

---

[a] Gul. Neubrig. Book i. Ch. 27.   [b] Pascal's Life. Locke of Educ. &c.

secting them at equal Angles, so as to form the whole Superficies
into squares. But, in the midst of all these Improvements, a stop
was put to his learning the *Alphabet,* nor would he let him proceed to Letter D, till he could truly and distinctly pronounce C
5 in the ancient manner, at which the Child unhappily boggled for
near three months. He was also obliged to delay his learning to
write, having turn'd away the Writing Master because he knew
nothing of Fabius's Waxen Tables.

Cornelius having read, and seriously weigh'd the methods by
10 which the famous Montaigne was educated, and resolving in
some degree to exceed them, resolv'd he should speak and learn
nothing but the learned Languages, and especially the Greek; in
which he constantly eat and drank, according to Homer. But
what most conduced to his easy attainment of this Language,
15 was his love of Ginger-bread; which his Father observing, caused
it to be stampt with the Letters of the Greek Alphabet; and the
child the very first day eat as far as Iota. By his particular application to this language above the rest, he attain'd so great a profi-
cience therein, that Gronovius ingenuously confesses he durst
20 not / confer with this child in Greek at eight years old; and at   33
fourteen he composed a Tragedy in the same language, as the
younger ^e Pliny had done before him.

He learn'd the Oriental Languages of Erpenius, who resided
some time with his father for that purpose. He had so early a
25 Relish for the Eastern way of writing, that even at this time he
composed (in imitation of it) the *Thousand and One Arabian
Tales,* and also the *Persian Tales,* which have been since translated into several languages, and lately into our own with particular elegance, by Mr. Ambrose Philips. In this work of his
30 Childhood, he was not a little assisted by the historical Tradi-
tions of his *Nurse.*

^e Plin. Epist. Lib. 7.

CHAP. V.

A Dissertation upon Play-things.

HERE follow the Instructions of Cornelius Scriblerus concerning the Plays and Play-things to be used by his son Martin.
5 *"Play* was invented by the *Lydians* as a remedy against "Hunger. Sophocles says of Palamedes, that he invented *Dice* to "serve sometimes instead / of a dinner. It is therefore wisely con- 34 "trived by Nature, that Children, as they have the keenest *Ap-* "petites, are most addicted to *Plays.* From the same cause, and 10 "from the unprejudic'd and incorrupt simplicity of their minds "it proceeds, that the Plays of the Ancient Children are preserv'd "more entire than any other of their Customs. In this matter I "would recommend to all who have any concern in my Son's "Education, that they deviate not in the least from the primitive 15 "and simple Antiquity.

"To speak first of the *Whistle,* as it is the first of all Play- "things; I will have it exactly to correspond with the ancient "Fistula, and accordingly to be compos'd, *septem paribus dis-* "juncta cicutis.

20 "I heartily wish a diligent search may be made after the true "Crepitaculum or *Rattle* of the Ancients, for that (as *Archytas* "Tarentinus was of opinion) kept the children from breaking "Earthen Ware. The *China* Cups in these days are not at all the "safer for the modern *Rattles;* which is an evident proof how far 25 "their *Crepitacula* exceeded ours.

"I would not have Martin as yet to scourge a *Top,* till I am bet- "ter informed whether the *Trochus* which was recommended "by *Cato* be really our present *Top,* or rather the *Hoop* which "the boys drive with a stick. Neither *Cross and Pile,* / nor *Ducks* 35 30 *"and Drakes* are quite so ancient as *Handy-dandy,* tho' Macro- "bius and St. Augustine take notice of the first, and Minutius "Felix describes the latter; but *Handy-dandy* is mention'd by "Aristotle, Plato, and Aristophanes.

"The Play which the Italians call *Cinque,* and the French 35 *"Mourre,* is extremely ancient; it was play'd at by *Hymen* and "Cupid at the Marriage of *Psyche,* and term'd by the Latins, "digitis micare.

"Julius Pollux describes the *Omilla* or *Chuck-farthing:* tho'
"some will have our modern *Chuck-farthing* to be nearer the
"*Aphetinda* of the Ancients. He also mentions the *Basilinda,* or
"*King I am;* and *Myinda,* or *Hoopers-Hide.*

5 "But the *Chytindra* described by the same Author is certainly
"not our *Hot-cockle;* for that was by pinching and not by strik-
"ing; tho' there are good authors who affirm the *Rathapygismus*
"to be yet nearer the modern *Hot-cockles.* My son Martin may
"use either of them indifferently, they being equally antique.

10 "*Building of Houses,* and *Riding upon Sticks* have been used
"by children in all ages, *Ædificare casas, equitare in arundine*
"*longa.* Yet I much doubt whether the Riding upon Sticks did
"not come into use after the age of the *Centaurs.*

"There is one Play which shews the gravity of ancient Educa-
15 "tion, call'd the *Acinetinda,* in which / Children contended who   36
"could longest *stand still.* This we have suffer'd to perish en-
"tirely; and, if I might be allow'd to guess, it was certainly first
"lost among the *French.*

"I will permit my son to play at *Apodidiascinda,* which can be
20 "no other than our *Puss in a Corner.*

"Julius Pollux in his ninth book speaks of the *Melolouthe* or
"the *Kite;* but I question whether the Kite of Antiquity was the
"same with ours: And tho' the Ὀρτυγοκοπία or *Quail-fighting*
"is what is most taken notice of, they had doubtless *Cock-*
25 "*matches* also, as is evident from certain ancient Gems and
"Relievo's.

"In a word, let my son Martin disport himself at any Game
"truly Antique, except one, which was invented by a people
"among the Thracians, who hung up one of their Companions
30 "in a Rope, and gave him a Knife to cut himself down; which if
"he fail'd in, he was suffer'd to hang till he was dead; and this
"was only reckon'd a sort of joke. I am utterly against this, as
"barbarous and cruel.

"I cannot conclude, without taking notice of the beauty of the
35 "*Greek* names, whose Etymologies acquaint us with the nature
"of the sports; and how infinitely, both in sense and sound, they
"excel our barbarous names of Plays.

Notwithstanding the foregoing Injunctions of Dr. Cornelius,
he yet condescended to allow the Child / the use of some few   37

modern Play-things; such as might prove of any benefit to his mind, by instilling an early notion of the sciences. For example, he found that *Marbles* taught him *Percussion* and the *Laws of Motion; Nut-crackers* the use of the *Leaver; Swinging* on the ends of a Board, the *Balance; Bottle-screws,* the *Vice; Whirligigs* the *Axis* and *Peritrochia; Bird-cages,* the *Pully;* and *Tops* the *Centrifugal* motion.

Others of his sports were farther carried to improve his tender soul even in Virtue and Morality. We shall only instance one of the most useful and instructive, *Bob-cherry,* which teaches at once two noble Virtues, Constancy and Patience; the first in adhering to the pursuit of one end, the latter in bearing a disappointment.

Besides all these, he taught him, as a Diversion, an odd and secret manner of *Stealing,* according to the Custom of the Lacedæmonians; wherein he succeeded so well, that he practised it to the day of his death.

CHAP. VI.

Of the Gymnasticks; *in what Exercises* Martinus *was educated; something concerning* Musick; *and what sort of a Man his Uncle was.*

5   NOR was Cornelius less careful in adhering to the rules of the purest Antiquity, in relation to the *Exercises* of his Son. He was stript, powder'd, and anointed, but not constantly bath'd, which occasioned many heavy complaints of the Laundress about dirtying his linen. When he play'd at Quoits, he was allowed his
10 Breeches and Stockings; because the *Discoboli* (as Cornelius well knew) were naked to the middle only. The Mother often contended for modern Sports and common Customs, but this was his constant reply, "Let a Daughter be the care of her "Mother, but the Education of a Son should be the delight of his
15 "Father."
    It was about this time he heard, to his exceeding content, that the *Harpastus* of the Ancients was yet in use in *Cornwall,* and known there by the name of *Hurling.* He was sensible the common *Foot-ball* was a very imperfect imitation of that exercise;
20 and thought it necessary to send Martin into the West, to be initiated into that truly ancient and manly part of the *Gymnasticks.* The poor boy was / so unfortunate as to return with a broken   39 leg. This Cornelius look'd upon but as a slight ailment, and promis'd his Mother he would instantly cure it: He slit a green
25 Reed, and cast the Knife upward, then tying the two parts of the Reed to the disjointed place, pronounced these Words, [a] *Daries, daries, astataries, dissunapiter; huat, hanat, huat, ista, pista fista, domi abo, damnaustra.* But finding to his no small astonishment, that this had no effect, in five days he condescended to have it
30 set by a modern Surgeon.
    Mrs. Scriblerus, to prevent him from exposing her Son to the like dangerous Exercises for the future, propos'd to send for a Dancing-Master, and to have him taught the Minuet and Rigadoon. "Dancing (quoth Cornelius) I much approve, for *Socrates*

---

[a] Plin. Hist. Nat. lib. 17. in fine. *Carmen contra luxata membra, cujus verba inserere non equidem serio ausim, quanquam a Catone prodita.* Vid. Cato de re rust. c. 160.

"said the best Dancers were the best Warriors; but not those
"species of Dancing which you mention: They are certainly Cor-
"ruptions of the Comic and Satyric Dance, which were utterly
"disliked by the sounder Ancients. Martin shall learn the Tragic
5 "Dance only, and I will send all over Europe till I find an Anti-
"quary able to instruct him in the *Saltatio Pyrrhica*. [b] Scal-
"iger, / from whom my son is lineally descended, boasts to have 40
"perform'd this warlike Dance in the presence of the Emperor,
"to the great admiration of all Germany. What would he say,
10 "could he look down and see one of his posterity so ignorant,
"as not to know the least step of that noble kind of *Saltation*?"

The poor Lady was at last enur'd to bear all these things with
a laudable patience, till one day her husband was seized with a
new thought. He had met with a saying, that *"Spleen, Garter,*
15 "and *Girdle* are the three impediments to the *Cursus.*" Therefore
Pliny (lib. xi. cap. 37.) says, that such as excel in that exercise
have their *Spleen* cauteriz'd. "My son (quoth Cornelius) runs
"but heavily; therefore I will have this operation performed
"upon him immediately. Moreover it will cure that immoderate
20 "Laughter to which I perceive he is addicted: For laughter (as
"the same author hath it, ibid.) is caused by the bigness of the
"Spleen." This design was no sooner hinted to Mrs. Scriblerus,
but she burst into tears, wrung her hands, and instantly sent to
his Brother Albertus, begging him for the love of God to make
25 haste to her husband. /   41

Albertus was a discreet man, sober in his opinions, clear of Pedantry, and knowing enough both in books and in the world, to
preserve a due regard for whatever was useful or excellent,
whether ancient or modern. If he had not always the authority,
30 he had at least the art, to divert Cornelius from many extravagancies. It was well he came speedily, or Martin could not have
boasted the entire Quota of his Viscera. "What does it signify
"(quoth Albertus) whether my Nephew excels in the *Cursus* or
"not? Speed is often a symptom of Cowardice, witness Hares and
35 "Deer."—"Do not forget Achilles (quoth Cornelius) I know
"that Running has been condemn'd by the proud Spartans, as

---

[b] Scalig. Poetic. l. i. c. 9. *Hanc saltationem Pyrrhicam nos sæpe & diu, jussu Bonifacii patrui,
coram Divo Maximiliano, non sine stupore totius Germaniæ, repræsentavimus. Quo tempore vox
illa Imperatoris, Hic puer aut Thoracem pro pelle aut pro cunis habuit.*

"useless in war: and yet Demosthenes could say, ἀνὴρ ὁ φεύγων
"καὶ πάλιν μαχήσεται; a thought which the English Hudibras
"has well rendered,

For he that runs may fight again,
Which he can never do that's slain.

5

"That's true (quoth Albertus) but pray consider on the other
"side that Animals ᶜ spleen'd grow extremely salacious, an ex-
"periment well known in dogs. Cornelius was struck with this,
"and reply'd gravely; If it be so, I will defer the Operation, for
10 "I will not encrease the powers of / my son's body at the expence   42
"of those of his mind. I am indeed disappointed in most of my
"projects, and fear I must sit down at last contented with such
"methods of Education as modern barbarity affords. Happy had
"it been for us all, had we liv'd in the age of Augustus! Then my
15 "son might have heard the Philosophers dispute in the Porticos
"of the Palæstra, and at the same time form'd his Body and his
"Understanding." "It is true (reply'd Albertus) we have no *Ex-*
"*edra* for the Philosophers, adjoining to our Tennis-Courts; but
"there are Ale-houses where he will hear very notable argu-
20 "mentations: Tho' we come not up to the Ancients in the *Tragic*
"*dance,* we excel them in the κυβιστικὴ, or the art of *Tumbling.*
"The Ancients would have beat us at *Quoits,* but not so much
"at the *Jaculum* or *pitching the Bar.* The ᵈ *Pugilatus* is in as great
"perfection in England as in old Rome, and the *Cornish-Hug* in
25 "the ᵉ *Luctus* is equal to the *Volutatoria* of the Ancients." "You
"could not (answer'd Cornelius) have produc'd a more unlucky
"instance of modern folly and barbarity, than what you say of the
"*Jaculum.* ᶠ The Cretans wisely forbid their servants Gymnas-
"ticks, as well as Arms; and yet your modern Footmen exercise
30 "them- / selves daily in the *Jaculum* at the corner of *Hyde Park,*   43
"whilst their enervated Lords are lolling in their chariots (a
"species of Vectitation seldom us'd amongst the Ancients, except
"by old men.) You say well (quoth Albertus) and we have sev-
"eral other kinds of Vectitation unknown to the Ancients, par-
35 "ticularly flying Chariots, where the people may have the benefit
"of this exercise at the small expence of a farthing. But suppose

ᶜ Blackmore's Essay on Spleen.   ᵈ Fisty-Cuffs.
ᵉ Wrestling.   ᶠ Aristot. Politic. lib. 2. cap. 3.

"(which I readily grant) that the Ancients excel'd us almost in
"every thing, yet why this singularity? Your son must take up
"with such masters as the present age affords; we have Dancing-
"masters, Writing-masters, and Musick-masters."

5   The bare mention of *Musick* threw Cornelius into a passion.
"How can you dignify (quoth he) this modern fiddling with the
"name of Musick? Will any of your best Hautboys encounter a
"Wolf now-a-days with no other arms but their instruments, as
"did that ancient Piper Pythocaris? Have ever wild Boars, Ele-
10 "phants, Deer, Dolphins, Whales or Turbotts, shew'd the least
"emotion at the most elaborate strains of your modern Scrapers,
"all which have been as it were tam'd and humaniz'd by ancient
"Musicians? Does not ᵍ Ælian tell us how the Libyan Mares
"were ex- / cited to horsing by Musick? (which ought in truth to   44
15 "be a caution to modest Women against frequenting Operas;
"and consider, brother, you are brought to this dilemma, either
"to give up the virtue of the Ladies, or the power of your
"Musick.) Whence proceeds the degeneracy of our Morals? Is it
"not from the loss of ancient Musick, by which (says Aristotle)
20 "they taught all the Virtues? Else might we turn Newgate into
"a College of Dorian Musicians, who should teach moral Virtues
"to those people. Whence comes it that our present diseases are
"so stubborn? whence is it that I daily deplore my Sciatical
"pains? Alas! because we have lost their true cure, by the melody
25 "of the Pipe. All this was well known to the Ancients, as ʰ Theo-
"phrastus assures us (whence ⁱ Cælius calls it *loca dolentia de-*
"*cantare*) only indeed some small remains of this skill are pre-
"served in the cure of the Tarantula. Did not ᵏ Pythagoras stop a
"company of drunken Bullies from storming a civil house, by
30 "changing the strain of the Pipe to the sober Spondæus? and yet
"your modern Musicians want art to defend their windows from
"common Nickers. It is well known that when the Lacedæ-
"monian Mob were up, they ˡ commonly sent for a Lesbian Musi-
"cian to appease them, and they immediately grew calm as
35 "soon / as they heard Terpander sing: Yet I don't believe that   45
"the Pope's whole band of Musick, tho' the best of this age, could

ᵍ Ælian. Hist. Animal. lib. xi. cap. 18. and lib. xii. cap. 44.
ʰ Athenæus, lib. xiv.   ⁱ Lib. de sanit. tuenda, c. 2.
ᵏ Quintil. lib. I. cap. 10.   ˡ Suidas in Timotheo.

"keep his Holiness's Image from being burnt on a fifth of No-
"vember. Nor would Terpander himself (reply'd Albertus) at
"Billinsgate, nor Timotheus at Hockley in the Hole have any
"manner of effect, nor both of 'em together bring ^m Horneck to
5 "common civility." "That's a gross mistake (said Cornelius very
"warmly) and to prove it so, I have here a small Lyra of my own,
"fram'd, strung, and tun'd after the ancient manner. I can play
"some fragments of Lesbian tunes, and I wish I were to try them
"upon the most passionate creatures alive."—"You never had a
10 "better opportunity (says Albertus) for yonder are two Apple-
"women scolding, and just ready to uncoif one another." With
that Cornelius, undress'd as he was, jumps out into his Balcony,
his Lyra in hand, in his slippers, with his breeches hanging down
to his ankles, a stocking upon his head, and a waistcoat of
15 murrey-colour'd sattin upon his body: He touch'd his Lyra with
a very unusual sort of an Harpegiatura, nor were his hopes frustrated. The odd Equipage, the uncouth Instrument, the strangeness of the Man and of the Musick drew the ears and eyes of the
whole Mob that were got about the two female Champions, and
20 at last of / the Combatants themselves. They all approach'd the   46
Balcony, in as close attention as Orpheus's first Audience of Cat-
tle, or that of an Italian Opera when some favourite Air is just
awaken'd. This sudden effect of his Musick encouraged him
mightily, and it was observ'd he never touch'd his Lyre in such
25 a truly chromatick and enharmonick manner as upon that occasion. The mob laugh'd, sung, jump'd, danc'd, and us'd many odd
gestures, all which he judg'd to be caused by his various strains
and modulations. "Mark (quoth he) in this, the power of the
"Ionian; in that, you see the effect of the Æolian." But in a little
30 time they began to grow riotous, and threw stones: Cornelius
then withdrew, but with the greatest air of Triumph in the
world. "Brother (said he) do you observe I have mixed unawares
"too much of the *Phrygian;* I might change it to the *Lydian,* and
"soften their riotous tempers: But it is enough: Learn from this
35 "Sample to speak with veneration of ancient Musick. If this Lyre
"in my unskilful hands can perform such wonders, what must
"it not have done in those of a Timotheus or a Terpander?" Hav-

^m Horneck, a scurrilous Scribler who wrote a weekly paper, called *The High German Doctor.*

ing said this, he retir'd with the utmost Exultation in himself, and Contempt of his Brother; and, it is said, behav'd that night with such unusual haughtiness to his family, that they all had reason to wish for some ancient Tibicen to calm his Temper. /   47

Rhetoric, Logic, Metaphysics.

COrnelius having (as hath been said) many ways been disappointed in his attempts of improving the bodily Forces of his son,
5 thought it now high time to apply to the Culture of his Internal faculties. He judg'd it proper in the first place to instruct him in *Rhetorick*. But herein we shall not need to give the Reader any account of his wonderful progress, since it is already known to the learned world by his Treatise on this subject: I mean the ad-
10 mirable Discourse Περὶ Βάθους, which he wrote at this time but conceal'd from his Father, knowing his extreme partiality for the Ancients. It lay by him conceal'd, and perhaps forgot among the great multiplicity of other Writings, till, about the year 1727, he sent it us to be printed, with many additional examples drawn
15 from the excellent live Poets of this present age. We proceed therefore to *Logick* and *Metaphysick*.

The wise Cornelius was convinced that these, being *Polemical* Arts, could no more be learned alone, than Fencing or Cudgel-playing. He thought it therefore necessary to look out for some
20 Youth of pregnant parts, to be a sort of humble Companion to his son in those Studies. His good / fortune directed him to one of most singular endowments, whose name was Conradus Crambe, who by the father's side was related to the *Crouches* of Cambridge, and his mother was Cousin to Mr. *Swan*, Game-
25 ster and Punster of the City of London. So that from both parents he drew a natural disposition to sport himself with *Words,* which as they are said to be the counters of wise Men, and ready-money of Fools, Crambe had great store of cash of the latter sort. Happy Martin in such a Parent, and such a Companion! What
30 might not he atchieve in Arts and Sciences.

Here I must premise a general observation, of great benefit to mankind. That there are many people who have the use only of one Operation of the Intellect, tho' like short-sighted men they can hardly discover it themselves: They can form *single appre-*
35 *hensions,* but have neither of the other two faculties, the *judi-cium* or *discursus.* Now as it is wisely order'd, that people de-

priv'd of one sense have the others in more perfection, such people will form single Ideas with a great deal of vivacity; and
happy were it indeed if they would confine themselves to such,
without forming *judicia,* much less *argumentations.*

5   Cornelius quickly discovered, that these two last operations
of the intellect were very weak in Martin, and almost totally extinguish'd in Crambe; however he used to say that Rules of
Logick are / Spectacles to a purblind understanding, and there-   49
fore he resolved to proceed with his two Pupils.

10   Martin's understanding was so totally immers'd in *sensible
objects,* that he demanded examples from Material things of the
abstracted Ideas of Logick: As for Crambe, he contented himself
with the Words, and when he could but form some conceit upon
them, was fully satisfied. Thus Crambe would tell his Instructor,
15 that All men were not *singular;* that Individuality could hardly
be prædicated of any man, for it was commonly said that a man
is not the same he *was,* that madmen are *beside themselves,* and
drunken men *come to themselves;* which shews, that few men
have that most valuable logical endowment, Individuality. Cor-
20 nelius told Martin that a shoulder of mutton was an individual,
which Crambe denied, for he had seen it cut into commons:
That's true (quoth the Tutor) but you never saw it cut into
shoulders of mutton: If it could (quoth Crambe) it would be the
most lovely individual of the University. When he was told, a
25 *substance* was that which was *subject to accidents;* then Soldiers
(quoth Crambe) are the most substantial people in the world.
Neither would he allow it to be a good definition of *accident,*
that it could be *present or absent without the destruction of the
subject;* since there are a great many accidents that destroy the
30 subject, as burning does a house, and death a man. But as to /   50
that, Cornelius informed him, that there was a *natural death,*
and *a logical death;* that though a man after his natural death
was not capable of the least parish-office, yet he might still keep
his Stall amongst the logical prædicaments.

35   Cornelius was forc'd to give Martin sensible images; thus calling up the Coachman he ask'd him what he had seen at the Bear-
garden? The man answered he saw two men fight a prize; one
was a fair man, a Sergeant in the Guards, the other black, a
Butcher; the Sergeant had red breeches, the Butcher blue; they

fought upon a Stage about four o'clock, and the Sergeant
wounded the Butcher in the leg. "Mark (quoth Cornelius) how
"the fellow runs through the prædicaments. Men, *Substantia;*
"two, *quantitas;* fair and black, *qualitas;* Sergeant and Butcher,
5 "*relatio;* wounded the other, *actio & passio;* fighting, *situs;*
"Stage, *ubi;* two o'Clock, *quando;* blue and red Breeches, *habitus.*" At the same time he warn'd Martin, that what he now
learn'd as a Logician, he must *forget* as a natural Philosopher;
that tho' he now taught them that accidents inher'd in the sub-
10 ject, they would find in time there was no such thing; and that
colour, taste, smell, heat, and cold, were not in the things, but
only phantasms of our brains. He was forc'd to let them into this
secret, for Martin could not conceive how a habit inher'd in a
dancing-master, when he did not / dance; nay, he would de-   51
15 mand the Characteristicks of Relations. Crambe us'd to help him
out by telling him, a Cuckold, a losing gamester, a man that had
not din'd, a young heir that was kept short by his father, might
be all known by their countenance; that, in this last case, the Pa-
ternity and Filiation leave very sensible impressions in the *re-
20 latum* and *correlatum.* The greatest difficulty was, when they
came to the Tenth prædicament: Crambe affirmed, that his
Habitus was more a substance than he was; for his cloaths could
better subsist without him, than he without his cloaths.

Martin suppos'd an *Universal Man* to be like a Knight of a
25 Shire or a Burgess of a Corporation, that represented a great
many Individuals. His Father ask'd him, if he could not frame
the Idea of an Universal Lord Mayor? Martin told him, that
never having seen but one Lord Mayor, the Idea of that Lord
Mayor always return'd to his mind; that he had great difficulty
30 to abstract a Lord Mayor from his Fur, Gown, and Gold Chain;
nay, that the horse he saw the Lord Mayor ride upon not a little
disturb'd his imagination. On the other hand Crambe, to shew
himself of a more penetrating genius, swore that he could frame
a conception of a Lord Mayor not only without his Horse, Gown,
35 and Gold Chain, but even without Stature, Feature, Colour,
Hands, Head, Feet, or any Body; which he suppos'd was the abstract of a Lord / Mayor. Cornelius told him that he was a lying   52
Rascal; that an *Universale* was not the object of imagination, and

that there was no such thing in reality, or a *parte Rei*. But I can prove (quoth Crambe) that there are *Clysters a parte Rei,* but *clysters* are *universales; ergo.* Thus I prove my Minor. *Quod aptum est inesse multis,* is an *universale* by definition; but every
5 clyster before it is administered has that quality; therefore every clyster is an *universale.*

He also found fault with the Advertisements, that they were not strict logical *definitions:* In an advertisement of a Dog stolen or strayed, he said it ought to begin thus, *An irrational animal*
10 of the *Genus caninum,* &c. Cornelius told them, that though those advertisements were not fram'd according to the exact rules of logical definitions, being only *descriptions* of things *numero differentibus,* yet they contain'd a faint image of the *prædicabilia,* and were highly subservient to the common pur-
15 poses of life; often discovering things that were lost, both animate and inanimate. *An Italian Grey-hound, of a mouse-colour, a white speck in the neck, lame of one leg, belongs to such a Lady.* Grey-hound, *Genus;* mouse-colour'd, &c. *differentia;* lame of one leg, *accidens;* belongs to such a Lady, *proprium.*
20 Though I'm afraid I have transgress'd upon my Reader's patience already, I cannot help taking notice of one thing more extraordinary than any / yet mention'd; which was Crambe's 53 *Treatise of Syllogisms.* He suppos'd that a Philosopher's brain was like a great Forest, where Ideas rang'd like animals of several
25 kinds; that those Ideas copulated and engender'd Conclusions; that when those of different Species copulate, they bring forth monsters or absurdities; that the *Major* is the male, the *Minor* the female, which copulate by the Middle Term, and engender the Conclusion. Hence they are call'd the *præmissa,* or Predecessors
30 of the Conclusion; and it is properly said by the Logicians *quod pariunt scientiam, opinionem;* they *beget* science, opinion, &c. Universal Propositions are Persons of quality; and therefore in Logick they are said to be of the first *Figure:* Singular Propositions are Private persons, and therefore plac'd in the third or last
35 figure, or rank. From those Principles all the rules of Syllogisms naturally follow.

I.   That there are only three Terms, neither more nor less; for to a child there can be only one father and one mother.

II.   From universal premisses there follows an universal con-
        clusion; as if one should say that persons of quality always
        beget persons of quality.

III.   From singular premisses follows only a singular conclu-
5   sion; that is, if the parents be only private people, the issue
        must be so likewise. /   54

IV.   From particular propositions nothing can be concluded;
        because the *Individua vaga* are (like whoremasters and
        common Strumpets) barren.

10 V.   There cannot be more in the conclusion than was in the
        premisses; that is, children can only inherit from their
        parents.

VI.   The conclusion follows the weaker part; that is, children
        inherit the diseases of their parents.

VII.   From two negatives nothing can be concluded; for from
        divorce or separation there can come no issue.

VIII.   The medium cannot enter the conclusion; that being
        logical incest.

IX.   An hypothetical proposition is only a contract, or a prom-
20   ise of marriage; from such therefore there can spring no
        real issue.

X.   When the Premisses or parents are necessarily join'd (or
        in lawful wedlock) they beget lawful issue; but contin-
        gently join'd, they beget bastards.

25   So much for the Affirmative propositions; the Negative must
be defer'd to another occasion.

   Crambe us'd to value himself upon this System, from whence
he said one might see the propriety of the expression, *such a one
has a barren imagination;* and how common it is for such people
30 to *adopt* conclusions that are not the issue of their pre-/ misses: 55
Therefore as an Absurdity is a *Monster,* a Falsity is a *Bastard;*
and a true conclusion that followeth not from the premisses,
may properly be said to be *adopted.* But then what is an
Enthymem? (quoth Cornelius.) Why, an Enthymem (reply'd
35 Crambe) is when the Major is indeed married to the Minor, but
the Marriage *kept secret.*
   METAPHYSICKS were a large field in which to exercise the

Weapons *Logick* had put into their hands. Here Martin and Crambe us'd to engage like any prize-fighters, before their Father, and his other learned companions of the Symposiacks. And as Prize-fighters will agree to lay aside a buckler or some
5 such defensive weapon, so would Crambe promise not to use *simpliciter & secundum quid,* provided Martin would part with *materialiter & formaliter:* But it was found, that without the help of the defensive armour of those Distinctions, the arguments cut so deep, that they fetch'd blood at every stroke. Their
10 *Theses* were pick'd out of Suarez, Thomas Aquinas, and other learned writers on those subjects. I shall give the Reader a taste of some of them.

I.   If the Innate Desire of the knowledge of Metaphysics was the cause of the Fall of Adam; and the *Arbor Porphyri-*
15   *ana* the Tree of Knowledge of good and evil? *affirm'd.* /   56
II.   If transcendental goodness could be truly prædicated of the Devil? *affirm'd.*
III.   Whether one, or many be first? or if one doth not suppose the notion of many? *Suarez.*
20 IV.   If the desire of news in mankind be *appetitus innatus* not *elicitus? affirm'd.*
V.   Whether there are in human understandings potential falsities? *affirm'd.*
VI.   Whether God loves a *possible Angel* better than an *actu-*
25   *ally-existent flie? deny'd.*
VII.   If Angels pass from one extreme to another without going through the middle? *Aquinas.*
VIII.   If Angels know things more clearly in a morning? *Aquinas.*
30 IX.   Whether every Angel hears what one Angel says to another? *deny'd. Aquinas.*
X.   If temptation be *proprium quarto modo* of the Devil? *deny'd. Aquinas.*
XI.   Whether one Devil can illuminate another? *Aquin.*
35 XII. If there would have been any females born in the state of Innocence? *Aquinas.*
XIII.   If the Creation was finish'd in six days, because six is the most perfect number; or if six be the most perfect number

because the Creation was finished in six days? *Aquinas.*
There were several others of which in the course of the Life of
this learned person we may have occasion to treat, and one particularly that remains unde- / cided to this day; it was taken   57
5 from the learned Suarez.

XIV. *An præter* esse reale *actualis essentiæ sit aliud* esse necessarium *quo res actualiter existat?* ·In English thus.
Whether besides the real being of actual being, there be
any other being necessary to cause a thing to be?

10 This brings into my mind a Project to banish Metaphysicks
out of Spain, which it was suppos'd might be effectuated by this
method: That nobody should use any Compound or Decompound of the Substantial Verbs but as they are read in the common conjugations; for every body will allow, that if you debar a
15 Metaphysician from *ens, essentia, entitas, subsistentia,* &c. there
is an end of him.

Crambe regretted extremely, that *Substantial Forms,* a race
of harmless beings which had lasted for many years, and afforded a comfortable subsistance to many poor Philosophers,
20 should be now hunted down like so many Wolves, without the
possibility of a retreat. He consider'd that it had gone much
harder with them than with *Essences,* which had retir'd from the
Schools into the *Apothecaries Shops,* where some of them had
been advanc'd into the degree of *Quintessences.* He thought
25 there should be a retreat for poor *substantial Forms,* amongst the
Gentlemen-ushers at court; / and that there were indeed *sub-*   58
stantial forms, such as *forms of Prayer,* and *forms of Government,* without which, the things themselves could never long
subsist. He also us'd to wonder that there was not a reward for
30 such as could find out a *fourth Figure* in *Logick,* as well as for
those who shou'd discover the *Longitude.*

CHAP. VIII.

ANATOMY.

COrnelius, it is certain, had a most superstitious veneration
for the Ancients; and if they contradicted each other, his Reason
5 was so pliant and ductile, that he was always of the opinion of
the last he read. But he reckon'd it a point of honour never to be
vanquish'd in a dispute; from which quality he acquir'd the
Title of the *Invincible Doctor.* While the Professor of Anatomy
was demonstrating to his son the several kinds of *Intestines,*
10 Cornelius affirm'd that there were only two, the *Colon* and the
Aichos, according to Hippocrates, who it was impossible could
ever be mistaken. It was in vain to assure him this error proceeded from want of accuracy in dividing the whole Canal of the
Guts: Say what you please (he reply'd) this / is both mine and   59
15 Hippocrates's opinion. You may with equal reason (answer'd
the Professor) affirm that a man's Liver hath five Lobes, and
deny the Circulation of the blood. Ocular demonstration (said
Cornelius) seems to be on your side, yet I shall not give it up:
Shew me any viscus of a human body , and I will bring you a
20 monster that differs from the common rule in the structure of it.
If Nature shews such variety in the same age, why may she not
have extended it further in several ages? Produce me a man now
of the age of an Antediluvian, of the strength of Sampson, or the
size of the Giants. If in the whole, why may it not in parts of the
25 body, be possible the present generation of men may differ from
the Ancients? The Moderns have perhaps lengthen'd the chan-
nel of the guts by Gluttony, and diminished the liver by hard
drinking. Though it shall be demonstrated that modern blood
circulates, yet I will still believe, with Hippocrates, that the blood
30 of the Ancients had a flux and reflux from the heart, like a Tide.
Consider how Luxury hath introduced new diseases, and with
them not improbably alter'd the whole Course of the Fluids.
Consider how the current of mighty Rivers, nay the very chan-
nels of the Ocean are changed from what they were in ancient
35 days; and can we be so vain to imagine that the Microcosm of the
human body alone is exempted from the fate of all things? I /   60

question not but plausible Conjectures may be made even as to
the Time when the blood first began to circulate.—Such disputes as these frequently perplex'd the Professor to that degree,
that he would now and then in a passion leave him in the mid-
5 dle of a Lecture, as he did at this time.

   There unfortunately happen'd soon after, an unusual accident,
which retarded the prosecution of the studies of Martin. Having
purchas'd the body of a Malefactor, he hir'd a Room for its dissection, near the Pest-fields in St. Giles's, at a little distance from
10 Tyburn Road. Crambe (to whose care this body was committed)
carry'd it thither about twelve o'clock at night in a Hackney-
coach, few House-keepers being very willing to let their lodgings
to such kind of Operators. As he was softly stalking up stairs in
the dark, with the dead man in his arms, his burthen had like to
15 have slipp'd from him, which he (to save from falling) grasp'd
so hard about the belly that it forced the wind through the *Anus,*
with a noise exactly like the *Crepitus* of a living man. Crambe
(who did not comprehend how this part of the Animal Oecon-
omy could remain in a dead man) was so terrify'd, that he threw
20 down the body, ran up to his master, and had scarce breath to tell
him what had happen'd. Martin with all his Philosophy could
not prevail upon him to return to his post. You may say what
you please (quoth Crambe) no man / alive ever broke wind   61
more naturally; nay, he seemed to be mightily relieved by it. The
25 rolling of the corps down stairs made such a noise that it awak'd
the whole house. The maid shriek'd; the landlady cry'd out
Thieves; but the Landlord, in his shirt as he was, taking a candle
in one hand, and a drawn sword in the other, ventur'd out of the
Room. The maid with only a single petticoat ran up stairs, but
30 spurning at the dead body, fell upon it in a swoon. Now the landlord stood still and list'ned, then he look'd behind him, and ventur'd down in this manner one stair after another, till he came
where lay his maid, as dead, upon another corps unknown. The
wife ran into the street and cry'd out Murder! The Watch ran
35 in, while Martin and Crambe, hearing all this uproar, were coming down stairs. The Watch imagin'd they were making their escape, seiz'd them immediately, and carried them to a neighbouring Justice; where, upon searching them, several kind of knives
and dreadful weapons were found upon them. The Justice first

examin'd Crambe. What is your Name? says the Justice. I have
acquir'd (quoth Crambe) no great Name as yet; they call me
Crambe or Crambo, no matter which, as to myself; though it
may be some dispute to posterity.—What is yours and your Mas-
5 ter's profession;—"It is our business to imbrue our hands in
"blood; we cut off the heads, and pull out the hearts of / those 62
"that never injur'd us; we rip up big-belly'd women, and tear
"children limb from limb." Martin endeavour'd to interrupt
him; but the Justice being strangely astonish'd with the frank-
10 ness of Crambe's Confession, order'd him to proceed; upon
which he made the following Speech.

    "May it please your Worship, as touching the body of this
"man, I can answer each head that my accusers alledge against
"me, to a hair. They have hitherto talk'd like num-sculls without
15 "brains; but if your Worship will not only give ear, but regard
"me with a favourable eye, I will not be brow-beaten by the
"supercilious looks of my adversaries, who now stand cheek by
"jowl by your Worship. I will prove to their faces, that their foul
"mouths have not open'd their lips without a falsity; though
20 "they have shew'd their teeth as if they would bite off my nose.
"Now, Sir, that I may fairly slip my neck out of the collar, I beg
"this matter may not be slightly skin'd over. Tho' I have no man
"here to back me, I will unbosom myself, since Truth is on my
"side, and shall give them their bellies full, though they think
25 "they have me upon the hip. Whereas they say I came into their
"lodgings, with arms, and murder'd this man without their
"Privity, I declare I had not the least finger in it; and since I am
"to stand upon my own legs, nothing of this matter shall / be 63
"left till I set it upon a right foot. In the vein I am in, I cannot for
30 "my heart's blood and guts bear this usage: I shall not spare my
"lungs to defend my good name: I was ever reckon'd a good
"liver; and I.think I have the bowels of compassion. I ask but
"justice, and from the crown of my head to the soal of my foot
"I shall ever acknowledge myself your Worship's humble Serv-
35 "ant."

    The justice stared, the Landlord and Landlady lifted up their
eyes, and Martin fretted, while Crambe talk'd in this rambling
incoherent manner; till at length Martin begg'd to be heard. It
was with great difficulty that the Justice was convinc'd, till they

sent for the Finisher of human laws, of whom the Corps had been purchas'd; who looking near the left ear, knew his own work, and gave Oath accordingly.

No sooner was Martin got home, but he fell into a passion at
5 Crambe. "What Dæmon, he cried, hath possessed thee, that thou "wilt never forsake that impertinent custom of punning? "Neither my counsel nor my example have thus misled thee; "thou governest thyself by most erroneous Maxims." Far from it (answers Crambe) my life is as orderly as my Dictionary, for
10 by "my Dictionary I order my life. I have made a Kalendar of radical words for all the seasons, months, and days of the year: Every day I am / under the dominion of a certain Word: But   64 this day in particular I cannot be misled, for I am govern'd by one that rules all sexes, ages, conditions, nay all animals rational
15 and irrational. Who is not govern'd by the word *Led?* Our Noblemen and Drunkards are pimp-led, Physicians and Pulses fee-led, their Patients and Oranges pil-led, a New-married Man and an Ass are bride-led, an old-married Man and a Pack-horse sad-led; Cats and Dice rat-led, Swine and Nobility are sty-led, a
20 Coquet and a Tinder-box are spark-led, a Lover and a Blunderer are grove-led. And that I may not be tedious—Which thou art (reply'd Martin, stamping with his foot) which thou art, I say, beyond all human toleration—Such an unnatural, unaccountable, uncoherent, unintelligible, unprofitable—There it is now
25 (interrupted Crambe) this your Day for *Uns.* Martin could bear no longer—however composing his Countenance, Come hither —he cry'd, there are five pounds, seventeen shillings and nine pence: thou hast been with me eight months, three weeks, two days, and four hours. Poor Crambe upon the receipt of his Salary,
30 fell into tears, flung the money upon the ground, and burst forth in these words: "O Cicero, Cicero! if to pun be a crime, 'tis a "Crime I have learned from thee: O Bias, Bias! if ,to pun be a "crime, by thy example was I / bias'd." Whereupon Martin   65 (considering that one of the greatest of Orators, and even a Sage of Greece had punned) hesitated, relented, and re-instated Crambe in his Service.

CHAP. IX.

How Martin *became a great Critic.*

IT was a most peculiar Talent in Martinus, to convert every Trifle into a serious thing, either in the way of Life, or in Learn-
5 ing. This can no way be better exemplified, than in the effect which the Puns of Crambe had on the Mind and Studies of Martinus. He conceiv'd, that somewhat of a like Talent to this of Crambe, of *assembling parallel sounds,* either *syllables,* or *words,* might conduce to the Emendation and Correction of
10 *Ancient Authors,* if applied to their Works, with the same *dili-gence,* and the same *liberty.* He resolv'd to try first upon Virgil, Horace, and Terence; concluding, that, if the *most correct* Authors could be so served with any reputation to the Critick, the amendment and alteration of *all the rest* wou'd easily follow;
15 whereby a new, a vast, nay boundless Field of Glory would be open'd to the true and *absolute Critick.*

This Specimen on Virgil he has given us, in the / Addenda 66 to his Notes on the Dunciad. His Terence and Horace are in every body's hands, under the names of Richard B—ley, and
20 Francis H—re. And we have convincing proofs that the late Edition of Milton publish'd in the name of the former of these, was in truth the Work of no other than our Scriblerus.

CHAP. X.

Of Martinus*'s Uncommon Practice of* Physick, *and how he applied himself to the* Diseases *of the* Mind.

BUT it is high time to return to the History of the Progress
5 of Martinus in the Studies of Physick, and to enumerate some at
least of the many Discoveries and Experiments he made therein.
   One of the first was his Method of investigating latent Distempers, by the sagacious Quality of *Setting-Dogs* and *Pointers.*
The success, and the Adventures that befel him, when he walk'd
10 with these Animals, to smell them out in the Parks and public
places about London, are what we would willingly relate; but
that his own Account, together with a *List of those Gentlemen
and Ladies* at whom they made a *Full Sett,* will be publish'd in
time convenient. There will also be added the Repre- / sentation, 67
15 which on occasion of one distemper which was become almost
epidemical, he thought himself oblig'd to lay before both Houses
of Parliament, intitled, *A Proposal for a General Flux,* to exterminate at one blow the P—x out of this Kingdom.
   He next proceeded to an Enquiry into the *Nature* and *Tokens*
20 of *Virginity,* according of the Jewish Doctrines, which occasion'd that most curious Treatise of the *Purification* of [a]*Queen
Esther,* with a *Display* of her *Case* at large; speedily also to be
published.
   But being weary of all practice on *foetid Bodies,* from a certain
25 niceness of Constitution (especially when he attended Dr.
Woodward thro' a Twelve-month's course of Vomition) he determined to leave it off entirely, and to apply himself only to
diseases of the *Mind.* He attempted to find out Specifics for all
the *Passions;* and, as other Physicians throw their Patients into
30 sweats, vomits, purgations, &c. he cast them into love, hatred,
hope, fear, joy, grief, &c. And indeed the great Irregularity of
the Passions in the English Nation, was the chief motive that induced him to apply his whole studies, while he continued among
us, to the Diseases of the Mind.
35   To this purpose he directed, in the first place, his late acquir'd
   [a] Vid. Esther, chap. ii. v. 12.

skill in *Anatomy*. He consider'd *Virtues* and *Vices* as certain
Habits which proceed from / the natural Formation and Struc-   68
ture of particular parts of the body. A Bird flies because it has
Wings; a Duck swims because it is web-footed; and there can be
5   no question but the aduncity of the pounces, and beaks of the
Hawks, as well as the length of the fangs, the sharpness of the
teeth, and the strength of the crural and Masseter-muscles in
Lions and Tygers, are the cause of the great and habitual Immorality of those Animals.

10   1st, He observ'd that the Soul and Body mutually operate upon
each other, and therefore, if you deprive the Mind of the outward Instruments whereby she usually expresseth that Passion,
you will in time abate the Passion itself; in like manner as Castra-
tion abates Lust.

15   2dly, That the Soul in mankind expresseth every Passion by
the Motion of some particular *Muscles.*

3dly, That all Muscles grow stronger and thicker by being
much us'd; therefore the habitual Passions may be discerned in
particular persons by the *strength* and *bigness* of the Muscles us'd
20   in the expression of that Passion.

4thly, That a Muscle may be strengthen'd or weakned by
weakning or strengthening the force of its Antagonist. These
things premis'd, he took notice, /   69

That *complaisance, humility, assent, approbation,* and *civility,*
25   were express'd by nodding the head and bowing the body forward: on the contrary, *dissent, dislike, refusal, pride,* and *arrogance,* were mark'd by tossing the head, and bending the body
backwards: which two Passions of *assent* and *dissent* the Latins
rightly express'd by the words *adnuere* and *abnuere.* Now he ob-
30   serv'd that complaisant and civil people had the Flexors of the
head very strong; but in the proud and insolent there was a
great over-balance of strength in the Extensors of the Neck and
Muscles of the Back, from whence they perform with great facil-
ity the motion of *tossing,* but with great difficulty that of *bowing,*
35   and therefore have justly acquir'd the title of *stiff-neck'd.* In
order to reduce such persons to a just balance, he judg'd that the

pair of Muscles call'd *Recti interni,* the Mastoidal, with other flexors of the head, neck, and body must be strengthen'd; their Antagonists, the *Splenii Complexi,* and the Extensors of the Spine, weaken'd: For which purpose Nature herself seems to
5 have directed mankind to correct this Muscular Immorality by tying such fellows *Neck-and-heels.*

Contrary to this is the pernicious Custom of Mothers, who abolish the natural Signature of Modesty in their Daughters by teaching them *tossing* and *bridling,* rather than the bashful pos-
10 ture of *stooping,* and *hanging down the head.* Martinus charg'd all / husbands to take notice of the *Posture of the Head* of such   70 as they courted to Matrimony, as that upon which their future happiness did much depend.

Flatterers, who have the flexor Muscles so strong that they are
15 always bowing and cringing, he suppos'd might in some measure be corrected by being tied down upon a Tree by the back, like the children of the Indians; which doctrine was strongly confirm'd by his observing the strength of the *levatores Scapulæ:* These Muscles are call'd the Muscles of *patience,* because in that
20 affection of Mind people shrug and raise up the shoulders to the tip of the ear. These Muscles also he observed to be exceedingly strong and large in *Henpeck'd Husbands,* in *Italians,* and in *English Ministers.*

In pursuance of his Theory, he suppos'd the *Constrictors* of the
25 *Eye-lids* must be strengthen'd in the supercilious, the *abductors* in drunkards and contemplative men, who have the same steddy and grave motion of the eye. That the *buccinatores* or blowers up of the *Cheeks,* and the *dilators* of the *Nose,* were too strong in Cholerick people; and therefore Nature here again directed us to
30 a remedy, which was to correct such extraordinary dilatation by *pulling by the Nose.*

The rolling amorous Eye, in the Passion of Love, might be corrected by frequently looking thro' glasses. Impertinent fellows that jump upon tables, and cut capers, might be cur'd by relax-
35 ing / medicines applied to the *Calves* of the *legs,* which in such   71 people are too strong.

But there were two cases which he reckon'd extremely difficult. First, *Affectation,* in which there were so many Muscles of the bum, thighs, belly, neck, back, and the whole body, all in a

false tone, that it requir'd an impracticable multiplicity of applications.

The second case was immoderate *Laughter:* When any of
that risible species were brought to the Doctor, and when he
5 consider'd what an infinity of Muscles these laughing Rascals
threw into a convulsive motion at the same time; whether we regard the spasms of the Diaphragm and all the muscles of respira-
tion, the horrible *rictus* of the mouth, the distortion of the lower
jaw, the crisping of the nose, twinkling of the eyes, or sphærical
10 convexity of the cheeks, with the tremulous succussion of the
whole human body; when he consider'd, I say, all this, he used to
cry out, *Casus plane deplorabilis!* and give such Patients over.

*The Case of a young Nobleman at Court, with
the Doctor's Prescription for the same.*

AN eminent instance of Martinus's sagacity in discovering
5 the distempers of the Mind, appear'd in the case of a young
Nobleman at Court, who was observ'd to grow extremely affected in his speech, and whimsical in all his behaviour. He began to ask odd questions, talk in verse to himself, shut himself
up from his friends, and be accessible to none, but Flatterers,
10 Poets, and Pickpockets; till his Relations and old Acquaintance
judged him to be so far gone, as to be a fit Patient for the Doctor.

As soon as he had heard and examined all the symptoms, he
pronounced his distemper to be *Love*.

His friends assured him that they had with great care observ'd
15 all his motions, and were perfectly satisfied there was no Woman
in the case. Scriblerus was as positive that he was desperately in
love with some person or other. "How can that be? (said his
"Aunt, who came to ask the advice) when he converses almost
"with none but himself?" Say you so? (he replied) why then he
20 is in love with Himself, one of the most common / cases in the   73
world. I am astonish'd, people do not enough attend this disease,
which has the same causes and symptoms, and admits of the
same cure, with the other: especially since here the case of the Patient is the more helpless and deplorable of the two, as this un-
25 fortunate passion is more blind than the other. There are people
who discover from their very youth a most amorous inclination
to themselves; which is unhappily nurs'd by such Mothers, as,
with their good will, wou'd never suffer their children to be
cross'd in love. Ease, luxury, and idleness, blow up this flame as
30 well as the other: Constant opportunities of conversation with
the person beloved (the greatest of incentives) are here impossible to be prevented. Bawds and Pimps in the other love, will
be perpetually doing kind offices, speaking a good word for the
party, and carry about Billet-doux. Therefore I ask you, Madam,
35 if this Gentleman has not been much frequented by Flatterers,
and a sort of people who bring him dedications and verses? "O

"Lord! Sir, (quoth the Aunt) the house is haunted with them."
There it is (replied Scriblerus) those are the bawds and pimps
that go between a man and himself. Are there no civil Ladies,
that tell him he dresses well, has a gentlemanly air, and the like?
5 "Why truly, Sir, my Nephew is not aukward— Look you,
Madam, this is a misfortune to him: In former days this sort of
lovers were happy in one respect, / that they never had any   74
Rivals, but of late they have all the Ladies so— Be pleased to answer a few questions more. Whom does he generally talk of?
10 Himself, quoth the Aunt. Whose wit and breeding does he most
commend? His own, quoth the Aunt. Whom does he write
letters to? Himself. Whom does he dream of? All the dreams I
ever heard were of himself? Whom is he ogling yonder? Himself in his looking-glass. Why does he throw back his head in that
15 languishing posture? Only to be blest with a smile of himself as
he passes by. Does he ever steal a kiss from himself, by biting his
lips? "Oh continually, till they are perfect vermillion." Have you
observ'd him to use Familiarities with any body? "With none
"but himself: he often embraces himself with folded arms, he
20 "claps his hand often upon his hip, nay sometimes thrusts it into
"—his breast."
    Madam, said the Doctor, all these are strong symptoms, but
there remain a few more. Has this amorous gentleman presented
himself with any Love-toys; such as gold Snuff-boxes, repeating
25 Watches, or Tweezer-cases? those are things that in time will
soften the most obdurate heart. "Not only so, (said the Aunt)
"but he bought the other day a very fine brilliant diamond Ring
"for his own wearing— Nay, if he has accepted of this Ring, the
intrigue is very forward indeed, and it is high time for friends to
30 interpose. Pray, Madam, a word or two / more— Is he jealous   75
that his acquaintance do not behave themselves with respect
enough? will he bear jokes and innocent freedoms? "By no
"means; a familiar appellation makes him angry; if you shake
"him a little roughly by the hand, he is in a rage; but if you chuck
35 "him under the chin, he will return you a box on the ear."—
Then the case is plain: he has the true Pathognomick sign of
Love, *Jealousy;* for no body will suffer his mistress to be treated
at that rate. Madam, upon the whole this Case is extremely dangerous. There are some people who are far gone in this passion

of self-love, but then they keep a *very secret Intrigue* with themselves, and hide it from all the world besides. But this Patient has
not the least care of the Reputation of his Beloved, he is down-
right scandalous in his behaviour with himself; he is enchanted,
5 bewitch'd, and almost past cure. However let the following
methods be tried upon him.

First, let him *** *Hiatus.* *** Secondly, let him wear a Bob-wig.
Thirdly, shun the company of flatterers, nay of ceremonious people, and of all Frenchmen in general. It would not be amiss, if
10 he travel'd over England in a Stage-coach, and made the Tour of
Holland in a Track-scoute. Let him return the Snuff-boxes,
Tweezer-cases (and particularly the Diamond Ring) which he
has receiv'd from himself. Let some knowing friend represent
to / him the many vile Qualities of this Mistress of his: let him   76
15 be shewn that her Extravagance, Pride, and Prodigality will infallibly bring him to a morsel of bread: Let it be prov'd, that he
has been false to himself, and if Treachery is not a sufficient cause
to discard a Mistress, what is? In short, let him be made to see
that no mortal besides himself either loves or can suffer this Crea-
20 ture. Let all Looking-glasses, polish'd Toys, and even clean
Plates be removed from him, for fear of bringing back the admired object. Let him be taught to put off all those tender airs,
affected smiles, languishing looks, wanton tosses of the head,
coy motions of the body, that mincing gait, soft tone of voice, and
25 all that enchanting woman-like behaviour, that has made him
the charm of his own eyes, and the object of his own adoration.
Let him surprize the Beauty he adores at a disadvantage; survey
himself naked, divested of artificial charms, and he will find
himself a forked stradling Animal, with bandy legs, a short neck,
30 a dun hide, and a pot-belly. It would be yet better if he took a
strong purge once a week, in order to contemplate himself in
that condition; at which time it will be convenient to make use
of the Letters, Dedications, &c. abovesaid. Something like this
has been observed by Lucretius and others to be a powerful rem-
35 edy in the case of Women. If all this will not do, I must e'en leave
the poor man to his destiny. / Let him *marry himself,* and, when   77
he is condemn'd eternally to himself, perhaps he may run to the
next pond to get rid of himself, the Fate of most violent Self-
lovers.

CHAP. XII.

How Martinus *endeavoured to find out the* Seat *of the* Soul, *and of his Correspondence with the* Free-Thinkers.

IN this Design of Martin to investigate the Diseases of the
5 Mind, he thought nothing so necessary as an Enquiry after the
Seat of the *Soul;* in which at first he labour'd under great uncer-
tainties. Sometimes he was of opinion that it lodg'd in the Brain,
sometimes in the Stomach, and sometimes in the Heart. Afterwards he thought it absurd to confine that sovereign Lady to one
10 apartment, which made him infer that she shifted it according
to the several functions of life: The Brain was her Study, the
Heart her State-room, and the Stomach her Kitchen. But as he
saw several offices of life went on at the same time, he was forc'd
to give up this Hypothesis also. He now conjectured it was more
15 for the dignity of the Soul to perform several operations by her
little Ministers, the *Animal Spirits,* / from whence it was natural to conclude, that she resides in different parts according to
different Inclinations, Sexes, Ages, and Professions. Thus in Epi-
cures he seated her in the mouth of the Stomach, Philosophers
20 have her in the Brain, Soldiers in their Hearts, Women in their
Tongues, Fidlers in their Fingers, and Rope-dancers in their
Toes. At length he grew fond of the *Glandula Pinealis,* dissecting many Subjects to find out the different Figure of this Gland,
from whence he might discover the cause of the different Tem-
25 pers in mankind. He suppos'd that in factious and restless-
spirited people he should find it sharp and pointed, allowing no
room for the Soul to repose herself; that in quiet Tempers it was
flat, smooth, and soft, affording to the Soul as it were an easy
cushion. He was confirm'd in this by observing, that Calves and
30 Philosophers, Tygers and Statesmen, Foxes and Sharpers, Pea-
cocks and Fops, Cock-Sparrows and Coquets, Monkeys and
Players, Courtiers and Spaniels, Moles and Misers, exactly resemble one another in the conformation of the *Pineal Gland.* He
did not doubt likewise to find the same resemblance in High-
35 way-men and Conquerors: In order to satisfy himself in which,
it was, that he purchased the body of one of the first Species (as

hath been before related) at Tyburn; hoping in time to have the
happiness of one of the latter too, under his anatomical knife. / 79
    We must not omit taking notice here, that these Enquiries into
the *Seat* of the *Soul* gave occasion to his first correspondence with
5 the society of *Free-Thinkers,* who were then in their infancy in
England, and so much taken with the promising endowments of
Martin, that they order'd their Secretary to write him the following Letter.

To the learned Inquisitor into Nature, MARTINUS SCRIBLERUS,
10 *The Society of* Free-Thinkers *greeting.*

                              Grecian Coffee-House, May 7.
    IT is with unspeakable joy we have heard of your inquisitive
Genius, and we think it great pity that it should not be better
employed, than in looking after that Theological Non-entity
15 commonly call'd the *Soul:* Since after all your enquiries, it will
appear you have lost your labour in seeking the Residence of such
a Chimera, that never had being but in the brains of some dreaming Philosophers. Is it not *Demonstration* to a person of your
Sense, that, since *you cannot find it,* there is *no such thing?* In
20 order to set so hopeful a Genius right in this matter, we have sent
you an answer to the ill-grounded Sophisms of those crack-
brain'd fellows, and likewise an easy *mechanical Explication* of
Perception or *Thinking.*/   80
    One of their chief Arguments is, that *Self-consciousness* can-
25 not inhere in any system of Matter, because all matter is made up
of several distinct beings, which never can make up one individual thinking being.
    This is easily answer'd by a familiar instance: In every *Jack*
there is a *meat-roasting* Quality, which neither resides in the
30 Fly, nor in the Weight, nor in any particular wheel of the Jack,
but is the result of the whole composition: So in an Animal, the
Self-consciousness is not a real quality inherent in one Being
(any more than meat-roasting in a Jack) but the result of several

modes or qualities in the same subject. As the fly, the wheels, the chain, the weight, the cords, &c. make one Jack, so the several parts of the body make one Animal. As perception or consciousness is said to be inherent in this Animal, so is meat-roasting said
5 to be inherent in the Jack. As sensation, reasoning, volition, memory, &c. are the several Modes of thinking; so roasting of beef, roasting of mutton, roasting of pullets, geese, turkeys, &c. are the several modes of meat-roasting. And as the general Quality of meat-roasting, with its several modifications as to beef,
10 mutton, pullets, &c. does not inhere in any one part of the Jack; so neither does Consciousness, with its several modes of sensation, intellection, volition, &c. inhere in any one, but is the result from the mechanical composition of the whole Animal. /   81

Just so, the Quality or Disposition in a Fiddle to play tunes,
15 with the several modifications of this *tune-playing* Quality in playing of Preludes, Sarabands, Jigs, and Gavotts, are as much real Qualities in the Instrument, as the thought or the imagination is in the mind of the Person that composes them.

The Parts (say they) of an animal body are perpetually
20 chang'd, and the fluids, which seem to be subject of consciousness, are in a perpetual circulation; so that the same individual particles do not remain in the Brain; from whence it will follow, that the idea of Individual Consciousness must be constantly translated from one particle of matter to another, whereby the
25 particle A, for example, must not only be conscious, but conscious that it is the same being with the particle B that went before.

We answer, this is only a fallacy of the imagination, and is to be understood in no other sense than that maxim of
30 the English Law, that the *King never dies*. This power of thinking, self-moving, and governing the whole Machine, is communicated from every Particle to its immediate Successor; who, as soon as he is gone, immediately takes upon him the Gov-

ernment, which still preserves the Unity of the whole System.

They make a great noise about this Individuality: how a man is conscious to himself that he is the same Individual he was twenty years ago; not- / withstanding the flux state of the Parti- 82
5 cles of matter that compose his body. We think this is capable of a very plain answer, and may be easily illustrated by a familiar example.

Sir John Cutler had a pair of black worsted stockings, which his maid darn'd so often with silk, that they became at last a pair
10 of silk stockings. Now supposing those stockings of Sir John's endued with some degree of Consciousness at every particular darning, they would have been sensible, that they were the same individual pair of stockings both before and after the darning; and this sensation would have continued in them through all the
15 succession of darnings; and yet after the last of all, there was not perhaps one thread left of the first pair of stockings, but they were grown to be silk stockings, as was said before.

And whereas it is affirm'd, that every animal is conscious of some individual self-moving, self-determining principle; it is
20 answered, that as in a House of Commons all things are deter- min'd by a *Majority,* so it is in every Animal system. As that which determines the House is said to be the reason of the whole assembly; it is no otherwise with thinking Beings, who are de- termin'd by the greater force of several particles; which, like so
25 many unthinking Members, compose one thinking System.

And whereas it is likewise objected, that Punishments cannot be just that are not inflicted upon the / same individual, which 83
cannot subsist without the notion of a spiritual substance. We reply, that this is no greater difficulty to conceive, than that a
30 Corporation, which is likewise a flux body, may be punished for the faults, and liable to the debts, of their Predecessors.

We proceed now to explain, by the structure of the Brain, the several Modes of thinking. It is well known to Anatomists that

the Brain is a *Congeries* of Glands, that separate the finer parts
of the blood, call'd Animal Spirits; that a Gland is nothing but a
Canal of a great length, variously intorted and wound up together. From the Arietation and Motion of the Spirits in those
5 Canals, proceed all the different sorts of Thought: Simple Ideas
are produced by the motion of the Spirits in one simple Canal:
When two of these Canals disembogue themselves into one, they
make what we call a Proposition; and when two of these propositional chanels empty themselves into a third, they form a Syllo-
10 gism, or a Ratiocination. Memory is perform'd in a distinct
apartment of the brain, made up of vessels similar, and like situated to the ideal, propositional, and syllogistical vessels, in the
primary parts of the brain. After the same manner it is easy to explain the other modes of thinking; as also why some people
15 think so wrong and perversely, which proceeds from the bad
configuration of those Glands. Some, for example, are born
with- / out the propositional or syllogistical Canals; in others   84
that reason ill, they are of unequal capacities; in dull fellows, of
too great a length, whereby the motion of the spirits is retarded;
20 in trifling genius's, weak and small; in the over-refining spirits,
too much intorted and winding; and so of the rest.

   We are so much persuaded of the truth of this our Hypothesis,
that we have employ'd one of our Members, a great Virtuoso at
Nuremberg, to make a sort of an Hydraulic Engine, in which a
25 chemical liquor resembling Blood, is driven through elastic
chanels resembling arteries and veins, by the force of an Embolus
like the heart, and wrought by a pneumatic Machine of the nature of the lungs, with ropes and pullies, like the nerves, tendons
and muscles: And we are persuaded that this our artificial Man
30 will not only walk, and speak, and perform most of the outward actions of the animal life, but (being wound up once a
week) will perhaps reason as well as most of your Country
Parsons.

We wait with the utmost impatience for the honour of having you a Member of our Society, and beg leave to assure you that
we are, &c.

What return Martin made to this obliging Letter we must
5 defer to another occasion: let it suffice at present to tell, that
Crambe was in a great rage at them, for stealing (as he thought)
a hint from his *Theory of Syllogisms,* without doing him / the   85
honour so much as to mention him. He advis'd his Master by no
means to enter into their Society, unless they would give him
10 sufficient security, to bear him harmless from any thing that
might happen after this present life.

CHAP. XIV.

The Double Mistress.

N. B. *The style of this Chapter in the* Original Memoirs *is so*
singularly different from the rest, that it is hard to conceive
5 *by whom it was penn'd. But if we consider the particular Re-*
gard which our Philosopher had for it, who expresly directed
that not one Word of this Chapter should be alter'd, *it will be*
natural to suspect that it was written by himself, at the Time
when Love (*ever delighting in* Romances) *had somewhat*
10 *tinctur'd his Style; and that the Remains of his first and strong-*
est Passion gave him a Partiality to this Memorial of it. Thus
it begins.

BUT now the successful Course of the Studies of Martin was
interrupted by *Love:* Love, that unnerves the Vigour of the
15 Hero, and softens the Severity of the Philosopher. It chanced,
that as Martin was walking forth to inhale the fresh / breeze   86
of the Evening, after the long and severe Studies of the day, and
passing through the Western confines of the famous Metropolis
of Albion, not far from the proud Battlements of the Palace of
20 Whitehall, whose walls are embraced by the silver Thames; his
eyes were drawn upwards by a large square piece of Canvas,
which hung forth to the view of the passing Citizens. Upon it
was pourtrayed by some accurate pencil, the Libyan Leopard,
more fierce than in his native Desert; the mighty Lion, who
25 boasted thrice the bulk of the Nemæan monster; before whom
stood the little Jackall, the faithful spy of the King of beasts:
Near these was placed, of two Cubits high, the black Prince of
Monomotapa; by whose side were seen the glaring Cat-a-mountain, the quill-darting Porcupine, and the Man-mimicking
30 Manteger. Close adjoining to this, hung another piece of Canvas
on which was display'd the pourtrait of two Bohemian Damsels,
whom Nature had as closely united as the ancient Hermaphroditus and Salmacis; and whom it was as impossible to divide, as
the mingled waters of the gentle Thames and the amorous Isis.
35 While Martin stood in a meditating posture, feasting his eyes

on this Picture, he heard on a sudden the sonorous notes of a
Clarion, which seem'd of the purest crystal: In an instant the
passing multitude flock'd to the sound, as when a Drum summons the straggling soldiers to the ap- / proaching Battle. The   87
5 youthful Virtuoso, who was in daily pursuit of the Curiosities of
Nature, was immediately surrounded by the gazing throng. The
doors, for ever barr'd to the penny-less populace, seem'd to open
themselves at his producing a silver Six-pence, which (like
Æneas's golden bough) gain'd him admission into that Scene
10 of Wonders. He no sooner enter'd the first apartment, but his
nostrils were struck with the scent of Carnage; broken Bones
and naked Carcases bestrow'd the floor. The majestick Lion
rouz'd from his bed, and shook his brindled Mane; the spotted
Leopard gnash'd his angry teeth, and walking to and fro, in in-
15 dignation rattled his chains. Martin with infinite pleasure heard
the History of the several Monsters, which was courteously
open'd to him by a Person of a grave and earnest mien; whose
frank behaviour and ready answers discover'd him to have been
long conversant with different Nations, and to have journey'd
20 through distant Regions. By him he was informed, that the Lion
was hunted on the hills of Lebanon, by the Basha of Jerusalem;
that the Leopard was nurs'd in the uninhabited woods of Libya;
the Porcupine came from the kingdom of Prester-John, and the
Manteger was a true descendant of the celebrated Hanniman
25 the Magnificent. Sir, said Mr. Randal (for that was the name of
the Master of the Show) the whole World cannot match these
prodigies; twice have I sail'd round the Globe, / these feet have   88
travers'd the most remote and barbarous nations; and I can with
conscience affirm, that not all the Deserts of the four Quarters
30 of the Earth furnish out a more complete set of Animals than
what are contain'd within these walls. Friend (answer'd Martin)
bold is thy Assertion, and wonderful is the knowledge of a Traveller. But didst thou ever risque thyself among the ᵃ Scythian
Cannibals, or those wild men of Abarimon, who walk with their
35 feet backwards? hast thou ever seen the Sciapodes, so called because when laid supine, they shelter themselves from the Sun-
beams with the shadow of their feet? canst thou procure me a
Troglodyte footman, who can catch a Roe at his full speed? hast

ᵃ Pliny, lib. 7. cap. 2.

thou ever beheld those Illyrian damsels who have two sights in
one eye, whose looks are poisonous to males that are adult? hast
thou ever measur'd the gigantick Ethiopian, whose stature is
above eight cubits high, or the sesquipedalian Pigmey? hast thou
5 ever seen any of the Cynocephali, who have the head and voice of
a Dog, and whose [b] milk is the only true specifick for Consumptions? Sir (replied Mr. Randal) all these have I beheld, upon my
honour, and many more which are set forth in my Journal: As
for your dog-fac'd men, they are no other than what stands be-
10 fore you; that is naturally the fiercest, but by art the tamest
Manteger in the world. / That word (replies Martin) is a cor- 89
ruption of the [c] Mantichora of the Ancients, the most noxious
Animal that ever infested the earth; who had a Sting above a
cubit long, and would attack a rank of armed men at once, fling-
15 ing his poisonous darts several miles around him. Canst thou
inform me whether the Boars grunt in Macedonia? Canst thou
give me a Certificate that the Lions in Africa are afraid of the
scolding of Women? hast thou ever heard the sagacious Hyæna
counterfeit the voice of a shepherd, imitate the vomiting of a
20 man to draw the dogs together, and ev'n call a shepherd by his
proper name? Your Crocodile is but a small one, but you ought
to have brought with him the bird Trochilos, that picks his teeth
after dinner, at which the silly animal is so pleased, that he gapes
wide enough to give the Ichneumon, his mortal enemy, an en-
25 trance into his belly. Your modern Ostriches are dwindled to
mere Larks in comparison with those of the Ancients; theirs
were equal in stature to a man on horseback. Alas! we have lost
the chaste bird Porphyrion! the whole Race was destroy'd by
Women, because they discover'd the infidelity of wives to their
30 husbands. The Merops too is now no where to be found, the only
bird / that flew backward by the tail. But say, canst thou inform 90
me, what Dialect of the Greek is spoken by the birds of Diomedes' Island? for it is from them only we can learn the true pro-
nunciation of that ancient language.—Mr. Randal made no satis-

[b] Pliny, l. 16.

[c] Ælian, lib. 4. cap. 2.   Ælian, lib. 1. cap. 2.
Pliny, lib. 8. cap. 30. lib. 8. cap. 25.   Pliny, lib. 11. cap. 51.
Ælian, lib. 3. cap. 42.   Ælian, lib. i. cap. 49.

factory answer to these demands, but harangued chiefly upon
modern Monsters, and seem'd willing to confine his instances
to the Animals of his own collection, pointing to each of them in
order with his Rod.

5   After Martin had satisfied his curiosity here, he was conducted
into another Apartment. Just at the entrance of the door appear'd a Negroe Prince. His habiliments bespoke him royal; his
head was crown'd with the feather of an Ostrich, his sable feet
and legs were interlaced with Purple and Gold, spangled with
10 the Diamonds of Cornwall, and the precious stones of Bristol.
Though his stature was of the lowest, yet he behav'd himself
with such an Air of Grandeur, as gave evident tokens of his
Regal Birth and Education. He was mounted upon the least Palfrey in the Universe; a Palfrey whose natural Beauty stood not
15 in need of those various colour'd Ribbons which braided his
Mane, and were interwoven with his Tail. Again the crystal
Clarion sounded, and after several courteous speeches between
the black Prince and Martin, our youthful Philosopher walk'd
into the midst of the room, to bless his sight with the most beauti-
20 ful Curiosity of Nature. / On a sudden enter'd at another door   91
the two Bohemian Sisters, whose common parts of Generation,
had so closely allied them, that Nature seem'd here to have conspired with Fortune, that their lives should run in an eternal
Parallel.

25   The Sun had twice eight times perform'd his annual course,
since their Mother brought them into the world with double
pangs. Lindamira's eyes were of a lively blue; Indamora's were
black and piercing. Lindamira's cheeks might rival the blush of
the morning; in Indamora the Lilly overcame the Rose. Linda-
30 mira's tresses were of the paler Gold, while the locks of Indamora were black and glossy as the Plumes of a Raven.

How great is the power of Love in human breasts! In vain has
the Wise man recourse to his Reason, when the insinuating
Arrow touches his heart, and the pleasing Poison is diffused
35 through his veins. But then how violent, how transporting must
that passion prove, where not only the Fire of Youth, but the un-
quenchable Curiosity of a Philosopher, pitch'd upon the same
object! For how much soever our Martin was enamour'd on her
as a beautiful Woman, he was infinitely more ravish'd with her

as a charming Monster. What wonder then, if his gentle Spirit, already humaniz'd by a polite Education to receive all soft impressions, and fired by the sight of those beauties so lavishly expos'd to his view, should prove unable to resist at / once so pleas-   92
5 ing a Passion, and so amiable a Phænomenon?

Martin, who felt the true emotions of Love, blush'd that the object of his flame should be so openly prostituted to vulgar eyes. And though he had been permitted to peruse her most secret charms, yet his honourable passion was so strong, that it ran into 10 the extreme of bashfulness; so that at the first interview he made no Overtures of his Love. Pensive he return'd, and flinging himself on his Couch, pass'd away the tedious hours of the night in the utmost Inquietude. The rushy Taper afforded a glimm'ring light, by which he contemplated the tender lines of Ovid; but 15 alas! his Remedy of Love was no cure for our unhappy Lover's Anxiety! He closed the amorous volume, sigh'd, and casting his eyes around on the Books that adorned his room, broke forth in this pathetic Apostrophe.

O ye Spirits of Antiquity, who yet live in those sacred leaves! 20 why do I make you conscious of my shame? Yet why should I depreciate the noble Passion of Love, and call it Shame? your Heroes have felt it, your Poets and Orators have prais'd it. Were I enamour'd on some gaudy Virgin, did I doat on vulgar Perfection, the Lustre of an Eye, or the Rose of a Cheek; with reason 25 might I blush before you, most learned Inquisitors into Nature! most reverend Pliny, Ælian, and Aldrovandus! Yet sure you cannot disapprove of this, which is / no wanton Passion, but ex-   93
cited by so unparallel'd a Production; a flame, that may not only justify itself to the Severity of a Philosopher, but even to the 30 Avarice of a Parent; since she who causes it carries a most plentiful Fortune in the sole Exhibition of her person. Heavens! how I wonder at the Stupidity of mankind, who can affix the opprobrious Name of Monstrosity to what is only Variety of Beauty, and a Profusion of generous Nature? If there are charms in one face, 35 one mouth, one body; if there are charms in two eyes, two breasts, two arms; are they not all redoubled in the Object of my Passion? What tho' she be the common Gaze of the multitude, and is follow'd about by the stupid and ignorant; does she not herein resemble the greatest Princes, and the greatest Beauties?

only with this difference, that her Admirers are more numerous, and more lasting.

Thus sigh'd he away the melancholy Night; but no sooner had Aurora, with blushes in her cheeks (as conscious that she 5 was just risen from the embraces of Tithon) advanc'd through the purple gates of the east, but Martin rose: He rose indeed, but Melancholy, the companion of his slumbers, rose and wak'd with him. This was the first day that he amused himself with the gaudy Ornaments of the body; that with secret pleasure he con- 10 templated his Face, and the symmetry of his limbs in a looking- glass. And now forsaking his solitary apartment, / he walked   94 directly to the habitation that confin'd the Object of his desires. But as it is observ'd that the Curious never wander into the City to indulge their thirst of knowledge 'till about the hours of eleven 15 or twelve; the Morning has ever been the season of Repose for all those Animals, who (trepann'd by the frauds of Men) have been oblig'd to change their Woods and Wildernesses for Lodgings in Cities at the rate of four shillings a week. Therefore Martin at this early hour was neither saluted by the sound of the 20 Trumpet, nor were his eyes feasted as before with the pleasing picture of his Mistress; but he walked to and fro before the door with folded arms, from the hour of five to eleven, humming in a low and melancholy tune.

The Trumpet no sooner sounded, but his heart leapt for joy, 25 and a second six-pence gain'd him a second admittance into her apartment. Yet this day also, he only own'd his Passion in the language of his Eyes: But alas! this language is only understood by those that love, and Lindamira remain'd still ignorant of his Passion.

30   In the mean time it was no small cause of wonder to Mr. Randal, that this Gentleman should come every day to behold the same show. He, no less covetous than the Guardian of a rich Heiress, entertain'd a suspicion that Martin had a design of steal- ing the Ladies. He thereupon issued out strict Orders, not to ad- 35 mit our Lover on any pretence / whatsoever. What Torments   95 must this occasion in the raging fever of Love? Martin had now recourse to Stratagem, and by a Bribe (which often even the Ermine and Scarlet Robe cannot resist) gain'd the Dwarf who

kept the gates of the Show-room, to promote his Amour. He promis'd to convey a Letter to Lindamira the same Evening, if he would bring it him when darkness favour'd his design, at the apartment next the Monsters. Martin overjoy'd, hasted home,
5 and after having consulted all the Authors that treat of Love, composed his Billet-doux, and at the time appointed went to entrust it to the hands of his Confident. Softly he stole up stairs, approach'd the door, and gave a gentle rap; when on a sudden a small hand was thrust through a little hole at the bottom of the
10 door, whence issued an unintelligible squeaking voice. Martin concluding it to be the Signal, delivered his Epistle, and made his retreat unobserv'd. He was no sooner retir'd, but Mr. Randal enter'd, and (as it was his usual custom before he went to bed) took a view if all were safe in the Show-room. At his coming in,
15 he saw his Monkey exceedingly busy in picking the Seal-wax by little bits from a Letter, which he turn'd over and over with infinite satisfaction. Mr. Randal, not thinking it a breach of honour to pry into the secrets of his own family, took the Letter from him, and read as follows. /   96

20   *To the most amiable* LINDAMIRA.

WHile others, O darling of Nature, look upon thee with the eyes of Curiosity, I behold thee with those of Love. Since I have been struck with thy most astonishing Charms, how have I call'd upon Nature to make a new head, new arms, and a new body to
25 sprout from this single Trunk of mine, and to double every member, so to render me a proper Mate for so lovely a Pair! but think to how little purpose it will be for thee to stay till Nature shall form another of thy kind! In such beauties she exhausts her whole art, and cannot afford to be prodigal. Ages must be num-
30 bred, nay perhaps some Comet may vitrify this Globe on which we tread, before we behold a Castor and a Pollux resembling the beauteous Lindamira and Indamora. Nature forms her wonders for the Wise, and such a Master-piece she could design for none but a Philosopher. Cease then to display those beauties to the pro-
35 fane Vulgar, which were created to crown the desires of

                           Your Passionate Admirer,

                        MARTINUS SCRIBLERUS. / 97

The Dwarf enter'd as he was reading the Letter, and, perceiving his Master mov'd with passion, immediately fell on his knees and confess'd the whole affair. Mr. Randal, bent on revenge, caused him to hasten to Martin's house, with assurances that
5 Lindamira had read his Letter with infinite satisfaction, and conjured him that he would immediately favour her escape. Martin over-joy'd at the news, flew thither on the Wings of Love. The perfidious Dwarf conducted him up stairs in the dark, gently open'd the door, and bad him enter. How happy was
10 Martin in that instant, who thought of nothing but leaping into the four soft arms of his Mistress! when lo, on a sudden he saw at the farther end of the Room two glitt'ring balls of Fire, which roll'd to and fro in a most terrible manner. Immediately his ears were invaded with horrid hissings and spittings, the balls of
15 Fire drew nearer him, and the noise redoubled as he approach'd. Our Philosopher, bold and resolute with love, ventur'd towards it; when all at once he perceiv'd something grasp him hard by the throat, and fix as it were sharp lancets in his cheek, so that blood trickled amain down his chin. Thrice Martin essay'd to
20 free himself, but vain were all his endeavours: till at length, to save his life, he was forced to betray his Intrigue, and alarm the house with reiterated cries of Murder. The apartment of the Bohemian Beauties being the adjoining Room, they / were the first   98
that enter'd with a light to his assistance. Martin all bloody as he
25 was, a most fierce Cat-a-mountain hanging at his chin (which Mr. Randal had maliciously plac'd there on purpose) at the sight of Lindamira forgot his distress. Ah, my Love! (he cried) how like is thy fate to that of Thisbe! who staying but a moment too late, found, as she thought, her miserable Lover torn in pieces by
30 a Savage beast! The affrighted Damsels shriek'd aloud; Mr. Randal with all his Retinue rush'd into the room; and now every hand conspired to free his under-jaw from the sharp teeth of the enraged Monster. But the Lady, whose heart melted at the piteous Spectacle, was so zealous in this office of Humanity,
35 that the Cat-a-mountain, provok'd at her good-natur'd diligence, leap'd furiously on her, and wounded three of her hands and her two noses, to such a barbarous degree, that she was not fit to be shown publickly for the space of three weeks. The generous Lover, more wounded at this Spectacle than by all the scratches

he had himself receiv'd, charg'd the monster again with the utmost Intrepidity, and rescued his mangled Mistress. Then (having taken her by the hand, and given it a gentle grasp) he re-
treated with his eye fixed upon her, and just as he left the room
5 (in a low and tender Accent) thus breath'd forth his Soul: "Be-
"hold, all this have I suffer'd for you." /   99

Such, and so modest was the first Declaration of Love, made
on this eminent occasion by our youthful Philosopher. Nor was
it ungently receiv'd by the simple and innocent Lindamira; who,
10 hitherto unus'd to the soft Protestations of adoring Slaves, had
rather been wonder'd at than belov'd; and received but imperfect
notions of that tender language, from the Addresses only of the
black Prince or the Dwarf.

Martin, notwithstanding this unfortunate adventure, still pur-
15 sued his wishes. His Letters were now no more intercepted.
Lindamira read them, and behav'd like other courteous dames
when they receive those amorous Testimonials; conceal'd them
from her Guardian, and return'd the most engaging answers. In
short, she was so far captivated as to resolve no longer to be gaz'd
20 at like a publick Beauty in her own Assembly; but retire from
the world, and become the virtuous Mistress of a Family.

But Fate had so ordain'd, that Martin was not more enamoured on Lindamira, than Indamora was on Martin. She, jealous
that her Sister had the greatest share in this conquest, resented
25 that an equal application had not been made to herself. She
teiz'd Lindamira to such a degree on this subject, as made her
promise to see Martin no more. But then again might Indamora
be deem'd the unhappiest of Women, whom her Passion and
Imprudence / had robb'd of the sight of her Lover. Yet shame 100
30 caused her to conceal those anxieties from her Sister. And let the
Reader judge how unhappy the Nymph must be, who was even
depriv'd the universal Relief of a *Soliloquy*. However, thus she
thought, without being allow'd to tell it to any Grove or purling
Stream.

35   Wretched Indamora! if Lindamira must never more see Martin, Martin shall never again bless the eyes of Indamora. Yet why
do I say wretched, since my Rival can never possess my Lover
without me? The pangs that others feel in Absence, from the
thought of those Joys that bless their Rivals, can never sting thy

bosom; nor can they mortify thee by making thee a Witness, without giving thee at the same time a share, of their Endearments. Change then thy proceeding, Indamora; thy Jealousy must act a new and unheard-of part, and promote the interest 5 of thy Rival, as the only way to the enjoyment of thy Lover.

From that moment she studied by all methods to advance her Sister's Amour, and in that her own. And thus there appeared in these three Lovers as extraordinary a Conjunction of Passions as of Persons: Love had reconcil'd himself to his mortal foes, to 10 Philosophy in Martin, and to Jealousy in Indamora.

And now flourish'd the Amour of Martin; Success even prevented his wishes, the Marriage was / agreed on, and the day 101 appointed. Sunday was the time, when Mr. Randal's Absence favour'd their hopes, who never on that day omitted taking the 15 fresh air in the fields: The key of the door he always took with him. Crambe was ready laid at a convenient distance, who accommodated them with a ladder of ropes. The ladder was thrown up, and the Signal given at the window. Lindamira hasten'd to the Alarm of Love, when behold a new Disaster! As 20 she was getting out of the window, the weight of her body on one side, and that of Indamora's on the other, unluckily caused them to stick in the midway: Lindamira hung with her coats stript up to the navel without, and Indamora in no less immodest posture within. The Manteger, who for his gentleness was al- 25 lowed to walk at large in the house, was so heightened at this sight, that he rushed upon Indamora like a barbarous Ravisher. Indamora cried aloud for help. Martin flew to revenge this insolent attempt of a Rape on his wedding-day. The lustful Monster, driven from our double Lucrece, fled into the middle of the 30 room, pursued by the valorous and indignant Martin. Three times the hot Manteger, frighted at the furious menaces of his Antagonist, made a circle round the chamber, and three times the swift-footed Martin pursued him. He caught up the *Horn* of a *Unicorn*, which lay ready for the entertainment of the curious 35 spectator, / and brandishing it over his head in airy circles, 102 hurled it against the hairy son of Hanniman; who wrinkling his brown forehead, and gnashing his teeth in indignation, stoop'd low: The horny Lance just ras'd his left shoulder, and stuck into the tapestry hangings. Provok'd at this, the grinning Offspring

of Hanniman caught up the pointed *Horn* of an *Antelope,* and
aim'd a blow against his undismay'd Adversary. Our heroic
Lover, who held his hat before him like a shield, receiv'd the
weapon full on the Crown; it pierc'd the beaver, and gave a small
5 rent to his breeches. Then the human Champion flung with
mighty violence the hinder *foot* of an *Elk,* which hit the bestial
Combatant full on the nether jaw. He reel'd, but soon recover-
ing, and his skill in war lying rather in the close fight than in
projectile weapons, he endeavour'd to close with him: Forth-
10 with assailing him behind unawares, he clamber'd up his back,
and pluck'd up by the roots a mighty grasp of hair—but Martin
soon dismounted him, and kept him at a distance. Love not only
inspired his breast with Courage, but gave double strength to his
Sinews; he heav'd up the *hand* of a prodigious *Sea-Monster;*
15 which when the chatt'ring Champion beheld, he no less furious,
wielded the pond'rous *Thigh-bone* of a *Giant.* And now they
stood opposed to each other, like the dread Captain of the seven-
fold Shield and the redoubted Hector. The Thigh- / bone miss'd 103
its aim; but the hand of the Sea-Monster descended directly on
20 the head of the Sylvan Ravisher. The Monster chatter'd horrible;
he stretch'd his quiv'ring limbs on the floor; and eternal sleep
lock'd fast his eyelids.

The lady from the window, like another Helen from the
Trojan wall, was witness of the Combat caused by her own
25 beauty. She saw with what gracefulness her Hero enter'd the
Lists, admir'd his activity and courage in the combat, and was a
joyful witness of his Triumph: She gave a spring from the window, and with open arms and legs embraced the neck and
shoulders of her Champion. Our Philosopher received her with
30 his Face turn'd modestly from her, and in that manner convey'd
her into the street. He call'd a Chair with all haste, but no chair-
man would take her; which obliged him to bear his extraordinary burden till he found a Coach, in which he carried her off,
and was happily united to her that very evening, by a Reverend
35 Clergyman in the Fleet, in the holy Bands of Matrimony.

CHAP. XV.

Of the strange and never to be parallel'd Process *at* Law *upon the Marriage of* Scriblerus, *and the Pleadings of the Advocates.*

BUT Nemesis, who delights in traversing the best-laid designs
5 of Cupid, maliciously contrived the means to make these three
Lovers unhappy. No sooner had the Master of the Show received
notice of their flight, but he seiz'd on the Bohemian Ladies by a
Warrant; and not content with having recover'd the Possession
of them, resolved to open all the Sluices of the *Law* upon Martin.
10 So he instantly went to Counsel to advise upon all possible
methods of revenge.

The first point he proceeded on was the *Property* of his Monster, and the question propounded was, (1) "Whether Slaves
"could marry without the consent of their Master?" To this he
15 was answer'd in the Affirmative, but told at the same time, "That
"(2) the Marriage did not exempt them from Servitude." /
This put him in no small hopes of having Martin added to his
Show, and acquiring a property in his *Bodily issue* by the Ladies.
But his joy was soon dash'd, when he was informed, that, since
20 Martin was a Free Man, (3) "The Children must follow the con-
"dition of the Father: or, that indeed, if they were to follow that
"of their Mother, the Case would be the same, there being no
"slavery in England." Then his Counsel judg'd it more advise-
able to plead for a *Dissolution* of the *Marriage,* upon the impos-
25 sibility of Conjugal dues in the Wife. But then the *Canon Law*
allow'd a *Triennial Cohabitation,* which entirely ruined this
Project also. Besides it was evident by the same Law, that "Mon-
"strosity could not incapacitate from Marriage," witness the Case
of Hermaphrodites, who are allow'd *"Facultatem Conjugii,* pro-
30 "vided they *make Election* before the *Parish Priest,* in *what sex*
"they will act, and take an Oath never to perform in the other
"Capacity." (1)
It was next consulted whether Martin should not be permitted

1 *An Servi possint, invitis Dominis, Matrimonium contrahere?*
2 *An Servus Matrimonio eximitur a Domini obsequio?*
3 *An Liberi sequuntur Conditionem Patris, an Matris?*
1 Sanchez, Hostiens. Sylvest.

to *take away* his Wife? since, upon his so doing, "he might be "sued for a *Rape* upon the body of her *Sister,* there being plainly "the / *four conditions* of a (2) Rape." But then again they con- 106 sider'd, that Martin might answer, he claim'd nothing but his 5 own; and if another person had fix'd herself to his Wife, he must not for that cause be debarr'd the use of his Property.

Yet still, upon the same head of Martin's possessing his spouse, a Suit might be devis'd in the name of Lindamira, on this account; (3) That a *"Wife* was not obliged to live with a *Concu-* 10 *"bine,* and such her Sister Indamora must be accounted to Martin "from the common (4) Proofs." To this too it was replied, that the Law order'd the Wife to *reside* with the *Husband* if there were sufficient security given to expel the Concubine. So Martin might say he was ready to accomplish his part of the Covenant, if 15 his wife would perform hers, and consent to the (5) Incision. But this being an impossibility on the side of the Wife, it could no way be exacted of the Husband.

At length Mr. Randal, being vex'd to the heart, to have been so long and so quaintly disappointed, determin'd to commence a 20 Suit against Martin for / *Bigamy* and *Incest.* Mean while he left 107 no Artifice or Address untried to perplex the unhappy Philosopher: He even contriv'd with infinite cunning, to alienate Indamora's affections from him; and debauch'd her into an intrigue with a Creature of his own, the black Prince; whom he secretly 25 caus'd to marry her, while her Sister was *asleep.*

Hereupon Martin was reduc'd to turn *Plaintiff,* and commenc'd a Suit in the *Spiritual Court* against the black Prince, for Cohabitation with his said wife. He was advised to insist upon a new Point, (viz.) "That Lindamira and Indamora *together* 30 "made up but *one* lawful wife."

The Monster-master, further to distress Martin, forc'd Lindamira to petition for Aliment, *lite pendente:* which was no sooner allow'd her by the Court, but he obliged her to alledge, that "it "was not sufficient to maintain both herself and her Sister; and 35 "if her Sister perish'd, she could not live with the dead body "about her."

2 *Violentia, Causa Libidinis, Traductio ad Locum, Mulier honesta.*
3 *Uxor non tenetur vivere cum viro Concubinam tenente.*
4 *Tactus, amplexus, cohabitatio.*
5 *An Uxor tenetur Incisionem pati?* Sanchez *de* Matrimonio.

Martin now began to repent that he had not executed a resolution he formerly conceived, of marrying Crambe to Indamora, as an Expedient to have made all secure. Moreover, it was insisted on, that the other also had a right to *Aliment,* "because, if Mar-
5 "tin's Wife should prove with child, the said Sister must neces-
"sarily perform the *Offices* of a *wife,* in contributing to the *Nu-*
"*trition* and *Gestation* of the said child." A / Jury of Physicians 108 being impannel'd, declar'd, that as to Nutrition they were doubtful, whether any blood of Lindamira circulated through
10 Indamora: But as to Gestation, it was evidently true. And upon this, Martin was order'd to allow Aliment to both, the Black Prince appearing *insolvent.*

Then the Court proceeded to the Trial. And as both the Cause and the Pleadings are of an extraordinary Nature, we think fit
15 here to insert them at length.

Dr. Penny-feather thus pleaded for Martinus Scriblerus the Plaintiff.

Dr. Penny-feather.

"I appear before your Honour in behalf of Martinus Scri-
20 "blerus, Batchelor of Physick, in a Complaint against Ebn-Hai-
"Paw-Waw, commonly call'd the black Prince of Monomotapa;
"Inasmuch as the said Ebn-Hai-Paw-Waw, hath maliciously,
"forcibly, and unlawfully seiz'd, ravish'd, and detain'd Linda-
"mira-Indamora, the wife of the said Martin, and the body of
25 "the said Lindamira-Indamora, from time to time ever since,
"hath wickedly, leudly, and indecently us'd, handled, and evil
"entreated. And in order to make this his Villany more lasting,
"hath presum'd to marry this Our Wife, pretending to give his
"wickedness the Sanction of a / Law. And forasmuch as the 109
30 "Adulterer doth not deny the fact, but insists upon his said Mar-
"riage as lawful, we cannot open the Case more plainly to your
"Honour, than by answering his Reasons, which indeed, to men-
"tion, is to confute.

"He maintains no less an absurdity than this, that *One* is *Two;*
35 "and that Lindamira-Indamora, the individual wife of the Plain-
"tiff, is not one, but two Persons: And that the said Ebn-Hai-
"Paw-Waw is not marry'd to Lindamira, the wife of the said
"Martin, but to his own lawful wife Indamora, another individ-

"ual Person distinct from the said Lindamira, tho' join'd to her
"by a strong Ligament of Nature.

In answer whereunto, we shall prove three things: *"First,* That
"the said Lindamira-Indamora, now our lawful wife, makes but
5 "one individual Person.

"*Secondly,* That if they made two individual persons, yet they
"constitute but one wife,

"*Thirdly,* That supposing they made two individual persons,
"and two wives, each lawfully married to her own husband, yet
10 "Prince Ebn-Hai-Paw-Waw hath no right to detain Lindamira
"our lawfully wedded wife, on pretence of being married to
"Indamora."

"As to the first point: It will be necessary to determine the
"*constituent Principle* and *Essence* / of *Individuality,* which, in 110
15 "respect to mankind, we take to be one simple identical soul, in
"one simple identical body. The individuality, sameness, or iden-
"tity of the body, is not determin'd (as some vainly imagine) by
"one head, and a certain number of arms, legs, and other mem-
"bers; but in one simple, single αἰδοῖον, or member of Genera-
20 "tion.

"Let us search Profane History, and we shall find Geryon with
"three heads, and Briareus with an hundred hands. Let us search
"Sacred History, and we meet with one of the sons of the Giants
"with six Fingers to each Hand, and six Toes to each Foot; yet
25 "none ever accounted Geryon or Briareus more than one Person:
"and give us leave to say, the wife of the said Geryon would have
"had a good Action against any women who should have es-
"pous'd themselves to the two other heads of that Monarch. The
"Reason is plain; because each of these having but one simple
30 "αἰδοῖον, or one Member of Generation, could be look'd upon as
"but one single person.

"In conformity to this, when we behold this one member, we
"distinguish the Sex, and pronounce it a *Man,* or a *Woman;* or,
"as the Latins express it, *unus Vir, una Mulier; un Homme, une*
35 "*Femme; One Man, One Woman.* For the same Reason Man
"and Wife are said to be one Flesh, because united in that part
"which constitutes / the Sameness and Individuality of each sex. 111

"And as where there is but one Member of Generation, there is
"but one body, so there can be but one Soul; because the said

"organ of Generation is the Seat of the Soul; and consequently,
"where there is but one such Organ, there can be but one Soul.
"Let me here say, without Injury to truth, that no Philosopher,
"either of the past or present age, hath taken more pains to dis-
5 "cover where the Soul keeps her residence, than the Plaintiff, the
"learned Martinus Scriblerus: And after his most diligent en-
"quiries and experiments, he hath been verily persuaded, that
"the Organ of Generation is the true and only *Seat of the Soul*.
"That this part is seated in the middle, and near the Centre of the
10 "whole body, is obvious to your Honour's view. From thence,
"like the sun in the Centre of the world, the Soul dispenses her
"warmth and vital influence: Let the Brain glory in the Wisdom
"of the aged, the Science of the learned, the Policy of the states-
"man, and the Invention of the witty; the accidental Amuse-
15 "ments and Emanations of the Soul, and mortal as the Possessors
"of them! It is to the Organs of Generation that we owe Man
"himself; there the Soul is employed in works suitable to the
"Dignity of her Nature, and (as we may say) sits brooding over
"ages yet unborn. /   112
20   "We need not tell your Honour, that it has been the opinion of
"many most learned Divines and Philosophers, that the Soul, as
"well as Body, is produced *ex traduce*. This doctrine has been de-
"fended by arguments irrefragable, and accounts for difficulties,
"without it, inexplicable. All which arguments conclude with
25 "equal strength, for the Soul's being seated in the Organs of Gen-
"eration. For since the whole man, both Soul and body, is *there*
"form'd, and since nothing can operate but where it *is,* it follows,
"that the Soul must reside in that individual place, where she
"exerts her generative and plastic Powers.
30   "This our Doctrine is confirm'd by all those Experiments,
"which conspire to prove the absolute Dominion which that part
"hath over the whole body. We see how many Women, who are
"deaf to the persuasions of the Eloquent, the insinuations of the
"Crafty, and the threats of the Imperious, are easily governed by
35 "some poor Logger-head, unfurnish'd with the least art, but that
"of making immediate application to this *Seat of the Soul*. The
"impressions made by the Ear are so distant, and transmitted
"thro' so many windings, that they lose their Energy: But your
"Honour, by immediately applying to the Organ of Generation,

"acts like a bold and wise Petitioner, who goes strait to the *very*
"*Throne* / and *Judgment-Seat* of the Monarch.   113
  "And whereas it is objected that here are *two Wills,* and there-
"fore *two* different *Persons;* we answer, if multiplicity of Wills
5 "implied multiplicity of Persons, there are few Husbands but
"what are guilty of *Polygamy,* there being in the same Woman
"great and notorious diversity of Wills: A Point which we shall
"not need to insist upon before any married person, much less
"of your Honour's Experience.
10   "Thus we have made good our first and principal Point; That
"if the wife of the Plaintiff, Lindamira-Indamora, hath but *one*
"Organ of Generation, she is but *one individual Person,* in the
"truest and most proper sense of Individuality. And that the
"matter of Fact is so, we are willing to put upon a fair Trial by a
15 "Jury of Matrons, whom your Honour shall think fit to nominate
"and appoint, to inspect the body of the said Lindamira-Inda-
"mora.
  "*Secondly,* We are to prove, that though Lindamira-Indamora
"were *two* individual Persons, consisting each of a Soul and
20 "Body, yet, if they have but one Organ of Generation, they can
"constitute but one wife. For, from whence can the *Unity* of any
"thing be denominated, but from that which *constitutes* the *Es-*
"*sence* or principal *Use* of it? Thus, if a knife or hatchet have but
"one blade, though two handles, it will properly / be denomi- 114
25 "nated but one knife, or one hatchet; inasmuch as it hath but one
"of that which constitutes the Essence or principal Use of a knife
"or hatchet. So if there were not only one, but twenty *Supposita*
"*Rationalia* with one common Organ of Generation, that one
"System would only make one Wife. Upon the whole, let not a
30 "few Heads, Legs, or Arms extraordinary, biass your Honour's
"Judgment, and deprive the Plaintiff of his legal Property: In
"which right our Client is so strongly fortified, that allowing
"both the former Propositions to be false, and that there were
"two Persons, two Bodies, two Rational Souls, yea, and two
35 "Organs of Generation, yet would it still be plain in the third
"place,
  "That the Defendant, Prince Ebn-Hai-Paw-Waw, can have no
"Right to detain from the Plaintiff his lawfully wedded *Wife,*
"Lindamira. For, abstracting from the *Priority* of the marriage

"of our Client, by which it would seem he acquir'd a property in
"his Wife and *all other Matter inseparably annex'd unto her,*
"it is evident Prince Ebn-Hai-Paw-Waw, by his marriage to
"Indamora, could never acquire any Property in Lindamira; nor
5 "can produce any Cause why both of them should live with him-
"self, rather than with the other? Therefore, we humbly hope
"your Honour will / order the body of Our said Wife to be re- 115
"stor'd to us, and due Censure past on the said Ebn-Hai-Paw-
"Waw.

10   Dr. Pennyfeather having thus ended his Pleading was thus
answer'd by

Dr. Leatherhead.

"I will not trouble your Honour with any unnecessary Pre-
"amble, or false Colours of Eloquence, which Truth hath no
15 "need of, and which would prove too thin a Veil for Falshood
"before the penetrating eyes of your Honour. In answer there-
"fore to what our learned brother, Dr. Pennyfeather, hath as-
"serted, we shall labour to demonstrate,
       "*First,* That though there were but one Organ of Generation,
20 "yet are there two distinct persons.
       "*Secondly,* That although there were but one Organ of Gen-
"eration, so far would it be from giving the Plaintiff any right
"to the body of Indamora, the wife of Ebn-Hai-Paw-Waw, that
"it will subject the Plaintiff to the penalty of Incest, or of Bigamy.
25   "*Thirdly,* We doubt not to prove that the said Lindamira-
"Indamora hath two distinct parts of Generation. /   116
       "And, *First,* we will shew, That neither the individual Essence
"of mankind, nor the Seat of the Soul, doth reside in the Organ
"of Generation; and this first from Reason. For unreasonable
30 "indeed must it be, to make that the Seat of the Rational Soul,
"which alone sets us on a level with beasts; or to conceive, that
"the Essence of Unity and Individuality should consist in that
"which is the Source of Discord and Division. In a word, what
"can be a greater absurdity, than to affirm Bestiality to be the Es-
35 "sence of Humanity, Darkness the Centre of Light, and Filthi-
"ness the Seat of Purity?
       "We could, from the authority of the most eminent Philoso-

"phers of all ages, confirm this our Assertion; few of whom ever
"had the impudence to degrade this Queen, the Rational Soul,
"to the very lowest and vilest Apartment, or rather Sink of her
"whole Palace. But we shall produce still a greater Authority
5 "than these, to manifest that personal Individuality did subsist,
"when there was no such generative Carnality.

"It hath been strenuously maintain'd by many holy Divines
"(and particularly by Thomas Aquinas) that our first Parents,
"in the state of Innocence, did in no wise propagate their species
10 "after the present common manner of men and beasts; but that
"the propagation at that time must have / been by Intuition, Co- 117
"alition of Ideas, or some pure and spiritual manner, suitable to
"the dignity of their station. And though the Sexes were distin-
"guish'd in that state, yet it is plain it was not by parts, such as
15 "we have at present; since, if our First Parents had any such, they
"must have known it; and it is written, that they discover'd them
"not till after the Fall; when it is probable those parts were the
"immediate Excrescence of Sin, and only grew forth to render
"them fitter companions for those Beasts among which they
20 "were driven.

"It is a Maxim in Philosophy, that *generatio unius est cor-*
"*ruptio alterius;* whence it is apparent that the Paradisaical Gen-
"eration was of a different nature from ours, free from all Cor-
"ruption and Imbecillity. This is farther corroborated by the
25 "Authority of those Doctors of the Church who have asserted,
"that before the Fall, Adam was endow'd with a continual un-
"interrupted Faculty of Generation; which can be explain'd of
"no other than of that *Intuitive Generation* abovesaid: Since it is
"well known to all, the least skill'd in Anatomy, that the present
30 "(male) part of Generation is utterly incapable of this continual
"Faculty.

"We come now to our *second* point, wherein the Advocate for
"the Plaintiff asserteth, that if / there were two persons, and one 118
"Organ of Generation, this System would constitute but one
35 "Wife. This will put the Plaintiff still in a worse condition, and
"render him plainly guilty of Bigamy, Rape, or Incest. For if
"there be but one such Organ of Generation, then both the per-
"sons of Lindamira and Indamora have an equal property in it;
"and what is Indamora's property cannot be dispos'd of without

"her consent. We therefore bring the whole to this short issue;
"Whether the Plaintiff *Martinus Scriblerus* had the *Consent* of
"Indamora, or *not?* If he hath *had* her consent, he is guilty of
"*Bigamy;* if *not,* he is guilty of a *Rape,* or *Incest,* or *both.*
5   "The Defendant, Prince Ebn-Hai-Paw-Waw, having been
"lately baptiz'd, hath with singular modesty abstain'd from Con-
"summation with his said Wife, until he shall be satisfied from
"the opinion of your Honour, his learned Judge, how far in Law
"and Conscience he may proceed; and therefore he cannot affirm
10 "much, nor positively, as to the structure of the Organ of Genera-
"tion of this his wife Indamora. Yet make we no doubt, that it
"will upon inspection appear, that the said Organ is distinct from
"that of Lindamira: Whereupon we crave to hear the Report of
"the Jury of Matrons, appointed to inspect the body of the said
15 "gentlewoman. /   119
     "And if the Matter of Fact be thus, give me your Honour's per-
"mission to repeat what hath been said by the Advocate for the
"Plaintiff; to wit, that *Martinus Scriblerus,* Batchelor in Physick,
"by this his Marriage with *Lindamira,* could in no wise acquire
20 "any property in the body of Indamora, nor shew any Cause why
"this duplicated Wife Lindamira-Indamora, should abide with
"him, rather than with the Defendant, Prince Ebn-Hai-Paw-
"Waw of Monomotapa.

     The Jury of Matrons having made their Report, and it appear-
25 ing from thence that the Parts of Generation in Lindamira and
Indamora were distinct, the Judge took time to deliberate, and
the next Court-day he spoke to this effect.

     GENTLEMEN,
     "I am of opinion that Lindamira and Indamora are distinct
30 "persons, and that both the Marriages are good and valid: There-
"fore I order you, Martinus Scriblerus, Batchelor in Physick,
"and you, Ebn-Hai-Paw-Waw, Prince of Monomotapa, to co-
"habit with your wives, and to lie in bed each on the side of his
"own wife. I hope, Gentlemen, you will seriously consider, that
35 "you are under a stricter Tye than common Brothers-in law; that
"being, as it were, joint Proprietors of / one common Tenement, 120
"you will so behave as good fellow lodgers ought to do, and with
"great modesty each to his respective sister-in-law, abstaining

"from all farther Familiarities than what Conjugal Duties do
"naturally oblige you to. Consider also by how small Limits the
"Duty and the Trespass is divided, lest, while ye discharge the
"duty of Matrimony, ye heedlesly slide into the sin of Adultery.

5   This Sentence pleas'd neither Party; and Martin appeal'd from
the Consistory to the *Court of Arches,* but they confirm'd the
Sentence of the Consistory.

It was at last brought before a *Commission of Delegates;* who,
having weigh'd the Case, revers'd the Sentence of the inferior
10 Courts, and disannull'd the marriage, upon the following Reasons; "That allowing the manner of Cohabitation enjoin'd to be
"practicable (though highly inconvenient) yet the *Jus petendi*
"*& reddendi Debitum conjugale* being at all times equal in both
"husbands and both wives, and at the same time impossible in
15 "more than one; two persons could not have a Right to the entire
"possession of the same thing, at the same time; nor could one so
"enjoy his property, as to debar another from the use of his, who
"has an equal right. So much as to the *Debitum petendi;* and as
"to the *Debitum reddendi, nemo tene- / tur ad impossibile."* 121
20 Therefore the Lords, with great Wisdom, dissolv'd both Marriages, as proceeding upon a natural, as well as legal Absurdity.

CHAP. XVI.

Of the Secession of Martinus, *and some Hint of his* Travels.

THIS affair being thus unhappily terminated, and become
5 the whole Talk of the Town; Martinus, unable to support the
Affliction, as well as to avoid the many disagreeable Consequences, resolv'd to quit the Kingdom.

But we must not here neglect to mention, that during the
whole Course of this Process, his continual Attendance on the
10 Courts in his own Cause, and his invincible Curiosity for all that
past in the Causes of others, gave him a wonderful insight into
this Branch of Learning, which must be confess'd to have been
so improved by the Moderns, as beyond all comparison to exceed
the Ancients. From the day his first Bill was filed, he began to
15 collect *Reports;* and before his Suit was ended, he had time
abundantly sufficient to compile a very consi- / derable Volume. 122
His Anger at his ill success caus'd him to destroy the greatest part
of these *Reports;* and only to preserve such, as discover'd most of
the Chicanery and Futility of the practice. These we have some
20 hopes to recover, if they were only mislaid at his Removal; if not,
the world will be enough instructed to lament the loss, by the
only one now publick, viz. The *Case of* Stradling *and* Stiles, *in
an Action concerning certain* black *and* white Horses.

We cannot wonder that he contracted a violent Aversion to the
25 *Law,* as is evident from a whole Chapter of his Travels. And perhaps his Disappointment gave him also a Dis-inclination to the
Fair Sex, for whom on some occasions he does not express all
the Respect and Admiration possible. This doubtless must be the
Reason, that in no part of his *Travels* we find him belov'd by any
30 *strange Princess;* nor have we the least account that he ever re-
laps'd into this Passion, except what is mention'd in the Introduction, of the *Spanish Lady's Phænomenon.*

It was in the year 1699 that Martin set out on his *Travels.* Thou
wilt certainly be very curious to know what they were? It is not
35 yet time to inform thee. But what hints I am at liberty to give, I
will. /

123

Thou shalt know then, that in his first Voyage he was carried by a prosperous Storm, to a Discovery of the Remains of the ancient *Pygmæan* Empire.

That in his second, he was as happily shipwreck'd on the Land
5 of the *Giants,* now the most humane people in the world.

That in his third Voyage, he discover'd a whole Kingdom of *Philosophers,* who govern by the *Mathematicks;* with whose admirable Schemes and Projects he return'd to benefit his own dear Country, but had the misfortune to find them rejected by the en-
10 vious Ministers of *Queen Anne,* and himself sent treacherously away.

And hence it is, that in his fourth Voyage he discovers a Vein of Melancholy proceeding almost to a Disgust of his Species; but above all, a mortal Detestation to the whole flagitious Race of
15 *Ministers,* and a final Resolution not to give in any *Memorial* to the *Secretary of State,* in order to subject the Lands he discover'd to the *Crown* of *Great Britain.*

Now if, by these hints, the Reader can help himself to a farther discovery of the Nature and Contents of these Travels, he is wel-
20 come to as much light as they afford him; I am oblig'd by all the tyes of honour not to speak more openly. /   124

But if any man shall ever see such very extraordinary Voyages, into such very extraordinary Nations, which manifest the most distinguishing marks of a Philosopher, a Politician, and a Leg-
25 islator, and can imagine them to belong to a *Surgeon of a Ship,* or a *Captain* of a *Merchant-man,* let him remain in his Ignorance.

And whoever he be, that shall farther observe, in every page of such a book, that cordial *Love of Mankind,* that inviolable *Re-*
30 *gard* to *Truth,* that *Passion* for his *dear Country,* and that particular attachment to the excellent Princess Queen *Anne;* surely that man deserves to be pitied, if by all those visible Signs and Characters, he cannot distinguish and acknowledge the Great *Scriblerus.*

CHAP. XVII.

Of the Discoveries and Works of the Great Scriblerus, *made and to be made, written and to be written, known and unknown.*

AND here it seems but natural to lament the unfortunate End
of the Amour of our Philosopher. But the Historian of these
Memoirs on the contrary cries out, "Happy, thrice happy day!
"which dissolved the Marriage of the great Scriblerus! let it be
"celebrated in every language, learned and unlearned! let the
"Latin, the Greek, the Arabian, the Coptic, let all the Tongues
"of many-languag'd men, nay of Animals, be employ'd to re-
"sound it! since to this we owe such immense discoveries, not
"only of Oceans, Continents, Islands, with all their Inhabitants,
"minute, gigantick, mortal and immortal, but those yet more en-
"larged and astonishing Views, of worlds philosophical, phys-
"ical, moral, intelligible and unintelligible!"

Here therefore, at this great Period, we end our first Book.
And here, O Reader, we entreat thee utterly to forget all thou
hast hitherto read, and to cast thy eyes only forward, to that
boundless Field the next shall open unto thee; the fruits of
which / (if thine, or our sins do not prevent) are to spread and 126
multiply over this our work, and over all the face of the Earth.

In the mean time, know what thou owest, and what thou yet
may'st owe, to this excellent Person, this Prodigy of our Age; who
may well be called *The Philosopher of Ultimate Causes,* since by
a Sagacity peculiar to himself, he hath discover'd Effects in their
very Cause; and without the trivial helps of Experiments, or Observations, hath been the Inventor of most of the modern Systems and Hypotheses.

He hath enrich'd Mathematics with many precise and Geometrical *Quadratures* of the *Circle.* He first discover'd the *Cause*
of *Gravity,* and the intestine *Motion* of *Fluids.*

To him we owe all the observations on the *Parallax* of the
Pole-Star, and all the new *Theories* of the *Deluge.*

He it was, that first taught the right use sometimes of the *Fuga
Vacui,* and sometimes of the *Materia Subtilis,* in resolving the
grand Phænomena of Nature.

He it was, that first found out the *Palpability* of *Colours;* and by the delicacy of his Touch, could distinguish the different Vibrations of the heterogeneous Rays of Light.

His were the Projects of *Perpetuum Mobiles, Fly-* / *ing En-* 127
5 *gines,* and *Pacing Saddles;* the Method of discovering the *Longitude* by *Bomb-Vessels,* and of increasing the *Trade-Wind* by vast plantations of *Reeds* and *Sedges.*

I shall mention only a few of his Philosophical and Mathematical Works.

10 1. A complete Digest of the Laws of Nature, with a Review of those that are obsolete or repealed, and of those that are ready to be renew'd and put in force.

2. A Mechanical Explication of the Formation of the Universe, according to the Epicurean Hypothesis.

15 3. An Investigation of the Quantity of real Matter in the Universe, with the proportion of the specifick Gravity of solid Matter to that of fluid.

4. Microscopical Observations of the Figure and Bulk of the constituent Parts of all fluids. A Calculation of the proportion
20 in which the Fluids of the earth decrease, and of the period in which they will be totally exhausted.

5. A Computation of the Duration of the Sun, and how long it will last before it be burn'd out.

6. A Method to apply the Force arising from the immense
25 Velocity of *Light* to mechanical purposes.

7. An answer to the question of a curious Gentleman; How long a *New Star* was lighted up be- / fore its appearance to the 128
Inhabitants of our earth? To which is subjoin'd a Calculation, how much the Inhabitants of the *Moon* eat for Supper, consider-
30 ing that they pass a Night equal to fifteen of our natural days.

8. A Demonstration of the natural Dominion of the Inhabitants of the Earth over those of the Moon, if ever an intercourse should be open'd between them. With a Proposal of a *Partition-Treaty,* among the earthly Potentates, in case of such discovery.
35 9. Tide-Tables, for a Comet, that is to approximate towards the Earth.

10. The Number of the Inhabitants of London determin'd by the Reports of the Gold-finders, and the Tonnage of their Car-

riages; with allowance for the extraordinary quantity of the *In-gesta* and *Egesta* of the people of England, and a deduction of what is left under dead walls, and dry ditches.

It will from hence be evident, how much all his Studies were
5 directed to the universal Benefit of Mankind. Numerous have been his Projects to this end, of which *Two* alone will be suffi- cient to show the amazing Grandeur of his Genius. The first was a Proposal, by a general contribution of all Princes, to pierce the first crust or *Nucleus* of this our *Earth,* quite through, to the next
10 concentrical Sphere: / The advantage he propos'd from it was, 129 to find the *Parallax* of the *Fixt Stars;* but chiefly to refute Sir Isaac Newton's Theory of *Gravity,* and Mr. Halley's of the *Vari- ations.* The second was, to build *Two Poles* to the *Meridian,* with immense Light-houses on the top of them; to supply the defect
15 of Nature, and to make the Longitude as easy to be calculated as the Latitude. Both these he could not but think very practicable, by the Power of all the Potentates of the World.

May we presume after these to mention, how he descended from the sublime to the beneficial parts of Knowledge, and par-
20 ticularly his extraordinary practice of *Physick.* From the Age, Complexion, or Weight of the person given, he contrived to prescribe at a distance, as well as at a Patient's bedside. He taught the way to many modern Physicians to cure their Patients by *Intuition,* and to others to cure *without looking on them at all.*
25 He projected a Menstruum to dissolve the Stone, made of Dr. Woodward's *Universal Deluge-water.* His also was the device to relieve Consumptive or Asthmatick persons, by bringing fresh Air out of the Country to Town, by pipes of the nature of the Recipients of Air-pumps; and to introduce the native Air of a
30 man's country into any other in which he should travel, with a seasonable Intromission of such Steams as were most familiar to / him; to the inexpressible comfort of many Scotchmen, Lap- 130 landers, and white Bears.

In *Physiognomy,* his penetration is such, that, from the *Picture*
35 only of any person, he can write his *Life;* and, from the features of the Parents, draw the Portrait of any Child that is to be born.

Nor hath he been so enrapt in these Studies as to neglect the Polite Arts of Painting, Architecture, Musick, Poetry, &c. It was

he that gave the first hint to our modern *Painters,* to improve the *Likeness* of their Portraits by the use of such *Colours* as would faithfully and constantly accompany the *Life,* not only in its present state, but in all its alterations, decays, age, and death
5 itself.

In *Architecture,* he builds not with so much regard to present symmetry or conveniency, as with a Thought well worthy a true lover of Antiquity, to wit, the noble effect the Building will have to posterity, when it shall fall and become a Ruin.

10 As to *Music,* I think Heidegger has not the face to deny that he has been much beholden to his Scores.

In *Poetry,* he hath appear'd under a hundred different names, of which we may one day give a Catalogue.

In *Politicks,* his Writings are of a peculiar Cast, for the most
15 part Ironical, and the Drift of them often so delicate and refin'd as to be mistaken by the vulgar. He once went so far as to write a Per- / suasive to people to eat their own Children, which was 131 so little understood as to be taken in ill part. He has often written against *Liberty* in the name of *Freeman* and *Algernoon Syd-*
20 *ney,* in vindication of the Measures of *Spain* under that of *Raleigh,* and in praise of *Corruption* under those of *Cato,* and *Publicola.*

It is true that, at his last departure from England, in the Reign of Queen *Anne,* apprehending lest any of these might be
25 perverted to the Scandal of the weak, or Encouragement of the flagitious, he cast them all, without mercy, into a Bog-house near *St. James's.* Some however have been with great diligence recover'd, and fish'd up with a hook and line by the Ministerial Writers, which make at present the great Ornaments of their works.
30 Whatever he judg'd beneficial to Mankind, he constantly communicated (not only during his stay among us, but ever since his absence) by some method or other in which Ostentation had no part. With what incredible Modesty he conceal'd himself, is known to numbers of those to whom he address'd sometimes
35 Epistles, sometimes Hints, sometimes whole Treatises, Advices to Friends, Projects to First Ministers, Letters to Members of Parliament, Accounts to the Royal Society, and innumerable others.

All these will be vindicated to the true Author, in the Course

of these Memoirs. I may venture to / say they cannot be unac- 132
ceptable to any, but to those, who will appear too much concern'd
as *Plagiaries,* to be admitted as *Judges*. Wherefore we warn the
publick, to take particular notice of all such as manifest any in-
5 decent Passion at the appearance of this Work, as Persons most
certainly involved in the Guilt.

FINIS.

PIECES *of* Scriblerus (*written in his Youth*)
already published.

An Essay on the *Origin* of *Sciences,* written from the
5 Deserts of *Nubia.*

Περὶ ΒΑΘΟΤΣ: Martinus Scriblerus his *Rhetoric,* or, Of the *Art of Sinking* in Poetry.

10 VIRGILIUS RESTAURATUS: Seu Martini Scribleri, summi Critici, Castigationum in Æneidem Specimen.

Annus Mirabilis, or The wonderful Effects of the Conjunction of *Jupiter, Mars,* and *Saturn.*

The *Report* of a *Case* in an *Action at Law* concerning certain *Pyed,* or *Black* and *White* Horses.

Notes and Prolegomena to the *Dunciad.*

Bentley's Milton.

Others not yet published, mentioned in the MEMOIRS.

15 The Case of Queen *Esther,* with the whole Process of her *Purification.*

An Account of the wonderful Discovery of divers Diseases
20 by *Setting-Dogs,* with a List of those Gentlemen

and Ladies at whom they *sett.*

A Proposal humbly offer'd to both Houses of Parliament, for a *General Flux.*

Scriblerus's REPORTS of certain extraordinary Cases in Law.

ADVERTISEMENT.

THere will be publish'd with all convenient speed, The SECOND BOOK of these MEMOIRS, Being the TRAVELS of *M. SCRIBLERUS,* Vindicated to their True Author. And the THIRD BOOK
5 never before publish'd, Containing his Journey thro' the Desarts of *Nubia* to the Court of *Æthiopia:* His Friendship with the Bishop of *Apamæa,* and their joint Voyage upon *Cunturs,* to *China;* with an account of all the *hidden Doctrines* of Religion, and the *refined Policy* of those Empires.
10 With these Travels will be intermix'd at proper intervals, the *Journal* of a High and Mighty Prince, styled in his own Country *Son of the Morning, Lord of the Air and Fire,* and *Elder than all the Kings of the Earth;* who hath long travel'd, and is yet travelling *Incognito,* thro' all the Courts of *Europe.*

THE NOTES

In the Foreword to this edition it was suggested that apart from its very considerable literary merit the *Memoirs* is significant: 1) for the light which it throws upon several important aspects of the intellectual and cultural history of the period, 2) for the insight it gives into the minds and characters of the six famous men who worked on it, 3) for the background it provides for many of the individual works of the Scriblerians, 4) for the effects that the Scriblerus project in all its ramifications had on the literature of the early eighteenth century, and 5) for its historical interest as the product of an unusual collaboration carried out under exceptionally colorful circumstances. It is with these broad points in mind that the notes and discussions which follow have been prepared.

In order to obviate the need for frequent and distracting reference back and forth between the text and notes, each note is preceded by a sufficient quotation from the text to make clear the point in question and, where desirable, the context in which it appears. It is hoped that as the result of this policy the reader, after having read through a chapter of the *Memoirs,* will be able to follow the notes to it with only an occasional reference back to the text until he wishes to return to the chapter as a whole.

Wherever the Scriblerians have annotated their text their note has been given first and marked "(Scrib.)." Many of the notes added by Pope's literary executor and the first editor of the *Memoirs,* Bishop William Warburton, have also been included in this fashion. These notes are marked "(Warb.)." Otherwise the notes of previous editors have been included only when they directly contribute to an understanding of the text or its background.

When a translation of a classical text has been used repeatedly, volume and page numbers are given without identification following the reference to the original text (e. g., Pliny vii. 2; II, 132). Bibliographical data on the translation may be obtained by consulting the list of works which follows.

WORKS CITED BY ABBREVIATIONS

In this book, works published in London are listed with dates of publication only.

Aitken—George A. Aitken. *The Life and Works of John Arbuthnot.* Oxford, 1892.

Bailey—N. Bailey. *An Universal Etymological English Dictionary.* 2 vols. (the second being a supplement). 1721–27.

Bayle—Pierre Bayle. *An Historical and Critical Dictionary.* Translated by several hands. 4 vols. 1710.

Beattie—Lester M. Beattie. *John Arbuthnot Mathematician and Satirist.* Cambridge, Mass., 1935.

Blount—Thomas Blount. *Glossographia.* 1656; 4th ed., 1674.

Brand—John Brand. *Observations on the Popular Antiquities of Great Britain.* 3 vols. Bohn Library. 1869.

Chambers—E. Chambers. *Cyclopædia: or, an Universal Dictionary of Arts and Sciences.* 2 vols. 1728; 4th ed., 1741.

Clarke—Samuel Clarke. *Works.* 4 vols. 1738.

DNB—Dictionary of National Biography. Sir Leslie Stephen and Sidney Lee, eds. 66 vols. 1885–1901.

Diogenes Laertius—*Lives of Eminent Philosophers.* R. D. Hicks, tr. 2 vols. Loeb Classical Library. 1925.

ELH—A Journal of English Literary History.

Galen—*Claudii Galeni opera omnia.* D. C. G. Kühn, ed. 20 vols. Leipzig, 1833.

Gay—John Gay. *Poetical Works.* G. C. Faber, ed. 1926.

Griffith—R. H. Griffith. *Alexander Pope. A Bibliography.* 2 vols. Austin, Texas, 1922–27.

Gunther—R. T. Gunther. *Early Science in Oxford.* 14 vols. Oxford, 1923–45.

Hearne—Thomas Hearne. *Remarks and Collections.* C. E. Doble, D. W. Rannie, and others, eds. 11 vols. Oxford, 1885–1921.

Hobbes—*The English Works of Thomas Hobbes.* Sir William Molesworth, ed. 11 vols. 1839–45.

Irving—W. H. Irving. *John Gay, Favorite of the Wits.* Durham, N. C., 1940.

King—William King. *Original Works.* John Nichols, ed. 3 vols. 1776.

Locke—John Locke. *An Essay concerning Human Understanding.* A. C. Fraser, ed. 2 vols. Oxford, 1894.

—— *Some Thoughts concerning Education,* in *The Educational Writings of John Locke.* J. W. Adamson, ed. 1912.

Misson—Henri Misson. *Memoirs and Observations in His Travels over England.* John Ozell, tr. 1719.

MLN—Modern Language Notes.

Monk—J. H. Monk. *The Life of Richard Bentley, D. D.* 2d ed. 2 vols. 1833.

Moréri—Louys Morery. *Le grand dictionaire historique.* 9th ed. Jean Le Clerc, ed. 4 vols. Amsterdam, 1702.

MP—Modern Philology.

NED—A New English Dictionary. James A. H. Murray and others, eds. 10 vols. Oxford, 1888–1928.

Parnell—Thomas Parnell. *Poetical Works.* G. A. Aitken, ed. Aldine Edition of British Poets. 1894.

Phil. Trans.—The Philosophical Transactions of the Royal Society. 1665/66–.

Pliny—*The Natural History of Pliny.* John Bostock and H. T. Riley, trs. 6 vols. Bohn Library. 1855–57.

Plutarch—*Plutarch's Lives. Translated from the Greek by Several Hands.* John Dryden and others. 5 vols. 1683–1703.

Pollux—Julius Pollux. *Onomasticon.* J. H. Lederlinus and T. Hemsterhuis, eds. 2 vols. Amsterdam, 1706.

Pope, E. & C.—Alexander Pope. *Works.* W. Elwin and W. J. Courthope, eds. 10 vols. 1871–89.

Port Royal Logic—A. Arnauld and P. Nicole. *Logic; or, The Art of Thinking.* Translated by several hands. 2d ed. 1693.

RES—Review of English Studies.

Sherburn—George Sherburn. *The Early Career of Alexander Pope*. Oxford, 1934.
SP—*Studies in Philology*.
Spence—Joseph Spence. *Anecdotes, Observations, and Characters, of Books and Men*. 2d ed. 1858.
Summa Theologica—Thomas Aquinas. Translated by the Fathers of the English Dominican Province. 2d ed., revised. Three parts. 1920–27.
Swift
    Corres.—The Correspondence of Jonathan Swift, D. D. F. Elrington Ball, ed. 6 vols. 1910–14.
    Works—The Prose Works of Jonathan Swift, D. D. Temple Scott, ed. 12 vols. 1897–1908.
    Poems—The Poems of Jonathan Swift. Harold Williams, ed. 3 vols. Oxford, 1937.
    Journ.—Journal to Stella. Works, 11.

INTRODUCTION

It is the function of the introductory chapter to set in motion the machinery not only of the *Memoirs* but of the whole Scriblerus project. The style of the chapter is that of burlesque romance, and the means employed for introducing Martinus is the familiar device of the accidental meeting with the shabby but obviously "noble" character who tells a strange story of persecution and, having left the narrator an important document vindicating himself, disappears under mysterious circumstances.[1] The device lent itself extremely well to the Scriblerian purposes. By making the character of the document which Martinus leaves somewhat nebulous and by following the plan of drawing materials from it rather than publishing it as it stands,[2] the Scriblerians provide themselves with a flexible and inexhaustible source for Martinus' exploits. The only addition necessary to complete the Scriblerus machinery is the fact that Martinus continues to correspond with his biographer, sending him new treatises from time to time and informing him of the true Scriblerian authorship of other pieces and projects assumed by his rivals.

The character and appearance given Martinus border on the fantastic; indeed, his figure is described as "so utterly unlike any thing of this world, that it was not natural for any man to ask him a question without blessing himself first." Nonetheless, in his chief characteristics—his macerated form, his piercing eye, his contempt of worldly affairs, his neglect of his person, and his jealous and secretive disposition—he was not without significant parallels within the memory of the audience for which the *Memoirs* was written. During the 1690's when Arbuthnot and Swift first began to take part in the intellectual life of London, the most prominent figures in the field of science were Boyle, Hooke, and Newton. The first two

1. Cf. *Huon de Bordeaux* and other medieval romances. Sir Thomas More uses the interesting-looking stranger with a story to tell as the opening mechanism for the *Utopia*.

2. Cf. below, p. 180, n. 13. There is one exception to this plan. The Double Mistress episode, which is one of the later additions to the *Memoirs*, is declared to be printed without change from the "Original Memoirs." P. 143.

of these were picturesque and eccentric characters. According to Burnet, Robert Boyle "neglected his person, despised the world, and lived abstracted from all pleasures, designs, and interests." [3] It was, however, of Robert Hooke that the intended readers of the description of Martinus would have been most strongly reminded. Hooke was thus described, shortly after his death, by Richard Waller, his first biographer:

As to his Person he was but despicable, being very crooked, tho' I have heard from himself, and others, that he was strait till about 16 Years of Age when he first grew awry, by frequent practicing, turning with a Turn-Lath, and the like incurvating Exercises. . . . He was always very pale and lean, and laterly nothing but Skin and Bone, with a meagre Aspect, his Eyes grey and full, with a sharp ingenious Look whilst younger; his Nose but thin, of a moderate height and length; his Mouth meanly wide, and upper Lip thin; his Chin sharp, and Forehead large; his Head of a middle size. He wore his own Hair of a dark Brown colour, very long and hanging neglected over his Face uncut and lank, which about three Year before his Death he cut off, and wore a Periwig.[4]

Like Martinus', Hooke's linen was questionable [5] and his living conditions were poor to an extreme, though in Hooke's case their poorness was occasioned not by want, since he possessed a very considerable estate, but by avarice.[6] In character, too, Hooke was somewhat like Martinus, he being, according to Waller,

. . . of an active, restless, indefatigable Genius even almost to the last, and always slept little to his Death, seldom going to Sleep till two three, or four a Clock in the Morning, and seldomer to Bed, oftener continuing his Studies all Night, and taking a short Nap in the Day. His temper was Melancholy, Mistrustful and Jealous, which more increas'd upon him with his Years.[7]

In common with Martinus, Hooke was extremely secretive about his work and anxious to claim credit for discoveries which others published first. As a result, his career was marred by a long series of bitter quarrels with fellow scientists, which left him cordially detested by most of the learned world.

The fact that the Scriblerians may have been satirizing the unkempt appearance and personal idiosyncrasies of Hooke and Boyle should not be misinterpreted into a belief that they wished to satirize the brilliant scientific achievement for which both were renowned.

Two previous editors believed that this introductory section was written in 1739.[8] Their opinion seems to have been based on Warburton's comment on the reference in the text to "some British Ship (whose Colours no Spaniard dares approach)" [9] that "This marks the time when the Introduction was written" and on the statement in the text that several years have elapsed since Martinus was last heard from on the occasion of his "Strictures on the Dunciad." [10]

3. Gilbert Burnet, *History of His Own Time* (1724–34), I, 193.
4. *The Posthumous Works of Robert Hooke,* Richard Waller, ed. (1705), pp. xxvi–vii.
5. *Ibid.*
6. *Ibid.*, p. xxvii.
7. *Ibid.*
8. Bowles, *Works of Pope* (1806), VI, 53 n., and Aitken, p. 310, n. 1.
9. Text, p. 93, l. 23.
10. Text, p. 93, l. 38.

Neither of these references provides a really solid basis for accepting so late a date for the original composition of a section which, though not an integral part of the framework of the *Memoirs,* contains ideas basic to the whole Scriblerus scheme, and the date seems in general to conflict with Pope's statement to Spence in the period 1734–36 that he had the *Memoirs* so nearly ready he could finish the first part in three or four days.[11] The reference to Spanish aggression against British shipping and to the *Dunciad Variorum* could easily have been slipped into an otherwise completed text. Moreover, Warburton's statement is enigmatic. Read one way it says the Introduction was written in the days of Queen Anne when Spaniards really did fear to molest British ships; read another it says it was written when such an ironic statement was appropriate. The intended satire of the text argues for the latter interpretation, but Warburton's notes were in general of such a character as to leave the suspicion that he was trying to make an ironical point in his footnote.

There are two periods when it seems most likely that satire on Walpole's regime might have been introduced. The first was during the time of Scriblerus activity from 1726 to 1729. During this period the first organized opposition to Walpole began to take shape. With this opposition in which two of their friends, Bolingbroke and Chesterfield, had leading parts, the Scriblerians were in active sympathy. Arbuthnot and Pope probably contributed quietly to the *Craftsman,* the leading antiministerial paper, and Gay stung Walpole with allusions in his *Beggar's Opera.* The attack on Walpole's hireling writers at the end of the seventeenth chapter was almost certainly added at this time and the allusions to his administration in the Introduction may very well have been. However, Spanish outrages against the English, especially the well-publicized affair of Jenkins' ear, stirred up public feeling to a war pitch in 1739–40 and Pope, who was at that time active against Walpole, might have introduced the reference to British shipping into the text during his last editing of the *Memoirs.*

Note (1)—page 91, line 5. *In the Reign of Queen Anne (which, notwithstanding those happy Times which succeeded, every Englishman has not forgot)* . . .
The quarto reads "(. . . every Englishman may remember) . . ."
An ironic understatement aimed at Walpole's administration. The tendency to idealize the reign of Queen Anne within a generation is illustrated by the description of it in the anonymous *Life and Reign of Queen Anne* (1738) as "so full of Wonders, (as the two Houses have observed) so fraught with Variety of great Events, no Age or Reign could ever parallel." P. iv.

(2) 91, 7. . . . *the Palace of St. James's;* . . .
St. James's Palace became, after the burning of the Palace of Whitehall in 1698, the royal town residence. Here Arbuthnot, as physician to Queen Anne, had his quarters when the Queen was in London. Being subject to call and hence less free than the other Scriblerians, Arbuthnot probably was host to the club on many occasions during the time when the *Memoirs* was being written. The immediacy

11. Spence, p. 133.

of the palace setting on such occasions was no doubt largely responsible for its use as a setting in the *Memoirs*.

(3) 91, 8. . . . *who, by the Gravity of his Deportment and Habit, was generally taken for a decay'd Gentleman of Spain.*

The stateliness and gravity of the Spaniards, like the wit and frivolity of the French, the bluntness of the Germans, etc., was a common characterization (cf. *Spectator*, No. 135, by Addison). The picture that the word "Spaniard" brought to mind in the early eighteenth century is suggested by Macky's description of the Earl of Nottingham as "In his Habit and Manners very formal; a tall, thin, very black man like a *Spaniard* or *Jew* . . ." (*Characters of the Court of Great Britain* [2d ed., 1733], p. 26) and the directions in *The Quack's Academy* to "walk with *Spanish Gravity*, as in deep contemplation upon an Arbitrament between life and death." *The Harleian Miscellany; or, A Collection of Scarce, Curious, and Entertaining Pamphlets and Tracts, as Well in Manuscript as in Print, Found in the Late Earl of Oxford's Library* (8 vols., 1744–46; 12 vols., 1808–11), II, 33. In another of their pieces, the *Origine of Sciences,* the Scriblerians again refer to the "grave and sullen temper" of the Spaniards. Aitken, p. 367.

(4) 91, 13. *Pythagoras was not more silent,* . . .

The Scriblerians erred here; Pythagoras himself was not notable for his silence. On the contrary, according to the account of Diogenes Laertius, his chief biographer, he seems to have been of a sociable disposition (viii.1.16) and to have possessed an extraordinary eloquence. Cf. Bayle. His disciples, however, were obliged to keep silence for five years, during which time they listened to his discourses. Diogenes Laertius, viii.1.10. The mistake on the part of the Scriblerians does not seem to have been accidental, as in their *Origine of Sciences* they refer to his reputed love of solitude. Aitken, p. 360.

(5) 91, 13. . . . *Pyrrho more motionless,* . . .

A reference to the philosophic creed of Pyrrho, who argued that all perceptions are of questionable validity and that therefore the wise man should regard the external circumstances of life as unimportant and seek above all to preserve the tranquility of his mind. He apparently did not attempt to carry his "motionlessness" into his private life, since his biographer, Diogenes Laertius, tells of his washing a pig. ix.11.66.

(6) 91, 14. . . . *nor Zeno more austere.*

Of Zeno's austerity there is no question. Diogenes Laertius says he was sour in disposition and of a frowning countenance, with niggardly habits, unworthy of a Greek, which he clung to on the plea of economy, vii.1.17. He also describes him as showing the greatest endurance and most extreme frugality, his food being uncooked and his cloak thin. Sec. 27.

(7) 91, 18. . . . *whether or no he had any other cloaths (much less any linen) under it, I shall not say;* . . .

In his *Letter of Advice to a Young Poet* Swift says: "I have always a secret veneration for any one I observe to be a little out of repair in his person, as supposing him either a poet or a philosopher; because the richest minerals are ever found under the most ragged and withered surface of earth." *Works*, xi, 105.

(8) 91, 20. . . . *his sword appear'd a full yard behind him, and his manner of wearing it was so stiff, that it seem'd grown to his Thigh.*

The fashion of wearing very long swords came in toward the end of the reign of Queen Anne and was sharply satirized in Nos. 143 and 145 of the *Guardian* (for August 25 and 27, 1713). Martinus' manner of wearing his indicates that he shared with Dr. Woodward, Dr. Freind, and other scientists of the period a disposition to argue scientific theories in mortal combat.

(9) 91, 24. *Those who never saw a* Jesuit *took him for one, and others believed him some* High Priest of the Jews.

The proverbial insularity of the English and their suspicious attitude toward anyone of strange appearance or manner was frequently complained of by travelers, who were its most frequent victims. Cf. Sorbière, Misson, Muralt, and others; also *Spectator*, No. 432. It also operated, however, against Englishmen who, like Martinus, did not conform. The Spectator declared that he had once been arrested for a Jesuit "for no other reason but my profound Taciturnity." *Spectator*, No. 4, by Steele. Few Englishmen of Queen Anne's time had ever seen either a Jesuit or a rabbi and the popular conception of their appearance suggested in the text was based on old hatreds and fears surviving, in the case of the Jesuits, from the days of the Popish Plot. For some evidence of the extent and character of the attack on the Jesuits from the Restoration to the Revolution see Arber's reprint of the *Term Catalogues, passim*. There is a notable absence of such attacks in the catalogues for the reign of Queen Anne.

In his "versified" version of Donne's *Satires*, Pope made use of the same way of characterizing a strange, outlandish figure, altering Donne's original lines,

> One, who for a Dane,
> In the Danes Massacre had sure beene slaine,
> If he had liv'd then; . . . Sat. iv, ll. 23–5.

to

> One whom the mob, when next we find or make
> A Popish plot, shall for a Jesuit take,
> And the wise justice starting from his chair
> Cry, "By your priesthood tell me what you are?" ll. 34–7.

(10) 91, 29. . . . *a scorn of doing or suffering the least thing beneath the dignity of a Philosopher.*

A common charge against the scientific "virtuosos" during the late seventeenth and early eighteenth centuries. The charge was generally made on the basis of their supposed refusal to be practical or to study problems of general interest and value. The attitude satirized is illustrated by Sir Nicholas Gimcrack and his friends in Shadwell's *The Virtuoso*:

Sir *Nic*. I content my self with the speculative part of Swiming, I care not for the Practick. I seldom bring any thing to use, 'tis not my way, Knowledge is my ultimate end.

Bruce. You have reason, Sir: Knowledge is like Vertue, its own reward.
Sir *Form.* To study for use is base and mercenary, below the serene and quiet temper of a sedate Philosopher. Act II; *Complete Works of Thomas Shadwell,* Montague Summers, ed. (1927), III, 127.

Sir Nicholas later declares, " 'Tis below a *Virtuoso,* to trouble himself with Men and Manners. I study Insects; . . ." Act II; *ibid.,* p. 142.

(11) 91, 36. *He declin'd speaking to any one, except the Queen, or her first Minister, to whom he attempted to make some applications;* . . .

For this satiric touch the Scriblerians did not have to resort to their imaginations. Like all prime ministers, the Earl of Oxford suffered from a plague of projectors and solicitors who daily plied him with their schemes for the benefit of the nation—and of their proposers. Cf. Swift's *Corres.,* I, 280. In their eagerness some of these projectors, unlike Martinus, turned to men like Swift who were known to have the ear of the chief minister. *Works,* II, 363.

(12) 92, 7. *. . . was walking about dinner-time alone in the Mall,* . . .

During the lives of the Scriblerians the Mall, the long, shaded promenade in St. James's Park, was in the height of its fashion. Because influential people could be met there casually, people in the position of Martinus as well as social climbers discreetly haunted it. Here, though they could hardly hope to see Oxford, they might meet Bolingbroke, or, failing some person of immediate power, such an influential man as Dr. Swift, who could speak to the prime minister on any subject he had a mind to and who could be met in the Mall now and then taking a turn with a friend or walking for exercise. Cf. *Journ., Works,* II, 142, 211, 229, 348–9, 406, 443.

(13) 92, 12. *. . . inscribed with these words,* Codicillus, seu Liber Memorialis, Martini Scribleri.

The exact character of this *Little Book, or the Memoirs of Martinus Scriblerus* and its relation to the present *Memoirs* is never made clear. Martinus' reference to it (p. 93) as his "Commentaries" (in the sense of a history written by the chief actor in the events described—cf. Bailey, II) and the later statements of his "historiographer" that the facts concerning Martinus' geniture are derived from it (p. 97) and that the Double Mistress episode is being reprinted from it without change (p. 143) indicate that, like other commonplace or memory books (e. g., *Thraliana*), it contained a good deal of autobiographical material. In view of the limited use made of it by the "historiographer," however, we may assume that this material was in fragmentary and episodic form. Vagueness concerning the particular character and contents of the book was no doubt deliberate on the part of the Scriblerians in order to keep the situation flexible.

(14) 92, 18. *. . . (as he stood under the Piazza by the Dancing-room in St. James's)* . . .

The piazza was a covered arcade in the first court of St. James's Palace. At the end of the piazza were the great stairs leading directly to the royal apartments. These stairs were guarded by a company of Foot Guards. *The Foreigner's Guide* (1729), p. 20. The dancing room is presumably the one marked as being on the south side of the court in the plan of the palace drawn by Simon Burgis in 1689. Reproduced in E. Sheppard's *Memorials of St. James's Palace* (1894), II, 13. Martinus' presence near the great stairs is, of course, a further indication of his efforts to speak to the Queen.

(15) 92, 26. . . . *for either the Stars and my Art are deceitful, or the destin'd time is come* . . .

Martinus' statement indicates that he is a follower of judicial astrology. In making him such, both here and in Chapter 1 (p. 97, l. 37), the Scriblerians were not consistent, for the activities of Martinus described later in the *Memoirs* mark him definitely as one of the "new" scientists, who had ever since the time of Bacon scorned and rejected astrology, palmistry, and such pseudo sciences. Astrological beliefs are much more appropriately ascribed to Cornelius (cf. text, p. 102, l. 35), who, as the representative of the older school of "philosophers" and a steadfast adherent of the ancients, would naturally cling to them.

(16) 92, 33. . . . *in this Island (a soil fruitful of Philosophers)* . . .

In 1667, in his *History of the Royal Society,* Sprat had boasted that

even the Position of our Climate, the Air, the Influence of the Heaven, the Composition of the *English* Blood; as well as the Embraces of the Ocean, seem to join with the Labours of the *Royal Society,* to render our Country a Land of *experimental Knowledge.* And it is a good Sign, that Nature will reveal more of its Secrets to the *English,* than to others; because it has already furnish'd them with a Genius so well proportion'd, for the receiving and retaining its Mysteries. (3d ed., 1722), pp. 114–15.

By the time of Queen Anne the work of Newton, Locke, Halley, Boyle, and other great leaders in science and learning had given weight to this boast and the fruitfulness of the English soil in producing philosophers had become a matter of national pride. Cf., for example, Addison, *Tatler,* No. 130, and Voltaire, *Letters concerning the English Nation* (1733), letter XIV.

(17) 92, 34. . . . *but my complexion is become adust, and my body arid* . . .

According to the medical theory of the early eighteenth century, which was still strongly influenced by the old theory of the four humors, when the body becomes excessively heated, as in climates "near the sun," the thinner parts of the blood steam away in vapors, leaving the remainder black and full of dregs. The medical term for this condition, a symptom of which was found in swarthy, parchmentlike complexions, was "adust." Cf. Bailey, II, Chambers, etc. The effect of this condition on the character is indicated by Swift's statement that the Earl of Nottingham's "adust complexion disposeth him to rigour and severity." *Works,* x, 29. In his *Humble Petition* Arbuthnot has the colliers and other interested parties object to "catoptrical cookery" in part on the grounds that "sunbeams taken inwardly render the humours too hot and adust, occasion great sweatings, and dry up the rectual moisture." Aitken, pp. 376–7.

(18) 92, 35. . . . *by visiting lands (as the Poet has it)* alio sub sole calentes.

Horace's phrase is *alio sole calentes,* "warmed by another sun." Odes ii.16.18.

(19) 92, 38. . . . *of the* Arcanum Magnum.

The *arcanum magnum* was the "great secret" of nature, by the discovery of which alchemists believed they would be able to effect the transmutation of metals, the prolongation of life, and other long-sought ends. The term was practically synonymous with the philosopher's stone. Though severely ridiculed by the skeptical in the reign of Queen Anne, the "great secret" still had the power to entrap such men as Sir Isaac Newton (Spence, p. 54; Sir David Brewster, *Memoirs of . . . Sir Isaac Newton* [1855], II, 371-6) and Sir Richard Steele (G. A. Aitken, *Life of Richard Steele* [1889], I, 141-5). The continued popularity of alchemy on the Continent is described by Lady Mary Wortley Montagu; in a letter written in Vienna on January 2, 1717, she says:

. . . there is indeed a prodigious number of alchymists at Vienna; the philosopher's stone is the great object of zeal and science; and those who have more reading and capacity than the vulgar, have transported their superstition (shall I call it?) or fanaticism from religion to chymistry; and they believe in a new kind of transubstantiation, which is designed to make the laity as rich as the other kind has made the priesthood. This pestilential passion has already ruined several great houses. There is scarcely a man of opulence or fashion, that has not an alchymist in his service; and even the Emperor is supposed to be no enemy to this folly in secret, though he has pretended to discourage it in publick. *Letters and Works,* W. Moy Thomas, ed. (Bohn Lib., n. d.), I, 142-3.

(20) 93, 2. . . . *the Revenge of a cruel Spaniard, . . .*

Like their gravity, the vengeful jealousy of the Spaniards was proverbial. Hence, Spain was sometimes used instead of Italy as a setting for comedies and tragedies of love intrigue and revenge. E.g., Dryden's *Love Triumphant* and *Spanish Fryar,* Cibber's *Heroick Daughter,* Congreve's *The Mourning Bride,* and Young's *The Revenge.*

(21) 93, 24. . . . *a safe passage to Jamaica, for that benefit.*

Jamaica was, during the time of Queen Anne, famous for its earthquakes, largely as the result of a particularly devastating one on June 7, 1692, which killed hundreds and destroyed most of the buildings on the island. The horrors of this disaster were luridly described in a number of pamphlets, such as *A Sad and Terrible Relation of the Dreadful Earthquake that happened at Jamaica* (1692), *The Truest and Largest Account of the Late Earthquake in Jamaica* (1693), etc. A more sober account by Sir Hans Sloane was published in *Phil. Trans.* XVIII, No. 209 (1694), 77 ff.

Later, in his famous *Voyage to the Islands of Madera . . . and Jamaica* (1707), Sloane, who was a friend of Arbuthnot, commented on the frequency of earthquakes in the region and declared that "the Inhabitants expect one every Year, and some of them think they follow their great Rains." I, xliv. He tells of one that he himself had experienced on February 19, 1688. Pp. xliv-v.

(22) 93, 37. *He sent me some of his Writings, and recommended to my care the recovery of others, straggling about the world, and assumed by other men.*

This idea, which serves as a basis for the brilliant chapter on the "Discoveries and Works" of Martinus and is neatly turned against Bentley and Hare in the chapter on Martinus as a critic, was given color at the time of the *Memoirs* by the numerous quarrels arising out of conflicting attributions and claims of authorship that marked the period. Swift himself was involved in one of these over his *Tale of a Tub;* Arbuthnot had the doubtful pleasure of having his anonymous *John Bull* pamphlets commonly attributed to Swift; and Pope and Gay were on several occasions involved in questions of authorship. Most such cases, like those of the Scriblerians, were the result of complete anonymity on the part of the authors, but some confusion arose from the use of pseudonyms such as Isaac Bickerstaff (which was used by Swift, Steele, Addison, Congreve, and others), Nestor Ironsides, and Wagstaffe. The greatest confusion of all, however, arose from the borrowing of names of living people who might conceivably have been the authors, as in the case of Wagstaffe and Bentley (whose name the Scriblerians attached to notes in the *Dunciad* written in burlesque of his style). Under such circumstances the public for whom the *Memoirs* was written might have been expected to have taken a keen pleasure in the "vindicating" of various well-known works to Martinus.

(23) 93, 38. *The last time I heard from him was on occasion of his Strictures on the Dunciad; . . .*
This refers to *The Dunciad Variorum. With the Prolegomena of Scriblerus,* which was published in April, 1729. Cf. above, p. 56.

(24) 94, 8. *. . . in which I dare promise the Reader, that, whenever he begins to think any one Chapter dull, the style will be immediately changed in the next.*
Since the Scriblerians felt obliged to take some cognizance of the different style employed in the Double Mistress episode (cf. text, p. 143, ll. 3–5), it seems possible that this promise to the reader was added with that episode particularly in mind. In any case, it serves the purpose of turning the varied and episodic character of the *Memoirs* to advantage.

CHAPTER I

Perhaps the most striking feature of the chapter, which burlesques the traditional "vita" in the grand manner, are the names of the famous learned men from whom Martinus is descended. These men, obviously chosen with considerable care by the Scriblerians in order to provide exactly the right background for their hero, fall into two groups, the natural philosophers and the critics, the first being much the larger.

From the group as a whole Martinus might be expected to inherit a number of good qualities. All the men mentioned were notable for their great brilliance of mind and their wide range of interests. With these qualities went a tremendous energy and endurance which enabled them to labor prodigiously in their fields. All were filled with an extraordinary zeal for knowledge, some traveling widely and enduring great hardship to acquire information and others beggaring themselves and their families to acquire material for study and rarities for their collections. And all were copious authors, their works in some cases filling a score of folio volumes.

With their good qualities, Martinus would, of course, be expected to acquire some of their faults. These were on something of the same scale as their virtues. In their eagerness for learning they were often overenthusiastic and credulous. This fault appeared perhaps most clearly in the field of natural history, where, as Bacon complained, there was not

that choice and judgment used as ought to have been; as may appear in the writings of Plinius, Cardanus, Albertus, and divers of the Arabians; being fraught with much fabulous matter, a great part not only untried but notoriously untrue, to the great derogation of the credit of natural philosophy with the grave and sober kind of wits.[1]

They were also on occasion given to rash speculation and theorizing on the basis of inadequate evidence and to making claims which they could not always support, so that some, like Paracelsus, came to be looked upon as charlatans.

Most of the group were also notable for a number of extreme personal failings. These include arrogance, pettiness, inconstant temper, neglect of worldly affairs, and—especially in the case of Paracelsus, the Scaligers, and Cardan—extreme vanity and quarrelsomeness. These last resulted in a number of famous squabbles which were carried on in public with the greatest rancor and recrimination.

It is interesting, in view of Martinus' activities as a critic[2] and the strong Scriblerian bias against them, that critics, editors, and commentators are not more numerous in Martinus' ancestry. Scriverius and Barthius obviously were selected primarily because of the story about Barthius' mistress, so that the Scaligers stand out as the chief representatives of this side of Martinus' background. They, too, appear to have been chosen as much for their personal failings as for their excessive erudition and pedantry, though the individual Scriblerians displayed animus against them only on the latter score.[3] Missing entirely from the Scriblerus family tree are the names of men who would foreshadow Martinus' activities in theology, logic and metaphysics, and the arts. The first two of these are represented in the ancestry given in the 1723 *Memoirs* and it may be, if that curious document was in fact written up from discarded manuscript fragments, that the Scriblerians at one time planned to stress this side of Martinus' character more.

In the margin of his copy of Jeremy Collier's translation of D'Acier's life of Marcus Aurelius, Coleridge wrote, "This translation is ridiculed by Pope in his Martinus Scriblerus."[4] The similarities of style on which he based this opinion occur chiefly in this first chapter of the *Memoirs* and the corresponding section of Collier's translation. They are illustrated in the following passage:

He loved Wrastling, Foot-Races, Tennis, and Hunting, not so much for the sake of the Diversion, as because he look'd upon them as a sort of innocent Preservatives of Health. Nay he went somewhat farther, and was of *Socrates* and *Aristippus's* Opinion, that Exercise of the Limbs was not unserviceable to Virtue it self. Before his Constitution was weaken'd with Fatiguing and constant Business, he

1. *Philosophical Works*, J. M. Robertson, ed. (1905), p. 57.
2. In Chap. ix of the *Memoirs* and in the Scriblerian pieces, *Virgilius Restauratus* and the *Dunciad Variorum.*
3. Cf. below, p. 186, n. 5.
4. Quoted in a letter by B. Ifor Evans, *Times Literary Supplement*, May 29, 1937.

used Hunting, and would frequently ride singly at the biggest Wild Boars, and attack them with great Dexterity and Courage. But his Passion for Philosophy, got the Ascendant, and made him cool in other Diversions. This Passion seiz'd him so strongly in his very Infancy, that when he was but twelve Years Old, he put on the *Habit* of the *Stoick* Philosophers, practis'd their Austerities, and lay upon the Ground with nothing but his Cloak under him.[5]

Despite the resemblance it seems doubtful that a direct parody was intended. The variety of the materials in the *Memoirs* and the extensive revising and editing it went through would have made it almost impossible to maintain a burlesque of a specific style with any consistency or effectiveness. The "crude vigour" and the "vulgarities" of language which impressed Coleridge in Collier's style were by no means peculiar to him. It seems safer to conclude that this part of the *Memoirs* ridicules a type of style of which Jeremy Collier's is an outstanding example.

(1) 95, 9. *In the City of Munster in Germany* . . .
The name of Münster brought to mind the extravagances and atrocities committed by the Anabaptists when they seized the city in 1534 and set up a Kingdom of Zion in which, until they were besieged and defeated by the Bishop of Münster in the following year, they practiced community of goods and polygamy. Their leader, Jack of Leyden, who on attaining power proclaimed himself King of Justice and of Israel, was a Swiftian "hero" as a prime example of a fanatic.

(2) 95, 13. . . . *a Skin of the true Pergamenian Parchment, which hung at the upper-end of his hall.*
This was the first known parchment. It was supposed to have been invented in the second century B.C. for the transcription of books for the great library at Pergamum as the result of an embargo on the exportation of papyrus from Egypt which Ptolemy had ordered in an attempt to prevent Eumenes from making a library as valuable and as choice as that at Alexandria. Cf. Pliny xiii.21; Bayle, *s.v.* "Pergamum." The reference serves a double purpose in calling to mind a supreme rarity and an extremely early example of jealousy and pettiness between collectors.

(3) 95, 15. . . . *all their Alliances and collateral Relations (among which were reckon'd Albertus Magnus,* . . .
At the time of the *Memoirs* very little was known about Albertus Magnus (d. 1280), though his works had been collected in twenty-one enormous folio volumes at Lyon in 1651. He was famous chiefly as an astrologer and alchemist. Bayle, i, 145 (misnumbered 147), n. E; cf. J. A. Fabricius, *Bibliotheca Graeca* (Hamburg, 1708–28), xi, 45. Addison, in attacking the Aristotelians for speaking unintelligibly of substantial forms, says:

I shall only instance *Albertus Magnus,* who in his Dissertation upon the Loadstone observing that Fire will destroy its Magnetick Virtues, tells us that he took particular Notice of one as it lay glowing amidst an Heap of burning Coals, and

5. *The Emperor Marcus Antoninus His Conversation with Himself* (1702), pp. viii–ix.

that he perceived a certain blue Vapour to arise from it, which he believed might be the *substantial Form,* that is, in our West-Indian Phrase, the *Soul* of the Loadstone. *Spectator* No. 56, for May 4, 1711.

(4) 95, 16. . . . *Paracelsus Bombastus, . . .*

The reputation of Philippus Aureolus Theophrastus Paracelsus Bombastus von Hohenheim (1493–1541) during the late seventeenth and early eighteenth centuries was a very mixed one. The value of some of his medical discoveries and of his fight against the rigid Galenist tradition of his day was recognized (cf. Moréri), but his boasting, his follies, and his false promises of cures were also remembered. Butler satirizes him in *Hudibras* (II, iii, 299–300, 627–30; III, iii, 475–6). Charles Patin, in his *Relations Historiques et Curieux de Voyages, en Allemagne, . . .* (Rouen, 1676), p. 237, says he found Paracelsus much esteemed in Germany, whereas in France he had come to regard him as a charlatan whose unfulfilled boasts of making gold and prolonging life had caused doubt both as to his probity and his erudition.

Swift, who owned a set of his works (3 vols., Geneva, 1658; H. Williams, *Dean Swift's Library* [Cambridge, 1932], No. 596), made use of his name for satirical purposes in the *Tale of a Tub* and the *Battle of the Books. Works,* I, 10, 107, 115, 116, 172, 177.

(5) 95, 17. . . . *and the famous Scaligers in old time Princes of Verona) . . .*

Both the Scaligers, Julius Caesar (1484–1558) and his son Josephe Juste (1540–1609), were famous for their vanity and quarrelsomeness as well as for their great erudition. The father was particularly notorious for his brutal and rancorous attacks on fellow scholars, notably Erasmus and Cardan. Cf. Moréri; Bayle, I, 857a; Warburton in his commentary on Pope's *Essay on Criticism,* E. & C., II, 99; and *Mr. Le Clerc's Judgment* (1713), pp. 15–16.

The phrase "in old time Princes of Verona" refers to the claim, vigorously maintained by both father and son, that they were descended from the noble Della Scala family of Verona—a boast much ridiculed by their enemies.

Swift cited the elder Scaliger in the *Tale of the Tub* and the *Battle of the Books* (*Works,* I, 11, 140, 183) and later made use of him as a stock example of a pedant. *Works,* XI, 81; cf. below, Chap. IX, p. 268, n. 1. In a letter to Parnell in 1714, Pope .mentions one of the Scaligers, presumably the younger, among a group of authorities with whom he is struggling in connection with his translation of the *Iliad.* E. & C., VII, 452. Gay refers to one of them in the Introduction to *The Mohocks* (1712).

(6) 95, 17. . . . *and deduced even from the Times of the Elder Pliny . . .*

Both the personal character and the work of the elder Pliny (23–79 A.D.) come well within the scope of the Scriblerians' satire. As his nephew, the younger Pliny (whose *Epistles,* the chief biographical source for the elder Pliny, were in Swift's library) declared, "his Wit was acute, his Study incredible, his Vigilance extraordinary." *Pliny's Epistles and Panegyrick,* translated by several hands (1724), I, 115. His industry was herculean. Even on journeys, "he took along with him by his side, an Amanuensis, with a Book, and Writing-Tables, whose Hands in Winter were guarded with Gloves, that the inclemency of the Air it self might not invade the Time of Study; upon which Account, in *Rome* he was carry'd in a Sedan." *Ibid.,* p. 116. Like the other scholars whose names appear in the text, his curiosity was insatiable and his credulity vast. His curiosity reached a fitting conclusion in an investigation at close range of an unusual eruption of Mount Vesuvius —an adventure that cost him his life. *Ibid.,* pp. 283–7. The fact that the Scriblerian genealogy goes back to the "times" of the elder Pliny rather than to the man himself is explained by the fact that he had no direct descendants and that the nephew who bore his name was of a very different character.

There is ample evidence in their individual works to indicate that all the Scriblerians were familiar with Pliny, as indeed were all well educated men of the time.

(7) 95, 23. . . . *she was undoubted daughter either of the great Scriverius, . . .*

Peter Scriverius (1576–1660) was a famous Dutch poet, philologist, and historian. Though some of his activities brought him within the scope of the satire in the *Memoirs,* he is obviously made use of here chiefly because of the story of his affair with the mistress of Barthius.

(8) 95, 23. . . . *she was undoubted daughter . . . or of Gaspar Barthius.*

Gaspar Barthius (1587–1658), "one of the most Learned Men of his Age" (Bayle, I, 511), is notable chiefly for a number of ably executed translations from Spanish and French and for his learned commentaries on Statius and Claudian. He was qualified to belong among Martinus' ancestors by his voluminous writings. Of these Bayle said (pp. 512–13):

The Manuscript Books he left behind him, those that were printed, those which he lost in the burning of his House, and those that he writ, and which are not to be found, I say all those Writings make such a prodigious bulk, that it is hard to conceive how one Man could be sufficient for so many things.

(9) 95, 31. *I am not ignorant of what Columesius affirms, that the learned Barthius was not so overtaken but he perceiv'd it, and in Revenge suffer'd this unfortunate Gentlewoman to be drowned in the Rhine at her return:*

"Columesius relates this from Isaac Vossius, in his Opuscul. p. 102." (Scrib.)

The Scriblerians apparently found this whole story in Bayle's *Dictionary,* where the passage from Columesius is translated as follows:

"Mr. *Vossius* told me one Day that *Barthius* being come from *Germany* to *Harlem* to see *Scriverius,* he brought a very fine Lady along with him; and that *Scriverius* had no sooner seen her, but he found the means to get *Barthius* drunk, that he might entertain that Lady with more liberty, which succeeded according to his desire. Nevertheless, he could not do it so well, but that *Barthius* being recovered from his Drink, had some suspicion of what had past, which increas'd in such a manner, that he carry'd the Lady back again, and suffer'd her to be drown'd in the Rhine." I, 513, n. N.

Bayle adds, "It must not be deny'd that *Barthius* had a bad Reputation as to his Morals. One of his best Friends confesses it; but he maintains that this is illgrounded." Bayle gives the same reference in the *Opuscula* of Columesius as the Scriblerians use, adding the edition, "edit. Ultraject. 1669."

(10) 96, 4. . . . *was related to Cardan on the father's side,* . . .

Jerome Cardan was a sixteenth-century physician and teacher, who was also noted for his fantastic character and copious writings. He was the author of some two hundred twenty-two tracts, and in the edition of Lyons, 1663, his works fill ten folio volumes. His most famous work, which appeared in 1550, was *De Subtilitate,* a vast mélange of physics, metaphysics, and natural history, much of the last of which he drew from Pliny and Aristotle. The adverse side of his reputation is indicated by Bayle's statement (p. 856): "His Poverty contributed to his Voluminous Writings, where his Digressions and Obscurity very often put his Readers to a Non-plus. He did not write so many Volumes without borrowing from others."

(11) 96, 5. . . . *and to Aldrovandus on the mother's:*

Ulysses Aldrovandus, a sixteenth-century professor of philosophy and physic at Bologna was, according to Bayle (1, 168),

one of the most curious Men in the World with respect to Natural History. His Cares, his Labours, and his Expences on that Account are incredible. He travell'd into the remotest Countries, without any other Motive than to inform himself of the things that Nature produc'd there: Minerals, Metals, Plants, and Animals were the Objects of his Enquiries, and of his Curiosity: But he applied himself chiefly to the Knowledge of Birds. . . .

Bayle (1, 169) adds that "Antiquity does not afford any Examples of such a large and laborious Design as that of our *Ulysses* in regard of Natural History." In the *Battle of the Books,* Swift refers to the monumental work on which he spent his life, fortune, and health as "Aldrovandus's Tomb." *Works,* 1, 183.

(12) 96, 19. *He ordered his diet according to the prescription of Galen, confining himself and his wife for almost the whole first year to Goat's Milk and Honey.*

"Galen Lib. de Cibis boni & mali succi. cap. 3." (Scrib.)

The passage cited in Galen (the reference for which should be to chapter 4 instead of 3, according to the four editions examined) merely points out that the use of goat's milk among his countrymen was widespread and that its mediocre quality as a food should be improved by the addition of honey. *Opera Omnia* (Leipzig, 1823), vi, 765–6.

(13) 96, 29. *However he disdained not to treasure up the Embryo in a Vial, among the curiosities of his family.*

One of the conventional points of attack on the scientific virtuosos of the time was their supposed habit of treasuring up repugnant and useless curiosities. This particular satiric touch had been partially anticipated by Addison, who in "The Will of a Virtuoso" (*Tatler,* No. 216) not only lists an "Embryo-Pickle" among the rarities disposed of but carries the same sort of jest further by adding this clause to the Virtuoso's testament:

My eldest son *John,* having spoke disrespectfully of his little Sister, whom I keep by me in Spirits of Wine, and in many other Instances behaved himself undutifully towards me, I do disinherit, and wholly cut off from any Part of this my personal Estate, by giving him a single Cockle-Shell.

(14) 96, 35. . . . *this Author asserting that the grossness and moisture of the southerly winds occasion the procreation of females, and not of males.*

"Arist. 14 Sect. Prob. 5." (Scrib.)

The source cited is not sufficient for all that is here attributed to Aristotle. In the *Problems,* the author does not mention winds, being only concerned with the effects of a damp climate on procreation. Later in the same work, however, he refers to the moistness of the south wind (xxvi. 2) and it is possible that the Scriblerians also had this in mind. In an authentic work Aristotle says that if the wind is northward during copulation sheep and goats produce males, and if it is southward, females. *Historia Animalium.* vi.19.

This last statement is quoted by Thomas Aquinas in his *Summa Theologica* (Quest. xcix, art. 2, reply 2) in a passage which the Scriblerians used for other purposes (cf. below, Chap. vii, p. 259, n. 56)—a circumstance which suggests that the idea was thus called to their attention. Aquinas fails to note that the statement he quotes refers to sheep and goats.

(15) 96, 38. . . . *a wind on which that great Philosopher bestowed the Encomiums of Fatner of the Earth, Breath of the Elysian Fields, and other glorious Elogies.*

There appears to be no direct source for these phrases in Aristotle. They are, however, in keeping with what, in general, the philosopher says of the west wind.

(16) 97, 3. *For our learned man was clearly of opinion, that the Semina out of which Animals are produced, are Animalcula ready formed, and received in with the Air.*

"Religion of Nature, Sec. 5. Parag. 15." (Scrib.)

"The seriousness with which this strange opinion, on so mysterious a point, is advanced, very well deserved this stroke of ridicule." (Warb.)

This theory, which appears to have grown out of observation of plants and to have been original with him, was advanced by William Wollaston in the following passage in his *The Religion of Nature Delineated* (1722):

If then the *semina* out of which animals are produc'd, are (as I doubt not) *Animalcula* already formed; which being distributed about, especially in some opportune places, are *taken in* with aliment, or perhaps the very air; being separated in the bodies of the *males* by strainers proper to every kind, and then lodged in *their* seminal vessels, do *there* receive some kind of addition and influence; and being thence transferred into the wombs of *females,* are *there* nourished more plentifully, and grow, till they become too big to be longer confined: . . . 1731 ed., p. 89.

The book had a considerable vogue, largely, according to Warburton, because the Queen became fond of it, which "made the reading of it, and the talking of it, fashionable." *Works of Alexander Pope* (1751), viii, 149 n. Pope apparently became familiar with it early. E. & C., ix, 149. His interest in it is suggested by the possibility that he may have drawn on it for some lines in his *Essay on Man.* Cf. E. & C., ii, 285, 349, 438, 446. Swift owned a copy of the 1726 Dublin edition.

(17) 97, 14. . . . *the recovery of* Manuscripts, . . .

It will be recalled that one of the greatest collectors of manuscripts in the period was the Earl of Oxford, whose splendid collection eventually became part of the nucleus of the British Museum library.

(18) 97, 14. . . . *set apart several annual Sums, for . . . the effossion of Coins, . . .*

Effossion, i.e. "digging out."

Numismatics from both an antiquarian and collector's point of view had flourished vigorously for more than a century. On the Continent enormous treatises on the subject had long been supplanting and supplementing each other regularly. In England, the widespread interest had come somewhat later, but had been kept at a high point by the continued discovery of Roman coins in various parts of the country. It infected many who were not professed antiquarians. Arbuthnot devoted his spare time for a quarter of a century to the study of the comparative value of ancient coins (cf. his *Tables* [1705 and 1727]), Addison wrote a series of *Dialogues upon the Usefulness of Ancient Medals* (pub. posthumously in Tickell's edition of his *Works* in 1721), and even Swift was led into some interest in the subject by his collector friend, Sir Andrew Fountaine. *Corres.,* I, 154; III, 286.

Keen rivalry and interest in a field already elaborately developed naturally led to an enthusiasm and a specialization in its minutiae which, unsympathetically viewed, offered excellent opportunities for ridicule, and satire on the virtuosi in this field had begun long before the *Memoirs* (as, for example, in the "characters" of John Earle, Samuel Butler, etc.).

The Scriblerians were possibly given a particular impetus toward satire on numismatics by the fact that Dr. Woodward, their favorite butt, was deeply interested in it, as well as in other antiquities. Echoes of the Scriblerian attitude appeared later in Pope's *Epistle to Addison,*

> With sharpen'd sight pale Antiquaries pore,
> Th' Inscription value, but the Rust adore:
> This, the Blue vernish, that, the Green endears,
> The sacred Rust of twice ten hundred years.
> To gain Pescennius one employs his schemes;
> One grasps a Cecrops in ecstatic dreams:
>
> .   .   .   .
>
> And Curio, restless by the fair one's side,
> Sighs for an Otho, and neglects his Bride. ll. 29–38,

and in the fourth book of the *Dunciad,* ll. 346–94.

(19) 97, 15. . . . *the procuring of Mummies; . . .*

One of the supreme marks of the comic virtuoso of the time was the possession of an Egyptian mummy. Cf., for example, *Tatler,* No. 216, for August 26, 1710, and Mrs. Centlivre's *A Bold Stroke for a Wife* (1718), Act III, sc. 1. The public was well acquainted with mummies during this period as the result of visits to the collection of rarities of the Royal Society at Gresham College, where one, given by Henry, Duke of Norfolk, had a prominent place. Cf. Ned Ward, *The London Spy* (1698–1700; 1924 ed.), p. 60; *New View of London* (1708), II, 666; *British Curiosities* (1721), p. 44; and other guidebooks of the period. Apparently there were a number of others in private collections in London, and one well-known anti-quarian, John Kemp (cf. Chap. IV, p. 213, n. 3), had two. *Memoirs for the Curious* (1708), II, 260. One of Lady Mary Wortley Montagu's first acts on arriving in Constantinople in 1717 was to "bespeak" a mummy. *Letters and Works,* W. Moy Thomas, ed. I, 206.

Mummy wrappings were also in high demand because of their supposed medic-inal value. "Powdered mummy" was a standard ingredient in pharmaceutical compounds and was regarded as a sovereign remedy for "all bruisings, spitting of blood, and diverse other diseases." Blount's *Glossographia;* cf. Chambers.

The Scriblerians exploited the popular attitude toward mummies in their comedy, *Three Hours after Marriage* (1717).

(20) 97, 17. . . . *and for all those curious discoveries by which he hoped to be-come (as himself was wont to say) a second* Peireskius.

For generations after his death, the name of Nicholas Fabrici de Peiresc (1580–1637) was mentioned with reverence by collectors, antiquarians, and scientists. Bayle said of him "that no man was ever more useful to the Republic of Letters than our Peiresc." Bayle, *s.v.* How much his name and his collections were re-spected in England is shown by John Evelyn's advice in 1656/7 to a young friend traveling in France:

I must believe that when you are in those parts of France you will not pass Beau-gensier without a visit; for, certainly, though the curiosities may be much dis-persed since the time of the most noble Peireskius, yet the very genius of that place cannot but infuse admirable thoughts into you. But I suppose you carry the *Life* of that illustrious and incomparable virtuoso always about you in your mo-tions; not only because it is so portable, but for that it is written in such excellent language by the pen of the great Gassendus, and will be a fit Itinerary with you. *Diary and Correspondence of John Evelyn,* W. Bray, ed. (n.d.), p. 575.

Even in 1698 his name had a certain magic in it: Lister in his *Journey to Paris* says, "But nothing pleased me more than to have seen the remains of the cabinet of the noble Peiresc, the greatest and heartiest Maecenas, to his power, of learned men of any of this age." John Pinkerton, *A General Collection of Voyages and Travels* (1809–14), IV, 39.

(21) 97, 21. . . . *he had composed two Treatises of Education: the one he called* A Daughter's Mirrour, *and the other* A Son's Monitor.

The titles were apparently not intended to satirize any particular works, though they call to mind Francis Osborne's famous *Advice to a Son* (1656–58), the Mar-quis of Halifax' *Advice to a Daughter* (1689), and many other tracts with some-what similar titles.

(22) 97, 25. *This is all we can find relating to Martinus, while he was in his Mother's womb; excepting that he was entertained there with a Consort of Musick once in twenty four hours, according to the Custom of the Magi;* . . .

"Ramsey's Cyrus." (Scrib.)

This is not exactly what the Chevalier Ramsay says of the Magi, but is, perhaps, a legitimate inference from the following passages:

Other men begin not the education of their children till after they are born, but the Magi seem'd to do it before: While their wives were with child, they took care to keep them always in tranquillity, and a perpetual chearfulness, by sweet and innocent amusements, to the end that from the mother's womb the fruit might receive no impressions, but what were pleasing, peaceful and agreeable to order. *The Travels of Cyrus*, N. Hooke, tr. (1728; 4th ed., 1730), I, 79–80.

These Philosophers looked upon musick as something heavenly, and proper to calm the passions, for which reason they always began and finished the day by concerts. *Ibid.*, 78–9.

Both of these statements were drawn by Ramsay from the seventeenth book of Strabo.

To the original citation of Ramsay, Warburton added the following note:

It was with judgment, that the Authors chose rather to ridicule the modern relator of this ridiculous practice, than the Antients from whence he took it. As it is a sure instance of folly, when amongst the many excellent things that may be learned from antiquity, we find a modern writer only picking out their absurdities.

Andrew Ramsay, a Scotchman, wrote *The Travels of Cyrus,* an imitation of Fénelon's famous *Les avantures de Télémaque,* in French and published it in Paris in 1727. An English translation in the following year by N. Hooke achieved a great success and won the Chevalier many friends, among them Swift (cf. *Corres.,* III, 405–6; IV, 79; V, 267; VI, 65) and Pope. Cf. E. Audra, *L'Influence française dans l'oeuvre de Pope* (Paris, 1931), pp. 84–6.

(23) 97, 27. . . . *the first of April, the birth-day of the great* Basilius Valentinus.

The alchemical works of Basilius Valentinus (ca., 1450) were first published in the seventeenth century, several editions of the more important ones being published on the Continent. In England, attention was probably directed to him by the publication in 1657 of his supposed last will under the following title, which both reveals the nature of his work and explains why All Fools' Day was chosen by the Scriblerians as his birthday: *Basilius Valentinus . . . His last Will and Testament. . . . Wherein he sufficiently declareth the wayes he wrought to obtain the Philosopher's stone, and taught them also to his fellow Collegians, all of whom attained also to the having of the Philosopher's stone: whereby not onely the leprous bodies of the impure, and inferiour metals are reduced unto the pure and perfect body of Gold and Silver, but also all manner of diseases whatsoever are cured in the bodies of unhealthfull men, and kept thereby in perfect health unto the prolonging of their lives.* This work was reprinted in 1671.

Almost nothing seems to have been known about him and references to him in seventeenth- and early eighteenth-century works are rare. Boyle takes notice of his "excellent Treatise of *Antimony*" and notes with approval his excuse for leaving many things undone in his study "that the Shortness of Life makes it impossible for one Man thoroughly to learn Antimony in which every Day something of new is discovered." *Some Considerations Touching the Usefulnesse of Experimental Naturall Philosophy* (Oxford, 1663), pp. 13–14.

(24) 97, 32. . . . *he had the common frailty of old men, to conceal his age; . . .*

This was a favorite jest of the time. Cf. *Spectator*, Nos. 136, 359, 530. It was usually attached to the "Old Beau" and was one of the stock devices for the characterization of this much-used figure.

(25) 97, 34. . . . *he first saw the light in St. Giles's Parish.*

St. Giles's Parish was one of the poorest and most degraded quarters in London. Its narrow, dirty streets, dilapidated buildings, and tiny courts made a rabbit-warren in which the most vicious and unfortunate classes were crowded under the worst conditions. It is thus described, in part ironically, by a contemporary guide-book:

St. Giles *in the Fields,* is a most wealthy and populous Parish, and is said to furnish His Majesty's Plantations in America [i.e. by transportation for criminal offenses] with more Souls than all the rest of the Kingdom besides. 'Tis very rare that the *Executioner* fails of being a Native as well as an Inhabitant hereof. Of the lower Sort there go two just Proverbs, Viz. *St. Giles's Breed, Better to hang than feed: fat, ragged,* and *sawcy,* as abounding in *Pedlars, Fish-women, News-cryers,* and *Corn-cutters.* . . . I am told, that thro' the Diligence of Messieurs *Wild* and *Ketch,* a good deal of trouble is taken off their (the Gentlemen in the Commission of the Peace) Hands in *Lewk-rs Lane, Park-s Lane, St. Thom-s's Street:* and that a Person may now venture to travel thro' at Mid-day without Pistols. *A New View of London and Westminster* (1725), pp. 12–13.

(26) 97, 36. *For one day, as I was passing by the* Seven Dials, . . .

The fame of the Seven Dials, a circus in the parish of St. Giles-in-the-Fields, as a place in which people became muddled and lost, and hence its appropriateness as the birthplace of Martinus, is suggested in Gay's *Trivia:*

> Where fam'd *St. Giles's* ancient limits spread,
> An inrail'd column rears its lofty head,
> Here to sev'n streets sev'n dials count the day,
> And from each other catch the circling ray.
> Here oft the peasant, with enquiring face,
> Bewilder'd, trudges on from place to place;
> He dwells on ev'ry sign with stupid gaze,
> Enters the narrow alley's doubtful maze,
> Tries ev'ry winding court and street in vain,
> And doubles o'er his weary steps again. Bk. II, ll. 73–81.

(27) 98, 9. . . . *to Mr. Neale's Will.*

Thomas Neal, who achieved fame as a speculator without losing his post as Master of the Mint, built the Seven Dials project not long before his death in 1699. He had been a familiar figure in London, his picturesque appearance being suggested by Prior's description of the Old Pretender as "lean, worn, and riv'led, not unlike Neal the projector." Hist. MSS Comm., Bath MSS, III, 259.

(28) 98, 13. *LOC. NAT. INCLUT. PHILOS. MAR. SCR.*

I. e. the birthplace of the illustrious philosopher, Martinus Scriblerus.

(29) 98, 19. *Mrs. Scriblerus dream'd she was brought to bed of a huge Ink-horn* . . .

This dream is the only direct link between the genuine *Memoirs* and the 1723 *Memoirs*, where it appears in a considerably elaborated version. See Appendix VI.

(30) 98, 25. *Likewise a* Crab-tree *that had been hitherto barren, appeared on a sudden laden with a vast quantity of Crabs: This sign also the old gentleman imagined to be a prognostic of the acuteness of his Wit.*

"Virgil's Laurel Donat." (Scrib.)

This is a burlesque of the prophetic incidents attending Virgil's birth as described by Aelius Donatus in the following passage:

His mother Maia, being great with childe with him, & dreaming that she was delivered of a Lawrell bough, which prickt into ye ground, grew forthwith to a great tree, replenished with sundrie kindes of fruits, and flowers: The next morning walking forth into the countrey with her husband, stept aside, and was delivered thereby in a ditch. The report goeth, that the childe so soone as he was borne, never cried, but looked so pleasantly, that he gave an assured hope, that by his birth some notable thing should chance. "Virgil's Life, Set forth . . ." in *The Thirteene Bookes of Aeneidos,* translated into English verse by Thomas Phaer (1600 ed.), p. [v].

(31) 98, 28. *A great swarm of* Wasps *play'd round his Cradle without hurting him, but were very troublesome to all in the room besides: This seemed a certain presage of the effects of his Satire.*

"Plato, Lucan, &c." (Scrib.)

The swarm of wasps is a burlesque of what is said to have happened to Plato and Lucan when they were young. The story about Plato appears in Aelian (*Variae Historiae* x.21; Lugd. Bat. [1731], p. 677), and is repeated by Stanley as follows:

Whilst *Plato* was yet an Infant, . . . his Father went to *Hymettus* . . . to sacrifice to the Muses or Nymphs, taking his Wife and Child along with him; as they were busied in the divine *Rites,* she laid the Child in a Thicket of Myrtles hard by; to whom, as he slept (*in cunis dormienti* [Cic. divinat. lib. I]) came a Swarm of Bees, Artists of *Hymettian* Honey, flying and buzzing about him, and (as it is reported) made a Honey-comb in his Mouth. This was taken for a Presage of the singular Sweetness of his Discourse; his future Eloquence foreseen in his Infancy. *History of Philosophy* (4th ed., 1743), p. 163.

The same story is told of Lucan (cf. James Welwood's account of Lucan in his preface to Rowe's translation of the *Pharsalia* [2d ed., 1722], I, iii) and of Pindar. Aelian xii.45.

Pope had previously made satiric use of the famous fable in his "To the Author of a Poem entitled 'Successio' " (1712), ll. 5–8.

(32) 98, 31. *. . . but the Father was of another opinion.*

Satire on dreams touched not only those who took the opinions of the ancients on that subject too seriously but the credulous and superstitious of the time. Belief in the prophetic character of dreams was widespread not only among the vulgar (cf. Brand's *Antiquities* [Bohn Lib., 1849], III, 127–41) but even among the educated. The completely uncritical attitude among some of the latter is illustrated by John Aubrey's essay on "Dreams." *Miscellanies* (1696).

Among the dreams most regarded were those of a mother before childbirth, of which there were many varieties and interpretations. Cf. e.g., Brand, III, 132–3; *The Interpretation of Dreams* (1722 ed.), p. 122. One of these prophetic dreams had already been used for humorous biographical purposes by Addison in the *Spectator*, No. 1. Prophetic dreams of all sorts were more and more coming to be regarded as superstitious folly. Cf., e.g., *Spectator*, No. 505.

(33) 99, 3. . . . *it was indeed a Paper kite which had broke its leash* . . .

If, as Lord Chesterfield has reported (*Letters*, Lord Mahon, ed. [1845], II, 447), Arbuthnot's children "frequently made kites of his scattered papers of hints," the inspiration for this incident may well have come from the doctor's home.

(34) 99, 5. *His back was armed with the Art Military, his belly was filled with Physick*, . . . [*etc.*]

It is to be noted that the parts of the kite closely foreshadow Martinus' fields of activity as set forth in the *Memoirs*. Physic is dealt with in chapters viii and x; rhetoric and poetic in chapters vii and ix (and in the *Peri Bathous*); logic and metaphysics in chapter vii; casuistry and polemical divinity in chapter xii; and common law in chapter xv.

In view of this, the inclusion and prominent place of "the Art Military" is highly significant. It will be remembered that the *Memoirs* were begun not long after the signing of the Peace of Utrecht, at a time when there was still the keenest feeling among the Tories against Marlborough and the war—a feeling which most of the Scriblerians shared and had been active in diffusing throughout the country. That this feeling, which had ruled them so long and which had occasioned some of the most brilliant and vigorous work of Arbuthnot and Swift (to say nothing of Oxford), should find an echo in any general satire in which they collaborated seems to the highest degree both fitting and probable. Further, the appropriateness of including in a satire on stupidity, folly, and misapplied effort an attack on an activity which they heartily believed to be the highest and purest form of these (see the bitter attacks on war in *Gulliver's Travels* and *John Bull*) could hardly have failed to appeal to them.

A military episode would not have been out of keeping with the character of Martinus. The elder Scaliger, one of the ancestors of Martinus, was an active soldier until forced into retirement and study by the gout. Moreover, active participation in fighting for Martinus would not have been necessary for effective satire. There had been many improvements in the art of warfare in the last half-century, and a large number of books on both the theoretical and practical sides of war had recently been published. Cf. *Term Catalogues, passim*. Thus the Scriblerians had at hand a rich field in which Martinus might display his pedantry and folly. Some faint hints as to the possible character of a Scriblerian satire on war may be gathered from Arbuthnot's discussion of the uses of geometry in war in his *Essay on the Usefulness of Mathematical Learning* (Aitken, pp. 426–7) and Swift's sketch of the officer in a coffee shop in his *Essay on Modern Education. Works*, XI, 52–3; cf. Pope's *Satires of Dr. Donne*, Sat. IV, l. 54.

If such an episode, or fragment of one, was actually written, its absence from the present version is not hard to explain. The death of the Queen and the coming of George to the throne distracted the people's attention from their old problems. The unpleasant aspects of the last war were forgotten, and as time passed England's successes during it stood out in memory with increasing brilliance. Marlborough, no longer feared, was once again idolized. The time for such a satire had passed; and another opportunity never came. As has been pointed out, the difficulties with Spain led to an increasingly martial spirit among the English people, which Pope's friends in the opposition took the greatest care to foster. When Pope finally arrived at putting the finishing touches on the *Memoirs* for publication this situation was at its height and the nation was on the verge of an actual declaration of war. In these circumstances its suppression would have been almost inevitable.

(35) 99, 6. . . . *his wings were the wings of Quarles and Withers,* . . .

That is, they were poems, such as Francis Quarles (1592–1644) and George Withers (1588–1667) had written, whose variously long and short lines made a pattern of wings. This kind of figure poetry, which had been written even in antiquity, was popular among some poets of the time of Charles I. Among the many shapes used were cups, crosses, altars, eggs, tombs, and portrait heads. After the Restoration, all such "conceits" were looked upon with increasing disfavor. Dryden indicates his contempt of such verse in *Mac Flecknoe* (ll. 205–08) and Addison devotes a *Spectator* paper (No. 58) to condemning this "obsolete" kind of "false Wit."

Neither Quarles nor Withers was particularly addicted to figure poetry, but their poems are full of other sorts of conceits for which the "wings" are made to stand. Pope's particular animus against these two, which does not seem to have been shared to an equal extent by other critics of the time, and his later use of them as examples of extremely bad poets (e.g., E. & C., III, 260, n. 6, 371; IV, 113; x, 379; and IV, 123; x, 370) point to him as the author of this satiric bit.

(36) 99, 10. . . . *with a* Lanthorn *of* Jacob Behmen.

"The enthusiastic founder of the German and English Methodists, Muggletonians, Hernhuters, and the illuminated Devotees on the Continent. He was called the German Theosophist. He was a Taylor at Gorlitz." (Warton)

This is a burlesque of the "inner light" or "spiritual illumination" which characterized the teaching of Behmen (1575–1624) and the other mystics of the seventeenth century. Swift had used the comparison to a lantern before in his *Mechanical Operation of the Spirit. Tale of a Tub,* A. C. Guthkelch and D. Nichol Smith, eds. (Oxford, 1920), pp. 280–1; *Works,* I, 202.

The lantern which children attached to kites when they were flown at night was a small affair of cardboard and paper with a lighted candle inside. Cf. Butler's *Hudibras,* II, iii, 413–22.

(37) 99, 15. . . . *as soon as he was born he uttered the voice of nine several animals. He cry'd like a Calf, bleated like a Sheep, chattered like a Mag-pye,*

grunted like a Hog, neighed like a Foal, croaked like a Raven, mewed like a Cat,
gabbled like a Goose, and bray'd like an Ass.

This passage is a burlesque of what is supposed to have happened at Homer's
birth. According to a story which Eustathius ascribes to Alexander the Paphian
and discredits (Leo Allatius, *De Patria Homeri* [Lyons, 1640], p. 45), Homer was
the son of the Egyptian Dmasagora, a descendant of Aethra and Isis. From
Dmasagora's breasts honey dropped into the mouth of the infant Homer, who
that night emitted nine voices, of a swallow, peacock, dove, crow, partridge,
prophyrian, starling, nightingale, and blackbird.

(38) 99, 21. *And the next morning he was found playing in his bed with two Owls,*
which came down the chimney. His Father greatly rejoyced at all these signs,
which betokened the variety of his Eloquence, and the extent of his Learning; but
he was more particularly pleased with the last, as it nearly resembled what hap-
pen'd at the birth of Homer.

According to the same story, Homer was later discovered in bed, jesting with
nine doves. All these prodigies were taken by his delighted mother as tokens of the
future greatness of the boy. *Ibid.*

To the word "Homer" in the first edition of the *Memoirs* there is attached the
following footnote: *Vid. Eustat. in Odyss. l. 12. ex Alex. Paphio. & Leo Allat. de*
patr. Hom. pag 45.

CHAPTER II

The chapter continues the satire on uncritical reverence for the ancients, this
attitude being burlesqued to the highest degree in Cornelius' rapture at the discovery that his son is afflicted with many of the bodily deformities of the great
ancients. In addition a number of other interesting themes of satire are introduced, the chief of them being philosophic pride, man's "wanting the perfections"
of various animals, the lying traveler, and what for want of a better title may perhaps be called the virtuoso-explorer theme. Of these the most interesting and important is that of philosophic pride or the overvaluing of man's capacities and
his place in creation. Though touched upon only briefly—in Cornelius' question,
"Is not man the lord of creation?"—this theme is fundamental to much of the remainder of the chapter and is an important element in the whole Scriblerian
philosophy.

By Scriblerian times the error and evil effects of the great pride in man's nature
and in his superior place in the great scheme of things that had become prevalent
during the Renaissance had been a favorite subject of essays, sermons, and satires
for more than a century. The major attacks on it came from three sources, the
first and most insistent being the church. Pride in all its manifestations had of
course always been regarded as one of the cardinal sins, and attacks on that form
of it which led man to look upon himself as the "lord of creation" had been vigorous.[1] Another source of attack was the anti-intellectualist movement, led by

1. Cf., for example, Thomas Aquinas, *Summa Theologica*, Pt. II, 2d part, Quest. CLXII, art. 5.

Montaigne, which sought to persuade man to proper humility by pointing out the limitations of the power of reason on which much of man's pride rested and by challenging his vaunted superiority over the animals.[2] A third had come from scientific circles during the late Renaissance and seventeenth century. The adoption of the Copernican system brought about a great revolution of man's concept of himself in relation to nature. The telescope and microscope were used to show man that the universe was vaster and more complex than his mind could comprehend,[3] and the Newtonian concept of the universe as a vast impersonal mechanism was used to show man how small and trifling his affairs were in the mind of the Creator.[4]

Attacks on philosophic pride from all these points of view appear in the works of the individual Scriblerians and of their friend and associate, Bolingbroke.[5] Gay's fable of "The Man and the Flea" is aimed at man's egoistical concept of the purpose of the world [6] and the theme of man's false pride in himself and his abilities is the basis of Arbuthnot's philosophical poem *Know Yourself*.[7] Satire on man's vanity in his reason and in his supposed superiority over the animals appears in several places in Swift,[8] most importantly, of course, in the fourth book of *Gulliver's Travels*. The most elaborate philosophical treatment of the theme among the Scriblerians is in Pope's *Essay on Man*.[9] Here all the major grounds of attack on man's egoism are restated with such force and clarity that the poem may be regarded as something like a climax in the development of this theme.

2. Montaigne, "Apologie de Raimond Sebond," *Essais*, Bk. ii, chap. xii. His ideas were echoed and enlarged upon down through the seventeenth century in such works as: Joseph Hall, *Satires*, Bk. iii, Sat. 1; Blaise Pascal, *Thoughts* (New York, 1859), pp. 161, 164, 270, etc.; Earl of Rochester, "A Satyr against Mankind," *Poems on Several Occasions* (1705), p. 89; Robert Gould, "A Satire on Man," *Poems* (1689), p. 196; Matthew Prior, "An Ode Written in 1688, as an Exercise at St. John's College, Cambridge," *Poems on Several Occasions* (Cambridge, 1905), p. 1; and William King, *De Origine Mali* (1702), chap. iv, sec. 2, subsec. 5. See also A. O. Lovejoy, " 'Pride' in Eighteenth-Century Thought," *MLN*, xxxvi (1921), 31–7.

3. For the very interesting results of the first impact of the telescope and microscope on English thought see Marjorie Nicolson, "Milton and the Telescope," *ELH*, ii (1935), 1–32; "The 'New Astronomy' and English Literary Imagination," *SP*, xxxii (1935), 428–62; and "The Microscope and English Imagination," *Smith College Studies in Modern Languages*, xvi, No. 4 (Northampton, Mass., 1935), 82 ff.

4. Reflections on man's insignificance in relation to the universe are too numerous to list; for typical expressions see William Derham's *Astro-Theology* (1715), pp. 26, 30–2, 33, 40–1, 50, 198–9, 220–8.

5. Bolingbroke's views on this subject are of particular interest because of his close connection with the *Essay on Man*, with the views of which in relation to man's pride he is in close agreement. See his *Works* (1793), iii, 312–13, 328; v, 338, 345, 347, 465.

6. *Fables* (1st series, 1727), No. xlix; *Poetical Works*, G. C. Faber, ed. (Oxford, 1926), p. 273.

7. ΓΝΩΘΙ ΣΕ'ΑΥΤΟΝ. *Know Yourself* (1734).

8. See his *Ode to Dr. William Sancroft* (stanza iv), *The Elephant, or the Parliament Man*, *The Day of Judgment*, and *The Beasts' Confession to the Priest*.

9. Man's belief that the universe was created for him is dealt with in Ep. i, ll. 131–40, and Ep. iii, ll. 27–48; pride as an evil because it makes man dissatisfied with his state in Ep. i, ll. 123–6; man's false estimate of his reason and its true limits in Ep. ii, ll. 19–52; and his relationship to the animals now and in the original state of nature in Ep. iii, ll. 79–98, 147–70.

(1) 100, 7. . . . *the Child had the Wart of Cicero,* . . .

". . . the *Latins* call a Vetch *Cicer,* and a flat Excresence in the resemblance of a Vetch on the tip of his Nose, gave him the sirname of Cicero." Plutarch, v, 292.

(2) 100, 8. . . . *the wry Neck of Alexander,* . . .

"The Statues that most resembled *Alexander,* were those of *Lysippus,* . . . [which] express'd the Inclination of his Head a little on one side towards his left Shoulder . . . with incomparable exactness." Plutarch, IV, 227.

(3) 100, 8. . . . *knots upon his legs like Marius,* . . .

". . . both his Legs [were] full of great Tumors, called *Varices* . . ." Plutarch, III, 73.

(4) 100, 9. . . . *and one of them shorter than the other like Agesilaus.*

"He had one Leg shorter than another; which Deformity he easily hid by a good Mien, and Briskness in his Behaviour, he being the first always to pass a Jest upon himself." Plutarch, IV, 3.

(5) 100, 11. *The good Cornelius also hoped he would come to stammer like Demosthenes, in order to be as eloquent;*

Plutarch says of Demosthenes that "he had (it seems) a Weakness in his Voice, a perplex'd and indistinct utterance, and a shortness of Breath, which by breaking and disjoynting his Sentences, much obscur'd the Sense and Meaning of what he spoke." Plutarch, v, 250.

(6) 100, 12. . . . *at many other Defects of famous men.*

The list of defects that Martinus shares with the great men of antiquity can with some confidence be assigned to Pope's principal authorship, since his friends would hardly introduce the subject. Pope bitingly satirizes those who draw such parallels in order to pay a compliment in his *Epistle to Dr. Arbuthnot:*

> There are who to my person pay their court:
> I cough like Horace, and, though lean, am short.
> Ammon's great son one shoulder had too high,—
> So Ovid's nose,—and, "Sir, you have an eye."
> Go on, obliging creatures, make me see
> All that disgraced my betters met in me. ll. 115–20.

(7) 100, 27. *Not so the Ancients, they could move them at pleasure,* . . .

The evidence for such an assertion had been discussed in all seriousness by John Bulwer in his *Pathomyotomia* (1649), a work with which there is some reason to believe the Scriblerians were familiar. Cf. Chap. x, p. 277, n. 13. Bulwer cites Galen, Athenaeus, St. Augustine, Casaubon, and others (pp. 181–2). Bayle has a typically long note in his *Dictionary* on men who could move their ears. *S.v.* "Hercules," p. 1646, n. G.

(8) 100, 28. . . . *and accordingly are often describ'd* arrectis auribus.

That is, "with raised ears"—a play on the Latin idiom *aures arrigere,* "to be attentive."

(9) 100, 31. . . . *why should he not have the perfection of a Drill, or of any other animal?"*

This complaint of man regarding his own imperfections, especially those of his senses in comparison with animals, birds, etc., was another favorite subject of satire among the Scriblerians and gave rise to the famous answer of Pope in his *Essay on Man:*

> Why has not man a microscopic eye?
> For this plain reason, man is not a fly.
> Say what the use, were finer optics giv'n,
> T'inspect a mite, not comprehend the heav'n?
> Or touch, if tremblingly alive all o'er,
> To smart and agonize at ev'ry pore?
> Or quick effluvia darting through the brain,
> Die of a rose in aromatic pain?
> If nature thundered in his op'ning ears,
> And stunned him with the music of the spheres,
> How would he wish that heav'n had left him still
> The whisp'ring zephyr, and the purling rill? Ep. i, ll. 193–204.

Like his pride, with which it is closely associated, this desire of man for greater natural endowments than those which he possesses had been much discussed and satirized in the century preceding the *Memoirs.* The conventional theological answer was that man's capacities had been determined by the wisdom of God and that man should therefore be content. Pope's argument that they are exactly fitted to his real needs had been very vigorously and clearly stated by Locke. *Essay concerning Human Understanding,* Bk. ii, chap. xxiii, sec. 12.

(10) 101, 9. *Let other Mortals . . . swallow the legends of lying travellers; . . .*

The age-old skepticism concerning the tall tales of travelers was particularly strong in the early eighteenth century when the new science was vigorously trying to sort out truth from fiction and to get rid of the idea that, as Lady Mary put it, it is the privilege of the traveler to lie. *Letters and Works,* W. Moy Thomas, ed. (Bohn Lib., n. d.), i, 109, 143, 146. Pope mentions the theme (*Satires of Dr. Donne,* Sat. iv, l. 31) and Swift, of course, makes excellent use of it in *Gulliver's Travels. Works,* viii, 117, 152, 302–04.

A real factor in the contemporary attitude was the exposure of the famous impostor Psalmanazar. George Psalmanazar (1679–1763), a Frenchman by birth, hit upon the idea of making a living by pretending to be a Formosan. In the company of a disreputable chaplain by the name of Innes, he came to London in 1704 and soon got in the good graces of Bishop Compton, who offered to send him to Oxford. Before going to the university, Psalmanazar, who lived up to his part by taking huge quantities of opium and eating his meat raw, published an account of Formosa which, supposedly, he had written in Latin and Innes had translated into English.

After less than a year at Oxford, Psalmanazar returned to London to superintend the publication of a second edition of his work, which he published under the title of *An Historical and Geographical Description of Formosa, an Island Sub-*

ject to the Emperor of Japan (1704). In the long preface to the edition, however, he overreached himself by declaring that about a year previously he had had the honor of meeting Halley (the Savilian professor of mathematics at Oxford) "with some other gentlemen at a tavern," and that he had returned satisfactory answers to all their questions regarding the position of the sun at midday and the length of the twilight in Formosa. When this statement was called to the attention of Halley, Mead, and Woodward (the last two of whom were the "other gentlemen"), they gave it the lie direct and declared they were convinced that he was an impostor. Psalmanazar, thus exposed, gave up his false claims and spent the rest of his long life as a hack writer for London booksellers. His memoirs were published in 1765 under the title of *Memoirs of* ———. For an account of his life see these *Memoirs;* W. C. Sidney, *England in the Eighteenth Century* (1892), I, 290–2; King, II, 133 n.

(11) 101, 12. . . . *from the peak of Derby* . . .
A punning jest based upon the name of a somewhat rugged region in the northwest part of Derbyshire. Though known as the "Peake," none of the summits within the district is especially remarkable for height. The region was famous for a number of curious geological formations, especially several grottoes or caverns, which were celebrated by Thomas Hobbes in his *De Mirabilibus Pecci Carmen* (1636) and by Charles Cotton in a poem entitled *The Wonders of the Peake* (1681). It appears from Defoe's disparaging comments that the "wonders" were regarded as considerably overrated by many travelers. *A Tour through England and Wales,* Everyman Lib., II, 157–79.

(12) 101, 13. . . . *to the peak of Teneriff;* . . .
The absurd height still ascribed to this mountain in the early eighteenth century is indicated by the statement in the *New Geographical Dictionary* (1737): "The famous Mountain called the *Pike of Teneriffe* is in the middle of this Island (i.e., one of the Canaries) which is by some said to be 15 miles high; the French Account is 15 Leagues. The least is high enough, & that may very well be questioned too." Earlier estimates had ranged from nine to seventy miles. Burton's *Anatomy of Melancholy* (1621), Pt. II, sec. 2, memb. 3. As one of the highest peaks yet scaled by man it was the object of much scientific attention during the last half of the seventeenth century. Accounts of climbing it sent in by travelers were published by Sprat (*History of the Royal Society* [1667], 200–13), Hooke (*Lectures* [1678]), and by Boyle. *Works* (1772), III, 226; V, 706. These accounts were not far wrong in their estimates of its true height; according to that published by Sprat the height was "vulgarly esteem'd to be two miles and a half. *Ibid.,* p. 204. The figure accepted today is 12,190 feet.

(13) 101, 13. . . . *visited the top of Taurus,* . . .
Taurus and the names which follow were apparently chosen because little was known about them and they conveyed the idea of great remoteness and danger. Taurus, now limited to the range of mountains running parallel to the seacoast in the southeastern part of Asia Minor, was the general name given to the supposed chain of mountains extending from Asia Minor to the China Sea. How-

ever, according to the *New Geographical Dictionary*, "It keeps its name only in *Caramania* & *Aladuli* in *Natolia;* some part of them are called *Caucasus,* & some *Dalanguer,* & *Imaus,* & *Altay.*" The highest point of the Taurus range is about 11,500 feet.

(14) 101, 13. . . . *Imaus* . . .
    The name is the one used by the ancients for the mountains dividing Scythia, which Alexander crossed (i.e. the western Himalayas). In the early eighteenth century the name was applied to the whole eastern part of the range supposed to extend entirely across Asia. The western part, according to the *New Geographical Dictionary*, "is to this day called Mount Caucasus, & the other is called *Altay,* that separates the *Calmuck Tartars* from the *Mogul Tartars.*"

(15) 101, 15. . . . *he may take a slight view of the snowy Riphaeans;* . . .
    These are apparently the southern part of the Ural Mountains. The *New Geographical Dictionary* says they lie "on the left side of the River *Irtis* & South of the City of Tobalski, & are called the Mountains of *Vergotur* or of *Pojas Semino.*"

(16) 101, 19. . . . *the burning mountain of Java,* . . .
    This probably refers to Gede. Pat Gordon, in his *Geography Anatomiz'd* (1693), says, "In the same Island [of Java] is a remarkable *Vulcano,* which sometimes burns with great Rage." P. 289.

(17) 101, 20. . . . *but chiefly Hecla the greatest rarity in the Northern Regions.*
    "The name of a mountain in Isleland; where there is a terrible abyss, or deep place, where nothing but the lamentable cries of persons, as is supposed extremely tormented, are heard for the compass of a League round about it." Phillips, *New World of Words* (3d ed., 1671). It had long been famous as a fabulous natural wonder and had been seriously enquired into by the Royal Society. Cf. Ethel Seaton, *Literary Relations of England and Scandinavia in the Seventeenth Century* (Oxford, 1935), pp. 275–8.

(18) 101, 21. . . . *the wonders of the Mephitick cave.*
    This is the cave mentioned by Virgil in the *Aeneid* (vii.83). Since until recently the cave was not known to exist, it seems probable that the Scriblerians were making fun of Cornelius for taking Virgil too literally.

(19) 101, 30. . . . *those fountains of fresh water that are at the bottom of the Ocean.*
    Apparently those mentioned by Lucretius (*De Rerum Natura,* vi. 890),
                As little streams, that cut their secret way,
                And rise up sweet i' th' bottom of the sea;
                Beat off the salt, and the resisting flood
                To thirsty sailors proves a mighty good.
                    Thomas Creech, tr. (1682), ll. 879–82.
    In discussing the operation of an "Ark for submarine Navigations," Bishop Wilkins says, "The many fresh springs that may probably be met with in the bottom of the sea, will serve for the supply of drink and other occasions. *Mathematical Magick* (1648), Bk. ii, chap. v.

CHAPTER III

In this chapter we encounter the first of a series of Scriblerian satires on Dr. John Woodward, a contemporary scientist and antiquarian, whose unenviable distinction it is to have been the individual most frequently and severely satirized by our club of wits. The episode of the shield was designed to ridicule Dr. Woodward's extravagant claims for an old embossed shield which he believed to be of great antiquity and value but which the most skeptical antiquarians of his time regarded as a worthless modern imitation.

Though aimed primarily at Woodward, the satire touches all excessive antiquarianism and zeal for collecting. Interest in antiquities had become widespread in the early eighteenth century, and not only wealthy noblemen and improvident scholars collected ancient objects, but professional men such as Dr. Mead, Dr. Sloane, and Dr. Woodward devoted considerable portions of their earnings to the purchase of ancient as well as modern rarities. The Scriblerians themselves were not exempt from the current taste. The Earl of Oxford and his son built up a large collection; Pope, though he confined his collecting to objects for his garden and grotto, told Spence he had once developed enough interest in antiquities to write a treatise in Latin on the old buildings in Rome; [1] Swift showed in occasional references in his letters and in his purchase of books that he was attracted by the ancient and curious; and Arbuthnot displayed in his *Tables of Ancient Coins* and other writings a strong interest in various aspects of ancient life and learning. We may safely assume, therefore, that the intention here, as in other cases in the *Memoirs,* is not to ridicule the subject itself but to satirize those who carried their enthusiasm for all things connected with the ancients to the point of folly.

The career of John Woodward may legitimately be called distinguished.[2] In 1692, at the age of twenty-seven, he was elected professor of physic at Gresham College. In the following year he became a member of the Royal Society and two years later received the degree of M.D. both from Archbishop Tenison and from Cambridge University. In 1698 he was admitted a candidate of the College of Physicians and in 1703 was elected to full fellowship and to the post of Censor, an honor which was again conferred upon him in 1714. He died in 1728, after having held his chair at Gresham for a period of thirty-six years.

Like most scientists of the period, Woodward did not confine his activities to one field. His first major interest was in what has become the modern sciences of geology and paleontology. In 1695 he published a treatise entitled *An Essay*

1. Spence, p. 154.
2. A full biography of Woodward yet remains to be written. The most important accounts of him are to be found in Beattie, pp. 190–262; J. W. Clark and T. M. Hughes, *The Life and Letters of the Reverend Adam Sedgwick* (1890), I, 166–86; the *Dictionary of National Biography; General Dictionary* (1741), *s.v.* "Woodward (John)," art. by Thomas Birch; and John Ward, *The Lives of the Professors of Gresham College* (1740), pp. 282–301. Mr. Beattie's account deals chiefly with Woodward's contemporary reputation and the controversial pamphlets and satires written against him by Arbuthnot and others; it is therefore particularly useful for those interested in this side of his career. It is with pleasure that I acknowledge my indebtedness both to Mr. Beattie's published work and to him personally for much information about Woodward and his shield.

toward a Natural History of the Earth in which he advanced the theories that fossil remains were not, as had been generally agreed, merely "sports" of nature but were instead the true remains of once living creatures and that the stratification of rock, of which he was one of the first scientific observers, was the result of the settling of solid matter after the Flood. Another interest was antiquities, and though his publication in this field was confined to a slender monograph on some Roman remains uncovered in London, he carried on a wide correspondence with the leading antiquarians throughout Europe and achieved a considerable reputation as a collector. Still a third field of activity was his professional one of "physick." Here his attention became centered on the nature and function of the bile, and he eventually propounded the theory that disorder of the "biliose salts" was the chief cause of disease in mankind.[3]

Woodward's virtues as a scientist lay in his intense interest in his various activities, his indefatigable energy, and his conscientious attempt to gather primary data by observations and collections. These virtues, however, were overbalanced and the value of his work nearly totally destroyed by his tendency to pursue the apparent direction of his findings far beyond the evidence into fantastic theories and by his refusal to retreat from or modify his position in the face of overpowering argument and strong contrary evidence. Thus his genuine achievements in geology and paleontology were buried under the folly of his theory of the Deluge; his antiquarian studies vitiated by his absurd conclusions, and his observations concerning the bile largely discredited as a result of his belief that all disease could be cured by vomits.

His faults as a scientist were much enhanced by a number of personal failings. He was extraordinarily rude, ill-tempered, arrogant, suspicious, jealous, and combative. As a result, every stage of his career was marked by violent and disgraceful quarrels,[4] which in the end won him, despite strong competition, Hooke's mantle as the most detested scientist of his generation. Even his friends and defenders, such as Hearne and Thoresby, found themselves at times irritated almost beyond endurance.[5]

It is probable that Arbuthnot was chiefly responsible for the satire on Woodward in the *Memoirs*. The genial doctor's interest in and contempt for the Greshamite

3. Of comparatively minor importance in his career, but of considerable interest in the history of science, was a paper he read before the Royal Society in 1697 entitled "Some Thoughts and Experiments concerning Vegetation." On the basis of this paper he has an indubitable claim to be called one of the founders of experimental plant physiology and the discoverer of transpiration. It is to be noted that the Scriblerians make no attempt to ridicule his sound work along this line.

4. Woodward's most protracted quarrel was with Sir Hans Sloane. The quarrel first came into the open when Woodward, stung by a rumor that he was the author of *The Transactioneer,* a satire on Sloane's editorship of the *Philosophical Transactions* (actually written by William King), issued a broadside demanding apologies and broadly hinting that he thought the attacks on Sloane's editorship justified. The result was, in the words of a contemporary, "a great fray betwixt the Virtuosi." Beattie, p. 211. The feud, after an interim, was renewed by an altercation in a Royal Society meeting, which led eventually to the expulsion of Woodward from the council. Another famous quarrel of Woodward's was with Freind and Mead over his theory of vomits and led to a ridiculous street quarrel and duel.

5. Beattie, pp. 217, 220–22.

dated back to Woodward's publication of his theory of the Deluge. Arbuthnot's first bow in the learned world was made in a little tract printed in 1697 in which he, with good humor but devastating effectiveness, pointed out the absurdities of Woodward's theory and his unacknowledged indebtedness to Steno for some of the sounder parts of his work.[6] Having made his points, Arbuthnot, characteristically, refused to be drawn into a quarrel on the subject; he did not, however, cease to be critical, and as Woodward in the passing years advanced to new follies and further revealed his vain and intemperate character the doctor's amusement and scorn were given ample exercise.[7]

Even if one of their members had not been so well acquainted with Woodward, the Scriblerians could hardly have overlooked him in their search for material. Within the year preceding the first drafting of the *Memoirs* Woodward achieved new prominence by the publication of an elaborated and pretentious version of his theory of the Deluge,[8] by his election as Censor of the College of Physicians for a second time, by the authorship of one account of some recently discovered Roman remains[9] and a reputed share in another,[10] and by the publication of an elaborate treatise on his famous shield written by Henry Dodwell.[11] Satire on him had, therefore, the additional merit of being highly topical.

The treatment of Woodward in the *Memoirs* is notable not only for its wit but for its good nature and its use of implication rather than direct attack. Apart from the episode of the shield, the satire on him is limited to a reference to his theory of vomits[12] and a jest based on his theory of the Flood.[13] Each satirical allusion, however, touches a vital point in Woodward's work and all together they are as effective as a formal indictment.

The Scriblerian satire on Woodward was not confined to the *Memoirs*. The Greshamite's habit of building elaborate theories on slender evidence was burlesqued in *An Essay on the Origine of Sciences,* and his character as a collector and antiquarian was ridiculed in the play *Three Hours after Marriage.* He was also used in a poem written as a sequel to *Annus Mirabilis,* entitled *An Epistle to the Most Learned Doctor W—d—d* (1722),[14] and was twice satirized by Pope— once for his "love of rust" and later for his theory of vomits.[15] In addition he was

6. *An Examination of Dr. Woodward's Account of the Deluge.* For a further account of it see below, p. 329, n. 6.

7. Arbuthnot was kept in constant contact with Woodward through the meetings of the Royal Society, which until 1710 met at Gresham College. Though positive evidence is lacking, it may be assumed that Arbuthnot took the side of his friend Sloane in his quarrels with Woodward.

8. *Naturalis Historia Telluris* (1714). Cf. below, p. 330, n. 6.

9. *An Account of Some Roman Urns* (1713).

10. Hearne, IV, 253.

11. See below, p. 207, n. 3.

12. Text, p. 130; cf. below, p. 274, n. 3.

13. Text, p. 168; cf. below, p. 344, n. 33.

14. Probably by Gay assisted by Arbuthnot, or vice versa. Cf. Irving, pp. 195–6; Beattie, pp. 240–1.

15. *Epistle to Addison,* ll. 41–2 (cf. below, p. 209, n. 11) and *Satires of Dr. Donne,* Sat. IV, ll. 152–3.

satirized in two rather coarse pamphlets in connection with the smallpox controversy which have, on slender and dubious evidence, been attributed to Arbuthnot.[16]

The fame of Woodward's shield was in part the result of the great contemporary interest in the Roman remains being uncovered in London and other parts of England, but in a still larger measure the result of the widespread publicity which Woodward managed to obtain for it. According to his own account, Woodward bought his treasure "of M[rs] Conyers, after y[e] Death of her Father, who found it in a Smiths shop near Tower Hill." [17] The shield was a small one (about fourteen inches in diameter), richly embossed with a large fantastic head in the center, a perspective of landscape and ruined buildings in the upper part, and an elaborate battle scene in the lower.[18] Having convinced himself of its genuineness and great value, Woodward had a full-sized engraving of it made, copies of which he distributed among leading antiquaries.[19] In the main the antiquarians, particularly those who were friends of the doctor, agreed with him, and differed only as to whether the shield was a *Parma equestris* or one of the *Clypei votivi*.[20] Hearne published a note about it in his edition of Livy,[21] and before his death the learned Dr. Henry Dodwell wrote a dissertation in which, on the basis of the clothes worn by the figures and style of architecture in the buildings, he "demonstrated" the shield to be a true *Parma equestris*.[22]

From the start, however, there were, in Hearne's words, "not wanting some ill-natur'd men who run it down as a Banter," [23] and Woodward and his defenders were heartily laughed at for their credulity. In the long run the victory lay with the skeptics; the shield declined sharply in value after Woodward's death and eventually found a home in the British Museum, where at the present time it is little regarded, being judged to be of late sixteenth-century German origin.[24]

16. *An Account of the Sickness and Death of Dr. W---dw---rd* and *The Life and Adventures of Don Bilioso de L'Estomac*. Both were published in 1719 and reprinted in the 1751 edition of the *Miscellaneous Works of the Late Dr. Arbuthnot*. It is doubtful if Arbuthnot had any connection with either; cf. Beattie, pp. 251–6.

17. Hearne, III, 499.

18. Its subject was supposed to be the taking of Rome by Brennus as told by Livy. Hearne, II, 13.

19. Cf. Chap. IV, p. 213, n. 4; Hearne, *loc. cit.*

20. Hearne and Woodward believed it to be a *Clypeus votivus*. Hearne, IV, 74 and John Ward, *op. cit.*, p. 140. Woodward's confidence in the general acceptance of the authenticity of the shield and his irritatingly arrogant manner are both illustrated in his statement to Hearne, in a letter dated October 28, 1712: "I do not think You'll think fitt to enter into Dispute wth a few trifleing People who pretend to doubt of y[e] Antiquity of y[e] Shield; since there's not a Man, who is a Judg, all over Europe, who doubts of it." Hearne, III, 476.

21. *Titi Livii Historiarum Editio altera, cum diversis annotationibus* (Oxford, 1708), VI, 195.

22. Cf. below, p. 207, n. 3.

23. Hearne, II, 13. Hearne cites particularly Dr. David Gregory, a friend of Arbuthnot's (Aitken, p. 31), who died in 1708.

24. Cf. F. H. Cripps-Day, *Record of Armour Sales, 1881–1924* (1925), p. xxxi. The opinion of its origin was expressed in a letter from Mr. A. B. Tonnochy, assistant keeper of the Department of British and Medieval Antiquities, to Mr. Beattie.

(1) 102, 6. *The day of the Christ'ning being come, and the house filled with Gossips, the Levity of whose conversation suited but ill with the Gravity of Dr. Cornelius, . . .*

For a somewhat earlier description of the customs of a christening, of the "gossips" who attended them, and of the type of conversation which distressed Dr. Cornelius, see Ned Ward's elaborate account of his adventures as a godfather. *The London Spy*, pp. 407–22.

(2) 102, 11. *He remembered to have read in Theocritus, that the Cradle of Hercules was a Shield; . . .*

This statement occurs in *Idyllium* xxiv, 1–5:

> *Alcides* ten months old, a vigourous Child,
> *Alcmena* fed, and laid him on a Shield,
> (The Shield from *Pterilus Amphitryo* won
> A great auspicious Cradle for his Son); . . .
>   Thomas Creech, tr. (1684), ll. 1–4.

(3) 102, 19. *. . . had caused him formerly to compile a Dissertation concerning it, proving from the several properties, and particularly the colour of the Rust, the exact chronology thereof.*

This is a reference to the dissertation on Dr. Woodward's shield written by Dr. Dodwell, who also comes within the scope of the Scriblerians' satire in another field. Cf. general note to Chapter xii. The dissertation was begun not long before Dodwell's death on the insistence of Dr. Woodward. Francis Brokesby, *The Life of Mr. Henry Dodwell; with an Account of his Works* (1715), I, 494.

In the dissertation, Dodwell attempted to establish the date of the shield by observing the garments and arms of the soldiers, the trappings of their horses, the architecture of the temples and theaters in the background, and especially the nature of the iron in the shield as shown by its patina and the absence of deep rust. He accompanied all this with such a wealth of classical references that the dissertation achieved fame as an important document with regard to the dress and habits of the Romans.

After the death of Dodwell on the seventh of June, 1711, the manuscript was turned over to Thomas Hearne, under whose editorship it was published in Oxford in 1713 under the title, *Henrici Dodwelli de Parma Equestri Woodwardiano Dissertatio* (Hearne, III, 426, 456, 463, 473, 476, 497–9; IV, 89, 95, 100–02, *et passim*).

(4) 102, 27. *. . . cover'd with a mantle of blue Sattin.*

It was the custom on these occasions to wrap the child in a rich robe. Cf. Ned Ward, whose godson is "wrap'd up in so Rich a Mantle, as if both *Indies* had Club'd their utmost Riches to furnish out a Noble covering for my little Kinsman, . . ." *The London Spy*, p. 411.

(5) 102, 29. *. . . they entered into a warm Debate about the* Triclinium . . .

Arbuthnot was himself interested in the manner in which the Romans ate, though we may be sure he did not discuss the matter at the christening of his children. In his *Tables of Ancient Coins, Weights and Measures* (1727) he says, in the course of a description of the Roman dining room:

About the Table there were three Beds (the *triclinium*) at most: after the time of Vespasian, there were often but two; from whence they were called *Biclinia;* and the Table was in the figure of a Semicircle, from which it was called *Sigma;* the Space before was open for Waiters. P. 134.

(6) 102, 30. . . . *and the manner of the* Decubitus *of the Ancients,* . . .
    Arbuthnot also discussed the manner of the *decubitus,* or reclining at the table, in his *Tables of Ancient Coins* (pp. 134–5).

(7) 102, 34. *Let the Physiognomists examine his features;* . . .
    Cornelius is here again following his beloved ancients, who displayed great interest, and considerable credulity, in the "art" or "science" of physiognomy. Hippocrates and Galen both wrote on the subject, but the ancients who were regarded as the authorities on physiognomy were Aristotle (in the *Physiognom-onica*—a work of doubtful authenticity) and the fifth-century Greek physician and Sophist, Adamantius. According to Chambers (*s.v.* "Physiognomy"), the "top modern authors" in the field were the Neapolitan, Giovanni Baptista della Porta (ca. 1539–1615), and the Englishman, Robert Fludd (1574–1637). However, several other men produced interesting treatises on the subject in the seventeenth century.
    In modern times physiognomy, like astrology, tended to split into two branches, one consisting of the pseudo-science of divining character and foretelling futures, even in babies, from the cast of the features and the lines of the face, and the other of a rational, if fumbling, study of facial expression and the effects of character, temperament, and various activities on the lineaments of the features. By the times of the Scriblerians, the "judicial" (to borrow the word from astrology) branch of physiognomy had long been looked upon by the educated as a vicious form of quackery. As early as 1597–98, "all persons fayning to have knowledge of Phisiog-nomie or like Fantastical Imaginacions" had been declared by law liable to be "openly whipped untill his body be bloudye." 39 Eliz. c. 4. That the "art" still continued to be practiced, however, is shown by the modifications of this old law made in 1713. 13 Anne c. 26.

(8) 102, 34. . . . *let the Chirographists behold his Palm:* . . .
    The Scriblerians here demonstrate their own innocence with regard to such subjects by using the wrong word for it—the commonly accepted term for those practicing palmistry being "chiromancer." Cf. the dictionaries of Blount, Phillips, Coles, Kersey, and Bailey. Chiromancy, like physiognomy, was of the greatest antiquity and the highest contemporary disrepute. Hippocrates, Aristotle, and Galen deal with it; and it is frequently mentioned by other ancient writers. There was some controversy over it in the seventeenth century—one advocate going so far as to ask, *"who but a* Mad-Man, *or* Foole *dare say, That the like Signes in the Hand of Man, are* Idle *and* Vain?*"* (J. Rothmann, *Chiromantia,* George Wharton, tr. [1652], "Epistle Dedicatory" to Elias Ashmole, p. [x]), but most people looked upon it, as Bacon had, as a "vain imposture." *De Augmentis,* Bk. IV, chap. i. It is satirized by Addison in *Spectator,* Nos. 505 and 518.

(9) 103, 5. . . . *I purchas'd that invaluable piece of Antiquity at the great (though indeed inadequate) expence of all the Plate of our family,* . . .

The idea of a "virtuoso" beggaring himself and his family to purchase some worthless curiosity or relic was a common one in the satire of the time. Cf., e.g., *Tatler*, No. 216 and Young, *Universal Passion*, Sat. i, ll. 175–84, iv, ll. 113–22.

(10) 103, 8. . . . *it broke the heart of the great Melchior Insipidus!"*
The name Melchior Insipidus is probably a concoction of the Scriblerians. It is remarkable in that it seems to be the sole occasion in the *Memoirs* on which the Scriblerians resort to fiction in referring to scholars, scientists, and antiquarians. The name Melchior was borne by a number of German theologians of the sixteenth and seventeenth centuries, notably by Melchior Hosman, a heretic whose followers were known as Melchiorites. The epithet "Insipidus" had been used in connection with several figures during the Middle Ages.

(11) 103, 15. . . . *Behold this Rust,—or rather let me call it this precious Ærugo, —behold this beautiful Varnish of Time,—this venerable Verdure of so many Ages—*
Another favorite point of attack on antiquarians was their supposed love of rust for its own sake. Durfey, *Madame Fickle* (1677), Act III, sc. i; King, "Journey to London" (1698), in *Works*, I, 203; Pope, *Epistle to Addison*, ll. 35–8, *Imitations of Horace*, Bk. II, Ep. i, ll. 35–6; etc.

(12) 103, 24. . . . *had scoured it as clean as her Andirons.*
This piece of satire had been used previously by William King in his parody of Lister's *Journey to Paris in the Year 1698*, where he says, "He presented me with a Roman tea-dish and a chocolate-pot; which I take to be about Augustus's time, because it is very rusty. My maid, very ignorantly, was going to scour it, and had done me 'an immense' damage." King, I, 203.

(13) 103, 29. . . . *Hungary Water, Hartshorn*, . . .
"*Hungary water* is one of the distilled waters of the shops; and is directed in the college dispensatory, to be made of Rosemary flowers infused some days in rectified spirit of wine, and thus distilled." Chambers. Rosemary flowers were a standard ingredient in all prescriptions for epilepsies, apoplexies, palsies, etc. Chambers, *s.v.* "Rosemary." Hartshorn was a form of smelling salts, which got its name from the fact that it was originally prepared from the horns of harts, and its efficacy from its large ammonia content. These two were the conventional remedies of the time for hysteria and fainting fits.

(14) 104, 2. . . . *the* Cuspis *of a sword*, . . .
I.e. the point.

(15) 104, 4. . . . *others accounting the* Insignia Virilia, *pronounc'd to be one of the* Dii Termini; . . .
Apparently the reference is to one of the statues of the god Terminus which the Romans used for marking boundaries. Since the subject of the scene on Woodward's shield was thought to be the sacking of Rome, the presence of a statue of Terminus, whose principal duty it was to protect the state from foreign invasion, would be particularly appropriate. The engraving of the shield published in Dodwell's treatise, however, does not portray any object that seems to fit the speculations in the text and the point of the jest is not clear.

(16) 104, 6. . . . *well may I say with Horace,* non bene relicta Parmula."

The phrase, which should read *relicta non bene parmula*—"I shamefully threw away my shield"—appears in *Odes* ii.7.10.

(17) 104, 11. . . . *a tight cleanly wench* . . .

"Tight, [in *Dress*] not slatternly," Bailey.

(18) 104, 15. . . . *'tis nothing but a paultry old* Sconce, *with the nozzle broke off.*

The same opinion was expressed by the author of the *Censor,* who in his fifth number, for April 20, 1715, declared:

I therefore profess that altho' I entertain a just veneration for the collections of *Celsus,* the Naturalist, I will no more suffer his Back of an old ill-fashioned *sconce* to pass under the name of a Roman shield. If notwithstanding my admonition he persists in the cheat, I shall publish certificates under the hand of the Broker who sold it and the Brazier who furbished it up to its present dignity. Pope; E. & C., x, 289, n. 1.

Seventeenth-century sconces, consisting of a shield to be fastened to the wall and one or more arms for holding candles, were sometimes so large and so elaborately embossed with scenes and figures that without the arms they might really be mistaken for shields. Cf. R. Holme, *Academy of Armoury* (Chester, 1688), iii, 381–2.

CHAPTER IV

The section on nutrition continues the satire on the uncritical following of the ancients, but the principal theme around which it turns is the theory that diet determines character. In having Cornelius express the opinion that differences in temperament between the peoples of various nations are to be attributed to their different diets, the Scriblerians are burlesquing, though in this case probably without the intention of ridiculing, current theories on the cause of national character, a topic of considerable interest in the seventeenth and early eighteenth centuries. It was generally agreed by writers who discussed the subject that along with social, religious, and political influence certain physical factors probably had an important effect. The factor generally agreed upon was not diet but climate, and statements expressing the belief that nations owe their character in a large measure to their climate are to be found scattered through the literature of the period, including the works of such men as Sprat, Boyle, and Temple. Arbuthnot subscribed to this theory.[1]

1. In his *Essay concerning the Effects of Air* (1733), he says, "It seems agreeable to Reason and Experience that the Air operates sensibly in forming the Constitutions of Mankind, the Specialities of Features, Complexion, Temper, and consequently the Manners of Mankind, which are found to vary much in different Countries and Climates." P. 146. He therefore concludes it probable that "the Genius of Nations depends upon that of their Air" (p. 148), a view he develops at some length. Passing references in the works of the other Scriblerians would seem to indicate their general agreement. Cf. e. g., Swift, *Works*, iii, 68; ix, 318; and Pope, *Essay on Criticism,* ll. 398–401, and Moral Essays, Ep. i, ll. 172–3. However, in one passage, in direct

The possible effects of diet were not wholly overlooked. Congreve, for example, in discussing English character in *Concerning Humour in Comedy* (1695), says, "I believe something considerable . . . may be ascribed to their feeding so much on Flesh, and the Grossness of their Diet in general." [2] Arbuthnot in his *Effects of Air* notes that aliment is among the factors to be reckoned with in accounting for temperament [3] and in his *Nature of Aliments* says, in connection with the characteristics of carnivorous and herbivorous animals, that "I know of more than one Instance of irascible Passions being subdu'd by a vegetable Diet." [4] He goes no further, however, and obviously both he and his contemporaries would regard Cornelius' use of diet as a complete explanation of why nations differ as the height of absurdity.

The most fundamental of the educational theories on which Cornelius operates in the second section of the chapter is that learning should be made pleasant for children so that they will become fond of it. This "progressive" view he shares with all the most enlightened writers on education since antiquity, but particularly with a distinguished series of modern writers including Erasmus, Ascham, Montaigne, and Comenius, all of whom strongly opposed the tyrannical "rule of the rod" and deadening grind of formal drill in languages and in other subjects which characterized the education of their time and which, despite their efforts, continued in force down to (and long after) the time of the Scriblerians.

The most recent and influential statement of this attitude had come from John Locke, in his famous *Some Thoughts concerning Education* (1693). That children should not be driven to learning but should be led to look upon it as a pleasure is a cardinal point in Locke's theory of education:

Children should not have anything like work, or serious [study], laid on them; neither their minds nor bodies will bear it. It injures their healths; and their being forced and tied down to their books, in an age at enmity with all such restraint, has, I doubt not, been the reason why a great many have hated books and learning all their lives after: it is like a surfeit, that leaves an aversion behind, not to be removed. [5]

The burlesque in the *Memoirs,* however, is less on the general idea of making education pleasant than on several well-known methods of attempting to carry this theory into practice. One method, which Montaigne says his father used with great success in teaching him Latin and which Cornelius also employs, was that of allowing only the learned language to be spoken in the presence of the child. [6] Another was the association of learning with play, particularly in the form of

contrast to Arbuthnot's observation that the temper of the French is much like that of the Gauls (*Effects of Air*, p. 149), Swift notes that Gauls, Britons, and others have retained "very little of the characters given them in ancient writings." *Works*, xi, 180.

2. *Comedies*, Bonamy Dobrée, ed. (Oxford, 1925), p. 11. Cf. Prior's *Alma*, in *Poems*, A. R. Waller, ed. (Cambridge, 1905), p. 245.

3. P. 147.

4. *An Essay concerning the Nature of Aliments* (1731; 3d ed., 1735), p. 226.

5. *Thoughts*, sec. 149; cf. secs. 72–4, 103, 128, 147–9, 155, 167, 202. Montaigne had taken a very similar stand; cf. *Essais*, Bk. i, chap. xxvi; ii, viii, xxvi.

6. Cf. below, p. 218, n. 20.

teaching children the alphabet by means of games. This ancient device [7] was strongly recommended by Locke. With alphabet dice, he suggests, a score of games might be invented which would help children to learn how to read.[8] Cornelius, who adopts the idea with uncritical enthusiasm, will, however, have no such "modern" improvements as Locke's dice; he follows an old Roman custom [9] by having the Greek alphabet stamped on gingerbread.

A more general and important method that is burlesqued is the pedagogical approach which was first introduced by John Amos Comenius, the great educational leader of the seventeenth century. It was one of Comenius' basic theories that children should not be taught merely by rote but as far as possible should have things presented directly to their senses so that they might be clearly and easily understood. He recommended that school and reading rooms should be furnished, as far as possible, with the objects being studied, or pictures of them, and he himself prepared an elaborate picture book, the *Orbis Pictus* (1657), containing a series of engravings of objects and scenes accompanied by short descriptions in simple and easy sentences.

Comenius' theories were at first received with great enthusiasm and his books were widely used both on the Continent and in England.[10] Unfortunately, as an early eighteenth-century advocate of the "Comenian Method" lamented, "by an indiscreet use of them, and want of a thorow acquaintance with his Method, or unwillingness to part from their old road, they began to be quite left off." [11] By the Scriblerian times Comenius' name was almost forgotten and all that was remembered of his doctrines was that once somebody had suggested teaching children by showing them pictures and having them talk about objects instead of "really making them learn."

It is, however, the extravagant and foolish applications which Cornelius devises rather than the theory of making education more pleasing and effective by an appeal to the senses that the Scriblerians are satirizing. We have no more reason for believing that the passage is intended to suggest that Comenius and his followers would approve teaching Biblical history by puppet shows, political his-

7. Quintilian knew of a device for making a game of the alphabet. *Institutio Oratoria*, Bk. I, chap. i, sec. 26. A similar scheme was recommended by St. Jerome (Epistle to Laeta; *Lettres de S. Jerome* [Paris, 1713], I, 167–8) and by Erasmus in his *De Pueris statim ac liberaliter instituendis. Opera Omnia*, Lugd. Bat. (1703–06), I, 511D-F. Montaigne tells how his father attempted, apparently without very great success, to teach him Greek "by a Trick; but a new one, and by way of sport; tossing our Declensions to and fro, after the manner of those, who by certain Games at Tables and Chess, learn Geometry and Arithmetick: for he, amongst other Rules, had been advis'd to make me relish Science and Duty by an unforc'd Will, and of my own voluntary motion." *Essais*, I, 26; Charles Cotton, tr. (1693), I, 270.

8. *Thoughts*, secs. 153–4.

9. Cf. Erasmus, *loc. cit.*

10. "J. H." in "An Advertisement Concerning this Edition," prefixed to the 1728 edition of the *Orbis Pictus*, says Comenius' "works carried that Esteem, that in his own Life-time some part of them were not only translated into 12 of the usual Languages of Europe, but also into the *Arabic, Turkish, Persian,* and *Mogolic* (the common Tongue of all that part of the *East-Indies*) and since his death, into the *Hebrew* and some others. Nor did they want their due Encouragement here in *England,* some Years ago." Reprinted in Syracuse, N. Y., 1887, p. xxx.

11. *Ibid.*

tory by raree shows, and natural history by signposts than we have for thinking the final chapter is meant to suggest that Bacon, Boyle, and Newton would admire Martinus' follies in modern science.

Arbuthnot's special qualifications suggest that he was the principal author of the chapter. His medical training, his knowledge of the classics, and his long standing interest in the subject of "aliment" fitted him especially well for writing the section on nutrition and his possession of a family of young children at the time when the *Memoirs* was being written might well have provided some of the incentive and ideas for the part on education. As a matter of fact, however, there is very little if anything in either section that might not have been contributed by the others and at least one reference in the first section points toward Pope.[12]

(1) 105, 8. . . . *"Wisely was it said by Homer, that in the Cellar of Jupiter are two barrels, the one of good, the other of evil, which he never bestows on mortals separately, but constantly mingles them together.*

> Two Urns by *Jove*'s high Throne have ever stood,
> The Source of Evil one, and one of Good;
> From thence the Cup of mortal Man he fills,
> Blessings to these, to those distributes Ills;
> To most, he mingles both: . . .
> *Iliad,* Bk. xxiv; Pope's translation, ll. 663–7.

(2) 105, 19. . . . *Dr. Woodward,* . . .
See general note to Chapter III.

(3) 105, 20. . . . *by the assistance of Mr. Kemp* . . .
John Kemp was a wealthy antiquarian and collector. He possessed a remarkable museum of antiquities which he had purchased from Lord Carteret. This museum, which was described briefly in the *Memoirs for the Curious* for September, 1708 (II, 259–61), and more elaborately, after Kemp's death, by Robert Ainsworth in *Monumenta vetustatis Kempiana* (1719–20), was offered, on Kemp's death in 1717, to the Earl of Oxford for £2,000. The offer was refused and the collection was eventually sold at auction in 1721 for £1,090. Kemp had been a fellow of the Royal Society since 1712.

(4) 105, 21. . . . *whereof a Cut hath been engraved, and exhibited* . . .
In 1705 Dr. Woodward had a handsome, full-sized engraving of his shield made by P. van Gunst of Amsterdam and presented copies of it to various antiquaries. Cf. J. Nichols, *Illustrations of the Literary History of the Eighteenth Century* (1817–58), IV, 100; *Letters to Ralph Thoresby* (Leeds, 1912), p. 142. A smaller engraving was used by Hearne in his edition of Livy (1708) and a very poor one by Benedict Baldwin in his *Calceus Antiquus* (2d ed., 1711). Cf. Hearne, IV, 74. Hearne later reprinted his engraving as a frontispiece to Dodwell's dissertation on the shield. Cf. Chapter III, p. 207, n. 3. I am indebted to Mr. Beattie for much of this information.

12. See below, p. 215, n. 11.

(5) 105, 22. . . . *to the great Contentation of the learned.*
    I.e. "Satisfaction of mind," Bailey. The word was becoming obsolete in Scriblerian times.

(6) 105, 34. *Beef, it is true, may confer a Robustness on the limbs of my son, but will hebetate and clogg his Intellectuals.*
    Hebetate—"to make dull or blunt," Bailey.
    That beef, though it builds the body, dulls the mind, was an old and common-place idea. Cf. Shakespeare, *Twelfth Night:*

> *Sir Andrew Aguecheek.* . . . but I am a great eater
>   of beef and I believe that does harm to my wit.
> *Sir Toby Belch.* No question. Act I, sc. 3.

(7) 106, 3. . . . *or as Horace expresses it, a Short Madness.*
    "*Ira furor brevis est*"—Horace, *Epistles* i.2.62.

(8) 106, 14. "*Lacedæmonian black Broth, thou would'st say,* . . .
    A famous dish of the Spartans, composed of little pieces of meat, blood, salt, and vinegar, which the older men, trained to extreme frugality, used as the sole item of their diet at their common messes. Plutarch, I, 152; *Morals,* W. W. Good-win, ed. (1870), I, 83. Its nature and reputation are suggested by a story told by Plutarch of a certain king of Pontus, who hired a cook at great expense to prepare some of it for his table. When he tasted it, however, he found it so nauseous that he spat it out; whereupon the cook, undaunted, told him that to enjoy it he should have prepared himself by long and hard labor and by bathing in the river Eurotas. *Ibid.,* I, 84; *Plutarch,* I, 152.
    King, with Bentley in mind, had already satirized the "virtuoso" who, with more regard for ancient customs than modern stomachs, would serve it at a modern table. *Dialogues of the Dead,* Dial. VI; King, I, 159. When Gulliver is in Glubb-dubdrib he has "a helot of Agesilaus" make him a dish, but he "was not able to get down a second spoonful." Swift, *Works,* VIII, 207.

(9) 106, 17. . . . *since it was recommended by the Divine Lycurgus.*
    The use of this dish and the common messes at which it was eaten were a part of the reforms introduced by Lycurgus to root out luxury and to train the Spartans in frugality and temperance. *Plutarch,* I, 146.

(10) 106, 28. *Consider Woman, the different Temperaments of different Nations: What makes the English Phlegmatick and melancholy . . . suck in with their food the intolerable Vice of Pride.*
    See the general note to this chapter. The temperamental characteristics ascribed to each of the nations were, of course, well-worn conventionalities which might as easily be illustrated from Shakespeare as from the *Spectator.* For an amusing tabular view of national "characters" in a long list of fields, including affection, clothes, conversation, learning, love, speech, temper, horses, and diseases, intended for the benefit of young gentlemen traveling abroad, see Jean Gailhard, *A Treatise Concerning the Education of Youth* (1678), II, 178–82. In his list Gailhard gives:

In Diet	In Tempers
French delicate	French jester and injurious
Spaniard sparing	Spaniard grave and respectful
Italian sober	Italian pleasant and jealous
German loves to drink	German lofty and fantastical

(11) 106, 37. . . . *according to a Prescription he had met with somewhere in Eustathius upon Homer.*

In his commentary on line 519 of the tenth book of the *Odyssey*. The allusion was probably introduced into the *Memoirs* during the 1726–29 period of Scriblerus activity since it seems likely that Pope first noticed the prescription in the autumn of 1724 when working with Broome on the notes for the tenth book of his translation of the poem.

(12) 107, 11. . . . *teaching him the Catechism: But Cornelius look'd upon this as a tedious way of Instruction, . . .*

Though Locke inveighed against tedious ways of instruction (see general note to chapter) and said that, "As for the Bible, which children are usually employed in to exercise and improve their talent in reading, I think the promiscuous reading of it, though by chapters as they lie in order, is so far from being of any advantage to children, either for the perfecting their reading, or principling their religion, that perhaps a worse could not be found" (*Thoughts,* sec. 158; cf. secs. 157, 159), he declared that it was necessary that the child learn the Lord's Prayer, the Creeds, and the Ten Commandments by heart (sec. 157) and recommended John Worthington's difficult *A Form of Sound Words, or A Scripture Catechism* (1673) in which all the answers were in the precise words of the Bible.

(13) 107, 14. *He would frequently carry him to the* Puppet-Shew *of the Creation of the world, . . .*

Such a puppet show was actually being exhibited in London and other parts of England during the reign of Queen Anne. A contemporary handbill advertising it begins:

At Crawley's Booth, over against the *Crown Tavern* in *Smithfield*, during the time of *Bartholomew Fair*, will be presented a little *opera,* called the *Old Creation of the World,* yet newly revived; with the addition of *Noah's flood;* also several fountains playing water during the time of the play. Harleian MSS 5931; reprinted in John Strutt's *Glig Gamena* (1801), pp. 128-9.

In the *Tatler,* No. 16, for May 17, 1709, there is an amusing description of the presentation of this puppet show at Bath in which the supposed educational value of the show is touched upon. During the performance "Old Mrs. Petulant" desires "both her Daughters to mind the Moral" and "Mrs. Mayoress" whispers, *"This is very proper for young People to see."*

The popularity of puppet shows is reflected in Arbuthnot's *History of John Bull.* In upbraiding her husband Mrs. Bull declares, "You sot, . . . you loiter about ale-houses and taverns, spend your time at billiards, ninepins, or puppet-shows . . . never minding me nor your numerous family," and the second Mrs.

Bull complains of Esquire South that "the whole generation of him are . . . in love with bagpipes and puppet-shows!" Aitken, pp. 202, 219. Swift apparently went to them occasionally. Cf. *Works*, II, 72; III, 133.

(14) 107, 18. *His first rudiments in profane history were acquired by seeing of* Raree-shews, *where he was brought acquainted with all the Princes of Europe.*

It is difficult to discover much about these entertainments, despite the fact that they were common. In the seventeenth century they seem usually to have consisted of a single scene, of a dramatic or risqué nature, mounted in a box small enough to be carried about. Judith Drake, *An Essay in Defence of the Female Sex* (2d ed., 1696), p. 101. By Scriblerian times, however, some had become very elaborate, as is shown by the following contemporary advertisement of one to be "exhibited at the great house in the Strand, over against the Globe Tavern, near Hungerford Market," at the price of one shilling for the best seats and six pence for the others:

To be seen, the greatest piece of curiosity that ever arrived in England, being made by a famous engineer from the camp before Lisle, who, with great labour and industry, has collected into a MOVING PICTURE the following figures: first, it doth represent the confederate camp, and the army lying intrenched before the town; secondly, the convoys and the mules with prince Eugene's baggage; thirdly, the English forces commanded by the duke of Marlborough; likewise, several vessels laden with provisions for the army, which are so artificially done as to seem to drive the water before them. The city and citadel are very fine, with all its outworks, ravelins, hornworks, counterscarps, half-moons, and palisados; the French horse marching out at one gate, and the confederate army marching in at the other; the prince's travelling coach with two generals in it, one saluting the company as it passes by; then a trumpeter sounds a call as he rides, at the noise whereof a sleeping sentinel starts, and lifts up his head, but, not being espyed, lies down to sleep again; besides abundance more admirable curiosities too tedious to be inserted here. In short, the whole piece is so contrived by *art,* that it seems to be *life* and *nature.* Strutt, *op. cit.,* p. 130.

(15) 107, 33. *In Natural history he was much assisted by his Curiosity in* Sign-Posts, *insomuch that he hath often confess'd he owed to them the knowledge of many Creatures which he never found since in any Author, such as White Lions,* Golden Dragons, &c.

Since all addresses in London at the time were given by landmarks, which were usually marked by signs, there were an enormous number and variety of symbols in use. Among these, animals and monsters were especially popular. In addition to golden dragons (the traditional signs of apothecary shops) and white lions, Martinus might also have seen white bears (one was a silk mercer's shop and another a tavern), unicorns (used by chemists and goldsmiths), blue boars, brazen serpents, two-necked swans, a golden buck, a flying fox (at Colchester), a mermaid, a phoenix, a green dragon, and others of the sort, to say nothing of the more conventional creatures such as apes, crocodiles, civets, hedgehogs, stags, bulls, ravens, dolphins, ostriches, magpies, and others—of which there was an enormous number. Cf. J. Larwood and J. C. Hotten, *The History of Signboards* (1866), *passim.* The great size and magnificence of these signs in London were a source of wonder to foreigners and disgust and concern to some residents who charged that they weakened the buildings, obstructed the free passage of air, and constituted a fire hazard. *Freethinker*, No. 35, for July 21, 1718. One traveler, Muralt, said he had seen some tavern signs in villages that were worth nearly as much as the taverns themselves. Béat de Muralt, *Letters Describing the Character and Customs of the English and French Nations* (1726), p. 83.

(16) 107, 36. *He once thought the same of Green Men, but had since found them mention'd by Kercherus, and verify'd in the History of William of Newbury.*
   "Gul. Neubrig. Book i, Ch. 27." (Scrib.)
   The wording here, that he had *since* found them in Kercherus and William of Newburgh, suggests that this sentence was added to the chapter after the original composition—a suggestion that is to a certain extent confirmed by the fact that the only edition of William of Newburgh's chronicle published within a century was that which appeared in Oxford under the editorship of Thomas Hearne in 1719. Since it is highly improbable that the Scriblerians made any formal search for this sort of material, the references illustrate the way in which the Scriblerians kept the *Memoirs* in mind and picked up pertinent material in the course of their reading.
   The story which William tells, after recounting how his own doubts of it had been swept away by the overwhelming weight of many competent witnesses, is that, during the reign of King Stephen, a group of reapers in East Anglia saw two children, a boy and a girl, emerge from some ancient pits. These children, who did not speak English, were dressed in clothes of a strange color and texture and were, moreover, completely green in their persons. However, after several months, they lost their green color. When they had learned to converse, they were questioned about their native country. This, they replied, was Christian, but never had any more of the sun's rays than would make English twilight.
   Kercherus, in describing a number of his experiments with light, tells how he discovered that when he placed a green glass or a vial of colored water in front of a shaded lamp the whole room and the faces of the men in it became green or the color of the water in the vial. A. Kercherus, *Ars Magna Lucis et Umbrae* (Rome, 1646), p. 819.

(17) 108, 2. *His disposition to the Mathematicks was discover'd very early, by his drawing parallel lines on his bread and butter, and intersecting them at equal Angles, so as to form the whole Superficies into squares.*
   "Pascal's Life. Locke of Educ. &c." (Scrib.)
   This precocity on the part of Martinus is a burlesque of that displayed by Pascal in his early youth, as related by his sister. According to this story, Pascal's father, noticing in him a disposition toward matters of reason, and being afraid that any introduction to mathematics would cause him to neglect his Latin, locked up all the books in his library on this subject and was careful never to mention it in his presence. Pascal, however, became interested in geometry "and being alone in a Hall, where he used to divert himself, he took a piece of Charcoal and drew Figures upon the Squares of the pavement, trying the ways of making, for example, a Circle perfectly round, a Triangle, the Sides and Engles whereof were equal, and

other Things of the like Nature." Edward Jesup, *Life of the Celebrated M. Pascal. Collected from the Writings of Madame Perier, His Sister* (1723), p. 8. Lacking any knowledge of the vocabulary of geometry, he was forced to make his own definitions. From these "he laid himself down some Axioms, and formed from them at Length perfect Demonstrations." Discovered at work on these by his father, he explained that he was "seeking after such a thing, which it seems was the very 32d Proposition of the first Book of *Euclid*" and showed his father that he had proved all the propositions leading up to it. *Ibid.*

This story, which first appeared in the preface (pp. [9]–[12]) to the *Traitez de l'equilibre des liqueurs* (Paris, 1663) and was reprinted in subsequent editions of that work, was also available to the Scriblerians in Adrien Baillet's *Des enfans devenus célèbres par leurs études* (Paris, 1688), in Bayle ("Pascal," n. C), and in the English translation cited above.

Warburton's statement that this passage also refers to "some trifling directions given for the introduction to the elements of Science, in Mr. Locke's book of Education" is not supported by an examination of Locke's treatise.

(18) 108, 5. . . . *nor would he let him proceed to Letter D, till he could truly and distinctly pronounce C in the ancient manner,* . . .

This touches one of the conventional educational ideas of the time, that a child should thoroughly master one thing before being allowed to take up any other. Cf. e.g., "Let them not take a new Lesson untill they have well learned the old; . . . Let them give every Letter his true sound distinctly, not sounding e as ee; nor confounding pb, bv, vf, cg, gj, td, mn, sz, jch, Chsh." George Robertson, *Learning's Foundation firmly laid in a Short Method of Teaching to Read English* (1651), p. 8.

(19) 108, 8. . . . *turn'd away the Writing Master because he knew nothing of Fabius's Waxen Tables.*

The test given the poor writing master was a severe one. The editor confesses that he has been unable to discover exactly what the Scriblerians had in mind.

(20) 108, 10. . . . *the methods by which the famous Montaigne was educated,* . . .

According to Montaigne, his father, "having made the most precise Enquiry that any man could possibly make amongst Men of the greatest Learning and Judgment" and having been made to believe by them "that the tedious time we applyed to the learning of the Tongues of them who had them for nothing, was the sole cause we could not arrive to that Grandeur of Soul, and Perfection of Knowledge with the ancient *Greeks* and *Romans,*" decided to put him, while he was still an infant, in the care of a German who was totally ignorant of French but very fluent in Latin. As a result, declares Montaigne, "I was above six years of Age before I understood either French or Perigordin, any more than Arabick, and without Art, Book, Grammar, or Precept, Whipping, or the expence of a Tear, had by that time learn'd to speak as pure Latin as my Master himself." (*Essais,* 1, 26; Charles Cotton, tr. (1693), 1, 268–9.

The same method was recommended by Locke (*Thoughts,* secs. 165–7) and by the anonymous author of *An Essay upon Education; shewing how Latin, Greek, and other Languages may be Learn'd more easily, quickly, and perfectly, than they commonly are* (1711), p. 5.

(21) 108, 16. *But what most conduced to his easy attainment of this Language, was his love of Ginger-bread; which his Father observing, caused it to be stampt with the Letters of the Greek Alphabet;* . . .

Cf. above, p. 212. Prior, too, uses this somewhat ancient jest in *Alma*, in *Poems*, A. R. Waller, ed., p. 236.

(22) 108, 19. . . . *Gronovius* . . .

Jacobus Gronovius was a famous contemporary Greek scholar. In the course of his wide travels, he had visited England and was acquainted with several of the learned men there. He published many editions of the classics and a number of original works, the most famous of which was his *Thesaurus Antiquitatum Graecarum* (1697–1702), which was published in Leyden in thirteen folio volumes. A copy of this, presented by Lord Bolingbroke, was in Swift's library. H. Williams, *Dean Swift's Library* (Cambridge, 1932), p. 46. The reputation of Gronovius was marred by his quarrelsomeness. He was, says Hearne, "a learned, but a very ill-natured man, and his stile so very intricate and obscure, that it is hard to know what he drives at." *Remains* (1869), II, 51. He was born in 1645 and died in Leyden, October 21, 1716. The use of the present tense in the text, in "ingenuously confesses," suggests that this passage was written during the first period of the composition of the *Memoirs*.

(23) 108, 20. . . . *he durst not confer with this child in Greek at eight years old;* . . .

This is a parody of Montaigne's statement that various learned men had "often told me, that I had in my Infancy that Language [Latin] so very fluent and ready, that they were afraid to enter into Discourse with me." *Essais*, I, 26; Cotton, tr. (1693), I, 270.

(24) 108, 22. . . . *and at fourteen he composed a Tragedy in the same language, as the younger Pliny had done before him.*

"Plin. Epist. Lib. 7" (Scrib.) Epistle IV, "To Pontius."

"To trace the Matter to the heighth, I was never averse to Poetry, nay, at the Age of Fourteen, I compos'd a Greek Tragedy. What sort of one was it, you will say? That I do not know, but it was call'd a Tragedy." *Pliny's Epistles. Done into English by Several Hands* (1724), II, 327.

(25) 108, 24. *He learn'd the Oriental Languages of Erpenius, who resided some time with his father for that purpose.*

The Scriblerians erred here in chronology, as Thomas Erpenius (b. 1584), the great Oriental scholar, to whom they refer, died in 1624, nearly half a century before we can suppose Martinus to have been born. His most famous publications were: *Grammatica Arabica* (1613), *Rudimenta linguae Arabicae* (1620), *Grammatica Ebraea generalis* (1621), and *Grammatica Chaldaica et Syria* (1628). The first of these, with additions and corrections, remained the standard work on the subject for more than a century and a late reprint of it may have led the Scriblerians to believe that he had lived more recently than he had.

(26) 108, 27. . . . *he composed . . . the* Thousand and One Arabian Tales, . . .

An English translation of the *Arabian Nights,* based on the French version of Antoine Galland, had appeared in 1707–08, and had been popular enough to be reprinted in 1711. Two of the stories are retold in the *Spectator,* Nos. 195 and 535. Though popular among certain types of readers, the tales offended some of the critics by their improbability and lack of regularity. Warburton, for example, says of them,

The collection in question is so strange a medley of sense and nonsense, that one would be tempted to think it the compilation of some coffee-man, who gathered indifferently from good and bad. The contrivance he has invented of tying them together is so blunderingly conducted, that after such an instance of the want of common sense one can wonder at no absurdity we find in them. Pope, E. & C., IX, 23 n.

(27) 108, 29. . . . *and also the* Persian Tales, *which have been since translated into several languages, and lately into our own with particular elegance, by Mr. Ambrose Philips.*

The popularity of the *Arabian Nights* in France led to an imitation by Petit de la Croix under the title of *Contes persans.* A poorly translated English version of this was published in 1709, and in 1713 or 1714 Ambrose Philips was commissioned to make a new translation at, according to Pope, half-a-crown a tale. E. & C., III, 255. The first volume of Philips' translation was announced as "This Day published" in the *Daily Courant* for July 6, 1714. It thus appeared during the first period of the composition of the *Memoirs.*

The *Persian Tales* received the same popular approval and critical denunciations as had the *Arabian Nights.* Philips' translation reached its sixth edition in 1783, but when, in 1720, Pope sent a copy to Bishop Atterbury for his comment, the Bishop replied:

Ill as I have been, almost ever since they came to hand, I have read as much of them as ever I shall read while I live. Indeed they do not please my taste; they are writ with so romantic an air, and, allowing for the difference of eastern manners, are yet, upon any supposition that can be made, of so wild and absurd a contrivance, (at least to my northern understanding,) that I have not only no pleasure, but no patience, in perusing them. E. & C., IX, 22–3.

The barb of the satire in the *Memoirs* was probably aimed less at the genre than at the translator. Despite a certain amount of critical disapproval of such stories the Scriblerians had something of a taste for them. Swift notes in his *Journal* for January 29, 1711/12 that he had borrowed "one or two idle books of *Contes de Fées*" and has been "reading them these two days, although I have much business upon my hands." After reading the *Persian Tales,* Pope thought for a time of writing a Persian fable himself in which he could have "given a full loose to description and imagination" (Spence, p. 105); and many allusions and echoes in Gay's *Fables* and other verse make it clear that he, too, was well acquainted with this type of literature.

Against Ambrose Philips, the Whig poet, two of the Scriblerians had a distinct animus. Both Pope and Swift were once very friendly with Philips, along with the other Whig writers surrounding Addison. Pope's break with him came in the spring of 1713, after the appearance of the *Guardian* paper (No. 40, for April 27, 1713) in which Pope ironically compared the merits of the Philips' pastoral with his own. Philips was furiously angry and, according to rumor, hung up a rod in Button's with which to chastise his rival. The quarrel was at its height in the spring of 1714 when the *Memoirs* were being written; on April 15 Gay published a burlesque of Philips' style of pastoral writing in *The Shepherd's Week*, and on June 8 Pope felt obliged to write to his friend Caryll explaining that many of the rumors regarding the quarrel were false. E. & C., VI, 209–10. Pope's animus continued throughout his life. Twenty years later in the *Epistle to Dr. Arbuthnot* he slipped in a reference to

> The Bard whom pilfered Pastorals renown,
> Who turns a Persian tale for half-a-crown. ll. 179–80.

Swift's coolness toward Philips was based chiefly on political differences and was of somewhat longer standing. Swift had become well acquainted with Philips in 1708, when both were seeing much of Addison. After Swift joined the Harley ministry, Philips' strong Whiggism led to an estrangement. *Journ.*, June 30, 1711; cf. December 27, 1712.

CHAPTER V

This little dissertation, which continues the satire on Cornelius' slavish following of the ancients and on the serious study of trivial aspects of ancient life by classical scholars, no doubt profited much from Arbuthnot's long search through classical literature for material on ancient weights, coins, and measures.[1] It was such evidence as that presented in this chapter which led him to make his well-known statement that *"Men* might talk what they pleased of the safe conveyance of *Tradition;* but it was no where preserved pure and uncorrupt but amongst Children, whose Customs and Plays . . . were delivered down invariably from one generation to another." [2]

Though its treatment is fresh, much of Cornelius' treatise on ancient games had been anticipated in William King's *Useful Transactions in Philosophy and Other Sorts of Learning* (1709). In the first issue of this burlesque version of the *Philosophical Transactions of the Royal Society* King included two letters from "Dr. Playford" to "Dr. Littlebrand" giving accounts of two treatises by Meursius which had just arrived from Holland, where they had been published (almost a century before).[3] The first of these treatises is on Grecian dances and the second on the "plays of the Grecian Boys." [4] The letters are, in burlesque of their prototypes in the learned journals, less an account of what is contained in Meursius' treatises than a display of the letter writer's own erudition.

1. Cf. Chap. I, p. 190, n. 18.
2. Recorded by William Warburton, *Works of Alexander Pope*, VI, 115 n.
3. King, II, 77–85.
4. Johannes van Meurs (1579–1639), *De saltationibus veterum*, Lugd. Bat. (1618), and *De ludis Graecorum*, Lugd. Bat. (1622).

"Dr. Playford's" humor is much broader than that of the Scriblerians. He begins his account of the treatise on the plays of Grecian boys by declaring, "It is wonderful to consider what things great men have and do employ themselves in." [5] Some of the plays, he admits with heavy irony, are very useful; for example, *Ascoliasmus,* which consists in hopping on one leg and beating other boys with a strap and is called by moderns "Fox, to thy Hole," requires "great cunning, exercise, and patience." [6] The ancients, he notes, had their *chytrinda, myinda,* and *basilinda,* corresponding to the present-day "Hot-cockles," "Blind-man's buff," and "King I am." [7] Like Cornelius, he is much impressed with the beauty of the Greek names for the various games in comparison with the barbarous-sounding modern equivalents, and he anticipates Cornelius' recognition of the moral and educational value of certain games [8] by declaring,

It would be very useful, if some Virtuoso would put our childrens plays in a true light; for, amongst other things, would appear their truth and justice, in "going halves in birds nests"; their foresight and parsimony, in "hoarding apples"; and the great benefits, as to the increase of secrecy, fidelity, and friendship, that may be gained by robbing of orchards, as Mr. Osborn, in the beginning of his "Advice to a Son," has extremely well observed.[9]

The similarities between these letters and the chapter in the *Memoirs* are so striking that we must either recognize a very specific debt on the part of the Scriblerians (which they failed to acknowledge) or suspect that Arbuthnot was the author of the Playford letters. The latter is a tempting theory not only because Arbuthnot obviously had the learning, the humor, and the stimulus toward an interest in games provided by young children in the family (King was not married) but because it has always seemed possible that the doctor might have engaged in some unidentified activities of this sort between 1706 and 1710. Very little has been discovered about the circumstances under which King produced the *Useful Transactions;* so we do not know whether he had contributors or wrote the whole of the various issues himself. Since aid was customary in such ventures and the *Transactions,* if issued monthly as King planned, would require a great variety of fresh material, it seems likely that contributions were welcomed. If Arbuthnot wrote the Playford letters he must have known King very well, since the letters appeared in the first issue. There is, of course, some question whether the doctor would contribute even under a pseudonym to a project which might be regarded as offensive by his friends in the Royal Society.

Though Arbuthnot was probably the principal author of the chapter on playthings, there is no reason to believe that the other Scriblerians did not have a part in its composition. The two chief sources of information regarding ancient games, Minucius Felix and Pollux,[10] were both well known and readily available.

5. King, II, 82.
6. *Ibid.,* p. 83.
7. *Ibid.*
8. Cf. p. 111, ll. 8–13 in the text and below, p. 228, n. 31.
9. King, II, 84.
10. Cf. below, p. 224, n. 12, p. 225, n. 17. There is, however, no mention of the two in the writings of Swift and Pope. Gay cites Minucius Felix in a note on *Cloacina* in his *Trivia,* Bk. II, n. to l. 115.

(1) 109, 6. Play *was invented by the* Lydians *as a remedy against* Hunger.

This statement is based on Herodotus, who says:

During the Reign of *Atys* the son of *Manes* King of *Lydia,* a Scarcity of Provisions spread over the Kingdom, which the People for a Time supported with Patience and Industry. But when they saw the Evil still continuing, they applied themselves to find out a Remedy; and some inventing one Game and others another, they gradually introduc'd Dice, Balls, Tables, and all other Plays, Chess only excepted . . . And to bear this Calamity better, they us'd to play one whole Day without Intermission . . . eating and drinking on the next Day. i. 94; Isaac Littlebury, tr. (1709), i, 61–2.

(2) 109, 7. *Sophocles says of Palamedes, that he invented* Dice *to serve sometimes instead of a dinner.*

Palamedes, though not mentioned by Homer, is celebrated as a great tragic hero of the Trojan wars by Sophocles, Euripides, Xenophon, Ovid, and others. Sophocles' reference to his invention of dice in time of famine appears in a four-line fragment, a Latin translation of which was published in England in 1694 in Thomas Hyde's "De Ludis Orientalium," an essay in his *Mandragorias, seu Historia Shahiludi* (pp. 110–15). Hyde here discusses the question of whether Palamedes could have been the inventor of dice. The question had also been discussed by Meurs in his famous *Græcia Ludibunda* (Leyden, 1625). Both of these were no doubt familiar to Arbuthnot and perhaps to the others.

(3) 109, 12. . . . *the Plays of the Ancient Children are preserv'd more entire than any other of their Customs.*

Cf. Arbuthnot's similar statement quoted in the general note to the chapter, above, p. 221.

(4) 109, 19. . . . *correspond with the ancient* Fistula, *and accordingly to be compos'd,* septem paribus disjuncta cicutis.

The ancient fistula, according to Chambers, was a flute or flageolet made of reeds or other stuff. Ovid mentions one composed of seven parts. *Met.* i. 688 *et seq.;* ii. 682; xiii. 784; cf. Pliny vii. 56, 57. The ancient poets call the shepherd's pipe, or pipes of Pan, a fistula.

(5) 109, 23. . . . *the true* Crepitaculum *or* Rattle *of the Ancients, for that (as* Archytas Tarentinus *was of opinion) kept the children from breaking Earthen Ware.*

This is drawn from Aristotle's *Politics,* but has been emended for the special purpose for which it is used. Aristotle simply says that since children must have something to do, the rattle of Archytas, which people give to children in order to amuse them and keep them from breaking things in the house, is a very useful device. *Politics* viii.6.2. Archytas, a famous philosopher, mathematician, general, and statesman, was a contemporary of Plato.

(6) 109, 29. . . . *whether the* Trochus *which was recommended by* Cato *be really our present* Top, *or rather the* Hoop *which the boys drive with a stick.*

The nature of the "trochus," which is referred to by Cato in his precepts (*Disticha*), has been a matter of genuine dispute. Cato's *troco lude* was rendered "play with the toppe" by Caxton (*Parvus Cato*) and this meaning of the word is the only one given by Ainsworth, *Latin Dictionary* (1736; 1823 ed.). Kersey defines it as "a Wheel, a Top for Children to play with" (Edward Phillips' *The New World of Words,* John Kersey, ed. [1706]) and Bailey calls it "a Wheell; also a little round lump of anything."

(7) 109, 29. . . . Cross and Pile, . . .

Cross and pile took its name from the old terms for the upper and under side of coins and is our present game of "heads and tails." Swift mentions a familiar version of the game, "Cross I win, and pile you lose," as boys' play. *Works,* v, 138.

(8) 109, 30. . . . *nor* Ducks and Drakes . . .

Swift was aware of the antiquity of the game of skipping stones on water, saying in his *Vindication of Carteret,* "Scipio and Laelius . . . often played at duck and drake with smooth stones on a river." *Works,* vii, 240.

(9) 109, 30. . . . Handy-dandy . . .

A children's game in which a small object is shaken between the two hands of one player, the hands being then suddenly closed and the other player required to guess in which hand the object remained. Sometimes a rhyme was said while the object was between the two hands. A. B. Gomme, *Traditional Games of England, Scotland, and Ireland* (1894–98), i, 189.

(10) 109, 31. . . . *Macrobius* [takes notice of Cross and Pile] . . .

Theodosius Macrobius, a fifth-century grammarian, mentions the game as popular among boys attending the Saturnalian festival. The boys, according to his account, throw their coins high into the air and call out *"capita aut navia."* *Saturnalia,* i, 7. The works of Macrobius were easily available to the Scriblerians in an edition published in London in 1694.

(11) 109, 31. . . . *St. Augustine* [takes notice of Cross and Pile] . . .

Unless they had some very obscure and metaphorical jest in mind, the Scriblerians are in error. Perhaps in the course of editing or transcribing, the allusion became garbled.

(12) 109, 32. . . . *Minutius Felix describes the latter* [Ducks and Drakes]; . . .

In his *Octavius,* Minucius Felix, a Roman lawyer who lived about 230 A.D., wrote:

And when we came to the *Drydock,* where the Ships are drawn ashore, and placed upon dry Planks, we observ'd a company of Boys very eager at play. They gather'd each of them a heap of round Shells, made smooth by the Waves, and stooping down, skimm'd them upon the Water, and he that had made them bound oftenest upon the Surface, was the Conqueror. *Those Two Excellent Monuments of Ancient Learning and Piety, Minucius Felix's Octavius, and Tertullian's Apology for the Primitive Christians, Render'd into English,* P.B., tr. (1708), p. 4.

(13) 109, 33. . . . *but* Handy-dandy *is mention'd by Aristotle, Plato, and Aristophanes.*

The handy-dandy of Aristotle, Plato, and Aristophanes was called "par impar," "even and odd," and differs from the English game in that it was, according to Julius Pollux (of whom, see below), played with nuts, dice, knucklebones, or coins—the players guessing odd or even. Aristotle mentions games with knucklebones among other sports and contests in his *Rhetoric* i.11.15–19. The mention by Plato occurs in his *Lysis* (sec. 206), where he speaks of some people being at a game of odd and even in a corner of the disrobing room, with a heap of knucklebones. In the *Plutus* of Aristophanes Cario says, "I and the other Gentlemen my Fellow-servants play at Even or Odd with Broad Pieces." 816–17; Lewis Theobald, tr. (1715), p. 38.

(14) 109, 35. *The Play which the Italians call* Cinque, *and the French* Mourre, *is extremely ancient;* . . .

The game, which was generally regarded as an Italian game (cf. Kersey, Richelet, *Dictionnaire de Trévoux,* and other dictionaries) was a very simple one, played by two persons, who rapidly and simultaneously hold up their right hands with one or more fingers extended—each player immediately calling out the number of fingers which he guesses the other has extended. As the Scriblerians say, the game was known in France by the name of *"Mourre,"* but they err in saying the Italians called it *"Cinque."* It was known in Italy under the name of *"mora"* —the name adopted for it in England.

The game is an ancient one, being mentioned by Cicero, Suetonius, and others. Cf. *micare* in various dictionaries. It does not appear to have been common in Greece, however, and is not included in Pollux' comprehensive list (for which see below).

(15) 109, 36. . . . *it was play'd at by* Hymen *and* Cupid *at the Marriage of* Psyche, . . .

It seems possible that the authors invented the allusion to illustrate the great antiquity of the game. The association of the game with Cupid may have been suggested to them by a definition of it as a "Play of Love." E.g., Edward Phillips, *op. cit.* Or they may have based it on the postures of Cupid and Hymen in a drawing from some Greek relief or vase, like the famous vase painting in Munich which shows Eros and Anteros playing the game while Cupid hovers over them. Cf. *Archaeologische Zeitung* xxix (Berlin, 1872), taf. 56.

(16) 109, 37. . . . *term'd by the Latins,* digitis micare.

Digitis micare, "to raise the fingers," is the name used by Cicero (*de Off.* iii. 19.17) and other Roman writers for the game.

(17) 110, 1. *Julius Pollux* . . .

Julius Pollux (second century A.D.) is the author of the famous encyclopedia of Greek culture, the *Onomasticon*. This work was probably known to the Scriblerians in the Amsterdam edition of 1706 (J. H. Lederlinus and T. Hemsterhuius, eds.), which contained a Latin translation. (The references below are to this edition.) The serious and lengthy discussion, chiefly of euphoniously titled children's games in the seventh chapter of book nine was put to heavy use by the Scriblerians for the "classical" games they mention.

(18) 110, 3. . . . *the* Omilla *or* Chuck-farthing: *tho' some will have our modern* Chuck-farthing *to be nearer the* Aphetinda *of the Ancients.*

According to Pollux' descriptions, either the *omilla* or the *aphentinda* (note the misspelling in the *Memoirs*) might be the ancient parent of chuck farthing, for in *omilla,* nuts are pitched into a circle drawn on the ground or into a hole (*Pollux* ix. 7. 102), and in *aphentinda* bits of pottery are used. *Ibid.,* sec. 117. The nice point over which the Scriblerians say there is a disagreement is whether the pitching of farthings is "nearer" to the pitching of nuts or to the pitching of bits of pottery.

(19) 110, 4. *He also mentions the* Basilinda, *or* King I am; . . .

Pollux says that in *basilinda* one boy is chosen by lot to serve as king, the others carrying out all the king's commands. *Ibid.,* sec. 111. "Dr. Playford" (see general note to this chapter) also identifies the game with "King I am" or "Questions and Commands." King, II, 83.

(20) 110, 4. . . . *and* Myinda, *or* Hoopers-Hide.

Pollux describes two varieties of *myinda.* In one the blindfolded boy searches for the others, who have hid themselves; in the other, the blinded one guesses who touches him. ix.7.113. *Myinda* is thus rightly the Greek equivalent of "Hoopers-Hide," the old name for blindman's buff and hide-and-seek.

(21) 110, 7. *But the* Chytindra *described by the same Author is certainly not our* Hot-cockle; *for that was by pinching and not by striking;* . . .

The players of *chytrinda* (note the misspelling in the text) might, according to Pollux, either pull (*vellere*), drag around (*circumtrahere*), or strike (*verberare*) the one who sits in the middle until he catches one of them Sec. 117. In hot cockles, the players strike a blindfolded person, who is lying down, until he guesses who has struck him. Strutt, *Sports and Pastimes of the English People,* W. Hone, ed. (1876), p. 501. Gay mentions the sport in his *Shepherd's Week,*

> As at *Hot-cockles* once I laid me down,
> And felt the weighty hand of many a clown;
> *Buxoma* gave a gentle tap, and I
> Quick rose, and read soft mischief in her eye.
>   "Monday," ll. 99–102.

(22) 110, 8. . . . *the* Rathapygismus *to be yet nearer the modern* Hot-cockles.

The name *rathapygismus* is derived from the verb meaning "to slap the buttocks." Pollux does not say whether guessing is included with it or not. The scholarly point involved in whether it or *chytrinda* is closer to hot cockles is parallel to the previous *omilla-aphentinda* problem.

(23) 110, 12. . . . Aedificare casas, equitare in arundine longa.

These phrases are probably drawn from the *Satires* of Horace (ii.3.247–9), where they appear in the passage: "If a Man in Years shou'd make Clay Houses . . . [or] ride upon a Hobby-Horse . . . wou'd not every one that saw him pronounce him mad?" S. Dunster, tr. (2d ed., 1712), p. 169.

(24) 110, 18. . . . Acinetinda . . . *first lost among the* French.

Pollux (ix.7.115) defines *acinetinda* as a contest to prove the players' skill in standing immobile. The reference to the French is based on the traditional English view of their neighbors as a volatile, talkative, and capering race. Cf. e.g, *Spectator*, Nos. 29, 45, 435, 556.

(25) 110, 20. . . . Apodidiascinda . . . *our* Puss in a Corner.
The spelling in Pollux is *apodidrascinda*. The game as described by Pollux differs from the modern puss in a corner in that the boy in the center has his eyes covered while searching for his corner.

(26) 110, 23. *Julius Pollux in his ninth book speaks of the* Melolouthe *or the* Kite; *but I question whether the Kite of Antiquity was the same with ours:*
The Scriblerians' doubt is a burlesque one; the *melolonthe* (note the misspelling in the text) is a comparatively large beetle, which, according to Pollux (secs. 124–5), Greek boys played with by attaching a long string to one of its legs and allowing it to fly in circles overhead. The kite of the times of the Scriblerians was, of course, a paper one flown in the wind.

(27) 110, 26. *And though the* 'Ορτυγοκοπία *or* Quail-fighting *is what is most taken notice of, they had doubtless* Cockmatches *also, as is evident from certain Gems and Relievo's.*
The Scriblerians' hasty study of the subject made them overly cautious; there was much evidence available to them that cockfighting was common in Greece and Rome in the earliest times not only in the form of pictorial representations but in references and descriptions of classic historians and authors. Cf. Samuel Pegge, "A Memoir on Cock-fighting," *Archaeologia* (1775), III, 132–50. They were probably influenced by Pollux, who describes quailfighting (secs. 107–08), but does not mention the use of cocks. For the popularity of cockfighting during the reign of Queen Anne see John Ashton, *Social Life in the Reign of Queen Anne* (1882), I, 300–02 and Strutt, *op. cit.*, pp. 375–7.

(28) 110, 30. . . . *Game . . . invented by a people among the Thracians, who hung up one of their Companions in a Rope, and gave him a knife to cut himself down;* . . .
Since it has not been possible to identify the source of this statement one is led to suppose that the Scriblerians violated their policy by inventing it.

(29) 110, 37. . . . *how infinitely, both in sense and sound, they excel our barbarous names of Plays.*
Cf. "Dr. Playford's" statement:

I have made it my general remark, that whereas the English plays have barbarous sounding names, as, "Almonds and Raisins," "Puss in a Corner," "Barley-break," "Push-pin," "Chicken-a-train-trow," and the like; those of the Grecian seem all as if they were ladies in romances, as *ecsustinda, elcustinda, chytrinda, ephesinda, basilinda,* which [with?] several others. King, II, 84.

(30) 111, 6. . . . Peritrochia; . . .
The peritrochium is "a wheel, as constituting part of the mechanical power called the wheel-and-axle." *NED.*

(31) III, 9. *Others of his sports were farther carried to improve his tender soul even in Virtue and Morality.*

This idea had been anticipated by "Dr. Playford." See the general note to this chapter.

(32) III, 13. . . . Bob-cherry, *which teaches at once two noble Virtues, Constancy and Patience; the first in adhering to the pursuit of one end, the latter in bearing a disappointment.*

The game consists in attempting to seize in the teeth or mouth a cherry which has been suspended by a string so that it is on a level with the mouth or, in more difficult forms of the game, high enough to require jumping. The Scriblerians' humorous statement as to its educational virtues was quoted, apparently seriously, by Johnson in his *Dictionary*.

(33) III, 16. . . . *an odd and secret manner of* Stealing, *according to the Custom of the Lacedæmonians;* . . .

The Scriblerians drew this from Plutarch's *Morals*. The passage dealing with this custom in the contemporary English rendering of it by John Pulleyn reads:

Though it might seem very strange and unaccountable in this wise nation, that anything which had the least semblance of baseness or dishonesty should be universally approved, commended, and encouraged by their laws, yet so it was in the case of theft, whereby their young children were allowed to steal certain things . . . whereby they were rendered more apt to serve them in their wars. . . . And if at any time they were taken in the act of stealing, they were most certainly punished with rods and the penance of fasting; not because they esteemed the stealth criminal, but because they wanted skill and cunning in the management and concealing of it. *Plutarch's Morals, Translated from the Greek by Several Hands* (1684–94); corrected and revised by W. W. Goodwin (1870), I, 89–90.

Goodwin says of Pulleyn's part, the "Account of the Laws and Customs of the Lacedemonians," that it is not strictly a translation but rather "an essay by Mr. Pulleyn based upon the text of Plutarch's brief notes on the customs of the Lacedemonians." P. 82.

CHAPTER VI

In this chapter the Scriblerians bring their satire on the followers of the ancients to a climax. The chapter falls into three main divisions. The first section deals with Martinus' training in gymnastics and dancing—Cornelius insisting, as he had in connection with childhood games, that his son occupy himself with only those pastimes and exercises practiced in antiquity. A new turn is then given to the narrative by Cornelius' determination to have Martinus' spleen removed. This amusing folly serves as a means of introducing his brother Albertus as a foil.

An interesting feature of the argument between the brothers is the character of Albertus. In ridiculing the followers of the ancients it was not the purpose of the Scriblerians to give comfort to the moderns; hence they made of Albertus not a partisan of the modern group but "a discreet man, sober in his opinions, clear of Pedantry, and knowing enough both in books and in the world, to preserve a due regard for whatever was useful or excellent, whether ancient or modern." Albertus' tactics with his brother are not to try to argue with him or to convert him to a contrary view but to divert his extravagances and to lessen his uncritical enthusiasm for all things ancient by the use of ironic and unflattering modern parallels. Albertus' mention of music, however, stirs Cornelius to his most amusing extravagance in praise of the ancients.

In taking up the relative merits of ancient and modern music the Scriblerians were tapping a rich field which had previously been little exploited by satirists. Moreover, music was an aspect of the great "Quarrel" which was still very much alive at the time the *Memoirs* were written. Though the long delay in the appearance of their satire kept it from exerting contemporary influence, the decisiveness of the stand which the Scriblerians took makes this chapter an important document in the history of the controversy.

The ancient-modern controversy in music has been neglected by scholars. Though it did not arouse as much contemporary interest as some of the broader phases of the whole argument, it was in many ways exceptionally interesting and significant. Very little was known about ancient music; hence, in contrast with literature, art, and architecture where each individual might judge for himself by comparing the masterpieces of antiquity with the corresponding ones of modern times, it was necessary in this field for critics to base their decisions primarily on the many testimonials of ancient authors as to the almost miraculous effects of ancient music. Thus despite a number of incidental issues, such as whether the ancients had harmony and whether by music they meant poetry and music, or melody alone, the issue at bottom was a simple one of reverence and credulity. If one believed what the ancients said, modern music was obviously much inferior, since not even Lully or Purcell could charm rocks or noticeably raise the ethical level of his audiences; if, on the other hand, one was irreverent enough to doubt the veracity of the ancients or to believe their accounts mere fable or hyperbole, the greater variety, complexity, and harmonic richness of modern music clearly tipped the scales equally far in its favor.

In general, the quarrel over music followed the lines of the major controversy.[1] It was, however, later in starting. Considerably after the hegemony of the ancients in other fields had been challenged, their superiority in music remained undisputed.[2] And, curiously enough, the quarrel over music was begun not by a modern attacking the ancients, but by an "ancient" attacking the moderns. In 1673 Isaac Vossius published at Oxford a treatise with the title *De Poematum Cantu et Viribus Rythmi* in which he harshly attacked modern music and extravagantly praised that of the ancients. The gist of his arguments was that the "rythmus" which the

1. Cf. H. Gillot, *La Querelle des anciens et des modernes en France* (Paris, 1914); R. F. Jones, *Ancients and Moderns: a Study of the Background of the Battle of the Books* (St. Louis, 1936); A. H. Rigault, *Histoire de la querelle des anciens et des modernes* (Paris, 1856).

2. The established view is represented by Vives (cf. *Opera Omnia* [Valent., 1782–90], III, 6; VI, 207, etc.) and Pancirollus (*Rerum Memorabilium* [Ambergae, 1599], I, iii, I). It is repeated by Meric Casaubon in his *Letter to Peter du Moulin* (1669), p. 29. One of the most easily accessible collections of statements concerning the powers of music, drawn chiefly from ancient writers, was provided by Abraham Cowley in the 32nd note to the first book of his *Davideis* (1656).

ancients took such care to develop was lost, that the intimate relationship between poetry and melody of antiquity was no longer practiced, being in fact impossible in modern times as the result of the harshness of modern languages, and that for these and other reasons modern music was wholly incapable of producing the great effects on listeners that ancient music was universally allowed to have had. The great fame of Vossius as a classical scholar both in England and on the Continent caused his work to be widely read and admired.[3]

The first to take up the defense of modern music was the brother of Charles Perrault, the famous defender of the moderns in other fields. In 1680 Claude Perrault published a short essay entitled *De la Musique des Anciens*. In this he took the position that the music of antiquity was inferior to that of modern times because the ancients, being nearer to the early ages, had, like other primitive peoples (he cites the "Irogois"), little knowledge of the physics of sound on which a true understanding of music must be based. In theory, he granted, the ancients had harmony but their harmony was entirely different from that of the moderns, consisting either of simple chanting in unison, or, as with the Hebrews, in a confusion of voices governed in an impromptu fashion by a known subject and a common cadence. Further, he maintained, their simple melody must have lacked the sweetness of ours because of the absence of half-tones, and must equally have lacked the variety since its entire range did not exceed that of the human voice, or two octaves. The marvelous effects ascribed to music by the ancient writers he brushed aside as incredible. Within the limits of its extreme simplicity, the ancients may have brought their music to a high pitch of delicacy and emotional power, but this "perfection" was relative to the simple tastes of the people of the time. In sum, he concluded that ancient music was simply *"un bruit fort convenable a l'enfance du monde"* and not comparable to the infinitely more complex and rich music of modern times.[4]

These early statements laid down the lines along which the later disputants carried on the war. On the side of the ancients the most famous successor of Vossius was Sir William Temple. In his *Essay upon the Ancient and Modern Learning* (1690) he once again echoed the old charge that the power of ancient music was lost.

What are become of the Charms of Musick, by which Men and Beasts, Fishes, Fowls, and Serpents, were so frequently enchanted, and their very Natures changed; by which the Passions of Men were raised to the greatest Height and Violence, and then as suddenly appeased, so as they might be justly said to be turned into Lyons or Lambs, into Wolves or into Harts, by the Powers and Charms of this admirable Art? 'Tis agreed by the Learned, that the Science of Musick so admired of the Ancients is wholly lost in the World, and that what we have now is made up out

3. It is strange that Isaac Vossius (1618–1689) does not figure directly in the *Memoirs* as he was, in some ways, an example of the kind of scholar whom the Scriblerians were ridiculing. Though a man of great industry and learning, Vossius was childishly credulous with regard to reputed marvels, especially those of the ancient world and of China. In his *Variarum Observationum Liber* (1685) Vossius declared that ancient Rome was twenty times larger than Paris and London together and that it contained fourteen million inhabitants.

4. *Oeuvres diverses de physique et de mechanique* (Leyden, 1721), pp. 295–321.

of certain Notes that fell into the Fancy or Observation of a poor *Fryar*, in chanting his Mattins.[5]

And the same plaint was repeated with variations by such men as Jeremy Collier,[6] Shaftesbury,[7] and the Abbé de Chateauneuf,[8] while on the side of the moderns, Perrault's charges that the ancients lacked harmony and counterpoint and that the stories of the tremendous and dramatic effects of ancient music were mere fables received powerful support from John Wallis,[9] Burette,[10] Malcolm,[11] and others.

One important figure in the large controversy attempted to straddle the issue of music by dividing the honors. William Wotton in his *Reflections upon Ancient and Modern Learning* (1694) was in general a vigorous champion of the moderns. In the field of music, however, he felt the odds were against him and was inclined to be apologetic for even bringing up the subject, saying: "It may seem improper to speak of *Musick* here, which ought rather to have been ranked amongst those Sciences, wherein the Moderns have, upon a strict Enquiry, been found to have been outdone by the Ancients." [12]

But he is not willing to resign the field entirely. Ancient music probably had all that affects "common Hearers" and the ancients were probably "very perfect" in swaying the emotions, but modern music appeals to the intellectual skill and judgment of the hearers. And though the music of antiquity perhaps served better the great end of music, that of pleasing the audience, still a "Modern Master" would be dissatisfied with ancient symphonies, because the chanting in unison in which ancient "harmony" consisted "cannot discover the Extent and Perfection of the Art" so much as the modern operas.[13]

From all this [he declares] it may, perhaps, be not unreasonable to conclude, that though [as Temple had said] *those Charms of* Musick, *by which Men and Beasts, Fishes, Fowls and Serpents, were so frequently enchanted, and their very Natures changed,* be really and irrecoverably lost; yet the Art of *Musick,* that is to say, of Singing, and Playing upon Harmonious Instruments, is, in it self, much a perfecter Thing, though, perhaps, not much pleasanter to an unskilful Audience, than it ever was amongst the Ancient *Greeks* and *Romans.*[14]

5. *Works* (1720), I, 162.

6. "Of Musick," *Essays upon Several Moral Subjects* (5th ed., 1702), II, 17–26. The essay was first published in 1695.

7. *Characteristicks* (1711), III, 263.

8. *Dialogue sur la musique des anciens* (Paris, 1725). Chateauneuf composed the *Dialogue* about the year 1705.

9. In an appendix to his *Claudii Ptolemaei Harmonicōrum Libri Tres* (Oxford, 1682), III, Wallis argued that the ancients did not have harmony in the modern sense and in a letter published in the *Phil. Trans.*, xx (1698), 297–303, he analyzed and effectively discounted the extravagant statements made by the ancients concerning the powers of music.

10. For Burette on ancient harmony see *Memoires de Litterature Tires des Registres de L'Academie Royale des Inscriptions et Belles-Lettres* (The Hague, 1724), v, 151–72, and (Amsterdam, 1736), XI, 100–27; for his attack on the supposed powers of ancient music see the same work (Amsterdam, 1731), VIII, 205–35.

11. Alexander Malcolm, *A Treatise of Musick* (Edinburgh, 1721), pp. 569–608.

12. Wotton, *op. cit.*, pp. 282–3.

13. *Ibid.*, pp. 285–8.

14. *Ibid.*, pp. 288–9.

There is no such shilly-shallying on the part of the Scriblerians. Their scorn of the supposed great power of ancient music was complete—and devastating.

Of the Scriblerians, Arbuthnot and Gay were the ones most interested in music. Arbuthnot made of it a lifelong hobby and was a figure of some importance in the musical circles of London,[15] while Gay wrote librettos for several operas (one of which, *Acis and Galatea,* was set to music by Handel) and himself selected and adapted the airs for his lyrics in the *Beggar's Opera.*[16] Parnell, too, had a well developed taste for music [17] and Swift, though he confessed he knew no more of it "than an ass," [18] was obliged to devote a good deal of time to it by his desire to improve and maintain the quality of his choir in St. Patrick's.[19] Like Swift, Pope knew nothing of the subject, but he fancied that he had "a very good ear" and, according to his own account, "often judged right of the best compositions in music by the force of that" [20]—a boast upon which his reported querying of Arbuthnot as to whether the applause bestowed on Handel was really deserved throws much doubt.[21]

In treating gymnastics and music together the Scriblerians are following the practice of the ancients, who looked upon these two as complementary parts of education—"gymnastics for the body and music for the soul." [22]

(1) 112, 7. *He was stript, powder'd, and anointed, . . .*
In accordance with the ancient custom; e.g., Ovid's *Metamorphoses,* x, 176–7.

(2) 112, 9. *. . . play'd at Quoits, . . .*
The word "quoits" (more commonly spelled "coits" in the early eighteenth century; cf. Bailey's and Kersey's dictionaries; *Spectator,* No. 56; etc.) might refer either to the ancient discus throwing or to its modern offspring, the pitching of an iron circle or a horseshoe at a peg, but presumably the Scriblerians refer to the latter, which was more common and popular. Bailey, for example, mentions only the latter in his *Dictionary,* and Johnson in his says, "The discus of the ancients is some times called in English *quoit,* but improperly."

(3) 112, 17. *. . . the* Harpastus *of the Ancients . . .*
The *harpastum* of the Romans was a ball of wool covered with cloth or leather which several opponents endeavored to catch at once. Ainsworth's *Latin Dictionary.*

(4) 112, 18. *. . . yet in use in* Cornwall, *and known there by the name of* Hurling.
Defoe in his *Tour through England and Wales* (1724–27) says,

15. Cf. Aitken, p. 113. On November 27, 1719, he was elected one of the court directors of the Academy of Music, the board which supervised the production of opera. A. Nicoll, *History of Early Eighteenth Century Drama* (Cambridge, 1925), p. 286.
16. Spence, p. 237, n.
17. See his poem "On the Death of Mr. Viner."
18. "Dr. Swift to Himself on St. Cecilia's Day," *Poems,* I, 300; cf. *Works,* II, 222, 253.
19. See his correspondence with Gay and Arbuthnot on the subject, *Corres.,* II, 298; III, 340, 342; IV, 16, 21; V, 106.
20. Spence, p. 237.
21. *Ibid.,* n.
22. Plato, *Republic* ii. 376.

The game called the *Hurlers,* is a thing the *Cornish* Men value themselves much upon; I confess, I see nothing in it, but that it is a rude violent Play among the *Boors,* or Country People; brutish and furious, and a sort of an Evidence, that they were, once, a kind of Barbarians. II, 6.

Though Defoe speaks of it as being played with "whirlebats," other accounts indicate that it more commonly consisted of a group of players trying to shove a ball over their opponents' goal. A description of the game was added by a later editor of the *Tour* (7th ed., 1769), II, 77–80. Its reputation for breaking bones is indicated by Prior's reference to it in his "Essay upon Opinion," *Dialogues of the Dead,* A. R. Waller, ed. (Cambridge, 1907), p. 201.

(5) 112, 28. *He slit a green Reed, . . . then . . . pronounced these Words,* Daries, daries, astataries, dissunapiter; huat, hanat, huat, ista, pista fista, domi abo, damnaustra.

"*Pliny Hist. Nat. lib.* 17. *in fine. Carmen contra luxata membra, cujus verba inserere non equidem serio ausim, quanquam a Catone prodita.*" (Scrib.)

"*Vid. Cato de re rust,* c. 160." (Scrib.)

The quotation from Pliny, which in standard texts reads: *Quippe cum averti carmine grandines credant plerique: cujus verba inserere non equidem serio ausim, quanquam a Catone prodita, contra luxata membra jungenda harundinum fissurae,* may be translated as follows: "Many believe that hail is averted by a charm, the words of which I do not dare to include seriously, although those charms which are used in connection with sprained limbs being joined to a splint were recorded by Cato."

The charms, *daries, daries,* etc., which are drawn from Cato (in the source cited in the Scriblerus note), are not quoted in the text in their entirety. Further, the charm, *huat, hanat,* etc., which follows the semicolon is a separate one. The various texts of Cato disagree somewhat in the spelling of the words but there is a general agreement that the second word of the first charm is *dardaries,* not the *daries* of the *Memoirs* text. The use of the obscure passage in Cato does not necessarily indicate special knowledge or effort on the part of the Scriblerians, as all the annotated editions of Pliny after Dalechampius' commonly printed his note citing chapter 160 in *De Re Rustica* below the passage in Pliny used in the *Memoirs.*

Both the Earl of Oxford and his son had an interest in such ancient superstitious practices. In a letter to Lord Harley, dated June 28, 1711, Dr. William Stratford, his former tutor, said:

I know your love of antiquities makes you a little superstitious. I have an elder stick that was cut in the minute that the sun entered Taurus. Such a planetary cutting of it gives it a virtue to stop bleeding to which you know you are subject. If you desire to know more of the time and manner of cutting it, of its virtues, and of the manner of applying it, you must consult Aubrey's *Miscellanies.* You may meet with it without doubt amongst your father's collection of mad books. Hist. MSS Comm., *Portland MSS,* VII, 36.

(6) 112, 34. *. . . Rigadoon . . .*

The rigadoon, a light and lively Provencal dance, was introduced into England during the last quarter of the seventeenth century and attained a considerable vogue. Purcell and other English composers used the form.

(7) 113, 1. . . . Socrates *said the best Dancers were the best Warriors;* . . .
    The statement goes beyond anything Socrates is reported to have said, but represents his general attitude toward gymnastic dancing.

(8) 113, 4. . . . *the Comic and Satyric Dance, which were utterly disliked by the sounder Ancients.*
    Plato, for example, says that there are some dances of the bacchic sort in which drunken men are imitated and others in which purifications are made or mysteries celebrated which are distinct from both warlike and peaceful dances and are not suited for a city at all. *Laws,* viii. 815.

(9) 113, 6. . . . *in the* Saltatio Pyrrhica.
    The *saltatio pyrrhica* was a violent military dance performed in military costume with a shield and weapons. Scaliger describes it and gives an account of its origin. Julius Caesar Scaliger, *Poetices libri septem* (3d ed., 1586), i. 18. In discussing dancing in the *Spectator,* No. 67, Budgell repeats Lucian's statement (in his *Dialogue on Dancing*) that Pyrrhus gained more reputation by inventing the dance which is called after his name than by all his other actions.

(10) 113, 7. *Scaliger, from whom my son is lineally descended,* . . .
    Cf. above, p. 186, n. 5.

(11) 113, 9. [Scaliger] *boasts to have perform'd this warlike Dance in the presence of the Emperor, to the great admiration of all Germany.*
    "*Scalig. Poetic l. i. c. 9. Hanc saltationem Pyrrhicam, nos saepe & diu, jussu Bonifacii patrui, coram Divo Maximiliano, non sine stupore totius Germaniae, repraesentavimus. Quo tempore vox illa Imperatoris, Hic puer aut Thoracem pro pelle aut pro cunis habuit.*" (Scrib.)
    The reference given is incorrect; it should be *Poetices, lib.* i, *cap.* 18. Further, in accordance with the practice of the Scriblerian notes, the opening part of the quotation has been revised to make it complete in itself. Properly, it reads: "*Hanc* [*saltationem Pyrrhicam*] *nos & saepe & diu coram Divo Maximiliano, iussu Bonifacii patrui,* . . ." J. C. Scaliger, *loc. cit.* i. 18. The passage may be rendered: "This [pyrrhic saltatio] we both often and long presented before the divine Maximillian, at the command of Boniface, the uncle, not without the astonishment of the whole of Germany. At the same time [came] the voice of the emperor, 'This boy was either born with a corselet or cradled in one.' "

(12) 113, 17. *Therefore Pliny (lib.* xi, *cap.* 37) *says, that such as excel in that exercise* [the Cursus] *have their* Spleen *cauteriz'd.*
    According to Pliny (xi. 80) the spleen sometimes offers a special impediment in running, and therefore the region of the spleen is cauterized in runners who are troubled with pains there.

(13) 113, 22. *For laughter (as the same author hath it, ibid.) is caused by the bigness of the Spleen.*

Pliny says (xi. 80) that some people believe that if a man loses his spleen he loses the power of laughing, and that excessive laughter is caused by the enlargement of it.

(14) 114, 1. . . . *I know that Running has been condemn'd by the proud Spartans, as useless in war:*
The Scriblerians may have had in mind Galen's attack on running as an exercise useless as training for war. The Spartans, says Galen, won their many victories not because they were able to run swiftly but because they could stand firmly against the enemy. *De Parvae Pilae Exercitio*, v, 899–910. Plutarch tells an anecdote to illustrate this reputation of the Spartans. *Plutarchi Chaeronensis, Quae Supersunt Omnia,* Iacobus Reiske, ed. (12 vols., Leipzig, 1774–82), vi, 813–14.

(15) 114, 1. . . . *Demosthenes could say, . . .*
This saying was attributed to Demosthenes by Aulus Gellius as his excuse for running away and leaving his shield in the battle between Philip of Macedon and the Athenians at Chaeronea. *Noct. Attic.* xvii. 21. The saying has been paraphrased many times.

(16) 114, 5. . . . *a thought which the English Hudibras has well rendered.*

> For he that runs may fight again,
> Which he can never do that's slain.

The quotation was apparently written down from memory, as Butler's couplet actually reads:

> For those that fly may fight again,
> Which he can never do that's slain.
>   *Hudibras,* iii, iii, 243–4; cf. i, iii, 607–10.

(17) 114, 8. . . . *Animals spleen'd grow extremely salacious, an experiment well known in dogs.*
"Blackmore's Essay on Spleen." (Scrib.)
Blackmore says, "This Hypothesis is supported by the Observation of the learned Dr. *Purcell,* who assures his Reader, in his Treatise of the Cholick, that he found that Dogs, after the exsection of the Spleen, were more salacious and prone to Venery than before." Sir Richard Blackmore, "An Essay upon the Spleen," *A Treatise of the Spleen and Vapours* (1725), p. 230.

(18) 114, 16. . . . *the Palæstra, . . .*
The *palestrae* were the *gymnasia* or ordinary schools in which boys were trained in gymnastic exercises.

(19) 114, 18. . . . Exedra . . .
The *exedrae* were halls, equipped with seats, in which rhetoricians, philosophers, and others met for disputation and conversation.

(20) 114, 20. . . . *there are Ale-houses where he will hear very notable argumentations.*
The ale houses of the time, which were frequented by servants and rowdies, were famous for their drunken arguments and brawls. Cf. J. Ashton, *Social Life in the*

Reign of Queen Anne, I, 214–36; J. Timbs, *Clubs and Club Life in London* (n.d.), *passim; Spectator,* No. 88, etc.

(21) 114, 21. . . . *we excel them in the* κυβιστικὴ, *or the art of* Tumbling.

The success of the moderns in tumbling was a sore point with dramatic critics. After centuries of popularity in connection with fairs and exhibitions (cf. Strutt, *Sports and Pastimes,* pp. 291–327) tumbling, posturing, and acrobatics began near the end of the seventeenth century to invade the theaters, much to the consternation of the dramatists and critics. "Mr. *Collier* may save himself the trouble of writing against the theatre," wrote Tom Brown in 1699, "for, if these lewd practices are not laid aside, and sense and wit don't come into play again, a man may easily foretel, without pretending to the gift of prophecy, that the stage will be short-liv'd, and the strong *Kentish* man will take possession of the two playhouses, as he has already done of that in *Dorset-Garden." Works* (1730), I, 194. Both the practices and the protests continued, however. In 1702, for example, in a pamphlet entitled *A Comparison between the Two Stages,* the character of Sullen says, "It has always been the Jest of all the Men of Sense about Town; not that the Fellows perform'd ill, for in their way they did admirably; but that the Stage that had kept it's purity a hundred Years (at least from this Debauchery) shou'd now be prostituted to Vagabonds, to Caperers, Eunuchs, Fidlers, Tumblers, and Gipsies." P. 46. The popularity of acrobatic acts in the theaters continued for a decade, the theaters frequently advertising loudly these added attractions. By 1710 the rage apparently died down, for in 1711 Steele wrote in the *Spectator* that "The Method, some time ago, was to entertain that Part of the Audience who have no Faculty above Eyesight, with Rope-Dancers and Tumblers; . . ." No. 141, for August 11, 1711; cf. No. 258, for December 26, 1711.

(22) 114, 23. . . . *but not so much at the* Jaculum *or pitching the Bar.*

The *jaculum* of the Romans was a light dart or spear. Strutt points out that pitching the bar and hammer, a favorite pastime of Henry VIII, appears to have fallen from favor among the nobility by the beginning of the seventeenth century. *Op. cit.,* p. 140. Peacham in his *Compleat Gentleman* (1634; Oxford, 1906) says, "For throwing and wrestling, I hold them exercises not so well beseeming Nobility, but rather soldiers in a Campe, or a Princes guard." P. 215.

(23) 114, 24. *The* Pugilatus *is in as great perfection in England as in old Rome,* . . .
  "Fisty-Cuffs." (Scrib.)

Any Thing that looks like Fighting, is delicious to an *Englishman.* If two little Boys quarrel in the Street, the Passengers stop, make a Ring round them in a Moment, and set them against one another, that they may come to Fisticuffs. . . . These Combats are less frequent among grown Men than Children, but they are not rare. If a Coachman has a Dispute about his Fare with a Gentleman that has hired him, and the Gentleman offers to fight him to decide the Quarrel, the Coachman consents with all his Heart. *M. Misson's Memoirs and Observations in his Travels over England,* J. Ozell, tr. (1719), pp. 304–05.

Professional boxing, however, remained second in favor to sword fighting as a public spectacle until later in the century.

(24) 114, 25. . . . *and the* Cornish-Hug *in the* Luctus *is equal to the* volutatoria *of the Ancients."*

"Wrestling." (Scrib.)

"The Cornish," says Thomas Fuller, "are Masters of the Art of Wrestling, so that if the Olympian Games were now in fashion, they would come away with the victory. Their Hugg is a cunning close with their fellow combitant, the fruits whereof is his *fair fall." Worthies of England* (1662), I, 197–8. Defoe says that the hug has made Cornish men "eminent in the wrestling rings all over England." *Tour* (1724–27), II, 6. A book by Sir Thomas Parkyns on the art of wrestling called *The Inn-Play or, Cornish-Hugg Wrestler. Digested in a Method which teacheth to break all Holds, and throw most Falls Mathematically,* a second and enlarged edition of which was published in 1714, may have provided the stimulus for the allusion in the *Memoirs.*

The *volutatoria* of the Romans was a type of throwing or tumbling used in wrestling.

King, in his dialogue on ancient and modern sports (see general note to Chapter V), has his modern Butcher say to Hercules, "In truth, Sir, I believe the Cornish hugg would have puzzled the *art* of your philosophers; . . ." King, I, 151.

(25) 114, 29. *The Cretans wisely forbid their servants Gymnasticks, as well as Arms; . . .*

"Aristot. politic. lib. 2. cap. 3." (Scrib.)

". . . the ingenious policy of the Cretans, who give their slaves the same institutions as their own, but forbid them gymnastic exercises and the possession of arms." B. Jowett, tr. (Oxford, 1885), p. 36.

(26) 114, 31. . . . *their enervated Lords . . .*

The progressive degeneration, enervation, and effeminacy of the nobility, a frequent theme of satire ever since ancient times, was a favorite subject with Swift, who, in common with Bolingbroke and other Tory leaders, believed the nation should be governed by a vigorous, well-trained aristocracy and therefore strongly deplored the fact that ever since the Restoration the degeneracy of the nobility had forced the government to entrust the conduct of affairs to commoners or "new" men. Swift laid the blame for the decline of the old aristocracy on luxury and idleness, declaring that many great families had come to an end "by the sloth, luxury, and abandoned lusts, which enervated their breed through every succession, producing gradually a more effeminate race wholly unfit for propagation." *Works,* XI, 57; cf. VIII, 211, and *Letters of Jonathan Swift to Charles Ford,* D. Nichol Smith, ed. (Oxford, 1935), p. 83. Swift felt that the best means of correcting the situation lay in the improvement of the training and education of the children of the aristocracy. See his *Essay on Modern Education* in *Works,* XI, 49–57. For the contemporary attack on luxury as the cause of enervation and weakness among the aristocracy see above, p. 265, n. 6.

(27) 114, 34. . . . *(a species of Vectitation . . .*

"Vectitation" is an extremely rare word, meaning "being carried frequently," or, as Blount has it, "an often carriage." *Glossographia* (1656; 4th ed., 1674). The word was not included in their dictionaries by either Kersey or Bailey.

(28) 114, 36. . . . *flying Chariots, where the people may have the benefit of this exercise at the small expence of a farthing.*

The price of a farthing indicates that these "flying Chariots" must have been something in the nature of a merry-go-round. The fares for coaches and chairs in London was regulated by act of Parliament and was during this period never less than a shilling, even, as Misson points out, if a passenger went "but a hundred Steps." P. 39. They probably derived their name from the "flying coaches" that were introduced in the reign of Charles II for rapid journeys between cities.

(29) 115, 4. *Your son must take up with such masters as the present age affords; we have . . . Musick-masters.*

According to Pope the *Memoirs* once contained an episode, written by Anthony Henley, dealing with the life of Martinus' music master, Tom Durfey. See Appendix III.

(30) 115, 7. . . . *Hautboys . . .*

This woodwind instrument with a double reed (the modern oboe) was particularly valued in the early eighteenth century for its soft beauty of tone; cf. Gay's "My boxen haut-boy sweet of sound," in Prologue to the *Shepherd's Week*.

(31) 115, 9. . . . *that ancient piper Pythocaris?*

The only mention of Pythocaris seems to be in Aelian (xi.28), who gives no information about him aside from the statement that he repelled an onrush of wolves by the sound of his flute.

(32) 115, 14. . . . *Ælian tells us how the Lybian Mares were excited to horsing by Musick?*

"Ælian Hist. Animal. lib. xi, cap. 18. and lib. xii. cap. 44." (Scrib.)

Only the second of the references to Aelian is pertinent. The first does not mention the effects of music and deals with the allaying of passion among mares rather than the exciting of it. In book twelve, where he discusses the effects of music on horses, saying that music can make Lybian mares docile and even move them to tears, Aelian credits Euripides with the statement that marriage tunes incite mares to venery.

(33) 115, 20. . . . *Musick, by which (says Aristotle) they taught all the Virtues?*

Aristotle does not appear to have made such a statement. He does, however, declare that music has a power of forming the character and should therefore be introduced into the education of the young. *Politics* viii.5.

(34) 115, 22. . . . *turn Newgate into a College of Dorian Musicians, who should teach moral Virtues to those people.*

The Dorian was a mode of ancient Greek music which was characterized by solemnity and simplicity. Plato chose it as most becoming to valiant, sober, and temperate men. *Republic* iii. 399. According to Athenaeus, it was described by Heraclides in his treatise on music as a manly and high-sounding strain of a rather stern and vehement character, without any great variations or any sudden changes. *The Deipnosophists* xiv.20. Aristotle calls it the gravest and manliest of the modes. *Politics* viii. 7.

(35) 115, 26. . . . *as Theophrastus assures us* . . .
"Athenaeus, lib. xiv. [cap. 19]." (Scrib.)

Athenaeus quotes Theophrastus as saying that music can heal diseases and cites a passage in his treatise on enthusiasm which declares that men with diseases in the loins lose their pain if a Phrygian air is played opposite to the part affected. Theophrastus' cure is also mentioned by Appolonius Dyscolus (*Historia Commentitia,* "De Musica," cap. xliv) and by Aulus Gellius (*Noctes Atticae* iv. 13), both of whom quote Theophrastus as associating the remedy more specifically with sciatic gout.

(36) 115, 27. . . . (*whence Caelius calls it* loca dolentia decantare) . . .
"Lib. de sanit. tuenda c. 2." (Scrib.)
Loca dolentia decantare—"to enchant [or sing away] the afflicted places."

The statement is drawn from the fifth book of *De Morbis Chronicis* (i. 23) by Caelius Aurelianus, a celebrated Latin physician, probably of the time of Galen. Caelius explains that the pain is relieved by causing a vibration in the fibers of the afflicted part (*quae cum saltum sumerent palpitando, discusso dolore mitescerent*).

(37) 115, 28. . . . *some small remains of this skill are preserved in the cure of the Tarantula.*

The superstition that venomous bites can be cured by music probably goes back to the ancient theory, expressed by Theophrastus and Democritus (Aulus Gellius iv. 13), that the sound of the flute was a specific for the bite of a viper. The modern superstition with regard to the bite of the tarantula, which appears to have first come from Apulia in Italy, was widely believed in the seventeenth and early eighteenth centuries. "M. Burette, with our Dr. Mead, Baglivi, and all the learned, of their time, throughout Europe, seem to have entertained no doubt of this fact," says C. Burney in his *History of Music* (1776–89), i, 186 n. Cf. Sir Thomas Browne, *Pseudodoxia Epidemica,* Bk. iii, chap. xxviii; Pepys's *Diary* for February 4, 1661/2; Addison, *Spectator,* No. 582. *The British Apollo* for March 24–29, 1710, in response to a query on the subject, says,

. . . the Success of Musick in such Cases is allow'd of by the best Authors, and is attributed to the swift Motion impressed upon the Air by Musical Instruments, and Communicated by the Air to the Skin, and so to the Blood and Spirits, which does in some measure dissolve and dispel their growing Coagulations; the Effects of the Dissolution encreasing as the Sound it self encreases, till at last the Humours receive their Primitive Fluid State; upon which the Patient gradually Revives, Moves and Jumps about with Violence, till the Sweat breaks out and carries off the Seeds of the Poyson.

The supposed cure of tarantula bites by music was frequently cited in the ancient-modern controversy over the power of music. Cf. e.g., Abbé de Chateauneuf, *Dialogue sur la musique des anciens* (Paris, 1725), p. 24.

(38) 115, 30. *Did not Pythagoras stop a company of drunken Bullies from storming a civil house, by changing the strain of the Pipe to the sober Spondæus?*
"Quintilian lib. i. cap. 10 [sect. 32]." (Scrib.)

According to Quintilian, Pythagoras calmed the passions of a party of young men, who were about to offer violence to a respectable family, by requesting a female musician to change her strain to a spondaic measure.

John Brown in his *Dissertation on the Rise . . . of Poetry and Music* (1763) says the ridicule of this story in the *Memoirs* is based on "an entire Misapprehension, or Misrepresentation, of the true nature of *ancient* Music" and that the ridicule vanishes when it is explained that "the Melody was accompanied by a *poetic Exhortation* suited to the Numbers [i.e. the Dorian mode]." P. 94. It seems doubtful, however, that the Scriblerians would have found the idea of a group of drunken bullies being halted in their nefarious project by an ethical song any less ridiculous than their being chastened by simple melody.

(39) 115, 32. . . . *defend their windows from common Nickers.*

Nickers were rowdy youths who startled people within houses by throwing coins at windows—often with disastrous results to the glass. Gay mentions them in his *Trivia,*

> His scatter'd pence the flying *Nicker* flings,
> And with the copper show'r the casement rings. Bk. iii, ll. 323–4.

(40) 115, 35. . . . *when the Lacedæmonian Mob were up, they commonly sent for a Lesbian Musician to appease them, and they immediately grew calm as soon as they heard Terpander sing:*
"Suidas in Timotheo." (Scrib.)

The reference to Suidas is an error; the story of Terpander's quelling the Lacedemonian mob comes from Plutarch's *De Musica,* chap. 42; R. Volkmann, ed. (Leipzig, 1856), p. 49. Suidas' *Lexicon* has accounts of both Timotheus and Terpander, but its account of Timotheus does not connect him in any way with Sparta and its account of Terpander does not contain the story of his quelling the mob. Terpander was said to have been born in Lesbos.

(41) 116, 2. . . . *his Holiness's Image from being burnt on a fifth of November.*

The allusion probably dates from one of the later periods of composition. From the days of the Popish Plot until near the end of the reign of Queen Anne the more customary time for burning the pope's image was on November 17, the anniversary of the accession of Queen Elizabeth. The occasions were often dangerously riotous and when in 1711 the Whigs, as a political move to arouse public feeling against the Jacobites and the Oxford ministry, planned a particularly elaborate demonstration (Swift's *Works,* ii, 283 ff.), it and subsequent public celebrations of the day were suppressed. The practice of burning the pope's image then reverted to November 5, Guy Fawkes Day. During the early years of George I, when the threat of the Pretender was strong, this day was celebrated with great enthusiasm.

(42) 116, 3. . . . *Billinsgate, . . .*

The quarrelsomeness and vigorous language of "the Ladies of the *British* Fishery" (to use Addison's phrase—*Spectator,* No. 247), while displaying their wares at the fish market in Billingsgate, seem to have become proverbial during the seventeenth century.

(43) 116, 3. . . . *Timotheus* . . .

One of the great musicians of the ancients, famous as the man whose music moved Alexander the Great. Suidas, *Lexicon,* III, 475. Dryden mentions him in *Alexander's Feast* (ll. 20 ff.) and Pope celebrates him in the *Essay on Criticism* (ll. 374–9). It has been pointed out (W. O. Christie, *Poetical Works of Dryden* [1870], p. 373 n.) that the most famous Timotheus died before Alexander was born and that Dryden (and, hence, Pope who followed him) must be referring to the musician of Boeotia who was a favorite of Alexander, but it seems more likely that the poets simply confused the two.

(44) 116, 3. . . . *Hockley in the Hole* . . .

Hockley-in-the-Hole was a bear garden and arena, situated slightly to the north-west of Clerkenwell Green. It was notorious for ferocious bear and bull baiting, dog fights, prize fights of all kinds, and cock matches within the arena and for battles between supporters of various contestants and drunken brawls among the spectators. The fights were chiefly attended by the butchers (who seem to have been the chief dog fighters), the drovers, and the common mob, but the gentry and nobility not infrequently occupied the expensive seats. The district around the arena was notorious as the home of thieves, bullies, and prostitutes and was frequently the scene of impromptu fights. Cf. W. J. Pinks, *The History of Clerkenwell,* E. J. Wood, ed. (1865), pp. 158–64; H. B. Wheatley, *London Past and Present* (1888), *s.v.;* Walter Thornbury, *Old and New London* (1897), II, 306–09; etc.

The place and the fights which occurred there were frequently made use of for satiric purposes by the Scriblerians and other writers of the time. In the *Beggar's Opera,* Mrs. Peachum says: "You should go to *Hockley in the hole,* and to *Marybone,* child, to learn valour. These are the schools that have bred so many brave men." Act I, sc. vi. Gay also refers to the fights there in *Trivia* (Bk. II, ll. 410–12) and in his *Fables* (xxxiv, 27–8). Pope mentions it in the *Dunciad* (Bk. I, ll. 222, 326) and in his *Imitations of Horace* (Sat. I, l. 49).

Cf. below, p. 250, n. 19.

(45) 116, 5. . . . *bring Horneck to common civility."*

"Horneck, a scurrilous Scribler who wrote a weekly paper, called *the High German Doctor."* (Scrib.)

Little is known about Philip Horneck except that he was an attorney who in 1716 became Solicitor to the Treasury. *Diary of Mary Countess Cowper* (1864), p. 64. *The High German Doctor* was a trashy and vituperative weekly, which lasted from May 4, 1714, until May 12, 1715. The general character of the paper was sufficient to warrant the mention in the *Memoirs* of its author, but it is more likely that he won his place by an attack on Pope and Gay in connection with *The What D'ye Call It* in 1715. In a joint letter with Pope to Parnell, dated March 18 [1715]—a short time after the appearance of the play, Gay says, "I find success, even in the most trivial things, raises the indignation of scriblers: for I, for my What-d'ye-call-it, could neither escape the fury of Mr. Burnet, or the German Doctor." Pope, E. & C., VII, 455. Pope, as might be expected, did not forget the attack and found a place in the *Dunciad* to mention "Horneck's fierce eye." Bk. III, l. 152.

(46) 116, 15. . . . murrey-colour'd . . .

"A colour like that of the mulberry; a purple-red or blood colour." *NED*.

(47) 116, 16. . . . *Harpegiatura*, . . .

The spelling in the *Memoirs* is an unusual one which is not listed in the *NED*. The word is not given by Phillips, Blount, Kersey, Coles, Bailey (1721), etc. Later editions of Bailey give two spellings, *Harpeggio* and *Harpeggiato*.

(48) 116, 19. . . . Mob . . .

The use of the word "mob" here and elsewhere in this chapter may be evidence that Swift had no direct part in the writing or editing of it, for Swift displayed a constant and vigorous aversion toward the term as a vulgar contraction. Under his influence, Addison attacked such abbreviations in the *Spectator*, No. 135, saying, "It is perhaps this Humour of speaking no more than we needs must, which has so miserably curtailed some of our Words, . . . as in *mob. rep. pos. incog,* and the like . . ." Swift returned to the charge in his *Proposal for Correcting . . . the English Tongue* in 1712 and later attacked Burnet sharply for admitting this vulgarism into his *History. Works*, x, 329. In 1738, in *Polite Conversation*, he struck at "abbreviations exquisitely refined; as, *pozz* for *positive; mobb* for *mobile; phizz* for *physiognomy; . . .*" *Works*, xi, 217.

(49) 116, 25. . . . *he never touch'd his Lyre in such a truly chromatick and enharmonick manner* . . .

Of the three genera of ancient music, the enharmonic, chromatic, and diatonic, which were determined by the various ways of dividing the tetrachord, Cornelius typically uses the two which were rarely used by the ancients and had been wholly rejected by the moderns. In his *Treatise of Musick* (Edinburgh, 1721), Malcolm says: "The *Enharm.* was by all [the ancients] acknowledged to be so difficult, that few could practise it, if indeed any ever could do it accurately; and they own much the same of the *Chromatick.* Such Inequalities in the Degrees of the *Scale,* might be used for attacking the Fancy, and humouring some disorderly Motions: But what true Melody could be made of them, we cannot conceive. All acknowledged, that the *Diatonick* was the true Melody which Nature had formed all Mens Ears to receive and be satisfied with; and therefore it was the general Practice . . ." P. 517.

(50) 116, 29. . . . *the power of the Ionian;* . . .

Plato in the *Republic,* which, with Aristotle's *Politics,* provides the chief source of knowledge of the modes of Greek music, describes the Ionian mode as slow and peaceful. He disapproves of it because it is "lax." *Republic* iii. 399.

(51) 116, 29. . . . *the effect of the Æolian."*

The Aeolian was described as like the Thessalians, bold and gay but hospitable and chivalrous. D. B. Monro, *The Modes of Ancient Greek Music* (Oxford, 1894), p. 9.

(52) 116, 33. . . . *too much of the* Phrygian; . . .

The Phrygian is described by Aristotle as the most exciting and inspiring of the modes—the one suitable for warriors. *Politics* viii. 5.

(53) 116, 33. *. . . change it to the* Lydian, . . .

Plato says that some Lydian modes are soft and lax and are not to be used in the training of warriors (*Republic* iii. 399), and Aristotle declares the Lydian to be suited to children because it possesses elements of order and education. *Politics* viii. 7. Cf. Milton's "Lap me in soft Lydian airs." *L'Allegro,* l. 136.

(54) 117, 4. *. . . for some ancient Tibicen . . .*
Tibicen—"a flute-player."

CHAPTER VII

Though as usual there are a number of interesting side issues, the principal subjects of satire in the chapter are the logic and metaphysics of the schoolmen. In attacking these parts of the "old philosophy," the Scriblerians were following what had become by their time a well-worn tradition. Ever since Bacon had led the revolt against the cramping bonds of the old established forms of thought and given direction to the search for a new and more fruitful approach to the study of nature, attacks on Aristotelian logic and metaphysics had been a standard element in the writings of those who favored the "new learning." Wilkins, Hobbes, Descartes, Sprat, Glanvil, Boyle, and Locke were but a few of the intellectual leaders of the seventeenth century to excoriate what they believed to be the empty subtleties and the endless, futile wranglings of the logicians and Schoolmen. Nor was the "new learning" the sole banner under which the war against the old forms of thought was waged; Puritans and educational reformers fiercely attacked the dominance of peripateticism in theology and in the universities.

In scientific and learned circles the revolters soon achieved a considerable and eventually a sweeping victory but in the universities they accomplished little. Under the Caroline Code, sponsored by Archbishop Laud and inaugurated in 1636, much of the students' time at the universities had been allotted to training in formal logic. All students at Oxford had to attend disputations several times a week from the end of their first year until they obtained their degrees. At the end of two years they were obliged to respond *pro forma,* upon which they became General Sophisters. Thereafter they were required to dispute *in parvise* at least once each term until they were graduated.[1] Reverence for the doctrines of Aristotle was maintained by statute, the penalty of disputing his authority in a public exercise being failure in that exercise and a fine of five shillings.[2] Despite generations of student protest,[3] the system remained substantially the same more than three-quarters of a century later under George I,[4] as indeed it was to continue to under

1. Sir Charles E. Mallett, *History of the University of Oxford* (1924–27), II, 323–4.
2. N. Amhurst, *Terrae-Filius,* No. 21, for March 28, 1721.
3. Locke declared that because of his aversion to the disputatious method of training he spent a good part of his first years at the University in reading romances. Spence, p. 81. Amhurst, who was at Oxford from 1716 to 1719, devoted several issues of *Terrae-Filius* to a bitter attack on the system. "The whole business of our Education," he declared, "seems to be to defend those absurdities and impositions which we have, long ago, renounced." No. 20, for March 24, 1721.
4. In 1728, David Gregory, first Regius Professor at Oxford, informed Lord Townshend that "the methods of education in the two Universities had been in some measure defective

several of his successors. Hence, though the theme was not a fresh one, attacks on formal logic were still timely in Scriblerian days. The group did not have to go far for material and inspiration since three members had gone through the training, Swift and Parnell at Trinity College, Dublin, and Arbuthnot at Oxford.[5]

In the course of the chapter, the Scriblerians cover most of the commonly expressed objections to logic and metaphysics as they had been practiced by the Schoolmen and as they were taught in the universities. Both are presented as "polemical arts" in which the primary purpose is not to discover truth but to beat down and conquer an opponent and in which arguments are carried on through "barbarous terms," monstrous quibbles, and sophistical reasoning.[6] In the field of logic, the chief attack of the Scriblerians is on the formal Aristotelian method of defining, with its elaborate scale of predicaments, and on reasoning by means of syllogisms.

Both of these parts of formal logic were special objects of attack by the anti-Aristotelians in the seventeenth century. The ten predicaments of Aristotelian logic were declared to be of little use and formed rather for the birth of mysteries than true enlightenment,[7] while reasoning by means of syllogisms was regarded as empty and profitless. The rejection of syllogistic reasoning was an important part of the creed of the new scientists. Here, as in other aspects of the "new philosophy," Bacon was the great leader; he found this sort of reasoning unfit for use in science on the grounds that

syllogisms consist of propositions, and propositions of words; and words are but the current tokens or marks of popular notions of things; wherefore if these notions (which are the souls of words) be grossly and variably collected out of particulars, the whole structure falls to pieces. And it is not the laborious examination either of consequences of arguments or of the truth of propositions that can ever correct that error.[8]

The climax of the attack on syllogistic reasoning came at the end of the century in John Locke. A large part of the chapter on "Reason" in the fourth book of his

since they were obliged to adhere so much to the rules laid down by their forefathers," and that "the old scholastic learning had been for some time despised, but not altogether exploded because nothing had been substituted in its place." N. Sykes, *Edmund Gibson* (1926), p. 106.

5. Arbuthnot entered University College as a Fellow-commoner in 1694, at the age of twenty-seven, and remained there two years before beginning the study of medicine at St. Andrews. As an older man, he was doubtless more than ordinarily critical of the formal philosophical training he was getting.

6. A colorful attack on formal logic on these grounds is to be found in John Webster's *Academiarum Examen* (1654). Webster says, "As it is now used in the *Schools,* it is meerly *bellum intestinum Logicum,* a civil war of words, a verbal contest, a combat of cunning, craftiness, violence and altercation, wherein all verbal force, by impudence, insolence, opposition, contradiction, derision, diversion, trifling, jeering, humming, hissing, brawling, quarreling, scolding, scandalizing, and the like, are equally allowed of, and accounted just, and no regard had to the truth, so that by any means, *per fas aut nefas* they may get the Conquest, and worst their adversary, and if they can entangle or catch one another in the Spider Webs of *Sophistical* or fallacious argumentations, then their rejoicing and clamour is as great as if they had obtained some signal Victory." P. 33; quoted by R. F. Jones, *Ancients and Moderns* (St. Louis, 1936), pp. 107–08.

7. Cf. below, p. 251, n. 22.

8. *De Augmentis,* v, ii; *Philosophical Works,* J. M. Robertson, ed. (1905), p. 503. Cf. *De Augmentis,* v, iv and *Novum Organum,* I, 13–14; Robertson, pp. 515 and 260.

Essay concerning Human Understanding is devoted to showing the uselessness and futility of reasoning in this manner. This futility he attributes to two general causes; that one can perceive connections and proofs "as easily, nay, perhaps better" without the aid of syllogisms,[9] and that "those scholastic forms of discourse are not less liable to fallacies than the plainer ways of argumentation," as is demonstrated by "common observation, which has always found these artificial methods of reasoning more adapted to catch and entangle the mind, than to instruct and inform the understanding."[10] In sum, he declares,

Syllogism at best is but the art of fencing with the little knowledge we have, without making any addition to it. And if a man should employ his reason all this way, he will not do much otherwise than he, who having got some iron out of the bowels of the earth, should have it beaten up all into swords, and put into his servants' hands to fence with, and bang one another. Had the king of Spain employed the hands of his people, and his Spanish iron so, he had brought to light but little of that treasure that lay so long hid in the entrails of America. And I am apt to think that he who shall employ all the force of his reason only in brandishing of syllogisms, will discover very little of that mass of knowledge which lies yet concealed in the secret recesses of nature; and which, I am apt to think, native rustic reason (as it formerly has done) is likelier to open a way to, and add to the common stock of mankind, rather than any scholastic proceeding by the strict rules of mode and figure.[11]

The Scriblerian satire in the field of metaphysics is aimed at the Scholastic theologians and their doctrine of substantial forms. No part of the "old philosophy" was more attacked in the seventeenth century than the metaphysics of the Schoolmen. The works of the philosophers, scientists, essayists, and satirists are filled with harsh attacks on "frivolous distinction," "crabbed Notions," "vulgar disputes," "perplexing Subtilties," "bombastic phrases," "sophistical Chimeras," and "insignificant trains of strange and barbarous words" of the school divines who, in the words of Hobbes,

striving to make good many points of faith incomprehensible, and calling in the philosophy of Aristotle to their assistance, wrote great books of school-divinity, which no man else, nor they themselves were able to understand; as any man may perceive that shall consider the writings of Peter Lombard, or Scotus, or of him that wrote commentaries upon him, or of Suarez, or any other school divine of later times.[12]

9. Bk. iv, chap. xvii, sec. 4.
10. *Ibid.*
11. *Ibid.*, sec. 6.
12. *The English Works of Thomas Hobbes,* Sir William Molesworth, ed. (1839), vi, 185; cf. iii, 17–70, *passim,* 108, 669–93; v, 256 ff.; i, 34, 531. For some other typical expressions by various types of critics see J. Wilkins, *Mathematical and Philosophical Works* (1708), p. 146; Samuel Butler, *Hudibras,* i, i, 150–8, *Satires,* R. Lamar, ed. (Cambridge, 1928), pp. 159–64, *Characters,* A. R. Waller, ed. (Cambridge, 1908), p. 283; T. Sprat, *History of the Royal Society* (3d ed., 1722), pp. 15–22; J. Gailhard, *Treatise concerning the Education of Youth* (1678), pp. 20–1; *The Petty-Southwell Correspondence,* the Marquis of Lansdowne, ed. (1928), pp. 309, 323–4; John Locke, *Essay concerning Human Understanding* (1690), Bk. iii, chap. x, sec. 6, *et seq.;* W. Freke, *Select Essays* (1693), pp. 61 ff.; and R. F. Jones, *Ancients and Moderns,* chaps. v and vi.

Nor was there any slackening in these attacks after the turn of the century; the contemporaries of the Scriblerians were equally vehement in their condemnation of the doctrine of abstractions and the "mysterious jargon of Scholasticism, than which there could never have been contrived a more effectual method to perplex and confound human understanding," that "our youth spend several years in acquiring" at the universities.[13]

Though the Scriblerians agreed in condemning what they believed were the abuses of the Aristotelians, they arrived at this common ground from somewhat different points of departure. Pope's attitude, and presumably that of Parnell, Gay, and Oxford, was simply a reflection of the popular view.[14] Arbuthnot's opposition was that of the scientists; the refinements of formal logic were useful, and perhaps necessary, in overcoming obstinate and perverse opponents, "but in the search of truth, an imitation of the method of the geometers will carry a man further than all the dialectical rules." [15] Swift's position was more complex. His pronounced dislike of subtle speculations and philosophical intricacies of all sorts, and particularly those which seemed to him to obscure the simple truths of the Christian religion, led him to share the general scorn for the perplexities, abstractions, and involved terminology of Aristotelian logic and Scholastic theology.[16] On the other hand, his admiration for Aristotle, particularly for his *Politics*,[17] by which he was greatly impressed, tempered his views somewhat [18] and led him to distinguish perhaps even more sharply than was customary between Aristotle and his followers.[19]

(1) 118, 10. . . . *I mean the admirable Discourse* Περὶ Βάθους, *. . .*
  The Art of Sinking in Poetry, which was published in the Swift-Pope *Miscellanies,* "The Last Volume," in 1727. See above, pp. 54–6.

(2) 118, 10. . . . *which he wrote at this time . . .*
  The suggestion contained in the above statement that the *Art of Sinking* had

13. George Berkeley, *Works,* A. C. Fraser, ed. (Oxford, 1901), II, 224; cf. I, 249. See also Shaftesbury, *Characteristicks* (1711 ed.), I, 289–90, II, 354–5, III, 61, 80; Sir R. Blackmore, *The Lay Monastery* (2d ed., 1714), p. 11; M. Tindal, *The Rights of the Christian Church* (2d ed., 1706), p. 226; J. Addison, *Spectator,* No. 239: N. Amhurst, *Terrae-Filius* (2d ed., 1726), I, 114–17.

14. Cf. *Essay on Criticism,* ll. 440–5 and *Essay on Man,* Ep. II, ll. 81–4.

15. Aitken, p. 411.

16. Cf. *Works,* I, 66, 164; III, 97; VIII, 140; and XI, 53.

17. Cf. *Works,* III, 65, 99, 114; XI, 38; *Corres.,* II, 150.

18. Swift's most interesting statement on the subject appears in his *Remarks* on Tindal's *The Rights of the Christian Church:* "We [the clergy of the Church of England] have exploded schoolmen as much as he, and in some people's opinion too much, since the liberty of embracing any opinion is allowed. They following Aristotle, who is doubtless the greatest master of arguing in the world: But it hath been a fashion of late years to explode Aristotle, and therefore this man hath fallen into it like others, for that reason, without understanding him. Aristotle's poetry, rhetoric, and politics, are admirable, and therefore, it is likely, so are his logics." *Works,* III, 114.

19. When, during his stay in Glubbdubdrib, Gulliver calls up the spirits of some of the great ancients, he finds that "Aristotle was out of all patience with the account I gave him of Scotus and Ramus, as I presented them to him; and he asked them whether the rest of the tribe were as great dunces as themselves." *Works,* VIII, 206–07.

been planned and started long before it was published—in fact, commenced during the first period of the composition of the *Memoirs*—is supported by other evidence. Cf. Swift, *Corres.*, ii, 160.

(3) 118, 12. . . . *but conceal'd from his Father, knowing his extreme partiality for the Ancients.*

This statement, coupled with the one below that in the final version many additional examples were added "from the excellent live poets of this present age," is clearly intended to suggest that in the original version of the *Art of Sinking* the examples of bad poetry were drawn from the writings of the ancients. The slight evidence we have regarding the composition of the piece does not support this suggestion, and such indirect evidence as can be educed from the plans of the Scriblerus Club and from the individual literary activities of its members—especially Arbuthnot and Pope, who seem to have been chiefly responsible for the *Art of Sinking*—is against it. It therefore seems probable that Pope—who was known to have much revised the piece before it was published and was said to have added the initials and names which particularized the attacks against the wishes of Arbuthnot and who was, at the time of publication, finishing the *Dunciad,* in the presentation of which he wished to pose as having been for many years the victim of attacks from Grub Street writers without his having attacked them—added these statements to disguise the fact that thirteen years before the appearance of the *Dunciad* he had had a large share in a project for satirizing contemporary poets.

(4) 118, 15. . . . *drawn from the excellent live Poets of this present age.*

The poets most severely satirized in the *Art of Sinking* are Blackmore, Ambrose Philips, Theobald, Broome, Lee, Cooke, John Philips, Dennis, and Welsted. More than a score of other writers, however, are mentioned or quoted.

(5) 118, 18. . . . *these* [*i.e.* logic and metaphysics], *being* Polemical *Arts,* . . .
See general note to the chapter.

(6) 118, 23. . . . *whose name was Conradus Crambe,* . . .
"CRAMBE, a Repetition of Words, or saying the same Thing over again." Bailey. The word was commonly associated with the popular game of crambo, a play in rhyming in which a person repeating a word used before is forced to pay a forfeit. The game is mentioned in the *Spectator*, Nos. 63 and 504. In his *Letter of Advice to a Young Poet*, Swift says, " 'Crambo' is of extraordinary use to good rhyming . . ." *Works*, xi, 101. Newcastle and Shadwell had used the name Crambo for one of the characters in their play *The Triumphant Widow* (1674).

(7) 118, 24. . . . *was related to the* Crouches *of Cambridge,* . . .
The allusion is probably to the numerous family of Crouches who became active as writers and printers during the middle of the seventeenth century. The best known were Humphrey, a ballad writer, and John, the author of a series of doggerel eulogies and florid panegyrics. The link between this family and Cambridge has not been established and it may be that the Scriblerians are combining alliteration with a passing dig at the great rival of the university to which Arbuthnot and Swift felt allegiance.

(8) 118, 24. . . . *and his mother was Cousin to Mr.* Swan, *Gamester and Punster of the City of London.*

Captain Swan, a frequenter of Will's Coffee-house, was celebrated for his low humor and plays on words. He is mentioned in the *Spectator,* No. 61, by Addison, as "the famous Punnster." Swift, in making fun of the supposed political implications of a famous couplet which began, "Turn up the mistress," says,

I could, if it were proper, demonstrate the very time when those two verses were composed, and name the author, who was no other than the famous Mr. Swan, so well known for his talent at quibbling, and was as virulent a Jacobite as any in England. Neither could he deny the fact, when he was taxed for it in my presence . . . at the Smyrna coffee-house, on the 10th of June, 1701. *Works,* VII, 280; cf. III, 108.

John Dennis dedicated his letter on quibbling to him. *Letters upon Several Occasions* (1696), p. 65.

(9) 118, 28. . . . *with* Words, *which as they are said to be the counters of wise Men, and ready-money of Fools,* . . .

This quotation, perhaps already common at the time, is from Hobbes's *Leviathan,* Pt. I, chap. iv, where it appears as, "For words are wise mens counters, they do but reckon by them; but they are the money of fools, that value them by the authority of an Aristotle, a Cicero, or a Thomas, or any other doctor whatsoever, if but a man." *Works,* III, 25.

(10) 118, 35. . . . *They can form* single apprehensions, . . .

When a learned Friend once urged to our Author the Authority of a famous Dictionary-maker against the latinity of the expression *amor publicus,* which he had used in an inscription, he replied, that he would allow a Dictionary-maker to understand a single word, but not two words put together. (Warb.)

In later editions the "learned Friend" was identified as Dr. Mead and the "Dictionary-maker" as Dr. Patrick (the editor of Ainsworth's *Latin Dictionary*); "our Author" is, of course, Pope. The inscription was for Shakespeare.

(11) 118, 36. . . . *but have neither of the other two faculties, the* judicium *or* discursus.

The Scriblerians are following the scholastic tradition. The division of the faculties of the mind into simple apprehension, judgment, and discourse comes from Aquinas. *Opuscu.* 48, *Tractatus Primus De Syllogismo Simpliciter in S. Thomae Aquinatis Praeclarissima Commentaria in Libros Aristotelis Perihermenias & Posteriorum Analyticorum* (Venice, 1553), f. 116. The Port Royal logicians added a fourth, disposition or method. Port Royal Logic, pp. 37–8.

(12) 119, 1. *Now as it is wisely order'd, that people depriv'd of one sense have the others in more perfection,* . . .

A commonplace which Steele had previously used to characterize the "Spectator" (*Spectator,* No. 4).

(13) 119, 7. . . . *these two last operations of the intellect were . . . almost totally extinguish'd in Crambe;* . . .

I. e. among people given to punning and plays on words. For the attitude of the Scriblerians and their contemporaries toward this form of "wit," see general note to Chapter VIII.

(14) 119, 19. . . . *for it is commonly said that a man* is *not the same he* was, *that madmen are* beside themselves, *and drunken men* come to themselves; *which shews, that few men have that most valuable logical endowment, Individuality.*

Warburton pointed out (*Works of Pope*, VI, 127 n.) that this is a satire on the following passage in Locke's *Essay concerning Human Understanding:*

But if it be possible for the same man to have distinct incommunicable consciousness at different times, it is past doubt the same man would at different times make different persons; which, we see, is the sense of mankind in the solemnest declaration of their opinions, human laws not punishing the mad man for the sober man's actions, nor the sober man for what the mad man did,—thereby making them two persons: which is somewhat explained by our way of speaking in English when we say such an one is 'not himself' or is 'beside himself;' in which phrases it is insinuated, as if those who now, or at least first used them, thought that self was changed; the self-same person was no longer in that man. Bk. II, chap. 27, sec. 20; Fraser, ed., I, 460–1.

Locke's theory is that individuality is based on identity of consciousness or memory. *Ibid.*, secs. 10–27.

The difficulties involved in Locke's definition of individuality were first called to general attention not by the immediate opponents of Locke but by Samuel Clarke in his famous quarrel with Collins over the materiality of the soul (for an account of this see the general note to Chapter XII, below). During the course of the quarrel Collins, who was maintaining the material nature of the soul, made use of Locke's argument. In answer Clarke said:

A Man, you say, who, during *a short Frenzy, kills* another, *and then returns to himself, without the least Consciousness of what he has done; cannot attribute that Action to himself;* and *therefore the mad Man and the sober Man are really two as distinct Persons as any two other Men in the World, and will be so considered in a Court of Judicature.* Extraordinary Reasoning indeed! Because in a *figurative* Sense a Man, when he is mad, is said *not to be himself;* and in a *forensick* Sense, is looked upon as not answerable for his *own Actions;* therefore in the *natural and philosophical* Sense also, *his Actions* are not *his own Actions,* but *another Person's;* and the *same Man is really two distinct Persons!* Clarke, *Works* (1738), III, 902.

Clarke also attacks Locke directly for this view. *Ibid.*, pp. 903–04.

In view of the interest which the Scriblerians took in this quarrel and their use of material from it later in the *Memoirs,* it does not seem improbable that the humorous possibilities in Locke's view were thus called to their attention and even that the satire here is aimed principally at Collins, of whom they were contemptuous, rather than at Locke.

(15) 119, 21. . . . *for he had seen it cut into commons:*

"COMMONS, a Proportion of Victuals, especially the Regular Diet of a College or Society," Bailey. Swift uses the word in the sense of a meal. "Imitation of Horace, Epist. I, vii, To Lord Oxford, A.D. 1713," l. 74.

(16) 119, 24. . . . *it would be the most lovely individual of the University.*

A double pun on "individual" and "university"; the phrase meaning in one sense "the loveliest indivisible thing in the whole, or universe" (cf. Bailey's definition— "UNIVERSITY, the whole in general, generality") and in another "the loveliest person among the colleges." Still other meanings might be read into the phrase, as "the loveliest problem of individuality among the logicians at the university" and "the loveliest individual portion served at the commons of the university," but as these are more farfetched it is doubtful if they were intended.

(17) 119, 25. . . . *a* substance *was that which was* subject to accidents; . . .

"A Substance is a Being subsisting of its self, and subject to Accidents." *Monitio Logica: or, an Abstract and Translation of Burgersdicius his Logick* (1697), p. 8.

(18) 119, 29. . . . *a good definition* of accident, *that it could be* present or absent without the destruction of the subject; . . .

"*A common Accident, is an universal, which may or may not inhere in the subject, without the destruction of the subject,* as *man* is the subject of *whiteness,* but the not *being* [white] doth not presently make him not to be a *man.*" J. Newton, *The Art of Logick* (1671), p. 13. The definition was the commonly accepted one based on Aristotle. *Topics,* I, v; cf. *ibid.,* Bks. II and III; Port Royal Logic, I, vi; Bailey, II, *s.v.*

(19) 119, 37. . . . *what he had seen at the Bear-garden?*

The bear garden was an amphitheater in Hockley-in-the-Hole where bear and bull baiting, dog fights, prize fights, and all sorts of rough sports took place. It was very popular not only among the lower classes but among some of the gentry. A contemporary description of the place is to be found in Preston's *Aesop at the Bear-garden, a Vision* (1715). This bear garden is not to be confused with the old one on the Bankside in Southwark, which was destroyed toward the end of the reign of William and Mary. Cf. above, p. 241, n. 44.

(20) 119, 37. . . . *he saw two men fight a prize;* . . .

One of the most popular exhibitions at the bear garden were prize fights, carried on by "two masters of the noble science of self-defence" as they were commonly called. Sometimes the fighting was done with fists, but more commonly with swords, daggers, staffs, cudgels, or other weapons. The following is a typical advertisement for one of these spectacles:

At the Bear Garden, in Hockley-in-the-Hole

A trial of skill to be performed between two profound masters of the noble science of defence, on Wednesday next, the 13th of July, 1709, at two o'clock precisely. I, George Gray, born in the City of Norwich, who has fought in most parts of the West Indies, viz., Jamaica, Barbadoes, and several other parts of the world, in all twenty-five times upon the stage, and was never yet worsted; and am now lately come to London, do invite James Harris to meet, and exercise at the following weapons,—back-sword, sword and dagger, sword and buckler, single falchon [a large broadsword like a scimitar], and case of falchons. I, James Harris, master of the said noble science of defence, who formerly *rid* in the Horse Guards, and hath fought 110 prizes, and never left a stage to any man, will not fail (God willing) to meet this brave and bold inviter, at the time and place appointed, desiring sharp swords, and from him no favour. No person to be upon the stage, but the seconds. Vivat Regina. Quoted by W. J. Pinks, *History of Clerkenwell,* p. 159.

A good description of one of these battles is given in the *Spectator,* No. 436, for July 21, 1712, by Steele.

(21) 120, 2. . . . *wounded the Butcher in the leg.*

The details given here are the conventional ones. It will be noted that in the advertisement given above, and in the account written by Steele, one of the combatants is a military man. In Steele's description, also, the combatants are distinguished by the colors red and blue and the fight ends with the sergeant's opponent being wounded in the leg. The only difference is in the time, which in the *Memoirs* is four o'clock and in the *Spectator* two.

(22) 120, 3. . . . *how the fellow runs through the prædicaments.*

The ten predicaments or categories of Aristotle in English are: substance (what a thing is), quantity, quality, relation (of one thing to another), action, passion (suffering or receiving), position (e.g., standing or sitting), where, when, and possession (as of a man having clothing). The value of these categories had been sharply attacked by seventeenth-century logicians. They were, say Arnauld and Nicole,

formed for the Birth of so many Mysteries, though, to say truth, of very little use, and so far from rectifying of Judgment, which is the Scope of Logic, that they frequently do much mischief; and that for two Causes which it will be worth while to display in this place.

The first is, That these Predicaments are things look'd upon as Things grounded upon Reason and Truth, whereas they are Things meerly Arbitrary, and which have no ground but in the Imagination of a Man, that has no Authority to prescribe Laws to others, who have as much Right as he, to dispose in the same, or any other Order, the Objects of Thinking, according to the Rules of Philosophy, which every one Embraces. . . .

The other Reason why we think this Series of Predicaments to be pernicious is this, because it occasions Men to satisfie themselves with the outward Rind of Words, instead of Profiting by the wholesom Fruit, and to believe they know all things, so they are able to say by rote certain Names of *Arbitrary* Signification, which yet imprint no clear or distinct *Ideas,* as we shall afterwards demonstrate." Port Royal Logic, pp. 58–60.

Chambers (1728) says,

These ten *Categories* of Aristotle, which logicians make such mysteries of, are now almost out of doors; and, in effect, are of little use: the less, as being things purely arbitrary, without any foundation, but in the imagination of a man, who had no authority to prescribe laws for ranging the objects of other peoples ideas. *S.v.* "Category."

(23) 120, 8. *At the same time he warn'd Martin, that what he now* learn'd *as a Logician, he must* forget *as a natural Philosopher;* . . .

This statement is worth noting as an especially succinct expression of the attitude toward formal logic that characterized the followers of the "new philosophy" from Bacon onward.

(24) 120, 12. . . . *that tho' he now taught them that accidents inher'd in the subject, they would find in time there was no such thing; and that colour, taste, smell, heat, and cold, were not in the things but only phantasms of our brains.*

In opposition to the scholastic tradition, the "new philosophers" of the seventeenth century maintained, as had Democritus and the Epicureans, that secondary qualities, such as color, taste, and smell, inhere not in objects but in the perceiver. Galileo declared,

But that external bodies, to excite in us these tastes, these odours, and these sounds, demand other than size, figure, number, and slow or rapid motion, I do not believe; and I judge that, if the ears, the tongue, and the nostrils were taken away, the figure, the numbers, and the motions would indeed remain, but not the odours nor the tastes nor the sounds, which, without the living animal, I do not believe are anything else than names, just as tickling is precisely nothing but a name if the armpit and the nasal membrane be removed; . . . *Opere,* IV, 336 ff.; quoted by E. A. Burtt, *Metaphysical Foundations of Modern Physical Science* (1925), p. 78.

The distinction between primary and secondary qualities here introduced was vigorously advanced by Descartes (*Principia Philosophiæ* [Amsterdam, 1644], III, 69–71), Hobbes (*English Works,* Sir William Molesworth, ed. [1839], III, 2 ff.), Boyle (*Origine of Formes and Qualities* [1666], pp. 10, 43, 100–01; cf. "An Introduction to the History of Particular Qualities," *Tracts* [1671], p. 18), Malebranche (*De la Recherche de la vérité* [1674], VI, ii), and Locke, by whom it was expounded at length (*Hum. Understand.* [1690], Bk. II, chap. viii, sec. 9 *et seq.*). Its acceptance after Locke is illustrated by Samuel Clarke's statement that "the Vulgar thinks Colours and Sounds to be properties inherent in Bodies, when indeed they are purely Thoughts of the Mind (*Demonstration of the Being and Attributes of God* [1704], prop. viii, sec. 2) and his treatment of Collins when the latter failed to make it (*Works,* III, 759, 796). That the distinction was being taught in the universities is suggested by Jack Lizard's attempt to persuade his mother, who had burned her fingers in lighting the lamp for her teapot, that there is no such thing as heat in fire and his other fooleries during his visit home after a year and a half at Oxford as described by Steele in the *Guardian,* No. 24.

(25) 120, 15. . . . *he would demand the Characteristicks of Relations.*

He would, in other words, demand to know those things by which we distinguish relationships, or, more simply, the nature of relation. The phrase merely serves to introduce Crambe's burlesque examples based on Locke's definition.

(26) 120, 18. . . . *a Cuckold, a losing gamester, a man that had not din'd, a young heir that was kept short by his father, might all be known by their countenance;* . . .

These examples are ridiculous applications of Locke's definition of relation as the *extension* of the mind from a particular thing to an associated one. The faces and expressions of these men bring up associated ideas which identify them as being cuckolds, gamesters, etc. Cf. *Hum. Understand.*, Bk. II, chap. xxv, sec. 1.

(27) 120, 23. *. . . when they came to the Tenth prædicament: Crambe affirmed, that his Habitus was more of a substance than he was; for his cloaths could better subsist without him, than he without his cloaths.*

The jest at bottom turns on two senses in which the word "accident" was used by logicians. In one sense the word was used to refer to "Whatsoever does not essentially belong to a Thing, tho' it be a Substance in it self, but casually, as the Cloths a Man has on, the Mony in his Pocket, &c." (Bailey) and in another it was used "In opposition to Substance, when it is in its Essence or Nature to adhere or subsist in some Substance, and cannot be [i.e. exist] alone . . ." *Ibid.*; cf. Port Royal Logic, I, vi (vii); J. Newton, *The Art of Logick,* p. 13; Chambers, *s.v.* In order to fit their jest into the context, however, the Scriblerians express the problem in terms of the tenth predicament, *habitus*—"a Manner, after which Clothes, or any thing like Clothes, are put about the Body, *appended* or any other way adjoined to it." *Monitio Logica* (1697), p. 30; cf. M. Blundeville, *The Arte of Logicke* (1619), p. 44, Port Royal Logic, I, iii.

The logical problem of the double nature of clothes as both substance and accident had been solved by the recognition of the possibility of substances assuming the character of accidents by modifying other substances or of two substances, such as *man* and his *clothes,* combining to make a new whole. Port Royal Logic, I, vi.

(28) 120, 32. *Martin told him, that never having seen but one Lord Mayor, the Idea of that Lord Mayor always return'd to his mind; that he had great difficulty to abstract a Lord Mayor from his Fur, Gown, and Gold Chain; . . . disturb'd his imagination.*

Martinus is here illustrating the doctrine of Locke, whose theory of abstraction is that man's mind extracts from the observation of a series of particular or individual things of the same type a composite of common characteristics to which he applies a general or "universal" name. *Hum. Understand.* Bk. II, chap. xi, sec. 9, *et seq.*, III, iii. It follows that since Martinus has seen only one lord mayor he cannot make a composite of the common characteristics of lord mayors, and hence cannot achieve an abstract idea of one.

(29) 120, 37. *On the other hand Crambe, to shew himself of a more penetrating genius, swore he could frame a conception of a Lord Mayor not only without his Horse . . . but even without stature, . . . or any body; which he suppos'd was the abstract of a Lord Mayor.*

Crambe takes the scholastic view that there exists a *substantial form* of a lord mayor which can be conceived independently of any or all of the *accidents,* such as the horse, gown, gold chain, etc., commonly associated with it. For the seventeenth and early eighteenth century attacks on the doctrine of *substantial forms* see below, p. 260, n. 62.

To this passage Warburton appended the following note:

This is not a fair representation of what is said in the *Essay on Human Understanding* concerning *general and abstract ideas*. But serious writers have done that Philosopher the same injustice.

Warburton's opinion is, of course, mistaken. The passage, far from being a satire on Locke, is a burlesque of the views which Locke himself derided.

(30) 121, 1. . . . *an* Universale *was not the object of imagination, and that there was no such thing in reality, or a* parte Rei.
  Cornelius here takes the view of Locke, who declares:

It is plain, by what has been said that *general* and *universal* belong not to the real existence of things; but are the inventions and creatures of the understanding, made by it, for its own use and concern only signs, whether words or ideas. Words are general, as has been said, when used for signs of general ideas, and so are applicable indifferently to many particular things: and ideas are general, when they are set up as the representatives of many particular things; but universality belongs not to things themselves, which are all of them particular in their existence; even those words and ideas which in their signification are general. *Hum. Understand.*, Bk. iii, chap. iii, sec. 11.

(31) 121, 2. . . . Clysters . . .
  "CLYSTER, a fluid Medicine of different Qualities injected into the Bowels by the Fundament," Bailey.

(32) 121, 4. Quod aptum est inesse multis, . . .
  I.e. that which is fitting to belong to many.

(33) 121, 8. . . . *they were not strict logical definitions:*
  According to seventeenth-century books of logic a proper definition of a thing should include a statement of the genus and of the differences. Cf. R. Crakanthorp, *Logicae* (1641), p. 35; J. Le Clerc, *Logica* (1692), pp. 93–4; *Monitio Logica* (1697), ii, 6; Chambers, *s.v.* "Definition," etc.
  Like other parts of formal logic, definitions were attacked sharply in the seventeenth century as useless intricacies. Locke casts them aside for clear and practical explanations, saying, "For definitions . . . being only the explaining of one word by several others, so that the meaning or idea it stands for may be certainly known; languages are not always so made according to the rules of logic, that every term can have its signification exactly and clearly expressed by two others [i.e. one of *genus* and one of *differentia*]. *Hum. Understand.*, Bk. iii, chap. iii, sec. 10. Further, Locke declares that simple ideas are undefinable. *Ibid.*, chap. iv.

(34) 121, 9. . . . *In an advertisement of a Dog stolen or strayed,* . . .
  Such advertisements appeared frequently in the newspapers of the time. Their wording is illustrated by these typical examples:

Run away from the Duke of Rutland's at Southampton-House, on Thursday the with Brown, Yellow, and White Spots, his Eyes of different Colours, and his Tail 14th Instant in the Evening, a little Danish Dog: He is spotted all over like Marble turning upon his Back . . . [for the return of which a guinea reward is offered]. *Daily Courant*, Saturday, January 16, 1714.

A Fine Black Greyhound Bitch, lost the 24th of March, at Night, near New-gate: Her Face is Black, with a Scald a little below her Eye (with the Hair off) the Breadth of a Sixpence, a white Breast, 4 white Feet, one Fore-leg white, a little White on the end of her Tail. Whoever brings her to Henry Patry, Seed-Man, at the Frying-pan in Newgate street, London, or discovers where she is, or has been since that time, so she may be had again, shall have 20s Reward. *Post Boy,* May 8-11, 1714.

(35) 121, 14. . . . *yet they contain'd a faint image of the prædicabilia,* . . .

The predicables (or universals), according to seventeenth-century books of logic, are five: genus, species, proprium, differentia, and accidens. M. Blundeville, *op. cit.,* p. 6; R. Crakanthorp, *Logicae* (1641), p. 3; Port Royal Logic, I, vi; *Monitio Logica* (1697), p. 30; Chambers and Bailey, etc.

(36) 121, 16. . . . *and were highly subservient to the common purposes of life; often discovering things that were lost, both animate and inanimate.*

A comparable revelation of the much-satirized pedantic and patronizing atti-tude of the "learned" toward practical affairs is made by Sir Nicholas Gimcrack in Shadwell's *Virtuoso.* Cf. above, p. 179, n. 10.

(37) 121, 31. . . . *and it is properly said by the Logicians* quod pariunt scientiam, opinionem, *they* beget *science, opinion,* &c.

The quotation seems to have been made up by the Scriblerians for their pur-pose.

(38) 121, 33. . . . *and therefore in Logick they are said to be of the first* Figure.

Crambe's love of punning here carries him too far. The first figure is that in which the middle term is the subject in the major proposition and the attribute in the minor. It is one of the rules of this figure that the major proposition must be a universal; hence Crambe can say that universal propositions are "of the first *Figure.*" But universal propositions must also be the majors of the second figure and are used in the third figure so that Crambe's statement means nothing from the point of view of logic.

(39) 121, 35. . . . *and therefore plac'd in the third or last figure, or rank.*

The third figure is that in which the middle term is twice taken as the sub-ject; e.g.,

There are wicked Men in the most flourishing Fortunes—
All wicked Men are miserable;
Therefore there are Men miserable in the most flourishing fortunes. Port Royal Logic, III, vii.

Crambe's point is based on the fact that by the rules of this figure one of the propositions, and hence the conclusion, must be particular—i.e. "singular"— Bailey. *Ibid.*

(40) 121, 36. . . . *all the rules of Syllogisms naturally follow.*

In laying out Crambe's ten rules for syllogisms, the Scriblerians were not bur-lesquing any coherent body of logic but simply were drawing from the vast body of axioms and rules of syllogistic reasoning such as fitted their purpose.

(41) 122, 8. . . . *the* Individua vaga . . .

"INDIVIDUUM *vagum* (in Logick) is that which though it signifies but one Thing, yet may be any of that Kind; as when we say, *a Man, a certain Person,* or *one did so,*" Bailey.

(42) 122, 34. . . . *an Enthymen?*

"An Enthymen *is an imperfect Syllogism, inferring the conclusion from some one proposition only; as, a man is a living creature, therefore he hath a soul.* . . . [It] is a perfect *Syllogism* in respect of the *firm proof,* and *imperfect* in respect of the *evidence* of the *conclusion,* one of the premises being understood, but not expressed." Newton, *op. cit.,* pp. 101–02. In his *History of John Bull,* Arbuthnot has John say: "I desire to know whether you will have it by way of Syllogism, Enthymen, Dilemma, or Sorites." Aitken, p. 276.

(43) 123, 7. . . . *not to use* simpliciter & secundum quid, *provided Martin would part with* materialiter & formaliter:

These distinctions were employed by the scholastic metaphysicians. *Simpliciter* indicates that a thing is being referred to either simply and absolutely or totally; *secundum quid* that the reference to the thing is in some respect. By *materialiter* is meant the consideration of a thing in itself or in its proper nature and by *formaliter* the consideration of it under a special point of view or in certain connections. Cf. Pierre Nova, *Dictionnaire de terminologie scholastique* (Paris, 1885). The satire of the Scriblerians lies, of course, in the suggestion that these distinctions were merely defensive armor with which antagonists could parry the blows of their adversaries.

(44) 123, 10. . . . *Suarez,* . . .

Francisco Suarez (1548–1617), a Jesuit and professor of theology in several of the leading Spanish universities, was the last great representative of Scholasticism. In his own day he enjoyed an enormous reputation for wisdom. His general philosophical position was that of a moderate Thomist, and on the question of universals, the point on which the Scriblerians satirize him, he endeavored to maintain something of a middle ground between the extreme realism of Duns Scotus and the nominalism of William of Ockham. His greatest and most lasting work was his huge *Tractatus de legibus ac Deo legislatore,* and it is chiefly as a philosophical jurist that he is now remembered. He was a voluminous writer, the first collected edition of his works (Venice, 1740–57) filling twenty-three folio volumes.

His general reputation in England at the time of Queen Anne (references to him are comparatively rare) is indicated by Swift's inclusion of him in the phrase ". . . the most perplexed and perplexing follower of Aristotle from Scotus to Suarez . . ." *Works,* III, 97. Sir William Petty, a scientist and modern, however, had some time earlier included him among the ten greatest modern geniuses. *The Petty-Southwell Correspondence,* Marquis of Lansdowne, ed. (1928), p. 158.

(45) 123, 10. . . . *Thomas Aquinas,* . . .

The reputation of St. Thomas Aquinas (c. 1225–1275) in the first half of the eighteenth century is indicated by Bishop William Warburton's description of him, in his commentary on Pope's *Essay on Criticism,* as

a truly great genius, who, in those blind ages, was the same in theology, that our Friar Bacon was in natural philosophy; less happy than our countryman in this, that he soon became surrounded with a number of dark glossers, who never left him till they had extinguished the radiance of that light, which had pierced through the thickest night of monkery . . . Pope's *Works,* I, 112; E. & C., II, 108.

Swift owned a copy of the *Summa Theologica* printed in 1585. H. Williams, *Dean Swift's Library,* No. 257.

(46) 123, 12. . . . *a taste of some of them.*
The list given is varied in character. Somewhat more than half of the entries are genuine topics of discussion drawn from Aquinas or Suarez. Of the remainder, some are burlesques of questions in Aquinas, some were apparently suggested by the discussion in the *Summa Theologica,* and others were probably pure inventions of the Scriblerians introduced to fill out the list and heighten the satire.

(47) 123, 15. . . . *the* Arbor Porphyriana . . .
The "Porphyrian Tree," whose identity with the tree of knowledge in the Garden of Eden Martinus and Crambe are to debate, was a figure employed by the Schoolmen for diagramming a scale of being. It consists of three columns of words, the middle of which contains the genera and species, while the outer columns contain the differences. It was frequently drawn in the form of a tree. The following is a common form:

SUBSTANCE

Thinking   Extended

BODY

Inanimate   Animate

ANIMAL

Irrational   Rational

MAN

This   That

PLATO

The *arbor porphyriana* is also called *scala praedicamentalis.* Cf. Chambers.

(48) 123, 19. III. *Whether one, or many be first? or if one doth not suppose the notion of many?* Suarez.
This thesis is drawn from Suarez only in a general way. Suarez discusses the question of the one and the many at considerable length, reviewing the previously expressed opinions of Aquinas, Cajetan, Scotus, and others and developing the problem in various directions. *Metaphysicarum Disputationum* (Venice, 1605), Dis. IV. He does not take up the exact problem posed by the Scriblerians. Unity, he declares, is primary and basic, but the concept is negative in character since it says no more about a thing than that it is not many. *Ibid.,* sec. 2. In another connection he explains that a thing may have both unity and multiplicity, since unity may be considered as an act and multiplicity as a power. *Ibid.,* sec. 4, No. 4.

(49) 123, 23. V. *Whether there are in human understanding potential falsities?* affirm'd.

This burlesque problem was probably suggested to the Scriblerians by Aquinas' discussion of the question "Whether there can be falsehood in the intellect of an Angel?" *Summa Theologica,* Quest. LVIII, art. 5; Pt. I, No. 2, p. 372.

(50) 123, 25. VI. *Whether God loves a* possible Angel *better than an* actually-existent flie? deny'd.

A burlesque of Aquinas' Quest. XX, arts. 2, 3, and 4: "Whether God loves all things? Whether God loves all things equally? Whether God always loves more the better things?" *Ibid.,* No. 1; pp. 286–93.

(51) 123, 27. VII. *If Angels pass from one extreme to another without going through the middle?* Aquinas.

In answer to his Quest. LIII, art. 2, "Whether an Angel passes through intermediate space?" Thomas concludes that ". . . if an angel's motion be not continuous, it is possible for him to pass from one extreme to another without going through the middle." *Ibid.,* No. 2; p. 319.

(52) 123, 29. VIII. *If Angels know things more clearly in a morning?* Aquinas.

Aquinas' question is "Whether there is a 'Morning' and an 'Evening' knowledge in the Angels?" Quest. LVIII, art. 6. To this he answers,

The expression "morning" and "evening" knowledge was devised by Augustine; who interprets the six days wherein God made heaven and earth, not as ordinary days measured by the solar circuit, since the sun was only made on the fourth day, but as one day, namely, the day of angelic knowledge as directed to six classes of things. As in the ordinary day, morning is the beginning, and evening the close of the day, so, their knowledge of the primordial existence of things is called morning knowledge; and this is according as things exist in the Word. But their knowledge of the very existence of the thing created, as it stands in its own nature, is termed evening knowledge; because the existence of things flows from the Word, as from a kind of primordial principle; and this flow is terminated in the existence which they have in themselves. *Ibid.,* pp. 374–5.

(53) 123, 31. IX. *Whether every Angel hears what one Angel says to another?* deny'd. Aquinas.

Aquinas' reply to this question (Quest. CVII, art. 5) is that

. . . a thing can be ordered through some cause to one thing and not to another; consequently the concept of one (angel) may be known by one and not by another; and therefore an angel can perceive the speech of one angel to another; whereas others do not, not through the obstacle of local distance, but on account of the will so ordering, as explained above. *Ibid.,* No. 3; pp. 424–5.

(54) 123, 33. X. *If temptation be* proprium quarto modo *of the Devil?* deny'd. Aquinas.

The question in Aquinas reads simply *Utrum tentare sit proprium diaboli*— "Whether to tempt is proper [i.e. peculiar] to the devil?" Quest. CXIV, art. 2, p. 498. By making the question one of *proprium quarto modo* the Scriblerians narrow it sharply, this mode being that in which the predication is a characteristic peculiar to a species and common to all individuals in it (as laughing is to man), though not necessarily at any determinate time (as man has always the faculty of laughing but an individual man may not be doing so at any given moment). Aquinas does not discuss the question in this specific form, but it is clear from what he says that he would deny it.

(55) 123, 34. XI. *Whether one Devil can illuminate another?* Aquin.

This punning question was no doubt suggested by Aquinas' discussion of *Utrum unus angelus illuminet alium*—"Whether one Angel can enlighten another?"—Quest. cvi, art. 1, p. 408.

(56) 123, 36. XII. *If there would have been any females born in the state of Innocence?* Aquinas.

The problem in Aquinas reads "Whether, in the Primitive State, women would have been born?" Quest. xcix, art. 2. His answer is that "In the state of innocence, both sexes would have been begotten." *Ibid.*, p. 344.

(57) 124, 1. XIII. *If the Creation was finish'd in six days, because six is the most perfect number; or if six be the most perfect number because the Creation was finished in six days?* Aquinas.

Aquinas does not appear to have discussed this specific problem. It may have been suggested to the Scriblerians by his "Treatise on the Work of the Six Days."

(58) 124, 7. XIV. An præter *esse reale* actualis essentiæ sit aliud *esse necessarium* quo res actualiter existat?

The question, which illustrates better than any of the other theses devised or selected by the Scriblerians the type of metaphysical problem which they and the other antischolastics thought mere futile quibbling, was drawn directly from Suarez' *Metaphysicarum Disputationum*, Dis. xxxi, sec. 5. In his discussion Suarez takes up the problem of the relation between the existence and essence of a thing. He thinks that the two cannot be separated, one being intrinsically a part of the other. Sec. 12. On this point he disagreed with the Thomists.

(59) 124, 11. . . . *banish Metaphysicks out of Spain,* . . .

The proverbial gravity and propensity toward philosophical profundities of the Spaniards, as illustrated in Suarez, probably accounts for the selection of Spain as the country in which the project is to be tried.

(60) 124, 14. . . . *nobody should use any Compound or Decompound of the Substantial Verbs, but as they are read in the common conjugations;* . . .

By "substantial verbs" the Scriblerians mean verbs of substance or being, i.e. the copulas *is, was,* etc. After explaining the process of abstraction, or separating accidents from any body or substance, Hobbes says,

From the same fountain spring those insignificant words, *abstract substance, separated essence,* and the like; as also that confusion of words derived from the Latin verb *est,* as *essence, essentiality, entity, entitative;* besides *reality, aliquiddity, quiddity, &c.* which could never have been heard of among such nations as do not copulate their names by the verb *is,* but by adjective verbs, as runneth, readeth, &c. or by the mere placing of one name after another; and yet seeing such nations compute and reason, it is evident that philosophy has no need of those words *essence, entity,* and other the like barbarous terms. *Elements of Philosophy,* Pt. I, sec. 3, No. 4; *Works,* Sir William Molesworth, ed. (1839–45), I, 34.

By "decompound" is meant a compound composed of parts which are themselves compounds.

(61) 124, 16. . . . *if you debar a Metaphysician from* ens, essentia, entitas, subsistentia, &c. *there is an end of him.*

Ens is a Scholastic term signifying being—i.e. all that exists or can exist either in reality or in our intelligence. Cf. *Summa Theologica,* Pt. I, Quest. III, art. 4; Pierre Nova, *op. cit., s.v;* Chambers, *s.v. Essentia* had two meanings among the Schoolmen, the first denoting "the whole essential perfection of a being, and consequently its entity, with all its intrinsic, or essential, and necessary attributes taken together," and the other denoting "the principal, and most intimate of all the attributes of a thing; or that which agrees to every such thing, and such alone, and that always, and in such manner, as that the mind, with all its attention cannot perceive any thing prior thereto," Chambers. The *Entitas* is "a physical ens, or being, considered according to what it is in its natural capacity," Chambers; cf. Nova. *Subsistentia* is the mode by which a thing exists in itself and not in another. Cf. Nova.

(62) 124, 20. . . . *that* Substantial Forms, *a race of harmless beings which had lasted for many years, and afforded a comfortable subsistence to many poor Philosophers, should be now hunted down like so many Wolves* . . .

According to St. Thomas, two conditions are necessary to a substantial form.

One of them is that the form be the principle of substantial being to the thing of which it is the form: and I speak not of the effective but of the form principle, whereby a thing is, and is called a *being.* Hence follows the second condition, namely that the form and matter combine together in one being, which is not the case with the effective principle together with that to which it gives being. This is the being in which a composite substance subsists, which is one in being, and consists of matter and form. *Summa Contra Gentiles* ii. 68; English Dominican Fathers, tr. (1923), II, 171.

No single part of Scholastic metaphysics was more sharply attacked in the seventeenth century than the doctrine of substantial forms; from Bacon to Locke (to remain within the boundaries of the century) condemnations of this doctrine increased steadily. Indeed, much of the complaint against the Schoolmen for their "barbarous terms," "unintelligible distinctions," "mysterious jargon," and so on referred to Scholastic disputes over the character and attributes of substantial forms.

Of the doctrine of substantial forms, Pierre Bayle says,

There is no Question in Natural Philosophy, that is a clearer Proof of the Power of Prejudices than this. They must needs darken the Mind with respect to the most evident Notions, since there are so many People, who can't see the Impossibility of extracting a Substance from the Bosom of matter, unless it was there before, or unless it be produc'd by a true Creation. The Peripateticks tell you very coldly, or rather they passionately maintain, that Forms do not exist in their Subject, and that nevertheless they are produc'd by an Action which must not be call'd Creation but Education. This Opinion would be the most monstrous thing in the World, if it were not a more amazing Prodigy to see such a Number of Learned and Ingenious Men, espouse still at this Day, the Doctrine of Substantial Forms. Bayle, "Heidanus," n. E; cf. "Gorlaeus," A, "Morin," M.

For some other hostile opinions see Descartes, *Discours de la methode,* E. Gilson, ed. (Paris, 1925), pp. 341–2, 384, 454; Hobbes, *Works,* I, 34, III, 32, 381–2, IV, 61; Boyle, *Works,* I, 411, III, 7–49, IV, 451, V, 518, VI, 223; Malebranche, *De la recherche de la vérité,* I, xvii, 3–4, T. Taylor, tr. (2d ed., 1700), pp. 38–9; Locke, *Essay concerning Human Understanding,* Bk. III, chap. vi, sec. 10; Shaftesbury, *Characteristicks* (1711), I, 289–90, II, 354–5; and Chambers, *s.v.* "Form."

(63) 124, 26. . . . *the Gentlemen-ushers at court;* . . .

The gentlemen-ushers were minor functionaries whose duties consisted in the arrangement and observance of small court formalities and in attendance on the person of the sovereign or other member of the royal family to whom they were attached. In the time of George II, the annual salary ranged from £200 for the gentleman-ushers of the Privy-Chamber down to £100 for those attached to the princesses. Cf. *The True State of England. Containing the Particular Duty, Business and Salary Of Every Officer . . . In All the Publick Offices . . . ,* (1734).

As one would expect, the Scriblerians were contemptuous of this post and its holders. Swift, after dining with a group of gentlemen-ushers at Windsor, called them "scurvy company" (*Journ.,* August 7, 1711), and later used them as illustrations of pedantic concern over empty form and ceremony. *Works,* XI, 79 ff.; cf. V, 403. In 1727, Gay, with the approval of his friends, indignantly rejected an offer of the post of gentleman-usher to the three-year-old Princess Louisa (Swift's *Corres.,* III, 426–7, 431), though he was seriously in need of the salary.

(64) 124, 31. . . . *a reward for such as could find out a* fourth Figure *in* Logick, *as well as for those who shou'd discover the* Longitude.

Like the squaring of the circle, the problem of a fourth figure in logic has been a favorite exercise with ingenious minds since antiquity. In the course of time many solutions have been offered, but on strict examination all of these have been discovered either to be unsound or, more commonly, simply a disguised or inverted version of one of the three standard figures. The most common form offered for a fourth figure is that in which the middle term serves as the predicate in the major and the subject in the minor. This mode was rejected by Aristotle and his followers as not a valid figure (cf. *Organon,* O. F. Owen, tr. [1889], I, 89, n. 2; 137); it was, however, accepted by many, including the Port Royal logicians. Port Royal Logic, pp. 234–6. Chambers says some prefer this figure before all others on the ground that in it the medium has its natural situation. *S.v.,* "Figure."

For the contemporary offer of a reward for the discovery of a practical means of working out the longitude and the many futile efforts to solve this problem satisfactorily, see below, p. 334, n. 13.

CHAPTER VIII

The present chapter is the most purely facetious in the *Memoirs*. Apart from a final and very good satire on Cornelius' obedience to ancient authority, it is given over to Crambe's exploits as a punster. Punning, though frowned upon by judicious critics such as Addison,[1] was exceptionally popular in the early eighteenth century. All the Scriblerians were given to it, but none so much as Swift. All his life the Dean delighted in puns and word plays of all sorts,[2] and during the years of his Irish "exile" he devoted a great deal of time and energy to "pun-ick wars" and collaborations with Tom Sheridan, a redoubtable punster whose *The Art of Punning; or, the Flower of Languages* (1719) was the most ambitious effort at this kind of humor in the period. In the autumn of 1716 Arbuthnot, Pope, and Gay were apparently in a punning mood. One or more of them published a little pamphlet entitled *God's Revenge Against Punning, Shewing the Miserable Fates of Persons addicted to this Crying Sin, in Court and Town*.[3] And it seems possible that at the same time Arbuthnot was responsible for *An Heroi-Comical Epistle From a certain Doctor To a certain Gentle-Woman, In Defence of the most Antient Art of Punning*.[4]

This chapter as it now stands is a combination of two chapters in the original manuscript—chapter eight, "Anatomy," and chapter nine, "How Crambe had some Words with his Master." Fortunately, through a printer's mistake in preparing several copies of one (Griffith, No. 566) of the two issues of Volume III, Part II, of the 1742 octavo edition of Pope's works, enough of the missing chapter has been preserved to indicate its nature and suggest what may have happened to it. In this issue the original chapter nine [5] occupied half of page 61, all of pages 62–3, and half of page 64. Apparently after the sheets were printed it was decided to cut out a large part of the chapter and combine the remainder with chapter eight. Consequently a separate sheet was printed containing the last paragraph of chapter eight, which appears on the top of page 61, and, without a chapter break, a condensed version of chapter nine. This is followed by chapter ten and the regular text beginning halfway down the verso side of the sheet. Since this substitute leaf was to take the place of two leaves, it was numbered page 61 on the recto and page 64 on the verso. In preparing several of the copies,[6] however, the printers seem to have assumed that only one leaf was to be canceled; they therefore introduced the

1. *Spectator*, No. 61; cf. *Tatler*, No. 32, *Spectator*, No. 504; also *Guardian*, No. 36, *Spectator*, No. 396.

2. Cf. *Corres., Works*, and *Poems, passim*. For an account of his punning with Pembroke, the Berkeleys, and others see *Corres.*, I, 373–4.

3. Reprinted in The Third Volume of the Swift-Pope *Miscellanies* (1732), pp. 52–6. It is listed in the 1742 *Miscellanies* as by Mr. Pope and Mr. Gay.

4. Irving, pp. 145–6.

5. The situation is confused by the fact that in the 1741 quarto and the companion issue of the one referred to (i.e. Griffith, No. 567) chapter ten has been numbered chapter nine in the text, though not in the tables of contents. No attempt was made in the editions published in Pope's lifetime to revise the tables of contents or to correct all the subsequent chapter numbers.

6. Copies of this issue are comparatively rare and I have been able to examine only three. All these three contain the printer's mistake described, but it seems likely that the error was caught and the cancellation made properly in part of the issue.

revised leaf in place of the second of the two leaves (pp. 63–4) in the text and left the first leaf (pp. 61–2) untouched. The result is that in these copies both the revised version and half of the original version appear.

Pope may have decided to cut down chapter nine because of something contained in the part which we do not have, or he may have decided that much of the punning was not especially brilliant and could be eliminated without loss. A plausible and somewhat more satisfactory explanation, however, is perhaps to be found in Crambe's queries as to "what governs all England but the words Passive Obedience and Liberty?" and "what divides good Christians but the words Transubstantiation, Consubstantiation, and No-substantiation." Though innocently meant, Crambe's questions might be taken by the hypercritical to imply that these were merely empty shibboleths—a suggestion highly offensive to serious-minded patriots and Christians and one which Pope, who had been under attack from both Catholics and Protestants for the deistical tendencies of his *Essay on Man* and *Universal Prayer,* would therefore be anxious to avoid. Since the Scriblerians did not see this objection before, one suspects that if this were the true cause of the change the alteration is to be laid at the door of the Rev. William Warburton, D.D., who read the *Memoirs* before publication.[7]

Before the revision, chapter eight, containing Crambe's adventures with the corpse, concluded with the paragraph in the present text beginning "The Justice stared . . ." and ending with the sentence "It was with great difficulty that the Justice was convinc'd, till they sent for the Finisher of human laws, of whom the corps had been purchas'd; who looking near the left ear, knew his own work, and gave Oath accordingly." Such part of the unrevised text of the next chapter as was preserved in the manner described above follows:

How Crambe *had some Words with his Master.*

What hath possessed thee, Crambe (cry'd Martin) that thou wilt never forsake that impertinent custom of Punning? neither my counsel nor my example can reform thee; assuredly thou governest thy self by erroneous Maxims. Far from it (answers Crambe) my life is as orderly as my Dictionary, for by my dictionary I order my life. Order (reply'd Martin) is not only the beauty of all good writing, but the very Quintessence of all sound Morality. You have liv'd long enough with me to know mine and your own business through every hour and every day of the week. I no sooner rise but I—Crambe interrupts him—repeat your Latin prayer, play a tune on your Guitar, breakfast on water-gruel without sugar, dine punctually at half an hour after one, at three a clock take a quarter of an hours nap, and at nine are at the Club. Your Diet and Studies on Mondays, are Apple-pye and Astrology; Tuesdays, Natural history and Ling; Wednesdays, Poetry and fasting; Thursdays, Mutton and Mathematicks; Fridays, Divinity and more fasting; and on Saturdays you take physick.

As to my self, my method of life is neither borrow'd from the Ancients nor Moderns: Let it suffice to tell you, that I have made a

7. Cf. above, p. 64.

Kalendar of radical words for all the seasons, months, and days of the year, and that every day I am under the dominion of a certain Word. For example, this 24th of June, I am govern'd by the word Cord; I accord favours to such as ask them, live in concord with all the world, prevent discord among my neighbours, tune my harpsicord, cord my trunk, put on my corded drugget, and record the actions of famous men. Monstrous! (says Martin, lifting up his hands and eyes) such an unnatural, unaccountable, unintelligible, unpolite, unprofitable Jargon! There it is now (answers Crambe) this is your day for *Uns*: The whole world is govern'd by Words. What governs all England but the words Passive Obedience, and Liberty? What divides good Christians but the words Transubstantiation, Consubstantiation, and No-substantiation. Now

(1) 125, 8. . . . *he acquir'd the Title of the* Invincible Doctor.

Doctor Irrefragibilis was the title given to Alexander of Hales (d. 1245), a celebrated teacher of theology, who was the first to attempt a systematic exposition of the Catholic doctrine after the metaphysical and physical works of Aristotle had become known in the West. His greatest work, the *Summa Universæ Theologiæ* (begun in 1231 and left unfinished) provided a model both in method and arrangement for Aquinas' *Summa*.

(2) 125, 11. . . . *there were only two, the* Colon *and the* Aichos, *according to Hippocrates.*

Since Arbuthnot knew his Hippocrates thoroughly (see his essays on air and aliment and his "Dissertation concerning the Doses of Medicines given by Ancient Physicians" in his *Tables of Ancient Coins* [1727], pp. 282 ff.), it must be assumed that this statement is correct. It is not clear, however, on what it is based or from what work it is derived.

(3) 125, 20. . . . *and I will bring you a monster that differs from the common rule* . . .

Monsters and freaks of nature of all kinds held a peculiar fascination for both scientists and laymen in the seventeenth and early eighteenth centuries. The *Philosophical Transactions* during the period were filled with accounts of double births, giants, pygmies, strange growths, and abnormalities of all sorts, while public exhibitions of living freaks (like that in which Martinus first sees his double mistress) were exceptionally popular with the public. Sir Hans Sloane collected an astonishingly large number of handbills advertising freaks. H. Morley, *Memoirs of Bartholomew Fair* (1859), p. 315.

(4) 125, 24. *Produce me a man now of the age of an Antediluvian, of the strength of Sampson, or the size of the Giants.*

Cornelius is here echoing the challenge of the extreme followers of the ancients who maintained that all nature is decaying and cited statements in the Scripture and in the writings of the ancients concerning giants as evidence of the decline of man's stature. Cf. R. F. Jones, *Ancients and Moderns*, pp. 23–42. By the end of the century enough study had been made of the subject of giants to eliminate this argument. The contemporary scientific view was expressed by Dr. Thomas Molyneux in a paper on giants published in the *Philosophical Transactions of the Royal Society* in 1700. After discussing and describing modern giants, he considers those mentioned in the Scriptures and elsewhere and concludes that those for whom there was any evidence of size were not significantly larger than those of modern times. As for others still larger, he says he has not met with proof or authority of sufficient weight to convince him "and till some such evidence be produced, we may look upon all the stories of those extravagantly Gigantick men, to be little better than the Fables of the Poets of old, or the Whims and Romances of some modern Credulous and Inventive men." xx (1700–01), 507–08.

One of the best satires on the decline of man is, of course, to be found at the end of the seventh chapter of the second book of *Gulliver's Travels,* where he diverts himself by reading a Brobdingnagian treatise on the subject. *Works,* viii, 141–2.

(5) 125, 30. . . . *I will still believe, with Hippocrates, that the blood of the Ancients had a flux and reflux from the heart, like a Tide.*

The movement of the blood is not discussed in the works of Hippocrates, but the theory that it acted in the fashion of an *euripus,* or tide, was, of course, the commonly held view from the ancient times (cf. e. g., Galen, ii, 787–830, v, 149–80, 537 ff.) until Harvey announced his discovery in 1619.

(6) 125, 31. . . . *Consider how Luxury hath introduced new diseases,* . . .
Cf. Pope's

> But just disease to luxury succeeds,
> And ev'ry death its own avenger breeds.
> *Essay on Man,* Ep. iii, ll. 165–6.

The theme was a favorite one with pulpit reformers, who usually had in mind the pox, or "French disease," a malady which was strongly associated with luxury and licentiousness. Swift echoed the theme in *Gulliver's Travels;* when calling up the dead in Glubbdubdrib, Gulliver is shocked to observe how much the human race has degenerated in the past hundred years and reflects with melancholy upon

How the pox under all its consequences and denominations had altered every lineament of an English countenance, shortened the size of bodies, unbraced the nerves, relaxed the sinews and muscles, introduced a sallow complexion, and rendered the flesh loose and rancid.

For contrast he calls up "some English yeomen of the old stamp," who were "once so famous for the simplicity of their manners, diet and dress," and for their other virtues. *Works,* viii, 211.

(7) 126, 8. . . . *Having purchas'd the body of a Malefactor,* . . .
Tyburn and other gallows were the chief legitimate source of bodies for anatomical dissection. It was even the grisly custom for surgeons to visit the jail just before a hanging and bargain with the criminal for his body. Cf. *Spectator,* No. 504, by Steele.

(8) 126, 10. . . . *near the Pest-fields in St. Giles's, at a little distance from Tyburn Road.*

The Pest-fields was a piece of ground on the northern edge of London where, after the great plague of 1665, William, first Earl of Craven, founded a lazaretto consisting of thirty-six small houses for housing those afflicted with the plague. Near it, at the lower end of Marshall Street, was a cemetery, where, during the plague year, thousands were buried. Because of its associations with the dreaded plague, the spot was held in disgust and fear, no houses being built on it until the reign of George I. Cf. John Noorthouck, *A New History of London* (1773), p. 730. The spot was selected by the Scriblerians probably less on account of its conveniency for Martinus' experiments than for its thoroughly unsavory character.

(9) 126, 30. . . . *but spurning at the dead body,* . . .

The word "spurn," now obsolete in the meaning intended, meant to trip or stumble over. Cf. *NED.* Gay uses the word in this sense in his *Trivia,* ii, 333.

(10) 128, 11. . . . *radical words* . . .

"*Radical word,* a simple uncompounded word having the form of, or directly based on, a root," *NED, s.v.,* A, 5.

(11) 128, 32. . . . "*O Cicero, Cicero! if to pun be a crime, 'tis a Crime I learned from thee:*

Sheridan, in his *Ars Pun-ica* (1719), in which he was possibly aided by Swift, quotes Cicero in praise of puns.

Punning is extremely delightful, and oftentimes very profitable, in which, as far as I can judge, Caesar, you excel all Mankind; for which Reason you may inform me, whether there be an Art of Punning, or if there be, above all Things, I beseech you, to instruct me in it. Title page and p. ii.

Cicero's opinion and his own frequent use of verbal plays was commonly cited by those who sought to defend punning. Cf. *Spectator,* No. 61.

(12) 128, 33. . . . *O Bias, Bias! if to pun be a crime, by thy example was I bias'd.*

There is no evidence that the Greek sage Bias was given to punning. The Scriblerians are perhaps following Plutarch and others in confusing Bias with Bion Borysthenites, a philosopher of the fourth century b.c., who was famous for his jests and plays on words. Cf. Moreri and Bayle, *s.v.,* "Bion."

CHAPTER IX

Scriblerian satire in some ways is seen at its clearest and best in the two short paragraphs that compose this chapter. The person aimed at was no misguided fool whose crackbrained enthusiasms were to be laughed at and forgotten, but Richard Bentley, one of the most famous scholars of his age, and the follies ridiculed were not those personal weaknesses of arrogance, impatience, and vindictiveness of which Bentley was so notoriously guilty but the misguided ingenuity, unchecked virtuosity, and lack of judgment which marred some of his best works and led eventually to the fiasco of his edition of Milton.

The Scriblerians both individually and as a group had many reasons for hostility toward Bentley and their satires on him extended over nearly the whole of his long career. These attacks fall into three groups; the early satires of Swift, the Scriblerus burlesques, and the caustic ridicule of Pope during his and Bentley's final years. Swift's attacks came in the days of the Phalaris controversy. His sympathies were naturally strongly on the side of his patron, Sir William Temple, and the Oxford group; he therefore vigorously drubbed Bentley in both the *Tale of a Tub* and the *Battle of the Books*. More mature judgment, together perhaps with a realization that he was not in a position to quarrel with Bentley on equal terms, led him to be content with what he had written and he never formally satirized Bentley again.

Even if the Scriblerians had not been disposed to be hostile toward Bentley, they could hardly have overlooked him in 1714 when they were gathering material for their satire. His recent edition of Horace was an obvious mark for satire [1] and at the very time the club was meeting he was being tried for misconduct as master of Trinity. There were, however, other reasons why the group would not be likely to forego an opportunity for ridiculing him. Arbuthnot, like Swift, had been against Bentley in the Phalaris days,[2] and the major figures of the Christ Church group, Boyle (since become Lord Orrery), Atterbury (now Bishop of Rochester), and the two Freinds, were friends and associates of most of the Scriblerus group. Moreover, with his talent for making enemies, Bentley had managed to antagonize both the Earl of Oxford and Bolingbroke.[3]

In addition to the passage in the *Memoirs,* which was probably originally sketched out in 1714 and revised later to include the references to Bentley's later work, the Scriblerian satire on him included a very happy little burlesque of his methods of textual emendation entitled *Virgilius Restauratus,*[4] and the attaching of his name to a number of elaborate burlesque notes in the *Dunciad Variorum.* For all of these Arbuthnot seems to have been chiefly responsible and it is possible that he was also the author of two other satires on Bentley which, on very dubious evidence, have been attributed to him. The first of these was an amusing little supplement to *Gulliver's Travels* called *An Account of the State of Learning in the Empire of Lilliput; together with the History and Character of Bullum the Emperor's Library Keeper,* which was published in 1728,[5] and the other a pamphlet entitled *Critical Remarks on Capt. Gulliver's Travels. By Doctor Bantley,* which was not published until 1735, the year of Arbuthnot's death.[6]

1. Cf. below, p. 270, n. 6.
2. See Arbuthnot's letter to Dr. Charlett, dated January 25, 1697/98; Aitken, p. 23.
3. In 1711 Bentley appealed to Oxford and Bolingbroke in the Trinity controversy and succeeded in winning their sympathy. Oxford's attempts at mediation were, however, futile. Monk, I, 297 ff. Bentley's intransigeance in this matter, together with his later switch to the Whigs and perhaps other offenses, left the Oxford family very bitter against him. Cf. E. & C., VIII, 290. In 1713 Bentley offended Bolingbroke over the question of a scholarship. Monk, I, 353–6.
4. Cf. below, p. 269, n. 5.
5. Reprinted in *Miscellaneous Works* of Arbuthnot (1751), I, 141–51; Aitken, pp. 483–90.
6. Reprinted in *Miscellaneous Works,* I, 115–40; Aitken, pp. 491–506. The piece is dated at the end "Cambridge, Jan. 26, 1734-5."

Despite the fact that Bentley, on his own admission, had "talked against his Homer," [7] Pope did not attempt any serious satires against him until after 1732. Bentley's name appeared in one line of the manuscript of the *Dunciad,* but in the first edition it was replaced by two asterisks and in 1736 Welsted's name was substituted.[8] After the publication of Bentley's Milton, however (when Pope was on much safer ground than he would have been in connection with Bentley's classical studies), Pope began a series of attacks against the aging scholar. The line in the *Dunciad* was restored,[9] a bitter attack on textual critics published with the Atticus portrait in the 1727 *Miscellanies* [10] was revised to fit Bentley in part and introduced into the *Epistle to Dr. Arbuthnot* (1735),[11] his editing of Horace and Milton was ridiculed in the *Sober Advice from Horace* (1735),[12] and a sharp couplet against him was included in the *Imitations of Horace,* Bk. II, Ep. 1 (1737).[13] The climax of Pope's attack, however, came in the fourth book of the *Dunciad,* published in 1742, in which Bentley is made to figure heavily as Aristarchus, the

mighty Scholiast, whose unweary'd pains
Made Horace dull, and humbled Milton's strains.[14]

(1) 129, 5. . . . *to convert every* Trifle *into a serious thing, either in the way of* Life, *or in* Learning.

This comes very close to Swift's definition of pedantry. It was customary to define pedantry as a *pretence* to learning. Cf. *Tatler,* No. 244, by Steele and the dictionaries of the time. Swift went deeper and recognized that the basic fault of the pedant lies not so much in his lack of real learning as in his placing too high a value on the knowledge he does possess. "Pedantry," Swift declared, "is properly the over-rating any kind of knowledge we pretend to." "And," he added, "if that kind of knowledge be a trifle in itself, the pedantry is the greater. For which reasons I look upon fiddlers, dancing-masters, heralds, masters of the ceremony, &c. to be greater pedants than Lipsius, or the elder Scaliger." *Works,* XI, 81. It is in this sense that Cornelius, Martinus, and Richard Bentley were thought of as pedants by the Scriblerians.

(2) 129, 10. . . . assembling parallel sounds, . . . *might conduce to the Emendation and Correction of* Ancient Authors, . . .

The reference is to Bentley's practice of emending what he considered to be corrupt passages in the texts of ancient authors by substituting, on a purely con-

7. Monk, II, 372.

8. E. & C., IV, 283. The line, which reads "Bentley his mouth with classic flattery opes," referred to the adulatory dedication, in Latin, of his edition of Horace to the Earl of Oxford; cf. p. 270, n. 6.

9. In the "Vol. II" of Pope's *Works,* issued in 1735, Bk. II, l. 197. Still later, in the *New Dunciad* (1742), the line was assigned by Pope, in a note, to Thomas Bentley, the scholar's nephew. E. & C., IV, 145.

10. "The Last Volume," pp. 129–30.

11. Ll. 157–68.

12. Burlesque notes in the style of Bentley were appended to the Latin text and in the dedication there is a sneering reference to his Milton.

13. Ll. 104–05.

14. Ll. 211–12; cf. ll. 201–74.

jectural basis, words or phrases of similar sound but better sense or rhythm. His most famous applications of this practice, and the ones which the Scriblerians no doubt had in mind, occurred in his edition of Horace (1711). Bentley himself said that he owed more of the many hundreds of corrections he introduced into the text of Horace to such conjecture or "divination" than to the manuscripts he had collated. Richard Bentley, *Q. Horatius Flaccus, Ex Recensione & cum Notis* (Cambridge, 1711), "Præfatio ad Lectorem." Especially well-known among his corrections in this edition are his substitution of *male ter natos* (thrice shaped amiss) in the line *et male tornatos incudi reddere versus* (and put your ill-turned verses on the anvil again) in the *Art of Poetry* (v. 441), the line *Ut silvis folia privos mutantur in annos* (as woods have their leaves changed with each year) for *Ut silvae foliis pronos mutantur in annos* (as woods undergo change of leaves with each *declining year*) in the same poem (v. 60), and his altering *urbes* (cities) into *umbres* (shades) in *Odes* iii.4.45.

(3) 129, 12. *He resolv'd to try first upon Virgil, Horace, and Terence; . . .*
     See nn. 5, 6, and 7 below.

(4) 129, 16. *. . . the true and* absolute Critick.
     Swift, with Bentley in mind, had described this kind of critic in his *Tale of a Tub:*

THE Third, and Noblest Sort, is that of the TRUE CRITICK, whose Original is the most Antient of all. Every *True Critick* is a Hero born, descending in a direct Line from a Celestial Stem, by *Momus* and *Hybris,* who begat *Zoilus* [the ridiculer of Homer], who begat *Tigellius* [the satirist of Horace], who begat *Etcætera* the Elder, who begat *B—tly,* and *Rym-r,* and *W-tton,* and *Perrault,* and *Dennis,* who begat *Etcætera* the Younger. . . .
     NOW, from this Heavenly Descent of *Criticism,* and the close Analogy it bears to *Heroick Virtue,* 'tis easie to Assign the proper Employment of a *True Antient Genuine Critick;* which is, to travel thro' this vast World of Writings: to pursue and hunt those Monstrous Faults bred within them: to drag out the lurking Errors like *Cacus* from his Den; to multiply them like *Hydra's* Heads; and rake them together like *Augeas's* Dung. A. C. Guthkelch and D. Nichol Smith, eds. (Oxford, 1920), pp. 93–5; *Works,* i, pp. 71–2.

(5) 129, 18. *This Specimen on Virgil he has given us, in the Addenda to his Notes on the Dunciad.*
     As a satire on Bentley's textual methods the Scriblerians prepared a burlesque specimen showing how Virgil's *Aeneid* might be emended. This they entitled *Virgilius Restauratus: seu Martini Scribleri, Summi Critici, Castigationum in Aeneidem Specimen.* The piece, which is brilliantly executed, was probably largely, if not exclusively, prepared by Arbuthnot. Since its short, imperious decrees are much more like Bentley's manner in his ill-starred edition of the *Fables of Phaedrus* (cf. n. 8, below) than in his *Horace,* which was notable for its excessively long notes, it seems likely that it was written in 1726 or 1727.
     Not carried far enough to warrant independent publication (it contains only a score of emendations and goes no farther than the second book), it was published by Pope as part of the scholarly paraphernalia with which he surrounded the *Dun-*

ciad in the *Variorum* edition of 1729. Later it was republished in the fourth volume of the Swift-Pope *Miscellanies*. It was also included in the general collection of Scriblerus pieces in the second volume of Pope's prose works (1741) and in the revised and enlarged edition of the *Dunciad* which was published in 1743.

(6) 129, 19. *His Terence and Horace are in every body's hands, under the names of Richard B—ley,* . . .

For the editions of Terence see n. 7, below.

Bentley's *Horace* appeared on December 8, 1711. It was much ridiculed and attacked. Cf. Monk, I, 316–23; A. T. Bartholomew, *Richard Bentley, D.D., A Bibliography* (Cambridge, 1908), pp. 47–53. The most elaborate satire on the edition appeared in a translation of it by William Oldisworth, which appeared in a series of parts in 1712 and 1713 and was published in a collected form in 1713 under the title, *The Odes, Epodes, and Carmen Seculare of Horace, in Latin and English; With a Translation of Dr. Ben-ley's Notes. To which are added Notes upon Notes. By Several Hands.* In the "Notes upon Notes" Bentley's theories and manner were much satirized and burlesqued.

Bentley's edition was dedicated to the Earl of Oxford in the most fulsome terms of flattery—a fact which at the time strongly irritated the Whigs, it having been understood before Oxford's rise to power that it was to be offered to Halifax, and one which was later, when Bentley was associated with the Whigs, remembered with great bitterness by the Tories.

(7) 129, 20. . . . *and Francis H-re.*

Francis Hare was another old enemy of the Scriblerians, particularly of Swift. He was a violent Whig, and during 1711 and 1712 defended Marlborough and the war in several pamphlets, one of which, *The Allies and the Late Ministry Defended against France* (4 pts., 1711) was an answer to Swift's *Conduct of the Allies.* Swift, in turn, ridiculed a sermon preached by Hare on the ninth of September, 1711, on the subject of the taking of Bouchain, in his *A Learned Comment.* Hare became the subject of general ridicule and attack later by publishing a tract called, *The Difficulties and Discouragements which Attend the Study of the Scriptures in the Way of Private Judgment* (1714), which was taken to be ironical and was censured by the Convocation. He was also placed in an opposite camp from the Scriblerians in the days of the club by his then intimate friendship with Bentley, to whom, in 1713, he addressed *The Clergyman's Thanks to Phileleutherus* (Bentley's pseudonym) for his counterattacks on Anthony Collins in the Freethinker controversy.

Hare had a distinguished career in the church, becoming Bishop of Chichester in 1731 and being proposed by Walpole as Archbishop Wake's successor in 1736. He was personally unpopular, however, being known for his harsh disposition and tendency to become involved in acrimonious quarrels. Hervey describes him in later years as a "haughty, hard-natured, imperious, hot-headed, injudicious fellow" who was "thoroughly disliked in private, and feared in public life." *Memoirs of the Reign of George the Second* (1848), II, 110.

His edition of Terence, which is referred to in the text, was published in 1724. It was founded on that of Faërnus and contained a good deal of material drawn from a long correspondence with Bentley, from whom he had since become estranged. Furiously annoyed at being anticipated in the publication of the material which he had gathered and which he had intended to use himself, Bentley published in 1726 a rival edition, in the notes of which he bitterly attacked Hare. At the same time, in order to revenge himself further on his rival, Bentley hurried through an edition of the *Fables of Phaedrus,* a project which Hare had long been at work upon. The many follies and errors of this hastily prepared edition gave Hare ample opportunity for revenge, and in 1727, in his *Epistola Critica,* he subjected Bentley's work to a devastatingly thorough and rancorous examination.

It is at this stage, presumably, that the Scriblerians, who could not have failed to be delighted at this monumental exhibition of scholarly pettiness and at the way in which the two enemies were exposing each other, included this reference.

(8) 129, 21. . . . *the late Edition of Milton publish'd in the name of the former of these, . . .*

"Milton's Paradise Lost. A New Edition. By Richard Bentley, D.D." was published in 1732. In his preface Bentley explained that his edition was built on the theory 1) that Milton's amanuensis, in addition to making mistakes in spelling and punctuation, had written down wrong words of similar sound, 2) that "the Friend or Acquaintance, whoever he was, to whom *Milton* committed his Copy and the Overseeing of the Press, did so vilely execute that Trust, that *Paradise* under his Ignorance and Audaciousness may be said to be *twice* lost," the first edition being "polluted with such monstrous Faults, as are beyond Example in any other printed Book," 3) that "this suppos'd Friend . . . thought he had a fit Opportunity to foist into the Book several of his own Verses, without the blind Poet's Discovery," and 4) that Milton himself was responsible for "some Inconsistencies in the System and Plan of his Poem, for want of his Revisal of the Whole before its Publication."

On this compound basis Bentley scanned every line of the poem for errors, substitutions, interpolations, and even mistakes of judgment. The results, in the form of hundreds of suggested corrections and improvements, he offered in long footnotes. Typical of his proposed emendations are these from the opening lines (his suggestions being in brackets):

that on the secret [sacred] top
Of Horeb,   ll. 6–7.

I thence
Invoke thy aid to my adventrous Song [Wing],
That with no middle flight intends to soar
Above th' Aonian Mount, while *it pursues* [I pursue]
Things unattempted yet in Prose or *Rime* [Song].
ll. 12–6.

For some of the many harsh contemporary attacks on the edition see Monk, II, 322–3, and Bartholomew, *op. cit.,* pp. 77–9. Not long after it appeared Pope expressed his opinion very succinctly in a letter to Jacob Tonson: "As to Dr. Bentley and Milton, I think the one *above* and ye other *below* all criticism." E. & C., III, 530. However, in the margin of his copy he marked some comments with "recté, bené, pulchré, etc." E. & C., VIII, 294 n.

CHAPTER X

It would naturally be expected that any broad satire in which Dr. Arbuthnot took a leading part would contain a large section devoted to "Physick." That Arbuthnot was aware of the opportunity which the follies of the medical men of his time provided and did plan many exploits for Martinus in this field is indicated by the early "hints" he sent to Swift and his statement that "the ridicule of medicine is so copious a subject that I must only here and there touch it." [1]

Yet, on the whole, medicine plays a small role in the *Memoirs*. Two chapters, the present chapter and the one which follows it, are devoted to Martinus' "practice of physick," but both deal almost entirely with "diseases of the mind" and are primarily social satires, the ridicule not being aimed at the medical theories which Martinus puts into practice but the social vices which he attempts to cure. Satire on medicine as such is confined to Cornelius' subservience to the ancients in medicine as in all other fields and to a few miscellaneous jests at the start of this chapter and in chapter seventeen.

One reason for the absence of a larger amount of satire on current medical follies may be that Pope, in the course of his drastic editing and revising of the *Memoirs,* eliminated a good deal of it on one ground or another. But perhaps a better explanation is to be found in the difficulties which Arbuthnot must have encountered in writing such satire. If he had really found the ridicule of medicine the "copious subject" he believed it to be when he wrote to Swift, it seems likely that he would have written many non-Scriblerian pieces touching on it—and he did not. Apart from some satires on Dr. Woodward in connection with the vomits vs. purges war in 1719, which are of doubtful authenticity, he made little use of his powers of satire in his own professional field.

There were perhaps several reasons why Arbuthnot did not exert himself more on the subject, particularly in connection with the Scriblerus project. Since quackery as such fell outside the scope of the Scriblerian scheme, Arbuthnot was limited to more or less legitimate medicine. Here there were two difficulties. Extensive satire in this field could hardly avoid being excessively technical and it would be almost certain to embroil Arbuthnot seriously with many of his colleagues in the College of Physicians, a situation which his prudence, his good humor, and his long, painful experience with quarrels of this nature would equally counsel him to avoid.

Beneath such reasons, however, lay a more fundamental one in the "state of physick" in Arbuthnot's time. Unlike all the other fields with which the Scriblerians deal, medicine had undergone in the last generation no great changes or improvements. There was no real ancient-modern controversy in medicine, though both sides in the general quarrel had cited ancient and modern discoveries in this field to support their position. Harvey's discovery of the circulation of the blood had revolutionized one aspect of medicine and other parts of ancient medicine had long since been discarded, but the work of Hippocrates and of Galen still stood as the foundation of all medical learning, and in 1731 Arbuthnot could say in his

1. *Corres.,* II, 159.

Essay concerning the Nature of Aliments, without question of his status as an up-to-date physician, that

The Doctrine laid down in this *Essay,* . . . in most Particulars (I do not say in all) conform[s] to that of the divine *Hippocrates,* as appears by several Passages of his Works, particularly of his Books of Diet, of his Method of Diet in acute Diseases, and *Galen's* Commentaries both upon those Books, and some others of his Works.[2]

(1) 130, 18. . . . *A Proposal for a General Flux, to exterminate at one blow the P-x out of this Kingdom.*

The word "flux" was applied to the contemporary treatment of syphilis because of the heavy flow of saliva that resulted from the use of mercury.

In calling up the spirits of the dead in Glubbdubdrib, Gulliver is made melancholy by observing how in the past hundred years, "the pox under all its consequences and denominations had altered every lineament of an English countenance, shortened the size of bodies, unbraced the nerves, relaxed the sinews and muscles, introduced a sallow complexion, and rendered the flesh loose and rancid." *Works,* VIII, 211. That satire on such sweeping medical proposals was needed is illustrated by the fact that in 1739, after a public subscription had failed, Parliament passed a bill granting a Joanna Stephens £5000 for the secret of her remedy for the stone. When the great secret was revealed it was found to consist of a powder consisting of eggshells and snails, both calcined, a decoction made by "boiling some Herbs (together with a Ball, which consists of Soap, Swine's-Cresses burnt to a Blackness, and Honey)" and pills composed "of Snails calcined, Wild Carrot-Seeds, Burdock Seeds, Ashen-Keys, Hips and Hawes, all burnt to a Blackness, Soap and Honey." *Gentleman's Magazine,* IX (1739), 298; cf. IX, 49, 159; X, 142, etc.

(2) 130, 23. . . . *that most curious Treatise of the* Purification *of* Queen Esther *with a* Display *of her* Case *at large; speedily also to be published.*

This tract was apparently to be based on Esther ii.12:

Now when the turn of every maiden was come to go in to King Ahasuerus, after that it had been done to her according to the law for women, twelve months, (for so were the days of their purifications accomplished, *to wit,* six months with oil of myrrh, and six months with sweet odours, and with the things for the purifying of the women,) then in this wise came the maiden unto the King, . . .

Whether such a tract was actually contemplated by the Scriblerians cannot be determined. The manner in which it is referred to strongly suggests that the piece had been written and was among the Scriblerus papers. Its real existence is further suggested by the inclusion of the title in the list of the works of Scriblerus already

2. (3d ed., 1735), p. 227. Cf. his striking statement at the end of the *Essay:* "It would be easy to produce a great many Instances to prove the Conformity of the Doctrine of the *Essay,* with the Notions and Practice of *Hippocrates;* but those already mention'd are sufficient, and may be of use to some Readers to confirm by Authority, what they will not be at the Trouble to deduce by Reasoning" (pp. 238–9) as well as his frequent citations of, and references to, Hippocrates both in this essay and the one concerning the effects of air.

published and to be published given at the end of the *Memoirs*. On the other hand, there is no reference to any such work in any of the correspondence of the Scriblerians. However, this is a fact of doubtful importance since their correspondence contains no references to other pieces which were actually published. More significant perhaps is Pope's failure to mention it to Spence.

An important consideration with regard to it, whether it was actually written or not, must have been whether it was sacrilegious. It would have been almost impossible to handle the subject freely without offending some on this ground. This consideration would seem to rule out both Arbuthnot and Swift, who would have avoided even the appearance of ridiculing a part of the Bible. Pope and Gay were not, however, under such strong restraint, though Pope throughout his life displayed a concern for the feelings and opinions of his Catholic friends. In view of these circumstances, it seems likely that if Gay, or Pope and Gay, had written a humorous piece of this sort, its publication might have been temporarily checked by the other Scriblerians, further delayed by Pope's own scruples, and finally prevented by Warburton, who undoubtedly would have taken an unfavorable view of it. Such speculations, however, do not overcome the simple fact that no trace or mention of the piece other than the one noted is known.

The idea of such a treatise no doubt came to Pope or Arbuthnot while they were preparing the libretto for Handel's oratorio *Esther,* which was first produced on August 29, 1720. Cf. G. W. Sherburn, " 'Timon's Villa' and Cannons," *Huntington Library Bulletin,* No. 8 (1935), pp. 144–6.

(3) 130, 26. . . . *attended Dr. Woodward thro' a Twelvemonth's course of Vomition)* . . .

With his usual talent for developing absurd conclusions out of interesting and valuable investigations, Dr. Woodward, after having made a careful study of the nature and operations of the bile, concocted the theory that bile was the main spring or focal point of the bodily economy and that disturbances of the bile, and particularly those "biliose salts" that are collected in the stomach, were the cause of most of the diseases with which man is afflicted. On the basis of this theory he concluded that the sovereign remedy for disease was the evacuation of the overly sharp and hot or excessively weak salts from the stomach. He therefore instituted the practice of putting his patients through long and severe "courses of vomits."

The manner he took of presenting his views was equally in accordance with his character. In 1717 Dr. John Freind published an edition of Hippocrates' *De Morbis Popularibus,* to which he attached a commentary in which, following the best medical practice of his day, he recommended the use of purges under certain conditions at the start of the second fever in the confluent smallpox. Since in Woodward's eyes purges merely carried the dangerous salts down through the patient's system, he looked on this advice as little better than murder. In the following year he therefore published a book entitled *The State of Physick and of Diseases* in which he violently attacked Freind and expounded his own views. The result was a bitter pamphlet warfare over the respective merits of vomits and purges which exceeded in extent and personal acrimony all other medical quarrels of the period and which eventually led to a most absurd personal combat between Dr. Woodward and the great Dr. Mead. In this quarrel Arbuthnot's sympathies were naturally strongly against Woodward, and though the extent of his participation is doubtful he probably took an active part in ridiculing Woodward.

In his *Satires of Dr. Donne* Pope says:

> As one of Woodward's patients, sick and sore,
> I puke, I nauseate,—yet he thrusts in more:
>
> Sat. iv, ll. 152–3.

(4) 130, 29. *He attempted to find out specifics for all the* Passions; . . .

The idea of regulating the mind by means of medicines also appears in Swift's *The Right of Precedence between Physicians and Civilians,* which was published in 1720:

The force of physic goes further than the body, and is of use in relieving the mind under most of its disorders: And this I dare venture to affirm, having frequently made the experiment upon my own person with never-failing success; and this I did by the direction of my worthy parish minister, who is indeed an excellent divine, and withal an able physician; and a good physician only to be the better divine. That good man has often quieted my conscience with an emetic, has dissipated troublesome thoughts with a cordial, or exhilarating drops, has cured me of a love-fit by breathing a vein, and removed anger and revenge by the prescription of a draught, thence called bitter; and in these and other instances, has convinced me, that physic is of use to the very soul, as far as that depends on the crasis of the body. *Works,* xi, 42–3.

(5) 131, 6. . . . *the aduncity of the Pounces, . . . of the Hawks, . . .*

That is, the hookedness, or inward curve, of the claws or talons. Cf. Bailey.

(6) 131, 9. . . . *the crural and Masseter-muscles in Lions and Tygers, are the cause of the great and habitual Immorality of those Animals.*

The crural muscles are those of the leg and the masseters one of the principal masticatory muscles of the jaws. Cf. Chambers and Bailey. The "immorality" of the animals was proverbial. Cf. e.g., Pliny viii.17). Arbuthnot attributed the character of these animals in part to diet, their carnivorous habits leading to greater muscular strength and fierceness of passions. *Essay concerning the Nature of Aliments* (3d ed., 1735), pp. 225–6.

(7) 131, 16. . . . *the Soul in mankind expresseth every Passion by the Motion of some particular* Muscles.

The expression of passion by particular muscles, a subject of comment and inquiry among the ancients, had been discussed learnedly and fully (though credulously and at times foolishly) by John Bulwer, "Sirnamed the Chirosopher," in his *Pathomyotomia, or a Dissection of the significative Muscles of the Affections of the Minde* (1649). Cf. below, n. 13.

(8) 131, 20. . . . *the habitual Passions may be discerned in particular persons by the strength and bigness of the Muscles us'd in the expression of that Passion.*

The Scriblerians here apply to the whole body a theory commonly accepted in connection with physiognomy, of which, in some ways, this whole jest is a burlesque. Chambers says,

Now, if by repeated acts, or the frequent entertaining of a favourite passion, or vice, which natural temperament has hurried, or custom dragged one to, the face is often put in that posture which attends such acts; the animal spirits will make such patent passage through the nerves . . . that the face is sometimes unalterably set in that posture . . . or at least falls insensibly and mechanically into that posture, unless some present object distort it therefrom, or dissimulation hide it.

This reasoning, he declares, is confirmed by observation.

Hence we may account for the quakers expecting face, waiting the spirit, the melancholy face of most sectaries, the studious face of men of great application of mind, &c.

Were our observation a little more strict and delicate, we might doubtless not only distinguish habits and tempers, but even professions.—In effect, does there need much penetration to distinguish the fierce look of the veteran soldier, the contentious look of the practiced pleader, the solemn look of the minister of state, &c. "Physiognomy"; cf. below, nn. 10 and 11.

(9) 132, 23. *These Muscles [of patience] also he observed to be exceedingly strong and large in* . . . English Ministers.

Again it is to be remembered that one of the active members of the Scriblerus Club was the Earl of Oxford, the then Prime Minister of Great Britain.

(10) 132, 26. . . . *the* abductors *in Drunkards and contemplative men,* . . .

"ABDUCTOR *oculi,* a Muscle that draws the Eye from the Nose," Bailey.

The close-set eyes of drinkers was a conventionality which was taken quite seriously. Chambers in describing the effects of passions or vices on the face says, "We see great drinkers, with eyes generally set to the nose; the adducent muscles being oft employed to put them in that posture, in order to view their loved liquor in the glass in the time of drinking; whence those muscles are also denominated *bibitory muscles." S.v.* "Physiognomy."

(11) 132, 33. *The rolling amorous Eye, in the Passion of Love, might be corrected by frequently looking thro' glasses.*

The roving eye of the amorous was also a conventionality. Chambers says, "Thus also lascivious persons are remarkable for the *oculorum mobilis petulantia,* as Petronius calls it." *Ibid.*

By "glasses" is, of course, meant telescopes and microscopes.

(12) 132, 35. . . . *by relaxing medicines applied to the* Calves *of the* legs. . . .

Medical men in the early eighteenth century were much interested in muscular tension and devoted much effort to contracting and stiffening the "solids" of some of their patients and to relaxing and softening those of others. Arbuthnot in his *Essay concerning the Nature of Aliments* (1731) says that "The most common Diversities of Human Constitutions arise either from the solid Parts as to their different Degrees of Strength and Tension; in some being too lax and weak, in others too elastick and strong; or from the different State of the Fluids; . . ." 3d ed., 1735, p. 151. He classified the effects of all diets and medicines on the solid parts of the body as

First, Stimulating or increasing their Vibrations or oscillatory Motions. *Secondly,* Contracting, that is, diminishing their Length, and increasing their Thickness.

Thirdly, Relaxing, or making them more flexible in their less coherent Parts. And *Lastly,* Constipating, or contracting, or narrowing the Cavity of the capillary Tubes. P. 115.

"Relaxing the Fibres" he explains as "making them flexible, or easy to be lengthen'd without Rupture, which is done only in the capillary vascular Solids." *Ibid.,* p. 123. For another statement of relaxing medicines see J. Quincy, *A Complete English Dispensatory* (10th ed., 1736), p. 114.

(13) 133, 6. *The second case was immoderate* Laughter: . . . *what an infinity of Muscles these laughing Rascals threw into a convulsive motion* . . .

John Bulwer in his *Pathomyotomia* (1649) gives an elaborate anatomical description of immoderate laughter (pp. 104–26) which may possibly have provided suggestions for the passage in the text. Dr. Nehemiah Grew, in his *Cosmologia Sacra* (1701), points out that

No less than 40 or 50 Muscules, besides all other subservient Parts, go to execute that one Act of Laughter. Divers of those in the Nose, Lips, Cheeks, and Chin, for figuring the Face. Of those in the Weason, Chest, *Diaphragm,* and Belly, for making the Noise, by the Explosion of the Air. P. 28.

CHAPTER XI

Nowhere in the *Memoirs* or in any of the Scriblerus pieces is the influence of the *Tatler, Spectator,* and *Guardian* more apparent than in the "Case of the Young Nobleman at Court." Like the preceding chapter it is an excellent example of the ingenious and neatly turned pieces of social satire that had been the literary rage for the five years preceding the forming of the Scriblerus Club, which most of the wits of the time, including all the Scriblerians save Oxford and Arbuthnot, had taken a turn at composing. Not only does the "Case of the Young Nobleman" resemble many of the contributions to the famous periodicals in general conception but it is markedly like them in style and method of treatment.

Too late for inclusion in my discussion of the authorship and publication of the *Memoirs*[1] I have learned of the discovery by Mr. Vinton A. Dearing that Pope included the chapter in the third volume of a special set of his works which he presented to the Prince of Wales in 1738. It there appears among his *Guardian* papers with the heading, "A Letter of Martinus Scriblerus. M.D. To the Guardian. Being the Case of a young Lord at Court." The letter, which is dated April 1, 1713, begins and closes with a reference to "Dr. *Gnatho,*" who had described his successful use of an elixir of flattery in *Guardian* No. 11, for March 24, 1712/13, by Pope. Otherwise the text of the chapter appears as it does in the *Memoirs.*

Since the character of Martinus had not yet been created and there appears no strong reason why Pope should not have published the piece in the *Guardian* if it had been written at the purported time,[2] it seems likely that it was actually composed at a somewhat later date, possibly with some help from other Scriblerians. Pope's inclusion of it in the presentation copy may have been motivated by the

1. Above, pp. 60–1.
2. Contributions by Pope continued to appear until the following September 29.

thought that the subject might appeal particularly to the Prince of Wales and that the inclusion of an unpublished piece would add interest and value to the volume. Mr. Dearing's discussion of this and other interesting points about the presentation copy will appear in a forthcoming article in the *Harvard Library Bulletin*.

The long description of both the symptoms of love and the methods of its cure in Burton's *Anatomy of Melancholy*[3] offered an easy source for some of the ideas and references in the chapter.

(1) 134, 35. . . . *much frequented by Flatterers, . . .*

Cf. Steele's statement: "First we flatter our selves, and then the Flattery of others is sure of Success. It awakens our Self-love within, a Party which is ever ready to revolt from our better Judgment, and joyn the Enemy without." *Spectator*, No. 238.

(2) 135, 8. *In former days this sorts of lovers . . . never had any Rivals, but of late they have all the Ladies so . . .*

The liking of women for effeminate fops had been commented upon at some length by Addison in the *Spectator*, No. 128. The subject was taken up by Steele and carried on in essays Nos. 156 and 158.

(3) 135, 24. . . . *any Love-toys; such as gold Snuff-boxes, . . .*

Snuffboxes, watches, and tweezer cases were equally the "toys" of women and fops—fashionable women being given to the taking of snuff. Cf. *Spectator*, Nos. 37, 57, 58, 73, 91, 296, 344. Among the possession of a beau in John Hughes's "Inventory" are "Four pounds of scented snuff, with three gilt snuff boxes; one of them with an invisible hinge, and a Looking glass in the lid." *Tatler*, No. 113.

(4) 135, 25. . . . *repeating Watches, . . .*

These watches were so designed that when a string was pulled or the stem pressed they struck the hour, quarter hour, or minute. Clocks of this type were invented by a man named Barlow about the year 1676 and were refined into watches during the reign of James II. William Derham, *The Artificial Clockmaker* (1696), pp. 106–07.

(5) 135, 25. . . . *or Tweezer-cases?*

Another item in John Hughes's "Inventory of a Beau" is "A very rich Tweezer-case, containing twelve Instruments for the Use of each Hour in the Day." *Tatler*, No. 113. Some cases were apparently even more elaborate than this (Steele, *Tatler*, No. 142) and were regarded as sufficiently necessary and ornamental to be carried in the pocket or worn on the person. Cf. Arbuthnot, *History of John Bull*, Pt. II, chap. i; Aitken, p. 231, and Pope, *Rape of the Lock*, Canto v, l. 116.

(6) 136, 7. *First, let him* * * * *Hiatus.* * * *

Cf. Burton, *op. cit.*, Pt. III, sec. 2, memb. 5, subsec. 5.

(7) 136, 7. . . . *a Bob-wig.*

The "Bob" wig was a short, small one, either with very short curls on the side

3. Pt. III, sec. 2, membs. 3–5.

or trimmed to imitate the natural head of hair. It was commonly used by soldiers, tradesmen, and the lower orders, and was therefore highly unfashionable. James Stewart, *Plocacosmos* (1782), pp. 203–04; J. Ashton, *Social Life in the Reign of Queen Anne*, I, 146. Steele, in his *Lying Lover* (1704) has one of his characters speak ironically of "this smart Bob." Act IV, sc. I.

(8) 136, 9. *Thirdly, shun the company of flatterers, nay of ceremonious people, and of all Frenchmen in general.*

The addition of "ceremonious people" and "of all Frenchmen in general" is a reflection of the current attack on the imitation by Englishmen of the extravagant flattery and compliments that were believed to characterize the manners of foreigners and especially of Frenchmen. Archbishop Tillotson expressed the general view in saying:

The old English Plainness and Sincerity, that generous Integrity of Nature and Honesty of Disposition, which always argues true Greatness of Mind, and is usually accompany'd with undaunted Courage and Resolution, is in a great measure lost amongst us. There hath been a long Endeavour to transform us into Foreign Manners and Fashions, and to bring us to a servile Imitation of none of the best of our Neighbours, in some of the worst of their Qualities. The Dialect of Conversation is now-a-days so swell'd with Vanity and Compliment, and so surfeited (as I may say) of Expressions of Kindness and Respect, that if a Man that lived in an Age or two ago shou'd return into the World again, he would really want a Dictionary to help him to understand his own Language . . . "On Sincerity"; quoted with approval by Steele in the *Spectator*, No. 103.

(9) 136, 11. . . . *travel'd over England in a Stage-coach, and made the Tour of Holland in a Track-scoute.*

One of the cures which Ovid most strongly recommends for the lovesick, or "sick minds," is extensive and arduous travel. *Remedio amoris*, ll. 213–24; cf. Burton, *op. cit.*, Pt. III, sec. 2, memb. 5, subsec. 2. The Dutch "Track-scoute" (or more properly, Trekschuit) was a horse-drawn boat used for transporting goods and passengers on the canals of Holland. Cf. *Spectator*, No. 130.

(10) 136, 17. *Let some knowing friend represent to him the many vile Qualities of this Mistress of his: let him be shown that her Extravagance, Pride, and Prodigality will infallibly bring him to a morsel of bread: Let it be prov'd, that he has been false to himself,* . . .

It is to be feared that Martinus' cure would have a greater effect on the friendship than on the love affair. Ovid leaves the distasteful task to the patient himself. *Op. cit.*, ll. 297–341. Cf. Burton, Pt. III, sec. 2, memb. 5, subsec. 3.

(11) 136, 22. *Let all Looking-glasses, polish'd Toys, and even clean Plates be removed from him, for fear of bringing back the admired object.*

The sight of the loved one, Ovid points out, may cause a serious relapse. *Op. cit.*, ll. 609–34.

(12) 136, 28. *Let him surprize the Beauty he adores at a disadvantage; survey himself naked, divested of artificial charms,* . . .

Again this follows Ovid's advice. *Ibid.*, ll. 341–56; cf. Burton, Pt. iii, sec. 2, memb. 5, subsec. 3.

(13) 136, 33. *. . . at which time it will be convenient to make use of the . . . Dedications, . . .*
Condemnation of dedications for their abject servility and gross flattery was common in the early eighteenth century. Swift was particularly scornful of them and went somewhat beyond contemporary opinion by declaring, "I confess it is with some disdain that I observe great authors descending to write any dedications at all." *Works*, x, 195.

(14) 136, 35. *Something like this has been observed by Lucretius and others to be a powerful remedy in the case of Women.*
> And this our Misses know, and strive to hide
> Their Faults from those (the Cov'rings decent Pride)
> Whom they would cheat, and bind to an Amour;
> Tho' foul behind, they look all bright before.
>   Lucretius, *De Rerum Natura,* Thomas Creech, tr.,
>   Bk. iv, ll. 1187–90; 1714 ed., i, 410.
Cf. Burton, subsec. 1.

(15) 136, 36. *Let him* marry himself, . . .
Cf. Burton, subsec. 5.

CHAPTER XII

The chief subject of ridicule in the chapter is the sect of Freethinkers. More specifically the satire is directed at 1) attempts to find the seat of the soul, 2) arguments against the existence of an immaterial soul, and 3) attempts to explain thought on a purely mechanistic basis. The first and third of these were more or less common themes of satire in the period, the two having an element in common in that both touch in part on Descartes' theories and reflect the current English reaction against the French philosopher and scientist.[1] The second was a direct burlesque of a theological quarrel which took place several years before the *Memoirs* was begun.

In attacking the Freethinkers the Scriblerians were aiming at a rapidly growing group which held that the church had led men astray and that one should believe only what his freely exercised reason and judgment convinces him is true. Freethinking, properly speaking, was only an attitude of mind and a method which might, and did, lead to all sorts of conclusions from a mild doubt concerning certain Christian dogmas and mysteries to complete atheism. Commonly it resulted

1. For the English attitude toward Descartes see Sterling P. Lamprecht, "The Role of Descartes in Seventeenth Century England," in *Columbia University Studies in the History of Ideas* (New York, 1935), iii, 181–240, and M. Nicolson, "The Early Stage of Cartesianism in England," *Studies in Philology*, xxvi (1929), 356–75.
The Scriblerians were strongly opposed to Descartes both because of his outmoded scientific theories and his *a priori* and hypothetical reasoning; see Swift's *Works*, i, 116, 118, 166, 172, 177–8, viii, 207; and ll. 459–76 in the fourth book of the *Dunciad* which reflect in part on Descartes. Cf. below, p. 331, n. 8.

in a general rejection of revealed religion, but with at least a nominal acceptance of the idea of a divine power. It was therefore in the late seventeenth and early eighteenth centuries almost indistinguishable from deism and the two terms were practically synonymous in the public mind.

The movement, which was fostered by the works of Lord Herbert of Cherbury, Hobbes, and Blount, seems to have spread slowly until after the revolution of 1688 when, judging from the increasing flood of defenses of the Christian religion, it apparently began to grow rapidly. It is difficult to determine just how widespread it became. The press laws and public opinion made open advocacy of deism dangerous and only a few men such as Tindal, Toland, Coward, and Collins were rash enough to express themselves in print. Both the movement and the opposition to it seem to have grown steadily during the reign of Queen Anne until something like a crisis was reached in 1713 when Collins aroused such a storm by his *Discourse on Free-Thinking* that he was forced to flee to Holland.[2] Among those who took a leading part in arousing public opinion against him was Swift, who detested and feared Freethinkers as dangerous atheists, bent on pulling down the fabric of the church.[3]

The part of the Freethinkers' letter that is devoted to the question of the materiality of the soul is a satire on an argument between Samuel Clarke, the English metaphysician, and Anthony Collins. The quarrel, which extended through the years 1706, 1707, and 1708, is interesting less for its philosophical importance than as an illustration of the intellectual interests and temper of the time. It was an offshoot of a controversy growing out of a passage in the *Essay concerning Human Understanding* (1690) in which Locke raised doubts concerning man's ability to demonstrate certainly that the soul is immaterial.[4] The question was an old one, having been extensively discussed in ancient times and again brought up in the early seventeenth century largely as a result of Gassendi's revival of epicureanism. Arguments over it in England had been given a particularly strong impetus by Thomas Hobbes's sharp attack on the whole idea of immaterial substance.[5]

The immediate cause of the Clarke-Collins controversy was a pamphlet published in 1706 by the aged and learned nonjuror, Henry Dodwell, entitled *An Epistolary Discourse*.[6] In this tract Dodwell sought to revive the doctrine advocated by several of the early patristic writers that the soul is naturally mortal and is made immortal only through baptism by the successors of the apostles.[7]

2. Public attacks on Freethinking were particularly numerous and virulent during the period just before and while the *Memoirs* was being planned. The most famous answers to Collins were written by Richard Bentley under the pseudonym of "Phileleutherus Lipsiensis."

3. See the index to Swift's *Works* under "Collins" and "Freethinkers."

4. Bk. iv, chap. iii, sec. 6; cf. Bk. iv, chap. x, secs. 9–19. This controversy was part of a larger one in which Edward Stillingfleet, Bishop of Worcester, sought to prove that a number of Locke's principles were heretical.

5. Hobbes, iii, 32–4, 96–7, 381–3, 641–3; iv, 306, 313–14, 350–3.

6. Dodwell, it will be recalled, was the author of a very learned dissertation on Woodward's shield. Cf. general note to Chap. iii. The extent of his reputation for learning is suggested by Arbuthnot's reference to him in his *Essay on the Usefulness of Mathematical Learning* (1700) as "our incomparable historian." Aitken, p. 419.

7. Dodwell had previously expressed some of his views on the subject in his *Letter concerning the Immortality of the Soul against Mr. Henry Layton's Hypothesis* (1703).

His pamphlet, which was learned and temperate in tone, stirred up a host of angry replies.[8] One of the most prompt and vitriolic of these was *A Letter to Mr. Dodwell* by Samuel Clarke. Clarke, who at this time was chaplain to the Bishop of Norwich, had just won considerable fame by his series of Boyle lectures in 1704 and 1705. Flushed with success and eager to win further honors as a champion of religion, Clarke saw in Dodwell's pamphlet a chance to display his metaphysical and polemical skill. Undeterred by Dodwell's great age and indisputable piety, Clarke went through the *Epistolary Discourse* point by point with merciless thoroughness.

Against Clarke's harsh attack Dodwell was helpless; his answer, which was little more than a plea that he had been misunderstood, was more than a year in coming out.[9] But he was not long without a defender, though this champion was to prove even more embarrassing to him than Clarke had been. Almost as promptly as Dodwell had been answered, his opponent was attacked by Anthony Collins, who saw in the situation an opportunity to air his ultraliberal views under cover of a defense of the pious divine. Collins' challenge drew Clarke's attention to him and there began between the two a crossfire of "Defences" and "Replies."[10]

Since the letter from the Freethinkers follows parts of Clarke's arguments closely, a sketch of the main outlines of the Clarke-Collins controversy is necessary for an understanding of the text. In his attack on Dodwell, Clarke argued, among other things, that the soul must naturally be immortal because it is immaterial —its immateriality being proved both by authority and by reason. Since matter is divisible, he maintained, consciousness must inhere in every particle and not in any organization of particles and since consciousness is not a natural quality of individual particles it must be an immaterial substance added to them. If against

8. The list is too long to be given here; see Arber's *Term Catalogues* and Watt's *Bibliotheca Britannica.*

9. *A Preliminary Defence of the Epistolary Discourse, concerning the distinction between the Soul and Spirit, in two parts. 1st, Against the charge of favouring Impiety. 2d, Against the charge of favouring Heresy* (1707). He followed this by: *The Scripture Account of the Eternal Rewards or Punishments, without an Immortality necessarily resulting from the nature of the Souls themselves* (1708) and *The Natural Mortality of Humane Souls clearly Demonstrated from the Holy Scriptures* (1708).

10. A list of the pamphlets in the controversy follows. The months given are those of the term catalogues in which they were advertised.

1. 1706 (May). S. Clarke, *A Letter to Mr. Dodwell; wherein all the Arguments, in his 'Epistolary Discourse against the Immortality of the Soul' are particularly answered.*
2. 1706. A. Collins, *A Letter to the Learned Mr. Henry Dodwell; Containing some Remarks on a (pretended) Demonstration of the Immateriality and natural Immortality of the Soul.*
3. 1707 (February). S. Clarke, *A Defence of an Argument made use of in a Letter to Mr. Dodwell.*
4. 1707. A. Collins, *A Reply to Mr. Clarke's Defence of his Letter to Mr. Dodwell.*
5. 1707 (May). S. Clarke, *A Second Defence of an Argument . . . etc.*
6. 1707. A. Collins, *Reflections on Mr. Clarke's Second Defence.*
7. 1707 (November). S. Clarke, *A Third Defence of an Argument . . . etc.*
8. 1707. A. Collins, *An Answer to Mr. Clarke's Third Defence.*
9. 1708. S. Clarke, *A Fourth Defence of an Argument . . . etc.* Most of the tracts went through at least a second edition before 1712. Both Collins' and Clarke's pamphlets were reprinted in *The Works of Samuel Clarke, D.D.* (1738), III, 719–913.

this it were argued that God might superadd consciousness to united particles, it could be answered that the particles, being still distinct beings, could not be the subjects in which an individual, and therefore indivisible, consciousness inhered and hence that such a superadded consciousness must be immaterial.

In reply Collins argued that an individual power might reside in a system and that there could be in a system more than the sum of its parts. As an illustration of this he chose the unfortunate example of the odor of a rose. This argument brought up the question of primary and secondary qualities, and in his first *Defence* Clarke made short work of the rose analogy. There are, declared Clarke, three distinguishable qualities: 1) those that strictly inhere in a subject, such as magnitude and motion, 2) those that are "vulgarly" looked upon as residing in a system but are really only effects on and qualities of other subjects, as the odor of Collins' rose, and 3) other powers such as "magnetism," "electrical attraction," and gravity which are not real qualities residing in any subject but either, in the first category, merely names of the effects of "some determinate motions of streams of matter" or, in the second, the operations of some other being. Thinking, he maintained, must be reckoned among the first of these only.

Collins' answer was an elaborate one. Clarke, he said, had not proved that consciousness is not a power arising from a union of different kinds of power (as, for instance, in the case of an egg, which achieves consciousness by a change and development of particles), and he had begged the question in calling thinking an individual power. It is, he argued, as logical to maintain that matter gravitates as the result of powers originally placed in it by God as to assume that an immaterial being puts an object in motion and continues to keep it moving. He then attempted to refute, at some length, Clarke's contention that consciousness, in contrast to matter, is absolutely indivisible. In addition he maintained that the objections against matter's thinking apply also against an immaterial substance.

In his reply, his *Second Defence,* Clarke brought in a new element. A man, he pointed out, remembers things he has done many years before, yet the spirits and particles of the brain are known to be in a perpetual flux. Since no individual quality can be transferred from one subject to another, it follows that consciousness must be "a real Quality which subsists without inhering in any Subject at all." Collins' answer to this was to point out that in addition to remembering we also "half remember" and totally forget. In fact, he declared, it is known that memory is only maintained by periodic recollections which refresh it. These phenomena, he argued, can only be explained by the idea of a gradual flux and change of parts in the mind and, in the end, by the hypothesis that thinking is a mode of motion. If, answered Clarke, "the continued Addition or Exciting of like Consciousness in the newly acquired Parts" of the mind were true, there could be no justice, for it would obviously be unjust to punish this group of particles for what another group had done. Further, if, as Collins had maintained, thinking is a mode of motion, the doctrine of resurrection would be "inconceivable" and the "justice of future Rewards and Punishments impossible to be made out."

Such were the principal points on which the argument rested. Since both followed the policy of attempting to refute every point made by the other, the progress of the debate was marked by increasing complexities which threatened to be endless. Collins' answer to Clarke's *Third Defence,* however, was his last, and with his *Fourth Defence* Clarke was left in possession of the field.

From the point of view of their contemporaries, there can be no question that Clarke won—the rectorship of St. James's, a famous steppingstone, being a tangible acknowledgment of his victory. Regardless of whatever merits Collins' arguments may have possessed, a popular victory on his part was practically impossible. Clarke was maintaining an orthodox view which was backed by all the weight of the church, while Collins' position at least savored of heresy and at times bordered on atheism. Collins might at least have escaped ridicule for his part in the argument, however, had not his subsequent publications shocked and antagonized public opinion. Leaving Clarke's *Fourth Defence* unanswered, Collins, in 1709, published a work called *Priestcraft in Perfection* in which he attacked the power of the church to decree rites and ceremonies and its authority in controversies of faith. By this he marked himself as a deist and an opponent of the church. The climax came in 1713 when he published his famous *Discourse on Free-Thinking, Occasion'd by the Rise and Growth of a Sect call'd Free-Thinkers,* which aroused a tremendous outcry and turned his name into that of a pariah.

To the stir created by this last pamphlet is probably to be attributed the interest of the Scriblerians in the Clarke-Collins controversy. Although all the Scriblerians had been in London at some time during the quarrel, there is no reference to it either in their contemporary or later writings. Swift's lack of interest is, of course, to be traced to his detestation of metaphysical argument and religious speculation. Even Collins' attack on the authority of the church did not arouse him, though he must have been irritated by it. The *Discourse on Free-Thinking,* however, seemed to him open atheism and as such a menace which should not be allowed to pass. Leaving to others, notably Bentley, the task of answering Collins logically, Swift opened on him the full power of his satire and in a little tract entitled *Mr. C——n's Discourse of Free-Thinking, Put into Plain English* (1713) treated him with savage and effective irony.

The popular feeling against Collins, the harshness of which is illustrated by the verdict of the *Guardian* that "if ever Man deserved to be denied the common benefits of air and water, it is the Author of A Discourse on Free-Thinking," [11] made him an obvious subject for Scriblerian satire and it is probable that in searching for a way to attack him that would not parallel Swift's satire too closely the Scriblerians turned to the pamphlets which Collins and Clarke had written earlier, new editions of which were available.

The fact that in the letter from the "Society of Free-Thinkers" to Martinus the Scriblerians ridicule Collins' arguments does not mean that they were particularly sympathetic toward Clarke. Swift, rather curiously, never mentions Clarke in all his correspondence or works, and Pope, though he referred to him occasionally in later years, never displayed any special liking for him.[12] Clarke's scholastic methods and manners were not apt to please any one of the Scriblerians, and

11. No. 3, for March 14, 1713, by Steele or Berkeley.

12. It has been suggested that Pope attacked Clarke in ll. 459–92 of the fourth book of the *Dunciad.* The description of the "gloomy Clerk," however, is in several respects so far from Clarke's true character as a thinker that the identification remains doubtful.

his condemnation for Arianism by the Convocation in 1712 was certain to have antagonized the steadfastly devout Arbuthnot and the two churchmen, Swift and Parnell. It seems probable, therefore, that the Scriblerians wrote their burlesque argument with somewhat mixed feelings and that their purpose at bottom was as much to satirize the whole argument as to bring into contempt the atheistical arguer.[13]

In the Freethinkers' letter the Scriblerians take up Clarke's principal positions one after another and then answer them in a burlesque style. Unfortunately for the effectiveness of the satire on the Freethinkers, however, the answers which the Scriblerians put into their hands, though expressed in "low" terms and everyday examples, are so neat, so apt, and so clear that they actually excel much of Collins' reasoning and in practical effect fail to arouse the laughter and scorn they were intended to produce.

Swift's dislike of metaphysical reasoning and the lack of interest or training in philosophical matters on the part of all the others save Arbuthnot and possibly Parnell strongly suggest that the learned doctor had a principal share in the writing of the chapter. That he was actively engaged in working out ideas for the chapter is shown by the "hint" he sent to Swift for a ridicule on the German physicians "who set up a sensitive soul as a sort of first Minister to the rational." [14]

The date "May 7" attached to the letter of the Freethinkers corresponds to a period in the spring of 1714 when Scriblerian activity was at its height and may very well indicate the time when the letter was first drafted. Arbuthnot's "hint" to Swift noted above, which was contained in a letter dated June 26, 1714, makes it clear that the chapter was not put into its final form until some time later.

The first person to call attention to the fact that a part of the letter of the Freethinkers was a ridicule of the Clarke-Collins controversy was Bishop Warburton in his edition of Pope (1751).[15] He mistakenly declares, however, that the "whole chapter" refers to that quarrel.

(1) 137, 6. . . . *an Enquiry after the* Seat *of the* Soul; . . .

The seat of the soul was an old cause of dispute among philosophers. Plato, Aristotle, Pythagoras, and Hippocrates believed the soul to be divided among the various parts of the body, understanding having its seat in the brain, anger in the heart, sensuality in the liver, and so on. Others, notably Epicurus and Lucretius, believed that the principal part of the soul, that which comprehended the mind and the passions, resided in the heart while the inferior parts were diffused throughout the body. Still others placed it solely in the brain. The subject was revived again in the seventeenth century by Descartes' decision that its true seat was the pineal gland. See n. 3 below.

13. The Scriblerian attitude toward the problem is summed up in Swift's later statement that "The manner whereby the soul and body are united, and how they are distinguished, is wholly unaccountable to us. We see but one part, and yet we know we consist of two; and this is a mystery we cannot comprehend, any more than that of the Trinity." *Works,* IV, 133. See Arbuthnot's poem *Know Yourself* (1734).

14. *Corres.,* II, 159–60.

15. VI, 151 n. Warton, in reprinting the note, failed to credit Warburton. As a result, Courthope and Aitken, who followed Warton's text, erroneously attributed it to Warton.

Inquiries as to the seat of the soul are pleasantly ridiculed by Prior in the first canto of his *Alma: or, the Progress of the Mind* (written during his imprisonment, 1715-17), and by Swift in *The Right of Precedence between Physicians and Civilians Enquir'd into* (Dublin, 1720), in which he facetiously declares that he has always, "contrary to vulgar notions," regarded the stomach not only as the seat of honor "but of most great qualities of the mind, as well as of the disorders of the body." *Works*, xi, 34. It seems probable that both Prior and Swift were influenced by the Scriblerian considerations of the problem.

In chapter fifteen, in connection with the lawsuit over Martinus' marriage to the Double Mistress, the Scriblerians again take up the question, on that occasion suggesting that the seat of the soul lies in the genitals.

(2) 137, 16. . . . *the Soul to perform several operations by her little Ministers, the* Animal Spirits, . . .

The doctrine of animal spirits is one of the most curious and interesting aspects of medical theory in the Renaissance and early modern times. It was the almost universally accepted theory of the method by which the soul acted upon the material body. Though there was a general agreement as to what animal spirits were, there was, naturally, some doubt and confusion as to the means by which they performed their theoretically impossible but very necessary function.

Animal spirits were thus described, in answer to a query, in the *British Apollo* for June 16-18, 1708:

The Animal Spirits are Particles of the Blood so exceedingly Rarified, and by Mutual Collision so particularly Configurated, as to be Capable of a Swifter Motion, and of a free Passage thro' such Parts of the Body as are Impervious to the other Particles of the Blood.

Cumberland, in his *Treatise of the Laws of Nature,* says that by the name "animal spirits"

. . . I understand the *most active Parts of the Blood,* thence convey'd into the *Brain,* to assist the Imagination and Memory, and also into the Nerves and Muscular Fibres, there to be subservient to the Motions of the Animal, such as Harvey himself does not deny. The Manner *how* the Spirits, or more active Parts of the Blood, are *separated* from the rest, has not yet, perhaps, come to the Knowledge of those Curious Inquirers into Nature, the learned in Physick. J. Maxwell, tr. (1727), p. 146. Cf. Descartes, *Passiones Animae,* i, x; *Dioptre,* iv, i, *et seq.*

The doctrine of animal spirits seems to have been derived from the Epicurean theories concerning the nature of thought, which are described at some length in the *De Rerum Natura* of Lucretius. The grave theoretical difficulties involved in the doctrine led Malebranche and Leibnitz to reject it.

(3) 137, 23. . . . *he grew fond of the* Glandula Pinealis, *dissecting many Subjects to find out the different Figure of this Gland,* . . .

The pineal gland had been selected by Descartes as the seat of the soul. He said,

In examining the matter with care, it seems as though I had clearly ascertained that the part of the body in which the soul exercises its functions immediately is in nowise the heart, nor the whole of the brain, but merely the most inward of all its parts, to wit, a certain very small gland which is situated in the middle of its substance and so suspended above the duct whereby the animal spirits in its anterior cavities have communication with those in the posterior, that the slightest movements which take place in it may alter very greatly the course of these spirits; and reciprocally that the smallest changes which occur in the course of the spirits may do much to change the movements of this gland. *Passiones Animae*, I, xxxi; *The Philosophical Works of Descartes*, E. S. Haldane and G. R. T. Ross, trs. (Cambridge, 1911), I, 345–6.

Descartes also argues for the pineal gland on the ground that it alone of all parts of the brain is single and thus is the only place from whence thought, which is single, might emanate. *Ibid.*

Like most of Descartes' theories, this one was regarded with a good deal of skepticism and scorn in England during the early eighteenth century. The prevailing attitude is indicated by Elijah Fenton in his *The Fair Nun* (1717):

> We sage Cartesians, who profess
> Ourselves sworn foes to emptiness,
> Assert that souls a tip-toe stand
> On what we call the pineal gland;
> As weather-cocks on spires are plac'd,
> To turn the quicker with each blast. ll. 1–6.

(4) 137, 25. . . . *dissecting many Subjects to find out the different Figure of this Gland, from whence he might discover the cause of the different Tempers in mankind.*

Addison had previously made passing use of the idea that a dissection of the pineal gland would reveal the character of its owner. Describing, in a *Spectator* paper, the dissection of a beau's head, he said:

The Pineal Gland, which many of our Modern Philosophers suppose to be the Seat of the Soul, smelt very strong of Essence and Orange-Flower Water, and was encompas'd with a Kind of horny Substance, cut into a thousand little Faces or Mirrours, which were imperceptible to the naked Eye; insomuch that the Soul, if there had been any here, must have been always taken up in contemplating her own Beauties. No. 275, for January 15, 1712.

A year later Berkeley built an amusing *Guardian* paper (No. 35, for April 21, 1713) around the idea that by means of a magical snuff given him by a virtuoso he had been able to make a tour of the pineal glands of various people. While within the glands he was able to observe the ways in which their minds operated and he describes particularly the gland of a voluptuary he visited.

(5) 137, 35. *He did not doubt likewise to find the same resemblance in Highwaymen and Conquerors:*

Gay improved this idea into his famous comparison of highwaymen with statesmen in the *Beggar's Opera*.

(6) 138, 1. . . . *he purchased the body of one of the first Species (as hath been before related) at Tyburn;* . . .

See Chapter VIII.

(7) 138, 6. . . . *the Society of* Free-Thinkers, *who were then in their infancy in England*, . . .

Since Martinus is said to have departed on his travels in 1699 (cf. text, p. 164) the events of this chapter and the "infancy" of the Freethinkers are presumably to be dated in the 1690's.

(8) 138, 11. Grecian *Coffee-House*, . . .

The Grecian, one of the famous coffeehouses of the time, was located in Devereux Court in the Strand. During most of the reign of Queen Anne it was looked upon as the meeting place of the learned. The first *Tatler*, for example, declares that "all Accounts of Gallantry, Pleasure, and Entertainment, shall be under the Article of White's Chocolate-House; Poetry, under that of Will's Coffee-House; Learning, under the Title of Grecian; . . ." April 12, 1709; cf. No. 31, for September 4, 1710. In 1711 the Spectator in describing himself said, "My face is likewise very well known at the Grecian . . ." *Spectator*, No. 1, for March 1, 1711; cf. No. 49, for April 26, 1711. Members of the Royal Society were apparently accustomed to dropping into it after meetings of the society. *The Diary of Ralph Thoresby*, J. Hunter, ed. (1830), II, 99, 117, 145, etc.

In 1712, as the result of the presence of Anthony Collins and a group of his satellites, its reputation began to change and for a time it was looked upon as a center of atheism and kindred horrors. Cf. George Duckett's *A New Project, Dedicated . . . to the Unbelieving Club at the Grecian* (1712) and *An Account of a Discourse at the Grecian Coffee-House on February the 11th 1712/13 Occasion'd by Dr. B——y's Answer to the Discourse of Free-thinking* (1713).

The Grecian got its name from a Greek named Constantine who founded it. *Intelligencer* for January 23, 1664/65; Wheatley, *London Past and Present*.

(9) 138, 27. *One of their chief Arguments is, that* Self-consciousness *cannot inhere in any system of Matter, because all matter is made up of several distinct beings, which never can make up one individual thinking being.*

This is the position taken by Clarke in his *A Letter to Mr. Dodwell*. The soul cannot possibly be material, he says,

For *Matter* being a divisible Substance, consisting always of separable, nay of actually separate and distinct parts, 'tis plain, that unless it were essentially Conscious, in which case every particle of Matter must consist of innumerable separate and distinct Consciousnesses, no System of it in any possible Composition or Division, can be any individual Conscious Being. Clarke, III, 730.

Collins replied that he could not see why an individual power might not reside in a system.

Now if an Individual Power can be lodged by God in, or superadded to that which is not an Individual Being, or follows from the Composition or Modification of a Material System, consisting of actually separate and distinct Particles; the very Soul and Strength of Mr. *Clarke's* Demonstration is gone. And [the] Matter of Fact is so plain and obvious, that a Man cannot turn his Eye but he will meet with Material Systems, wherein there are Individual Powers which are not in every one, nor in any one of the Particles that compose them when taken apart, and considered singly. Let us instance for example in a *Rose*. *That* consists of several Particles, which separately and singly want a Power to produce that agreeable Sensation we experience in them when united. And therefore either each of the Particles in that Union contributes to the Individual Power, which is the external Cause of our Sensation; or else God Almighty superadds the *Power* of producing that Sensation in us upon the Union of the Particles. And this, for ought I can see, may be the case of Matter's Thinking. *A Letter to the Learned Mr. Henry Dodwell; Containing Some Remarks on a (pretended) Demonstration of the Immateriality and Natural Immortality of the Soul;* Clarke, III, 751.

In his reply Clarke pointed out that in his analogy of the rose Collins was confusing primary and secondary qualities. Clarke, III, 759–60.

(10) 139, 16. . . . *Sarabands, . . .*
Chambers defines the saraband as "a musical composition in triple time; being, in reality, no more than a minuet, whose motions are slow and serious" and also as a dance to the same measure.

(11) 139, 18. *Just so, the Quality or Disposition in a Fiddle to play tunes, . . . are as much real Qualities in the Instrument, as the thought or the imagination is in the mind of the Person that composes them.*
The analogy of a violin had been used by Collins to make the same point in a somewhat different way:

Does not a musical Instrument, by being operated on in a peculiar Manner, operate on us again, and produce in us several agreeable Sensations? And is not that *Power or Ability to be acted on by us, and to act on us,* peculiar to the Modification of that Body, and not the Results of Powers of the same kind, since there are Parts of that System of Matter absolutely necessary to the Continuance of that Power in them which produces our Sensations? For as the Strings of a Violin are not sufficient of themselves, so neither are the remaining Parts of that Instrument to produce in us those harmonious Sounds that are caused by the whole System of that Matter being modified into that peculiar Form. *Reflections on Mr. Clarke's Second Defence;* Clarke, III, 804.

(12) 139, 24. *The Parts (say they) of an animal body are perpetually chang'd, . . . from whence it will follow, that the idea of Individual Consciousness must be constantly translated from one particle of matter to another, . . .*
Clarke's position with regard to the continuity of consciousness and the nature of personal identity is seen more clearly in the next problem taken up by the Freethinkers. See the following note.

(13) 140, 5. *They make a great noise about this Individuality: how a man is conscious to himself that he is the same Individual he was twenty years ago; notwithstanding the flux state of the Particles of matter that compose his body.*
In answer to Collins' materialistic explanation of the continuity of consciousness, Clarke argued that,

if the Brain or Spirits be the Subject of Consciousness; and the Parts of the Brain or Spirits be (as they certainly are, whatever Question may be made concerning any original *Solid Stamina* of the Body,) in perpetual flux and change; it will follow that That Consciousness, by which I *not only Remember* that certain Things were done many Years since, but also *am Conscious that they were done by Me, by the very same Individual Conscious Being* who now remembers them; it will follow, I say, that That Consciousness is transferred from one Subject to another; that is to say, that it is a real Quality which subsists without inhering in any Subject at all. *A Second Defence;* Clarke, III, 787.

To this Collins replied that,

if we utterly forget, or cease to be conscious of having done many things in the former Parts of our Lives which we certainly did, as much as any of those things which we are conscious that we have done; and if in fact we do by degrees forget every thing which we do not revive by frequent Recollection, and by again and again imprinting our decaying Ideas; and if there be in a determinate Time a partial or total flux of Particles in our Brains: What can better Account for our total Forgetfulness of some things, our partial Forgetfulness of others, than to suppose the Substance of the Brain in a constant Flux? And what can better show that Consciousness is not transferred from one Subject to another, than our forgetting totally or partially, according to the Brain's being more or less in a Flux? *Reflections on Mr. Clarke's Second Defence;* Clarke, III, 809.

Locke had discussed the whole question of personal identity at some length in his *Essay concerning Human Understanding;* see Bk. II, chap. xxvii.

(14) 140, 8. *Sir John Cutler* . . .

Sir John Cutler was an astonishing combination of petty miserliness and large public generosity. He was made a knight by Charles II for his part in raising a subscription for the use of the king. In addition he founded a lectureship at Gresham College, built an anatomical theater for the College of Physicians at a cost of nearly £7,000 and gave money to other public projects.

Personally, however, he was extremely parsimonious and as he grew older the habit of saving small sums grew so pronounced that he became notorious for it. His reputation was further lowered after his death in 1693 by the discovery that he had entered his "gift" to the College of Physicians as a debt on which he expected interest. The College, of which Arbuthnot was later a member, eventually paid his heirs £2,000 but erased a grateful inscription which they had put on their building.

Wycherley addressed a poem to him entitled *The Praise of Avarice* (*Posthumous Works* [1728], Pt. II, 200–06) and Pope used him as an example of avarice in his *Epistle to Allen, Lord Bathurst,* ll. 315–34.

(15) 140, 19. *And whereas it is affirm'd, that every animal is conscious of some individual self-moving, self-determining principle;* . . .

Clarke did not advance this specific point, but it is a legitimate extension of his position.

(16) 140, 28. *And whereas it is likewise objected, that Punishments cannot be just that are not inflicted upon the same individual, which cannot subsist without the notion of a spiritual substance.*

Clarke made much of this point in his argument with Collins. A man, he declared, cannot be *really and truly* the *same Person,* unless the *same individual numerical Consciousness* can be transferred from one Subject to another. For, the continued Addition or Exciting of a *like Consciousness* in the new acquired Parts, after the Manner you suppose; is nothing but a Deception and Delusion, under the Form of Memory; a making the Man to seem to himself to be conscious of having done that, which really was not done by him, but by another. And such Consciousness in a Man, whose Substance is wholly changed, can no more make it Just and Equitable for such a Man to be punished for an Action done by another Substance; than the Addition of the like Consciousness (by the Power of God) to two or more new created Men; or to any Number of Men now living, by giving a like Modification to the Motion of the Spirits in the Brain of each of them respectively; could make them All to be one and the same individual Person, at the same time that they remain several and distinct Persons; or make it just and reasonable for all and every one of them to be punished for one and the same individual Action, done by one only, or perhaps by none of them at all. *A Third Defence;* Clarke, III, 844–5.

Collins' doctrine would, he pointed out, not only upset human justice but would make the doctrine of the Resurrection "inconceivable and incredible; and the Justice of future Rewards and Punishments, impossible to be made out." Clarke, III, 851.

In his answer Collins pointed out that since being consists of consciousness and consciousness consists of individual numerical acts which cease to exist after having occurred and can therefore never be resurrected together exactly as they were, resurrection or just punishment would be impossible on Clarke's basis and that the only reasonable method of explaining these was by explaining personal identity as consciousness and consciousness as a mode in a fleeting system of matter. *Answer to Mr. Clarke's Third Defence;* Clarke, III, 876–8.

The effect of the theory of changing particles on identity and hence on both civil and eternal punishments had been discussed by Locke in his *Essay concerning Human Understanding* (Bk. II, chap. xxvii, sec. 18 *et seq.*) and again in his replies to the Bishop of Worcester. In general Collins follows his position.

(17) 141, 2. *It is well known to Anatomists that the Brain is a* Congeries *of Glands, that separate the finer parts of the blood, call'd Animal Spirits;* . . .

The Scriblerians are simply stating the generally accepted theory as to the anatomy and functions of the brain. Chambers (under "Brain") declares:

From the whole, it appears past doubt, that the fibres of the *brain* are exceedingly minute canals; that they receive an humour, infinitely the most subtile, fluid, moveable, and solid of any in the whole body; prepared and secreted by the artful structure of the cortex, driven into these tubules by the force of the heart, and from every part hereof collected into the medulla oblongata.—And this is what some call *animal spirits,* others the *nervous juice;* the great instrument of sensation, muscular motion, &c.

For an earlier account of ancient and modern theories, see William Wotton's *Reflections upon Ancient and Modern Learning* (1694), pp. 195–9.

(18) 141, 4. . . . *the Arietation . . . of the Spirits* . . .

I.e., the butting, battering, or concussion of them. Cf. Bailey.

(19) 141, 5. *From the . . . Motion of the Spirits in those Canals, proceed all the different sorts of Thought:*

What follows is a burlesque of explanations of thought on a purely mechanical basis. The ridicule was probably directed primarily at Collins, who, in the course of his argument with Clarke, attempted to develop Locke's theories of the operations of the mind into an entirely mechanistic system, but it also falls, intentionally or otherwise, on the work of some contemporary medical men, notably that of the famous French physician, Jean Astruc. Astruc's theory, which was advanced in his *De Motus Fermentativi Causa* (Mons, 1702), is, however, so much more elaborate and absurd than the one advanced by the Scriblerians that it is difficult to believe that they were acquainted with it at the time that this passage was written—a plausible situation in view of the fact that Astruc did not acquire a wide reputation until many years later. His theory is summarized (sympathetically) by Chambers (under "Brain") as follows:

He lays it down as an axiom, that every simple idea is produced by the oscillation of one determinate fibre; and every compound idea from cotemporary vibrations of several fibres: that the greater or less degree of evidence follows the greater or less force where the fibre oscillates. Hence he proceeds to show, that the affirmation or negation of any proposition, consists in the equal or unequal number of vibrations, which the moving fibres, representing the two parts of the proposition, make in the same time: *i.e.* if the vibrations of the fibre that gives the idea of the subject, and those of the fibre which gives the idea of the attribute of a proposition, be isochronal, or make an equal number of vibrations in the same time, we are determined to the affirmation of the proposition; if heterochronal, or the vibrations be unequal, the soul will be determined to a negation, &c. Hence result consonant, dissonant, and harmonical fibres, &c.—The evidence and certainty of a judgment, whether affirmative or negative, he deduces from the greater or less consonance or dissonance of the fibres of the subject and attribute; and a right or wrong judgment from the natural or depraved tone of the fibres of the brain.

In his *A Discourse Concerning the Mechanical Operation of the Spirit* (1704) Swift ridiculed some of the current explanations of the nature of thought. It is, he says,

the opinion of choice *virtuosi,* that the brain is only a crowd of little animals, but with teeth and claws extremely sharp, and therefore, cling together in the contexture we behold, like the picture of Hobbes's Leviathan, or like bees in perpendicular swarm upon a tree, or like a carrion corrupted into vermin, still preserving the shape and figure of the mother animal. That all invention is formed by the morsure of two or more of these animals, upon certain capillary nerves, which proceed from thence, whereof three branches spread into the tongue, and two into the right hand . . . That if the morsure be hexagonal, it produces Poetry; the circular gives Eloquence; if the bite hath been conical, the person, whose nerve is so affected, shall be disposed to write upon Politics; and so of the rest. *Works,* I, 201–02.

(20) 141, 24. . . . *a great Virtuoso at Nuremberg, to make a sort of an Hydraulic Engine,* . . .

Nuremberg was famous for its mechanical figures and elaborate clocks. Cf. Moreri; Swift's *Corres.*, I, 160.

(21) 141, 27. . . . *by the force of an Embolus like the heart,* . . .
Embolus—a piston in a cylinder, as in a syringe. Cf. Bailey, II.

(22) 141, 31. . . . *our artificial Man will not only walk, and speak, and perform most of the outward action of the animal life,* . . .
The idea of an artificial man is in part a reflection on Descartes' theory that animals are only elaborate machines. This theory, which Descartes expressed and elaborated upon repeatedly during his lifetime, provoked an enormous amount of discussion and became so controversial that belief in animal automatism became one of the tests of orthodox Cartesianism in science. The concept did not gain much headway in England and was one of the phases of Cartesianism generally rejected by the English scientists of the generation of the Scriblerians. For an account of Descartes' views on the subject see Albert G. A. Balz, "Cartesian Doctrine and the Animal Soul," in *Columbia University Studies in the History of Ideas* (New York, 1935), III, and L. D. Cohen, "Descartes and Henry More on the Beast-machine," *Annals of Science* (1936), I, 48–61. An elaborate confutation of the idea appeared in the widely read *Turkish Spy* of the Italian writer Marana. Vol. II, Bk. I, letter 26; IV, III, 4; IV, IV, 7; and VII, III, 8.

(23) 141, 33. . . . *will perhaps reason as well as most of your Country Parsons.*
The poverty, ignorance, and servile character of country parsons were frequent subjects of satire in the seventeenth and eighteenth centuries. During the seventeenth century various factors had caused the lower clergy to fall in the economic and social scale until in country households they were often regarded as scarcely the equals of the better servants. Too poor to buy books, burdened with heavy parish duties, and usually tied down by large families, they frequently forgot whatever learning they once had and so lost all pretences to dignity or intellectual standing. A brilliant picture of their debased state appears in the third chapter of Macaulay's *History of England.*
Swift, who during a considerable part of his life belonged in the ecclesiastical if not the social and intellectual category of a country parson, felt very keenly about the condition of the lower clergy and both satiric and serious reflections upon it are to be found scattered through his works.

[CHAPTER XIII]

Although a "Chap. 13" is listed in the table of contents (p. 89), the original text contained no chapter with this number. Cf. p. 80.

CHAPTER XIV

In addition to its obvious merits as an individual piece, the episode of the Double Mistress contained in this and the succeeding chapter serves a very useful purpose in bringing to the *Memoirs* dramatic action and a change in the style of humor at a time when their need is beginning to be felt by the reader. After the often brilliant but somewhat static wit of the preceding chapters the broad humor and farcical action of Martinus' experience with the *"tender Passion"* come as a refreshing change. And when the last court of appeal has brought the strange romance to a close by dissolving the marriage, the reader returns to Martinus' intellectual adventures with renewed zest.

Besides burlesquing the plot of romantic novels, the Scriblerians travesty the high-flown style in which fiction of this sort was written. The love which interrupts Martinus' studies is that which "unnerves the Vigour of the Hero, and softens the severity of the Philosopher." This statement, whose counterpart could be found in a score of romantic novels or heroic plays,[1] sets the style of the chapter. The double heroine is described with the extravagant adjectives applied to her prototypes, the lovesick Martinus is made to read Ovid by the glimmering light of a rushy taper and to break forth into a pathetic soliloquy, his love note praises his mistress above all living creatures, and so on.

This burlesque style led to some difficulty in fitting the episode into the *Memoirs*. The narrator who supposedly composed the *Memoirs* as they stand was to be merely a sober and admiring biographer. To attribute the "high" style of the present episode to him would not only violate his character but raise a question as to whether the Scriblerians really intended to ridicule such writing or had themselves unconsciously slipped into it. Since the episode was not designed to meet this difficulty, it seems likely that it did not occur to the Scriblerians until the chapter had been written. Their solution of the problem by assigning the authorship of the piece to Martinus himself and saying that he expressly ordered that not one word of it should be changed, is ingenious, if not entirely plausible. The reader may be left in some wonderment at Martinus' having composed such an elaborate and literary account of his own romance, but the character given both him and the "little book" which he leaves the narrator is so nebulous and elastic that it is impossible to cavil at the possibility of the episode's having been contained in the "Original Memoirs."

The Scriblerians as usual drew on their knowledge rather than their imagination for the materials with which to fashion this episode. Not only were the ancient monsters to which Martinus refers during his discussion with Mr. Randal taken from Aristotle, Pliny, and Aelian, but the setting and several of the principal characters were drawn from life. The model for Martinus' double mistress was a famous set of twins exhibited in London some years before the founding of the Scriblerus Club. These twins, whose names were Helena and Judith, were born in Szony, in Hungary, on October 26, 1701.[2] They were bound together, back

1. Cf., e.g., John Dryden, *Tyrranick Love* (1669), Act III, sc. 2, *Conquest of Granada* (1670), Act II, sc. 1, *Aureng-Zebe* (1675), Act II, sc. 1; Nathaniel Lee, *Sophonisba* (1675), Act I, sc. 2; and Elkanah Settle, *Heir of Morocco* (1682), Act I, sc. 1.

2. A very interesting collection of materials on the twins was printed in the *Philosophical Transactions of the Royal Society* for the year 1757 (L, i, 311–22). The collection includes drawings of the twins as children and adults, an account of a postmortem examination of their bodies by Dr. J. J. Torkos (read before the Society on May 23, 1751), an extract from a letter by William Burnet to Sir Hans Sloane, dated from Leyden on May 9, 1708, in which they are described (read before the Society on May 12, 1708), another description of them taken from a manuscript volume (among Sloane's papers preserved in the British Museum) by J. P.

to back, by common ligaments in the region of the buttocks and were further united by the possession of common genital and rectal orifices. In accordance with the commonly accepted theory of the times, it was believed that their malformation was the result of their mother's having seen, during the formative period of gestation, a pair of monstrous dogs that were joined with their heads in opposite directions.[3]

The twins were exhibited all over Europe and excited a general interest comparable to that aroused at a later date by the celebrated Siamese twins. In the spring of the year 1708 they were seen at The Hague by William Burnet, the eldest son of the famous bishop. Young Burnet, in the best virtuoso tradition, sent a description and a print of them to Sir Hans Sloane, the letter being read before the Royal Society on May 12, 1708.[4]

Shortly after the letter was received, the twins themselves arrived in London and were placed on public exhibition. The exhibit was advertised with the usual handbills:

At Mr. John Pratt's, at the Angel in Cornhil . . . are to be seen two Girls, who are one of the greatest Wonders in Nature that ever was seen, being Born with their Backs fastn'd to each other, and the Passages of their Bodies are both one way. These Children are very Handsome and Lusty, and Talk three different Languages; they are going into the 7th year of their Age. Those who see them, may very well say, they have seen a Miracle, which may pass for the 8th Wonder of the World.[5]

The curious formation of the twins attracted the attention not only of scientists and vulgar sightseers but of the town wits, who promptly began to raise such questions as whether or not the twins possessed double souls and what their marital status would be if they reached adult life. On June 10, 1708, Swift wrote to Stearne, "Here is the sight of two girls joined together at the back, which, in the newsmonger's phrase, causes a great many speculations; and raises abundance of questions in divinity, law, and physic." [6] These questions poured in on *The British Apollo* (the successor to the Athenian Society in the attempt to provide answers to all sorts of queries) and, beginning with issue No. 36, for June 11–16, 1708, the authors of the journal attempted to answer a number of them.[7] Since among these questions were several which figure in the present episode,[8] it seems pos-

du Plessis entitled *A Short History of human Prodigies, etc.*, and a long passage concerning them from *Gerardi Cornelii Drieschii Historia magnae Legationis Caesareae, quam Caroli VI. auspiciis suscepit Damianus Hugo Virmondtius, etc.* (Vienna, 1729).

3. *Ibid.,* p. 311.

4. His description and a reproduction of the print are included in the above-mentioned collection, pp. 315–16.

5. Reprinted in John Ashton, *Social Life in the Reign of Queen Anne,* I, 279.

6. *Corres.,* I, 90.

7. Cf. No. 37, for June 16–18; No. 38, for June 18–23; No. 39, for June 23–25; No. 42, for July 2–7; No. 46, for July 16–21, and No. 69, for October 6–7, 1708. The twins had previously been mentioned in No. 8, the supernumerary paper for November, 1707.

8. Queries as to whether the twins had one or two souls and whether they might marry if they reached maturity were taken up in No. 36, and the question of whether marriage with one would result in incest with the other was discussed in No. 38. The answers given were vague and noncommittal.

sible that some of them were originally submitted, and perhaps answered, by Arbuthnot.

Added interest was given to the question of the twins' possible marriage by the fact that they were attractive both in manner and appearance. According to James Paris du Plessis, who saw them during their stay in London,

They were brisk, merry, and well-bred; they could read, write, and sing very prettily: they could speak three different languages, as Hungarian or High Dutch, Low Dutch, and French, and were learning English. They were very handsome, very well shaped in all parts, and beautiful faces . . . They loved one another very tenderly. Their clothes were fine and neat. They had two bodies, four sleeves; and one petticoat served to the bodies, and their shifts the same.[9]

Helena, the elder, who is to be identified with Lindamira, was considerably stronger and more healthy than Judith, and generally took the lead in common activities such as walking, where it was necessary for one to move backward. In her sixth year, Judith suffered a paralytic stroke in her left side and throughout her life was given to attacks, which, however, did not affect her sister.[10] On February 8, 1723, while the twins were in Posen, Judith began to suffer severely from convulsions. As she became worse, Helena too grew ill, and on the twenty-third of the same month both died.[11]

The remainder of Mr. Randal's show is modeled on two other real exhibits shown in London during Queen Anne's reign. One of these, which was on view in the latter part of the year 1711,[12] contained the little Black Prince who becomes Martinus' brother-in-law, as well as some of the animals listed by the Scriblerians. It is thus described in its handbill:

By Her Majesty's Permission. This is to give Notice to all Gentlemen, Ladies, and Others, that JUST over against the *Mews Gate* at *Charing Cross,* is to be seen a Collection of strange and wonderful Creatures from most Parts of the World, all alive.

The First being a little *Black Man,* being but 3 Foot high, and 32 Years of Age, strait and proportionable every way, who is distinguished by the Name of the *Black Prince,* and has been shown before most Kings and Princes in *Christendom.* The next being his Wife, the *Little Woman,* NOT 3 Foot high, and 30 Years of Age, strait and proportionable as any Woman in the Land, which is commonly call'd the *Fairy Queen,* she gives a General satisfaction to all that sees her, by Diverting them with Dancing, being big with Child. Likewise their little *Turkey Horse,* being but 2 Foot odd Inches High, and above 12 Years of Age, that shews several diverting and surprising Actions, at the Word of Command. The least Man, Woman and Horse that ever was seen in the World Alive. *The Horse being kept in a Box.* The next being a strange Monstrous Female Creature, that was taken in the Wood in the Desarts of ÆTIOPIA in Prestor *John's* Country, in the remotest parts of AFFRICA, being brought over from *Cape de Bon Esperance* alias *Cape of Good Hope;* from hir Head downwards she resembles Humane Nature, having Breasts, Belly, Navel, Nipples, Legs, and Arms like a Woman, with a long

9. *Phil. Trans.,* L (1757), i, 317–18.
10. *Ibid.,* p. 312.
11. *Ibid.,* p. 313.
12. The exhibit is mentioned in *Spectator,* No. 271, for January 10, 1711/12.

Monstrous Head, no such Creature was ever seen in this part of the World before, she showing many strange and wonderful Actions which gives great satisfaction to all that ever did see her. The next is the Noble *Picary* which is very much admir'd by the Learned. The next being the Noble *Jack-call,* the Lion's provider, which hunts in the Forest for the Lion's Prey. Likewise a small *Egyptian Panther,* spotted like a *Leopard.* The next being a strange monstrous Creature, brought from the *Coast* of *Brazil,* having a Head like a Child, Legs and Arms very wonderful, with a long Tail like a Serpent, wherewith he feeds himself, as an *Elephant* doth with his Trunk. With several other Rarities too tedious to mention in this Bill.—And as no such Collection was ever shewn in this Place before, we hope they will give you content and satisfaction, assuring you, that they are the greatest Rarities that ever was shewn alive in this Kingdom, and are to be seen from 9 a Clock in the Morning, till 10 at Night, where true Attendance shall be given during our stay in this Place, which will be very short. *Long live the* QUEEN.[13]

The other show contained the mantegar who attempts to ravish the double heroine and several of the curiosities which he and Martinus use as weapons in their great battle. Its handbill read:

By Her Majesty's Authority. Is to be seen, the Hand of a Sea Monster which was lately taken on the Coasts of *Denmark;* the whole Creature was very large, and weigh'd (according to Computation) at least fifty Tuns, and was seventy foot in length: His upper part resembled a Man; from the middle downwards he was a Fish, &c. Likewise there is a Man Teger, lately brought from the *East Indies,* a most strange and wonderful Creature, the like never seen before in *England,* it being of Seven several Colours, from the Head downwards resembling a Man, its fore parts clear, and his hinder parts all Hairy; having a long Head of Hair, and Teeth 2 or 3 Inches long; taking a Glass of Ale in his hand like a Christian, Drinks it, also plays at Quarter Staff. There is also a famous Porcupine, a Martin Drill, a Pecari from the Deserts of Arabia, the Bone of a Giant above a Yard long, with several other Monstrous Creatures too difficult to describe, all alive. This is to give notice that the *Man Teger* is removed from *Holborn Bars* to the sign of the *George* against the steps of *Upper More Fields.* Vivat Regina.[14]

Besides combining these three shows into one, the Scriblerians make several changes for dramatic purposes. For obvious reasons the Black Prince's wife is eliminated, as is the "strange Monstrous Female Creature" from Prester John's country. The peccary that appears in two of the exhibits and the Brazilian monster with a head like a child are also dropped. The other most notable changes are the alteration of the martin drill into the monkey who intercepts Martinus' love letter and the addition of a number of rarities to serve as missiles in the combat between Martinus and the mantegar.

As the result of the discovery by Professor Sherburn of a fragment of the manuscript of the Double Mistress episode among the Pope manuscripts preserved in the British Museum, it is possible to work out the authorship and the history of the composition of the present and the succeeding chapter more fully than of any other part of the *Memoirs.*[15] From the evidence gleaned from this bit of

13. Quoted up to the long dash from Ashton, *op. cit.,* I, 273–4, and the remainder from H. Morley, *Memoirs of Bartholomew Fair,* p. 325.
14. Ashton, *op. cit.,* I, 271–2.
15. See Appendix IV.

manuscript it appears that the episode was probably written in the spring of the year 1717, following the collaboration of Arbuthnot, Pope, and Gay on their farce *Three Hours after Marriage*. Added plausibility is given to this date by the small but, in view of the closeness with which Lindamira and Indamora are modeled on the Hungarian twins, significant fact that in the episode the double heroine is said to be sixteen years old,[16] the age of Helena and Judith at that time. Still further evidence that the episode and the play were written at about the same time is perhaps to be found in the farcical mood common to both (which is not found in their other collaborations) and in the allusions to such out-of-the-way wonders of the ancients as the marticora and the chaste bird porphyrion.[17]

The conjunction of the two suggests the possible source of inspiration for the episode. *Three Hours after Marriage* deals with the ill-fated marriage of a virtuoso. This virtuoso, Dr. Fossile, is so like Martinus that had not the name "Scriblerus" been too closely associated with the still-hated Oxford and his Tory ministry for safety,[18] they might very well have used it instead. This similarity must have led the three to think of their old hero and to plan a like romance for him. In the play Fossile mentions "monstrous twins."[19] Such a hint would be sufficient to start the ingenious mind of Arbuthnot working.

It is easy to discern Arbuthnot's hand in the episode; the learning, the ingenious reasoning in the second part, and the nice sense of the ridiculous shown throughout are typically his and suggest that in this, as in so many other parts of the *Memoirs*, he was the principal author. The fragment of manuscript bears this out. The original rough draft contained on the page is in Arbuthnot's handwriting. But this draft has been heavily corrected by another hand—that of Pope.[20] The corrections involved are considerable, the passage being much shortened and the style clarified and sharpened. If this small sample is typical of the whole, it would seem that the doctor drafted the episode and Pope was responsible for its finished form. Though perhaps broadly true, such a view oversimplifies the situation. Gay, who was with Pope and Arbuthnot, would certainly have a hand in any Scriblerus piece being written. The plot was no doubt talked over and developed in conversation, so that it cannot be assumed that Arbuthnot originated all the ideas for it even though he "held the pen." Pope's corrections were probably by no means so drastic throughout the piece as in this one passage. And finally it is to be observed that Pope's own version was subject to considerable correction by himself or others before the passage reached its present form.

We learn one other item of interest from the manuscript fragment. In the original draft the names of the twins are Tabitha and Tryphena.[21] In the course of Pope's revision these are changed to the much more romantic Lindamira and Inda-

16. Text, p. 146, ll. 25–7.
17. Text, p. 145, ll. 12 and 28; *Three Hours after Marriage*, Act III.
18. Oxford was not released from the Tower until July 1, 1717.
19. Act II.
20. See below, Appendix IV.
21. It seems probable that the names originally chosen for the twins by the Scriblerians were Tryphena and Tryphosa. These names appear together in the Bible (Romans 16:12) and some Biblical commentators have suggested that they were the names of twin sisters. There appear to be two possible reasons why the Scriblerians altered Tryphosa to Tabitha. One was that the

mora. These names were taken from a novel by Thomas Brown, *The Adventures of Lindamira*. Brown's novel consisted of a series of letters from Lindamira, "a Lady of Quality," to her friend Indamora in the country—Brown professing merely to have "revised and corrected" the letters for publication. Though the primary setting is in England and Brown declares in his preface that *"the weight of Truth, and the importance of real Matter of Fact"* ought to overbalance the *"feign'd Adventures of a fabulous Knight-Errantry,"* [22] *The Adventures of Lindamira* contains most of the usual clichés of plot and expression. It was first published in 1702 and was popular enough to warrant a second edition in the next year and a third in 1734. Added humor was given to the use of the names Lindamira and Indamora for the twins (whose "most secret Charms" might be viewed for six pence) by the fact that the modest behavior of the original Lindamira led to her being cited as a model of propriety.[23]

The Double Mistress episode continued to have its own history after being incorporated in the *Memoirs*. As has been noted,[24] the two chapters were left out without comment by Warburton and were not restored to the text until Warton's edition of Pope's works in 1797. Warton thought the episode "full of the most exquisite original humor." [25] Bowles, his successor, agreed [26] and retained the chapters, but the mid-nineteenth-century editors, Roscoe and Courthope, returned to Warburton's policy of ignoring them. Aitken, too, declined to print them in his *Life and Works of Arbuthnot,* but he at least felt obliged to inform his readers of their existence and to give them some hint of their character.[27]

(1) 143, 7. . . . our Philosopher . . . expresly directed that *not one Word of this Chapter should be alter'd,* . . .

The Scriblerians forgot that the "Original Memoirs" were written in Latin. Cf. Text, p. 92, ll. 11–12.

(2) 143, 20. . . . *not far from the proud Battlements of the Palace of Whitehall,* . . .

The Scriblerians place their show on the spot occupied by the exhibition of which the Black Prince was a part, the handbill for that show advertising it as being held "over against the *Mews Gate at Charing Cross.*" Cf. above, p. 296. The place does not seem to have been a usual one for such shows. The region is described in *The Foreigner's Guide* (1729) as "a large Square upon rising Ground,

---

strangeness of the names Tryphena and Tryphosa would tend to emphasize the extraordinary aspects of the twins at the expense of the pseudoromantic atmosphere which the Scriblerians were trying to develop and the other that the Biblical context in which these names appear ("Salute Tryphena and Tryphosa, who labour in the Lord.") was hardly appropriate to the character and activities of the twins in the *Memoirs*. The name Tabitha is also Biblical (Acts 9: 36–43) but was sufficiently common in England to make the twin who bore it seem more like an ordinary heroine.

22. Preface.
23. *Tatler*, No. 9.
24. Cf. above, pp. 66, 81–2.
25. *Works of Pope* (1797), VI, 150 n.
26. *Works of Pope* (1806), VI, 138 n.; I, [vii]–viii.
27. P. 354, n. 1.

with Statues and Coach Houses, . . . where the Horse and Grenadier Guards parade in the Morning to mount the Guard." P. 48.

The reference to the "proud Battlements of the Palace of Whitehall" is ironic. All that remained after the disastrous fire of 1691 was Inigo Jones's Palladian style Banqueting House, whose windows had been bricked up in order to make it into a chapel, and one court on the river side which, though crenelated, was only two stories high. The ruins were a regular·sight for visitors.

(3) 143, 21. . . . *his eyes were drawn upwards by a large square piece of Canvas, . . .*

In his *Part of the Seventh Epistle of the First Book of Horace Imitated* (*1713*), Swift says,

> Some few Days after, Harley spies
> The Doctor fasten'd by the Eyes
> At Charing-Cross, among the Rout,
> Where painted Monsters are hung out.
> Ll. 57–60; *Poems*, II, 172.

(4) 143, 25. . . . *thrice the bulk of the Nemæan monster; . . .*

A monstrous lion, born of the hundred-headed Typhon, which for many years terrorized the neighborhood of Nemaea. Slaying it was the first of Hercules' labors.

(5) 143, 26. . . . *the little Jackall, the faithful spy of the King of beasts:*

All the ancient writers on natural history describe the jackal as following the lion and spying out prey for him. See the same statement about him in the handbill for the Black Prince exhibit. Above, p. 297.

(6) 143, 28. . . . *of the two Cubits high, the black Prince of Monomotapa; . . .*

According to Arbuthnot's reckoning in his *Tables of the Grecian, Roman and Jewish Measures, Weights and Coins* (1705) two cubits equal three feet, the height given on the handbill.

As added glory for their character the Scriblerians have made him Prince of Monomotapa. The Kingdom of Monomotapa was a region in South Africa discovered and conquered by the Portuguese. It was said to extend from the Zambesi almost to the Cape of Good Hope, but its boundaries were never accurately defined. It was supposed to have been a great empire and the imperial palace in its capital, Banamatapa, is described in Moreri's dictionary as of great magnificence. Arbuthnot mentions the place in his poem "The Quidnuncki's," l. 18.

(7) 143, 29. . . . *the glaring Cat-a-mountain, . . .*

According to Pliny (viii. 32), all who behold the horrible eyes of this monster fall dead upon the spot. Aelian (vii. 5) describes it in some detail.

(8) 143, 29. . . . *the quill-darting Porcupine, . . .*

A porcupine was one of the exhibits in the show of which the mantegar was a part; cf. above, p. 297.

(9) 143, 30. . . . *the Man-mimicking Manteger.*

Though of a somewhat later date, the following description of a mantegar kept in the yard of the Tower of London in the middle of the eighteenth century brings out more clearly than most those characteristics of the animal which are put to use by the Scriblerians in the episode:

After this, you are shewn . . . a young *Manteger,* commonly called a *Man-Tiger,* a curious Animal, somewhat of the Baboon Kind, but of astonishing Strength, and very mischievous if affronted. He has a dextrous Art of throwing Stones, and will fling Lead or Iron, if it happens to be in his Reach, with such Force as to split Stools, Bowls, or other wooden Utensils, into a hundred Pieces. In his Passage hither he killed a poor Boy on Board the Ship that brought him by throwing a Shot of nine Pounds Weight at him, in some Disgust. . . . If you fling any Thing at him you cannot hit him, for he catches it with surprizing Dexterity. He is very young, but appears by his Motions, when Women approach him, to be exceeding leacherous. *London in Miniature* (1755), pp. 17–18.

The Scriblerians refer to the mantegar several times in the *Origine of Sciences.* E. & C., x, 418–20.

(10) 143, 33. . . . *as closely united as the ancient Hermaphroditus and Salmacis;*
The story is contained in the fourth book of Ovid's *Metamorphoses.*

(11) 143, 34. . . . *the mingled waters of the gentle Thames and the amourous Isis.*

This analogy is an echo of the "marriage of the rivers" motif popular with Elizabethan poets. The most famous example is the elaborate description of the marriage of the Thames and the Medway in the fourth book of Spenser's *Faerie Queene.* In his description of Oxfordshire Camden quotes at considerable length a poem, apparently of his own authorship, on the marriage of the masculine Isis with the feminine Thames. Cf. C. G. Osgood, "Spenser's English Rivers," *Transactions of Connecticut Academy of Arts and Sciences,* XXIII (1920), 71–2. The theme still persisted in Queen Anne's time, William King writing a short poem on the subject beginning,

> So the God Thame, as through some pond he glides,
> Into the arms of wandering Isis slides: King, III, 269.

Pope refers to "The winding Isis and the fruitful Thame" in *Windsor Forest,* l. 340.

(12) 144, 9. . . . *(like Æneas's golden bough)* . . .
The bough which enables Aeneas to visit the lower regions. Cf. the sixth book of Virgil's *Aeneid.*

(13) 144, 23. . . . *the Porcupine came from the kingdom of Prester-John* . . .
The kingdom of Prester John was set by some writers in Tartary or India and by others in Ethiopia. An elaborate account of it is given in the *Travels of Sir John Mandeville,* chaps. xx, xxx; (1905), pp. 122, 178–85. For a contemporary summary of the various theories of the origin of the name see Moreri's dictionary. It will be recalled that in the handbill for the Black Prince's show the "Monstrous Female Creature" was said to have been taken "in the Wood in the Desarts

of ÆTIOPIA in Prestor *John's* Country, in the remotest parts of AFFRICA."
Cf. above, p. 296.

(14) 144, 25. . . . *the Manteger was a true descendant of the Celebrated Han-*
niman the Magnificent.

Hanūmān (also spelled Hanumat, Harman, etc.) is an ape god of India, wor-
shiped as a protector of towns and as the personification of fertility and virile
strength. He figures in a number of ancient epics which were retold by European
travelers. Cf. *Les six voyages de Jean Baptiste Tavernier* (Paris, 1676), Bk. III,
chap. v; Churchill, *Collection of Voyages and Travels* (1704), III, 838–9, 862–3.

The Scriblerians also make humorous use of Hanūmān in their *Origine of*
Sciences. There they speak of his great knowledge and identify as his the tooth
which the Portuguese took in Bisnager in 1559 and which, according to Linschoten, various kings of India attempted to buy back for seven hundred thousand duc-
ats. Linschoten and others thought the tooth to be that of a monkey, but it seems
to have been a reputed tooth of Buddha. Cf. *The Voyage of John Huyghen van*
Linschoten, Hakluyt Society (1885), I, 292–3.

(15) 144, 34. *But didst thou ever risque thyself among the Scythian Canni-*
bals, . . .

"Pliny lib. 7. cap. 2." (Scrib.)

The reference is an illustration of the thorough way in which the authors
combed Pliny for material. In the passage cited, Pliny simply says that there are certain tribes of the Scythians and, indeed, many other nations which feed upon
human flesh.

(16) 144, 35. . . . *those wild men of Abarimon, who walk with their feet back-*
wards?

Pliny places Abarimon in a great valley of Mount Imaus, the modern Himalaya
range. He says (vii. 2) the inhabitants, whose feet are turned backwards, are
wonderfully quick and wander about freely with the wild beasts. Aulus Gellius
gives the same account (ix. 4), listing Aristeas and Isigonus as his authorities.

(17) 144, 37. . . . *hast thou ever seen the Sciapodes, so called because when laid*
supine, they shelter themselves from the Sun-beams with the shadow of their
feet?

Pliny vii. 2. Mandeville also gives an account of these people, though he does
not name them. In Ethiopia, he says, "be folk that have but one foot, and they go
so blyve that it is a marvel. And the foot is so large, that it shadoweth all the
body against the sun, when they lie and rest them." *Op. cit.,* chap. xvii; (1905),
p. 105.

(18) 144, 38. . . . *canst thou procure me a Troglodyte footman, who can catch*
a Roe at his full speed?

Pliny quotes Ctesias as saying that the Troglodytes live not far from the Sciapodes
(vii. 2) and Crates of Pergamus as saying that they dwell beyond Ethiopia and are
able "to outrun the horse." *Ibid.*

(19) 145, 2. . . . *hast thou ever beheld those Illyrian damsels who have two sights in one eye, whose looks are poisonous to males that are adult?*
Pliny vii. 2.

(20) 145, 4. . . . *hast thou ever measur'd the gigantick Ethiopian, whose stature is above eight cubits high,* . . .
Pliny vii. 2.

(21) 145, 4. . . . *the sesquipedalian Pigmey?*
Sesquipedalian, i.e. a foot and a half high. The pygmies described by Pliny (vii. 2) are three spans in height (twenty-seven inches). Homer refers to the war of the pygmies in the *Iliad*, Bk. III, l. 9; and Aristotle gives an account of them in *Hist. Animal.* viii.12. In 1699 Dr. Edward Tyson published (as an appendix to his *Orang-Outang, sive Homo Sylvestris*) a tract entitled "A Philological Essay concerning the *Pygmies*, the *Cynocephali*, the *Satyrs*, and the *Sphinges* of the Ancients," in which he endeavored to prove that the ancient pygmies were simply monkeys. With this work the Scriblerians were familiar, as they put it to heavy use in their *Origine of Sciences*.

(22) 145, 7. . . . *hast thou ever seen any of the Cynocephali, who have the head and voice of a Dog, and whose milk is the only true specifick for Consumptions?*
"Pliny 16." (Scrib.)
The Cynocephali, according to Aristotle, are like other apes in form except for their faces and teeth, which are like those of dogs. *Hist. Animal.* ii.5.1. Pliny refers to them as dog-headed apes (viii. 80) and says that a race of Ethiopian nomads, called the Memismini, live on their milk (vii. 2), but says nothing about the use of their milk for consumptions. Aelian gives much the same description as Aristotle, saying that they are natives of India, and adding that they keep sheep and goats whose milk they drink (iv. 46).
The value of their milk for curing consumptions seems to be an original idea of the Scriblerians based on the beliefs of the ancients (e.g., Pliny xxviii. 33; Galen, VI, 775) that various kinds of milk are used for this purpose.

(23) 145, 15. *That word (replies Martin) is a corruption of the Mantichora of the Ancients, the most noxious Animal that ever infested the earth; who had a Sting above a cubit long, and would attack a rank of armed men at once, flinging his poisonous darts several miles around him.*
"Aelian. lib. 4. cap. 2 [an error for 21]." (Scrib.)
Aelian says that the animal is called the marticora (the spelling in the text is an alternate one; cf. Chambers, *Supplement* [1753], *s.v.*) because it is of all beasts the most warlike and dangerous to men. According to his account, its sting, which is several cubits long, throws out poison in perpetual succession. He also says that it attacks men in groups rather than singly. His account, like that of Aristotle (*Hist. Animal.* ii. 3. 10) and Pliny (viii. 30) appears to have been drawn entirely from the *Indicae* of Ctesias.
Beneath the reference to Aelian noted above the Scriblerians list six references which are not attached to any particular part of the text. See Text, p. 145. Three

of these are to Pliny (xi. 51; viii. 30; viii. 25) and three are to Aelian (iii. 42; i. 49; i. 2). Since only two of these references cite material having anything to do with any of the eight prodigies (Aelian i. 49 refers to the merops and iii. 42 to the bird porphyrion [cf. note 29 and note 30, below]), it seems probable that these citations refer to passages in the text that were eliminated by Pope in the course of his revisions.

(24) 145, 16. *Canst thou inform me whether the Boars grunt in Macedonia?*

As an example of the effect of various localities on the noises of beasts, Pliny (xi. 112) notes merely in passing that it is said that in Macedonia both the frogs and the wild boars are dumb.

(25) 145, 18. *Canst thou give me a Certificate that the Lions in Africa are afraid of the scolding of Women?*

The Scriblerians here give a facetious twist to Pliny, who says that it is believed in Libya that lions understand pleas addressed to them and that he had been told that a slave woman when attacked by a number of lions had been able to calm their ferocity by explaining what unworthy prey she was for such noble beasts and by imploring their compassion (viii. 19). None of the other writers on natural history describes lions as fearing the scolding of women.

(26) 145, 21. *. . . hast thou ever heard the sagacious Hyæna counterfeit the voice of a shepherd, imitate the vomiting of a man to draw the dogs together, and ev'n call a shepherd by his proper name?*

Pliny viii. 44. Aristotle also says of the hyena that it secretly attacks men and that it hunts dogs by vomiting like men. *Hist. Animal.* viii. 7. 2.

(27) 145, 25. *Your Crocodile is but a small one, but you ought to have brought with him the bird Trochilos that picks his teeth after dinner, at which the silly animal is so pleased, that he gapes wide enough to give the Ichneumon, his mortal enemy, an entrance into his belly.*

This account of the crocodile, the trochilus, and the ichneumon is agreed upon by all the ancient naturalists. Pliny gives the most elaborate version (viii. 37). Aelian repeats the account of the crocodile and the trochilus in one place (iii. 11) and of the enmity between the crocodile and the ichneumon in another (x. 47). Aristotle tells of the trochilus cleaning the crocodile's mouth (*Hist. Animal.* ix. 7, 3) but does not say the ichneumon made use of the opportunity.

King, in *The Art of Cookery,* made humorous use of the cleaning of the crocodile's teeth by suggesting that observation of this natural wonder led the Egyptians to invent the toothpick. King, III, 47. He, however, confuses the trochilus with the ichneumon.

(28) 145, 27. *Your modern Ostriches are dwindled to meer Larks in comparison with those of the Ancients; theirs were equal in stature to a man on horseback.*

Pliny (x. i) gives this height for them.

(29) 145, 30. *Alas! we have lost the chaste bird Porphyrion! the whole Race was destroy'd by Women, because they discover'd the infidelity of wives to their husbands.*

The porphyrion, according to Aelian (iii. 42), watches married women and if he perceives that a wife has been ravished, he strangles himself.

(30) 145, 31. *The Merops too is now no where to be found, the only bird that flew backward by the tail.*
This description of the merops is drawn from Aelian, i. 49. Pliny's account (x. 51) says nothing of its flying backward.

(31) 145, 34. . . . *what Dialect of the Greek is spoken by the birds of Diomedes' Island?*
Pliny states (x.61) that these birds pursue any barbarians who land on the island with loud and clamorous cries but are courteous to Greeks and seem thus to honor them as fellow countrymen of Diomedes.

(32) 146, 10. . . . *spangled with the Diamonds of Cornwall,* . . .
Fuller says of them, "These of themselves sound high, till the *Addition* of *Cornish* substracteth from their Valuation. In *Blackness* and *Hardness,* they are far short of the *Indian.* Yet Set with a good *Foyle* . . . may at the first sight deceive no unskilfull Lapidary." *Worthies of England,* i, 193.

(33) 146, 10. . . . *and the precious stones of Bristol.*
"BRISTOW-STONES, a sort of soft Diamonds, which are found in abundance in a Rock near *Bristol,*" Bailey. In *Three Hours after Marriage,* Dr. Fossile, after discovering the true character of his bride, says, "But if I have a Bristol stone put upon me instead of a diamond, why should I by experiments spoil its lustre." Act I.

(34) 146, 14. *He was mounted on the least Palfrey in the Universe.*
In the real exhibit the Black Prince had a little turkey horse "but 2 Foot odd Inches High." Cf. above, p. 296.

(35) 146, 22. . . . *whose common parts of Generation, had so closely allied them,* . . .
See prefatory note to the following chapter.

(36) 146, 26. *The Sun had twice eight times perform'd his annual course, since their Mother brought them into the world* . . .
As has been noted (above, p. 298) the age given Lindamira and Indamora by the Scriblerians corresponds to the age of the real twins in 1717.

(37) 147, 1. . . . *he was infinitely more ravish'd with her as a charming Monster.*
The "passion" of the virtuosi for monsters and abnormalities was frequently ridiculed in the later seventeenth and early eighteenth centuries. However, in translating that "passion" into actual amorousness, as they do both here and in the case of the Spanish lady's phenomenon, the Scriblerians open up an entirely original vein of humor.

(38) 147, 15. . . . *but alas! his [Ovid's] Remedy of Love was no cure* . . .
For some of the means of curing love suggested by Ovid in his *Remedio Amoris* see above, p. 279, nn. 10–12.

(39) 147, 26. . . . *most reverend Pliny, Ælian, and Aldrovandus!*

For Pliny and Aldrovandus see p. 186, n. 6, p. 188, n. 11. Claudius Aelianus was a Roman writer and teacher of the third century A.D. His chief works, *De natura animalium,* a series of moral stories of animal life, and his *Variae historiae* are of value in large part because of the numerous quotations from older writers which they contain.

(40) 148, 22. . . . *he walked to and fro . . . from the hour of five to eleven, . . .*

In delaying the opening of Mr. Randal's show until eleven o'clock, the Scriblerians appear to have exercised dramatic license. The Black Prince's exhibit was advertised as opening at nine in the morning (above, p. 297) and this seems to have been the usual hour. It is, of course, possible that the twins, Helena and Judith, observed less taxing hours.

(41) 149, 30. . . . *some Comet may vitrify this Globe . . .*

Ever since the great comet of 1680 these celestial bodies had exercised a great effect on popular imagination, and the fear that some day a comet would destroy the earth, though laughed at by most scientists, appears to have been quite common. Some quasi-scientific grounds for this fear were provided by William Whiston, who, in February, 1714, in a work entitled *The Cause of the Deluge Demonstrated,* advanced a theory, previously advanced by Halley, that the comet of 1680 had brought about the great Deluge. The Scriblerians ridiculed Whiston's theory by having Martinus prepare tide tables for a comet that is to approach the earth. Cf. below, p. 341, n. 26. For a summary of the contemporary theories regarding the nature and movements of comets see Chambers.

(42) 151, 32. *But Fate had so ordain'd, that Martin was not more enamoured on Lindamira, than Indamora was on Martin.*

The passage which follows in the text is that which is covered by the fragment of manuscript discovered by Professor Sherburn. For an account of this and the earlier versions of the passage contained in it see Appendix IV.

(43) 151, 34. . . . *how unhappy the Nymph must be, who was even depriv'd the universal Relief of a* Soliloquy. *However, thus she thought, without being allow'd to tell it to any Grove or purling Stream.*

Cf. Shadwell's *The Virtuoso* (1676), Act III:

Bruce. Come, I see this way will not do: I'll try another with you. Ah, Madam! change your cruel intentions, or I shall become the most desolate Lover, that ever yet, with arms across, sigh'd to a murmuring Grove, or to a purling Stream complain'd. Savage! I'll wander up and down the Woods, and carve my passion on the Barks of Trees, and vent my grief to winds, that as they fly shall sigh and pity me.
Clarinda. How now! What foolish Fustian's this? you talk like an Heroick Poet.
Complete Works of Thomas Shadwell, M. Summers, ed., III, 134.

(44) 153, 16. . . . *he heav'd up the* hand *of a prodigious* Sea-Monster; . . . *wielded the pond'rous* Thigh-bone *of a* Giant.

These two articles were part of the mantegar exhibit; cf. above, p. 297.

(45) 153, 18. *And now they stood opposed to each other, like the dread Captain of the seven-fold Shield and the redoubted Hector.*

Cf. *Iliad*, Bk. xxii. The adjective "seven-fold" applied to Achilles' shield is somewhat curious as in the well-known description of its forging by Vulcan it is said to be composed of "five ample plates" (Bk. xviii; Pope translation, l. 555) and later in the account of the fatal combat between the two warriors it is referred to as his "four-fold cone" (Bk. xxii, l. 395), the "four-fold" probably being explained by the division of the shield into four concentric circles. Cf. Pope's dissertation on the shield in the fifth volume of his translation (1720), pp. 1442–66. A factor in the situation is that at the time the Scriblerians were working on the Double Mistress episode, Pope had progressed no further in his translation than book fifteen or sixteen and hence had not reached the passage describing the shield.

(46) 153, 25. *The lady from the window, like another Helen from the Trojan wall, was witness of the Combat caused by her own Beauty.*

A reference to the famous passage in the third book of the *Iliad*. See Pope's translation, ll. 165 *et seq.*

(47) 153, 35. *. . . happily united to her that very evening, by a Reverend Clergyman in the Fleet, in the holy Bands of Matrimony.*

"Marriage in the Fleet" was a highly disreputable marriage ceremony made use of by extremely poor couples and elopers. The Fleet was a debtors' prison standing on the east side of Farringdon Road in Clerkenwell. Before 1711 the marriages were performed in the prison chapel by any clergyman who happened to be confined in the prison for debt. No license or publishing of banns was required. In 1711 Parliament passed an act (10 Anne c. 19) prohibiting marriages in the Fleet chapel. The only effect of this law, however, was to drive the ceremonies outside the prison into the so-called "Liberty of the Fleet," a district where, because of the excessively crowded conditions in the prison, privileged debtors were allowed to reside. Here the marriages were performed in taverns and other buildings under conditions that were worse than before. The practice of these marriages was not stopped until 1774, when an act was passed declaring such marriages from that time on illegal and not binding.

CHAPTER XV

The Englishman's proverbial hatred of the complexities, trivialities, delays, worries, and costs of civil law was shared by the Scriblerians. Individual lawyers were among their valued friends, but they detested the breed and frequently satirized law in their writings. Swift was especially vigorous in his attacks on legal complexities and chicanery. Hostile reflections on law and lawyers appear in several places in his writings,[1] but most notably in *Gulliver's Travels*. Gulliver's attempts to explain English justice and law to the King of Brobdingnag and to his Master in Houyhnhnmland lead to some of the bitterest and, in the latter case, longest passages of

1. Cf., e.g., *Works*, iii, 74, 99; iv, 281; xi, 23–45; *Corres.*, iii, 277.

satire in the entire *Travels*.[2] The other Scriblerians were scarcely less harsh. Arbuthnot's *History of John Bull*, the original title of which was *Law Is a Bottomless Pit*, is filled with satirical strokes aimed against law and its analogical counterpart, war. Pope's works contain a score of sharp lines and passages [3] whose general tone is summed up in the well-known line,

> And (all the plagues in one) the bawling Bar; [4]

and Gay's *Fables* and his two operettas, the *Beggar's Opera* and *Polly*, contain equally biting attacks.[5] Parnell and Oxford did not treat the theme in a literary way, but there is no reason to believe that they differed from their colleagues in their attitude, the latter at least having had good cause to hate the costly intricacies of law. As a group, the Scriblerians, in addition to satirizing law in the present chapter and the first part of the succeeding one, also prepared a burlesque law case in the name of Martinus Scriblerus entitled *Stradling versus Stiles*.[6]

The chapter falls into four general parts: the advice of counsel, the arguments of Dr. Pennyfeather for Martinus, the counterarguments of Dr. Leatherhead, and the decisions of the various courts. The first of these is remarkable for its display of erudition on somewhat obscure points of marriage law. Since such matters were outside the professional provinces of the Scriblerians, the question naturally arises whether or not they received outside help in preparing it and perhaps other parts of the chapter. Such help would seem to have been easily available from their friend Fortescue, an able lawyer and judge who eventually became Master of the Rolls. Fortescue was on intimate terms with Gay, Pope, and Arbuthnot during the period when the Double Mistress episode was composed and we have Pope's word for the fact that he later helped them with *Stradling versus Stiles*.[7] Against the idea of help from Fortescue, however, it may be argued that since his career was in civil law he would probably be no better informed on questions of marriage law, which fell within the jurisdiction of the ecclesiastical courts, than a well-read outsider would be, that many chapters in the *Memoirs* give evidence of the willingness of Arbuthnot and the other Scriblerians to spend time and effort in collecting out-of-the-way material, and that the erudition displayed would not have been particularly difficult to collect.

The principal source used by the Scriblerians was the *Disputationum de Sancto Matrimonii Sacramento Libri III* [8] of Thomas Sanchez, a Spanish Jesuit (1551–1610). This vast, elaborate, and learned work, which deals with all aspects of matrimony, was reprinted several times in the seventeenth century and was there-

2. *Works*, VIII, 133–4, 140, 256–61, 272. The Scriblerians refer to the attack on law in *Gulliver's Travels* in the *Memoirs;* see Text, p. 164, ll. 24–25, and below, p. 321, n. 3.

3. Cf. A. Abbott, *A Concordance to the Works of Alexander Pope* (New York, 1875), under "Bar," "Law," and "Lawyers."

4. *Satires of Dr. Donne*, Sat. IV, l. 55.

5. *Fables*, 2d series, No. I, ll. 1–26, No. IX, ll. 19–22; see the two operettas *passim*.

6. Cf. above, p. 46.

7. Spence, p. 109.

8. It was first printed in Genoa in 1592, but better known are the Antwerp editions of 1607 and 1614. For a summary of the attacks on and defenses of the work, see the article on Sanchez in Bayle's *Dictionary*.

fore readily available to the Scriblerians.[9] The other works referred to in the chapter, the *Summa* of Cardinal Hostiensis and Sylvester's *De Sponsalibus,* were much more rare, especially the latter. They were, however, extensively quoted by Sanchez and it is quite possible that the Scriblerians derived their references to them from him.

Much of the humor and legal reasoning in the chapter turns on the physical structure of the twins. The real twins were independent in their structure and vital functions except in the pelvic region where they were joined. Here they possessed common genital and rectal orifices situated between the two bodies in a normal relationship to each other. Since it was impossible to determine their internal anatomy exactly during their lifetime, there was some question whether they also possessed common internal genitalia. Hence the contradictory verdicts of the jury of physicians, who decide that if Martinus' wife becomes pregnant Indamora must take part in the gestation,[10] and of the jury of matrons, who determine that the parts of generation in the two are distinct.[11]

All such questions regarding the real twins were resolved after their death in 1723. A post-mortem dissection revealed that each body had its own bladder, uterus with ovaries, Fallopian tube, and a portion of a vagina. These last coming together from both twins formed a common vagina with a single orifice.[12]

In this chapter the little Black Prince figures prominently as Martinus' brother-in-law and the defendant in the several lawsuits. Since the lawsuits made it necessary for him to have a name, the Scriblerians provided him with one. The one they chose, or rather devised, Ebn-Hai-Paw-Waw, though perfectly adequate in general character and sound, was concocted from somewhat incongruous elements, the first two parts of it being regular Arabic names and the last two probably being derived from the American Indian word "powwow"—meaning conjurer or medicine man. The Arabic names were sufficiently uncommon in early eighteenth century literature to make possible a tentative identification of the source from which the Scriblerians derived them as Simon Ockley's translation of an old Arabic treatise, *The Improvement of Human Reason, Exhibited in the Life of Hai Ebn Yokdhan,* which was published in 1708.[13]

Added plausibility and humor were given to the Black Prince's marriage to Indamora and to the charge of Martinus' lawyer that he had "wickedly, leudly, and indecently us'd, handled, and evil entreated" the twins by the fact that the real dwarf was widely advertised as being united in marriage to a midget woman, the "Fairy Queen"—"in which State," as S. T. declared in his facetious letter to the *Spectator,* "the little Cavalier has so well acquitted himself, that his Lady is with Child."[14] The condition of his wife was announced in the handbills.[15]

9. The Avignon edition of 1689 was the most recent edition.
10. Text, p. 156, ll. 7–10.
11. Text, p. 162, ll. 24–6.
12. *Phil. Trans.,* L, i (1757), 313–14.
13. A Latin and two English versions of Ibn al-Tufail's work had appeared previously, but the spelling of the name, as well as the later date, make Ockley's translation the most likely source.
14. No. 271.
15. Cf. above, p. 296.

To the end of the chapter the Rev. William Lisle Bowles appended the comment: "These pleadings have the *least humour,* as they certainly are the most offensive part of the history." [16] Others have thought this section a masterpiece of wit.

(1) 154, 14. . . . (1) *"Whether Slaves could marry without the consent of their Master?"*

"1. *An Servi possint, invitis Dominis, Matrimonium contrahere?"* (Scrib.)

The question was an important one in early works on marriage. Both Sanchez and Cardinal Hostiensis discuss it at some length. Sanchez, *De Sancto Matrimonii Sacramento* (Avignon, 1689), vii. 21. nn. 1–10; Henricus de Bartholomaeis, Cardinal Hostiensis, *Summa Hostiensis* (Lyons, 1517), iv. 365. Neither states the question exactly as the Scriblerians do in their footnote, Sanchez posing it as *"An servis integrum fit matrimonium invitis inire . . . ?"* and Hostiensis as *"An servis possit contrahere matrimonium . . . et an consensus domini reuiratur?"*

(2) 154, 15. *To this he was answer'd in the Affirmative,* . . .

The authority for the affirmative answer is Sanchez (*loc. cit.*), the *Summa Hostiensis* declaring that marriage contracted without the consent of the master may be dissolved (*loc. cit.*).

(3) 154, 16. . . . *"That (2) the Marriage did not exempt them from Servitude."*

"2. *An Servus Matrimonio eximitur a Domini obsequio?"* (Scrib.)

Again the Scriblerians give the question their own phrasing. The decision is drawn from Sanchez vii.21.11.

(4) 154, 21. . . . (3) *"The Children must follow the condition of the Father:*

"3. *An Liberi sequuntur Conditionem Patris, an Matris?"* (Scrib.)

Sanchez discusses this problem under the title *"Utrius parentis conditionem filij sequentur, quoad servitutem & honores,"* vii. 24. Like Cardinal Hostiensis (iv. 366) he decides that, except in special cases, the children follow the social status of the father.

(5) 154, 23. *". . . there being no slavery in England."*

Though this was a commonly voiced opinion, it was not, at the time of the *Memoirs,* strictly true. Returning travelers, traders, and colonials frequently brought slaves with them and kept them in bondage after their arrival in England. In this the masters were to a certain extent protected by the courts. For example, in 1690 in the case of Katherine Auker, a Negress who had been brought from the Barbadoes by Robert Rich and who, according to her complaint, had been tortured and turned out by her master without a discharge so that she could not get work elsewhere, the court merely ordered that she be freed from the imprisonment in which her master had caused her to be held and that she be free to serve anyone until her master returned to claim her.

An important case with regard to the legal aspects of the matter came up in the Middlesex Sessions of 1717. The basis of the case was the petition of the wife

16. *Works of Pope* (1806), vi, 171 n.

of John Caesar, who declared that she was destitute and that unless her husband was freed from slavery and enabled to provide for her she would become a parish charge. According to her complaint, Benjamin and John Wood, printers and embossers in Whitechapel, had kept her husband in slavery for fourteen years, during which time they had much abused him and for the greater part of the time held him imprisoned in their house, though he had been baptized and though "as the petitioner is advised, slavery is inconsistent with the laws of this realm." Middlesex Records (Cal.), September, 1717; quoted from Dorothy George, *London Life in the Eighteenth Century* (New York, 1925), p. 136. The decision of the court was that the masters should come to some reasonable agreement with regard to wages for Caesar. Since the Woods had failed to do this by the start of the next session, certain justices were ordered to determine the amount. George, *ibid*.

The whole question of slavery in England was not solved until later in the century, when as the result of the famous Somerset case (1771–72) the Scriblerians' statement became literally true.

(6) 154, 25. . . . Dissolution *of the* Marriage, *upon the impossibility of Conjugal dues in the Wife.*

Dissolution of a marriage or annulment was possible in England when the causes, such as consanguinity, impotency, frigidity, etc., were precedent to the marriage. Cf. Giles Jacob's *New Law Dictionary* (1729), under "Divorce."

(7) 154, 26. . . . *the* Canon Law *allow'd a* Triennal Cohabitation, . . .

In his disputation on the dissolving of marriages, Sanchez (vii. 99) upholds the requirement that, especially in cases of frigidity, there must be triennial cohabitation before a divorce is allowed. Cf. Jacob, *loc. cit.*

(8) 154, 32. . . . *the* Case *of* Hermaphrodites, *who are allow'd* "Facultatem Conjugii, *provided they* make Election *before the* Parish Priest, *in* what sex *they will act, and take an Oath never to perform in the other Capacity."* (1)

"1. Sanchez, Hostiens. Sylvest." (Scrib.)

Sanchez gives one of his disputations the title *"An hermaphroditus possit matrim, inire? & juxta quem sexum?"* He concludes that if either sex prevails in the hermaphrodite, he must choose to act only in that sex and that if both sexes are equal in him, he must choose either one before he enters marriage and remain in that sex. vii. 106. 1–7. He cites similar opinions from the *Summa Hostiensis* and from the *De Sponsalibus* of Sylvester.

(9) 155, 3. *". . . there being plainly the* four conditions *of a* (2) *Rape."*

"2. *Violentia, Causa Libidinis, Traductio ad Locum,* Mulier honesta." (Scrib.)

The four conditions listed are taken from Sanchez viii.12.3, who requires: (1) that it be the result of violence, (2) that the ravishing be done for the sake of lust, (3) that there be a carrying from one place to another, and (4) that the woman be honest.

(10) 155, 10. . . . (3) *That a* "Wife *was not obliged to live with a* Concubine . . ."

"3. *Uxor non tenetur vivere cum viro Concubinam tenente."* (Scrib.)

So says Sanchez, x.18.29.

(11) 155, 11. ". . . the common (4) Proofs."

"4. *Tactus, amplexus, cohabitatio.*" (Scrib.)

The four proofs, touching, kissing, embracing, and cohabitation (the Scriblerians' footnote omits *oscula*) are the basis for the discussion of adultery and divorce in the tenth book of Sanchez.

(12) 155, 13. . . . *the Law order'd the Wife* to reside *with the* Husband *if there were sufficient security given to expel the Concubine.*

Cf. Sanchez, x.18.20.

(13) 155, 15. . . . *and consent to the (5) Incision.*

"5. *An Uxor tenetur Incisionem pati? Sanchez de Matrimonio.*" (Scrib.)

The Scriblerians give a humorous twist to the question posed by Sanchez, who proposes the incision not for Siamese twins but for married women who are impotent because of physical obstructions. vii. 92–3.

(14) 155, 27. . . . *commenc'd a Suit in the* Spiritual Court . . .

The Spiritual Courts had jurisdiction in matrimonial cases; they also probated wills, settled questions of tithes, and tried cases of defamation. Cf. Jacob, *op. cit.*

(15) 157, 22. . . . *Geryon with three heads,* . . .

Geryon is represented by Hesiod, Virgil, and other poets as having three heads and three bodies. He was a shepherd who lived on the island of Gades and was slain by Hercules. Moreri, etc.

(16) 157, 22. . . . *and Briareus with an hundred hands.*

This famous giant had a hundred hands and fifty heads. He assisted the giants in their war against the gods and, according to some accounts, was thrown under Mount Aetna. Commonly called Aegeon by men, he was given the name Briareus by the gods. He is mentioned in the *Iliad* and the *Aeneid,* and by Hesiod. Moreri under "Egeon."

(17) 157, 24. *Let us search Sacred History, and we meet with one of the sons of the Giants with six Fingers to each Hand, and six Toes to each Foot;* . . .

This son of the giants is mentioned in 2 Samuel 21:20.

(18) 158, 6. . . . *no Philosopher,* . . . *hath taken more pains to discover where the Soul keeps her residence, than* . . . *the learned Martinus Scriblerus:*

See the first part of chapter twelve, "*How Martinus endeavoured to find out the Seat of the Soul.*"

(19) 158, 19. . . . *there [in the Organs of Generation] the Soul* . . . *(as we may say) sits brooding over ages yet unborn.*

It was believed by many in the early eighteenth century that God had created in Adam and Eve the seeds of all future mankind and that these were carried down from generation to generation. This theory, which was associated with traducianism (see the note below), was subscribed to by Arbuthnot. In his "An Argument for Divine Providence, taken from the constant Regularity observ'd in the Births of both Sexes," published in *Phil. Trans.,* xxvii (October–December, 1710), 189, he says, "There seems no more probable Cause to be assigned in Physicks for this

Equality of the Births, than that in our first Parents Seed there were at first formed an equal Number of both Sexes."

(20) 158, 24. . . . *it has been the opinion of many most learned Divines and Philosophers, that the Soul, as well as Body, is produced* ex traduce. *This doctrine has been defended by arguments irrefragable, and accounts for difficulties, without it, inexplicable.*

Dr. Pennyfeather does not make clear whether in using the phrase *"ex traduce"* he has specifically in mind traducianism, the doctrine that the soul of the offspring is derived by extension or division from that of the father and is transmitted during the physical act of procreation, or generationism, the nonmaterialistic doctrine that the soul of the child originates from that of the parent in some mysterious way somewhat analogous to the way in which the body of the child originates from the parent's organism. Both are opposed to creationism, according to which each soul is individually created by God.

The Scriblerians are, of course, being ironic in having the learned pleader declare that the *ex traduce* origin of the soul had been "defended by arguments irrefragable." Traducianism was maintained only by Tertullian, Apollinaris, and a few other heretics, and generationism, though advocated by St. Augustine, was also formally declared a heresy by the Church. Both were vigorously opposed by Aquinas and the Scholastics. Cf. *Contra Gentiles,* II, c. 86; *Summa Theologica,* Pt. I, No. 3, Quest. XC, art. 2 and Quest. CXVIII, art. 2; *Catholic Encyclopedia.*

The lawyer's statement that the doctrine accounts for difficulties otherwise inexplicable refers to the problem of transmission of original sin. St. Augustine was led to adopt generationism by the belief that the *ex traduce* origin of the soul provided the most satisfactory, if not the only, solution of this problem.

(21) 161, 10. *It hath been strenuously maintain'd by many holy Divines (and particularly by Thomas Aquinas) that our first Parents, in the state of Innocence, did in no wise propagate their species after the present common manner of men and beasts; . . .*

This is not a true statement of Aquinas' position. In Quest. XCVIII, art. 2, "Whether in the state of innocence there would have been generation by coition," he presents four arguments against coition in paradise. But he subsequently answers each of these objections and reaches the conclusion that generation was after the present manner, except that "in that state, fecundity would have been without lust." *Summa Theologica,* Pt. I, No. 3, pp. 337–40. In support of this view, Aquinas quotes Augustine's statement that "Intercourse would have been without prejudice to virginal integrity" and that "the union was one not of lustful desire but of deliberate action." *De Civ. Dei,* xiv. 26; *Summa Theologica,* Pt. I, No. 3, p. 340.

(22) 161, 18. . . . *not by parts, such as we have at present; . . . those parts were the immediate Excresence of Sin, . . .*

Paracelsus appears to have been the author, or one of the authors, of this curious idea. He believed that our first parents did not have the necessary parts for generation before they sinned, but that afterward the parts grew out as "Excresences, or like the King's Evil at the throat." Quoted from I. Vossius, *De Philosophia,* cap.

ix, p. 71, by Bayle, under "Adam," n. G. The idea was picked up and enlarged upon by Antoinette Bourignon, the founder of the Quietist sect. Her conception of Adam's anatomical structure and the mechanism of generation in paradise is exceedingly curious. Cf. Bayle, *loc. cit.* Her ideas, known as Bourignonism, created quite a stir in the early years of the eighteenth century, particularly in Scotland, and some acquaintance with the doctrine may have provided the material for the jest in the text. In discussing the approaching transformation of sexes in their piece *Annus Mirabilis* (1722), the Scriblerians say:

The Philosophy of this Transformation will not seem surprizing to People, who search into the *Bottom* of Things. Madam Bourignon, a devout *French* Lady, has shewn us, how Man was at first created Male and Female in one Individual, having the Faculty of Propagation within himself: A Circumstance necessary to the State of Innocence, wherein a Man's Happiness was not to depend upon the Caprice of another. It was not till after he had made a *faux pas,* that he had his Female Mate, (first join'd to him as the *Bohemian* Girls were join'd, and then separated.)

(23) 161, 22. *It is a Maxim of Philosophy, that* generatio unius est corruptio alterius; . . .

"The generation of one is the corruption of the other."—an Aristotelian maxim used especially by the Scholastics. Cf. Aquinas, *Summa Theologica,* Pt. 1, No. 2, Quest. cxiii, art. 6. Its application is illustrated by Swift's "the corruption of the senses is the generation of the spirit." *Works,* 1, 196; cf. Sir Thomas Browne, *Works,* C. Sayle, ed. (1904), 1, 342, and J. Dryden, *Dramatic Essays,* W. H. Hudson, ed. (1912), p. 66.

(24) 163, 6. . . . *Martin appeal'd from the Consistory to the* Court of Arches, . . .

The consistory was the common court for ecclesiastical causes, one being held in each diocese. It was presided over by the bishop's chancellor.

The Court of Arches, which belonged to the Archbishop of Canterbury, was the chief and most ancient of the consistory courts. It derived its name from the structure of St. Mary le Bow's Church in London, where it was once held. The court had extraordinary jurisdiction in all ecclesiastical causes, except those that belonged to the prerogative court. It was the court of appeal from the judgments of the consistory courts, the decisions of bishops, etc. Jacob's *New Law Dictionary.*

(25) 163, 8. *It was at last brought before a* Commission of Delegates; . . .

The court of delegates tried cases of appeal to the king and was the highest court for civil affairs that concerned the church. It derived its name from the fact that its judges sat by virtue of the king's commission, under the Great Seal. Jacob, *op. cit.*

(26) 163, 13. . . . *the* Jus petendi & reddendi Debitum conjugale . . .

That is, the right of seeking and of rendering the marital duty.

(27) 163, 19. . . . *as to the* Debitum reddendi, nemo tenetur ad impossibile."

That is, as to the duty of yielding, no one is held to the impossible. The twins, of course, were physically incapable of performing the conjugal duties with their respective husbands at the same time.

CHAPTER XVI

By identifying the travels of Captain Lemuel Gulliver as those of Martinus, this chapter raises the very interesting problem of the relationship of Swift's great work to the *Memoirs*. It was, of course, part of the Scriblerus scheme that individual pieces should be published by members of the group and later "vindicated" to the great Scriblerus. It is hardly surprising that the Scriblerians should devote almost the whole of a chapter to claiming so brilliant an offshoot of their scheme. The mere assertion of the claim, however, is not entirely satisfactory. The differences between the *Memoirs* and the *Travels* are so great, especially, of course, in the characters of the central figures, that the reader does not accept the identification easily. Obviously Swift developed his work to a very considerable extent along independent lines. The question for those interested in the Scriblerus project is how intimate the relationship between the two pieces really was and how the striking differences between the two are to be accounted for.

Though Swift never publicly said so, it seems likely that he actually began writing the travels as a direct contribution to the club scheme. From the time when the club first began to break up in the spring of 1714 he was under very strong pressure to give part of his time to their plan. In the middle of June, Pope wrote to Swift at Letcombe that Arbuthnot's theory of his retirement was that he was going to devote his full leisure to "the life and adventures of Scriblerus," [1] and later the doctor himself wrote, "Pray, remember Martin, who is an innocent fellow and will not disturb your solitude." [2] After Swift left for Ireland the pressure continued. At a meeting of the remnants of the group in November a "scrap of a letter" to him was begun "by the whole Society," [3] which apparently contained indications that they were expecting him to work on Scriblerus—a suggestion perhaps reinforced by messages carried by Parnell. In any case, in his first letter to Pope in the following spring, Swift felt obliged to excuse himself for his lack of activity. [4]

The passing of time brought what was for Swift comparative peace of mind, and news that Pope, Arbuthnot, and Gay had written a Scriblerian play and were working on new additions to the *Memoirs*[5] must have stirred him to consider what he might do to carry out part of the grandiose plan. It was about this time that he began writing the *Travels* and it is impossible to believe that he could have begun a work so close to the club scheme without considering his friends and wishing to give them pleasure by adding his part to the Scriblerus activity.

We need not consider at any length the question why, if Swift contemplated a contribution to the project, he did not consult his friends. Collaboration with them was impossible under the circumstances. Moreover, his moods were not stable and anything he attempted might come to nothing. Hence it was obviously wiser to surprise his friends with a completed piece than to have them waiting in impatient

---

1. Above, p. 37; *Corres.*, II, 155.
2. *Ibid.*, pp. 158–9.
3. *Ibid.*, p. 254.
4. *Ibid.*, p. 288.
5. Swift was not in active correspondence with his fellow Scriblerians at this time, but mutual friends who traveled between London and Dublin no doubt kept him well informed of their activities.

expectation for a work he might never complete or might not wish to acknowledge as his.

That of all the aspects of the Scriblerus scheme to which he might have contributed he should have chosen the travels of the hero is hardly surprising. Many subjects, such as philosophy, pedantry, and antiquarianism had been pretty well exhausted by his own early works and by the satiric sketches already blocked out or written by the club. Arbuthnot was obviously the one to treat recent activities in the learned world, especially in the field of science, and Pope had pre-empted the field of criticism with his "collection of high flights of poetry." Religion was, as Swift had bitter reason for knowing, a dangerous subject for an extended satire, and, moreover, one of the best topics, the Freethinkers, had already been ably dealt with in the *Memoirs* and in his own tract on Collins' *Discourse*. In short, at a distance and without consultation with his fellow Scriblerians the travels of Martinus were clearly the best subject available.

It is probable that the plan of taking Martinus on his travels began to be considered very early in the development of the Scriblerus project and that some ideas were developed at considerable length. The basic idea was almost inescapable; the very concept of Martinus as an extravagantly learned man carried with it the idea of his traveling to the far corners of the earth in search of knowledge, and the many writers of burlesque travel books, *voyages imaginaires,* and tales of humorous adventure in the past century had shown how successfully travel stories could be used for satiric purposes. Unfortunately we do not have very satisfactory evidence as to what these ideas were or how far they were carried. Pope told Spence that "There were pigmies in Schreibler's travels; and the projects of Laputa." [6] His statement would seem to imply that some kind of a book of travels had been at least sketched out.

Another indication that such a book was at one time contemplated and perhaps largely written is provided by the Advertisement attached to one of the early editions of the *Memoirs,* in which we are told that there will soon be published a third book of the *Memoirs* containing accounts of Martinus' trip through the Nubian desert to the court of Ethiopia and his voyage to China with the Bishop of Apamæa.[7] The general character of these two voyages is in harmony with what Pope told Spence. The Nubian desert was the reputed home of a race of pygmies and the Scriblerians labeled Martinus' *Origine of Sciences* as written from there. The "projects of Laputa" might well have been contained in the voyage to China, the general character of which is suggested by the statement in the Advertisement that the journey was made on the backs of condors.

If such a book of travels had been planned and perhaps even partly written before Swift left for Ireland, it must have exerted a great deal of influence over his early planning for Gulliver. We cannot, however, accept its existence as being satisfactorily proved by the evidence available. The Advertisement did not appear until a decade and a half after the publication of Gulliver and might have been inspired or influenced by it. Even if the two voyages described had been devised before *Gulliver's Travels* was printed, there is no internal evidence that they dated

6. Spence, p. 8; below, p. 363.
7. Cf. text, p. 172, and notes, pp. 349–50.

back to the club days and hence could have influenced Swift. Pope's statement to Spence seems support for their existence in the early period, but it is possible to argue that the pygmies he refers to are those in the *Origine of Sciences* and that by the "projects of Laputa" he meant the inventions of Martinus listed in chapter seventeen. But whether the Scriblerians had gone so far as to write some of Martinus' travels or not, it seems reasonably certain that the plans and discussions of the club must have given both direction and impetus to Swift's thinking.

If Swift actually began *Gulliver* as the travels of Martinus, the process by which it became altered into the famous *Travels* is not difficult to trace. At the very start of his thinking Swift would have been faced with a problem of literary craftsmanship the solution of which would have far-reaching effects on the character of the whole piece. Satire depends for its effect on a sharp contrast between the sensible, practical, or "right" on the one side and the foolish, abnormal, or "wrong" on the other. In formal satire and burlesque the normal or "right" generally remains in the reader's mind, but in extended narrative satire, especially of a pseudorealistic variety where the reader's credulity and sympathy may be insensibly aroused, thus destroying most of the effectiveness of the satire, it is desirable, if not absolutely necessary, that both contrasting elements be present in the action. This is usually accomplished by having the protagonist represent one element and the surrounding characters or environment the other. Thus, for example, in *Don Quixote, Hudibras,* and *Candide* the situation is that of the principal character acting foolishly in a normal and practical world, while in the *voyages imaginaires,* the *Connecticut Yankee,* and other satires of that type the hero is a sensible, normal person cast into a strange or fantastic environment. It is not necessary that the "normal" remain fixed; it may, as in Rabelais, shift between the protagonist and the other characters or the environment.

The Scriblerus project was built on the same situation as *Don Quixote.* Its hero is an abnormal figure operating in a normal, rational world. Hence the plan of taking him on his travels into strange and fantastic lands offered grave difficulties. Martinus in such a land as Lilliput might have been the basis for a brief fantastic skit, but it was an obviously unmanageable situation for a sustained narrative satire. One or the other had to be altered, and since the "strange countries" could not very well be made "normal," it was necessary for the hero to assume another character.

The change of Martinus Scriblerus into Lemuel Gulliver, ship surgeon and captain of a merchantman, did not in itself involve a repudiation of the Scriblerian scheme. The Scriblerians had deliberately made Martinus a very shadowy character in contemplation of just such a situation. Within the *Memoirs* itself Martinus acts a variety of roles involving somewhat conflicting characteristics. But the transformation of the learned virtuoso who illustrates all follies of learning into a plain, simple, normal, right-thinking English mariner did alter the literary scheme of the Scriblerians and genuinely change the character of the satire.

Had Swift fully accepted the implications of the differences between the character of his hero and that of Martinus, *Gulliver's Travels* could hardly have become the enduring masterpiece that it is. But he did not. Whether or not he began his work with Martinus as the principal character, the idea that the hero or narrator of the travels was himself to be an object of satire persisted in his mind. It led him to regard neither Gulliver nor his strange hosts as the exclusive representatives of the sensible, right, and normal. This attitude was to play a significant part in shaping the individual voyages and was a most important factor in producing the peculiarly individual and effective character of the *Travels* as a whole.

One of the effects of this attitude was to place certain limits on the design of most of the countries which Gulliver was to visit. Since the strange peoples with whom Gulliver was to come in contact were at least occasionally to represent the "right," they must not all be fantastic in conception. Some might differ from the normal in striking ways, but the culture and points of view of most of them must have much in common with Gulliver's and ours. The importance of this limitation need hardly be stressed. The large part that the basic normality of the Lilliputians and Brobdingnagians plays in the charm, the satiric effectiveness, and the story quality of *Gulliver's Travels* has been recognized from the first appearance of the book.

Swift's double attitude toward his hero and the peoples he visits produced a uniquely effective satiric pattern. An almost universal failing of long satires is that their rigid pattern tends to blunt the reader's appetite and keenness of appreciation. It must be confessed that the *Memoirs*, like *Hudibras*, suffers to some extent from this defect. By not making a clear-cut division of "right" and "foolish" between Gulliver and his successive hosts Swift avoided this weakness. He was aware of the advantage his flexible satiric pattern gave him and exploited it carefully. The reader of the *Travels* is seldom allowed to slip into a fixed attitude toward the characters and events and is not permitted to anticipate for any considerable length of time the character of the satire he is to encounter. In consequence the *Travels* remains challenging and fresh even on rereadings.

It is clear from a study of the various voyages that Swift did not work out the whole formula of the *Travels* before he began to write but developed it as he wrote. In the first book he obviously still had strongly in mind a burlesque travel book. That Swift should have written this burlesque in a simple, factual, and persuasive style rather than in a broad and ludicrous one is typical of him. He had employed the same general style with great success in such burlesque pieces as his *Meditation upon a Broom-Stick*, tracts on religion, and the Bickerstaff papers, and he was to use it again with equal effect in such Irish tracts as the *Modest Proposal*. In the later voyages the burlesque travel book element becomes less and less strong, reappearing only sporadically when Swift could use burlesque touches with effect.

The different handling of the satire in the four books also gives evidence of a gradual evolution of method. In the first voyage the satire is almost entirely directed at the Lilliputians. With only minor exceptions (obviously touches which Swift could not resist), Gulliver stands for sturdy common sense amidst the follies of the little people. In the following voyage, where the physical relationships are reversed, the roles become more complex. Neither side consistently or completely represents the rational and virtuous. The complexity of Gulliver's role reaches its greatest height in the last voyage to the land of the Houyhnhnms. Here both the good and bad are fully represented by the different beings which inhabit that land, the Houyhnhnms possessing reason and virtue to the highest degree and the Yahoos utterly lacking either. Gulliver himself stands halfway between, being physically and by instinct a Yahoo and by intellectual persuasion a Houyhnhnm.

The third book, containing the voyages to Laputa, Glubbdubdrib, etc., presents a special problem in connection with this evolution. Until recently it was assumed that these voyages were among the first written by Swift. We now know from the Ford letters and from the Nicolson-Mohler studies that they were probably the last to be completed.[8] Nonetheless, the mood and form of the third book are so obviously at variance with those of the voyage to the Houyhnhnm country that it seems probable that this book had been drafted some time earlier and that at the time he wrote to Ford, Swift was simply filling it out and polishing it. This assumption is supported by the wording of Swift's statement to Ford. Since this book is as long as any of the other three, he could hardly have expected to finish it so quickly if it had not been substantially complete. Moreover, his casual reference to the flying island would seem strongly to imply that Ford was well acquainted with the general character of the Laputa episode.

The voyage to Laputa is of particular interest in connection with the *Memoirs* because it, of all parts of the travels, bears the strongest traces of the Scriblerus project and because it was from the start recognized by Swift's fellow Scriblerians and the public at large as the weakest. Both of these aspects have a common root in the rather feeble satire on the virtuosi of the flying island and the academies of Lagado. Some of the feebleness is to be traced to Swift's lack of knowledge of the subjects he was attempting to satirize. But a more fundamental and pervasive cause of weakness lies in the general extravagance of the conception. The Laputians have none of those broad human characteristics that endear the Lilliputians, Brobdingnagians, and Houyhnhnms to us. They are too far removed from reality to allow us to slip into the state of half-credulity into which we are subtly beguiled by the other voyages. They are, in short, like most other strange and *outré* figures in the typical *voyages imaginaires,* too fantastic to be either highly amusing or satirically effective.

We have suggested that the division of the role of protagonist of the right and normal between Gulliver and the peoples he visits provided a check against excessive fancy in the other voyages. That check is here missing. With the exception of Lord Munodi, Gulliver's host in Balnibarbi, both the Laputians and the Balnibarbians are consistently cast in the role of the foolish, the extravagant, and the abnormal, while Gulliver is throughout the exponent of common sense. This sharp division suggests that this part of the travels was planned before the second and fourth books, and perhaps even before the first, for it is difficult to believe that after developing the very subtle and effective pattern of the other voyages Swift would have gone back to so elementary a stage. The fact that this voyage is much

8. *The Letters of Jonathan Swift to Charles Ford,* David Nichol Smith, ed. (Oxford, 1935), p. 101, and Marjorie Nicolson and Nora M. Mohler, "The Scientific Background of Swift's *Voyage to Laputa*," *Annals of Science,* II (1937), 302, n. 13.

the closest of the four to the Scriblerus project, its central theme like that of the *Memoirs* being "false taste in learning," also suggests that it was the first part of the voyages to be drafted.

If we assume that the Laputa episode was one of the first parts of the *Travels* to be planned, we can trace in the first, second, and fourth books the successive stages in the development of the character of Gulliver and of the whole pattern of satire. Since Swift revised and reworked his material extensively, he doubtless corrected his early drafts in the light of his final concept of the satire. This revision would account for certain characteristics in the voyages to Laputa and Lilliput which are not in keeping with our hypothesis of their having constituted intermediate steps between the inspiration and the completed product.

It is not necessary to point out how far beyond the original Scriblerus scheme *Gulliver's Travels* extends or how greatly superior Swift's work is to the *Memoirs* from a literary point of view. It is necessary to make clear, however, that the literary changes which Swift introduced were not matched by corresponding intellectual ones. *Gulliver's Travels* is thoroughly Scriblerian in its basic intellectual attitudes and even, with the exception of the references to Irish affairs, in its specific objects of satire. It therefore fits into the broad Scriblerus scheme without difficulty.

Since the chapter concludes the account of Martinus' adventures during the period of his life covered by the *Memoirs,* it was probably one of the last of the chapters in point of composition. The references in the chapter to Gulliver fix its earliest possible date as 1726, while the suggestion that more of Martinus' law cases may be recovered and published indicates that it was composed at a time when the Scriblerians still contemplated further activity. It seems probable, therefore, that the chapter was written during the period of Scriblerus activity from 1727 to 1729.

The text of the chapter has been mutilated in most editions. The elimination of the Double Mistress episode obliged Warburton also to drop the material in this chapter relating to Martinus' experiences at law. In his edition, therefore, the chapter commences with the paragraph beginning, "It was in the year 1699 that Martin set out on his *Travels."* Apparently on the ground that this curtailed version of the chapter fitted more exactly the title given it by the Scriblerians, Warton, while restoring the missing episode, still preserved Warburton's chapter break, attaching the first three paragraphs of the original chapter to the end of chapter fifteen.

Warton's decision was, to say the least, ill-advised. The transfer of the paragraphs destroys a much-needed continuity between the chapters and results in a still greater disparity in length between this chapter and those which surround it. Moreover, the revised version presents the connection between the *Memoirs* and *Gulliver's Travels* in a harsh and abrupt fashion which is clearly at variance with the author's intentions.

Bowles adopted Warton's version, but Roscoe, Courthope, and Aitken follow Warburton in dropping the three paragraphs along with the Double Mistress episode. The present edition is therefore the first since the death of Pope in which the chapter appears in its original form.

(1) 164, 2. Of the Secession of *Martinus* . . .

As used in the seventeenth and eighteenth centuries, the word "secession" signified the act of retiring from public view and living remote from one's accustomed home or neighborhood. In this sense, which is now obsolete, the word implied a revolt, but one of an informal and personal character. Cf. the dictionaries of the period and *NED*.

(2) 164, 23. . . . *the only one now publick, viz. The* Case of *Stradling* and *Stiles,* in an Action concerning certain *black* and *white* Horses.

For an account of the Scriblerian piece *Stradling versus Stiles,* see above, p. 46.

(3) 164, 25. *We cannot wonder that he contracted a violent Aversion to the* Law, *as is evident from a whole Chapter of his Travels.*

The reference is to the fifth chapter of the fourth book of *Gulliver's Travels,* in which Gulliver attempts to explain English law to his Houyhnhnm Master. The satire on law and the legal profession was so virulent that, to Swift's annoyance, Motte drastically revised the chapter before publishing it in the first edition of the *Travels.* Law is also satirized, but less harshly, in the second book. *Works,* VIII, 133–4, 140.

(4) 164, 28. *And perhaps his Disappointment gave him also a Dis-inclination to the* Fair Sex, *for whom on some occasions he does not express all the Respect and Admiration possible.*

The occasions occur chiefly in the voyage to Brobdingnag, where Gulliver's microscopic view makes even the fairest skins and cleanest bodies disgusting and where the Maids of Honor to the Queen treat him with notable indecorum. Pt. II, chap. v; *Works,* VIII, 120–1. Gulliver, however, consistently refers to the Queen and to his nurse Glumdalclitch with great respect and affection.

It will be recalled that during his stay in Lilliput Gulliver was accused by the gossip-mongers of having an affair with the Treasurer's wife and that for some time the court scandal had it that she had once visited him privately. But Gulliver indignantly denies all such aspersions and handsomely vindicates the excellent lady's reputation. Pt. I, chap. vi; *Works,* VIII, 66–7.

(5) 164, 33. *It was in the year 1699 that Martin set out on his* Travels.

"We set sail from Bristol, May 4, 1699 . . . ," says Gulliver in commencing his account of his voyage to Lilliput. Pt. I, chap. i; *Works,* VIII, 18.

According to his own account, however, Gulliver had actually set out on his travels many years before. Before his marriage he had been surgeon on the *Swallow* for three and a half years, "making a voyage or two into the Levant, and some other parts." And after failing in his London practice he "was surgeon successively in two ships, and made several voyages, for six years, to the East and West-Indies, . . ." *Ibid.*

(6) 165, 11. . . . *Kingdom of* Philosophers, . . . *whose admirable Schemes and Projects he return'd to benefit his own dear Country, but had the misfortune to find them rejected by the envious Ministers of* Queen Anne, *and himself sent treacherously away.*

The reference is to the *Memoirs* (Text, pp. 91–2) rather than the *Travels*, Gulliver making no mention of any attempt to introduce the scheme of the Laputans into England.

In the "Introduction" to the *Memoirs* it was said that Martinus attempted to make his applications to the Queen's "first Minister." By altering this to her "envious Ministers" the Scriblerians made the jest apply not only to their fellow club member, the late Earl of Oxford, but also to their currently intimate friend, Viscount Bolingbroke, the principal Secretary of State to Queen Anne.

(7) 165, 15. . . . *a mortal Detestation to the whole flagitious Race of* Ministers, . . .

The reference is, of course, to the bitter passage on ministers of state in the last part of the sixth chapter of the fourth book of the *Travels* (*Works*, VIII, 266–7) and to the extensive satire on ministers in the court of Lilliput. Swift had in mind specifically Walpole and the ministers of state under George I, but his distrust and dislike of political leaders in general went far back in his past and was frequently expressed even when he was on the most intimate terms with the ministry in the last years of Queen Anne. The other Scriblerians shared Swift's view, but felt much less intensely on the subject.

(8) 165, 17. . . . *a final Resolution not to give in any* Memorial *to the* Secretary of State, *in order to subject the Lands he discover'd to the* Crown *of* Great Britain.

In the last chapter of his *Travels*, Gulliver says that it was "whispered" to him that it was his duty as a subject of England to have given such a memorial to the secretary of state immediately on his return. Gulliver explains his decision not to do so in a passage which bitterly castigates the European nations for their harsh treatment and merciless exploitation of the primitive people discovered by their seamen. He exempts England from these charges, but with obvious irony. *Works*, VIII, 304–06.

(9) 165, 26. . . . *a* Surgeon of a Ship, *or a* Captain *of a* Merchant-man, . . .

Gulliver, it will be recalled, after having made the first three voyages described in the *Travels* in the capacity of a surgeon, was in the fourth entrusted with the command of the merchant ship *Adventurer*.

(10) 165, 31. . . . *that cordial* Love *of* Mankind, *that inviolable* Regard *to* Truth, *that* Passion *for his* dear Country, *and that particular attachment to the excellent* Princess Queen Anne; . . .

The marks by which Martinus is to be identified provide a puzzle for the reader. The reference to Gulliver's "*Love of Mankind*" is obviously ironic, since his visit among the Houyhnhnms leaves him with a profound aversion toward his fellow men. The reference to his "inviolable *Regard to Truth*" is also ironic, but in a different way, since Gulliver professes from the first to the last that he is no "lying traveller" and that every word of his account contains the simple unvarnished truth. On the other hand, the irony of the reference to his "*passion for his dear Country*" is somewhat doubtful. In his first three voyages he displays a marked attachment to his homeland, but in the fourth he returns to England most unwillingly. His unwillingness, however, arises out of his detestation of the whole race of Yahoos rather than a particular dislike of his own country and fellow countrymen. Most confusing of all is the reference to his "particular attachment to the excellent Princess Queen *Anne.*" In the context this, too, might be ironical, but it is difficult to believe that the Scriblerians, who held the memory of the late Queen in high regard, really intended it to be so. The confusion of the passage was probably deliberately designed by the Scriblerians as a jest upon the reader, but since the jest does not seem to have any particular point it can hardly be reckoned a good one.

CHAPTER XVII

During the decade and a half in which the Scriblerus project, though worked upon only intermittently, was never far from the mind of Arbuthnot and his collaborators, the Scriblerians must have collected a considerable number of "hints" which for one reason or another did not lend themselves to development within the *Memoirs* or as independent Scriblerus pieces. It was this reservoir of material which no doubt formed the basis of the list of discoveries and works which, in accordance with the custom of biographies in the period, brings to a close the account of the life of the great Scriblerus. The conclusion is a fitting one. The list is remarkable both for the range of its subject matter, which extends over a dozen fields in the arts and sciences, and for the variety and quality of its humor, which runs the gamut from the broadest puns and the most ludicrous burlesque to highly refined irony.

By far the largest and most interesting section of the list is devoted to Martinus' labors as a natural philosopher. Up to this point in the *Memoirs* satire on the follies of contemporary scientists has been slight. Cornelius' absurdities have provided us with a good deal of amusement at the expense of those who still slavishly followed the ancients, and there have been several passing references to the follies of some of Martinus' contemporaries, but at no time have we taken a real excursion into the field of contemporary science. This lack is now rapidly but effectively supplied. The more than two dozen theories, treatises, and inventions attributed to Martinus cover a large and representative section of early eighteenth-century science and leave us with a clear understanding of what the Scriblerians considered abuses of learning in the field of natural philosophy.

In general, the Scriblerian satire consists, on the one hand, in making Martinus the proponent of what the best contemporary opinion considered wrong attitudes and exploded theories and, on the other, in attributing to him a series of ridiculous activities and absurd or impractical inventions. Martinus is, we learn, what was anathema to the real scientists of the day, "a philosopher of ultimate causes," who is able to create hypotheses and whole "systems" of natural philosophy without the trivial helps of experiments and observations. Appropriately, though with more virtuosity than consistency, he still clings to the outmoded *fuga vacui* of the Aristotelians and *materia subtilis* of the Cartesians in accounting for the phenomena of nature and to the atomistic theory of the Epicureans in explaining the origin of the universe.

The inventions and activities assigned to Martinus fall into two general classes.

One class, which provides the most direct and powerful satire on the follies of contemporary scientists, consists in inventions and theories that had actually been proposed by various philosophers and projectors but which are now "vindicated to their true author, Martinus." Among these are the many solutions of such perennially favorite problems as perpetual motion, squaring the circle, flying engines, and new theories accounting for the Deluge. There are also a few references to specific inventions such as Sir William Petty's pacing saddle and the bomb-vessel system of discovering the longitude which was proposed by Whiston and Ditton.

The second and much larger group consists of a series of absurd treatises, calculations, and discoveries which are burlesque in character and ridicule a wide range of follies in contemporary science. These burlesques range all the way from direct satire on the work of individual scientists (as in the proposed use of Dr. Woodward's Universal Deluge Water to cure the stone) to broad ridicule, by the process of *reductio ad absurdum,* of certain current tendencies in the field of natural philosophy (as in the case of Martinus' investigation of the quantity of real matter in the universe and his complete digest of the laws of nature).[1]

The vigor, the range, and the directness of the Scriblerian satire put this section of the *Memoirs* in the very forefront of the satires dealing with science that were written during the period. Other satires dealt with science in greater detail, with richer humor, and perhaps with greater literary skill, but nothing written in the century following the founding of the Royal Society, not even the third voyage of *Gulliver's Travels,* can be said to surpass these few pages as a sharp, comprehensive, and authoritative review of the follies of contemporary scientists.

It should hardly be necessary to point out that in ridiculing these follies the Scriblerians were not attacking science itself. On the contrary, it is clear that the Scriblerians, far from seeking to hinder science, were attempting to aid it by combating errors and tendencies which they (and the best informed opinion of their time) believed to be impeding the forward progress of learning. As a study of their satire will show, they selected their subjects for ridicule with care and discrimination. The reader will search in vain for a single instance where their satire is directed at a valuable achievement or a thoroughly worthy effort. It is true that they ridicule several inventions or calculations (such as flying engines, the parallax of the pole star, and the effects of comets on tides) which have since been carried out successfully. If the contemporary background of these allusions is considered, however, it will be seen that their skepticism concerning what was then being attempted was thoroughly justified.

The description of Martinus' achievements in the fine arts is, as Warton pointed out, somewhat "flat, general, and unappropriated." The Scriblerians had already dipped into the field of poetry in their *Art of Sinking,* and no doubt any further

1. It is interesting to compare the Scriblerian methods of satire with those of Swift in the third voyage of Gulliver. As Miss Nicolson and Miss Mohler point out in their very enlightening studies of the scientific background of the voyage to Laputa, Swift's general method is to use actual titles and experiments which will seem absurd to the general reader; sometimes, however, he improves on real experiments by combining two or carrying one a step further. *Annals of Science,* II (1937), 322. A few of his experiments have a literary source in Rabelais and Tom Brown. *Ibid.*

ideas that occurred to them along this line were reserved for the text and burlesque notes to the *Dunciad*. But it is surprising that the other subjects did not receive more extensive and effective treatment. Pope studied painting for some time
under Jervas and was intimately acquainted with Kneller and the Richardsons. In
addition he was much interested in gardening and architecture, and looked upon
himself as a competent critic of both. In the light of these advantages, and the use
to which he put them in his famous *Epistle to the Earl of Burlington,* the jest
of painting portraits with colors which decay along with the subject and of de-
signing buildings so that they will have a noble effect when they become ruins,
though amusing, seem inadequate to the opportunities. Even more disappointing
is the treatment of modern music. The single pun on Heidegger's homely countenance serves only to remind us, on the one hand, of the rich humor of the treatment
of ancient music in chapter six of the *Memoirs* and, on the other, of the splendid
opportunities for satire in the current vogues in opera, the quarrels of the famous
opera singers, Bordoni and Cuzzoni, which "divided the town," and a dozen
other topics, with all of which Arbuthnot and Gay at least were thoroughly
familiar.[2]

The account of Martinus' activities as a political writer, though somewhat confusing, once again raises the level of the satire. Martinus' political writings, as the
Scriblerians explain, are for the most part ironical and are of such a refined and
delicate drift that they are frequently mistaken by the vulgar. The example they
cite is his suggestion that poor parents eat their own children—a reference, of
course, to Swift's *Modest Proposal*. The "vindication" of this piece to Martinus
is, it must be confessed, very disturbing. So far we have been led to suppose that
whatever irony appeared in his writings was wholly unconscious. The suggestion
that he is capable of consciously employing such powerful irony as is to be found
in Swift's piece would, if taken at its entire value, force us to readjust our whole
estimate of his character and our understanding of all of his works. We may, however, set aside this aspect of the paragraph as unintentional on the part of the
Scriblerians. It is clear from what follows that the purpose of this identification
was not to claim the *Modest Proposal* as a Scriblerus piece but merely to pave the
way for the very clever and satirically effective suggestion that the famous defenses
of the Walpole ministry which appeared in the public prints under the pseudonyms of "Cato," "Publicola," "Algernon Sidney," and "Freeman" were in reality
also ironical tracts written by Martinus. This amusing idea is further exploited by
the statement that Martinus has at one time written many ironical tracts of a political character but that on his departure from England, fearing that they might
be perverted to vicious uses during his absence, he had cast them into an outhouse
near St. James's, from whence they had been diligently fished out with a hook and
line by Walpole's hireling writers.

The inclusion of the name "Raleigh," one of the prominent contributors to the
Craftsman when the Scriblerians were closely associated with the group controlling
it, is interesting as reflecting Pope's disillusionment in the later thirties, when this
passage was written or revised, with some of the political leaders on whom the
Bolingbroke group had once fixed its hopes. The "Raleigh" letters were probably

2. Cf. Swift, *Corres.*, III, 154.

by Cartaret and in subsequent years Pope's associates came to regard him and Pulteney, the leaders of the anti-Walpole Whigs, as no less motivated by venality and expediency than the "Great Man" himself. During this period Pope began to attack the whole corrupt system of politics and in various verses dealt with these opposition leaders even more scathingly than he did the Prime Minister. The broader purpose of the passage is, of course, to ridicule all party writers, and by implication politicians, for seeking to achieve in fact the very opposite goals to the noble ones which they loudly proclaim.

The description of Martinus' political writings gives some indication of the time when the chapter achieved its present form. The reference to the *Modest Proposal* indicates that the chapter was still being worked on in 1729, since Swift's tract was not published until that year. This date would do much to explain the hasty treatment of the arts in the list of Martinus' activities. In the spring of that year Gay was busy with *Polly,* the sequel to the *Beggar's Opera,* while Pope, with Arbuthnot's help, was engaged in completing the Variorum edition of the *Dunciad.* None of these Scriblerians would therefore have much time to devote to the *Memoirs.*

A feature of the whole chapter which deserves comment is the literary skill with which it is handled. The presentation of literally dozens of satirical ideas which are all very much alike in general character in such a fashion that their humor will remain fresh and their bulk unoppressive constitutes a most difficult literary problem, which the Scriblerians solve with considerable success. The items are presented with a minimum of formality, there is no discernible progression to warn the reader what to expect next, and the patterns of presentation are carefully varied to prevent excessive uniformity and monotony. The sentence structure, too, is artfully varied and a very considerable degree of easy coherence is achieved with a minimum amount of purely transitional material.

The reference to the Double Mistress episode in the opening lines of the chapter caused Warburton to drop the first paragraph from his text. In restoring his predecessor's omissions Warton overlooked this one, with the result that the text of the chapter remained incomplete in his edition. Since all the nineteenth-century editors followed either Warton or Warburton, the omission has not been rectified until this present edition.

(1) 166, 24. . . . *may well be called* The Philosopher of Ultimate Causes, . . .
It was a cardinal tenet of the "new philosophy" that the concern with "first" and "ultimate" causes (i.e. how things came originally to be created and the final end or purpose for which they were designed), which were thought characteristic of the "old" or Scholastic philosophy, led merely to empty theorizing and futile disputation and that the pursuit of natural knowledge must be confined to a study of the efficient and material causes of phenomena. This attitude, which was part of the foundation of the new science laid down by Bacon (*Philosophical Works,* J. M. Robertson, ed., pp. 96, 266, 471, and 473), and which was subscribed to by all of his followers, was most fully expressed by Robert Boyle in his *A Disquisition about the Final Causes of Natural Things: Wherein it is Inquir'd, Whether, And*

(if at all) With what Cautions, a Naturalist should admit Them? (1688); *Philosophical Works,* T. Birch, ed. (1744), IV, 515-51.

Despite the general agreement among the new scientists in England, the issue of material and efficient versus final causes continued to be an open one well into the eighteenth century. In part this was due to the fact that on the Continent and in the universities the "old" philosophy still flourished, but it was also the result of certain tendencies among the new scientists themselves. Most of the new scientists were religious men 'and many of them were in orders. It was natural, therefore, for them to see the hand of the Creator in the phenomena they were observing and to attempt to discover divine will and purpose in the natural world about them. Moreover, the enthusiasm for natural knowledge, the fluid state of scientific opinion, and the absence of data resulted in a tendency toward philosophical-scientific speculation which constantly brought back the problem of first and final causes. Hence even in Scriblerian times satire on the "Philosophers of Ultimate Causes" remained pertinent and needed.

The attitude of the calmer scientists in the early eighteenth century is illustrated by Arbuthnot's discussion of the achievements of the new science in his *Essay on the Usefulness of Mathematical Learning* (1701). Regarding light he says:

How unsuccessful enquiries are about this glorious body without the help of geometry, may appear from the empty and frivolous discourses and disputations of a sort of men that call themselves philosophers; whom nothing will serve perhaps but the knowledge of the very nature and intimate causes of every thing: while on the other hand, the geometers not troubling themselves with those fruitless enquiries about the nature of light, have discovered two remarkable properties of it, in the reflection and refraction of its beams; . . . teaching us to manage this subtile body for the improvement of our knowledge, and useful purposes of life. Aitken, p. 415.

(2) 166, 30. *He hath enrich'd Mathematics with many precise and Geometrical* Quadratures *of the* Circle.

Despite a general agreement among the learned men of the time that efforts to discover a method of squaring the circle were as futile as attempts to find the philosopher's stone, the problem continued to attract men of mathematical talents. Hooke brought before the Royal Society a draft in perspective of a circle said to be equal to a square (Gunther, VII, 610) and three years later the Society received a letter from a foreigner, Georgius Rash, containing another proposed solution, which Hooke proved false. Gunther, VII, 694. Sloane printed an account of a method proposed by Abraham De Moivre in the *Philosophical Transactions* for March–April, 1702 (XXIII, 1113-27) and in 1705 Abraham Sharpe sent still another quadrature to the Society. Brewster's *Newton,* II, 167 n.

Quadratures of circles were a common subject of satire. Swift in his *Mechanical Operation of the Spirit* lists it, along with such things as the philosopher's stone, the grand elixir, and the planetary worlds, as a subject for enthusiasts and fanatics, and Pope refers to it satirically in the *Dunciad* (Bk. IV, l. 34).

(3) 166, 31. *He first discover'd the* Cause *of* Gravity, . . .

For several years after the appearance of Newton's *Principia* the cause of gravity was a subject of much speculation. Huygens published a treatise on it (*"Tractatum de Mutu et de Vi Centrifuga descriptionem Automatii Planetarii," Opuscula Posthuma* [Leyden, 1703]), and Hooke advanced the theory that it was caused by an internal motion in the body of the earth. *Posthumous Works of Robert Hooke,* R. Waller, ed. (1705), p. 181; cf. pp. 180, 184. Newton's own attitude (obviously shared by the Scriblerians) was clearly expressed in a letter to Richard Bentley, dated January 17, 1692/93, in which, in answer to Bentley's suggestion that perhaps gravity was essential and inherent to matter, he replied, "Pray do not ascribe that notion to me; for the cause of gravity is what I do not pretend to know . . ." *Works of Richard Bentley,* A. Dyce, ed. (1838), III, 210. In another letter to Bentley, dated February 25, 1692/93, Newton declared, "Gravity must be caused by an agent acting constantly according to certain laws; but whether this agent be material or immaterial, I have left to the consideration of my readers." *Ibid.,* p. 212. By 1714 the cause of gravity had been recognized to be one of those problems of first or ultimate causes which the new science had sworn to eschew.

The Scriblerians' attention may have been called to such theorizings by the argument between Clarke and Collins over the cause and nature of gravity in the course of their controversy over the immateriality of the rational soul. See notes to Chapter XII.

(4) 166, 31. *. . . and the intestine* Motion of Fluids.

This is aimed at the Cartesians, who, says Chambers (*s.v.* "Fluids"),

define a *Fluid* to be a body whose parts are in continual intestine motion; and Dr. Hooke, Mr. Boyle, and Boerhaave, though far from Cartesianism, subscribe to the definition: alledging arguments to prove that the parts of *Fluids* are in continual motion; and even that it is this motion, which constitutes Fluidity. . . .

The latter Newtonians dare not go so far: To say that the parts of a *Fluid* are in continual motion, is more than either our senses, experience, or reason will warrant; and to define a thing from a property that is disputable, is certainly bad philosophy."

(5) 166, 33. *To him we owe all the observations on the* Parallax *of the* Pole-Star, . . .

This is aimed principally at the work of the Rev. John Flamsteed. The possibility of observing a star from two points on the earth's surface or, better still, from two opposite points in the earth's orbit and thus by triangulation working out the distance of the star had been considered by Copernicus, Tycho Brahe, and Galileo, but so enormous is the distance to the nearest star, so crude were the astronomical instruments available, and so complex were the subsidiary problems involved that little progress was made until 1669 when Hooke, by means of a perfected telescope, detected an apparent parallax of between 27″ and 30″ in one star. Though his results were by no means generally accepted, they led Flamsteed to begin, in 1689, a series of observations on the Pole Star. These he continued until 1697, when he reached the conclusion that the parallax of the star was equal to about 40″. John Wallis, *Opera Mathematica,* III, 705. His work, however, was almost immediately upset by Cassini, who pointed out that his findings were incompatible with true parallax and that some other factor must have caused them. *Memoires de l'Academie des Sciences* (1699), p. 177. The nature of this factor became clear in 1728 when Bradley announced his epoch-making discovery of the aberration of light. *Phil. Trans.,* xxxv (1728), 637. In the meantime Wallis, Huygens, Bianchini, and many others had worked on the problem of the parallax of fixed stars with such unsatisfactory results that men such as Halley had reached the conclusion that the problem was beyond any known method of calculation. *Miscellanea Curiosa,* Edmund Halley, ed. (1705), i, 268.

It is probable that Flamsteed's failure was singled out for satire not because it was particularly egregious (his observations being extraordinarily accurate) but because it was well known and because Flamsteed had made himself extremely obnoxious to Arbuthnot and many other prominent scientists by his excessive jealousy and intransigeance with regard to the publication of his catalogue of the stars. Flamsteed quarreled bitterly with Newton, with a committee (of which Arbuthnot was a member) appointed by the Royal Society to superintend the publication of the work, and with Halley, who was to edit it. In the spring of the year 1711 Arbuthnot, acting as ambassador for the committee, carried on an extensive correspondence with Flamsteed, which must have left the genial doctor highly irritated. For an account of the controversy and Arbuthnot's part in it see F. Bailey, *An Account of the Rev. John Flamsteed* (1835), *passim.*

(6) 166, 33. . . . *and all the new* Theories *of the* Deluge.

During the last quarter of the seventeenth century a number of elaborate hypotheses were advanced to account for the Deluge. The two basic problems around which the various theories turned were the origin and disappearance of the waters and the cause of such geological phenomena as the stratification of rock and the presence of petrified marine bodies high above present sea levels. The first man to draw wide attention to the problems was Dr. Thomas Burnet. In the course of an elaborate two-volume history of the earth, published under the title of *Telluris Theoria Sacra* (1681–89; translated into English by the author in 1684–89), Burnet pointed out, as had others, that all the waters of the present oceans, even supposing them emptied, were not sufficient to cover the land to a point 15 cubits above the highest mountain as the Mosaic account had declared the Flood had done. To surmount this difficulty Burnet adopted Descartes' theory that the earth was once perfectly spherical, its surface being composed of a muddy solution which gradually settled according to the specific gravity of its elements. He then supposed that a hard crust had been formed, which in time cracked, plunging the pieces into the waters beneath. He also supposed that the shock had shaken the earth out of its central place under the heavens into an oblique position, thus causing the seasons, which he declared were not known in antediluvian times. In the ensuing discussion some opponents objected to his theory in part on the grounds that it appeared to run counter to the Biblical account, which mentions mountains in the account of the Flood (though for the first time) and tells of God's promise after the Deluge that there would continue to be seasons, with days and nights, as there had been before.

Other scientists, notably John Ray (*Three Physico-Theological Discourses* [1692; 3d ed., 1713], pp. 86–7), were inclined toward the theory that the center of the earth is unfixed and that its shiftings caused huge tides which successively over-whelmed parts of the land, but they were not entirely successful in meeting the objections that there did not appear to be sufficient water in the oceans to over-whelm the great continents near them and that this theory appeared to contradict the Biblical statement that the whole earth was covered at once.

A highly ingenious solution of the origin of the Flood waters was made public in 1696 by William Whiston. In a book entitled *A New Theory of the Earth,* Whiston developed a suggestion advanced by Edmund Halley in two brief papers presented to the Royal Society in 1694 that the *"Choc* of a *Comet* might account for some of the phenomena of the Flood." *Phil. Trans.,* xxxiii (1724–25), 118–25. Whiston supposed that a great comet, passing so close to the earth that it was under the moon, raised tremendous tides not only in the waters on the surface of the earth but in the abysses beneath and that these tides so stretched the earth out of shape that they caused the crust of land to break and allow the flood waters to pour out. In order to provide necessary additional water, he suggested that as the comet went by, the earth picked up from its atmosphere and its tail vast quan-tities of water vapor which, being rarefied by the sun, descended again on the earth in the form of the rain of which the Bible speaks. In his first publication Whiston treated this whole theory merely as an hypothesis; in February, 1714, however, he published a little tract entitled *The Cause of the Deluge Demonstrated,* in which he treated the theory as proved and identified the comet as the great comet of 1680.

The other great problem, that of the origin and nature of geological strata, marine bodies on land, etc., achieved an even more fantastic solution in the hands of Dr. John Woodward. In his *An Essay toward a Natural History of the Earth* (1695), Woodward suggested that the Flood carried the marine bodies on to land and left them there when it retired, that the flood waters were of such a nature that when they covered the land they dissolved all solid matters such as metals and rocks, that this solid matter then precipitated itself and settled according to its weight into regular strata around the surface of the globe, and that an internal force within the earth then caused various violent eruptions which broke up these strata into their present irregularities and by opening great cracks in the sur-face of the earth allowed the flood waters to subside into the abyss again. Like Whiston, Woodward first advanced his theory more or less tentatively, but, hav-ing later "perfected" it, maintained it unshaken throughout his life.

Woodward's theory was both attacked and defended. The most severe attack was Arbuthnot's. In a pamphlet entitled *An Examination of Dr. Woodward's Ac-count of the Deluge &c.* (1697), he courteously, but with devastating effect, pointed out the inconsistencies and improbabilities in Woodward's theory. Among the difficulties which he pointed out was the fact that the waters should have sustained much heavier substances such as minerals and rocks, that the abyss emptied of the waters should still sustain the weight of the land, that the abyss was of such unthinkably vast proportions as to contain sufficient water to cover the land 15 cubits above the highest mountains, and finally that the seeds of plants and other living matter which after the Flood grew on the earth should have swum un-harmed in a liquid which dissolved rocks.

For an account of the extensive discussions of cosmological problems during the period see Katharine Collier's *Cosmogonies of Our Fathers* (New York, 1934).

(7) 166, 35. . . . *taught the right use sometimes of the* Fuga Vacui, . . .

According to various ancient philosophers, ethereal space consists of a total void which nature constantly strives to fill. This tendency, called the *fuga vacui*, or abhorrence of a vacuum, was believed to be a fundamental natural law and was used to explain a wide variety of phenomena. Cf. Chambers, *s.v.* "Vacuum." Before the advent of the Cartesian and Newtonian systems, the *fuga vacui* was the commonly accepted explanation of the celestial mechanics pointed out by Copernicus, Kepler, and others. So firmly was this concept established that it yielded very slowly to the rival theories and still remained a matter of debate on the Continent long after English science had adopted the Newtonian theory of a thinly spread out ether.

The theory of the *fuga vacui* was not very extensively or effectively satirized in the period. The most common jest in connection with it, which Swift includes in the collection of saws that make up his *Tritical Essay,* is that the vacuum which the philosophers have argued about so long is to be found in a critic's head. *Works,* I, 294.

(8) 166, 36. . . . *and sometimes of the* Materia Subtilis, *in resolving the grand Phænomena of Nature.*

In opposition to the Aristotelian theory of a vacuum Descartes suggested that the whole universe was filled with a subtle matter so infinitely fine and so equally diffused throughout space that exactly the same amount of it is contained in any two equal volumes of space or any two bodies of the same size whether of air or of gold. *Oeuvres de Descartes,* C. Adam and P. Tannery, eds. (1897–1909), XI, 33. It was by means of enormous vortices or whirlpools in this subtle matter that Descartes explained the movements of celestial bodies. Despite the work of Newton and his followers, Descartes' theories dominated scientific thought on the Continent well into the eighteenth century. The English contempt for them is effectively described by Voltaire in his contrast of the two men and their systems in his *Letters concerning the English Nation* (1733, letter xiv).

(9) 167, 3. *He it was, that first found out the* Palpability of Colours; *and by the delicacy of his Touch, could distinguish the different Vibrations of the heterogeneous Rays of Light.*

Swift uses the same idea in *Gulliver's Travels.* In the Grand Academy of Lagado, according to Gulliver, "There was a man born blind, who had several apprentices in his own condition: their employment was to mix colours for painters, which their master taught them to distinguish by feeling and smelling." *Works,* VIII, 187.

In their study of the scientific background of *Gulliver's Travels,* Marjorie Nicolson and Nora Mohler point out that Swift probably got the idea from Robert Boyle's "Experiments and Observations upon Colours," which was first published in 1664 and reprinted in the 1725 edition of Boyle's *Philosophical Works,* edited by Peter Shaw, from which Swift obtained other material for the satire in the third voyage. *Annals of Science,* II (1937), 323–5. In his paper Boyle says that a "Dr. J. Finch, extraordinary anatomist to that great patron of the Virtuosi, the now Great Duke of Tuscany" had told him of a blind man at Maestricht, named John Vermaasen, who at certain times could distinguish colors by the touch of his fingers. Boyle accepted the story as true, though with some reluctance. *Philosophical Works,* T. Birch, ed., II, 13.

It seems probable that whoever contributed this bit to the *Memoirs,* presumably Arbuthnot, had the same source in mind.

(10) 167, 4. . . . Perpetuum Mobiles, . . .

Like the squaring of the circle, perpetual motion was a weed in the garden of science which no amount of discouragement and satire seemed able to kill. By the time of the Scriblerians, projects for perpetual motion were a jest of long standing; yet in 1721 Desaguliers published an article in the *Philosophical Transactions* (XXXI, 234–9) which treated the subject with great seriousness, and in the *London Journal* on January 12, 1722/23 there appeared the following item:

They write from Germany, that a Certain Professor of the Mathematicks, who has endeavour'd to find out what is call'd *Perpetuum Mobile,* with much loss of Time and Money, has given over his Search into a Mystery, which he owns to be unsearchable; saying only *Perpetuum Mobilum scio, sed modum nescio,* i.e. I am sensible there is such a thing as a Perpetual Motion, but I am ignorant of the Manner.

Interest in the problem was very keen in the seventeenth century. Bacon included some perpetual motion machines among the riches of Solomon's house described in the *New Atlantis* (*Philosophical Works,* J. M. Robertson, ed., p. 731) and many attempted to make this dream a reality. For some contemporary accounts of various machines see I. De Caus, *New and Rare Inventions of Water Works* (1659); the Marquis of Worcester, *Century of Inventions* (1663), No. 56; the diary of John Evelyn for Aug. 14, 1668, and the *Phil. Trans.,* XV (1685), 1240–1, XVI (1686), 138–9, 267–8.

For a brief statement of the current scientific views of the problem at the time this chapter was probably put together, see Chambers, *s.v.,* "Perpetual Motion." "In effect," says Chambers, "there seems but little in nature to countenance all this assiduity and expectation; among all the laws of matter and motion, we know of none yet, which seems to lay any principle or foundation for such an effect."

(11) 167, 5. . . . Flying Engines, . . .

Among the many wonders which the early advocates of the new science confidently expected it to perform was the invention of some means of carrying man through the air. In Bacon's *New Atlantis* the inhabitants of Solomon's house imitate the flights of birds and "have some degrees of flying in the air" (*Philosophical Works,* J. M. Robertson, ed. [1905], p. 731) and in Bishop John Wilkins' *A Discovery of a New World* (1638), the able but enthusiastic prelate declares:

. . . I do seriously, and upon good grounds, affirm it possible to make a Flying Chariot; in which a Man may sit, and give such a motion unto it, as shall convey him through the Air. And this perhaps might be made large enough to carry

divers Men at the same time, together with Food for their *Viaticum,* and com-
modities for Traffick. . . .

This Engine may be contrived from the same Principles by which *Architas* made
a wooden Dove, and *Regiomontanus* a wooden Eagle.

I conceive it were no difficult matter (if a man had leisure) to shew more particularly the means of composing it. (5th ed., 1684), p. 159.

In 1648 Wilkins discussed the problem at some length, and with undiminished
enthusiasm, in his *Mathematical Magick,* Bk. ii, chaps. vi–viii; (5th ed., 1707),
pp. 112–29.

Much of Wilkins' confidence and enthusiasm can be traced to Robert Hooke,
the brilliant secretary of the Royal Society, whose character and appearance so
strikingly resemble that of our own hero. Cf. general note to Introduction, pp.
175–6. In his youth Hooke invented no less than thirty different flying engines.
According to his own account,

I contriv'd and made many trials about the Art of flying in the Air, and moving
very swift upon the Land and Water, of which I shew'd several Designs to Dr.
Wilkins then *Warden* of *Wadham* College, and at the same time made a Module,
which, by the help of Springs and Wings, rais'd and sustain'd it self in the Air; but
finding by my own trials, and afterwards by Calculation, that the Muscles of a
Mans Body were not sufficient to do anything considerable of that kind, I apply'd
my Mind to contrive a Way to make artificial Muscles; diverse designs whereof I
shew'd also at the same time to Dr. *Wilkins,* but was in many of my Trials
frustrated of my expectations. *Posthumous Works of Robert Hooke,* Richard
Waller, ed., p. iv.

The inventions of a Frenchman, Sieur Besnier, and an Italian, Father Francisco
Lana, again interested Hooke in the problem, and in 1679 he read several papers
before the Royal Society on the subject. *Philosophical Collections* (1679), No. 1,
p. 18; Gunther, vii, 517, 518, 523, and vi, 247.

Popular interest in flying continued to be stimulated by publications dealing
with flights to the moon, such as the translation of Cyrano de Bergerac's *Comical
History* (1687), David Russen's *Iter Lunare: or, A Voyage to the Moon* (1703),
and Daniel Defoe's *A Journey to the World in the Moon* (1705), *A Letter from
the Man in the Moon* (1705), and *The Consolidator* (1705), and by occasional reports of new inventions, such as Bartholomeu de Gusmão's "Passarola," a model of
which was successfully demonstrated before the Portuguese court in 1709.

But the repeated failure of practical attempts, coupled with the highly imaginative
developments of the idea of flying by literary men, led to skepticism and satire.
Shadwell set the tone for the latter in his *The Virtuoso* (1676) by having Sir Nicholas Gimcrack declare:

You know a great many *Virtuoso's* that can fly; but I am so much advanc'd in the
Art of Flying, that I can already out-fly that pond'rous Animal call'd a *Bustard;*
nor should any Greyhound in *England* catch me in the calmest day, before I get
upon wing: Nay, I doubt not, but in a little time to improve the Art so far, 'twill
be as common to buy a pair of Wings to fly to the World in the Moon, as to buy
a pair of Wax Boots to ride into *Sussex* with. Act ii; *Complete Works of Thomas
Shadwell,* M. Summers, ed., iii, 126.

Swift apparently considered the subject of flying with some care in preparing the "Flying Island" episode in *Gulliver's Travels*. For a discussion of early interest in flying and of Swift's probable sources, see Marjorie Nicolson and Nora M. Mohler, "Swift's 'Flying Island' in the Voyage to Laputa," *Annals of Science,* II (1937), 419–30; and Miss Nicolson's *Voyages to the Moon* (New York, 1948).

(12) 167, 5. . . . Pacing Saddles; . . . ,

This is one of the most curious bits of satire in the whole *Memoirs*. The "Pacing Saddle" was a two-wheeled carriage or chariot invented by Sir William Petty in 1676. It was in general modeled on the calash, which had been introduced into England shortly after the Restoration. According to Sir William, the virtues of his invention were that it was cheap to construct ("not ⅓ the price of a comon chariott"), that it could be drawn with a load of three men by one horse or two men, that with the wheels removed it could be used as a sedan chair, and that it would be inexpensive to repair and maintain. *The Petty Papers*, Marquis of Lansdowne, ed. (1927), II, 149, 151. The name "Pacing Saddle" Petty declared he had chosen "as one that will best please those that smile at Inventions." *Petty-Southwell Correspondence*, Marquis of Lansdowne, ed. (1928), p. 14. In August, 1684, he wrote his friend Southwell that "The Chariot is done, and so as I verily believe can never be much improv'd." *Ibid.,* p. 125.

Shortly after he had invented it, Petty sent a model to London, where it was received with skepticism and amusement. Shadwell, in his comedy *The Virtuoso*, speaks of "Engines of as little use as Pacing Saddles" (*Works,* Montague Summers, ed., III, 106) and Samuel Butler apparently intended to satirize it in his *Elephant in the Moon* in the lines:

> No more our making old Dogs young
> Make Men suspect us still i' the Wrong;
> Nor new-invented Chariots draw
> The Boys to course us, without Law; . . . ll. 213–16.

How this invention, an obscure failure of thirty years' standing, came to be mentioned in the *Memoirs* is puzzling. If the Scriblerians were trying to satirize Petty as an inventor they would have succeeded far better by referring to his famous failure, the "double-bottom" or two-hulled ship, a model of which was kept in the museum of the Royal Society. Nehemiah Grew, *Musaeum Regalis Societatis* (1681), pp. 363–4.

(13) 167, 6. . . . *the Method of discovering the* Longitude *by* Bomb-Vessels, . . .

A system of working out the longitude by means of bomb vessels was actually proposed in the summer of 1714 by two distinguished scientists, William Whiston and Humphrey Ditton.

The discovery of some simple and accurate means whereby mariners might work out their longitude while at sea was perhaps the most popular single scientific problem in the century following the founding of the Royal Society. During the quarter century before 1714 more than a dozen systems were proposed in print, and no doubt many times that number had their hour on ship deck or in the coffeehouses. Among the many distinguished men to work on the problem was Robert Hooke. Gunther, VI, 235, 238–9; VII, 429, 680–1; and *Posthumous*

Works, R. Waller, ed., pp. 510–18. Another was Christian Huygens, who in 1689 published instructions in the *Philosophical Transactions* for the use of pendulum watches in working out the longitude.

Each proposer dreamed of making a vast fortune from his discovery. Hooke declined to reveal his 1675 proposal until he had been offered £1,000 or £150 a year for life (Gunther, VII, 429) and influential men were frequently plagued by projectors who wished to assure themselves of reward from the government. In the heyday of his power, Swift was among those whose help was solicited. *Corres.*, I, 324–5; cf. *Journ.* for March 28, 1711/12 and *Works*, XI, 400–1.

The question of reward was finally settled in 1714 when, in a large measure as the result of rumors concerning the Whiston-Ditton proposal, Parliament offered a reward of £20,000 (13 Anne c. 14). The first public announcement concerning the Whiston-Ditton scheme had been made in the *Guardian* for July 13, 1713, and this had been followed by subsequent announcements concerning it in the *Englishman* for December 10, 1713, and at the end of Ditton's treatise, *A New Law of Fluids,* which was published early in 1714. Despite these public statements the greatest secrecy had been preserved concerning the exact nature of the proposal. The fact that both men were known to be able scientists and that Newton, Halley, and others were said to have approved the scheme led the public to believe that the proposal was to be an epoch-making one.

In the face of this high expectation the actual proposal, when it was finally published on July 14, 1714, was very much of a letdown. In brief, the Whiston-Ditton scheme was that fireships should be anchored at each degree of the meridian and each day at exactly twelve noon should discharge huge cannon and set off tremendous rockets which would burst at known altitudes. By marking the length of time the sound took to reach his ship and noting the angle subtended by the bursting rocket, a mariner was to discover his distance from the known position of the ship.

Despite the unfavorable reception of the scheme, Whiston persisted in it for a time and even went to the expense of a public experiment. Hampstead was selected as the site for the trial and public notice was duly given a week in advance. It was definitely not a success. Whiston, though damped, offered other proposals in 1719 and 1738.

It happened that just before the publication of the Whiston-Ditton scheme Arbuthnot had been working on a satirical one for Martinus. On the appearance of the much-heralded proposal Arbuthnot wrote to Swift complaining that the superior absurdity of the Whiston-Ditton scheme had ruined his Scriblerian project. Cf. below, p. 343, n. 31. Apparently at this time Gay wrote the vulgar ditty on Whiston and Ditton which was published in the "Last Volume" of the Swift-Pope *Miscellanies*, pp. 172–3. Cf. Spence, p. 152 and Pope, E. & C., VI, 226–7. Prior included an amusing couplet on Whiston and his scheme in *Alma*, in *Poems*, A. R. Waller, ed., p. 248.

(14) 167, 7. . . . *and of increasing the* Trade-Wind *by vast plantations of* Reeds *and* Sedges.

This noble product of *non-sequitur* reasoning appears to have been built on a theory of Dr. Martin Lister, the distinguished scientist and physician. The theory appears in the following passage from an article by Lister published in the *Philosophical Transactions* (1684):

Among the known *Sea Plants* the *Sargosse* or *Lenticula Marina,* is not to be forgot; this grows in vast quantities from 36 to 18 Degrees Northern Latitude, and elsewhere upon the deepest Seas. And I think (to say something by the by of that great *Phænomenon* of the *Winds*) from the daily and constant Breath of that Plant, the *Trade* or *Tropic Winds* do in great part arise: because the matter of that Wind, coming (as we suppose) from the breath of only one *Plant,* it must needs make it constant and uniform: Whereas the great variety of *Plants* and *Trees* at Land must needs furnish a confused matter of *Winds:* Again the *Levant Breezes* are briskest about *Noon,* the *Sun* quickning the *Plant* most then, causing it to *breath* faster, and more vigorously; and that *Plants* mostly languish in the night is evident from many of them, which contract themselves and close at that time; also from the effects of our *Winters* upon them, which cause them to cast both fruit and leaves too; whereas they are said (the same *Plants* for kind) universally to flourish all the year alike within the *Tropicks*.
As for the *direction* of this *Breeze* from *East* to *West,* it may be owing to the *General current* of the *Sea,* for a gentle *Air* will still be lead with the *stream* of our *Rivers,* for example. Again every *Plant* is in some measure an *Heliotrope,* and bends it self, and moves after the *Sun,* and consequently emits its vapours thitherward, and so its *direction* is in that respect also owing in some measure to the *Course* of the *Sun.* XIV, 494–5.

The absurdity of Lister's theory was emphasized by the appearance in the *Philosophical Transactions* a few years later of an article by Edmund Halley entitled "An Historical Account of the Trade Winds, and Monsoons, observable in the Seas between and near the Tropicks, with an attempt to assign the Phisical cause of the said Winds." XVI (1686–87), 153–68. Halley's work, which was in keeping with the high standard of all his scientific activities, developed the theory that the winds arose out of differences in temperature and the movement of masses of air from high pressure to low pressure areas.

(15) 167, 2. *1. A complete Digest of the Laws of Nature, with a Review of those that are obsolete or repealed, and of those that are ready to be renew'd and put in force.*
This is a reflection on the rapid change of scientific concepts in the time of the Scriblerians. Within the lifetime of Arbuthnot and Swift, three major "systems of Nature" (the Aristotelian, Cartesian, and Newtonian) had vied for supremacy and literally hundreds of minor "laws" had been discovered, many of them promptly to be disproved or "repealed" by the work of abler and sounder scientists. The result was much skepticism regarding all supposed "laws" of nature. Swift very effectively expresses such skepticism in the scene where Gulliver, while in Glubbdubdrib, has the Governor call up the spirits of Descartes and Gassendi, whom he prevails upon to explain their systems to Aristotle:

This great philosopher freely acknowledged his own mistakes in natural philosophy, because he proceeded in many things upon conjecture, as all men must do;

and he found, that Gassendi, who had made the doctrine of Epicurus as palatable as he could, and the *vortices* of Descartes, were equally exploded. He predicted the same fate to *attraction,* whereof the present learned are such zealous asserters. He said, that new systems of nature were but new fashions, which would vary in every age; and even those who pretend to demonstrate them from mathematical principles, would flourish but a short period of time, and be out of vogue when that was determined. Pt. iii, chap. viii; *Works,* viii, 207.

Though Martinus' treatise does not seem to have been intended as a burlesque of any particular work, the Scriblerians no doubt had in mind such popular digests as William Derham's *Physico-Theology* (1713) and *Astro-Theology* (1715), as well as such works as Humphrey Ditton's *Treatise on the General Laws of Nature and Motion* (1705).

(16) 167, 14. 2. *A Mechanical Explication of the Formation of the Universe according to the Epicurean Hypothesis.*

One of the most embarrassing problems which the new science had to face was a public tendency to associate atomism and the concept of the mechanically ordered universe with Epicureanism. In their effort to keep the obloquy of atheism and materialism away from natural philosophy the scientists themselves took the lead in opposing and attempting to refute Epicureanism. On his death in 1691 Robert Boyle, one of the leading scientific atomists, left a sum of money to endow an annual series of lectures to carry on the campaign. In the next two decades many able men, including Bentley, Ray, Whiston, and Derham, wrote extended tracts to show how God's majesty and wisdom are revealed in the natural world, and for a time scientists rarely touched on the wonders of astronomy or the mechanics of nature without pausing to admire the greatness of the Supreme Being who created them.

For some account of atomism and Epicureanism in the seventeenth century see C. T. Harrison's "Bacon, Hobbes, Boyle and the Ancient Atomists," *Harvard Studies and Notes in Philology and Literature,* xv (1933), 191–218 and his "Ancient Atomists and English Literature of the Seventeenth Century," *Harvard Studies in Classical Philology,* xlv (1934), 1–80; G. B. Stones' "The Atomic View of Matter in the XVth, XVIth, and XVIIth Centuries," *Isis,* x (1928), 445–65; and T. F. Mayo's *Epicurus in England 1650–1725* (Dallas, Texas, The Southwest Press, 1934).

Typical expressions of the current attitude toward Epicureanism may be found in Swift. E.g., *Works,* i, 284, 291–2; iii, 186; iv, 177. Arbuthnot attacks it in his poem *Know Yourself* (1734).

(17) 167, 17. 3. *An Investigation of the Quantity of real Matter in the Universe, with the proportion of the specifick Gravity of the solid Matter to that of fluid.*

This investigation is a ridiculous extension of the striking calculations to be found in the third book of Newton's *Principia* regarding the quantity and specific gravity of the matter in the sun and all the planets which have satellites. The results of these calculations, which were based on the law of gravity, Adam Smith later declared to be "above the reach of human reason and experience." Sir David Brewster, *Memoirs of . . . Sir Isaac Newton* (Edinburgh, 1855), i, 322.

(18) 167, 19. 4. *Microscopical Observations of the Figure and Bulk of the constituent Parts of all fluids.*

This is pure burlesque. It was believed that fluids were composed of noncohesive particles or atoms which, because they were very round and smooth, tumbled over each other easily, but it was well known that these particles were so minute in size as to be far beyond the reach of the most powerful microscope.

Being troubled by dust once while traveling in a coach during the days of the Scriblerus Club, Arbuthnot composed the following epigram:

> The dust in smaller particles arose,
> Than those which fluid bodies do compose:
> Contraries in extremes do often meet,
> 'Twas now so dry, that you might call it wet.
>
> Swift's *Corres.*, ii, 160.

(19) 167, 21. *A Calculation of the proportion in which the Fluids of the earth decrease, and of the period in which they will be totally exhausted.*

This burlesque calculation seems to be aimed in part at those theories of the Deluge which hypothesized more water on the earth than is now present (cf. above, p. 329, n. 6, and Chambers, *s.v.* "Deluge") and in part at those who feared the gradual decay of such life-sustaining factors as the sun. See the following note.

(20) 167, 23. 5. *A Computation of the Duration of the Sun, and how long it will last before it be burn'd out.*

A satire on the Cartesian hypothesis that suns after expending the greater part of their energy become comets and that comets in turn degenerate into planets. This theory was flatly rejected by Newton as incompatible with known facts. See his letter to Bentley, December 10, 1692; Bentley's *Works* (1838), iii, 204. It was considered possible that the sun was gradually diminishing in power, but the rate was considered to be too slight for observation. Cf. Robert Hooke, *Posthumous Works*, R. Waller, ed., p. 94.

Swift in *Gulliver's Travels* satirizes those who fear the sun will burn out. The Laputians, says Gulliver, "are under continual disquietudes, never enjoying a minute's peace of mind" because they fear changes in the celestial bodies. Among their fears is the dread, "That the sun daily spending its rays without any nutriment to supply them, will at last be wholly consumed and annihilated; which must be attended with the destruction of this earth, and of all the planets that receive their light from it." *Works*, viii, 169; see Marjorie Nicolson and Nora M. Mohler, "The Scientific Background of Swift's *Voyage to Laputa*," *Annals of Science*, ii (1937), 310–11. Mrs. Centlivre also used the jest; one of the characters in her *A Bold Stroke for a Wife* (1718) boasts that he knows "what quantity of combustibles he [the sun] burns in a day, and how much of it turns to ashes and how much to cinders." Act iii.

(21) 167, 25. 6. *A Method to apply the Force arising from the immense Velocity of Light to mechanical purposes.*

Attempts to make practical use of the enormous heat generated by the rays of the sun when concentrated on a single spot first excited wide interest in the last half of the seventeenth century. Many devices for making use of this source of heat were suggested, a notable one being a large speculum invented in Germany and described in the *Acta Eruditorum* for January, 1686/87. This invention was brought to the attention of the Royal Society by its secretary, Robert Hooke, who (typically) had already considered the problem and suggested a somewhat similar device. *Phil. Trans.*, xvi (1686–87), 354. According to the German inventors, the force of their speculum was such "that even Chymists, who best know the Power of Fire, will hardly credit it, unless they see it with their own eyes." *Ibid.*, p. 353. It would, they declared, vitrify slate, earth, pumice stone, and bones, burn holes through steel, and perform other astonishing feats. *Ibid.*, pp. 353–4. A still more famous invention was a burning glass consisting of "7 Concave foiled Glasses, each of them 12 inches in diameter: which are so placed as to have their Foci concur in one point," which Sir Isaac Newton designed and presented to the Royal Society. W. Derham, *Astro-Theology* (1715), p. 153 n.

Additional interest in the phenomenon was aroused by Newton's discovery of the corpuscular nature of light and Römer's discovery of its immense velocity. The wonder and hopes excited by these discoveries are indicated by Jeremiah Wainewright's description of them in his *A Mechanical Account of the Non-Naturals* (1707). After telling of Römer's discovery, which was based on observations of the eclipses of the satellites of Jupiter, Wainewright says:

And if a *Bullet* moving with the same Celerity with which it leaves the Musle of the *Cannon,* require 25 years to pass from the Earth to the Sun, as *Hugens* has computed it, then will the velocity of Light, to that of a *Cannon Ball,* be as twenty five Years to ten Minutes, which is above a Million to one: So that the Particles of Light move above a Million of times swifter than a *Cannon Bullet;* and may we not expect proportionable effects from them, tho' they are so exceeding small? for the *Momentum* of any Body in motion against another, is as a *Rectangle* under the Magnitude and Celerity of the Moved Body. We may guess at the effects of the *Rays* of Light separately, by what we observe when collected together in the *Focus* of a Burning-Glass: For no *Body,* tho' never so compact, is able to resist its force. Gold it self may be *Vitrify'd* by the concenter'd Rays of the Sun, though it be unalterable by any *culinary Fire* whatever; as Mr. *Blondel* tells us, one part exhaling whilst the other is turned into Glass, and this in a few *Seconds* of time. Pp. 74–5.

How widespread the interest in burning glasses had become by the end of the reign of Queen Anne is suggested by Swift's pastime of burning holes in paper with one during the anxious days of his stay at Letcombe in the summer of 1714. Cf. the joint letter of Pope and Parnell to Arbuthnot; E. & C., vii, 469–70. In 1716 Arbuthnot issued a witty little satire on attempts to make use of sunlight for practical purposes in the form of a mock petition to the mayor and aldermen of the city of London by the "Colliers, Cooks, Cook-maids, Blacksmiths, Jackmakers, Braziers and others" against the practice of "catoptrical cookery." The petitioners maintain that catoptrical cookery will ruin them and urge that it be totally prohibited or heavily taxed and reserved to the Royal Society and to the "commanders of the bombvessels, under the direction of Mr. Whiston for finding out the longitude, who, by reason of the remoteness of their stations, may be reduced to straits for want of firing." Aitken, pp. 377–8; cf. above, p. 334, n. 13.

(22) 167, 28. 7. *An answer to the question of a curious Gentleman; How long a* New Star *was lighted up before its appearance to the Inhabitants of our earth?*

The satire here is aimed at calculations made on the basis of grossly insufficient evidence. The approximate speed of light was known, as the result of the work of Römer and Huygens—though so distinguished a scientist as Robert Hooke refused to accept their findings and declared that light is "(in all Probability, and as far as Experiments, Observations and Reasons can assist us) infinitely swift" and that "at the very instant the remotest Star does emit Light, in that very instant does the Eye upon the Earth receive it, though it be many Millions of Millions of Miles distant, so that in Probability no time is spent between the emitting and the reception" (*Posthumous Works*, p. 77) but as yet no method of working out the distance of stars had been developed (cf. above, p. 328, n. 5) and the nature of novae, faint or undetected stars which suddenly explode into visibility only to die out in a brief time, was, as it has remained, an unsolved puzzle. Newton thought these novae were fixed stars whose energy had become exhausted and then built up again by the accession of comets (*Principia*, lib. iii, prop. 42) while others believed them to be revolving stars with a dark side or merely planets of other systems. Cf. W. Derham, *Astro-Theology*, p. 45.

(23) 167, 30. . . . *a Calculation, how much the Inhabitants of the* Moon *eat for Supper, considering that they pass a Night equal to fifteen of our natural days.*

For an account of the many speculations concerning life in the moon and other planets by literary and scientific writers in the seventeenth and early eighteenth centuries see Marjorie Hope Nicolson, *Voyages to the Moon* (New York, 1948), "A World in the Moon," *Smith College Studies*, xvii, No. 2 (1936) and "Cosmic Voyages," *ELH*, vii (1940), 83–107; also Grant McColley, "The Seventeenth-Century Doctrine of a Plurality of Worlds," *Annals of Science*, 1 (1936), 385–430.

The Scriblerian satire was aimed not at the idea that life may exist on the moon or other planets, a theory which even Newton thought likely (Sir David Brewster, *Memoirs of . . . Sir Isaac Newton*, ii, 353), but at those scientists who in all seriousness attempted to reach highly specific conclusions concerning the nature and activities of the inhabitants of other worlds. A notable example of this type of speculation is to be found in a posthumously published book by the celebrated Christian Huygens entitled *Cosmotheoros* (1698), translated into English under the title *The Celestial Worlds Discover'd: or, Conjectures concerning the Inhabitants, Plants and Productions of the Worlds in the Planets* (1699). By piling supposition on analogy Huygens "demonstrates" that the planets are inhabited by beings, animals, and plants almost exactly like our own. He even undertakes to point out how much the peoples of these other worlds know, concluding that they are acquainted with navigation, music, astronomy, mathematics, and other sciences.

Perhaps the two best of the many satires on the scientists who were overly enthusiastic concerning the world in the moon were Samuel Butler's *The Elephant in the Moon* and Mrs. Aphra Behn's *The Emperor of the Moon* (1687). In Mrs. Behn's comedy, Dr. Baliardo, the chief character, is so moon-struck that, according to his daughter, "he discourses as gravely of the People, their Government, In-

stitutions, Laws, Manners, Religion, and Constitution, as if he had been bred a
Machiavel there." Act 1, sc. 1; *Works,* Montague Summers, ed. (1915), III, 399.

(24) 167, 33. *8. A Demonstration of the natural Dominion of the Inhabitants of
the Earth over those of the Moon, if ever any intercourse should be open'd between
them.*

The Scriblerian satire on the "natural Dominion of the Inhabitants of the Earth
over those of the Moon" stems from another aspect of lunar studies in the seventeenth century. As various astronomers "explored" and mapped the moon with
increasingly large telescopes, they formed the practice of complimenting their
rulers or patrons by naming various "continents" and "islands" after them. The
satirists laughed at this practice and compared it to the custom of explorers who laid
claim to all newly discovered lands in the names of their kings. Samuel Butler, for
example, sneers at the virtuosos who "sillyly" have "giv'n away whole Ilands in
the Moon." *Satires and Miscellaneous Poetry and Prosa,* R. Lamar, ed. (1928), p.
203.

(25) 167, 34. *With a Proposal of a* Partition-Treaty, *among the earthly Potentates,
in case of such discovery.*

A reference to the two partition treaties (of 1698 and 1700) by means of which
William III and Louis XIV, together with the Austrians and Dutch, sought to
solve the difficult problem of who should succeed to the throne of Spain on the
death of Charles II. The repudiation of the second treaty by Louis XIV led to the
War of the Spanish Succession.

William gravely offended the English people by negotiating these treaties without the knowledge or consent of his cabinet and Parliament. Later the Whigs
vigorously supported the treaties and the war which grew out of them, but to the
Tories they remained iniquitous. In 1714, only a year after the signing of the
treaty of peace, "partition treaties" were still an object of scorn and satire on the
part of Tory writers.

(26) 167, 36. *9. Tide-Tables, for a Comet, that is to approximate towards the Earth.*

A satire on the Halley-Whiston theory that the comet of 1680 had, in an earlier
visit, caused the Biblical Deluge by passing so close to the earth that it had caused
tremendous tides both in the oceans and in the subterranean waters with which
they and others supposed the abysses of the earth to be filled. Cf. above, p. 329,
n. 6. The satire also touches on the fear, which for several generations after the
appearance of the comet amounted almost to an obsession among both laymen and
scientists, that some day the earth would be destroyed by a comet. Cf. above, Chap.
XIV, p. 306, n. 41; cf. Marjorie Nicolson and Nora M. Mohler, "The Scientific Background of Swift's *Voyage to Laputa,*" *Annals of Science,* II (1937), 312–17.

(27) 168, 3. *10. The Number of the Inhabitants of London determin'd by the
Reports of the Gold-finders, and the Tonnage of their Carriages; with allowance
for the extraordinary quantity of the* Ingesta *and* Egesta *of the people of England,
and a deduction of what is left under dead walls, and dry ditches.*

Gold finders—a slang term for sewage collectors.

The proposed method of discovering the size of London's population, which reminds one of the Emperor Elagabalus' attempt to compute the number of the inhabitants of Rome by the quantity of spiders' webs, is a burlesque on the exceedingly dubious and roundabout methods by which population figures were arrived at in the early eighteenth century. So strong were fears, based on political, economic, and religious prejudice, of what a real census would reveal that it was not until the year 1800 that a census bill was passed by Parliament and the actual counting of the people was begun. Before the results of this census were available, people had only the vaguest ideas of the actual size of cities. In the middle of the seventeenth century estimates of the size of London actually varied all the way from 100,000 to 7,000,000, with the preponderance of opinion inclining toward the latter figure! Equally fantastic ideas as to the size of foreign cities were current.

In *Gulliver's Travels* the King of Brobdingnag laughs at Gulliver's "odd kind of arithmetic (as he was pleased to call it) in reckoning the numbers of our people by a computation drawn from the several sects among us in religion and politics." *Works*, VIII, 134-5).

The first man to attempt to develop a sound method of calculation for population figures was Sir William Petty. Cf. above, p. 334, n. 12. After experimenting with all sorts of data, Petty came to the conclusion that the best method of computing population was to compare calculations based on 1) the number of houses and probable number of people living in them, 2) the number of burials in healthful times and hence the probable number of people surviving, and 3) the number of deaths in plague years together with the available data on those that escaped. Since Petty's data were often little better than guesswork and he was forced to pile hypothesis on hypothesis, his method was highly fallible. On one occasion he reached the figure of 384,000 for London and on another 670,000. The Scriblerians, however, probably did not intend their satire to fall on Petty personally or to call into contempt the effort he and others were making. In his *Essay on the Usefulness of Mathematical Learning* (1701), Arbuthnot had written:

What Sir William Petty and several others of our countrymen have wrote in political arithmetic, does abundantly shew the pleasure and usefulness of such speculations. It is true, for want of good information, their calculations sometimes proceed upon erroneous suppositions; but that is not the fault of the art. Aitken, p. 422.

Swift possessed a copy of Petty's *Essays in Political Arithmetick,* the 1699 edition. H. Williams, *Dean Swift's Library.*

(28) 168, 11. . . . *to pierce the first crust or* Nucleus *of this our* Earth, *quite through, to the next concentrical Sphere: . . . to find the* Parallax *of the* Fixt Stars; . . .

The jest turns on Halley's theory that the earth is composed of an outer crust and an inner nucleus. Cf. below, p. 343, n. 30. The use of a shaft in finding the parallax of fixed stars seems merely to be a fantastically literal application of astronomers' practice in calculating parallaxes from a spot at the center of the earth.

The Scriblerians had already satirized efforts to calculate the parallax of fixed stars. Cf., above, p. 328, n. 5.

(29) 168, 12. *. . . but chiefly to refute Sir Isaac Newton's Theory of Gravity, . . .*

Is seems possible that this refers to an episode in Newton's quarrel with Hooke over the credit for discovering certain aspects of the law of gravity, particularly the law of duplicate proportion. During the quarrel Newton wrote to Edmund Halley, June 20, 1686, acknowledging that Hooke had told him of the law that the decrease of gravity is reciprocal as the squares of the distances from the center, but declaring that he regarded Hooke's views as erroneous because Hooke believed the effects of the rule "to reach down from hence to the center of the earth." Sir David Brewster, *Memoirs of . . . Sir Isaac Newton*, I, 309. Newton went on to say that "he himself had never extended the duplicate proportion lower than the superficies of the earth" and that "before a certain demonstration he found last year he suspected it did not reach accurately enough down so low." *Ibid.*

(30) 168, 13. *. . . and [to refute] Mr. Halley's [theory] of the Variations.*

Halley's theory was that the magnetic needle of the compass was under the influence of four magnetic poles, two fixed in the outer shell of the earth and two in an inner nucleus whose slower motion or drag with relation to the superficies of the earth resulted in an internal revolution during a period of approximately seven hundred years (for a contemporary account of the theory see Chambers, under "Variations"). Halley's theory explained the previously mysterious secular magnetic changes quite successfully. He first proposed his solution in 1683 and published further developments of it in 1692. *Phil. Trans.*, XIII (1683), 208 ff., and XVII (1692), 563–78. Halley was a friend of Arbuthnot's, the two being associated in the preparation for the press of Flamsteed's catalogue of the stars.

(31) 168, 16. *. . . to build Two Poles to the Meridian, with immense Lighthouses on the top of them; . . . to make the Longitude as easy to calculate as the Latitude.*

In a letter to Swift written on July 17, 1714, Arbuthnot said:

Whiston has at last published his project of the longitude; the most ridiculous thing that ever was thought on. But a pox on him! he has spoiled one of my papers of Scriblerus, which was a proposal for the longitude, not very unlike his, to this purpose: that since there was no pole for East and West, that all the Princes of Europe should join and build two prodigious poles, upon high mountains, with a vast light-house to serve for a pole-star. I was thinking of a calculation of the time, charges, and dimensions. Now you must understand, his project is by lighthouses, and explosion of bombs at a certain hour. *Corres.*, II, 186.

To this Swift replied, "It was a malicious satire of yours upon Whiston, that what you intended as a ridicule, should be anyway struck upon by him for a reality." *Corres.*, II, 197.

For an account of Whiston's and Ditton's scheme of bomb vessels see above, p. 334, n. 13.

(32) 168, 22. *From the Age, Complexion, or Weight of the person given, he contrived to prescribe at a distance, as well as at a Patient's bedside.*

The abuse which the Scriblerians are attacking is perhaps adequately illustrated by the following anecdote told about Dr. John Radcliffe, the most celebrated physician of the day, who was famous for his blunt speech.

The Apothecaries, and other Smatterers in the Art of Pharmacy, had in order to draw People to them, gave out, that they could as well cure People at a Distance, as by Personal Attendance, of all manner of Human Maladies, by a Sight of their Water; which would be of great Use to Patients, who, by Reason of their Infirmities, could not apply for Relief to theirs [i.e., them]; or, of their Poverty, could not pay for Visits at their own Homes. This had worm'd the Country out of many a sweet Penny, and Crouds of Men and Women went daily to them, with Vials, Bottles, &c for a definitive Sentence, in their Husbands, Wives, and Children's Cases. Amongst the rest, to whom should one of these credulous Women come, with an Urinal in her Hand, but to Dr. *Radcliffe:* The good Woman dropt a Courtezy, told him, that she had heard of his great Fame at *Stanton,* and that she made bold to bring him a Fee, by which she hop'd his Worship would be prevail'd with to tell her the Distemper her Husband lay sick of, and to prescribe proper Remedies for his Relief. *Where is he?* cries the Doctor, *Sick in Bed four Miles off,* says the Petitioner. *And that's his Water, no doubt,* cries the Querist. *Yes, and it please your Worship,* the Answerer replies: And being ask'd what Trade he was of, tells him, *that of a Shoemaker. Very well, Mistress,* cries the Examinant, and taking the Urinal, empties it into the Chamber-pot, and then filling it with his own Water, dismisses her, with this Advice: *Take this with you home to your Husband, and if he will undertake to fit me with a Pair of Boots, by the sight of my Water, I'll make no Question of Prescribing for his Distemper, by a Sight of his. Some Memoirs of the Life of John Radcliffe, M.D.* (1715), pp. 12–13.

Throughout the whole of the early eighteenth century there was vigorous warfare between reputable medical men on the one side and quacks and apothecaries on the other regarding the dispensing of drugs and prescriptions without medical training. The most famous literary piece growing out of the quarrel was Sir Samuel Garth's well-known poem *The Dispensary* (1699). In 1724 Arbuthnot aided the physicians' cause by a very clever pamphlet entitled *Reasons humbly offer'd by the Company exercising the Trade and Mystery of Upholders* [i.e. undertakers], *against part of the Bill, For the better Viewing, Searching, and Examining Drugs, Medicines, &c.*

(33) 168, 26. *He projected a Menstruum to dissolve the Stone, made of Dr. Woodward's* Universal Deluge-water.

This jest, which is one of the best in the whole of the *Memoirs,* is aimed primarily at Dr. John Woodward's theory, advanced in his *An Essay toward a Natural History of the Earth* (1695), that at the time of the Flood, waters welling up from inside the earth dissolved all stones and other material and that this dissolved material later settled according to its specific gravity, thus causing the present stratification of rock. See above, p. 329, n. 6. It also satirizes, however, the many quack nostrums for the cure of kidney and bladder stones from which the people of the time, as the result of their diet, very commonly suffered. Pepys, as readers of his diary will recall, once suffered from the stone and Arbuthnot himself suffered cruelly from recurrent attacks of this painful ailment. Cf. e.g., Swift, *Journ.*, October 4, 1711.

The versatile Robert Hooke seems to have inspired the search for a nostrum that would dissolve the stone in the body. In his *Micrographia* (1665) he tells of experiments in dissolving the stone by means of various liquids and suggests that physicians attempt to discover some effective remedy of this sort. Pp. 81–2. In later years one nostrum after another was advertised as the infallible remedy only to prove to be a fraud. In discussing the stone in his *Practical Rules of Diet* (1732; 3d ed., 1735–36) Arbuthnot says laconically: "As to Dissolvents of the Stone, all that have hitherto been propos'd are chimerical; *Helmont* talks of Bull's Blood; Goat's Blood is rather a better Dissolvent." P. 432.

After Arbuthnot's death Mrs. Joanna Stephens hoaxed £5,000 out of Parliament for a secret remedy which turned out to consist simply of calcined egg and snail shells, some burned herbs, and alicant soap. Cf. above, Chap. x, p. 273, n. 1. This last item was the chief element of another concoction of which Sir Robert Walpole was the victim. For many years he daily swallowed a mixture of this soap with lime water. On his death it was estimated that he had consumed at least one hundred eighty pounds of soap and twelve hundred gallons of lime water. Yet just before his death he had discharged thirty-two pieces of stone and after his death three whole stones were found in his bladder. Cf. *Letters of Horace Walpole*, Mrs. Paget Toynbee, ed. (Oxford, 1903–05), II, 71, 75.

(34) 168, 32. *His also was the device to relieve Consumptive or Asthmatick persons, . . . by pipes of the nature of the Recipients of Air-pumps; and to introduce the native Air of a man's country into any other in which he should travel, with a seasonable Intromission of such Steams as were most familiar to him; . . .*

The Scriblerians' memory here betrayed them. Shadwell had already thoroughly exploited this idea in his comedy *The Virtuoso* (1676). In Act IV of this play we learn about Sir Nicholas Gimcrack's ingenious scheme for taking the country air while still sitting at home in London. He employs men all over England to bottle up air. These bottles he keeps in his cellar and when he wishes to enjoy the air of a particular section of the country he merely closes the windows and doors of his room and opens the appropriate flasks. *Works of Thomas Shadwell*, Montague Summers, ed., III, 160, 164; cf. p. 144. Shadwell probably developed the jest by combining the idea of air pumps (in which there was a good deal of popular interest as the result of Boyle's experiments) with the idea of daily deliveries of Bath water which were widely advertised as making unnecessary the trip to Bath in order to enjoy the benefits of its famous water.

The repetition of the jest here is probably the result of Arbuthnot's interest in the effects of air on human bodies—a subject on which he published a treatise in 1733. He himself was a sufferer from asthma and in 1734 moved to Hampstead for the sake of the air. Aitken, p. 147. Pope, too, was a victim of this ailment, it being one of the causes of his death.

(35) 168, 33. *. . . to the inexpressible comfort of many Scotchmen, Laplanders, and white Bears.*

Both the rigors of the Scottish climate and the affection which Scotchmen away from home professed for it were common subjects of satire. The reference to Laplanders seems to have been inspired by the popular superstition that witches there could control the winds by incantations and would, for a sufficient sum, provide a merchant with any form of breeze he desired. This belief, which came down from the Middle Ages, was frequently referred to in the seventeenth century. Cf. Ethel Seaton, *Literary Relations of England and Scandinavia in the Seventeenth Century*, pp. 280–7. Swift mentions it jestingly in *Journ.*, for June 17, 1712.

(36) 168, 36. *In* Physiognomy, *his penetration is such, that, from the* Picture *only of any person, he can write his Life; and, from the features of the Parents, draw the Portrait of any Child that is to be born.*

The ancient "art" of physiognomy was as thoroughly exploded as was judicial astrology, but it held its sway among the vulgar. On a higher level, the subject continued to attract the attention of scientists. Cf., e.g., John Evelyn's "Digression concerning Physiognomy" in his *Numismata* (1697); Dr. Gwither's "Discourse of Physiognomy," *Phil. Trans.*, xviii (1694), 118–20; and Chambers, *s.v.* "Physiognomy." Addison speaks favorably of the art in *Spectator*, No. 86.

The reference to biographies written on the basis of a man's portrait was perhaps aimed obliquely at the disreputable Edmund Curll and other Grub Street writers who, on the death of any famous man, promptly published a biography without troubling to collect materials.

(37) 169, 5. *It was he that gave the first hint to our modern* Painters, *to improve the* Likeness *of their Portraits by the use of such* Colours *as would faithfully and constantly accompany the* Life, *not only in its present state, but in all its alterations, decays, age, and death itself.*

Martinus' proposal is, of course, a satire on painters who slavishly imitated nature and strove merely for likenesses in portraits instead of following the neoclassic ideal of delineating character and striving to present the universal qualities of grace, charm, spirit, etc.

It is also a painter's joke on the impermanent colors used by many artists. Since little was known about the underlying chemistry of pigments and what was known was often jealously preserved as trade secrets, it not infrequently happened that paintings by inferior artists showed changes of color and signs of darkening within a few years. Flesh tones built up with lake or carmine were particularly subject to decay. Inferior whites turned muddy or yellow; yellows turned brown; and greens darkened into black. Naturally in a time when hosts of minor and hack artists were clamoring for trade the charge of impermanent colors was a deadly weapon against rivals. It may be noted that some years later the great Sir Joshua Reynolds was complained against, with some justice, on this score.

Since Pope was especially interested in painting and was well acquainted with its problems, having studied for a year and a half with Charles Jervas, it seems reasonable to attribute this bit of satire to him. Several of the other Scriblerians, however, were well acquainted with Jervas and Sir Godfrey Kneller, and might therefore almost equally well have devised or picked up this jest.

(38) 169, 9. *In* Architecture, *he builds not with so much regard to present symmetry or conveniency, as with a Thought well worthy a true lover of Antiquity, to wit, the noble effect the Building will have to posterity, when it shall fall and become a Ruin.*

Behind this burlesque on the love of antiquity as such lay the growing current rage for ruins. This fad, which was to reach its height past the middle of the century, seems to have got its start in the 1720's in connection with the growing vogue of the "natural" garden, to which Pope contributed much by his patronage of Kent and by the example of his own famous miniature garden at Twickenham. Ruins were believed to give an air of picturesqueness "touched with melancholy" to otherwise placid country scenes and to bring to a romantic close the "prospects" which were the crowning glories of the new gardens. So great became the demand for picturesque ruins that estate owners not fortunate enough to own any and unable to wait for actual buildings to decay had architects design and build ruined towers, chapels, etc., all complete with tumbled-down stones, moss, and ivy. For those who could not afford to invest so heavily in ruins or who were not sure they would continue to like the same ruin in the same place, cheaper expedients were devised. Thus Batty Langley in *New Principles of Gardening* (1728) prints a series of plates (Nos. xix, xx, and xxi) illustrating "Views of *the Ruins of Buildings,* after the old *Roman manner,* to terminate such Walks that end in *disagreeable Objects,* which *Ruins* may either be *painted upon Canvas,* or actually built in that Manner with *Brick,* and cover'd with *Plaistering* in Imitation of Stone." P. xv.

(39) 169, 11. *As to* Music, *I think Heidegger has not the face to deny that he has been much beholden to his Scores.*

Count Heidegger, manager of the opera house in the Haymarket and Master of the Revels under George II, had the reputation of having the ugliest face of any man in England. Of his appearance he himself made a jest and he is said once to have laid a wager with the Earl of Chesterfield that within a given time the Earl could not discover an equally ugly face in all London. After much searching a hideous old woman was found who at first view seemed to surpass Heidegger. On being confronted with her, however, Heidegger snatched off her head-dress and put it on himself; whereupon "he was universally allowed to have won the wager." Chambers.

The Count, whose title was a courtesy one, came to England from Switzerland in 1708. In addition to his work in the opera he made an enormous success with his masquerade balls which, despite constant attacks on moral grounds, continued popular for many years and were even patronized by royalty. His ugliness was a frequent source of jest and comment. Fielding, in a poem called *The Masquerade* (1728), which he wrote under the pseudonym of Lemuel Gulliver, tells of a young masquerader who, on seeing Heidegger approach, inquired how it would ever occur to anyone to devise so horrible a masque. Pope mentions his appearance in the *Dunciad,* Bk. 1, l. 290. His features at their worst can be seen in Hogarth's caricature, "Heidegger in a Rage."

(40) 169, 18. *In* Politicks, *his Writings are of a peculiar Cast, for the most part Ironical, . . . He once went so far as to write a Persuasive to people to eat their own Children, which was so little understood as to be taken in ill part.*

The reference is, of course, to Swift's *A Modest Proposal For preventing the Children Of Poor People From being a Burthen to Their Parents or Country, And For making them Beneficial to the Publick,* which was first published in 1729 in Dublin. It has already been pointed out in the general note to this chapter that this "vindicating" of Swift's piece to Martinus is for the purpose of emphasizing the irony of the following ascriptions.

(41) 169, 20. *He has often written against* Liberty *in the name of* Freeman *and* Algernoon Sydney, . . .

"Ralph Freeman" and "Algernon Sidney" were pen names signed to articles appearing at intervals in the *Daily Gazetteer* between the years 1735 and 1738. According to the author of *An Historical View . . . of the Political Writers* (1740) the first was used by Raphael Courteville, the organist of the church of St. James's, Westminster, and the second by Francis Medley, a lawyer. Pp. 39–40. The reference is ironic, both writers strongly advocating liberty. "Algernon Sidney," of course, took his name from the famous advocate of republican doctrines who, after a trial under "Bloody Jeffreys," was beheaded for treason on December 7, 1683.

(42) 169, 21. *. . . in vindication of the Measures of* Spain *under that of* Raleigh, . . .

The name "Walter Raleigh" was signed to a series of letters appearing in the *Craftsman* (Nos. 125, 128, 135, 137, 139, 160, 162, 163, 164, 176) during the years 1728–29 in which Walpole's pusillanimous policy toward the aggressions of Spain was severely attacked. The "Raleigh" letters and one *Craftsman Extraordinary* all bore the identifying signature "A," except for the first, sixth, and last, which bore the letters "C.A.," "A.O.," and "C" respectively. The author has never been satisfactorily identified—Carteret being perhaps the most likely candidate in view of "Raleigh's" vehement defense of Stanhope, whose protégé Cartaret was.

(43) 169, 22. *. . . and in praise of* Corruption *under those of* Cato, *and* Publicola.

"Cato" was the name used by John Trenchard and Thomas Gordon in a famous series of letters in defense of Whig policies and the Walpole regime, which appeared in the *London Journal* in 1721 and 1722. "Publicola" was the name signed to another series appearing in the same journal during the years 1728 and 1729 in which Walpole was supported and the attacks of the *Craftsman,* especially those signed by "Walter Raleigh," were answered. Apparently several writers used the name. Cf. Bolingbroke's "Answer to the London Journal," *Works* (Philadelphia, 1841), I, 240.

(44) 169, 29. *. . . fish'd up with a hook and line by the Ministerial Writers, . . .*

All during his administration Sir Robert Walpole maintained a large staff of writers to defend himself and his ministry. These writers kept the presses busy with their Whig propaganda and their defenses of the ministry. On this "favorable press" Walpole spent large sums of secret service money, but since he was a believer in quantity rather than quality the money was for the most part spread among fourth-rate hacks. "No Minister," says a writer in the *Craftsman*, No. 210 (1731), VI, 234, "ever made Himself more remarkable by his Profusion of *Pensions* amongst the worst [writers]; which I think a much more generous and munificent Part; because *good Writers* may be able to support themselves by their *own Works*, whereas *bad Ones* must depend upon *his Protection*."

Walpole's hirelings naturally were objects of scorn in the eyes of the opposition writers, among whom were some of the most brilliant minds of the period. "Wretched Paper-stainers," "prostitute Scribblers," "pensionary writers," "invidious libellers," "mercenary and abandoned wretches," "shameless crew," and "little dirty Dabbler in Politicks" are but a few of the terms applied to these paid propagandists in the pages of the *Craftsman*.

THE ADVERTISEMENT

This advertisement appeared in only one edition of the *Memoirs*, No. 5, in the Bibliography of Principal Editions. Cf. above, p. 79. It is of considerable interest as suggesting how the Scriblerians may have intended to carry on their project. How significant it is naturally depends on how seriously it was meant. False advertisements and spurious proposals for books were a common jest of the period and one which the Scriblerians, notably Arbuthnot, had practiced before. Moreover, a humorous suggestion of future publications was directly in line with the Scriblerians' scheme.

On the other hand, Martinus' travels had previously been exploited in chapter sixteen by the suggestion that they were to be identified with those of Lemuel Gulliver and the present hint of still other travels is something in the nature of an anticlimax (a fact which probably accounts for Pope's having dropped it out of the final version of the text). Furthermore, unlike other Scriblerus proposals, this advertisement is not clearly humorous or satiric in itself. The idea of interlarding Martinus' account of what he and the Bishop of Apamaea saw in China with a Chinese prince's impression of Europe has considerable satiric possibilities, but these are hardly obvious enough to be entirely left to the reader's imagination. Moreover, as has been pointed out,[1] the character of the voyages agrees at least in a general way with what Pope told Spence about "the Schreibler's travels." It seems likely, therefore, that the works described were actually sketched out or drafted by the Scriblerians during the club days. If so, the manuscripts of them were doubtless among the Scriblerus manuscripts which Pope ordered destroyed.

The journey through the deserts of Nubia to the court of Ethiopia is associated with the Scriblerus piece *The Origine of Sciences,* which was written by Martinus from the deserts of Nubia and Ethiopia. The inspiration for the voyage to China is more difficult to identify. There was a good deal of interest in China in England during the latter part of the seventeenth and early part of the eighteenth centuries, though the wave of interest in all things Chinese did not develop until later. The most famous works on China were the accounts of the journeys of the Jesuit Father Le Comte, which was first published in London in 1697, and of Evert Ides, who

1. Above, pp. 316–17.

was an ambassador from Russia to China, which was translated into English in 1705. Both contained descriptions of the religion, politics, and social customs of the country.

The plan to publish the journal of the Chinese prince who is traveling incognito throughout Europe undoubtedly derives its general inspiration from the enormously popular *Turkish Spy* of the Italian writer Marana and its imitations. The Scriblerian proposal is interesting as anticipating the mechanism of Oliver Goldsmith's famous *Citizen of the World* essays.

(1) 172, 7. . . . *the Bishop of* Apamæa . . .

Why the Scriblerians selected the Bishop of Apamaea as Martinus' companion is not clear. Apamaea is the modern city of Hama on the Orontes River in Syria. In ancient times it was a rich and prosperous city which rivaled its neighbor Antioch. Cf. Pliny, Strabo, Ptolemy, etc. At one time its churches were presided over by archbishops under the patriarchate of Antioch.

(2) 172, 7. . . . *joint voyage upon* Cunturs, . . .

The cuntur is the South American condor. Cf. Bailey. The idea of the voyage upon the huge birds was probably borrowed from the *Arabian Nights*.

APPENDIX I

Rhymed Invitations to Scriblerus Meetings and Replies [1]

---

1. An Invitation [2]

In the handwriting of Swift

("Marc. 20: 1713/14") [3]

To the Lord High Treasurer

The Doctor and Dean, Pope, Parnell and Gay [4]
In manner submissive most humbly do pray,
That your Lordship would once let your Cares all alone
And Climb the dark Stairs to your Friends who have none:
To your Friends who at least have no Cares but to please you
To a good honest Junta that never will teaze you.
From the Doctor's Chamber [5]
past eight.

1. Cf. above, p. 27. Four of these sets of verses were first published by Hawkesworth among Swift's letters in 1766 (4to ed., x, 205–07) from manuscripts no longer known to exist. Manuscripts of eight, including one given by Hawkesworth, are among the Portland Papers at Longleat. Six of these have not previously appeared in print. They are printed here by the kind permission of the Marquis of Bath.

The verses reflect the very tense political situation during the month of April when the ministry was subjected to a series of sharp attacks in Parliament. On the basis of topical references and internal evidence, several of the pieces are now for the first time assigned tentative dates and the series is given in a more coherent order.

2. First printed by Elwin and Courthope (VIII, 225, n. 2); reprinted by H. Williams (*The Poems of Jonathan Swift* [Oxford, 1937], I, 185), both from the original manuscript. This consists of a folio sheet folded in half. Apparently as originally sent the outer surfaces were blank, with the verses appearing on the recto of the inner pages and the address to Oxford on the verso opposite. The manuscript has been turned inside out so that the verses are on p. 1 and the address on p. 4.

3. The date was added below the verses by Oxford.

4. During Swift's first return visit to England in 1726, the second Earl of Oxford wrote in a letter to Pope, "Now you three [Swift, Pope, and Gay] are together, I often think of the lines wrote in old times which begin,
    The Doctor and Dean, Pope, Parnell, and Gay.
Only poor Parnell is gone; . . ." E. & C., VIII, 224–5.

5. In St. James's Palace.

2. An Invitation [6]

Chiefly written by Swift [7]

[c. April 1?, 1714] [8]

Let not the whigs our tory club rebuke;
Give us our earl, the devil take their duke.[9]
Quaedam quae attinent ad Scriblerum,[10]
Want your assistance now to clear 'em.
    One day it will be no disgrace,
    In *Scribler* to have had a place.
Come then, my lord, and take your part in
The important history of *Martin.*

3. A Reply [11]

By Oxford? [12]

April 14[1?],[13] 1714. Back Stairs,[14] past Eight.

In a summons so *large,* which all clergy contains,

6. First printed by Hawkesworth; reprinted in *Swiftiana* (1804, I, 109) and by Sir Walter Scott (Swift's *Works,* 1814, xvi, 129), Aitken (*Life and Works of John Arbuthnot* [Oxford, 1892], p. 56, n. 1) without the first couplet, Ball (Swift's *Corres.,* II, 416), and Williams, *op. cit.*
7. Hawkesworth. Apparently Swift was aided by Parnell; cf. below.
8. The date is suggested by the reference in the second line to the Duke of Argyll, who, because of his opposition to the ministry, was deprived of his command in the Horse Guards by the Queen on April 1, and by the fact that it seems to be the invitation to which the verses which follow are a reply. The date falls on a Thursday.
9. John Campbell, Duke of Argyll and Duke of Greenwich, had served under the Oxford ministry, but in the spring of 1714, apparently actuated largely by his hatred of the Pretender, became hostile. He had been on terms of friendship with Swift but was the leader of the Scottish peers when they petitioned the crown against Swift's *Publick Spirit of the Whigs.* Cf. p. 36.
10. I.e., things which pertain to Scriblerus.
11. First printed by Hawkesworth and reprinted in *Swiftiana* and by Scott, Ball, and Williams.
12. Hawkesworth puts Gay's name at the head of these verses, but it seems more likely that Gay, in his capacity as secretary to the club, merely copied them. The phrase, "which all clergy contains," in the first line makes it seem likely that this reply is Oxford's answer to No. 2, which, as noted above, was probably by Swift with the aid of Parnell.
13. The date given by Hawkesworth seems clearly to be in error since there exists a reply from Oxford dated the fourteenth. The ascription to Gay and the date can be explained by suggesting that Gay may have sought to save Oxford the trouble of a reply by drafting one for him, but the likelihood is that Gay, or some later transcriber, simply made an error in the date by anticipating the "14" in the year and that the proper date is April 1.
14. In St. James's Palace.

I must turn *Dismal*'s [15] convert, or part with my brains,
Should I scruple to quit the back stairs for your blind ones,[16]
Or refuse your true juncto for one of ——

4. An Invitation and Reply [17]

Each couplet in the handwriting of its contributor

[April 10?,[18] 1714]

My Lord, forsake your Politick Utopians,
To sup, like Jove, with blameless Ethiopians.[19]

Pope.

In other Words, You with the Staff,
Leave John of Bucks,[20] come here and laugh.

Dean.

For Frolick Mirth give ore affairs of State,
To night be happy, be to morrow great.

Parnell.

Give Clans your money, us your smile
your Scorn to T—— end & Ar—ile [21]

Doctor.

15. The Earl of Nottingham, whose gloomy temperament and narrow clericalism led to this nickname. He had deserted the Tories at a critical juncture in 1711 and on March 17, 1714, joined with the Whigs in an attack upon the ministry.

16. Presumably those leading to the doctor's chamber mentioned in the first invitation.

17. The invitation was first printed by Williams; both are among the Longleat MSS.

18. The date is indicated by the reference in Arbuthnot's couplet and by the fact that the invitation seems to fill the obvious vacant space in dates before Pope left for Binfield on April 21. April 10 was a Saturday, a usual club day.

19. The couplet refers to a passage in the first book of the *Iliad*, on the translation of which Pope was then engaged. In his version it reads,

> The Sire of Gods, and all th' Etherial Train,
> On the warm Limits of the farthest Main,
> Now mix with Mortals, nor disdain to grace
> The Feasts of *Æthiopia*'s blameless Race. ll. 554–7.

20. John Sheffield, Duke of Buckingham and Normanby, a moderate Tory who had served as Lord President of the Council since June, 1711.

21. On April 9 Viscount Townshend moved that the House of Lords consider the ministry's action in remitting £4,000 annually to the clans of Scotland, whereupon the Duke of Argyll made a speech in which he argued that the ministry by this means was in effect subsidizing the Jacobites. The ministry was able to show that the subsidy had been a policy of long standing for the purpose of keeping the clans quiet and the House of Lords voted unanimously its approval of the ministry's action.

Leave Courts, and hye to simple Swains,
Who feed *no* Flock upon *no* Plains [22]

                                        Gay.

The Reply

By Oxford

                            Apr: 10: [1]714

You merry five who filled wth blisful nectar
Can Phillips sing as Homer chanted Hector
I wil attend to hear your tuneful Lays
And wish y^r merits meet with one who pays—

5. An Invitation [23]

Chiefly by Pope, Gay, and Swift? [24]

                            [April 14?, 1714] [25]

A Pox of [26] all Senders
For any Pretenders
Who tell us these troublesome stories,
In their dull hum-drum key
Of Arma Virumque
Hannoniae qui primus ab oris.[27]

22. The manuscript shows that Gay first wrote "come" for "hye" in the first line and "feeds *no* Flocks" in the second.

23. First printed by Hawkesworth; reprinted in *Swiftiana* and by Ball, Aitken, and Williams, the latter two from the Longleat manuscript. The Hawkesworth version differs from the manuscript in many points of spelling, capitalizing, punctuation, and italicizing, but in only four minor ways verbally. These are noted below.

24. The use of pseudo antique terms such as "Carle" and "Earle" are an indication that Gay wrote the second stanza, and the familiarity of the phrase "friend Mortimer," together with the rhyme "forty more," strongly suggest Swift in the third. Originally the invitation was followed by the names "A. Pope, J. Gay, J. Swift, J. Arbuthnot, T. Parnel"—not in their handwriting. Since his name led the list, Pope may have been the principal author of the first stanza. All the names have been scored out on the manuscript except that of Gay; cf. below, n. 32.

25. The date is indicated by the reference to Hanmer (see below, n. 28) and by the fact that it appears to be the invitation to which the dated verses of Oxford which follow are intended to be a reply. It will be noted that Oxford imitates the stanzaic form used here.

26. Hawkesworth gives "on."

27. This play on the opening lines of the *Aeneid* seems to be a tricky bit of fooling. The stanza

A fig too for H——r [28]
Who prates like his Grand mere
And all his old Friends would rebuke
In spite of the Carle
Give us but our Earle,
And the Devil may take their Duke.[29]

Then come and take part in
The Memoirs of Martin,
Lay by your White Staff & gray Habit,
For trust us, friend Mortimer [30]
Should you live years forty more
Haec olim meminisse juvabit.[31]
by order of y[e] Club
J. Gay [32]

---

refers to the current excitement in Parliament and in the metropolis over the rumors that the Pretender was arming, with the aid of the Duke of Lorraine, to invade England. These rumors were ridiculed in a pamphlet entitled *Hannibal Not at Our Gates,* said to have been written by the author of the *Examiner,* which consists of a dialogue between "Lord Panick" and "George Steady." In the course of the discussion Steady says, "I find some People of Foresight horribly startled at the *Duke* of *Lorrain's* Power: The profound *Daily Courant* and *Flying Post,* gave a dreadful Account of 25000 Men, of which 12000 are Horse, lately rais'd by that Prince, and I hear it whisper'd by good Hands, that he is fitting out a Fleet of 30 Men of War upon the *Moselle.* These Things indeed carry an ill Aspect. If the *Duke of Lorrain* should ship off those 13000 Foot and 12000 Horse, &c. If he should Sail over three or fourscore Leagues of Land, and come and catch us Napping, we might be finely serv'd, for *sleepy, senseless, stupid Dogs,* as the *Bishop of Sarum* thinks us." Quoted by A. Boyer, in his *Political State of Great Britain* for 1714, (2d ed., 1719), p. 332.

The lines of Latin seem to be a play on the idea of the Pretender sailing from his inland residence in Lorraine. The name of the neighboring duchy of Hainault was apparently used loosely to echo the sound of Vergil's words "cano Troiae." It will be recalled that succeeding lines in the *Aeneid* are appropriate to the jest, reading in part, as Dryden translated them,

His banish'd gods restor'd to rites divine
And settled sure succession in his line.

28. Sir Thomas Hanmer, the Speaker of the House of Commons, was a Hanover or "Whimsical" Tory who collaborated with the Oxford ministry for several years. When, however, the House was in committee on April 14 over the question of whether or not the Protestant succession was in danger, he spoke from the floor against the government and the following day, on the matter coming to a vote, led his followers into the opposition. The government carried the day by a reduced but safe margin.

In Hawkesworth the line reads, "A pox too on *Hanmer.*"

29. The Duke of Argyll.

30. Their friend was raised to the peerage as the Earl of Oxford and Earl Mortimer, the latter title being granted as protection against unforeseen claims to the previously extinct earldom of Oxford.

31. *Aeneid,* i, 203. The promise that one day it would "please him to remember these things" was fulfilled; cf. above, p. 49.

32. Gay, as secretary to the club, would properly sign the orders; hence the blotting out of the other names first listed on the manuscript. Cf. above, n. 24.

6. A Reply [33]

Written by Oxford [34]

April 14, 1714.

I *honour* the men, Sir,
Who are ready to answer,
When I ask them to stand by the queen;
In spite of orâtors,
And blood-thirsty praters,
Whose hatred I highly esteem.
Let our faith's defender
Keep out ev'ry pretender,[35]
And long enjoy her own;
Thus you four, five,[36]
May merrily live,
Till faction is dead as a stone.

7. An Invitation [37]

In the handwriting of Pope

("Saturday June [5], 1714") [38]

Tho the Dean has run from us in manner uncivil;
The Doctor, and *He that's nam'd next to the Devil,   *Pope.

33. First published by Hawkesworth, and reprinted in *Swiftiana* and by Scott, Ball, and Williams.

34. Hawkesworth.

35. It may be noted that Oxford here says only that the Queen should keep out every pretender. Swift always believed unquestioningly that Oxford was stoutly for the Protestant succession but we now know that he as well as Bolingbroke was in touch with the Pretender, though it is doubtful if his purpose was other than tentative and precautionary. G. M. Trevelyan, *England under Queen Anne* (1930–34), III, 267–9, 285–6, 336 *et seq.*

36. Ball, misled perhaps by Hawkesworth, who does not list Parnell among those writing the invitations, suggests that the line, which Oxford clearly meant to be interpreted as "four *or* five," is to be explained by the fact that Parnell, owing to his indolence, was considered an extra member of the group. Since Parnell was in fact in every way a full member, it is probably to be accounted for by the temporary absence of one of the members. Dr. Arbuthnot and Gay both had other duties which might prevent their attendance at a given session, but since Gay seems to have had a hand in the invitation to this one, the doctor was perhaps the missing person.

37. Now first printed from the manuscript at Longleat, Portland Papers, XIII, fol. 69.

38. So endorsed by Oxford; the fifth is the only possible Saturday.

With Gay, who Petition'd You once on a time,
And Parnell, that would, if he had but a Rhyme.[39]
(That Gay the poor Sec: and that arch Chap-
    -lain Parnell,
As Spiritual one, as the other is Carnal)
Forgetting their Interest, now humbly sollicit
You'd at present do nothing but give us a
    Visit.

<table>
<tr><td></td><td>A. Pope</td></tr>
<tr><td>That all this true is</td><td>T. Parnell</td></tr>
<tr><td> Witness E. Lewis [40]</td><td>Jo: Arbuthnott</td></tr>
<tr><td></td><td>J. Gay</td></tr>
</table>

8. A Reply [41]

By Oxford

June 5th: 1714

In these Dangerous times when Popery is Flagrant
And y[e] servants of Oxford would choose to be vagrant
When Mercury *Dukes* [42] set up for Physitians,
Or w[ch] is the same for state Polititians
He that cares not to rule will not fail to obey
When summoned by Arbuthnot, ~~A. Deacon~~ Pope, Parnel
                                     & Gay

39. Parnell was still hoping to be appointed chaplain to the Clarendon mission; cf. above, p. 37.

40. Erasmus Lewis, an undersecretary of state and long-time assistant to Oxford, with whom all of the Scriblerians were intimate.

41. Now first printed from the manuscript at Longleat, Portland Papers, XIII, fol. 71. The verses are in Oxford's handwriting and are endorsed "Answer to Dr. A: &c." In a letter to Swift dated June 12, Arbuthnot said, "The Dragon was with us on Saturday night last, after having sent us really a most excellent copy of verses. I remember the first part of his verse was complaining of ill usage, and at last he concludes:
         He that cares not to rule . . ." *Corres.*, III, 151.
The name "A. Deacon," deleted from the last line for metrical reasons, refers to Parnell.

42. The Duke of Argyll.

9. An Invitation [43]

To the Right Honble the
Earl of Oxford   June 12,
                                                  1714

The Dean to the plain,
& Gay to the main,
& Pope to the Mountains retires:
The Dean for his health
& Gay * for his wealth,
& Pope that the Muse may inspire.

Arbuthnot so tall,
& Parnell so small,
Perceiving their numbers decrease,
Woud have you resume
The chair in our room,
For you never must give up a Place [44]

*varii Codices from [45]

10. Scriblerian Verses, 1718—A Request [46]

In Pope's handwriting

[July 8, 1718] [47]

To the R^t. Honble
The Earl of Oxford.

Tuesday. 5. a clock

*One that should be a Saint   *Parnell
and *one that's a Sinner,   *Gay
And *one that pays reckning   *Pope

43. Now first printed from the manuscript at Longleat, Portland Papers, xiii, fol. 73.
44. The word is written in large letters; it refers, of course, to Oxford's office.
45. This footnote was added by another hand, perhaps by Gay. It refers to the fact that Gay was on the verge of leaving with the embassy to Hanover without the £100 Oxford had promised him. He got the money at the very last minute; cf. above, p. 37.
46. Now first printed from the manuscript at Longleat, Portland Papers, xiii, fol. 74.
47. The date is given on another copy of the verses among the Portland Papers, fol. 79.

but n'er eats a Dinner,[48]
In short Pope and Gay (as
    you'l see in the margin)
Who saw you in Tower, and since
    your enlarging,
And Parnell who saw you not since
    you did treat him,
Will venture it now—you have
    no Stick to beat him—
Since these for your Jury, good
    and true men, vous-avez;
Pray grant Us Admittance,
    and shut out Miles Davies.[49]

11. Scriblerian Verses, 1718—A Reply [50]

By Oxford

July 8: 1718

To my old friends
In Paper Course [coarse] [51]
This kindly comes to Greet you.
Let Parnel Pray
A Beau be Gay
And Pope Come heer to meet you.
'Till hower Eight
I Heer shal wait
But after Davies take you.

E. of Oxford

48. A reference to his frequent ill-health, which often forced him to be abstemious when with his friends, who were heavy eaters and drinkers.

49. Apparently the official who had charge of Oxford during his stay in the Tower.

50. Now printed for the first time from the manuscript at Longleat, Portland Papers, XIII, fol. 76. A draft of the reply is preserved among the same papers (fol. 78). On it, below the verses, Oxford wrote, "In answer to a Letter in verse Sent from the Ship Tavern, &c—received at the end of Dinner answered while the company was buy. Noted their Letter was wrote by them in Gilt papers. Superscribed 'Qui potest Capere Capiat.'" The paper is endorsed with the latter phrase.

51. In contrast to their gilt paper; see note above.

APPENDIX II

SCRIBLERUS IDEAS

While Swift was at Letcombe in the summer of 1714 Arbuthnot wrote him several letters containing news of political developments and ideas for the club project. The passages relating to the *Memoirs* follow:

June 26, 1714 [1]

Pray, remember Martin, who is an innocent fellow and will not disturb your solitude. The ridicule of medicine is so copious a subject that I must only here and there touch it. I have made him study physic from the apothecary's bill, where there is a good plentiful field for a satire upon the present practice. One of his projects was, by a stamp upon blistering-plasters, and melilot by the yard,[2] to raise money for the Government, and to give it to Radcliffe and others to farm.[3] But there was likely to be a petition from the inhabitants of London and Westminster, who had no mind to be flayed. There was a problem about the doses of purging medicines published four years ago, showing that they ought to be in proportion to the bulk of the patient.[4] From thence Martin endeavors to determine the question about the weight of the ancient men, by the doses of physic that were given them.[5] One of his best inventions was a map of diseases for the three cavities, and one for the external parts; just like the four quarters of the world. Then the great diseases are like capital cities, with their symptoms all like streets and suburbs, with the roads that lead to other diseases. It is thicker set with towns than any Flanders map you ever saw. Radcliffe is painted at the corner of the map, contending for the universal empire of this world, and the rest of the

1. *Corres.*, II, 158–60.
2. A satire on the excessive use of blistering plasters for a wide variety of disorders ranging from a weak stomach and asthma to the stone and gout, but especially the last of these. The frequent use of harsh irritants led to a demand for soothing plasters, the most popular being melilot, which was made from a species of clover of that name. "It is mostly employ'd," says J. Alleyne, "in dressing Blisters until they cease running, and skin over." *New English Dispensatory* (1733), p. 67.
3. Dr. John Radcliffe, famous for his frankness and wit as well as his successful treatment of patients, had the largest and by far the most lucrative practice of the day. Though disliked by many, including the Queen, and often at odds with his colleagues, he was much respected as a practitioner. Arbuthnot, of course, knew him and he had treated Pope in his youth and Swift in 1711. He was a High Churchman and Arbuthnot had opposed him to Dr. Garth, a Low Churchman and Whig, in an allegorical argument over the church in the second part of *John Bull*. Aitken, pp. 251–2. Here Garth is made to advocate the use of blisters, while Radcliffe, typically, according to the stories of the day, holds out no hope for the patient.
4. W. Cockburn, "The Practice of Purging and Vomiting Medicines, according to Dr. Cockburn's Solution of his Problem; with Tables shewing their Doses in particular Ages and Constitutions, *Phil. Trans.*, XXVI (1708), 46–53.
5. Dr. Arbuthnot had probably already begun to collect the material for his "A Dissertation Concerning the Doses of Medicines Given by Ancient Physicians," which he included in his *Tables of Ancient Coins, Weights and Measures* (1727), pp. 282–93.

physicians opposing his ambitious designs, with a project of a treaty of partition to settle peace.[6]

There is an excellent subject of ridicule from some of the German physicians, who set up a sensitive soul as a sort of first Minister to the rational.[7] Helmont calls him Archaeus.[8] Dolaeus calls him Microcosmetor.[9] He has under him several other genii, that reside in the particular parts of the body, particularly Prince Cardimelech in the heart; Gasteronax in the stomach; and the plastic Prince in the organs of generation. I believe I could make you laugh at the explication of distempers from the wars and alliances of those Princes, and how the first Minister gets the better of his mistress *Anima Rationalis*. The best is, that it is making a reprisal upon the politicians, who are sure to allegorize all the animal economy into state affairs. Pope has been collecting high flights of poetry, which are very good; they are to be solemn nonsense.[10]

I thought upon the following the other day, as I was going into my coach, the dust being troublesome:

> The dust in smaller particles arose,
> Than those which fluid bodies do compose:
> Contraries in extremes do often meet,
> 'Twas now so dry, that you might call it wet.[11]

I do not give you these hints to divert you, but that you may have your thoughts, and work upon them.

July 17, 1714 [12]

Whiston has at last published his project of the longitude; the most ridiculous thing that ever was thought on. But a pox on him! he has spoiled one of my papers of Scriblerus, which was a proposal for the longitude, not very unlike his, to this purpose: that since there was no pole for East and West, that all the Princes of Europe should join and build two prodigious poles, upon high mountains, with a vast light-house to serve for a pole-star.[13] I was thinking of a calculation of the time, charges, and dimensions. Now you must understand, his project is by lighthouses, and explosion of bombs at a certain hour.

6. The intent here, as above, is not so much to ridicule Radcliffe as to use his prestige and huge practice for the jest. The reference to the partition treaty likens him to Louis XIV, whose ambition to dominate Europe William III sought to check by means of secret treaties partitioning the Spanish empire. The Tories had satirized these for years. Cf. above, p. 341, n. 25.

7. Arguments over the nature and seat of the soul are ridiculed, above, in chapter XII of the *Memoirs*.

8. J. B. Van Helmont, *Ortus Medicinae*, F. M. Van Helmont, ed. (Amsterdam, 1652), pp. 33–5 *et passim*. The archeus, a separate entity containing the essential form or character of a substance or body, was an important element in his scientific as well as his philosophical speculations.

9. Johann Doläus (1651–1707) was a German doctor of considerable erudition and vast credulity, who was much influenced by Van Helmont. During the 1680's he published a number of medical works of cyclopedic character, but his contemporary fame was based less on these than on his claims to have developed secret remedies for various diseases. His collected works were published in 1690 and in 1703.

10. Cf. above, pp. 38, 41, 54, 246–7.

11. This idea was used in chapter seventeen of the *Memoirs*, see p. 338, n. 18.

12. *Corres.*, II, 186.

13. Cf. above, Chap. XVII, p. 343, n. 31.

APPENDIX III

MATERIAL ON THE *MEMOIRS* IN SPENCE'S *ANECDOTES*

Sometime in the period from 1728–30 [1] Pope discussed the *Memoirs of Scriblerus* in the presence of Spence. The account given by Spence in his *Anecdotes* [2] constitutes the fullest and most authoritative contemporary statement we have concerning the purpose and the authorship of the *Memoirs*. It contains, however, several facts which seem in direct conflict with other very strong evidence. Thus we can be reasonably sure that the Bishop of Rochester and William Congreve were not members of the club and we may doubt that Addison ever seriously contemplated becoming one.[3] Further, as has been pointed out, Anthony Henley, who in Spence's account is said to have written one of the episodes, had been dead more than two years before the club was founded.[4]

These mistakes, which have led to much confusion with regard to the club and the *Memoirs,* are not so extraordinary and so difficult to explain as appears on the surface. Though Spence was, on the whole, accurate and trustworthy,[5] he did not take stenographic notes and in preparing later a highly condensed version of what must have been a rambling and complex account of the Scriblerus project by Pope he could hardly avoid a certain amount of confusion and error of omission. As has been suggested, the inclusion of Atterbury, Congreve, and Addison is probably a confusion of Pope's original plan for a *Works of the Unlearned,* with the quite different Scriblerus project which developed out of it.[6] The posthumous activity of Henley is somewhat more difficult to account for, but it may, perhaps, be explained by the suggestion that Henley, a wit of distinctly Scriblerian flavor and an intimate friend of Swift [7] either wrote a burlesque sketch satirizing Tom Durfey which, with necessary alterations, the Scriblerians planned, out of honor to his memory, to introduce into the *Memoirs,* or in one of his characteristically witty letters drafted out a "hint" which the Scriblerians decided to develop.[8]

Particularly noteworthy in Spence's account is the statement with regard to the relationship of the *Memoirs* and *Gulliver's Travels*. In view of the source and date,

1. Very early in that period, if the position of the passage among Spence's notes is to be trusted.

2. Joseph Spence, *Anecdotes, Observations, and Characters, of Books and Men* (2d ed., 1858), p. 8.

3. Cf. above, pp. 18–19.

4. Cf. above, p. 62 and *Journ.,* August 22, 1711. Henley had a son of the same name, but he was a mere child at the time of the club and though in later years he became a Whig M.P., and something of a wit, there is no evidence that he had any literary pretensions or ability.

5. Cf. Austin Wright, "The Veracity of Spence's *Anecdotes,*" *PMLA,* LXII (1947), 123–9.

6. Cf. above, pp. 18–19.

7. The character of Henley's wit is indicated in his letters to Swift. *Corres.,* I, 112–14, 115, 160–5. For his friendship with Swift, see the references to him in the *Journ.* Probably Arbuthnot, and perhaps Pope, also knew him.

8. If either of these hypotheses is correct, the absence of the manuscript from Swift's correspondence could be accounted for by the fact that it probably would ·have been kept among the Scriblerus papers, which Pope eventually ordered destroyed.

as well as its inherent plausibility, this must be regarded as possessing the greatest weight. Cf. general note to Chapter XVI.

Pope's statements regarding the *Memoirs,* as recorded by Spence,[9] follow:

1. From Section I, 1728–30 [10]

The design of the Memoirs of Scriblerus was to have ridiculed all the false tastes in learning, under the character of a man of capacity enough; that had dipped into every art and science, but injudiciously in each. It was begun by a club of some of the greatest wits of the age. Lord Oxford, the Bishop of Rochester, Mr. Pope, Congreve, Arbuthnot, Swift, and others. Gay often held the pen; and Addison liked it very well, and was not disinclined to come in to it. The Deipnosophy consisted of disputes on ridiculous tenets of all sorts: and the adventure of the Shield was designed against Dr. Woodward and the Antiquaries. It was Anthony Henley who wrote "the life of his music master Tom Durfey;" a chapter by way of episode.—It was from a part of these memoirs that Dr. Swift took his first hints for Gulliver. There were pigmies in Schreibler's travels; and the projects of Laputa.— The design was carried on much farther than has appeared in print; [11] and was stopped by some of the gentlemen being dispersed or otherwise engaged (about the year 1715.) See the memoirs themselves.— *P.*

2. From Section IV, 1734–36 [12]

I have so much of the materials for the Memoirs of Scriblerus ready, that I could complete the first part in three or four days.— *P.*

3. From Section VIII, 1743–44 [13]

In the list of papers, ordered to be burnt, were the pieces for carrying on the Memoirs of Scriblerus; and several copies of verses by Dean Parnell. I interceded in vain for both. As to the latter, he said that "they would not add anything to the Dean's character."— *P.*

4. From Supplemental Anecdotes, 1755 [14]

The Episode on his Dancing-Master, and all the fragments of the Memoirs of Scriblerus, are destroyed.— *Dr. W[arburton].*

9. Notes regarding other Scriblerus pieces are to be found in Spence on pp. 109, 133, 152.

10. P. 8.

11. As yet neither the *Memoirs* nor *An Essay Concerning the Origine of Sciences* had been published. The *Origine of Sciences* was first printed in the Pope-Swift *Miscellanies* in 1732.

12. P. 133.

13. P. 219.

14. P. 279.

APPENDIX IV

A MANUSCRIPT FRAGMENT OF THE DOUBLE MISTRESS EPISODE

It was the custom of "paper-sparing Pope," as Swift called him, to preserve and make use of every scrap of paper which had a clean surface on it. Almost the entire first draft of his translation of the *Iliad* was on the backs of bills, envelopes, unimportant letters, and odd bits of paper. Among the miscellaneous papers thus accidentally saved, and now preserved in the British Museum,[1] Professor Sherburn discovered a sheet from what was apparently the first draft of the Double Mistress episode in the *Memoirs*.[2] This fragment of manuscript is of great interest both because it helps to set the approximate period when the Scriblerians were at work on the episode and because it gives a clue to the part Arbuthnot and Pope played in its composition.

Some idea of the general date of the fragment may be gathered from its place in the *Iliad* translation and from the dates of various notes and letters surrounding it. It appears in the part of the Homer manuscripts containing the translation of the sixteenth book, its clean side having been used by Pope for the passage containing lines 354 to 379 of his version. We do not know exactly when Pope was at work on this section, but since he wrote to Thomas Dancastle on October 16, 1717 that he had just finished book fifteen [3] and the passage is only a third of the way through the following book, it seems likely that it was some time during late November or December.[4]

In general, during the period of the *Iliad* translation, Pope seems to have kept up quite closely with his supply of paper and most of the scraps which bear dates were not more than a few months old when used again. It was possible, of course, for papers of earlier dates to get mixed in with Pope's current supply, and there are a number of instances of this in the Homer manuscripts, but the probabilities seem to be that a given sheet became available.for use at approximately the same time as those around it. Eight sheets before the *Memoirs* fragment (one of the sheets being a double leaf) appears an anonymous note dated September 17 and immediately preceding that is a letter from John Barber bearing the date October 16, while two pages after the Scriblerus fragment is a letter beginning, "Yours I rec'd dated Oct. 11th . . .". It seems likely, therefore, that the sheet of the Double Mistress draft got into Pope's pile sometime during the early autumn of 1717.

The first draft of the passage is in the handwriting of Arbuthnot and superimposed on it are drastic alterations in the hand of Pope. Later one or the other, probably Pope, produced a third version which was the one finally to appear in print. Why this page and no more of the manuscript appeared in Pope's scrap pile can only be surmised, but the extreme illegibility of the manuscript as the result of

1. Homer MSS, Add. MS 4808, fol. 132.
2. Sherburn, p. 80, n. 1.
3. E. & C., ix, 488.
4. Volume iv containing books thirteen to sixteen was not published until the following June, but the fact that Pope had finished three quarters of his task by October indicates that he was well ahead of publication schedule.

Pope's editing and the fact that both he and Arbuthnot made corrections and changes in their versions suggest either that Pope took the trouble to copy the page for the benefit of the person who was to make the fair copy for the press, or that, desiring to make the further changes that appear in the printed version, he was simply driven to using a clean sheet.

The three versions make possible an interesting comparison. It is difficult to judge literary merit on the basis of so short a passage, but there is a rich burlesque tone and an easy movement in Arbuthnot's version which makes it preferable to Pope's highly condensed revision and in some ways more successful than the polished version that was finally published.

An interesting aspect of the fragment is the fact that the names of the twins in the first version are Tabitha and Tryphena, and that these were changed to the more romantic ones of Lindamira and Indamora in the course of Pope's revision.[5]

The manuscript is so nearly illegible that the following transcription cannot be regarded as above dispute.

5. Cf. above, pp. 298–9.

I. ARBUTHNOT'S VERSION

But Tabitha was jealous of the [remainder of line trimmed off by binder]

thought still of fresh expedients to cross her love. She Remonstrated how just it was that she should have a vote ~~share~~ in the election of her husband [—] a person ~~who was~~ yt was her sisters husband was at least to be her constant companion ~~both~~ at bed & board. & indeed her argument had so far prevail'd with Tryphena, (who as I said before had not drunk so deep of the poyson of love) that she ~~pere~~ told her sister she would see

II. POPE'S REVISION

~~thought it her her sister~~ Lindamere   as to

for if ye person was her sisters husband he was at least to be her constant companion at bed & board.

In short she teizd Tryphena ~~her sister~~ to yt degree that she promis'd

III. 1741 EDITION

But Fate had so ordain'd, that Martin was not more enamoured on Lindamira, than Indamora was on Martin. She, jealous that her Sister had the greatest share in this conquest, resented that an equal application had not been made to herself.

She teiz'd Lindamira to such a degree on this subject, as made her promise to see Martin no more.

But then
again might Indamora be
deem'd the unhappiest of
Women, whom her Passion and
Imprudence had robb'd of the

sight of her Lover.

Yet
shame caused her to conceal
those anxieties from her

to see Martin no more.

~~But now again might~~   But now
~~Now it was that~~

again might Tabitha be justly
deem'd the unhappiest of
Mortals whom her own passion
& imprudence had robbd of the
him she loved.

sight of ~~her lover~~
~~the man she adored~~

Martin no more. Then it
was she began to repent of
her imprudent Measures her
passion had thrown her into
& in this place earnestly
wishd her self disjoyned
from her sister ~~in order to~~
~~flap~~ & regretted that she
was depriv'd
~~not capable~~ of the
comfort of a soliloquy so
necessary to distressed

lovers. Now it was that

Tabitha might be justly
deem'd the unhappiest of
lovers whom her passion &
imprudence had depryvd of

her lover & her close conjunction with her sister
had renderd incapable evn
of a soliloquy[,] the never
failing comfort of dispair-
ing damsells[;]

I. ARBUTHNOT'S VERSION

but thus she thought without being allowd to tell it to any grove or Murmuring stream. poor Tabitha! by what an eddy of passion art thou drivn to & fro jealousy which impells others to part their Rival from their Lover in thee must take the backward Course & strain all thy endeavours to bring them together if Try-phena will never any more see Martin—Martin must never more bless the eyes of Tabitha. but why do I say wretched since my Rival can never enjoy my lover without me, the pangs that other lovers feel

II. POPE'S REVISION

I leave it to ye Reader to judge how unhappy ye Lover must be who was even deprivd of ye benefit of a soliloquy

but thus she thought without being allowd to tell it to any grove or Murmuring stream wretched Tabitha! by what an eddy of passion are thou drivn? ~~jealousy~~ ~~which impells others to part~~ ~~their Rival from their~~ ~~Lover in thee must take the~~ ~~contrary Course~~ ~~to bring~~

~~them together~~ if Try-phena must never more see Martin—Martin must never more bless the eyes of Tabitha. Yet why do I say wretched since my Rival can never enjoy my lover without me? the pangs that others feel

III. 1741 EDITION

Sister. And let the Reader judge how unhappy the Nymph must be, who was even depriv'd the universal Relief of a *Soliloquy*.

However, thus she thought, without being allow'd to tell it to any Grove or purling Stream. Wretched Indamora!

if Linda-mira must never more see Martin, Martin shall never again bless the eyes of Indamora: Yet why do I say wretched? since my Rival can never possess my Lover without me. The pangs that others feel in Absence, from the thought of those Joys that bless their Rivals, can never sting thy bosom; nor can they mortify thee by making thee a Witness, without giving thee at the same time a share, of their Endearments. Change then thy proceeding, Indamora; thy Jealousy must act a new and unheard-of part, and promote the interest of thy Rival, as the only way to the enjoyment of thy Lover.

APPENDIX V

COLLATION OF TEXTS

A. Variant readings between the text of this edition (No. 6) and No. 5; cf. above, pp. 79–81:

Page	Line	No. 6	No. 5
91	9	visage long	visage was long
91	33	and he was	and was
91	36	but his real business	but what were his real business
92	20	Encomiums on	Encomiums of
92	27	this task	this great task
92	28	by the labours	in the labours
93	22–3	now, by means of some British ship (whose . . . approach) I impatiently expect a safe passage	now impatiently expect, by means of some British ship (whose . . . approach) a safe passage
93	30	I before related	I before hinted
95	1	Memoirs	The Memoirs
95	16	in old time Princes	anciently Princes
95	17	and deduced	deduced
95	24	time, the said	time, that the said
96	14	what exact Precautions	the many precautions
96	24	than to become	than become
96	34	and moisture	and mixture
96	34	occasion	occasions
96	36	was at West	was West
97	9	to England	into England
97	15	and for all	and all
98	1–2	that universal Genius	that prodigious man
98	3–4	which I found to be of equal	and finding them of equal
98	8–9	Codicil to Mr.	Codicil of Mr.
99	7	where the Doctor	Here the Doctor
101	27	the seven Gulphs	the seven great Gulphs
102	25–6	orders, that when the company was come she should lay	orders when the company was come to lay
103	31	opening his eyes, he saw	opening his eyes, and casting 'em round on the company, he saw
103	39	rude Touch	rude hand
104	11	a man makes	the man makes
104	16–17	this latter opinion	this opinion
105	20–1	same whereof a Cut hath been	same, a Cut of which hath been
106	26	as it might endue	as it indues
106	30–1	During this speech	During all this speech

Page	Line	No. 6	No. 5
106	35–7	be fed with Butter mix'd with Honey, according . . . Homer.	be fed (according . . . Homer) with Butter mixt with Honey:
107	1–2	But from thenceforth	From thenceforth
107	19	every thing contribute	every thing did contribute
107	26	Shoes were Spanish	Shoes Spanish
107	31	confess'd he owed	confess'd that he owed
109	6	that he invented	that invented
109	8	Children, as they have	Children who have
109	10	of their minds	of the minds of children,
111	9	only instance one	only instance in one
113	3	Satyric Dance	Satyrical Dance
114	11	of those of his mind	of his mind
114	31	lolling	softly lolling
116	4	Horneck	Henley [corrected in errata]
116	ftnote	Horneck, a scurrilous Scribler who wrote a weekly paper, called *The High German Doctor.*	[omitted from text but included in errata]
116	13	Lyra in hand	Lyra in his hand
116	20	last of the Combatants	last the combatants
116	26	danc'd	and danc'd
118	13	of other Writings	of his other Writings
118	24	and his mother	his mother
120	5–6	fighting, *situs;* Stage, *ubi;*	fighting—Stage, *ubi;*
121	19	Lady, *proprium.*	Lady, proprium; (though not *quarto modo proprium,* for the Lady had another dog).
123	2–3	their Father	the Father
123	20	mankind be	mankind is
124	2–3	several others of which in the course of the Life of this learned person we may have occasion	several others that we may perhaps in the course of the life of this learned person have occasion
126	1–2	made even as to the Time	made at the Time
128	4		[Beginning of the original Chap. IX, "How Crambe had some Words with his Master"—see general note to Chap. VIII.]
132	20	of Mind	of the Mind
132	39	the whole body	indeed the whole body
134	21	do not enough attend this	do not attend enough to this
134	34	and carry about	and carrying about
143	8	suspect that it	suspect, it
144	11–12	scent of Carnage; broken Bones and naked Carcases bestrow'd	scent of Carnage and Bones; and naked Carcasses that bestrow'd

Page	Line	*No. 6*	*No. 5*
144	13	rouz'd . . . , and shook	now rouz'd . . . , shook
144	21	on the hills	into the Toils
144	22	uninhabited	uninhabitable
144	30	of the Earth	of the World
145	29–30	to their husbands	to the husbands
146	3–4	in order	in their order
146	21–2	Generation, had so	Generation, to outward appearance, had so
146	27	eyes were	eye was
146	27	Indamora's were	Indamora's was
147	12	pass'd	he pass'd
147	30	she who causes it	this amiable Object
148	7–8	wak'd with him	walk'd with him
148	13	never wander	never walk forth
149	3	bring it him	bring it to him
149	8	approach'd	he approach'd
150	13	Immediately	Now
150	16	Our Philosopher	Yet our Philosopher
150	29	found, as she thought,	thought she found
151	11	and received but	and had but
151	12	from the Addresses only of the	having receiv'd no Addresses but from the
151	26	to such a degree	to that degree
151	26–7	as made her promise	that she promis'd
151	28	whom her Passion	whom her own Passion
152	33	He caught up	He now caught up
154	16–17	Servitude. This put him	Servitude; which put him
156	15	to insert them at length	to insert them
156	18	DR. PENNY-FEATHER	[omitted]
158	38	thro' so many windings	thro' many windings
160	7	Our said Wife	Our Wife
160	10–11	Pleading was thus answer'd by	Pleading, Dr. Leather-head began in this manner
160	12	DR. LEATHERHEAD	[omitted]
160	22	Generation, so far	Generation, and two distinct persons; so far
161	18	grew forth to render	grew forth in order to render
162	15	gentlewoman	gentlewomen
163	3	while	whilst
164	23	*concerning certain* black	*concerning* black
166	19	open unto thee;	open before thee;
166	26	and without the	and thus without the
168	8	The first was a Proposal by a general	The first by a general

B. The following table indicates the extent to which the punctuation and spelling of the folios and quarto (Nos. 1, 2, and 3) were altered for No. 6. The changes, for the most part, are obvious improvements.

Added comma	59	Capitals for lower case	33
Comma for semicolon	5	Lower case for capitals	17
Semicolon for comma	12	ed for 'd	26
Comma omitted	23	en for 'n	3
Semicolon for colon	18	Italic for roman	1
Period for colon	5	Roman for italic	3
Colon for period	10	Correction by plurals	2
Word left out	1	Correction of grammar	2

Correct spelling for incorrect or old-fashioned   37
Incorrect spelling for correct   1

C. Variant readings between the text of this edition (No. 6) and that of the folios and quarto (Nos. 1, 2, and 3):

Page	Line	No. 6	Nos. 1, 2, and 3
89	1	CONTENTS TO THE MEMOIRS	THE CONTENTS OF THE MEMOIRS
89	15	what a sort of a man	what sort of a man
91	4–5	Englishman has not forgot)	Englishman may remember)
111	11	Constancy and Patience	Patience and Constancy
115	27–8	skill are preserved	skill is preserved
120	13	a habit inher'd	a habit of dancing inher'd
123	22	there are in human	there is in human
124	11	which it was suppos'd	which was suppos'd
125	24–5	why may it not in parts of the body, be	why not in parts of the body, may it be
128	19	Dice rat-led	Dice are rat-led
132	19	These Muscles are call'd the Muscles of *patience,*	This Muscle is call'd the Muscle of *patience,*
132	21	These Muscles	This Muscle
132	35	of the *legs*	of their *legs*
137	20	in their Hearts	in their Heart
150	39	than by all	than at all
170	7	FINIS.	The END of the FIRST BOOK.

APPENDIX VI

THE 1723 *MEMOIRS*

One of the most puzzling of the many problems connected with the Scriblerus project is the appearance in February, 1723,[1] of the small pamphlet which is reprinted in the following pages. Practically nothing is known about any aspect of its publication, and there is no reference to it in any of the surviving correspondence of the Scriblerians. The piece itself is strange and stands in a very curious relationship to the true *Memoirs*. Its title, the basic idea of a satiric biography of a learned person who is to illustrate various follies, the "I" framework at the beginning and the mother's dream of being brought to bed of an inkhorn all suggest some direct connection with the original, while some other parts might be Scriblerian in origin.[2] On the other hand the background, the character, and some of the activities of the chief figure, as well as his name, are strikingly at odds with those of the club's hero. Timothy Scriblerus is not, like Martinus, a learned fool on the scale of Woodward and Whiston. He is, instead, a scrivener by training and a Grub Street author by profession. Much of the writing in the piece, too, is obviously different in character and quality from that in the original.

There are a number of internal oddities in the brief burlesque. Though it is labeled as by "Dr. S——t," Swift is satirized in the piece in a far from friendly way, and the biography of the hero is very fragmentary. A disproportionate part of the piece, almost a third, is devoted to Tim's parentage and birth; his apprenticeship is far from an adequate preparation for his activities; and the episodes at the end seem very inadequate in number.

The name on the title page has naturally led to an ascription of the piece to Swift and some scholars have believed him the true author, the satire on him being explained as fun at his own expense.[3] Even if one could accept the idea of the Dean satirizing his advancement and falsely attributing to himself three vulgar pieces which he almost certainly did not write,[4] it is impossible to believe that Swift would thus play false to his close friends, whom he had good reason to believe were still interested in the club project, or that he would produce such a poor piece. It is equally difficult to believe that Pope, Arbuthnot, or Gay would have written it or allowed it to be published. We are therefore driven to believe that it

1. It was advertised in the *Post Boy* on February 19 as "this day published."
2. The Satire on the Freethinkers, Richard Bentley, and John Dennis in the piece is consistent with Scriblerian attitudes, though it is unlikely that either Swift or Pope would have attacked Dennis just at this time. Swift was remote from and unconcerned with London critics, while Pope had recently made his peace with his old enemy (E. & C., x, 111–12). Another minor point of connection is the reference in the text to the fact that Tim's writings "have furnish'd this our noble City with its politest Conversation for ten Years past" a time that coincides with the existence of the Scriblerus scheme.
3. *Satires and Personal Writings by Jonathan Swift*, W. A. Eddy, ed. (1932), p. 142.
4. In one modern text the satire on Swift is made worse by the unwarranted substitution of his initials for those of Dennis in the mud-slinging episode.

was produced surreptitiously on the basis of some hints or material that in some way had got out of Scriblerian hands.

In the absence of evidence we are forced to call on conjecture in an attempt to account for what happened. One possibility, of course, is that some friend or acquaintance of the Scriblerians had heard enough about the *Memoirs* to write this piece as a jest on them. Another, somewhat more plausible, is that enough had been learned about the club and its project in Grub Street to enable some hack to turn a penny by writing up such hints as were available. In support of this theory it may be pointed out that the Scriblerians could hardly have kept their project entirely secret. The collaborations of the *Three Hours after Marriage* period were well-known to the town and it would be surprising if some whisper about the master plan had not gone the rounds. Both these explanations, however, meet a serious obstacle in their failure to explain how rumors about the *Memoirs* could at once be so limited and distorted as not even to have Martinus' name or true character right and yet be so highly specific as to have at least one episode in greater detail than the final version of the true piece.

It would seem as if the only way to account for the curious character of the piece is to assume that some actual pieces of Scriblerus manuscript fell into the hands of someone who otherwise knew practically nothing about the project. Since several such pieces would be required to make enough of a basis for a hack writer to work on and only part of the false *Memoirs* appears in the true version—and there in a much abbreviated form—it seems likely that any such fragments were bits that had been discarded by the Scriblerians. For an explanation of how such pieces got into the hands of the writer or the publisher, A. Moore, we might hazard a guess that Pope used their clean sides for copy or some hurried directions to a printer, as he had used the Double Mistress sheet for the Homer draft, and that some gleaner of trifles copied them before the manuscript was returned.

If this theory of the discarded fragments is sound, it would do much toward explaining the piece. On the basis of similarity to genuine Scriblerus material, the parts most likely to have been copied from fragments are the Joachim paragraph on through the inkhorn dream, the John Dennis episode, the "Bull" argument, and the Freethinker satire. The beginning and ending in which Swift is attacked and the very hurried and poorly conceived middle passage dealing with Timothy's apprenticeship and start in life would then be the filler provided by the Grub-Street writer. The inability of this hireling to carry out the project on the scale of the fragments would explain the over proportion of the parentage-birth section and the fragmentary character of the final episodes.

A strong indication that the piece had a very dubious origin is the fact that it was published by A. Moore. Not much is known about this bookseller except that he published many catchpenny pamphlets and scandalous pieces from 1719 to 1734 and gave his address as "near St. Paul's" until the latter year when it became "in Fleetstreet." [5] His name does not appear on the regular lists of printers or booksellers, and the only known clue to his identity, apart from his publications, is the

5. The appearance, about the year 1749, of a pamphlet entitled *A Letter to the Lord Viscount Bo———ke*, "Printed for A. Moore, near St. Paul's," indicates he was then still in business at the old site or that someone was using his imprint.

fact that an "Augustin Moore" is entered in the Apprentices' Registry Book of the Stationers Company as bound to Abel Roper on September 7, 1719. If this is he, it is not clear how he could in that year publish a pamphlet under his own name.

Most of Moore's pamphlets are wretched little things, vulgar or sensational in character and printed in large type on a poor quality of paper.[6] A few of his productions are of better caliber, an occasional one being a minor piece by a well-known author, such as Gay or Swift, which he had obtained surreptitiously or simply reprinted.[7] He did not hesitate to catch customers by attributing things to "Dr. S——t" or to say that they were reprinted from a Dublin copy whether they were or not. Two years before he had printed in this way *The Wonderful Wonder of Wonders,* which went through many editions, and a few days after the appearance of the false *Memoirs* he issued the spurious *A Supplement to Dean Sw——t's Miscellanies,* "By the Author." He seems to have been particularly active during the period 1722–23 and in 1728, during the latter year using the popularity of the Swift-Pope *Miscellanies* and the *Beggar's Opera* to foist off on the public a whole series of trashy bits.

The text which follows is reprinted from a copy in the possession of Professor R. H. Griffith. The copy in the British Museum, used by W. A. Eddy in reprinting the piece in *Satires and Personal Writings by Jonathan Swift* (1932), is identical except that defective type and rough paper make possible variant readings of a final letter in two skeletonized names.

6. The 1723 *Memoirs* is much above his usual level in quality of printing. The carelessness and haste with which it was got out, however, are illustrated by an advertisement for it in the *Post Boy* for March 7–9, which makes Joachim the hero and Tim his son instead of his descendant.

7. In 1729 he published *The Banish'd Beauty,* which has been attributed to Gay, and in 1730 he reprinted *The Mad Dog, A Tale* from Gay's 1720 *Poems.* In the early 1730's he printed a number of genuine Swift pieces, one of them, *The Grand Question Debated,* rather curiously being published as "London Printed for A. Moore, And, Dublin Re-printed by George Faulkner."

MEMOIRS

OF THE

LIFE

OF

SCRIBLERUS.

Scalpellum, Calami, Atramentum, Charta, Libelli.

By *D. S*———*t.*

[Emblem]

L O N D O N:

Printed from the Original Copy from
Dublin; and Sold by *A. Moore* near
St. *Paul's.* MDCCXXIII.

MEMOIRS, &c.
OF
SCRIBLERUS.

As I have a tender Regard to Men of great Merit, and small Fortunes, I shall let slip no Opportunity of bringing them to Light, when either through a peculiar Modesty, or some Unhappiness in their Per-/sonal Appearance, they have been unwilling to present themselves to the World, and have been consequently no otherwise remarkable in it, than by the Number or Size of their Performances. This Piece of Humanity was instilled into me by an accidental Turn in my own Fortunes, which was owing to the Discovery a Man of great Penetration and Power made of the Excellence and Superiority of my Genius; and reflecting how much it was obscur'd by a Thread-bare Coat, very graciously advanc'd me to a Station of good Profit and little Trouble, any farther than to provide others to do my Business. This gave me an Opportunity of cultivating my Person, which had lain long unregarded, in which Branch of my Profession I am so considerably advanced, that I often over-hear the Good Women, as I pass by, cry out, *L—d! how sleek our D——r is.*[1] This/ Piece of Flattery, with some other private Reasons, not very material to insert here, makes me advance twice a Year to shew my Person and Parts, for the Sake and Improvement of my Male and Female Auditors; this generally occasions Matter of mutual Compliment, and is the Support of a civil Correspondence the Year round.

Here you see an Instance of the Grand Foible in human Nature, for which I will not make any Apology, though I have the greatest Authority of my Side; my Design being at present to celebrate a Person, whose Merit will employ all the Stock of Genius I have collected, so that begging the gentle Reader to excuse these few Hints which I design one Day to extend into a sizable Volume, I shall, without farther Ceremony, conduct him out of the Entry to the Place of Entertainment./

I say, proceeding upon this Principle,
Haud ignara mali miseris succurrere disco.[2]
I have, in Justice to this worthy Gentleman, who (notwithstanding his Writings have furnish'd this our noble City with its politest Conversation for ten Years past) might otherwise have remain'd in Obscurity, collected some remarkable Circumstances of his Life, which I assure the Reader are related with all imaginable Truth and Accuracy.

The first of this antient Family that distinguish'd himself in the World was *Joachim Scriblerus,* a very learned Divine; he flourished in the Thirteenth and Fourteenth Centuries, and wrote an immense Quantity of very valuable Books in Divinity, of which there remain Thirty Two compleat Bodies, Seventy Six Commentaries, besides Two Thou-/sand Dissertations and separate Treatises; of which, a great Part were to be seen in a curious Collection of most rare Books, set forth in a neighbouring Metropolis, by that Ingenious Gentleman, *T—— R——.*[3]

This *Joachim* had Seven Sons, who were all educated under the Father till they came of Age, but were then turned out to the wide World with a sufficient Quantity of Quills, and other Implements, to get a Livelihood. But as the Father was to portion out his Stock into so many equal Parts, neither of these young Gentlemen were able to make any great Figure among the *Literati;* so that not one of the Family broke out in any remarkable Manner till the last Century, when the scattered Genius * of the Family was/ collected in the Hands of the   8 only Male Heir, to whose Life and History the curious Reader is desired to attend.

Timothy Scriblerus was the Son of an eminent Stationer, who for several Years after Marriage was in Expectation of a Male Heir; Daughters he had in Abundance, but his chief Concern was, least the Fame of the Family should dwindle for Want of a Son, and the World should not know he was any Relative of Old *Joachim*. This made him frequently very pensive,/ and one Day   9 when he was more than ordinary so, an elderly Woman observing the Concern in his Countenance, came up to the Shop Door, and shaking her Head, accosted him in the following Manner: I am very sorry for your Misfortune, my good Master, but if you will cross my Hand with a small Spill,[4] and follow my Advice, you shall have a Son to your Wish before the Year is out. The Mention of a Circumstance that he could not imagine how she came acquainted with, encouraged him to gratify her in any Request, whereupon he desired her to sit down and proceed. You are to know then, Sir, said she, that from my Acquaintance with the Stars I came by the Knowledge of your Wants; and by my great Skill in Natural Magick, to understand the Method of supplying them; provided you do your Part and follow this Direction: He promis'd strict Observance,/ and received the following Prescript: Take Seven of the fairest Sheets   10 of Paper, and upon each of them you must have Seven Alphabets of Seven different Languages varied Seventy Seven times, so that no one Letter stand twice in the same Posture; when you have done this, clip all these Letters asunder, and sew them up in a Pillowbier, and upon a certain critical Conjuncture —— —

— —

During this Operation the Pillow must be placed so, that she may incline herself towards the Right Side, I suppose from that Hint of the Poet's,

Virgam Dextra tenet ——[5]

The Good Man communicated this to his Wife, and they took the first Opportunity of following her Advice: Accordingly in Nine Months Time they were in daily Expectation of Success./ It happen'd one Evening they were amusing   11 themselves with the Prospect of their Bliss, and laying Schemes for the Education and Advancement of their promis'd Heir; the Conversation made such an Impression upon the Woman that she dreamt that Night the following Dream: She thought the Pains of Child-bearing were coming upon her, and order'd

---

* Here it may not be improper to remark/ the near Relation of Quills and Genius. When 7–8 a Man makes any bold Stroke in Rhime, don't we cry,—That's a fine Flight,—he soars;— that's a lofty Expression;—or,—his Fancy is upon the Wing; finding the Sentence always dignify'd by an Allusion to a Goose-Wing, which shews the Preeminence, tho' I compliment my Friend by making them signify the same.

the Midwife to be sent for, who no sooner enter'd the Room but ran to her Assistance, and immediately, with one dreadful Pang, out came a monstrous Thing, which the Midwife taking to the Light, in a great Fright, cry'd out, *L—d! what is this?* And laying it down upon the Table there issued from it a great Stream of Liquid, that divided itself into ten thousand little Branches, that spread themselves over the whole Room: This alarm'd the Company, which by this Time she thought was grown very/ numerous from the Flock of good 12 Women that came to assist at her Labour; every body crowded to see the young Progeny, when, to their horrid Amasement, they found it was a great black Ink-horn sending out innumerable Streams of Ink;[6] this so alarm'd her that she awaked.

In dreadful Consternation she continued the remaining Part of the Night, to think what could be the Event of so uncouth a Dream; but in the Morning advising with her Husband, they determined to go to a Man in the next Street, who had great Skill in Dreams, and other Misteries of Nature; accordingly up they got, and were heying to the Expounder, when they were met at the Door, by the same good Woman, whose advise they had followed with such Success; and immediately taking her by the Arm drew her in, and/ desired her Opinion 13 of the Dream that had created in them so many Fears, which they related as above, not omitting the least Circumstance. Here the Sallow Sorceress paus'd a while, then with a chearful Countenance, that dispersed half their Fears, began: The Inkhorn with those innumerable Streams issuing from it, are the Types, or Symbols of his Genius, and the Extent of it; by them are signify'd the great Variety of Productions in human Learning, that will render him the Admiration and Surprize of all the Universe; as to that Spout, it betokens the Sex, and that it will be a Son. Overjoy'd at this Interpretation they dismis'd her with a Reward, determining to wait the Event with Patience. In a few Days the Woman was brought to Bed of a Son, which assur'd them of the remaining Part; and now all their Hearts were set upon, was the proper Method/ of 14 educating it, least by any false Step they should mar the great Genius that was to be the Light of future Ages. Long Time they consulted together, at last determin'd to watch the little Motions of his Infancy, and learn from them how best to humour his Genius. They observ'd no Diversion took so much with him as the ratling of Paper, and dabling in Ink, and that young *Tim* was never better pleased than when up to the Elbows in it; this they look'd upon as an Earnest of what was promised in the Dream, and resolv'd to encourage him as far as their Stock would permit. One Day the Nurse, with great Joy, came running to the Father to tell him Master *Tim* call'd Papa, but the Father soon found the Mistake, and that the first Word *Tim* utter'd was, Paper. As *Tim* advanc'd in Years, the manifest bent of his Genius determin'd the Father to/ put him Apprentice to 15 a Scrivener, where he might learn to write a legible and swift Hand, that his Invention might not wait for his Pen; which was well judged, for I myself must acknowledge that in the Heat of my Imagination, I have had such a quick Succession of beautiful Thoughts, that for Want of Speed to reduce them to Pen, Ink, and Paper, the World has lost, I sigh to repeat it, a most valuable Treasure, both of Instruction and Entertainment. This was prudently avoided, for, by

incessant Practice, *Tim,* in a little Time, wrote as fast as he could think. The
Father propos'd to him Accounts, but *Tim* prudently told him, he was resolv'd
not to deal with this World any more than from Hand to Mouth, and begg'd
that [he] might not interrupt his Progress in Affairs of greater Moment. Thus
Tim sally'd out, and in the two first Years of his Ap-/prenticeship he apply'd 16
himself so diligently to his Improvement, that, without interrupting his Master's Business, he had transcrib'd 70 Volumes in Folio, of different Languages;
he could repeat by Heart all the *Seven Wise Masters* had said, he knew all the
Seven Champions Conquer'd, and *the History of the Seven Wonders of the
World.* He had dipp'd into 7 Sciences, and began now to be in Vogue among
the People of Letters. The distress'd of all Kinds came to him to have their Cases
drawn up, preferring *Tim* before his Master. He had such an easy Knack in the
Epistolary Way, that he could dress up the Complaint of a forsaken Chamber
Maid in the most affecting Terms, describe the Case of a poor Invalid, whether
directed to a General, or a Surgeon; in short, all Cases came before him, and
he grew intimate with the Town Intrigues, and learn'd be-/hind the Desk, in 17
a low Way, what he afterwards treated of in the sublime. *Tim* now began to
think that Servitude was an Enemy to Great Minds, that they should not be
cramp'd by low Indentures, left his Master, and returned to his Father, who
gave him Entertainment in his House, and, to keep his Genius in Play, allow'd
him a Rheam of Paper, and a Quartern of Ink every Day: Tho' this was an expensive Article, he was resolv'd to improve his Son's Talents at the Hazzard of
his own Fortunes. So unbounded was the Genius of our young Student that he
would one Day write a System of Physick; the next, a Comedy, or Copy of
Verses; a third, would make a Sermon; the next, a Tale of a Tub, or Romance;
but had this peculiar Turn in his Temper (whether it proceeded from natural
Modesty, or Policy, I will not venture to determine)/ that he never would own 18
his Productions, but always father'd them upon some body or other: I remember a Copy of his that appear'd under the Name of *P——e,* wherein he compliments a musical Lady,[7] but the World found him out here, and tho' they look'd
upon it as one of his Juvenile Performances, every body said it was prettily done
for one of his Bigness. *Tim* now apply'd himself to his Studies so strictly that his
Father was forced to encrease his Allowance: This fell so heavy upon him, and
the Stock wasted so fast, that in a short Time he had no Paper to serve his Customers; his Trade fell off, he run to Decay, and was forc'd to turn himself and
his Wife upon their Son for a Support from that Genius they had so carefully
indulg'd. *Tim* soon got him an Appartment, any thing contented him so he had
no Noise over his Head; but the/ Alteration in the Method of Life had such 19
Effect upon the good old Couple, that they were both seiz'd with an Atrophy,
and languishing a few Days, dyed. Now the young Man being more at large
than before, began to keep a little Company, and it was soon buzz'd about that
Tim was the greatest Genius of the Age, and the Booksellers began to hunt
after him; some offer'd Money, but he was so great a Contemner of Mammon
that he was never known to keep Company with more than a Tester [8] at once:
They attack'd him different Ways to no Purpose, *Tim* was resolv'd to stand
upon his own Bottom, knowing his Capacity would allow him to imitate the

sublimest Wits of his Time, and that a Title Page well countenanced would not
fail of selling Three Editions at least. It happen'd unluckily about this Time
that *Tim* fell sick of a Fever that set-/tled in his Head, and he would run up 20
and down in Alleys and Corners affronting every Body: In this Mood a Friend
of mine met him one Day, and *Tim* accosted him with an great Oath, Z——ds,
Sir, Don't you know me? Not I indeed, Sir, quoth my Friend, very civilly. No,
Sir, I am *J——n D——s* [9] Sir, the only Man alive that has a true Taste of the
Sublime. Sir, your most humble Servant, says my Friend, then you are not the
Man I took you for. To convince you that I am, quoth *Tim,* stooping down
to the Kennel, take that, and throws a great Handful of Mud all over his Cloaths.
My Friend acknowledg'd his Mistake, and got out of his Reach as fast as he
could. Another Time he collected a great Mob about him, and was telling
them that those Letters the World call'd Mr. *Bull's* [10] were not Mr. *Bull's,*
and that he could prove they were wrote/ Two Thousand Years before Mr. 21
Bull was ever thought of. Three or Four Gentlemen passing by over-heard
Tim talk in this extravagant Manner, and desired him to keep his Temper
a Minute and they wou'd convince him Mr. *Bull* was the Man that wrote those
Letters. How! says *Tim,* do you pretend to contradict a Master of a College,[11]
(for in those Vagaries he kept to his Humour of personating some Great Man)
I tell you, you are a Parcel of ignorant blockheadly Dunces: Here he fell a
kicking, and flouncing, and splashing, that the Company was glad to make the
best of their Way, for fear of worse Usage.[12] In these Resveries he continued
a good while, till Somebody put him into a Course of Physick, and recovered
him perfectly. Now he set himself to Work once more, very gravely,
for the Improvement of Mankind; and fell upon Two Things./ The 22
first was, to wipe out a Flaw in History that the World had passed by for near
1700 Years; and, as a Matter of great Importance, he studied Night and Day
to find Proofs to countenance this new and useful Invention. Having settled
the Thing to his Mind, he took an Opportunity to tell the World of what
Importance it was to be set right in the Affair under his Consideration; and
after opening the Mistake to them, began to Reason with them after this
Manner: Look ye, Gentlemen, at the Time he lived, the Places he dwell'd in
were under the *Roman* Jurisdiction, and were governed by Lord Lieutenants,
so that he could have no Kingdom under them; and if he had a Mind to one by
himself, he must have travelled a great Way, Three Parts of the known World
being then in their Dominions: But why stand I to prove this! Gentlemen, here
is my/ Hand upon it, I have considered the Thing seriously, and I protest to 23
you solemnly, *in verbo Sacerdotis,* as I hope to change this troublesome ——
Life for a better, he was so far from having a Kingdom, that he had not one
Foot of Land in all the World; and if either of us had been alive then, and in
the same Street, he would have had no more to do with us than the Emperor of
Russia has at this Moment.[13] Here *Tim* made his Bow, and left them to consider of it. Now, thinks he, I have made Way for a fine Argument; and observing he had set the People all agog, he thought this the critical Time to try
the Extent of his Genius by managing this whole Argument himself, *Pro* and
Con. Immediately he publish'd an Answer to his former Assertion, proving that

he was a King, and had great Authority upon Earth; and if he attempted to
as-/sert the Contrary, he would put him in the C——s,[14] and convince him to 24
his Cost. And now the Storm began to thicken; one Day he would publish *A
Vindication of, &c.* Another, *A Letter to, &c.* A Third, *A Defence of, &c.* Sometimes calling himself *——, or ——, or ——, or ——, or——, or——, giving
a new Name to every Treatise, and the whole Town began to be in an Uproar
for Fear of Daggers drawing, for he would give the Lye again and again, and
appeal to three or four at a Time, of each Side, to prove each lied. And tho' he
frequently used Language below a Porter, yet he reason'd so much like a
Divine, produc'd so many strong Arguments, and couch'd so much Ar-/tifice 25
on each Side the Question, that not one of them all refused to own his Productions; but every body swore their Adversaries were ——. The Town continu'd
in the Mistake, and least they should any longer, and in Honour to my Friend,
I take this Opportunity of assuring them they were every one wrote with his
own Hand.

The Second was, he having run through all Uviuersal Systems of Phylosophy,
and traced Nature in all her Intricacies, was so familiar with every Operation
she was Mistress of, knew the Necessity of her acting in the regular Manner she
does, that he had convinc'd himself there was no Occasion for a superior Power;
and that this Piece of useful Knowledge should not be kept a Secret from the
World, he oblig'd them with his Reasons in several very elaborate Discourses,
under/ the Names of *T——d,*[15] *C——s,*[16] *C——d,*[17] to which the *Beau Monde* 26
are vastly beholden for the most agreeable Set of Morals they ever put in Practice.

I have not been able to collect all the scatter'd Pieces of his, for Want of Time
and proper Correspondents, tho' I must not omit three curious little Tracts of
P——ns, F——ts, and D—d——ns,[18] all surprizing Pieces of Wit and Ingenuity; with these he complimented Dr. *S——ft,* which, tho' they were too gay
for one of his Cloth, might have set him up for a Wit, had not the World known
that his Talent lay more in sound Divinity that Rapartee.

I shall take my Leave of the Reader, intreating him, First, not to consider
these Memorandums as a perfect History; that was not what I promised, but
only look upon it as the To-/ken of a Heart full of Gratitude towards a Man 27
I acknowledge myself, to the last Degree, beholden to. That I could not write
for Fame he will be assur'd, when he reflects upon the Incapacity I have all
along discover'd to do Justice to my Friend, and I hope no body will descend
to suspect me of any Thing else.

I must obviate one Reflection I am aware of, *viz. That there is not one Word
in the whole Book in different Character,* by saying, that in true History there
is no Room for Humour or Wit; and I must own I have stifled several very
pretty Turns, for no other Reason than that they were below the Dignity of the
Subject.

FINIS.

* *Here was a List of Rt. Rds. Rds. and M. As. which the Bookseller thinks fit to leave out.*

1. [D——r] Doctor. Mr. Eddy reads the B.M. copy as "D——n.".

2. [*succerrere disco*] *Aeneid*, II, 325–7, 'Taught by my woes to succour the distressed'—Ogilby.

3. [T—— R——] Thomas Rawlinson, 1681–1725, a lawyer and bibliophile. He began his collecting in his youth and on inheriting a large estate in 1708 devoted himself to acquiring books, manuscripts, and paintings. While living in Gray's Inn he was obliged to sleep in a passage because his rooms were crowded by his possessions. He is said to have been the original from whom Addison drew his satiric portrait of Tom Folio in *Tatler*, No. 158. Having ruined himself financially by his purchases, he was before his death obliged to put some of his immense collection on sale, the first lot being offered to the public on March 7, 1721/22. Succeeding sales, among the most notable of the time, lasted until 1734.

4. [Spill] A slang term for gratuity that had apparently already become obsolete.

5. [*Dextra tenet* ——] The quotation seems to have been coined for the occasion.

6. [Streams of Ink] Cf. the text of the true *Memoirs*, p. 98.

7. [musical Lady] Pope's "Of her singing to a Lute," one of six "Verses in Imitation of Waller. By a Youth of Thirteen," which were published in *Poems on Several Occasions*, a minor miscellany issued by Lintot in 1717. There was no indication of Pope's authorship in the volume, but he later printed this poem among his accepted works.

8. [Tester] A corruption of *teston*, "an old silver coin formerly worth 12d. sinking by degrees to gilt brass and six pence." Coles' *Dictionary* (1692).

9. [J——n D——s] John Dennis, the critic, who was famous for his conceit, furious temper, and rough language. He had recently become embroiled with Sir Richard Steele and his friends as the result of his attack on *The Conscious Lovers*. His vigorous comments had, however, affronted so many writers that it is impossible to identify the particular cause of this ridicule.

10. [Bull's] *The Epistles of Phalaris*. An edition of this work by Charles Boyle, first published in 1695 and reprinted in 1718, led to the famous controversy between the Oxford wits and Richard Bentley, in the course of which Bentley proved to posterity, though not to all the partisans of the time, that the *Epistles* were a forgery produced many hundreds of years after their purported origin. The name of Phalaris, a tyrant of Agrigentum, is associated with a brazen bull in which he tortured many victims, including Perillus its inventor, and in which he was himself eventually put to death by his enraged subjects.

11. [Master of a College] Bentley was Master of Trinity College, Cambridge, an office he assumed on February 1, 1700.

12. [worse Usage] Bentley's contentious spirit, which caused him to produce his famous *Dissertation* (1699) in answer to Boyle, led to many other scholarly quarrels (cf. above, pp. 266–7) and kept his college in a turmoil for thirty-eight years.

13. [this Moment] This satire is aimed at the deists and freethinkers who had during the preceding three decades subjected various passages in the Bible to critical examination.

14. [C——s] In the courts, where, if proved guilty of blasphemy, he might be sentenced under the common law to fine, imprisonment, the pillory, etc.

15. [T——d] John Toland, the publication of whose *Christianity not Mysterious* in 1696 inaugurated the long controversy between the deists and the orthodox. Cf. above, pp. 280–1. A man of considerable ability who has since been recognized for his able work on the historical origin of creeds, he was the object of much scorn on the part of churchmen and was never able to earn more than a precarious existence as a political agent and hack writer. Early in 1714 he turned on his previous employer, Oxford, and in a sensational pamphlet, *The Art of Restoring*, which went through ten editions, accused him of planning to imitate Monck by bringing in the Pretender. Toward the end of his life he returned to ecclesiastical history and produced several works of a freethinking character. He died on March 11, 1721/22.

16. [C——s] Anthony Collins, 1676–1729, the author of *A Discourse of Free-Thinking* (1713) and other tracts in which he maintained the right of free enquiry in religious affairs. His long controversy with Samuel Clarke is burlesqued in Chap. XII of the true *Memoirs*. Cf. above, pp. 281–5. Like his fellow freethinkers, he was attacked with great fury by many opponents.

17. [C——d] William Coward, 1657?–1725, a physician and deistical writer, who in the first decade of the century wrote several works attacking the theory of a separate, immaterial soul. Though the least able of the group, he achieved great notoriety as the result of a House of Commons order that one of his books, *The Grand Essay; or a Vindication of Reason and Religion*

against Impostures of Philosophy (1704), be burned by the common hangman. One of Gay's early pieces, which he never later acknowledged, was a set of commendatory verses prefixed to Coward's *Licentia Poetica*, a minor critical work published in 1709. The B.M. copy of the *Memoirs* appears to read "C———o," but the "o" is probably a defective letter "d" in italic type.

18. [P–ns, F—ts, and D–d——ns] *Ars Pun-ica, sive Flos Linguarum; The Art of Punning; Or The Flower of Languages; In Seventy Nine Rules: For The Farther Improvement Of Conversation, And Help of Memory. By the Labour and Industry of Tom Pun-Sibi, &c.* (Dublin, 1719). It was reprinted in London in the same year by J. Roberts and went through several editions. Roberts' titlepage reads, "By . . . Tom Pun-Sibi, (i.e.) Jonathan Swift, D.D. &c."

The Benefit of Farting Explain'd: &c. Long-Fart: Printed by Simon Bumbubbard, At the Sign of the Wind-Mill opposite Twattling-Street (1722). This Irish edition was reprinted by A. Moore and went through at least ten editions in 1722.

A Dedication To A Great Man, Concerning Dedications. &c. (London, 1718). It was published by J. Roberts and went through seven editions in the first two years.

On March 13, 1721/22, Swift wrote to Knightley Chetwode, "Surely you in the country have got the London fancy, that I am author of all the scurvy things that come out here. The slovenly pages called the Benefit of — — was writ by one Dobbs a surgeon." *Corres.*, III, 125. The *Ars Pun-ica* has been attributed to Thomas Sheridan and *A Dedication* to Thomas Gordon.

INDEX

Italicized numbers refer to the *Scriblerus* text; roman numerals which immediately follow these refer to a note on the subject.